Teacher Wraparound Edition

GLENCOE FRENCH 

Bon voyage!

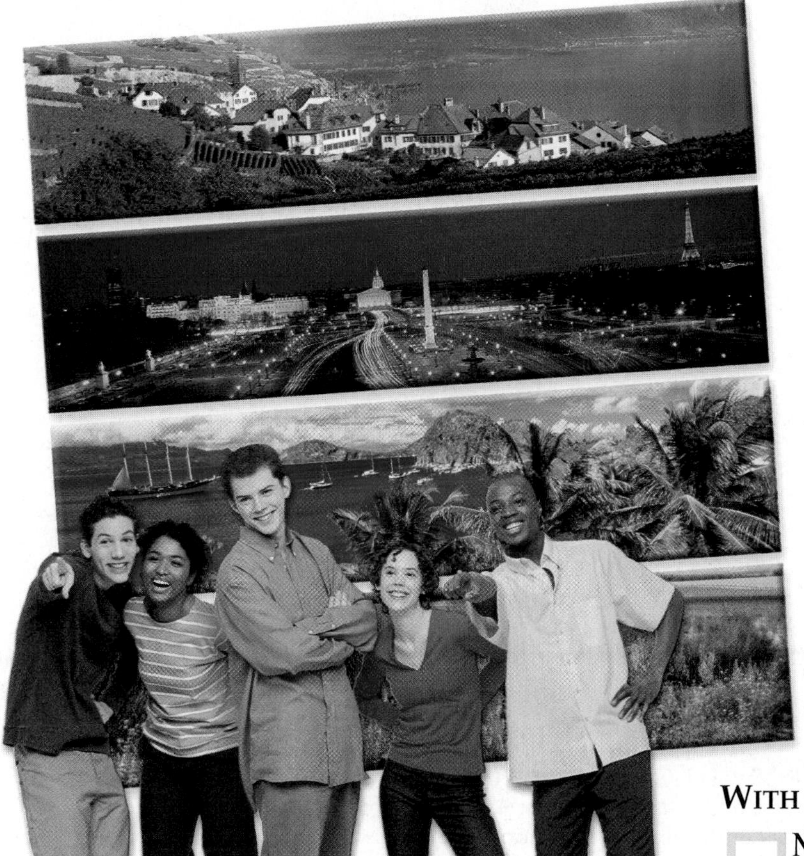

WITH FEATURES BY
NATIONAL GEOGRAPHIC SOCIETY

Conrad J. Schmitt • Katia Brillié Lutz

Glencoe McGraw-Hill

New York, New York   Columbus, Ohio   Chicago, Illinois   Peoria, Illinois   Woodland Hills, California

Glencoe/McGraw-Hill

A Division of The ***McGraw-Hill*** *Companies*

Send all inquiries to:
Glencoe/McGraw-Hill
8787 Orion Place
Columbus, Ohio 43240-4027

ISBN 0-07-821257-X (Student Edition)
ISBN 0-07-824343-2 (Teacher Wraparound Edition)

Printed in the United States of America

3 4 5 6 7 8 9 10 071/043 08 07 06 05 04 03

From the Authors

Itinerary for Success

- ✓ Exposure to Francophone culture
- ✓ Clear expectations and goals
- ✓ Thematic, contextualized vocabulary
- ✓ Useful and thematically linked structure
- ✓ Progressive practice
- ✓ Real-life conversation
- ✓ Cultural readings in the target language
- ✓ Connections to other disciplines . . . in French!
- ✓ Recycling and review
- ✓ **National Geographic Society** panoramas of the Francophone world

Dear French Teacher,

Welcome to Glencoe's **Bon voyage!** French program. We hope you will find that the way in which we have organized the presentation of the French language and Francophone cultures will make the French language more teachable for you and more learnable for your students.

Upon completion of each chapter of **Bon voyage!** your students will be able to communicate in French in a real-life situation. The high-frequency, productive vocabulary that is presented at the beginning of the chapter focuses on a specific communicative topic and covers key situations where students would have to use French to survive. The structure point that follows the vocabulary presentation will enable students to put their new words together to communicate coherently.

After students acquire the essential vocabulary and structure needed to function in a given situation, we present a realistic conversation that uses natural, colloquial French and, most importantly, French that students can readily understand. To introduce students to the culture of France and the Francophone world, the chapter topic is subsequently presented in a cultural milieu in narrative form. Each **Lecture culturelle** recombines known language and enables students to read and learn—in French—about the fascinating cultures of the people who speak French.

Any one of us who has taught French realizes the importance of giving students the opportunity to practice, a factor so often overlooked in many textbooks today. Throughout **Bon voyage!** we provide students with many opportunities to use their French in activities with interesting and varied, but realistic formats. The activities within each chapter progress from simple, guided practice to more open-ended activities that may use all forms of the particular structure in question. Finally, activities that encourage completely free communication enable students to recall and reincorporate all the French they have learned up to that point.

We are aware that your students have varied learning styles and abilities. For this reason we have provided a great deal of optional material in **Bon voyage!** to permit you to pick and choose material appropriate for the needs of your classes. In this Teacher Wraparound Edition we have clearly outlined the material that is required, recommended, or optional in each chapter.

Many resources accompany **Bon voyage!** to help you vary and enliven your instruction. We hope you will find these materials not only useful, but an integral part of the program. However, we trust you will agree that the Student Text is the lifeline of any program; the supporting materials can be used to reinforce and expand upon the themes of the main text.

Again, we hope that your yearlong journey with each of your classes will indeed be a **Bon voyage!**

Bien amicalement,

Conrad J. Schmitt • Katia Brillié Lutz

Teacher Edition

Student Edition

Expand your students' view of the Francophone world

Glencoe's **Le monde francophone** will take your students to the many places where they will be able to use their French.

Maps, facts, and figures will serve as a valuable resource for you and your students throughout your journey.

Awaken your students' interest with an introduction to the chapter theme in a cultural context

Itinerary for Success

- ✓ Exposure to Francophone culture
- ✓ Clear expectations and goals
- ✓ Thematic, contextualized vocabulary
- ✓ Useful and thematically linked structure
- ✓ Progressive practice
- ✓ Real-life conversation
- ✓ Cultural readings in the target language
- ✓ Connections to other disciplines . . . in French!
- ✓ Recycling and review
- ✓ **National Geographic Society** panoramas of the Francophone world

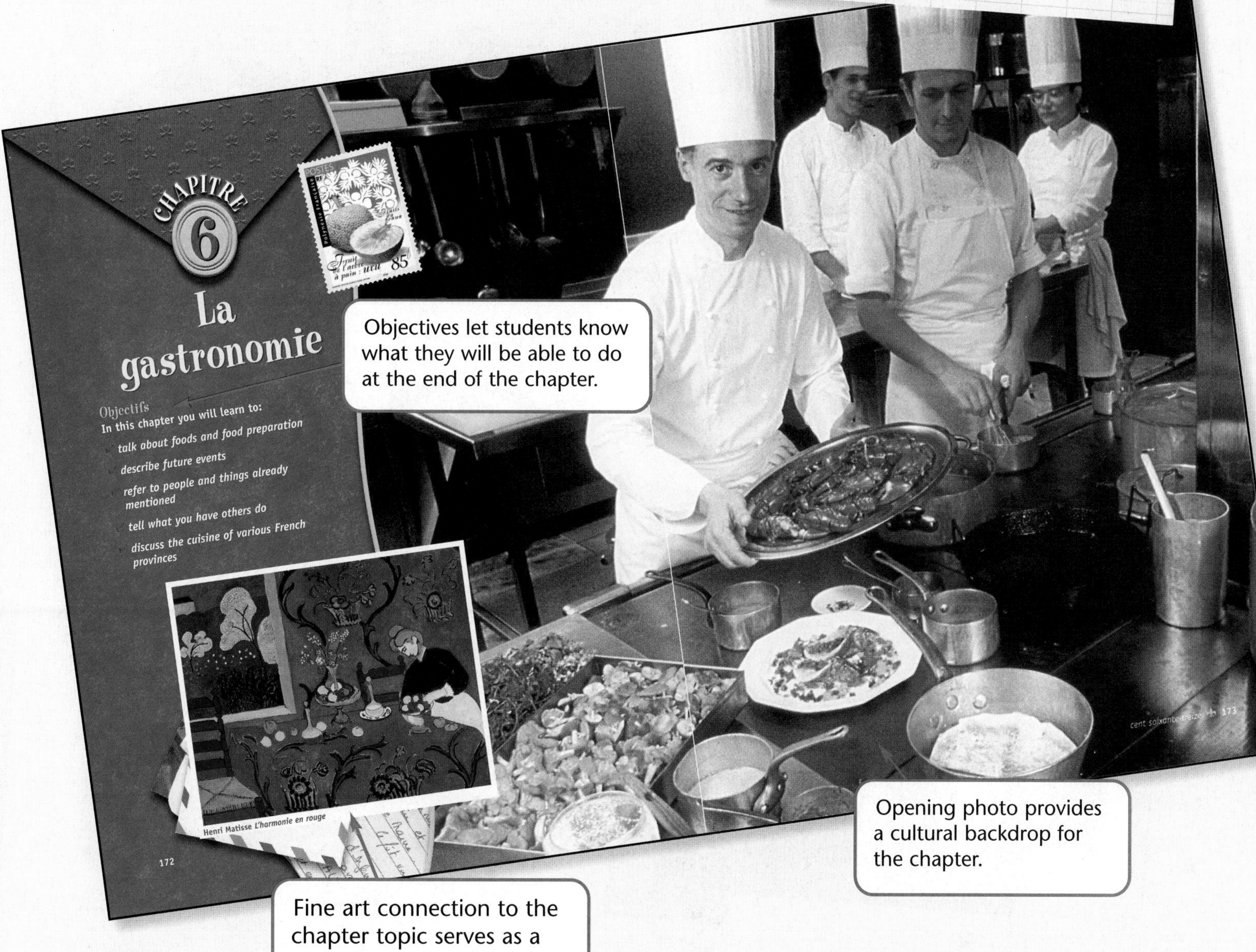

Objectives let students know what they will be able to do at the end of the chapter.

Fine art connection to the chapter topic serves as a springboard for discussion.

Opening photo provides a cultural backdrop for the chapter.

Give students something to talk about with thematic, contextualized vocabulary

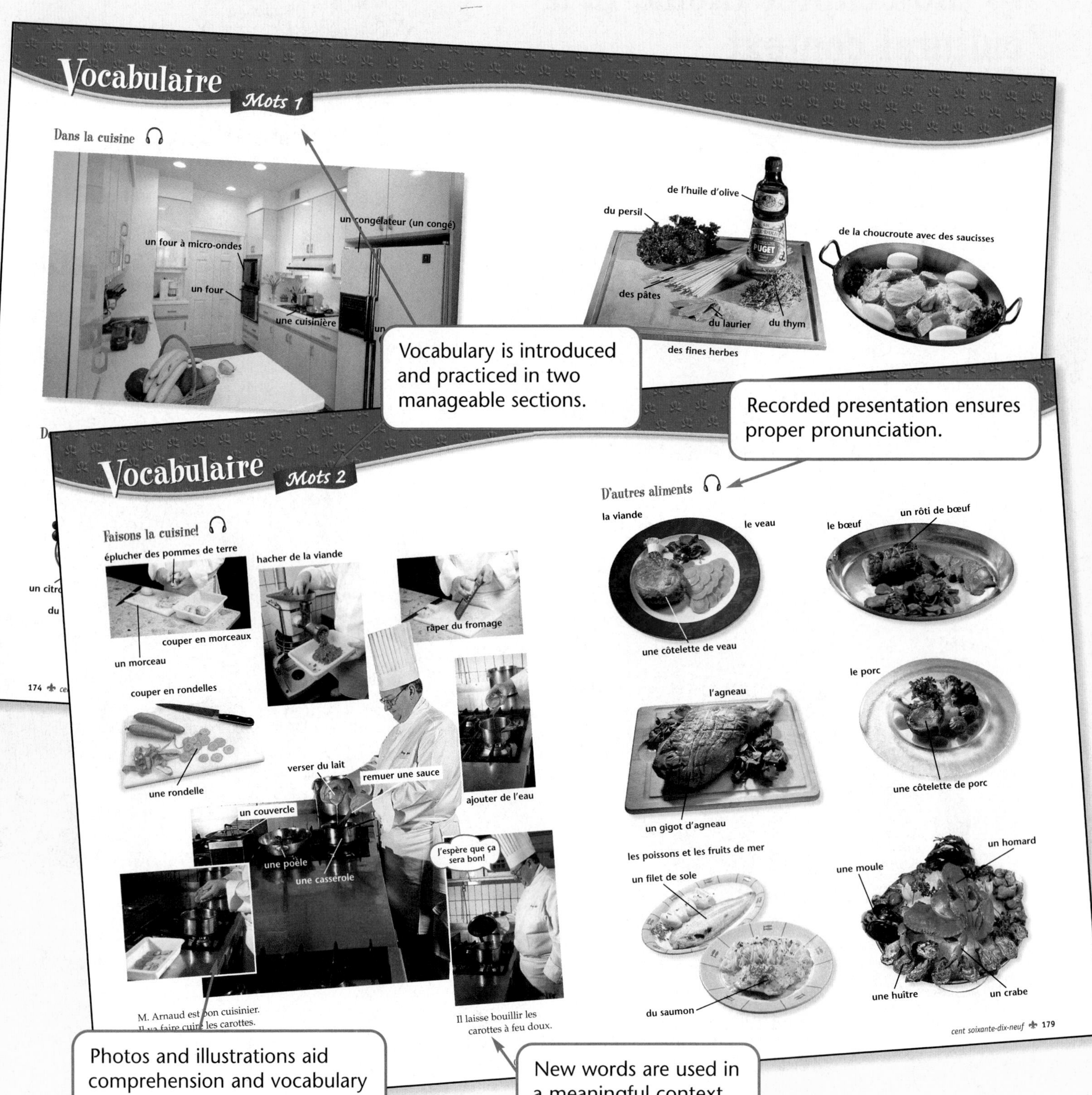

Vocabulary is introduced and practiced in two manageable sections.

Recorded presentation ensures proper pronunciation.

Photos and illustrations aid comprehension and vocabulary acquisition.

New words are used in a meaningful context.

Heighten students' cultural awareness

Itinerary for Success

- ✓ Exposure to Francophone culture
- ✓ Clear expectations and goals
- ✓ Thematic, contextualized vocabulary
- ✓ Useful and thematically linked structure
- ✓ Progressive practice
- ✓ Real-life conversation
- ✓ Cultural readings in the target language
- ✓ Connections to other disciplines . . . in French!
- ✓ Recycling and review
- ✓ **National Geographic Society** panoramas of the Francophone world

Recorded reading provides options for addressing various skills and learning styles.

Reading strategies help students read with ease.

Lectures culturelles

Un voyage gastronomique

Reading Strategy

Making connections When you read a piece of nonfiction, think about what you have already read on the subject, as well as your personal knowledge and experiences. Ask yourself if the information supports or refutes what you already know. How does the passage enhance your understanding of the topic? Can you make connections between what you've learned and other areas of knowledge?

Charles Smith est un étudiant américain à l'université du Michigan. Il fait du français parce qu'il s'intéresse au commerce international. Charles a toujours eu envie d'aller en France pour travailler son français. L'été prochain, il réalisera son rêve[1] quand il passera deux mois en France. Il voyagera dans toute la France.

Charles est un vrai gourmand, c'est-à-dire qu'il aime bien manger. Il sait que la France est connue dans le monde entier pour sa bonne cuisine. Chaque région a ses spécialités.

Alsace

Charles va commencer son voyage à Strasbourg, en Alsace, près de la frontière allemande. Là, il prendra sans doute une choucroute avec du jambon, des lardons[2] et des saucisses. La cuisine alsacienne ressemble à la cuisine allemande.

Provence

Ensuite, Charles ira dans le sud, en Provence. Quelle différence! En Provence on mange des pâtes et même de la pissaladière, un genre de pizza. Dans les plats provençaux, on utilise ce qu'on appelle les herbes de Provence: du thym, du laurier, du basilic, du romarin[3]. On utilise aussi des tomates, des oignons et de l'ail. La cuisine est toujours faite à l'huile d'olive. On n'utilise pas de beurre.

[1] rêve *dream*
[2] lardons *bacon bits*
[3] romarin *rosemary*

Alsace
Normandie
Bretagne
Bourgogne
Provence

Bourgogne

Après huit jours en Provence, Charles visitera la Bourgogne. La Bourgogne est une région de vignobles[4]. Les vins de Bourgogne sont très appréciés et on les utilise beaucoup dans la cuisine bourguignonne. Bien sûr, Charles va manger un bœuf bourguignon—une des spécialités de la région. On prépare le bœuf bourguignon avec du bœuf, bien sûr, mais aussi avec du vin rouge, des oignons, du thym et du laurier. On le sert avec des pommes de terre cuites à l'eau ou à la vapeur[5]. Un vrai régal[6]!

Bretagne

Ensuite Charles ira en Bretagne, dans le nord-ouest. Il visitera de jolis villages de pêcheurs, comme Cancale, par exemple. Et qu'est-ce qu'il va manger en Bretagne? Il aura l'occasion de manger les meilleurs fruits de mer du monde—des huîtres, des moules et des coquilles Saint-Jacques[7].

Normandie

Avant de rentrer à Paris, Charles passera par la Normandie. Comme la Normandie est une région de pâturages, il y a beaucoup de vaches[8]. Pour cette raison, les Normands préparent leurs sauces avec de la crème et du beurre. Une escalope[9] à la normande est une escalope de veau avec une sauce à la crème et des champignons. C'est délicieux!

Quand notre gourmand sera en France, il apprendra sans doute que «la cuisine en France, c'est un art». Et quand il rentrera aux États-Unis, il aura certainement pris quelques kilos de plus.

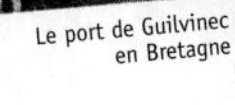

Le port de Guilvinec en Bretagne

[4] vignobles *vineyards*
[5] à la vapeur *steamed*
[6] régal *treat*
[7] coquilles Saint-Jacques *scallops*
[8] vaches *cows*
[9] escalope *cutlet*

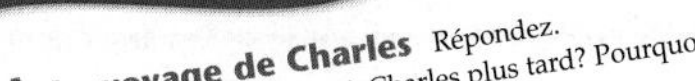

Après la lecture

A Le voyage de Charles Répondez.

1. Le français sera utile à Charles plus tard? Pourquoi?
2. Il ira en France quand?
3. Il visitera quelles régions?
4. Qu'est-ce qu'il apprendra quand il sera en France?

B Provinces et plats Donnez les informations suivantes.

1. le nom des provinces françaises que Charles visitera
2. un plat qu'il mangera dans chaque province

Cultural reading uses learned language to reinforce chapter theme.

Many visuals help students comprehend what they read.

Enrich students' cultural knowledge

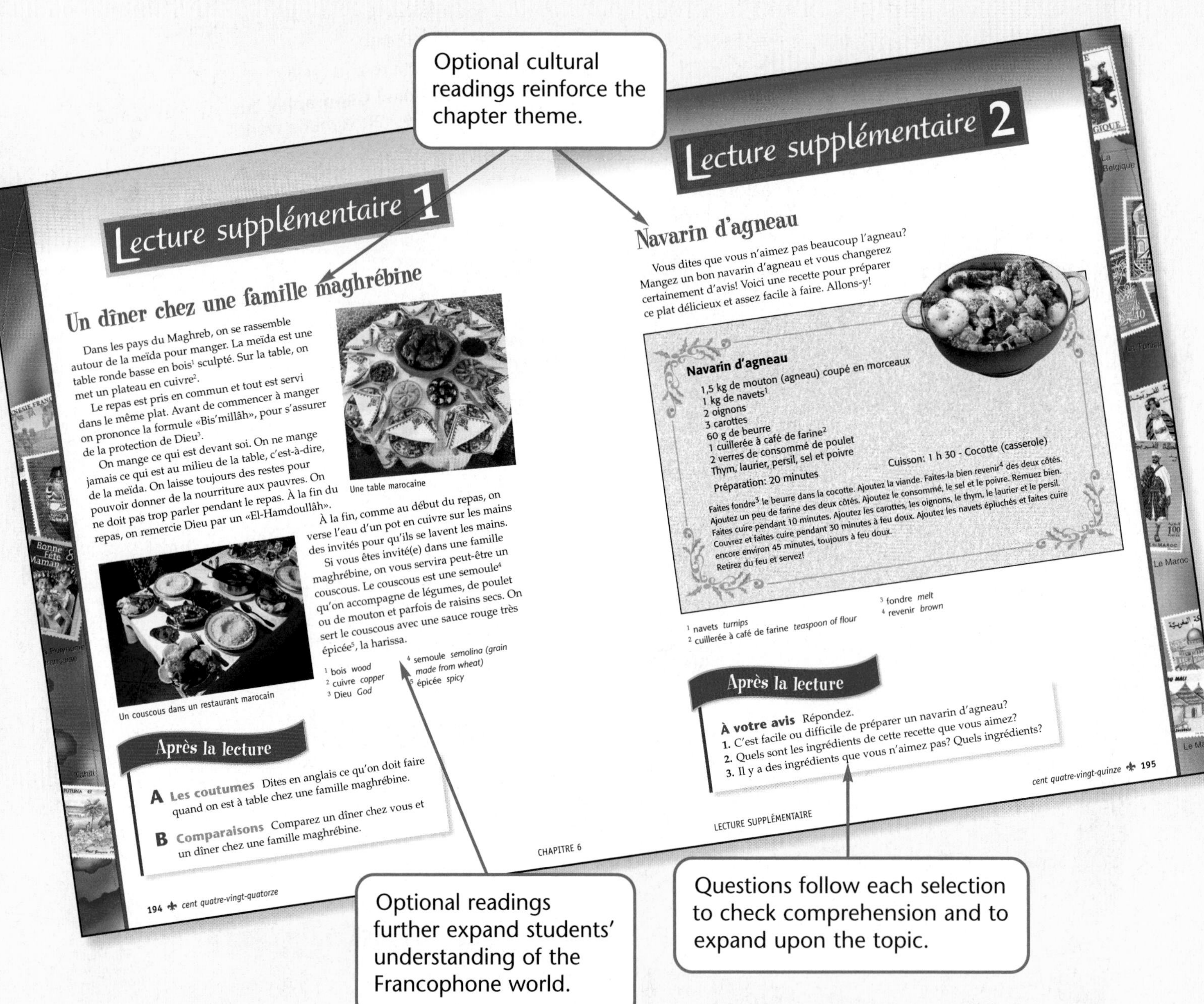

Lecture supplémentaire 1

Un dîner chez une famille maghrébine

Dans les pays du Maghreb, on se rassemble autour de la meïda pour manger. La meïda est une table ronde basse en bois[1] sculpté. Sur la table, on met un plateau en cuivre[2].

Le repas est pris en commun et tout est servi dans le même plat. Avant de commencer à manger on prononce la formule «Bis'millâh», pour s'assurer de la protection de Dieu[3].

On mange ce qui est devant soi. On ne mange jamais ce qui est au milieu de la table, c'est-à-dire, de la meïda. On laisse toujours des restes pour pouvoir donner de la nourriture aux pauvres. On ne doit pas trop parler pendant le repas. À la fin du repas, on remercie Dieu par un «El-Hamdoullâh».

À la fin, comme au début du repas, on verse l'eau d'un pot en cuivre sur les mains des invités pour qu'ils se lavent les mains.

Si vous êtes invité(e) dans une famille maghrébine, on vous servira peut-être un couscous. Le couscous est une semoule[4] qu'on accompagne de légumes, de poulet ou de mouton et parfois de raisins secs. On sert le couscous avec une sauce rouge très épicée[5], la harissa.

Une table marocaine

Un couscous dans un restaurant marocain

1 bois *wood*
2 cuivre *copper*
3 Dieu *God*
4 semoule *semolina (grain made from wheat)*
5 épicée *spicy*

Après la lecture

A Les coutumes Dites en anglais ce qu'on doit faire quand on est à table chez une famille maghrébine.

B Comparaisons Comparez un dîner chez vous et un dîner chez une famille maghrébine.

194 cent quatre-vingt-quatorze — CHAPITRE 6

Lecture supplémentaire 2

Navarin d'agneau

Vous dites que vous n'aimez pas beaucoup l'agneau? Mangez un bon navarin d'agneau et vous changerez certainement d'avis! Voici une recette pour préparer ce plat délicieux et assez facile à faire. Allons-y!

Navarin d'agneau

1,5 kg de mouton (agneau) coupé en morceaux
1 kg de navets[1]
2 oignons
3 carottes
60 g de beurre
1 cuillerée à café de farine[2]
2 verres de consommé de poulet
Thym, laurier, persil, sel et poivre

Préparation: 20 minutes — Cuisson: 1 h 30 - Cocotte (casserole)

Faites fondre[3] le beurre dans la cocotte. Ajoutez la viande. Faites-la bien revenir[4] des deux côtés. Ajoutez un peu de farine des deux côtés. Ajoutez le consommé, le sel et le poivre. Remuez bien. Faites cuire pendant 10 minutes. Ajoutez les carottes, les oignons, le thym, le laurier et le persil. Couvrez et faites cuire pendant 30 minutes à feu doux. Ajoutez les navets épluchés et faites cuire encore environ 45 minutes, toujours à feu doux. Retirez du feu et servez!

1 navets *turnips*
2 cuillerée à café de farine *teaspoon of flour*
3 fondre *melt*
4 revenir *brown*

Après la lecture

À votre avis Répondez.

1. C'est facile ou difficile de préparer un navarin d'agneau?
2. Quels sont les ingrédients de cette recette que vous aimez?
3. Il y a des ingrédients que vous n'aimez pas? Quels ingrédients?

LECTURE SUPPLÉMENTAIRE — cent quatre-vingt-quinze 195

Optional cultural readings reinforce the chapter theme.

Optional readings further expand students' understanding of the Francophone world.

Questions follow each selection to check comprehension and to expand upon the topic.

Connect with other disciplines

Itinerary for Success
- ✓ Exposure to Francophone culture
- ✓ Clear expectations and goals
- ✓ Thematic, contextualized vocabulary
- ✓ Useful and thematically linked structure
- ✓ Progressive practice
- ✓ Real-life conversation
- ✓ Cultural readings in the target language
- ✓ Connections to other disciplines . . . in French!
- ✓ Recycling and review
- ✓ **National Geographic Society** panoramas of the Francophone world

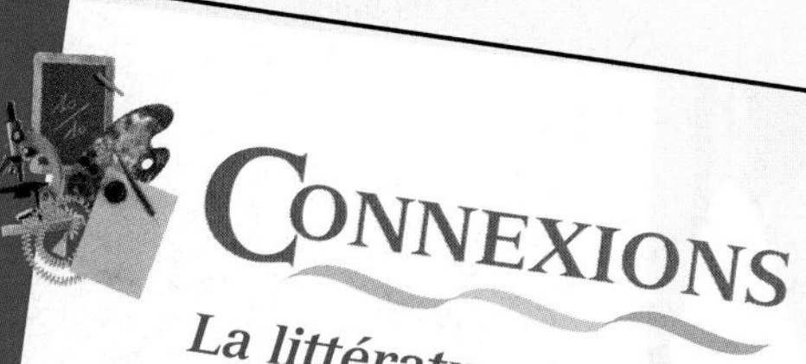

CONNEXIONS

La littérature

Gargantua de Rabelais

Introduction to the **Connexions** provides the background for students to understand the reading.

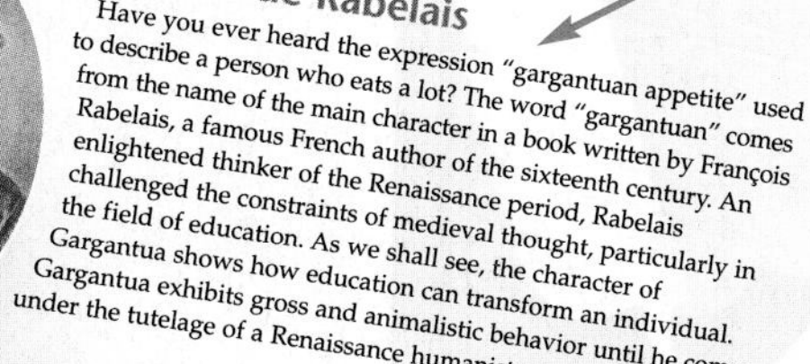

Have you ever heard the expression "gargantuan appetite" used to describe a person who eats a lot? The word "gargantuan" comes from the name of the main character in a book written by François Rabelais, a famous French author of the sixteenth century. An enlightened thinker of the Renaissance period, Rabelais challenged the constraints of medieval thought, particularly in the field of education. As we shall see, the character of Gargantua shows how education can transform an individual. Gargantua exhibits gross and animalistic behavior until he comes under the tutelage of a Renaissance humanist named Ponocrates.

François Rabelais, gravure d'un artiste inconnu

Gargantua.

M. D. XXXVII.

Gargantua

Gargantua est le fils de Grangousier et de Gargamelle. Tous deux sont des gros mangeurs et buveurs. Ils adorent manger et boire. Ce trait est transmis à leur fils. Dès l'instant[1] qu'il est né, il crie «À boire, à boire, à boire!» Son père l'entend et dit «Que grand tu as!»—et de là vient le nom de Gargantua. Le «petit» enfant a bu le lait de 17 913 vaches. Il s'est développé vite et il est devenu énorme—un véritable géant.

Quand il se réveillait, il sautait[2] dans son lit comme un mouton. Pour lui:

peigner, laver et nettoyer[3] était perdre son temps en ce monde. Puis rotait[4], crachait[5], toussait, éternuait, et déjeunait: belles tripes frites[6], belles carbonnades [grillades], beaux jambons.

[1] Dès l'instant *From the moment*
[2] sautait *jumped up and down*
[3] nettoyer *clean*
[4] rotait *burped*
[5] crachait *spit*
[6] tripes frites *fried tripe*

196 ✤ *cent quatre-vingt-seize*

CHAPITRE 6

Gargantua aime manger, mais il n'aime pas du tout faire de l'exercice. Quand on lui dit de faire de l'exercice, il répond:

Quoi! n'ai-je fait suffisant exercice?
Je me suis vautré[7] six ou sept tours
parmi le lit[8] avant de me lever.
N'est-ce assez?

La vie et le comportement de Gargantua changent complètement quand son père décide de confier son éducation au sage[9] humaniste Ponocrates. Gargantua apprend alors à se laver, se peigner, s'habiller et se parfumer. Il assouplit[10] son corps par toutes sortes d'exercices physiques. On stimule son esprit par des jeux. Il rend visite aux artisans et converse avec les savants.

[7] Je me suis vautré *I rolled around*
[8] tours parmi le lit *times in bed*
[9] sage *wise*
[10] assouplit *loosens up*

La Devinière, le village natal de Rabelais

Après la lecture

Gargantua Répondez.

1. Quel est un trait des parents de Gargantua?
2. Ce trait a été transmis à leur fils?
3. Quand Gargantua est né, qu'est-ce qu'il a crié?
4. On lui a donné quel nom?
5. Qu'est-ce qu'il a bu?
6. Qu'est-ce qu'il est devenu?
7. Qu'est-ce qu'il faisait quand il se réveillait?
8. Qu'est-ce qu'il mangeait?
9. Il aimait faire de l'exercice?
10. Quand est-ce que tout cela a changé?

cent quatre-vingt-dix-sept ✤ 197

Students further their knowledge of other disciplines—in French!

Encourage students to apply what they have learned

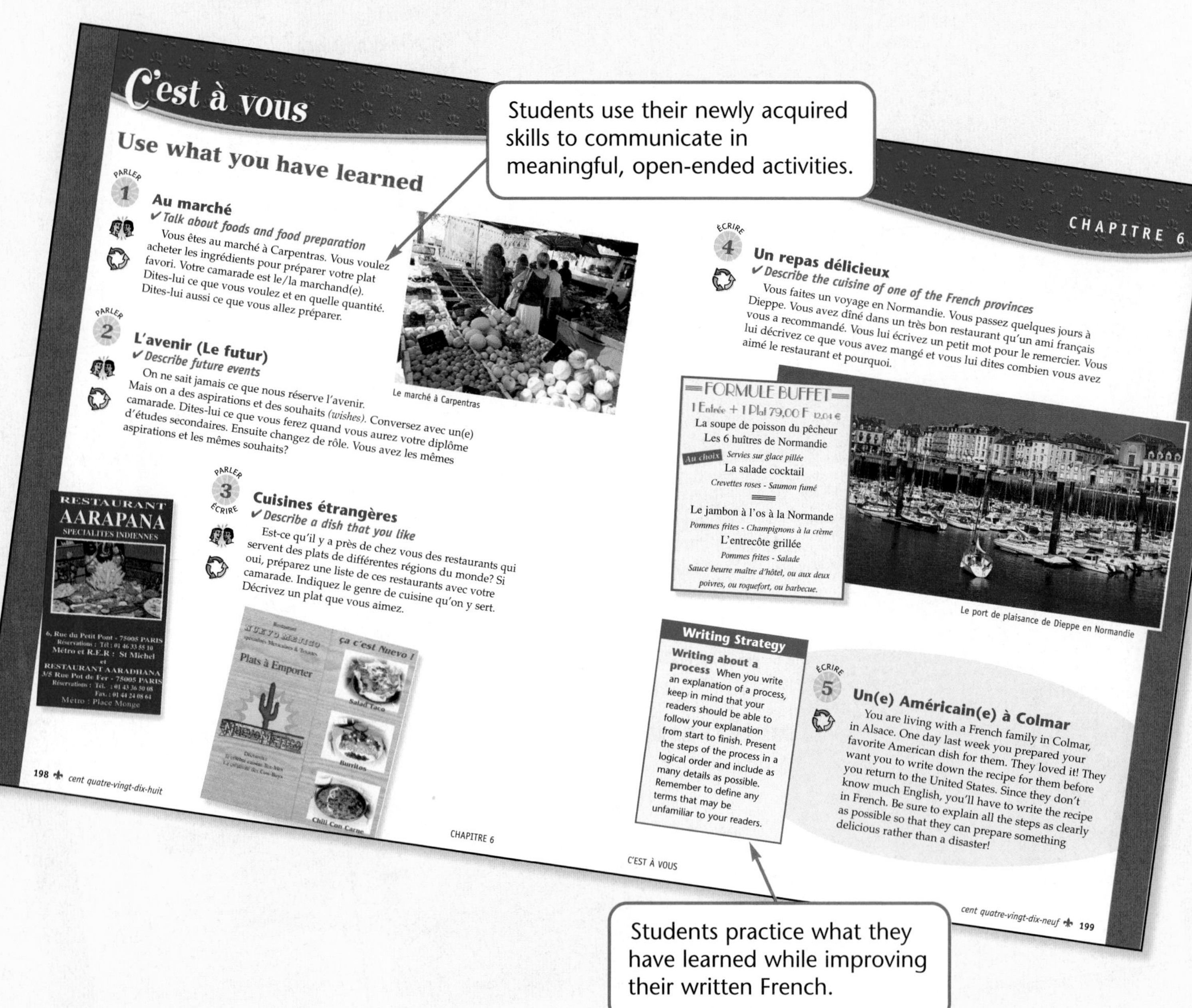

C'est à vous

Use what you have learned

PARLER **1** **Au marché**

✔ *Talk about foods and food preparation*

Vous êtes au marché à Carpentras. Vous voulez acheter les ingrédients pour préparer votre plat favori. Votre camarade est le/la marchand(e). Dites-lui ce que vous voulez et en quelle quantité. Dites-lui aussi ce que vous allez préparer.

Le marché à Carpentras

PARLER **2** **L'avenir (Le futur)**

✔ *Describe future events*

On ne sait jamais ce que nous réserve l'avenir. Mais on a des aspirations et des souhaits *(wishes)*. Conversez avec un(e) camarade. Dites-lui ce que vous ferez quand vous aurez votre diplôme d'études secondaires. Ensuite changez de rôle. Vous avez les mêmes aspirations et les mêmes souhaits?

PARLER ÉCRIRE **3** **Cuisines étrangères**

✔ *Describe a dish that you like*

Est-ce qu'il y a près de chez vous des restaurants qui servent des plats de différentes régions du monde? Si oui, préparez une liste de ces restaurants avec votre camarade. Indiquez le genre de cuisine qu'on y sert. Décrivez un plat que vous aimez.

CHAPITRE 6

ÉCRIRE **4** **Un repas délicieux**

✔ *Describe the cuisine of one of the French provinces*

Vous faites un voyage en Normandie. Vous passez quelques jours à Dieppe. Vous avez dîné dans un très bon restaurant qu'un ami français vous a recommandé. Vous lui écrivez un petit mot pour le remercier. Vous lui décrivez ce que vous avez mangé et vous lui dites combien vous avez aimé le restaurant et pourquoi.

Le port de plaisance de Dieppe en Normandie

Writing Strategy

Writing about a process When you write an explanation of a process, keep in mind that your readers should be able to follow your explanation from start to finish. Present the steps of the process in a logical order and include as many details as possible. Remember to define any terms that may be unfamiliar to your readers.

ÉCRIRE **5** **Un(e) Américain(e) à Colmar**

You are living with a French family in Colmar, in Alsace. One day last week you prepared your favorite American dish for them. They loved it! They want you to write down the recipe for them before you return to the United States. Since they don't know much English, you'll have to write the recipe in French. Be sure to explain all the steps as clearly as possible so that they can prepare something delicious rather than a disaster!

198 ✤ cent quatre-vingt-dix-huit

CHAPITRE 6 — C'EST À VOUS

cent quatre-vingt-dix-neuf ✤ 199

Students use their newly acquired skills to communicate in meaningful, open-ended activities.

Students practice what they have learned while improving their written French.

Check students' progress

Itinerary for Success

- ✓ Exposure to Francophone culture
- ✓ Clear expectations and goals
- ✓ Thematic, contextualized vocabulary
- ✓ Useful and thematically linked structure
- ✓ Progressive practice
- ✓ Real-life conversation
- ✓ Cultural readings in the target language
- ✓ Connections to other disciplines . . . in French!
- ✓ Recycling and review
- ✓ **National Geographic Society** panoramas of the Francophone world

Assessment activities give students a chance to see what they have really learned.

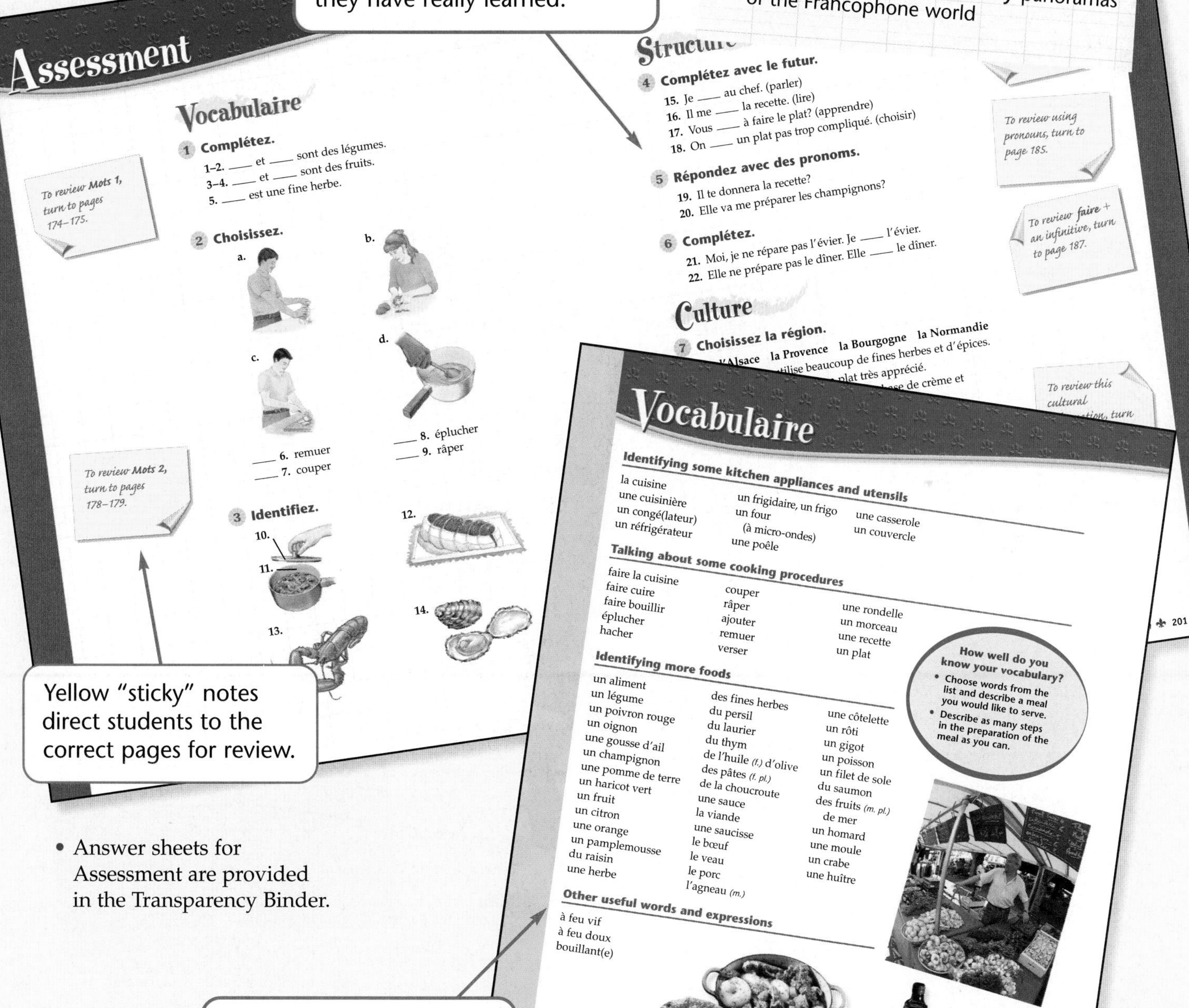

Assessment

Vocabulaire

1 Complétez.

1–2. ___ et ___ sont des légumes.
3–4. ___ et ___ sont des fruits.
5. ___ est une fine herbe.

To review ***Mots 1****, turn to pages 174–175.*

2 Choisissez.

a. b. c. d.

___ 6. remuer
___ 7. couper
___ 8. éplucher
___ 9. râper

To review ***Mots 2****, turn to pages 178–179.*

3 Identifiez.

10. 11. 12. 13. 14.

Structure

4 Complétez avec le futur.

15. Je ___ au chef. (parler)
16. Il me ___ la recette. (lire)
17. Vous ___ à faire le plat? (apprendre)
18. On ___ un plat pas trop compliqué. (choisir)

To review using pronouns, turn to page 185.

5 Répondez avec des pronoms.

19. Il te donnera la recette?
20. Elle va me préparer les champignons?

6 Complétez.

21. Moi, je ne répare pas l'évier. Je ___ l'évier.
22. Elle ne prépare pas le dîner. Elle ___ le dîner.

To review ***faire*** *+ an infinitive, turn to page 187.*

Culture

7 Choisissez la région.

l'Alsace la Provence la Bourgogne la Normandie

To review this cultural ...

201

Vocabulaire

Identifying some kitchen appliances and utensils

la cuisine, une cuisinière, un congé(lateur), un réfrigérateur, un frigidaire, un frigo, un four (à micro-ondes), une poêle, une casserole, un couvercle

Talking about some cooking procedures

faire la cuisine, faire cuire, faire bouillir, éplucher, hacher, couper, râper, ajouter, remuer, verser, une rondelle, un morceau, une recette, un plat

Identifying more foods

un aliment, un légume, un poivron rouge, un oignon, une gousse d'ail, un champignon, une pomme de terre, un haricot vert, un fruit, un citron, une orange, un pamplemousse, du raisin, une herbe, des fines herbes, du persil, du laurier, du thym, de l'huile (f.) d'olive, des pâtes (f. pl.), de la choucroute, une sauce, la viande, une saucisse, le bœuf, le veau, le porc, l'agneau (m.), une côtelette, un rôti, un gigot, un poisson, un filet de sole, du saumon, des fruits (m. pl.) de mer, un homard, une moule, un crabe, une huître

Other useful words and expressions

à feu vif, à feu doux, bouillant(e)

How well do you know your vocabulary?

- Choose words from the list and describe a meal you would like to serve.
- Describe as many steps in the preparation of the meal as you can.

202 deux cent deux

Yellow "sticky" notes direct students to the correct pages for review.

Vocabulary is categorized to help recall.

Students can use the list as a self-check at the end of the chapter.

- Answer sheets for Assessment are provided in the Transparency Binder.

Take students beyond the text to learn more about culture and language

The **Bon voyage!** Video Program reinforces the themes and language of the text, making it enjoyable and comprehensible for the students.

Students read a synopsis to set the stage for the video.

Students will love getting acquainted with the **Bon voyage!** video characters.

Online activities give students more opportunities to further explore the chapter topic.

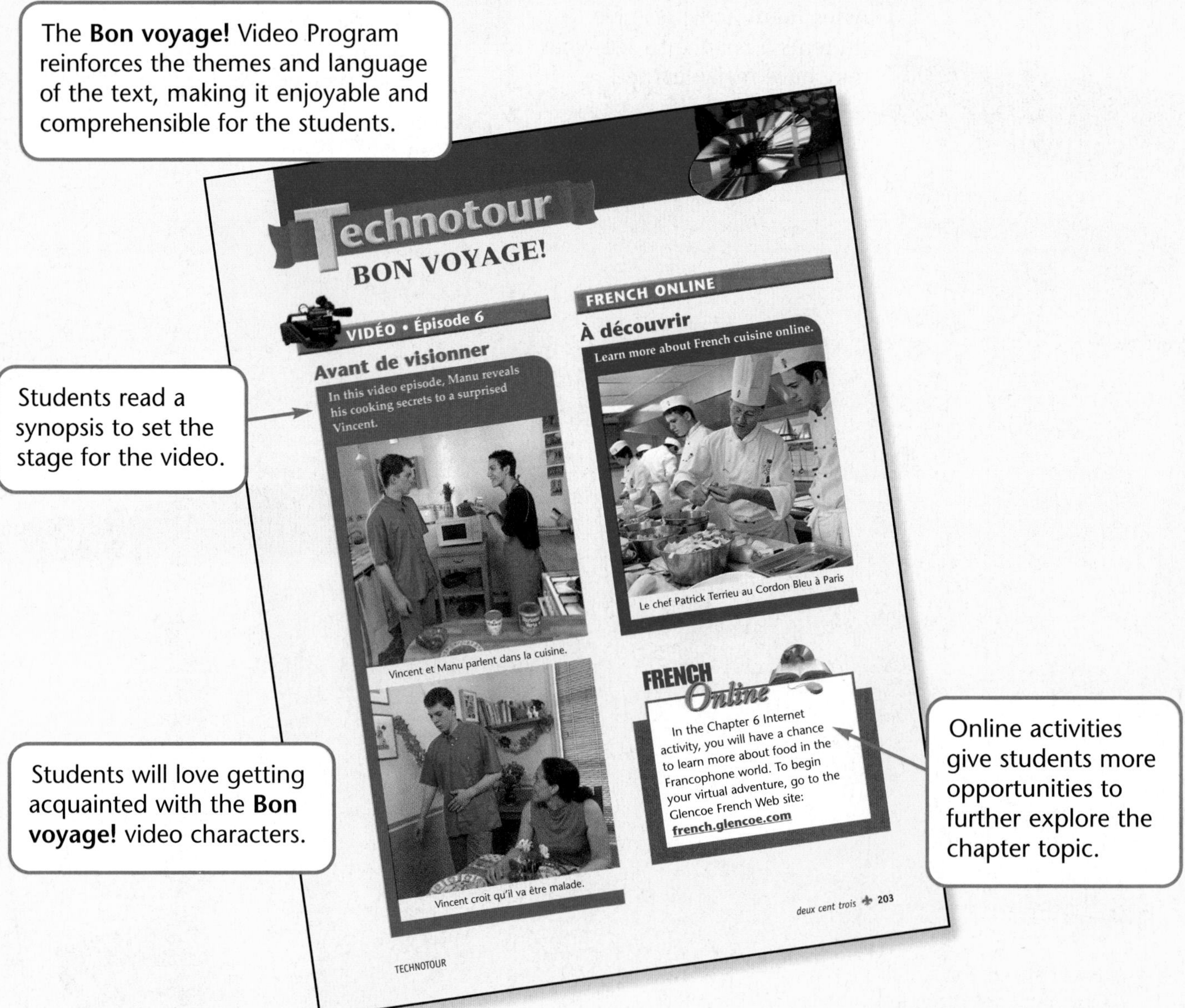

Technotour
BON VOYAGE!

VIDÉO • Épisode 6

Avant de visionner

In this video episode, Manu reveals his cooking secrets to a surprised Vincent.

Vincent et Manu parlent dans la cuisine.

Vincent croit qu'il va être malade.

FRENCH ONLINE

À découvrir

Learn more about French cuisine online.

Le chef Patrick Terrieu au Cordon Bleu à Paris

FRENCH Online

In the Chapter 6 Internet activity, you will have a chance to learn more about food in the Francophone world. To begin your virtual adventure, go to the Glencoe French Web site: **french.glencoe.com**

TECHNOTOUR

deux cent trois ✤ 203

Cultivate an appreciation of the diverse Francophone world with National Geographic Reflets

Itinerary for Success

- ✓ Exposure to Francophone culture
- ✓ Clear expectations and goals
- ✓ Thematic, contextualized vocabulary
- ✓ Useful and thematically linked structure
- ✓ Progressive practice
- ✓ Real-life conversation
- ✓ Cultural readings in the target language
- ✓ Connections to other disciplines . . . in French!
- ✓ Recycling and review
- ✓ **National Geographic Society** panoramas of the Francophone world

Students learn to appreciate the expanse of the Francophone world.

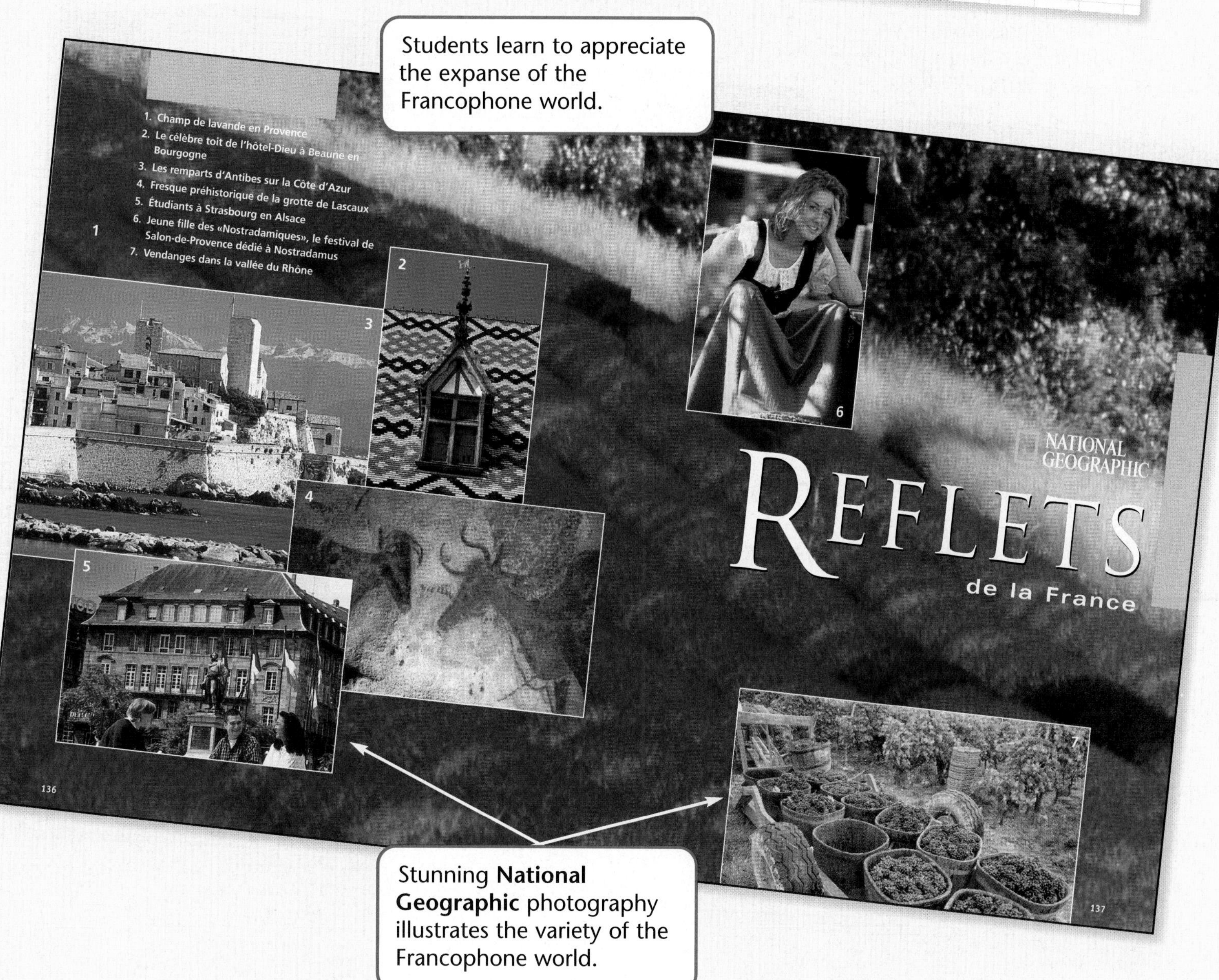

Stunning **National Geographic** photography illustrates the variety of the Francophone world.

Enhance appreciation of literature and culture

Itinerary for Success

- ✓ Exposure to Francophone culture
- ✓ Clear expectations and goals
- ✓ Thematic, contextualized vocabulary
- ✓ Useful and thematically linked structure
- ✓ Progressive practice
- ✓ Real-life conversation
- ✓ Cultural readings in the target language
- ✓ Connections to other disciplines . . . in French!
- ✓ Recycling and review
- ✓ **National Geographic Society** panoramas of the Francophone world

Literary Companion affords students yet another opportunity to apply their reading skills in French.

Literary selections present another view of Francophone culture.

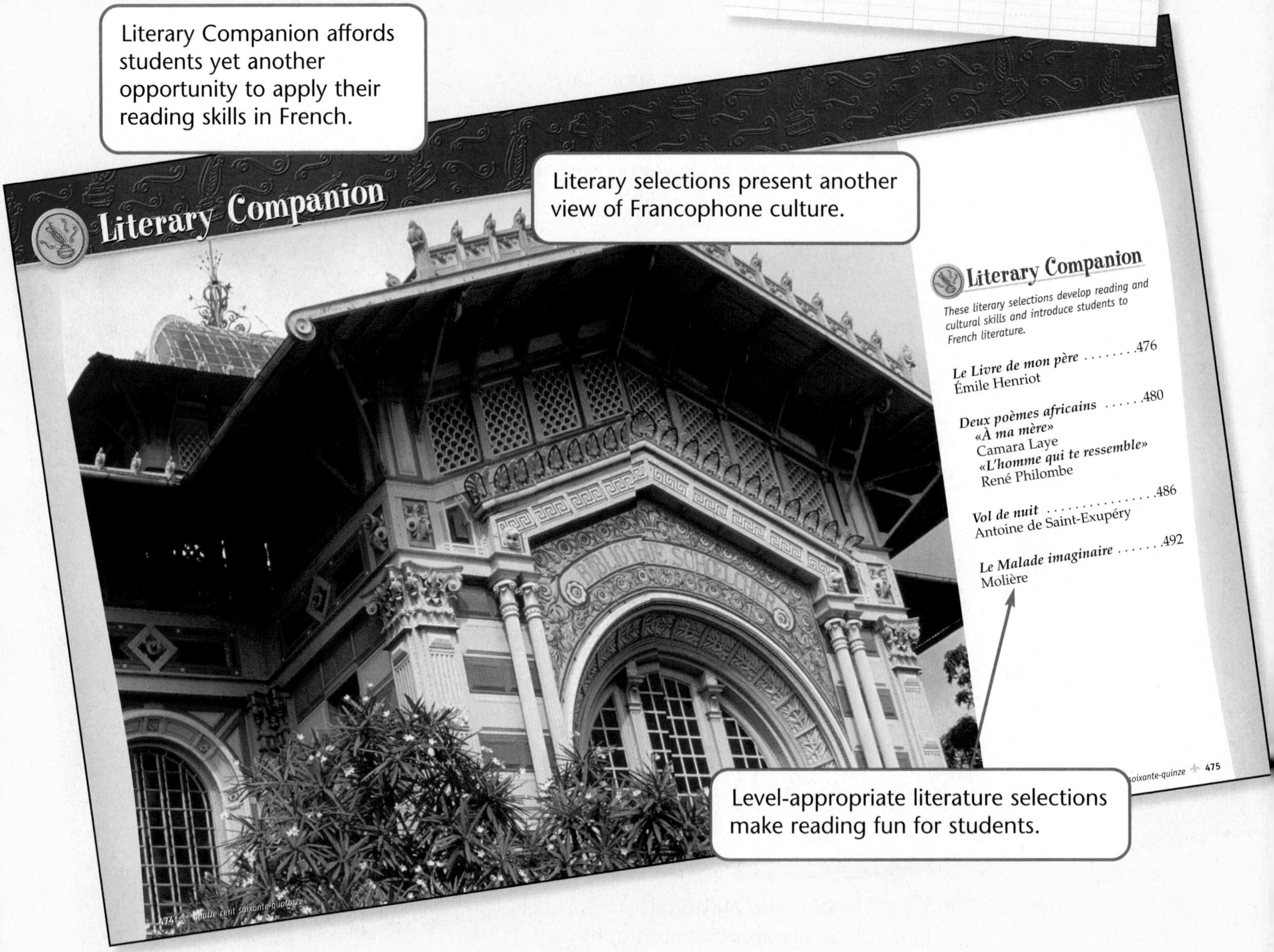

Literary Companion

Literary Companion

These literary selections develop reading and cultural skills and introduce students to French literature.

474 quatre cent soixante-quatorze

soixante-quinze 475

Level-appropriate literature selections make reading fun for students.

Bring French to life!

The **Bon voyage! Video Program** features teens from diverse parts of the Francophone world. The episodes follow the text thematically to aid comprehension and to reinforce what the students have learned. The **Video Activities Booklet** provides pre-viewing, viewing, and post-viewing activities for the students. It also contains the script for the entire video along with culture notes.

TPR Storytelling Booklet stories are written to reinforce the chapter themes and vocabulary. Once you have presented the chapter-specific story, your students will have fun acting it out and retelling it in their own words.

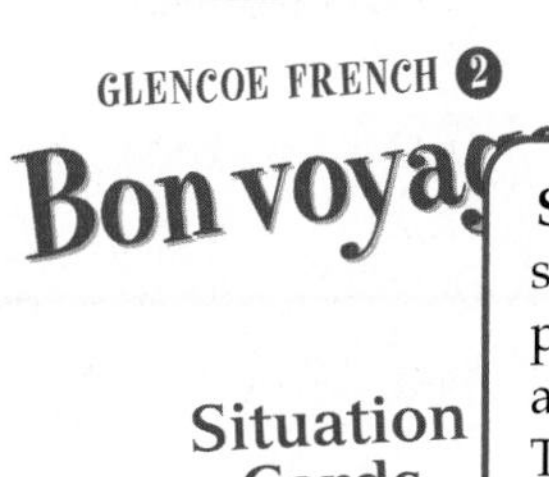

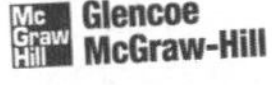

Situation Cards encourage students to communicate with a partner by suggesting a chapter-appropriate situation to discuss. The cards may be used for paired practice, assessment preparation, or assessment.

Interactive Conversation CD-ROM allows students to view the Conversation section of the text on video and to become an active participant in the conversation. They listen and record their own responses within the conversation.

Glencoe French Online gives students many opportunities to review, practice, and explore. There are chapter-related activities, online quizzes, and many links to Web sites throughout the vast Francophone world. Go to french.glencoe.com

Bon voyage! Resources

Assess what they have learned!

The MindJogger Videoquiz Program is a test preparation tool in gameshow format. Students "play" three rounds of the game to review the material they have learned in each chapter. Instructions for playing the game are included in the package.

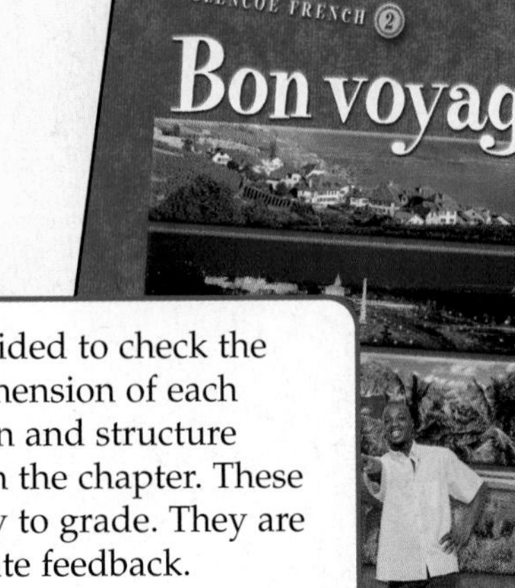

Quizzes are provided to check the students' comprehension of each vocabulary section and structure point presented in the chapter. These are short and easy to grade. They are ideal for immediate feedback.

Performance Assessment provides tasks such as interviews, research, presentations, and skits. Rubrics are provided to help you grade these reality-based tasks.

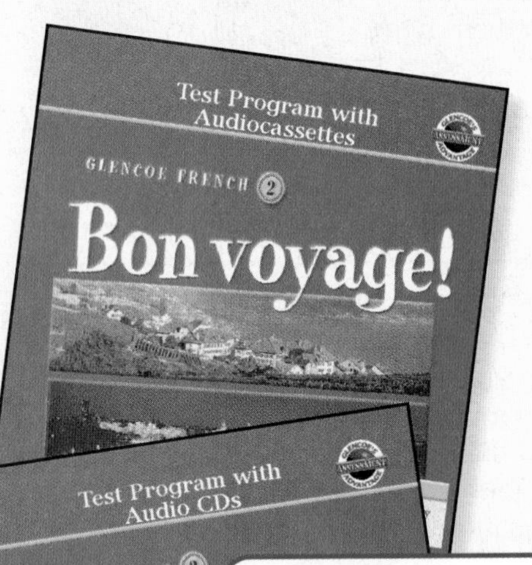

Test Booklet with Answer Key includes chapter tests for Reading, Writing, Listening, (an audio recording of the listening tests is available on CD or on cassette) and Speaking, which can be administered together or separately. In addition to the Chapter Tests, Unit Tests are included to follow each Revision section of the Student Edition. Also included are Chapter Proficiency Tests designed to measure the students' mastery on a more global level.

ExamView® Pro will allow you to choose from an existing bank of questions, edit them, or create your own test questions to make a test in a matter of minutes.

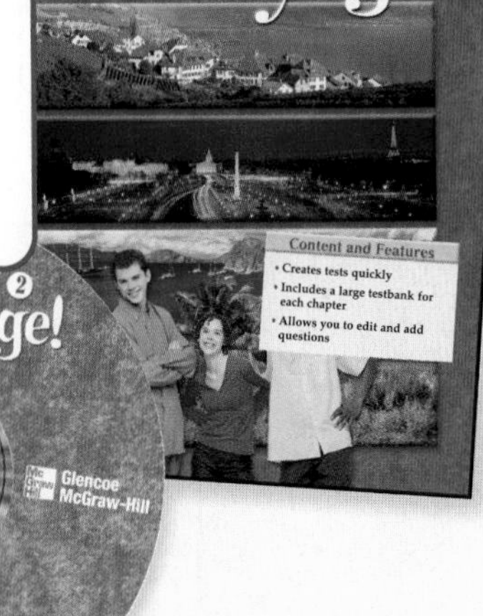

We can help make your job easier!

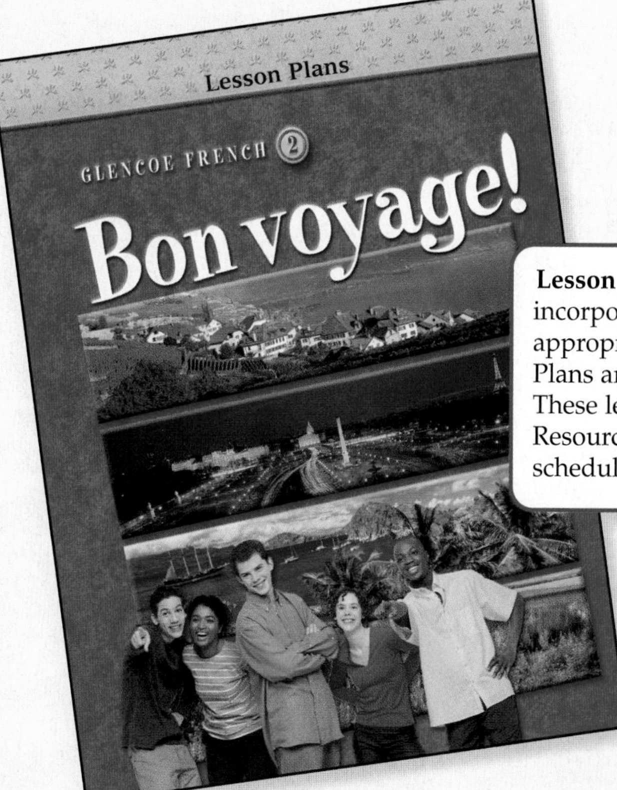

Lesson Plans are written for you. The lesson plans incorporate the Program Resources at their most appropriate point of use. Block Schedule Lesson Plans are provided for classes on the Block Schedule. These lesson plans also incorporate the Program Resources and are flexible for the various block-scheduling configurations.

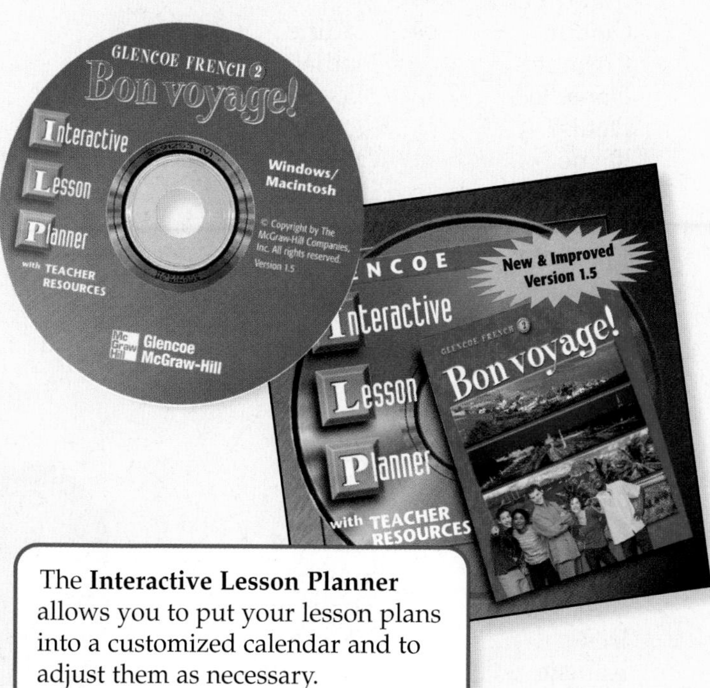

The **Interactive Lesson Planner** allows you to put your lesson plans into a customized calendar and to adjust them as necessary.

The **Bon voyage! Interactive Teacher Edition (ITE)** is your entire Teacher Wraparound Edition on disk. It includes your printed ancillaries as well. This tool will ease your preparation time and lighten your book bag.

French Names

The following are some French boys' and girls' names that you may wish to give to your students.

Garçons

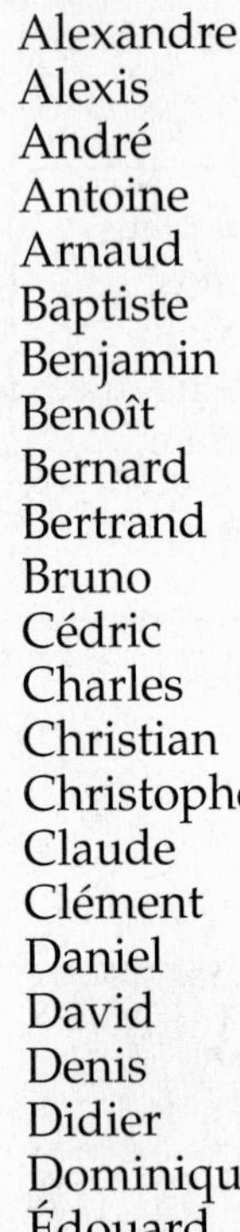
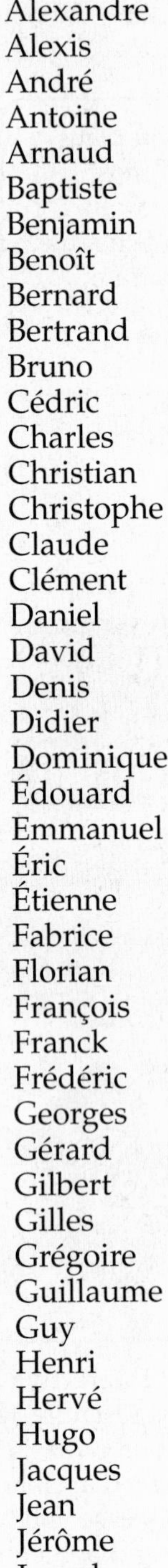

Alain
Albert
Alexandre
Alexis
André
Antoine
Arnaud
Baptiste
Benjamin
Benoît
Bernard
Bertrand
Bruno
Cédric
Charles
Christian
Christophe
Claude
Clément
Daniel
David
Denis
Didier
Dominique
Édouard
Emmanuel
Éric
Étienne
Fabrice
Florian
François
Franck
Frédéric
Georges
Gérard
Gilbert
Gilles
Grégoire
Guillaume
Guy
Henri
Hervé
Hugo
Jacques
Jean
Jérôme
Joseph
Julien
Laurent

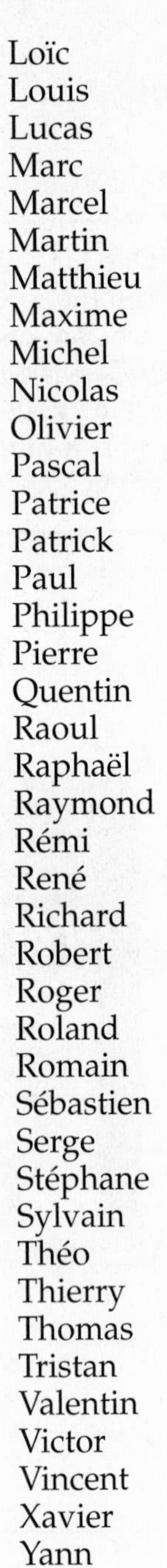

Loïc
Louis
Lucas
Marc
Marcel
Martin
Matthieu
Maxime
Michel
Nicolas
Olivier
Pascal
Patrice
Patrick
Paul
Philippe
Pierre
Quentin
Raoul
Raphaël
Raymond
Rémi
René
Richard
Robert
Roger
Roland
Romain
Sébastien
Serge
Stéphane
Sylvain
Théo
Thierry
Thomas
Tristan
Valentin
Victor
Vincent
Xavier
Yann
Yves

Filles

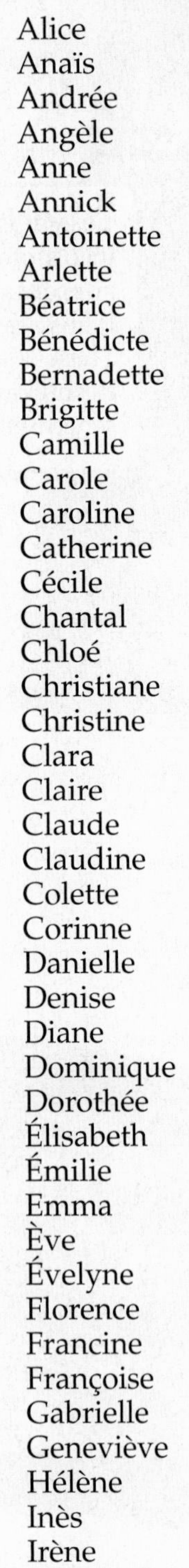

Alice
Anaïs
Andrée
Angèle
Anne
Annick
Antoinette
Arlette
Béatrice
Bénédicte
Bernadette
Brigitte
Camille
Carole
Caroline
Catherine
Cécile
Chantal
Chloé
Christiane
Christine
Clara
Claire
Claude
Claudine
Colette
Corinne
Danielle
Denise
Diane
Dominique
Dorothée
Élisabeth
Émilie
Emma
Ève
Évelyne
Florence
Francine
Françoise
Gabrielle
Geneviève
Hélène
Inès
Irène
Isabelle
Jacqueline
Janine
Jeanne

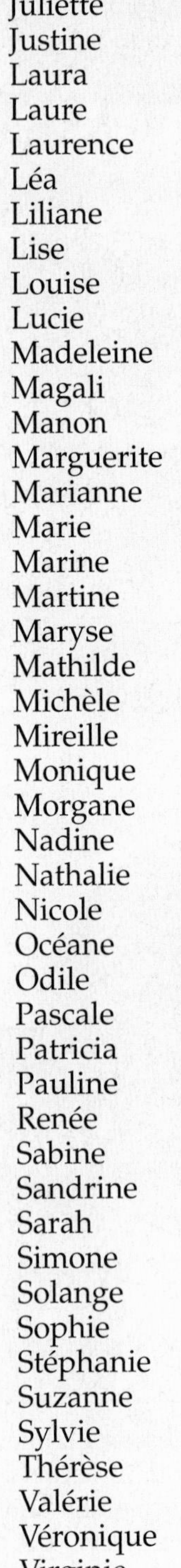

Julie
Juliette
Justine
Laura
Laure
Laurence
Léa
Liliane
Lise
Louise
Lucie
Madeleine
Magali
Manon
Marguerite
Marianne
Marie
Marine
Martine
Maryse
Mathilde
Michèle
Mireille
Monique
Morgane
Nadine
Nathalie
Nicole
Océane
Odile
Pascale
Patricia
Pauline
Renée
Sabine
Sandrine
Sarah
Simone
Solange
Sophie
Stéphanie
Suzanne
Sylvie
Thérèse
Valérie
Véronique
Virginie

Classroom Expressions

Below is a list of words and expressions frequently used when conducting a French class.

du papier	paper
une feuille de papier	sheet of paper
un cahier	notebook
un cahier d'exercices	workbook
un stylo	pen
un stylo-bille	ballpoint pen
un crayon	pencil
une gomme	(pencil) eraser
une craie	chalk
le tableau	chalkboard
une brosse	chalkboard eraser
la corbeille	wastebasket
un pupitre	desk
un rang	row
une chaise	chair
un écran	screen
un projecteur	projector
une cassette	cassette
un livre	book
une règle	ruler
un ordinateur	computer
une vidéo	video
un CD	CD

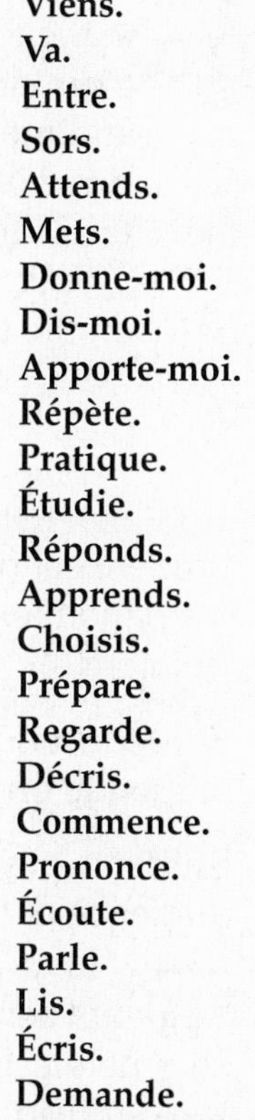

Viens.	**Venez.**	Come.
Va.	**Allez.**	Go.
Entre.	**Entrez.**	Enter.
Sors.	**Sortez.**	Leave.
Attends.	**Attendez.**	Wait.
Mets.	**Mettez.**	Put.
Donne-moi.	**Donnez-moi.**	Give me.
Dis-moi.	**Dites-moi.**	Tell me.
Apporte-moi.	**Apportez-moi.**	Bring me.
Répète.	**Répétez.**	Repeat.
Pratique.	**Pratiquez.**	Practice.
Étudie.	**Étudiez.**	Study.
Réponds.	**Répondez.**	Answer.
Apprends.	**Apprenez.**	Learn.
Choisis.	**Choisissez.**	Choose.
Prépare.	**Préparez.**	Prepare.
Regarde.	**Regardez.**	Look at.
Décris.	**Décrivez.**	Describe.
Commence.	**Commencez.**	Begin.
Prononce.	**Prononcez.**	Pronounce.
Écoute.	**Écoutez.**	Listen.
Parle.	**Parlez.**	Speak.
Lis.	**Lisez.**	Read.
Écris.	**Écrivez.**	Write.
Demande.	**Demandez.**	Ask.
Suis le modèle.	**Suivez le modèle.**	Follow the model.
Joue le rôle de...	**Jouez le rôle de...**	Take the part of . . .
Prends.	**Prenez.**	Take.
Ouvre.	**Ouvrez.**	Open.
Ferme.	**Fermez.**	Close.
Tourne la page.	**Tournez la page.**	Turn the page.
Efface.	**Effacez.**	Erase.
Continue.	**Continuez.**	Continue.
Assieds-toi.	**Asseyez-vous.**	Sit down.
Lève-toi.	**Levez-vous.**	Get up.
Lève la main.	**Levez la main.**	Raise your hand.
Tais-toi.	**Taisez-vous.**	Be quiet.
Fais attention.	**Faites attention.**	Pay attenion.

Attention.	Attention.
Attention, s'il vous plaît.	Your attention please.
Silence.	Quiet.
Encore.	Again.
Encore une fois.	Once again.
Un à un.	One at a time.
Tous ensemble.	All together.
À haute voix.	Out loud.
Plus haut, s'il vous plaît.	Louder, please.
En français.	In French.
En anglais.	In English.

Standards for Foreign Language Learning

Bon voyage! has been written to help you meet the Standards for Foreign Language Learning as set forth by ACTFL. The focus of the text is to provide students with the skills they need to create language for communication. Culture is integrated throughout the text, from the basic introduction of vocabulary to the photographic contributions of the National Geographic Society. Special attention has been given to meeting the standard of Connections with a reading in French in each chapter about another discipline. Linguistic and cultural comparisons are made throughout the text. Suggestions are made for activities that encourage students to use their language skills in their immediate community and more distant ones. Students who complete the **Bon voyage!** series are prepared to participate in the Francophone World.

Specific correlations to each chapter are provided on the teacher pages preceeding each chapter.

Communication

Communicate in Languages Other Than English	**Standard 1.1**	Students engage in conversations, provide and obtain information, express feelings and emotions, and exchange opinions.
	Standard 1.2	Students understand and interpret written and spoken language on a variety of topics.
	Standard 1.3	Students present information, concepts, and ideas to an audience of listeners or readers on a variety of topics.

Cultures

Gain Knowledge and Understanding of Other Cultures	**Standard 2.1**	Students demonstrate an understanding of the relationship between the practices and perspectives of the culture studied.
	Standard 2.2	Students demonstrate an understanding of the relationship between the products and perspectives of the culture studied.

Connections

Connect with Other Disciplines and Acquire Information	**Standard 3.1**	Students reinforce and further their knowledge of other disciplines through the foreign language.
	Standard 3.2	Students acquire information and recognize the distinctive viewpoints that are only available through the foreign language and its cultures.

Comparisons

Develop Insight into the Nature of Language and Culture	**Standard 4.1**	Students demonstrate understanding of the nature of language through comparisons of language studied and their own.
	Standard 4.2	Students demonstrate understanding of the concept of culture through comparisons of the cultures studied and their own.

Communities

Participate in Multilingual Communities at Home and Around the World	**Standard 5.1**	Students use the language both within and beyond the school setting.
	Standard 5.2	Students show evidence of becoming life-long learners by using the language for personal enjoyment and enrichment.

CHAPITRE  Les loisirs culturels

Objectifs

In this chapter you will learn to:

- ✔ *discuss movies, plays, and museums*
- ✔ *tell what you know and whom you know*
- ✔ *tell what happens to you or someone else*
- ✔ *refer to people and things already mentioned*
- ✔ *talk about some cultural activities in Paris*

CHAPITRE 2 La santé et la médecine

Objectifs

In this chapter you will learn to:

- ✔ *explain a minor illness to a doctor*
- ✔ *have a prescription filled at a pharmacy*
- ✔ *tell for whom something is done*
- ✔ *talk about some more activities*
- ✔ *give commands*
- ✔ *refer to people, places, and things already mentioned*
- ✔ *discuss medical services in France*

CHAPITRE 3 Les télécommunications

Objectifs

In this chapter you will learn to:

- ✔ *talk about computers, e-mail, the Internet, faxes, and telephones*
- ✔ *talk about habitual and continuous actions in the past*
- ✔ *narrate in the past*
- ✔ *discuss today's telecommunications*

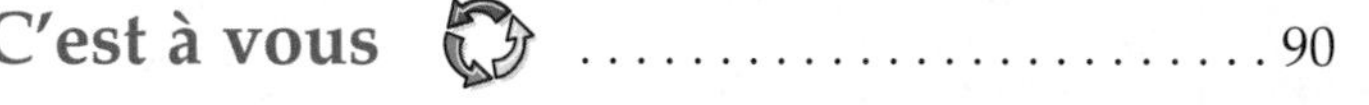

CHAPITRE  Des voyages intéressants

Objectifs

In this chapter you will learn to:

- ✔ *talk about train travel*
- ✔ *talk about air travel*
- ✔ *describe past events*
- ✔ *identify cities, countries, and continents*
- ✔ *discuss old and modern trains in France*

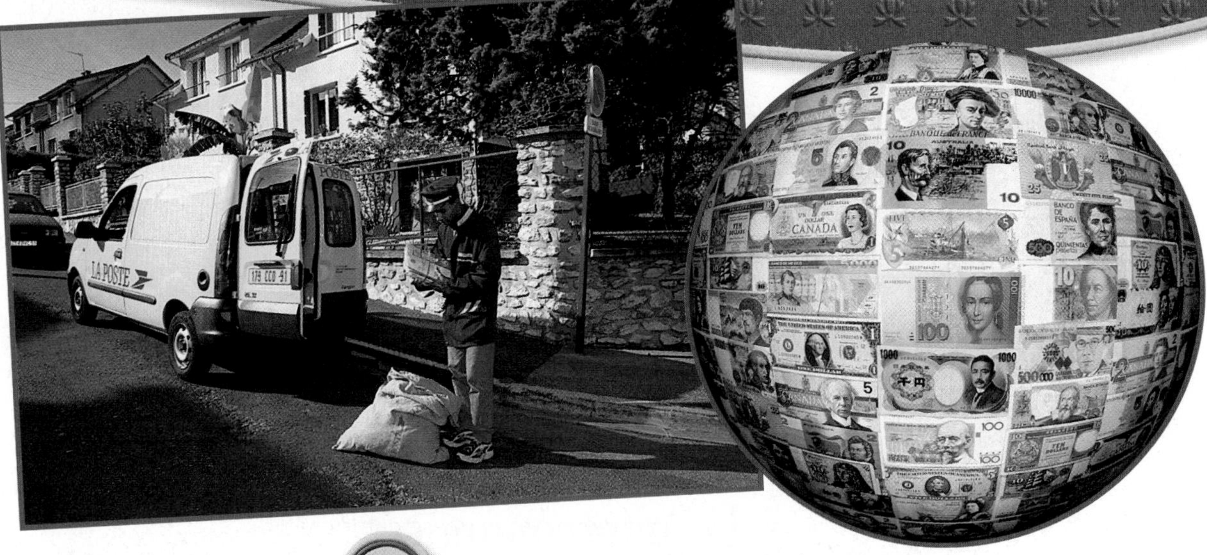

CHAPITRE 5 La banque et la poste

Objectifs

In this chapter you will learn to:

- ✔ *talk about using the services of the bank*
- ✔ *use words and expressions related to postal services*
- ✔ *give more information in one sentence*
- ✔ *refer to people and things already mentioned*
- ✔ *tell what you and others do for one another*
- ✔ *make negative statements*
- ✔ *talk about teen spending habits*

CHAPITRE 6 La gastronomie

Objectifs

In this chapter you will learn to:

- ✔ *talk about foods and food preparation*
- ✔ *describe future events*
- ✔ *refer to people and things already mentioned*
- ✔ *tell what you have others do*
- ✔ *discuss the cuisine of various French provinces*

CHAPITRE  La voiture et la route

Objectifs

In this chapter you will learn to:

- ✔ *talk about cars and driving*
- ✔ *give directions on the road*
- ✔ *talk about what would happen under certain conditions*
- ✔ *describe future events*
- ✔ *refer to something already mentioned*
- ✔ *talk about driving and highways in France*

CHAPITRE 8 Un accident et l'hôpital

Objectifs

In this chapter you will learn to:

- ✔ *talk about accidents and medical problems*
- ✔ *talk about emergency room procedures*
- ✔ *ask different types of questions*
- ✔ *tell people what to do*
- ✔ *compare people and things*
- ✔ *talk about a medical emergency in France*

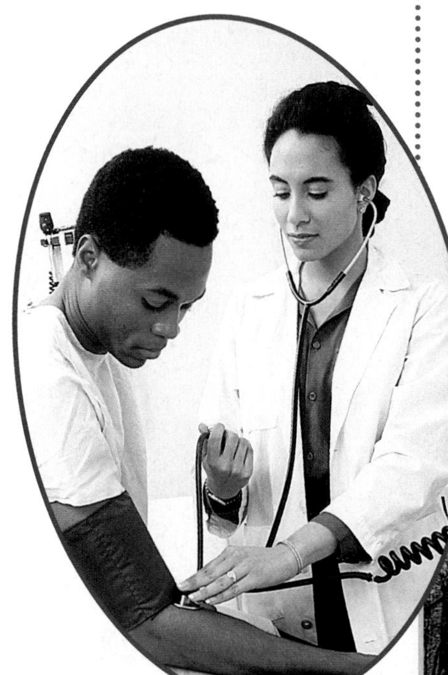

CHAPITRE 9 L'hôtel

Objectifs

In this chapter you will learn to:

- ✔ *check into and out of a hotel*
- ✔ *ask for things you may need while at a hotel*
- ✔ *talk about past actions*
- ✔ *refer to previously mentioned places*
- ✔ *talk about people and things already mentioned*
- ✔ *describe how you do things*
- ✔ *talk about hotels in France*

CHAPITRE  Les transports en commun

Objectifs

In this chapter you will learn to:

- ✔ *talk about public transportation*
- ✔ *request information formally and informally*
- ✔ *tell what you and others have just done*
- ✔ *find out how long someone has been doing something*
- ✔ *talk about taking the bus and subway in Paris*

CHAPITRE 11 À la ville et à la campagne

Objectifs

In this chapter you will learn to:

- ✔ *talk about life in the city and give directions*
- ✔ *talk about life in the country*
- ✔ *ask questions to distinguish between two or more people or things*
- ✔ *describe some more activities*
- ✔ *talk about life on a farm in France*

CHAPITRE 12 Les fêtes

Objectifs

In this chapter you will learn to:

- ✔ *talk about holidays and celebrations*
- ✔ *talk about things that may or may not happen*
- ✔ *express what you wish, hope, or would like others to do*
- ✔ *discuss some family celebrations*

CHAPITRE  Le savoir-vivre

Objectifs

In this chapter you will learn to:

- ✔ *talk about social etiquette*
- ✔ *introduce people to each other*
- ✔ *describe some feelings*
- ✔ *express opinions*
- ✔ *talk about more things that may or may not happen*
- ✔ *express emotional reactions to what others do*
- ✔ *compare etiquette in France and the United States*

CHAPITRE 14 Les professions et les métiers

Objectifs

In this chapter you will learn to:

- ✔ *talk about professions*
- ✔ *apply for a job*
- ✔ *express doubt*
- ✔ *express wishes about yourself and others*
- ✔ *express certainty and uncertainty*
- ✔ *discuss the advantages of learning French for future employment*

Literary Companion

xix

Handbook

Guide to Symbols

Throughout **Bon voyage!** you will see these symbols, or icons. They will tell you how to best use the particular part of the chapter or activity they accompany. Following is a key to help you understand these symbols.

Audio Link This icon indicates conversations in the chapter that are recorded on compact disk format and/or audiocassette.

Recycling This icon indicates sections that review knowledge from previous chapters and reading sections.

Paired Activity This icon indicates sections that you can read aloud and practice together in groups of two.

Group Activity This icon indicates sections that you can read aloud and practice together in groups of three or more.

Encore Plus This icon indicates additional practice activities that review knowledge from current chapters and reading sections.

Allez-y! This icon indicates the end of new material in each section and the beginning of the recombination section at the end of the chapter.

Literary Companion This icon appears in the review lessons to let you know that you are prepared to do the literature selection indicated if you wish.

Interactive CD-ROM This icon indicates that the material is also on an Interactive CD-ROM.

Métro

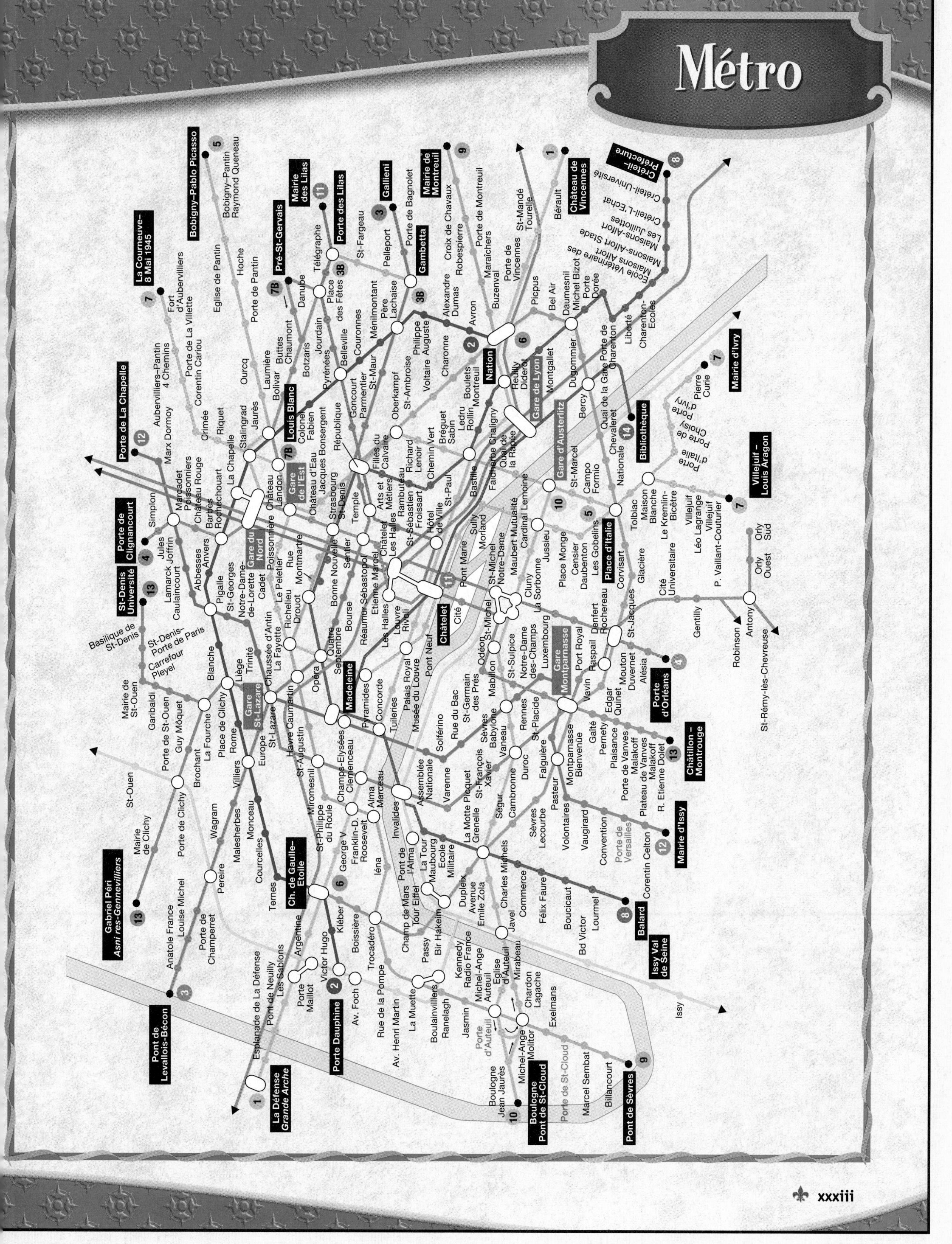

xxxiii

Le Canada

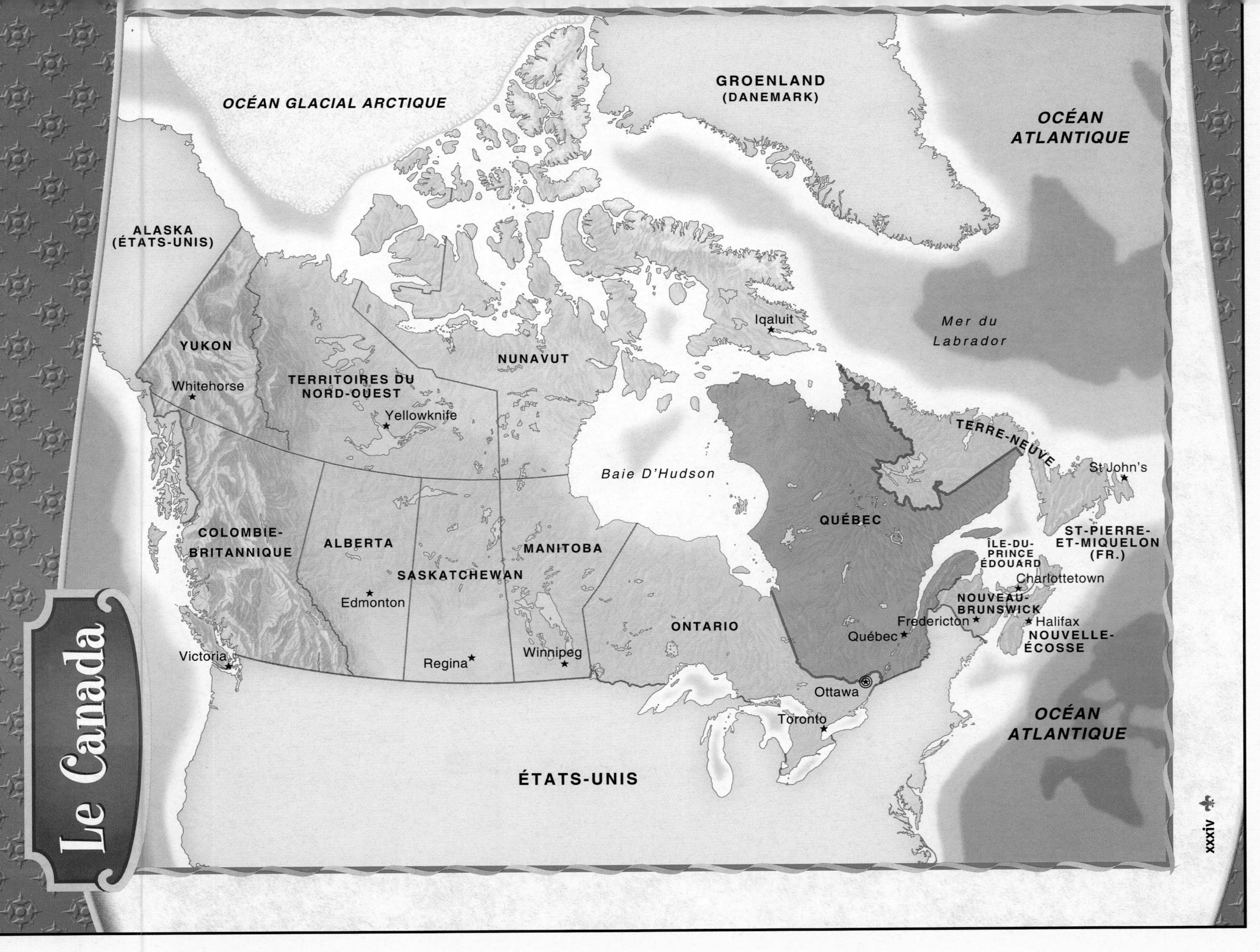

OCÉAN GLACIAL ARCTIQUE
GROENLAND (DANEMARK)
OCÉAN ATLANTIQUE
ALASKA (ÉTATS-UNIS)
YUKON
Whitehorse
TERRITOIRES DU NORD-OUEST
Yellowknife
NUNAVUT
Iqaluit
Mer du Labrador
TERRE-NEUVE
St John's
Baie D'Hudson
QUÉBEC
COLOMBIE-BRITANNIQUE
ALBERTA
SASKATCHEWAN
MANITOBA
ÎLE-DU-PRINCE ÉDOUARD
ST-PIERRE-ET-MIQUELON (FR.)
Charlottetown
NOUVEAU-BRUNSWICK
Fredericton
Halifax
NOUVELLE-ÉCOSSE
Edmonton
ONTARIO
Québec
Victoria
Regina
Winnipeg
Ottawa
Toronto
OCÉAN ATLANTIQUE
ÉTATS-UNIS

L'Afrique

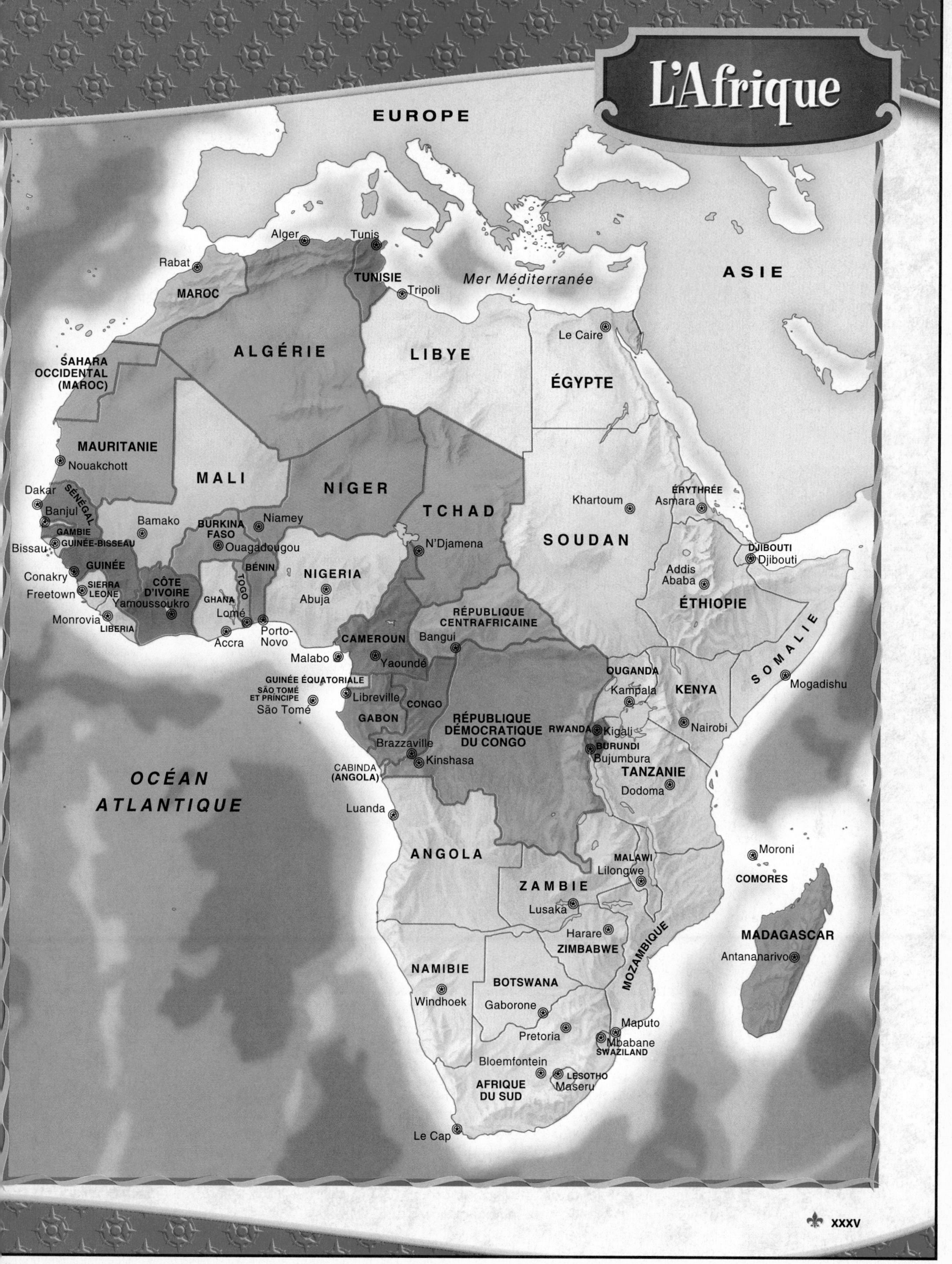
EUROPE
ASIE
Mer Méditerranée
OCÉAN
ATLANTIQUE
Alger
Tunis
Rabat
MAROC
TUNISIE
Tripoli
Le Caire
ALGÉRIE
LIBYE
ÉGYPTE
SAHARA
OCCIDENTAL
(MAROC)
MAURITANIE
Nouakchott
MALI
NIGER
TCHAD
SOUDAN
Khartoum
ÉRYTHRÉE
Asmara
Dakar
SÉNÉGAL
Banjul
GAMBIE
Bissau
GUINÉE-BISSEAU
Bamako
BURKINA
FASO
Niamey
Ouagadougou
N'Djamena
DJIBOUTI
Djibouti
GUINÉE
Conakry
SIERRA
LEONE
Freetown
CÔTE
D'IVOIRE
Yamoussoukro
BÉNIN
TOGO
GHANA
NIGERIA
Abuja
Addis
Ababa
ÉTHIOPIE
Monrovia
LIBERIA
Lomé
Accra
Porto-
Novo
RÉPUBLIQUE
CENTRAFRICAINE
Bangui
CAMEROUN
Yaoundé
Malabo
GUINÉE ÉQUATORIALE
SÃO TOMÉ
ET PRINCIPE
São Tomé
Libreville
GABON
CONGO
RÉPUBLIQUE
DÉMOCRATIQUE
DU CONGO
OUGANDA
Kampala
KENYA
SOMALIE
Mogadishu
Nairobi
RWANDA
Kigali
BURUNDI
Bujumbura
TANZANIE
Dodoma
Brazzaville
Kinshasa
CABINDA
(ANGOLA)
Luanda
ANGOLA
Moroni
COMORES
MALAWI
Lilongwe
ZAMBIE
Lusaka
Harare
ZIMBABWE
MOZAMBIQUE
MADAGASCAR
Antananarivo
NAMIBIE
Windhoek
BOTSWANA
Gaborone
Pretoria
Maputo
Mbabane
SWAZILAND
Bloemfontein
LESOTHO
Maseru
AFRIQUE
DU SUD
Le Cap

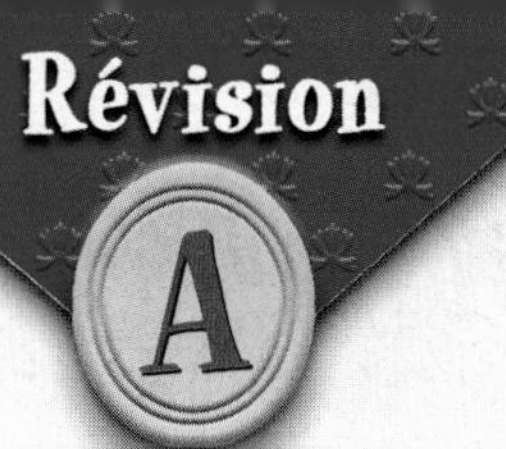

Preview

This review chapter covers vocabulary needed to describe people and school. These topics were first presented in **Bon voyage! Level 1.** The agreement of adjectives, the present tense of the verbs **être** and **aller,** and the contractions with **à** and **de** are also reviewed.

National Standards

Communication

In Review Chapter A, students will communicate in spoken and written French on the following topics:

- Describing people
- School activities

Students will also learn to narrate present events. They will obtain and provide information and engage in conversations about people and school as they fulfill the chapter objectives listed on this page.

Révision A

Les copains et l'école

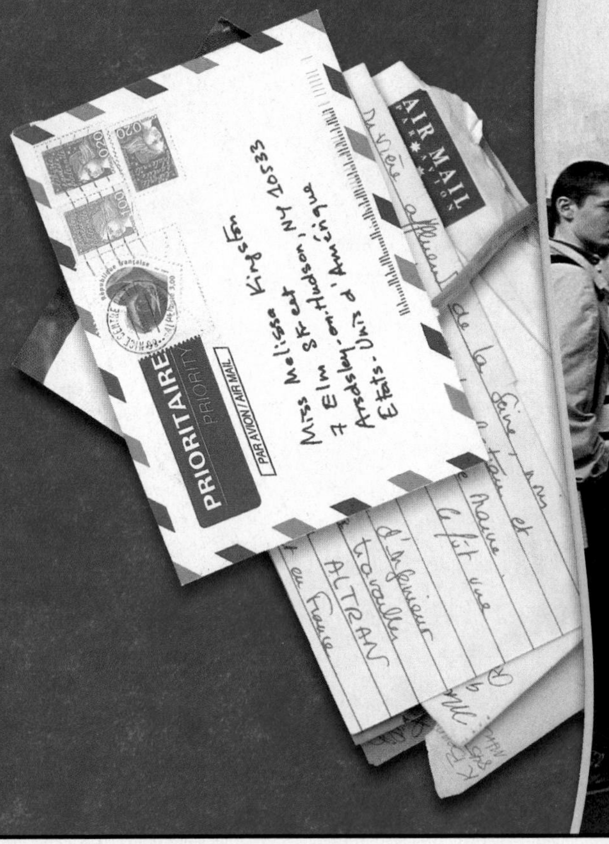

The **Glencoe Foreign Language Web site** (french.glencoe.com) offers several options that enable you and your students to experience the French-speaking world via the Internet:

- Games and puzzles afford students another opportunity to practice the material learned in a particular chapter.
- The *Enrichment* section offers students an opportunity to visit Web sites related to the theme of the chapter for more information on a particular topic.
- Online *Chapter Quizzes* offer students an opportunity to prepare for a chapter test.
- Visit our virtual **Café** for more opportunities to practice and explore the French-speaking world.

Révision

Spotlight on Culture

Photograph The Lycée Charlemagne is a typical Parisian lycée with a very good academic reputation.

Learning from Photos

(page R1) Have students describe as many students as they can in the photo.

Vocabulaire

Resource Manager

Workbook, page R1
Test Booklet
ExamView Pro®

Bellringer Review

Use BRR Transparency R.1 or write the following on the board.
Make a list of words that can be used to describe a person.

Presentation

Step 1 Have students open their books and repeat the sentences about Sandrine and Aurélien after you.

Step 2 Have the students identify the descriptive words used in the sentences.

Attention!

When students are doing the activities, accept any answer that makes sense. The purpose of these activities is to have students use the new vocabulary. They are not factual recall activities. Thus, it is not necessary for students to remember specific factual information from the vocabulary presentation when answering.

Vocabulaire

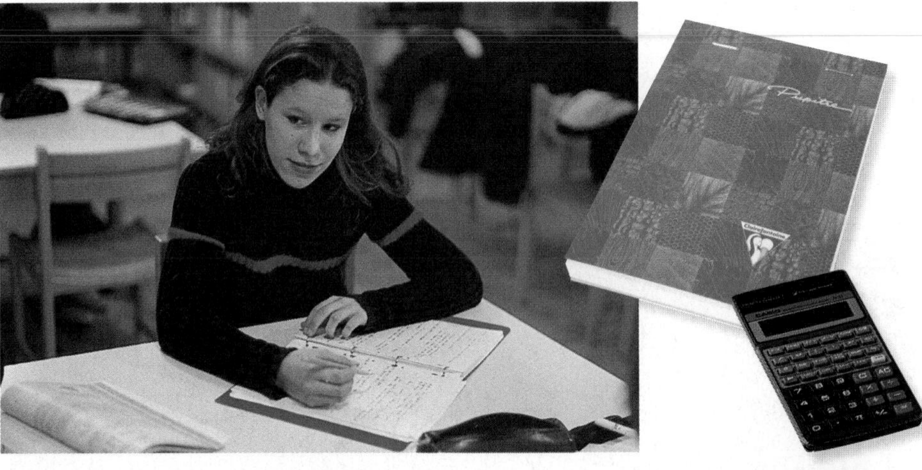

Voilà Sandrine.
Sandrine est française. Elle n'est pas américaine.
Elle est très intelligente.
Elle est élève au lycée Louis-le-Grand à Paris.
Elle va au lycée Louis-le-Grand.

Aurélien et Sandrine sont copains.
Ils vont tous les deux au même lycée.
Aurélien et Sandrine sont très amusants.

1 Historiette Une fille française

Inventez des réponses.

1. Caroline est française?
2. Elle est de Paris, la capitale de la France?
3. Elle est élève au lycée Louis-le-Grand?
4. Elle va au lycée Louis-le-Grand?
5. Caroline est intelligente?
6. Les copains de Caroline sont intelligents aussi?
7. Ils sont amusants?
8. Ils vont tous au même lycée?

Des copains au lycée

2 Historiette Guillaume

Répondez d'après les indications.

1. Guillaume est de quelle nationalité? (américain)
2. Il est d'où? (de New York)
3. Qui est élève? (Guillaume)
4. Il est élève où? (dans une école secondaire à New York)
5. Il va à l'école à quelle heure le matin? (à sept heures et demie)
6. Comment est Guillaume? (intelligent et amusant)

Révision A

Historiette Each time **Historiette** appears, it means that the answers to the activity form a short story. Encourage students to look at the title of the **Historiette,** since it can help them do the activity.

2 Expansion: Have students rewrite the questions in this activity in order to ask questions about a student in the class.

Writing Development

Have students write the answers to Activities 1 and 2 in paragraph form.

Learning from Photos

(pages R2–R3) Have students describe the students in the photos. Don't restrict them to adjectives; see if they can recall any clothing and colors, for example.

Reaching All Students

Additional Practice Have students make up questions about Sandrine or Sandrine and Aurélien to ask you or classmates.

Have students make up false statements about Guillaume. Their classmates will correct these statements.

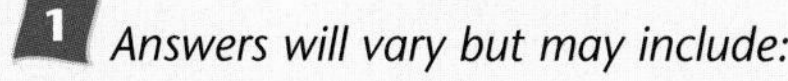

Answers to Révision

1 *Answers will vary but may include:*

1. Oui, Caroline est française.
2. Oui, elle est de Paris, la capitale de la France.
3. Oui, elle est élève au lycée Louis-le-Grand.
4. Oui, elle va au lycée Louis-le-Grand.
5. Oui, elle est intelligente.
6. Oui, ils sont intelligents aussi.
7. Oui, ils sont amusants.
8. Oui, ils vont tous au même lycée.

2

1. Guillaume est américain.
2. Il est de New York.
3. Guillaume est élève.
4. Il est élève dans une école secondaire à New York.
5. Il va à l'école à sept heures et demie.
6. Guillaume est intelligent et amusant.

Révision A

Conversation

Resource Manager

Workbook, page R1
Test Booklet

Presentation

Step 1 Review the expressions used for greeting people. Have the class repeat the conversation after you.

Step 2 Call on two students to read the conversation to the class.

Conversation

De bons copains

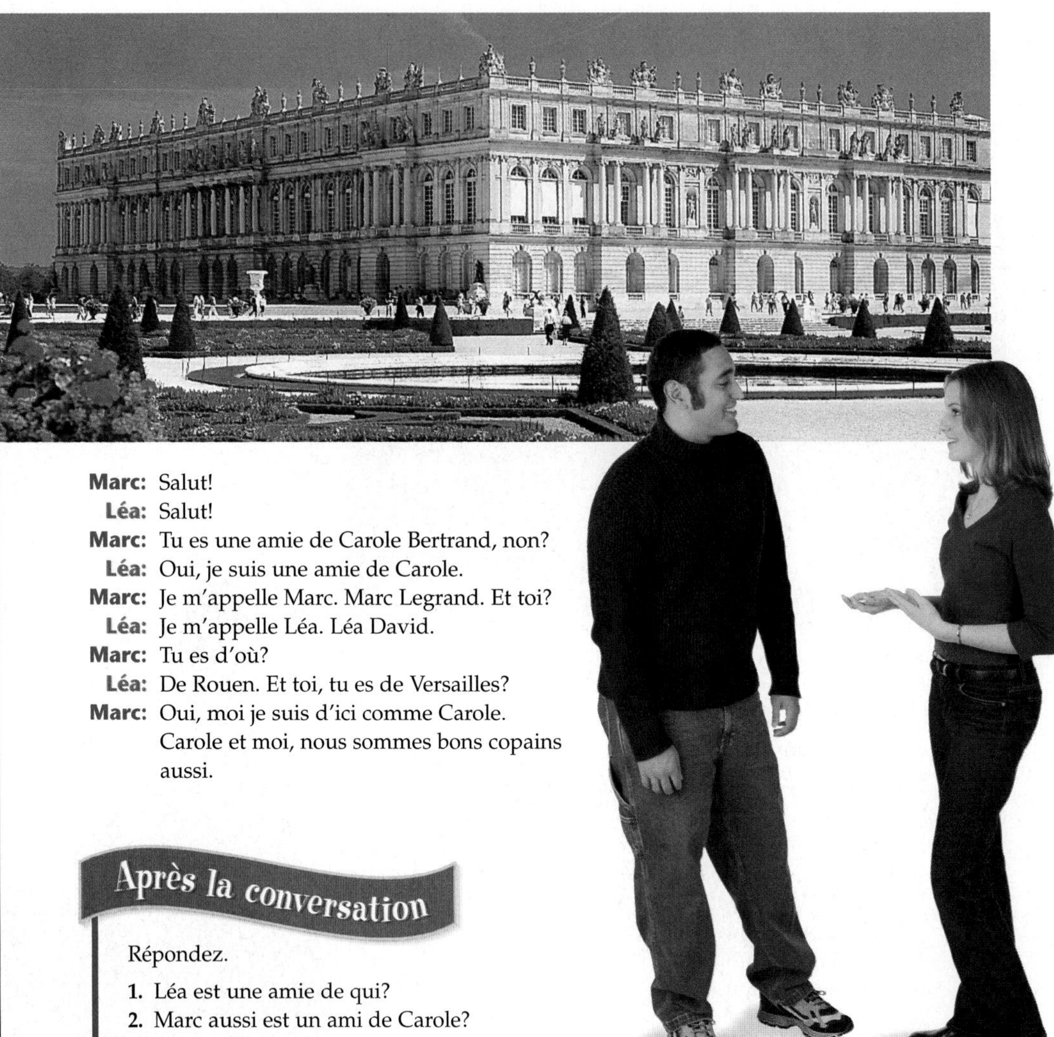

Marc: Salut!
Léa: Salut!
Marc: Tu es une amie de Carole Bertrand, non?
Léa: Oui, je suis une amie de Carole.
Marc: Je m'appelle Marc. Marc Legrand. Et toi?
Léa: Je m'appelle Léa. Léa David.
Marc: Tu es d'où?
Léa: De Rouen. Et toi, tu es de Versailles?
Marc: Oui, moi je suis d'ici comme Carole. Carole et moi, nous sommes bons copains aussi.

Après la conversation

Répondez.

1. Léa est une amie de qui?
2. Marc aussi est un ami de Carole?
3. Léa est d'où?
4. Et Marc et Carole, ils sont d'où?

Answers to Après la conversation

1. Léa est une amie de Carole Bertrand.
2. Oui, Marc aussi est un ami de Carole.
3. Léa est de Rouen.
4. Ils sont de Versailles.

Structure

L'accord des adjectifs

1. Adjectives must agree with the noun they describe or modify. Review the following.

	Féminin	Masculin
Singulier	une fille intelligente une amie timide	un garçon intelligent un ami timide
Pluriel	des filles intelligentes des amies timides	des garçons intelligents des amis timides

2. Note that adjectives such as **intelligent** that end in a consonant in the masculine form, change pronunciation in the feminine and have four written forms. Adjectives that end in **e,** such as **timide,** do not change pronunciation and have only two written forms.

Julie Décrivez Julie.

Les copains Décrivez les copains.

Julie Latour

Les copains

Révision A

Structure

Resource Manager

Workbook, pages R2–R6
Test Booklet
ExamView Pro®

Bellringer Review

Use BRR Transparency R.2 or write the following on the board.
Describe the student sitting closest to you.

Presentation

L'accord des adjectifs

Step 1 Read Item 1 to the class.

Step 2 Write the adjectives in the chart on the board. Cross out the **e** at the end of **intelligente** and remind students that the pronunciation changes. Have them repeat **intelligente/intelligent** after you. Then ask them what the difference is in pronunciation.

Step 3 Explain to students that adjectives that end in a consonant have four forms and those that end in **e** have two forms.

3 and 4 Encourage students to say as much as they can when doing these activities. After students do them orally, you may wish to have them write out their answers.

Note: Here is a list of some of the adjectives the students have learned through Chapter 7 of **Bon voyage! Level 1: petit, grand, brun, blond, amusant, patient, intelligent, intéressant, sympathique, timide, énergique, égoïste, dynamique, populaire, sociable, enthousiaste, français, américain, difficile, facile, strict, fort, mauvais, beau, nouveau, vieux, large, serré, habillé, sport, joli, favori.**

Answers to Révision

3 *Answers will vary but may include:*
Julie est une fille intelligente. Elle est française. Elle n'est pas américaine. Elle est élève dans un lycée français. Elle est amusante.

4 *Answers will vary but may include:*
Les copains sont amusants. Ils sont élèves au lycée Louis-le-Grand. Ils sont français. Ils sont intelligents et ils sont sympas aussi.

Révision A

Bellringer Review

Use BRR Transparency R.3 or write the following on the board.
Write five sentences telling where you like to go.

Presentation

Les verbes **être** et **aller**

Step 1 Have students repeat the verb forms after you.

Step 2 Remind students to make the liaison in **on est, vous êtes, nous allons, vous allez.**

Step 3 Have students read the example sentences after you.

5 Call on two students with good pronunciation to read the conversation in this exercise to the class.
Expansion: Call on a student to retell the story of the conversation in his or her own words.

Les verbes **être** et **aller**

1. Review the forms of the verbs **être** *(to be)* and **aller** *(to go)*.

ÊTRE	
je suis	nous sommes
tu es	vous_z_êtes
il/elle/on_n_est	ils/elles sont

ALLER	
je vais	nous_z_allons
tu vas	vous_z_allez
il/elle/on va	ils/elles vont

2. To make a sentence negative, you put **ne (n')... pas** around the verb.

Je suis française.	**Je ne suis pas américaine.**
Fabien est amusant.	**Il n'est pas timide.**

5 **Paul est de Montréal.** Répétez la conversation.

Maude: Bonjour Paul, ça va?
Paul: Ça va. Et toi?
Maude: Ça va... Paul, tu es américain, non?
Paul: Non, je suis canadien.
Maude: Ah oui, tu es d'où?
Paul: De Montréal.
Maude: Et tu vas à l'université à Montréal?
Paul: Non, je suis toujours à l'école secondaire.

6 **Historiette** **Américain ou canadien?**
Répondez d'après la conversation.

1. Paul est américain?
2. Il est de quelle nationalité?
3. Il est de quelle ville?
4. Il va à l'université?

Un lycée à Montréal

Answers to Révision

5 *Students will repeat the conversation.*

6

1. Non, il n'est pas américain.
2. Il est canadien.
3. Il est de Montréal.
4. Non, il ne va pas à l'université. Il est toujours à l'école secondaire.

7 **Moi!** Donnez des réponses personnelles.

1. Tu t'appelles comment?
2. Tu es d'où?
3. Tu es de quelle nationalité?
4. Tu vas à quelle école?
5. Tu vas à l'école avec des copains?
6. Tes copains et toi, vous allez à l'école à pied ou en car scolaire?
7. Où est votre école?
8. Comment sont les professeurs?

Des copains à Pointe-à-Pitre

8 **Historiette** **Au restaurant**

Complétez en utilisant le verbe **être** ou **aller.**

1. C'___ un petit restaurant. Il ___ vraiment bon.
2. Les serveurs ___ vietnamiens.
3. La cuisine vietnamienne ___ délicieuse.
4. Les copains de Mélanie ___ au restaurant.
5. Qui ___ demander l'addition au restaurant?
6. Qui ___ payer?
7. Vous ___ laisser un pourboire?

Un restaurant vietnamien à Paris

7 It is recommended that you do this activity once orally with books closed. **Expansion:** Call on a student to say as much as possible about his or her school.

8 This activity is more difficult than the preceding activities because students must determine which verb to use in addition to using the correct form.

Reaching All Students

Additional Practice Have students work in pairs. One student describes a famous person and the other tries to guess who it is.

Read the following to the class or write it on the board or on a transparency:

Fais une liste des caractéristiques que tu cherches dans un copain/une copine et que tu considères comme importantes.

Learning from Photos

(pages R7 left) Pointe-à-Pitre is the major city of Guadeloupe, **un departement français d'outre mer (un D.O.M.)** in the Caribbean.

(page R7 right) Ask the students the following questions about the photo: **C'est quelle sorte de restaurant? Le restaurant est en France? Il y a des restaurants vietnamiens dans ta ville? Tu aimes la cuisine vietnamienne? Tu aimes quelle sorte de cuisine?**

Vietnamese restaurants are as popular in France as are Chinese restaurants in the United States.

Answers to Révision

7 *Answers will vary but may include:*

1. Je m'appelle ___.
2. Je suis de ___.
3. Je suis américain(e).
4. Je vais à l'école ___.
5. Oui, je vais à l'école avec des copains.
6. Nous allons à l'école en car scolaire.
7. Notre école est dans la rue ___.
8. Les professeurs sont intelligents et sympas.

8

1. est, est
2. sont
3. est
4. vont
5. va
6. va
7. allez

Bellringer Review

Use BRR Transparency R.4 or write the following on the board.
Make a list of everything you associate with the following places.
l'école **le restaurant**

Presentation

Les contractions

Step 1 Write the contractions on the board.

Step 2 Have students read the example sentences aloud.

Step 3 Since the **au** and **du** forms present the greatest problem, you may wish to start by asking the following simple questions: **Tu vas au parc? Tu vas au restaurant? Tu vas au lycée? Tu vas au magasin? Tu vas au marché? Tu habites près du parc? Tu habites près du restaurant? Tu habites près du lycée? Tu habites près du marché?**

9 and **10** It is recommended that you go over the activities in class before assigning them for homework.

Learning from Photos

(page R8) Have students make up a dialogue between the teachers and the students in the photos.

(page R8 bottom) Ask the students the following questions regarding the photo:
Le prof est intéressant?
Les élèves aiment le cours?
Les élèves passent un examen?
Que font les élèves?

Les contractions

Le prof parle à un élève.

1. The preposition **à** can mean "in," "to," or "at." Remember that **à** contracts with the articles **le** and **les** to form **au** and **aux.**

à + la = à la	Je parle à la fille.
à + l' = à l'	Je parle à l'élève.
à + le = au	Je parle au professeur.
à + les = aux	Je parle aux élèves.

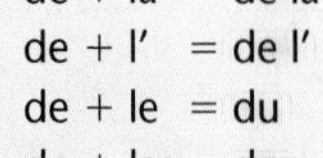

2. The preposition **de** can mean "of" or "from." **De** is also a part of longer prepositions such as **près de** and **loin de. De** contracts with **le** and **les** to form **du** and **des.**

de + la = de la	Il habite près de la station de métro.
de + l' = de l'	Il habite loin de l'université.
de + le = du	Il habite près du collège.
de + les = des	Il habite loin des magasins.

Une classe au lycée Janson de Sailly à Paris

9 On y va ou on n'y va pas?

Complétez.

Aujourd'hui on ne va pas __1__ parc; on ne va pas __2__ restaurant; on ne va pas __3__ maison; on ne va pas __4__ pâtisserie. Où est-ce qu'on va alors? On va __5__ école. On va __6__ cours de français. On va parler __7__ professeur et __8__ élèves.

Answers to Révision

1. au	5. à l'
2. au	6. au
3. à la	7. au
4. à la	8. aux

10 Tu habites où? Donnez des réponses personnelles.

1. Tu habites près ou loin de l'école?
2. Tu vas à l'école à quelle heure?
3. Tu habites près ou loin des magasins?
4. Tu vas souvent aux magasins?
5. Tu es un copain ou une copine du frère de Nathalie?
6. Tu habites près du magasin des parents de Nathalie?

La Martinique

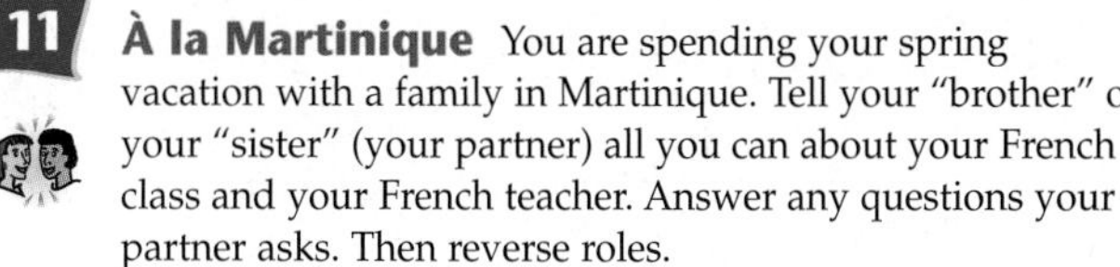

11 À la Martinique

You are spending your spring vacation with a family in Martinique. Tell your "brother" or your "sister" (your partner) all you can about your French class and your French teacher. Answer any questions your partner asks. Then reverse roles.

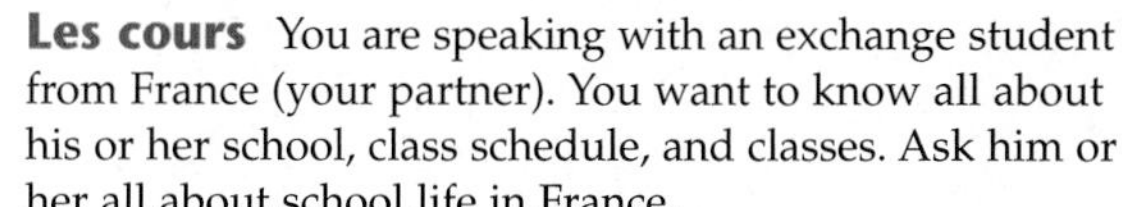

12 Les cours

You are speaking with an exchange student from France (your partner). You want to know all about his or her school, class schedule, and classes. Ask him or her all about school life in France.

Nom: BRILLIÉ
Prénom: Claire
Classe: 4e2
Ext. 1/2 P

	LUNDI	MARDI	MERCREDI	JEUDI	VENDREDI
8h - 8h 30					
8h 30 - 9h 30	HIST/GÉO	SC. NAT	MATH	PHYSIQUE	MATH/DESSIN
9h 30 - 10h 30	MATH	ALLEMAND	ED. CIVIQUE	ANGLAIS	HIST/GÉO
10h 30 - 11h 30	TECHNO	ANGLAIS		MUSIQUE	
11h 30 - 12h 30		LATIN	EPS/DESSIN	ALLEMAND	E.P.S.
12h 30 - 13h					
13h 30 - 14h					
14h - 15h	FRANÇAIS	4 er Semaine! 2e HIST/GÉO		FRANÇAIS	LATIN
15h - 16h	ALLEMAND	FRANÇAIS		LATIN	
16h - 17h	ANGLAIS			FRANÇAIS	
17h - 18h					

Signature: père mère Visa de la Direction

Révision A

11 and **12** These activities encourage students to use the language on their own. You may wish to let them choose the activities they would like to do.

Learning from Photos

(page R9) This photo is of Fort-de-France, the principal city of la Martinique, **un département d'outre mer (un D.O.M.)** in the Caribbean.

Learning from Realia

(page R9) Ask students the following questions about the class schedule: **Le cours de sciences naturelles est à quelle heure? Quel jour? Et le cours d'anglais? L'élève étudie combien de langues? Quels jours?**

Answers to Révision

10 *Answers will vary but may include:*

1. J'habite loin de l'école.
2. Je vais à l'école à sept heures et demie du matin.
3. J'habite loin des magasins.
4. Oui, je vais souvent aux magasins.
5. Non, je ne suis pas un copain (une copine) du frère de Nathalie.
6. Non, je n'habite pas près du magasin des parents de Nathalie.

11 *Answers will vary but may include:*

—J'aime beaucoup mon cours de français. Le professeur est très sympa et intéressant.
—Tu trouves le cours difficile?
—Non, je trouve le cours assez facile.
—Vous avez beaucoup d'examens?
—Oui, nous avons beaucoup d'examens. Il faut étudier!

12 *Answers will vary but may include:*

—Tu as combien de cours par semaine?
—J'ai treize cours.
—Tes cours sont difficiles?
—Le cours de maths et le cours d'allemand sont assez difficiles.
—Tu aimes ton cours d'anglais?
—Bien sûr!

Révision B

Preview

This review chapter covers vocabulary needed to describe home and family. These topics were first presented in **Bon voyage! Level 1.** The structures reviewed are the present tense of **-er** verbs, **avoir, faire,** and the partitive.

National Standards

Communication

In Review Chapter B, students will communicate in spoken and written French on the following topics:

- Describing their family
- Describing their home
- Food

Students will also learn to narrate present events. They will obtain and provide information and engage in conversations about home and family as they fulfill the chapter objectives listed on this page.

Révision B

La famille

R10

FRENCH Online

The **Glencoe Foreign Language Web site** (french.glencoe.com) offers several options that enable you and your students to experience the French-speaking world via the Internet:

- Games and puzzles afford students another opportunity to practice the material learned in a particular chapter.
- The *Enrichment* section offers students an opportunity to visit Web sites related to the theme of the chapter for more information on a particular topic.
- Online *Chapter Quizzes* offer students an opportunity to prepare for a chapter test.
- Visit our virtual **Café** for more opportunities to practice and explore the French-speaking world.

Révision C

8 **Au pluriel** Mettez au pluriel.

1. *Je prends* le car scolaire pour aller à l'école.
2. *Je prends* l'ascenseur pour monter au 6ᵉ étage.
3. *Tu prends* le bus ou le métro pour aller en ville?
4. *Tu prends* beaucoup de notes en classe?
5. *L'élève apprend* beaucoup de choses.
6. *Elle comprend* le professeur.

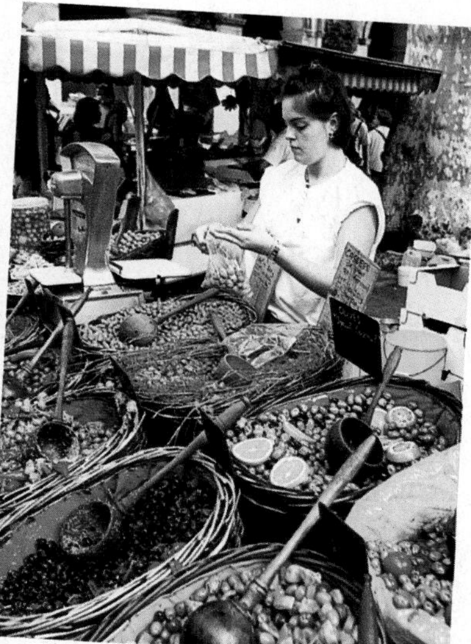

Un marché à Saint-Rémy-de-Provence

9 **Ce que je prends** Donnez des réponses personnelles.

1. Qu'est-ce que tu prends quand tu as soif?
2. Qu'est-ce que tu prends quand tu as faim?

10 **Qu'est-ce qu'on veut acheter?**
You and your friend are in an open-air market in France. Make a list of the items you want to buy. Take turns being the vendor and the customer as you shop for the items on your list.

11 **Qu'est-ce qu'on va manger?**
Work with a classmate. Prepare a menu in French for tomorrow's meals—**le petit déjeuner, le déjeuner et le dîner.** Based on your menus, prepare a shopping list. Be sure to include the quantities you need.

12 **C'est qui?** Work with a classmate. One of you describes what someone in the class is wearing and the other has to guess who it is. Take turns.

10 You may wish to supply props for the students to use for this activity.

12 Have the students use their description from the Bellringer Review to begin this game.

Answers to Révision

8

1. Nous prenons
2. Nous prenons
3. Vous prenez
4. Vous prenez
5. Les élèves apprennent
6. Elles comprennent

9 *Answers will vary but may include:*

1. Quand j'ai soif, je prends de l'eau minérale.
2. Quand j'ai faim, je prends un sandwich au jambon.

10 *Answers will vary depending upon what students want to buy. Some expressions that students know and can use are:* **un kilo de, une douzaine de, une boîte de, une bouteille de, ça fait combien, avec ça, c'est tout.**

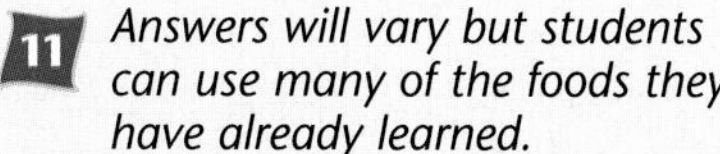

11 *Answers will vary but students can use many of the foods they have already learned.*

12 *Answers will vary but may include:*

—Il porte un jean et un polo rouge à manches courtes. Il porte des baskets.
—C'est Marc!

Preview

This review chapter covers vocabulary needed to describe traveling by train and plane. These topics were first presented in **Bon voyage! Level 1.** The present tense of **-ir** and **-re** verbs, and verbs like **partir** and **dormir,** are reviewed.

National Standards

Communication

In Review Chapter D, students will communicate in spoken and written French on the following topics:

- Traveling by train
- Traveling by plane

Students will also learn to narrate present events. They will obtain and provide information and engage in conversations about travel as they fulfill the chapter objectives listed on this page.

Révision D

En voyage

FRENCH Online

The **Glencoe Foreign Language Web site** (french.glencoe.com) offers several options that enable you and your students to experience the French-speaking world via the Internet:

- Games and puzzles afford students another opportunity to practice the material learned in a particular chapter.
- The *Enrichment* section offers students an opportunity to visit Web sites related to the theme of the chapter for more information on a particular topic.
- Online *Chapter Quizzes* offer students an opportunity to prepare for a chapter test.
- Visit our virtual **Café** for more opportunities to practice and explore the French-speaking world.

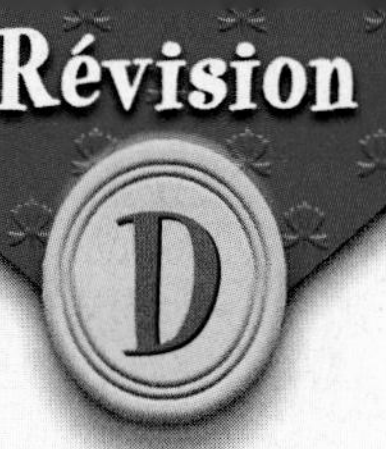

Spotlight on Culture

Photograph This photograph shows the **TGV (le train à grande vitesse)** in the La Rochelle train station.

R29

Révision D

Vocabulaire

Resource Manager

Workbook, pages R21–R22
Test Booklet
ExamView Pro®

Bellringer Review

Use BRR Transparency R.12 or write the following on the board.
Write down as many words and expressions as you can think of having to do with airports.

Presentation

Step 1 Have students share the words they wrote down for the Bellringer Review.

Step 2 Have students repeat the vocabulary words and sentences after you.

Learning from Photos

(page R30 top right) Ask the following questions about the train ticket:
Le train va partir de quelle ville? Il va arriver où? C'est un billet de quelle classe? Le billet est pour combien de personnes? Quel est le prix du billet? Quel est le prix pour chaque personne?

Vocabulaire

À la gare

Les voyageurs n'attendent pas le train.
Ils descendent du train sur le quai.

Le train part à l'heure.
Il arrive à l'heure.
Il n'a pas de retard.

À l'aéroport

Marie sort son billet de son sac à dos.
Elle choisit sa place dans l'avion.
Elle veut une place côté couloir.

Révision D

1 Historiette À la gare Inventez une histoire.

1. Il y a beaucoup de voyageurs dans la gare?
2. Il y a souvent une queue devant le guichet?
3. On vend des billets de train au guichet?
4. Les voyageurs entendent l'annonce du départ de leur train?
5. Le train arrive sur quelle voie?
6. Le train part à l'heure?

La gare de l'Est à Paris

Une hôtesse de l'air sert une collation.

2 À l'aéroport Vrai ou faux?

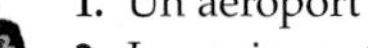

1. Un aéroport est toujours dans le centre d'une ville.
2. Les avions atterrissent sur une piste.
3. Les avions décollent d'une porte d'embarquement.
4. Les passagers ont une carte d'embarquement.
5. Les stewards et les hôtesses de l'air travaillent à l'aéroport.

Attention!

When students are doing the activities, accept any answer that makes sense. The purpose of these activities is to have students use the new vocabulary. They are not factual recall activities. Thus, do not expect students to remember specific information from the vocabulary presentation when answering. If you wish, have students use the photos on this page as a stimulus, when possible.

Historiette Each time **Historiette** appears, it means that the answers to the activity form a short story. Encourage students to look at the title of the **Historiette**, since it can help them do the activity.

2 Have students correct any false statements.

Writing Development

Have students write the answers to Activity 1 in paragraph form.

Learning from Photos

(page R31 right) Paris has six train stations. The **gare de l'Est** serves destinations in the east of France, as well as cities in Germany, Switzerland, and Austria.

Paired Activity

Have students work in pairs and make up a conversation about a trip to a French-speaking destination that interests them. Then ask for volunteers to present their conversations to the class.

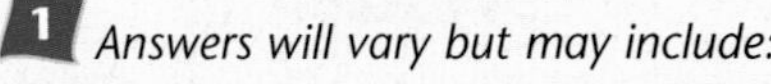

Answers to Révision

1 *Answers will vary but may include:*

1. Oui, il y a beaucoup de voyageurs dans la gare.
2. Oui, il y a souvent une queue devant le guichet.
3. Oui, on vend des billets de train au guichet.
4. Oui, les voyageurs entendent l'annonce du départ de leur train.
5. Le train arrive sur la voie numéro 5.
6. Oui, le train part à l'heure.

2

1. faux
2. vrai
3. faux
4. vrai
5. faux

Révision D

Conversation

Resource Manager

Workbook, pages R21–R22
Test Booklet

Presentation

Step 1 Have the class repeat the conversation after you.

Step 2 Call on two students to read the conversation to the class.

Geography Connection

Casablanca is the largest city in Morocco. The well-planned modern part of the city is crossed by attractive, wide, palm-lined avenues, which radiate from large central squares. Avenue Hassan II, shown in the photo on page R32, is the main inland artery (much of the city is very close to the coast). It skirts the large **parc de la Ligue Arabe,** which has a small stadium whose entrance is on Avenue Hassan II.

Conversation

Tu vas à Casablanca?

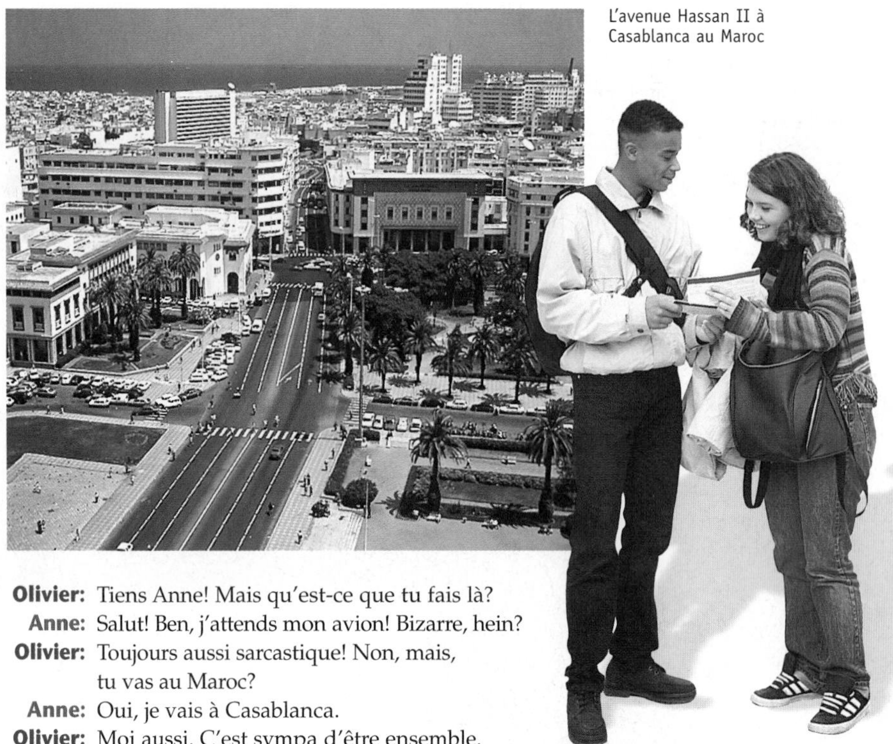

L'avenue Hassan II à Casablanca au Maroc

Olivier: Tiens Anne! Mais qu'est-ce que tu fais là?
Anne: Salut! Ben, j'attends mon avion! Bizarre, hein?
Olivier: Toujours aussi sarcastique! Non, mais, tu vas au Maroc?
Anne: Oui, je vais à Casablanca.
Olivier: Moi aussi. C'est sympa d'être ensemble.
Anne: Oui. Tu as quelle place?
Olivier: 22A. Et toi?
Anne: 15B.
Olivier: Oh, on va pouvoir changer après le décollage.
Anne: Oui. C'est sûr. Mais il faut d'abord partir!

Après la conversation

Répondez.

1. Où sont Olivier et Anne?
2. Qu'est-ce qu'ils attendent?
3. Ils partent pour quel pays?
4. Anne a quelle place? Et Olivier?
5. Est-ce qu'ils veulent être ensemble dans l'avion?
6. Est-ce qu'ils vont pouvoir changer de place?
7. D'après vous, l'avion va partir à l'heure?

Answers to Après la conversation

1. Ils sont à l'aéroport.
2. Ils attendent leur avion.
3. Ils partent pour le Maroc.
4. Anne a la place 15B. Olivier a la place 22A.
5. Oui, ils veulent être ensemble dans l'avion.
6. Oui, ils vont pouvoir changer de place.
7. Oui, l'avion va partir à l'heure. (Non, l'avion ne va pas partir à l'heure).

Structure

Les verbes en -ir et -re

Review the following forms of regular **-ir** and **-re** verbs in French.

FINIR				ATTENDRE			
je	finis	nous	finissons	j'	attends	nous‿attendons	
tu	finis	vous	finissez	tu	attends	vous‿attendez	
il/elle/on	finit	ils/elles	finissent	il/elle/on‿attend		ils/elles‿attendent	

3 **Un voyage en avion** Donnez des réponses personnelles.

1. Quand tu voyages en avion, tu choisis Air France comme compagnie?
2. Tu choisis une place côté couloir ou côté fenêtre?
3. En général, les passagers choisissent des places côté couloir?
4. Ta famille et toi, vous attendez longtemps à l'aéroport?
5. Vous remplissez vos cartes de débarquement avant l'arrivée?
6. Vous atterrissez en général à l'heure?

Un steward sert un café.

Révision D

Structure

Resource Manager

Workbook, pages R23–R26
Test Booklet
ExamView Pro®

Bellringer Review

Use BRR Transparency R.13 or write the following on the board.
Write down as many words related to train travel as you can.

Presentation

Les verbes en -ir et -re

Step 1 Write the verb forms on the board and have the students repeat them aloud.

Step 2 Other common **-ir** verbs the students know are **choisir, remplir,** and **atterrir.** Other **-re** verbs the students know are **vendre, entendre, répondre, perdre, descendre.**

3 Do this activity first with books open. Ask questions and call on individuals to respond. Students can then write the answers for homework.

Answers to Révision

3 *Answers will vary but may include:*

1. Oui, quand je voyage en avion, je choisis Air France comme compagnie.
2. Je choisis une place côté couloir.
3. Oui, en général les passagers choisissent des places côté couloir.
4. Non, nous n'attendons pas longtemps à l'aéroport.
5. Oui, nous remplissons nos cartes de débarquement avant l'arrivée.
6. Oui, nous atterrissons en général à l'heure.

Bellringer Review

Use BRR Transparency R.14 or write the following on the board.
Rewrite each sentence with the new subject.

1. **Ils vont en France.**
   Il ______.
2. **Ils choisissent un vol Air France.**
   Il ______.
3. **Nous voulons prendre le même vol.**
   Je ______.
4. **Nous répondons aux questions de l'agent.**
   Je ______.

Presentation

Les verbes **sortir, partir, dormir, servir**

Step 1 Have students repeat the verb forms after you. Remind students to drop the final sound of the **ils/elles** form to get the pronunciation for all singular forms.

5 and **6** Have students retell the stories in their own words.

Learning from Photos

(page R34) The **gare de Lyon** is one of the major train stations in Paris.

4 **À la gare** Complétez.

1. À la gare, on ____ les billets de train au guichet et on ____ des magazines et des journaux au kiosque. (vendre)
2. Quelques voyageurs ____ dans la salle d'attente et d'autres voyageurs ____ sur le quai. (attendre)
3. Nous, nous ____ sur le quai. (attendre)
4. Et vous, vous ____ le train où? (attendre)
5. J'____ l'annonce du départ de notre train. (entendre)

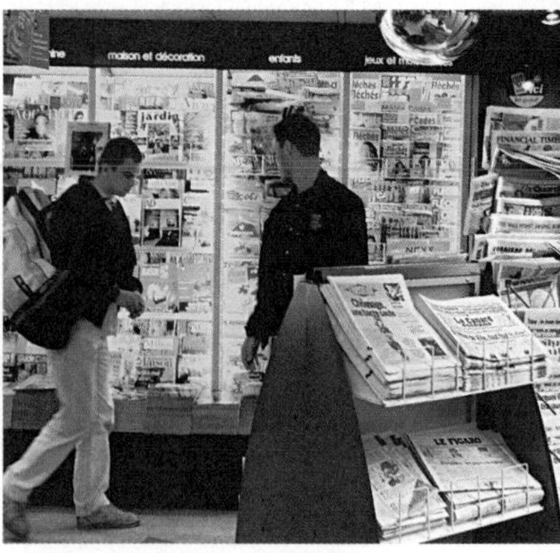

Un kiosque à la gare de Lyon à Paris

Les verbes **sortir, partir, dormir, servir**

Review the forms of the following **-ir** verbs.

SORTIR		PARTIR		DORMIR		SERVIR	
je	sors	je	pars	je	dors	je	sers
tu	sors	tu	pars	tu	dors	tu	sers
il/elle/on	sort	il/elle/on	part	il/elle/on	dort	il/elle/on	sert
nous	sortons	nous	partons	nous	dormons	nous	servons
vous	sortez	vous	partez	vous	dormez	vous	servez
ils/elles	sortent	ils/elles	partent	ils/elles	dorment	ils/elles	servent

5 **Historiette** **En voiture!** Répondez d'après les indications.

1. Le train part de quelle voie? (numéro deux)
2. Il part à quelle heure? (18 h 16)
3. On sert des repas dans le train? (oui)
4. Qui sert les repas? (des serveurs)
5. Les voyageurs dorment? (oui)
6. Quand le contrôleur arrive, tu sors ton billet? (oui)

Answers to Révision

1. vend, vend
2. attendent, attendent
3. attendons
4. attendez
5. entends

1. Le train part de la voie numéro deux.
2. Le train part à 18 h 16.
3. Oui, on sert des repas dans le train.
4. Des serveurs servent les repas.
5. Oui, les voyageurs dorment.
6. Oui, quand le contrôleur arrive, je sors mon billet.

Révision D

6 Historiette **Caroline fait un voyage.** Complétez.

Caroline est à la gare. Où est-ce qu'on __1__ (vendre) les billets? Ah, voilà le guichet. Caroline achète son billet. Elle __2__ (sortir) de l'argent de son sac à dos et paie. Son train __3__ (partir) de la voie numéro quatre. Tous les trains __4__ (partir) à l'heure. Beaucoup de voyageurs __5__ (dormir) dans le train. Mais Caroline ne __6__ (dormir) pas. Elle aime bien voyager en train.

L'Eurostar fait Paris-Londres.

7 En avion

Make a list of words associated with airline travel. Write a short paragraph using these words to describe a plane trip you'd like to take.

8 La gare

Describe the illustration in your own words.

FUN-FACTS

The Eurostar connects Paris and London by way of the new Eurotunnel between France and England. The trip takes a mere three hours.

Answers to Révision

6

1. vend
2. sort
3. part
4. partent
5. dorment
6. dort

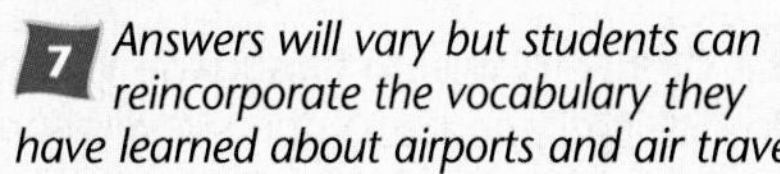

7 *Answers will vary but students can reincorporate the vocabulary they have learned about airports and air travel.*

8 *Answers will vary but students can reincorporate the vocabulary they have learned about train travel.*

Preview

This review chapter covers vocabulary related to seasons and a variety of sports. These topics were first presented in **Bon voyage! Level 1.** The **passé composé** of regular and irregular verbs is reviewed.

National Standards

Communication

In Review Chapter E, students will communicate in spoken and written French on the following topics:

- Seasons
- Individual and team sports

Students will also learn to narrate past events. They will obtain and provide information and engage in conversations about seasons and sports as they fulfill the chapter objectives listed on this page.

Révision E

Les sports

The **Glencoe Foreign Language Web site** (french.glencoe.com) offers several options that enable you and your students to experience the French-speaking world via the Internet:

- Games and puzzles afford students another opportunity to practice the material learned in a particular chapter.
- The *Enrichment* section offers students an opportunity to visit Web sites related to the theme of the chapter for more information on a particular topic.
- Online *Chapter Quizzes* offer students an opportunity to prepare for a chapter test.
- Visit our virtual **Café** for more opportunities to practice and explore the French-speaking world.

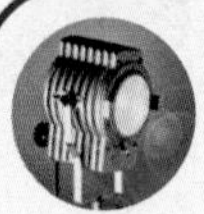

Spotlight on Culture

Photograph This photo shows France and Brazil competing in the 1998 World Cup final.

Learning from Photos

(pages R36–R37) Ask the students the following questions about the photo: **Il y a combien de joueurs sur la photo? Ils jouent au foot? Il y a combien d'équipes? Il y a des gradins?**

Vocabulaire

Resource Manager

Workbook, pages R27–R29
Test Booklet
ExamView Pro®

Bellringer Review

Use BRR Transparency R.15 or write the following on the board.
Write as many words as you can about the following sports.
le football
le basket-ball

Presentation

Step 1 Use gestures to reinforce the meaning of **nager, faire du ski nautique, prendre des bains de soleil, mettre de la crème solaire, faire du ski, faire du patin à glace, jouer au foot, donner un coup de pied dans le ballon.**

Step 2 Have students repeat the vocabulary words and sentences after you.

Paired Activity

Have students work in pairs and make up a conversation about a sport that interests them. Then ask for volunteers to present their conversations to the class.

Vocabulaire

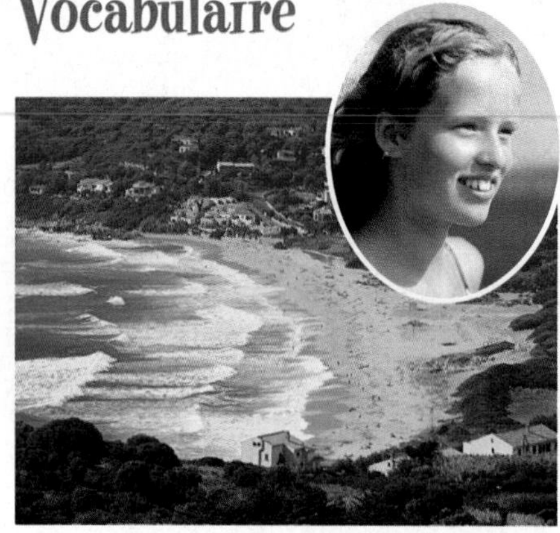

Julie a passé l'été dernier au bord de la mer.
Elle a pris des bains de soleil.
Elle a mis de la crème solaire.
Elle a bronzé.

L'hiver dernier Marc a appris à faire du ski.
Il a descendu la piste verte.

Samedi dernier, notre équipe a joué au foot.
Fabien a donné un coup de pied dans le ballon.
Il a marqué un but.
Notre équipe a gagné 6 à 4.
Nous avons joué contre Orsay.

Aimée a beaucoup nagé.

Lisette a fait du ski nautique.

Magali a fait du patin à glace.
Elle a eu un petit accident.

Geography Connection

The beach shown in the photo on page R38 is near the city of Ajaccio, on the island of Corsica **(la Corse)**. Corsica, the third largest of the Mediterranean islands, is officially **un département** of France. It is a very popular vacation spot, particularly for families. Corsica is a very mountainous island with many forests and sprawling beaches along the coast.

Learning from Photos

(page R38 top right) The ski resort of Avoriaz in the Mont-Blanc region is known for its chic clientele. No automobiles are allowed, and it is reached by cable car from the resort town of Morzine.

Révision E

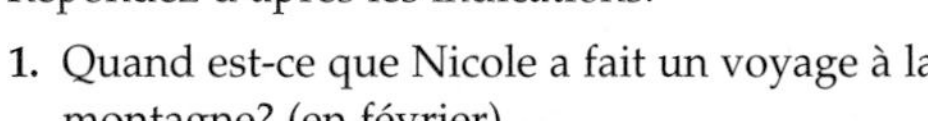

1 Historiette Un voyage à la montagne

Répondez d'après les indications.

1. Quand est-ce que Nicole a fait un voyage à la montagne? (en février)
2. Qu'est-ce qu'elle a pris? (des leçons de ski)
3. Elle a eu un moniteur? (oui)
4. Elle a beaucoup appris? (oui)
5. Elle a descendu quelle piste? (la piste verte)
6. Elle a eu un accident? (non)
7. Où est-ce qu'elle a fait du patin? (à la patinoire)

Une leçon de ski

Courchevel, France

2 Un match de foot

Répondez d'après les indications.

1. Vous avez joué au foot hier? (oui)
2. Lafitte a passé le ballon? (oui)
3. Garros a bloqué le ballon? (non)
4. Lafitte a marqué un but? (oui)
5. Les spectateurs ont applaudi? (oui)
6. L'équipe de Lafitte a perdu le match? (non)

Un match de foot

Historiette Each time **Historiette** appears, it means that the answers to the activity form a short story. Encourage students to look at the title of the **Historiette,** since it can help them do the activity.

1 Have students retell the activity in their own words.

Writing Development

Have students write the answers to Activity 1 in paragraph form.

Learning from Photos

(page R39 middle left) Courchevel is in the Savoie region. It is an upscale ski resort also known for its nightlife.

(page R39 middle right) Ask the students these questions about the skiing photo: **Ils font du ski alpin ou du ski de fond? Qu'est-ce qu'ils ont mis pour faire du ski? La neige est belle? Il fait beau ou il neige? Il fait froid? Ce sont des débutants?**

Answers to Révision

1

1. Nicole a fait un voyage à la montagne en février.
2. Elle a pris des leçons de ski.
3. Oui, elle a eu un moniteur.
4. Oui, elle a beaucoup appris.
5. Elle a descendu la piste verte.
6. Non, elle n'a pas eu d'accident.
7. Elle a fait du patin à la patinoire.

2

1. Oui, nous avons joué au foot hier.
2. Oui, Lafitte a passé le ballon.
3. Non, Garros n'a pas bloqué le ballon.
4. Oui, Lafitte a marqué un but.
5. Oui, les spectateurs ont applaudi.
6. Non, l'équipe de Lafitte n'a pas perdu le match.

Conversation

Resource Manager

Workbook, pages R27–R29
Test Booklet

Presentation

Step 1 Have the class repeat the conversation after you.

Step 2 Call on two students to read the conversation to the class. **Note:** Tell students that **avoir de la chance** is an expression meaning "to be lucky."

Learning from Photos

(page R40 right) The windsurfer is on the island of Guadeloupe in the French Antilles. Ask the following questions about the photo. **Qu'est-ce que cet homme fait? Tu aimes faire de la planche à voile? Tu fais de la planche à voile où? Qu'est-ce qu'il faut avoir pour faire de la planche à voile?**

Conversation

Au bord de la mer

Julie: Qu'est-ce que tu as fait pendant les vacances?
Sophie: J'ai passé un mois au bord de la mer.
Julie: Super! Tu as de la chance.
Sophie: Oui. J'ai passé tout mon temps à la plage. J'ai beaucoup nagé et j'ai appris à faire de la planche à voile.
Julie: Et je vois que tu as bien bronzé!

Après la conversation

Répondez.

1. Sophie a passé ses vacances d'été où?
2. Elle a passé combien de temps au bord de la mer?
3. Elle a beaucoup nagé?
4. Qu'est-ce qu'elle a appris à faire?
5. Elle a pris des bains de soleil?
6. Elle a bien bronzé?

Answers to Après la conversation

1. Elle a passé ses vacances au bord de la mer.
2. Elle a passé un mois au bord de la mer.
3. Oui, elle a beaucoup nagé.
4. Elle a appris à faire de la planche à voile.
5. Oui, elle a pris des bains de soleil.
6. Oui, elle a bien bronzé.

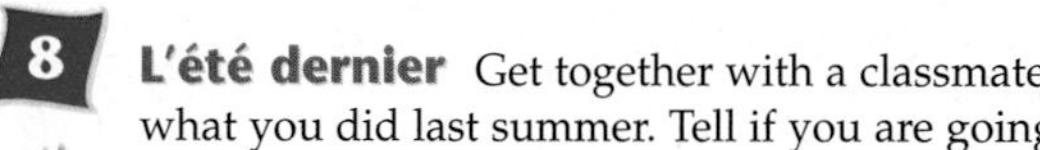

 **L'été dernier** Get together with a classmate. Tell one another what you did last summer. Tell if you are going to do the same things next summer **(l'été prochain).**

 **Ma saison préférée** Work with a classmate. Discuss your favorite season. Explain why you like it so much.

Des cyclistes en Provence

 **Jeu** **Les sports** Divide into small groups. Take turns describing a sport without mentioning its name. The others have to guess what sport is being described.

FRENCH Online

For more information about sports in the Francophone world, go to the Glencoe French Web site: french.glencoe.com

Révision E

8 and 9 These activities are more open-ended. You may wish to let students select the activity they wish to take part in. Encourage them to be as creative as possible.

Answers to Révision

 *Answers will vary but students can reincorporate all the beach vocabulary they have learned.*

 *Answers will vary depending upon the season students select.*

 *Answers will vary but may include the following sports:*

le football
le basket-ball
le volley-ball
le tennis
la natation
la planche à voile
le ski nautique
le ski alpin
le ski de fond

Révision

F

Preview

This review chapter covers vocabulary related to daily routines. This topic was first presented in **Bon voyage! Level 1.** The present and **passé composé** of reflexive verbs and the **passé composé** of verbs with **être** are reviewed.

National Standards

Communication

In Review Chapter F, students will communicate in spoken and written French on the following topics:

- Daily routines
- Home activities

Students will also learn to narrate present and past events. They will obtain and provide information and engage in conversations about daily routines as they fulfill the chapter objectives listed on this page.

Révision

F

La routine quotidienne

R46

The **Glencoe Foreign Language Web site** (french.glencoe.com) offers several options that enable you and your students to experience the French-speaking world via the Internet:

- Games and puzzles afford students another opportunity to practice the material learned in a particular chapter.
- The *Enrichment* section offers students an opportunity to visit Web sites related to the theme of the chapter for more information on a particular topic.
- Online *Chapter Quizzes* offer students an opportunity to prepare for a chapter test.
- Visit our virtual **Café** for more opportunities to practice and explore the French-speaking world.

R47

Révision F

Vocabulaire

Resource Manager

Workbook, pages R33–R34
Test Booklet
ExamView Pro®

Bellringer Review

Use BRR Transparency R.17 or write the following on the board.
Choose the correct completion.
du savon / du dentifrice / du shampooing / une brosse à dents / un peigne / un gant de toilette

1. **Je me lave la figure avec _____ et _____.**
2. **Je me lave les cheveux avec _____.**
3. **Je me brosse les dents avec _____ et _____.**
4. **Je me peigne avec _____.**

Presentation

Step 1 Have students repeat the vocabulary words and sentences after you.

Step 2 Intersperse questions to get students using the vocabulary. Examples are: **Laure s'est réveillée tôt ou tard ce matin? Elle s'est levée quand?**

Vocabulaire

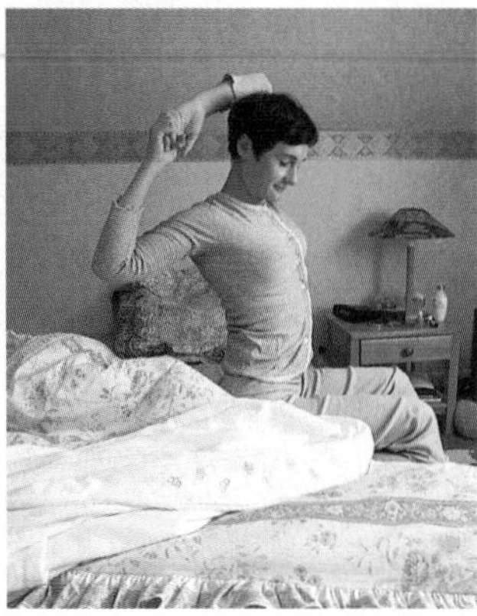

Laure s'est réveillée tôt ce matin. Elle s'est levée tout de suite.

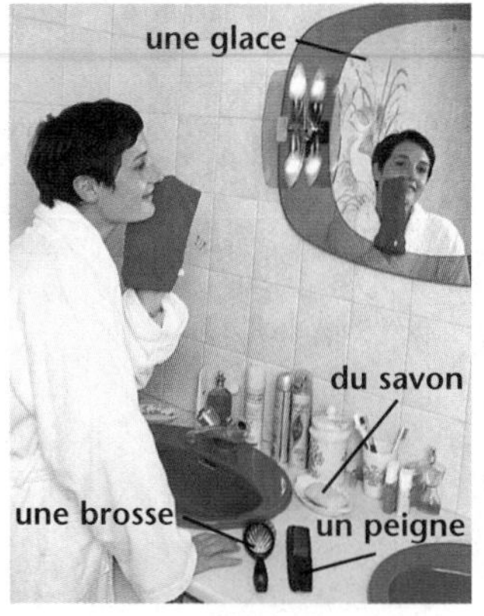

Elle s'est lavé la figure et les mains.

Ensuite, elle est sortie.

mettre la table

débarrasser la table

faire la vaisselle

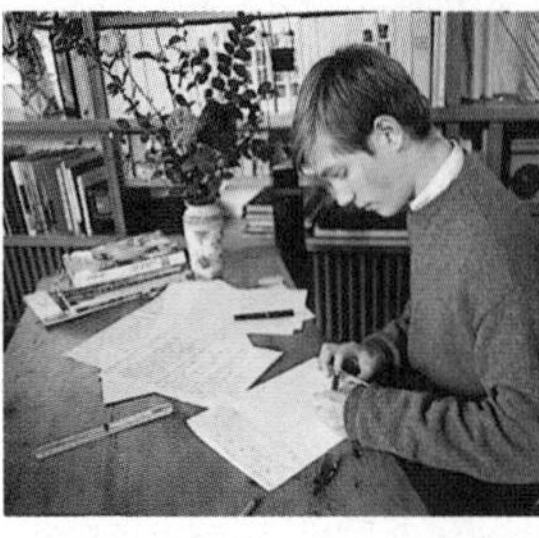

Après le dîner, Jean a fait ses devoirs.

Il a allumé (mis) la télévision.

À onze heures, il s'est couché.

Historiette Le matin

Inventez une histoire.

1. Ce matin, Cédric s'est réveillé tôt?
2. Il s'est levé tout de suite?
3. Il est allé dans la salle de bains?
4. Il s'est lavé les mains et la figure?
5. Il s'est lavé les dents?
6. Il s'est peigné?
7. Il s'est regardé dans une glace quand il s'est peigné?
8. Il est sorti?
9. Il est allé à l'école?
10. Il est arrivé à l'école à l'heure?

Les élèves arrivent à l'école à Paris.

Julie aide sa mère à faire la vaisselle.

Historiette Vrai ou faux? Répondez.

1. On met la table après le dîner.
2. Le lave-vaisselle est presque toujours dans la cuisine.
3. On débarrasse la table avant le dîner.
4. Pour regarder une émission il faut éteindre la télévision.
5. On peut zapper pour éviter les publicités à la télévision.

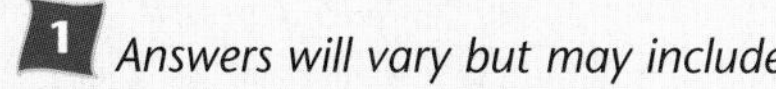

Answers to Révision

1 *Answers will vary but may include:*

1. Oui, il s'est réveillé tôt.
2. Oui, il s'est levé tout de suite.
3. Oui, il est allé dans la salle de bains.
4. Oui, il s'est lavé les mains et la figure.
5. Oui, il s'est lavé les dents.
6. Oui, il s'est peigné.
7. Oui, il s'est regardé dans une glace quand il s'est peigné.
8. Oui, il est sorti.
9. Oui, il est allé à l'école.
10. Oui, il est arrivé à l'école à l'heure.

2

1. faux
2. vrai
3. faux
4. faux
5. vrai

Révision F

Attention!

When students are doing the activities, accept any answer that makes sense. The purpose of these activities is to have students use the new vocabulary. They are not factual recall activities. Thus, do not expect students to remember specific information from the vocabulary presentation when answering. If you wish, have students use the photos on this page as a stimulus, when possible.

Historiette Each time **Historiette** appears, it means that the answers to the activity form a short story. Encourage students to look at the title of the **Historiette,** since it can help them do the activity.

1 After calling on students to answer individual questions, have students retell the information in the activity in their own words.

2 Have students correct any false sentences.

Writing Development

Have students write the answers to Activity 1 in paragraph form.

Learning from Photos

(page R49 middle) This photo shows some members of the Badez family in the kitchen of their suburban home in Brunoy on the outskirts of Paris.

Révision F

Conversation

Resource Manager

Workbook, pages R33–R34
Test Booklet

Presentation

Step 1 Have the class repeat the conversation after you.

Step 2 Call on two students to read the conversation to the class.

Learning from Photos

(page R50) Have students describe the two students. Have students identify the items.

Conversation

La matinée de Jean-Marc

Laurent: Tu te lèves à quelle heure le matin?
Jean-Marc: À quelle heure je me lève ou je me réveille?
Laurent: À quelle heure tu te lèves?
Jean-Marc: Je me lève à six heures et demie.
Laurent: Et tu quittes la maison à quelle heure?
Jean-Marc: À sept heures.
Laurent: Tu te laves, tu te laves les dents, tu te rases et tu prends ton petit déjeuner en une demi-heure!
Jean-Marc: Oui.
Laurent: Tu ne peux pas faire tout ça en une demi-heure!

Des lycéens devant le lycée Talma de Brunoy, près de Paris

Après la conversation

Répondez.

1. Jean-Marc se lève à quelle heure le matin?
2. Il quitte la maison à quelle heure?
3. Qu'est-ce qu'il fait avant de quitter la maison?
4. Il fait tout ça en combien de temps?

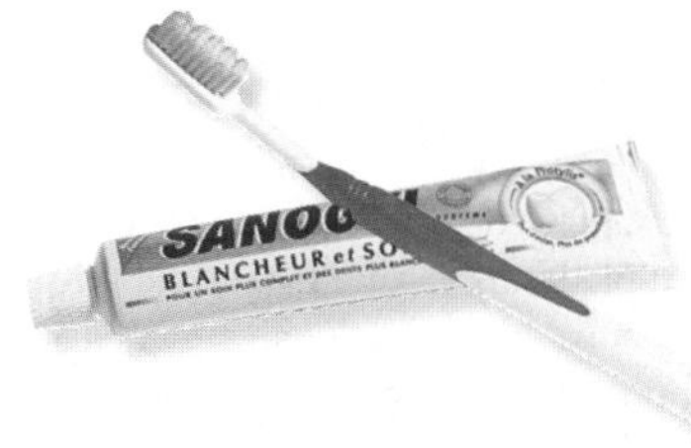

Answers to Après la conversation

1. Jean-Marc se lève à six heures et demie.
2. Il quitte la maison à sept heures.
3. Avant de quitter la maison il se lave, il se lave les dents, il se rase, et il prend son petit déjeuner.
4. Il fait tout ça en une demi-heure.

Structure

Les verbes réfléchis au présent

1. A verb is reflexive when the subject both performs and receives the action of the verb. Since the subject also receives the action, an additional pronoun is needed. This is called the reflexive pronoun. Review the following.

SE LAVER		S'HABILLER	
je	me lave	je	m'habille
tu	te laves	tu	t'habilles
il/elle/on	se lave	il/elle/on	s'habille
nous	nous lavons	nous	nous_zhabillons
vous	vous lavez	vous	vous_zhabillez
ils/elles	se lavent	ils/elles	s'habillent

Note that **me, te,** and **se** become **m', t',** and **s'** before a vowel or a silent **h.**

2. In the negative, **ne** comes before the reflexive pronoun. **Pas** follows the verb.

   Je me réveille, mais je ne me lève pas tout de suite.
   Il se lève, mais il ne s'habille pas tout de suite.

3. When a reflexive verb follows another verb, the reflexive pronoun agrees with the subject.

   Demain, nous allons nous lever tôt.
   Tu peux te réveiller tout seul?

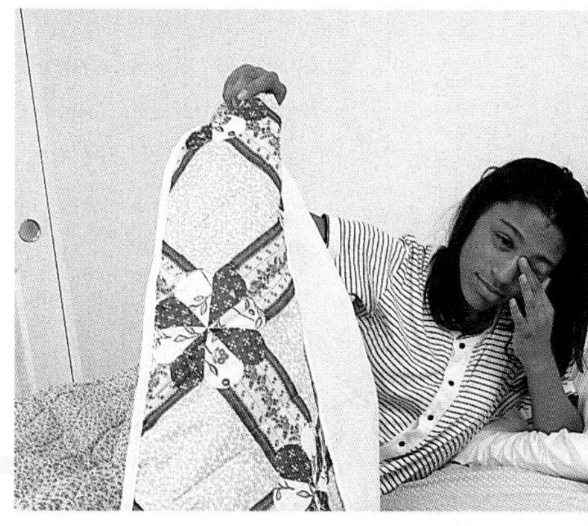

Structure

Resource Manager

Workbook, pages R35–R38
Test Booklet
ExamView Pro®

Bellringer Review

Use BRR Transparency R.18 or write the following on the board.
Write four things you do to help around the house.

Presentation

Les verbes réfléchis au présent

Step 1 Circle the reflexive pronoun. Underline the subject pronoun and draw a line from the reflexive pronoun to the subject to show that it is the same person.

Step 2 Practice word order by giving a few more sentences and having students change them to the negative.

Learning from Photos

(page R51) Ask the following questions about the photo:
La fille se réveille ou elle se couche?
Qu'est-ce qu'elle va faire avant d'aller à l'école?

4 **Expansion:** Have students compare their daily routine with that of Chloé.

3 Historiette **Mon horaire** Donnez des réponses personnelles.

1. Comment t'appelles-tu?
2. Tu te réveilles à quelle heure le matin?
3. Tu te lèves tout de suite?
4. Tu t'habilles avant ou après le petit déjeuner?
5. Quand est-ce que tu te laves les dents?
6. Tu te brosses les cheveux ou tu te peignes?
7. Tu te couches à quelle heure le soir?
8. Et ce soir, tu vas te coucher à quelle heure?
9. Demain matin tu vas te lever tôt ou tard?

4 Historiette **La matinée de Chloé** Complétez.

Bonjour! Je ___1___ (s'appeler) Chloé et mon frère ___2___ (s'appeler) Jérôme. Lui et moi, nous ___3___ (se lever) à sept heures du matin. Quand je ___4___ (se lever), je vais tout de suite dans la salle de bains. Là, je ___5___ (se laver), je ___6___ (se brosser) les dents et je ___7___ (se peigner). Le matin, je ___8___ (se dépêcher), je n'ai pas de temps à perdre. Je ne reste pas longtemps dans la salle de bains. Je sors, et tout de suite après, mon frère entre dans la salle de bains. Il ___9___ (se laver), ___10___ (se brosser) les dents et ___11___ (se raser).

À quelle heure est-ce que tu ___12___ (se lever) le matin? Tu as le même problème que nous? Tu ___13___ (se dépêcher) pour ne pas être en retard à l'école?

Answers to Révision

3 *Answers will vary but may include:*

1. Je m'appelle ______.
2. Je me réveille à six heures et quart.
3. Non, je ne me lève pas tout de suite.
4. Je m'habille avant le petit déjeuner.
5. Je me lave les dents après le petit déjeuner et avant de me coucher.
6. Je me peigne.
7. Je me couche à dix heures.
8. Ce soir je vais me coucher à onze heures.
9. Demain matin je vais me lever tard.

4

1. m'appelle
2. s'appelle
3. nous levons
4. me lève
5. me lave
6. me brosse
7. me peigne
8. me dépêche
9. se lave
10. se brosse
11. se rase
12. te lèves
13. te dépêches

Le passé composé avec **être**

1. Certains verbs form their **passé composé** with **être** instead of **avoir.** Many verbs that are conjugated with **être** express motion to or from a place.

ARRIVER	**Il est arrivé.**	PARTIR	**Il est parti.**
ENTRER	**Il est entré.**	SORTIR	**Il est sorti.**
MONTER	**Il est monté.**	DESCENDRE	**Il est descendu.**
ALLER	**Il est allé.**	RENTRER	**Il est rentré.**

2. The past participle of verbs conjugated with **être** must agree with the subject in number (singular or plural) and gender (masculine or feminine). Study the following forms.

Masculin	Féminin
je suis parti	je suis partie
tu es parti	tu es partie
il est parti	elle est partie
on est partis	on est parties
nous sommes partis	nous sommes parties
vous êtes parti(s)	vous êtes partie(s)
ils sont partis	elles sont parties

3. Although the following verbs do not express motion to or from a place, they are also conjugated with **être.**

RESTER	**Il est resté huit jours.**	*He stayed a week.*
TOMBER	**Il est tombé.**	*He fell.*
NAÎTRE	**Elle est née en France.**	*She was born in France.*
MOURIR	**Elle est morte en 1991.**	*She died in 1991.*

Bonnie est née à Paris.

Révision F

Bellringer Review

Use BRR Transparency R.19 or write the following on the board.
Rewrite each sentence in the **passé composé.**

1. **Je fais du ski.**
2. **Elle joue au tennis.**
3. **Ils répondent à toutes les questions du moniteur.**
4. **Je mets mon maillot et je nage dans la piscine.**

Presentation

Le passé composé avec **être**

Step 1 Have students pronounce the past participles in Item 1.

Step 2 Write the forms of the verb **être** on the board.

Step 3 Add a past participle after each of the forms of the verb **être** in order to form the **passé composé.** Then have the students repeat them after you.

Step 4 Underline the endings of the past participle.

Step 5 Have the students repeat the model sentences.

Step 6 Expansion: You may wish to write a verb conjugated with **avoir** on the board to contrast it with the **passé composé** formed with **être.** Point out the difference in agreement.

FUN-FACTS

Grenoble has grown faster than any other French city since World War II. It has many new skyscrapers in a valley that is surrounded by mountains. Important industries in Grenoble are electronics, engineering, and nuclear research.

5 **and** **6** These activities can be done with books closed, open, or once each way. **Expansion:** Call on an individual to retell all the information in his or her own words.

Writing Development

You can have students write any or all of these activities in paragraph form.

5 Historiette Un voyage à Grenoble

Répondez que oui.

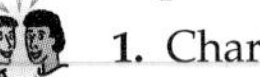

1. Charlotte est allée à Grenoble?
2. Elle est arrivée à la gare de Lyon à 10 h?
3. Elle est allée sur le quai?
4. Elle est montée dans le train?
5. Le train est parti à l'heure?
6. Le train est arrivé à Grenoble à l'heure?
7. Charlotte est descendue du train à Grenoble?
8. Elle est sortie de la gare?
9. Elle est allée chez ses amis?

La ville de Grenoble au pied des Alpes

6 Historiette À l'école

Donnez des réponses personnelles.

1. Tu es allé(e) à l'école ce matin?
2. Tu es arrivé(e) à quelle heure?
3. Tu es entré(e) immédiatement?
4. Tu es sorti(e) de l'école à quelle heure hier?
5. Tu es allé(e) manger quelque chose avec tes copains après les cours?
6. Tu es rentré(e) chez toi à quelle heure?

7 Historiette Où est-ce qu'elle est allée?

Complétez en utilisant le passé composé.

1. Marine ____ de la maison. (sortir)
2. Je ____ avec elle. (sortir)
3. Nous ____ au gymnase. (aller)
4. Nous ____ au deuxième étage. (monter)
5. Tu ____ au gymnase aussi, Hugo? (aller)
6. Tu y ____ avec un copain? (aller)
7. Vous ____ au gymnase à quelle heure? (arriver)
8. Marine a fait de l'aérobic et ensuite elle ____ à la piscine. (descendre)
9. Marine et moi, nous ____ du gymnase vers six heures. (sortir)
10. Elle ____ à la maison à six heures et demie et moi, je ____ à sept heures moins le quart. (rentrer)

Answers to Révision

5

1. Oui, Charlotte est allée à Grenoble.
2. Oui, elle est arrivée à la gare de Lyon à 10 h.
3. Oui, elle est allée sur le quai.
4. Oui, elle est montée dans le train.
5. Oui, le train est parti à l'heure.
6. Oui, le train est arrivé à Grenoble à l'heure.
7. Oui, Charlotte est descendue du train à Grenoble.
8. Oui, elle est sortie de la gare.
9. Oui, elle est allée chez ses amis.

6 *Answers will vary but may include:*

1. Oui, je suis allé(e) à l'école ce matin.
2. Je suis arrivé(e) à sept heures.
3. Oui, je suis entré(e) immédiatement.
4. Je suis sorti(e) de l'école à trois heures hier.
5. Oui, je suis allé(e) manger quelque chose avec mes copains après les cours.
6. Je suis rentré(e) chez moi à cinq heures et demie.

7

1. est sortie
2. suis sorti(e)
3. sommes allé(e)s
4. sommes monté(e)s
5. es allé
6. es allé
7. êtes arrivés
8. est descendue
9. sommes sorti(e)s
10. est rentrée, suis rentré(e)

RESOURCE GUIDE

Section	Pages	Section Resources
Vocabulaire *Mots 1*		
Au cinéma Au théâtre	2–3 3–5	Vocabulary Transparencies 1.2–1.3 Audiocassette 2A/CD 2 Audio Activities Booklet TE, pages 1–2 Workbook, pages 1–2 Quiz 1, page 1 ExamView Pro®
Vocabulaire *Mots 2*		
Au musée	6–9	Vocabulary Transparencies 1.4–1.5 Audiocassette 2A/CD 2 Audio Activities Booklet TE, page 3 Workbook, pages 3–4 Quiz 2, page 2 ExamView Pro®
Structure		
Les verbes **savoir** et **connaître** Les pronoms **me, te, nous, vous** Les pronoms **le, la, les**	10–11 12–13 14–17	Audiocassette 2A/CD 2 Audio Activities Booklet TE, pages 4–6 Workbook, pages 5–7 Quizzes 3–5, pages 3–5 ExamView Pro®
Conversation		
On va au cinéma?	18	Audiocassette 2A/CD 2 Audio Activities Booklet TE, page 7 CD-ROM
Prononciation		
Le son **/ü/**	19	Audiocassette 2A/CD 2 Audio Activities Booklet TE, page 8
Lectures culturelles		
Les loisirs culturels en France La musique africaine	20–21 22–23	Audiocassette 2A/CD 2 Audio Activities Booklet TE, pages 8–9 Test Booklet, Chapter 1
Connexions		
La musique	24–25	Test Booklet, Chapter 1
C'est à vous		
	26–27	**Bon voyage!** Video, Episode 1 Video Activities Booklet, Chapter 1 French Online Activities french.glencoe.com
Assessment		
	28–29	Communication Transparency C 1 Quizzes 1–5, pages 1–5 Test Booklet, Chapter 1 ExamView Pro® Situation Cards, Chapter 1 **Marathon mental** Videoquiz

Using Your Resources for Chapter 1

Transparencies

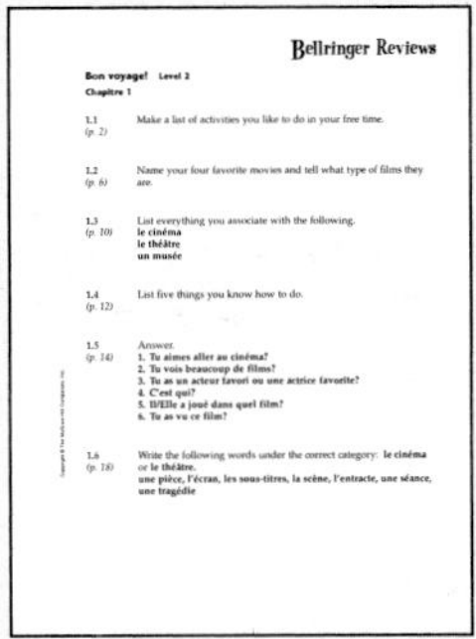
Bellringer Reviews

Bellringer 1.1–1.6

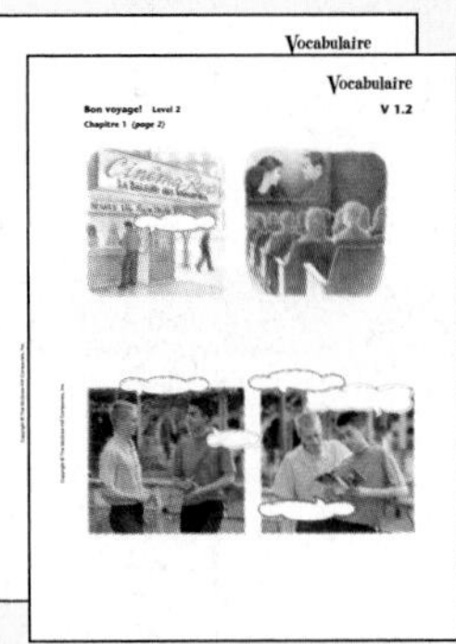
Vocabulaire
V 1.2

Vocabulary 1.1–1.5

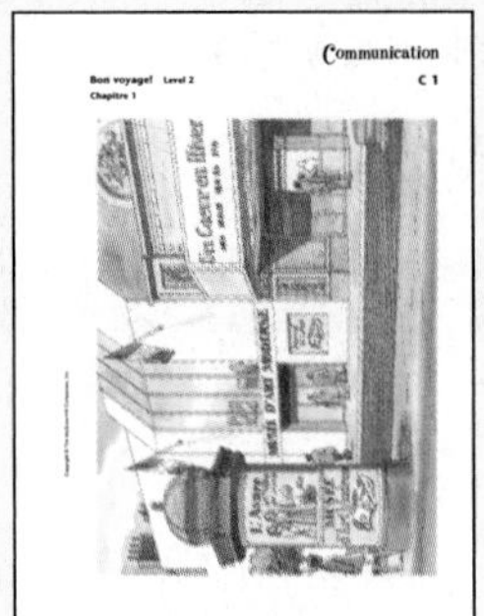
Communication
C 1

Communication C 1

Writing Activities Workbook

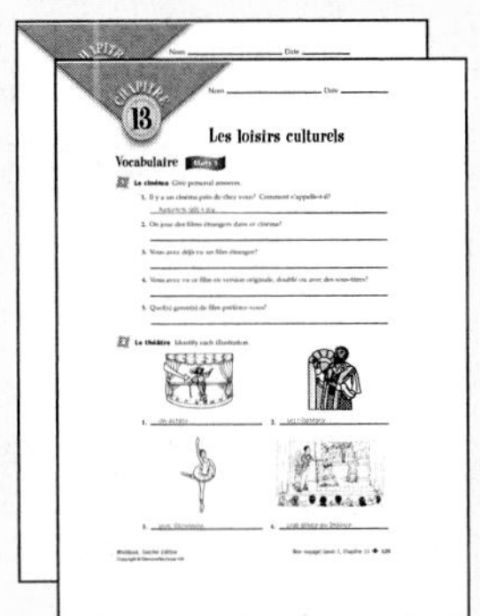
Les loisirs culturels

Vocabulary, pages 1–4

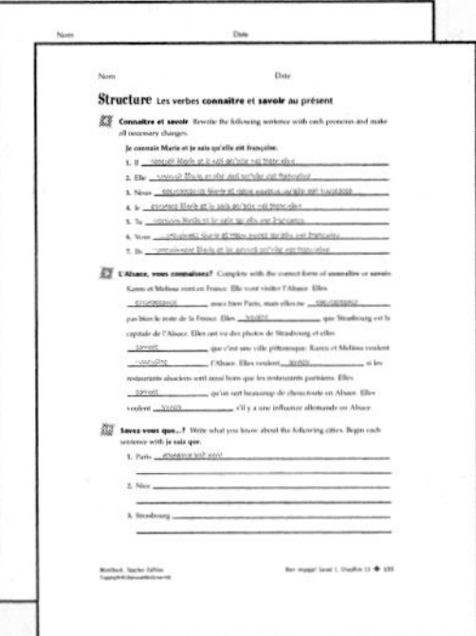

Structure, pages 5–7

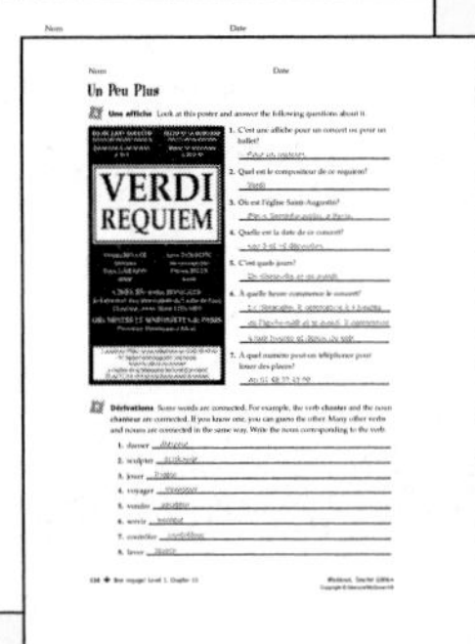

Enrichment, pages 8–10

Audio Program and Audio Activities Booklet

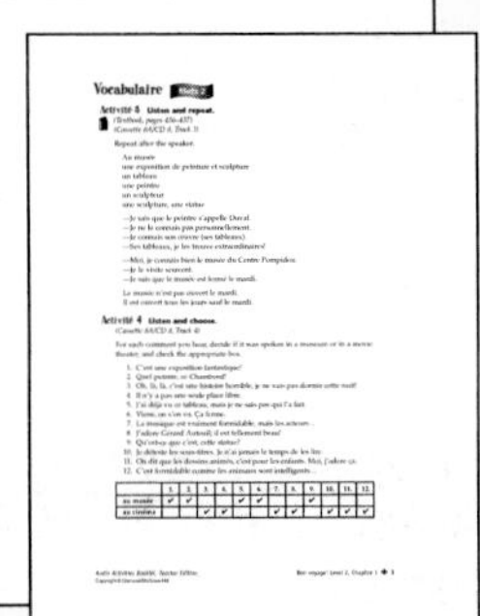
Vocabulaire

Vocabulary, pages 1–3

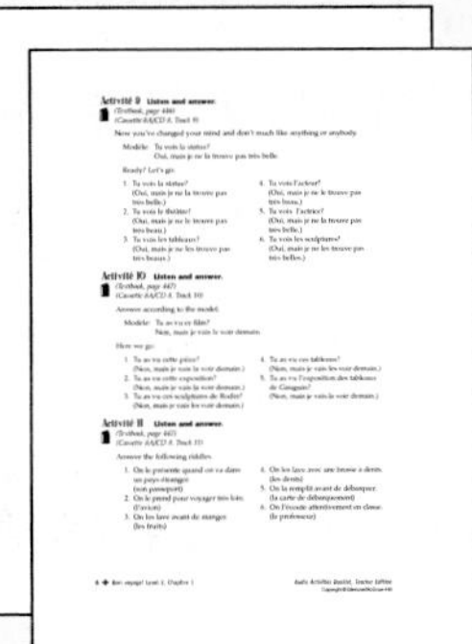

Structure, pages 4–6

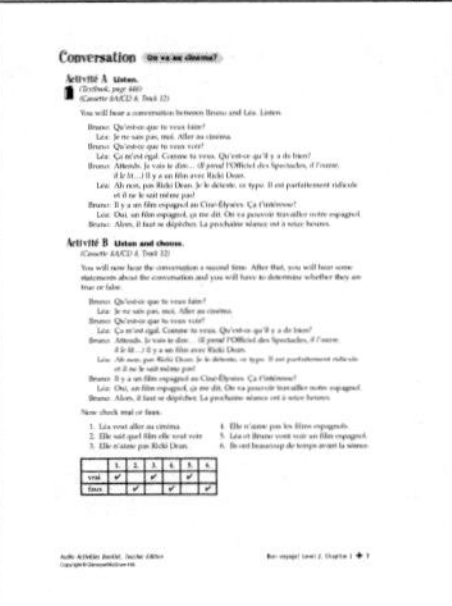

Conversation, page 7

Pronunciation, page 8

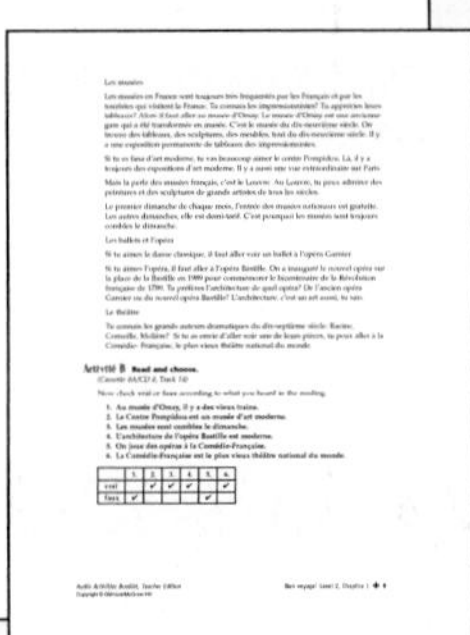

Cultural Reading, pages 8–9

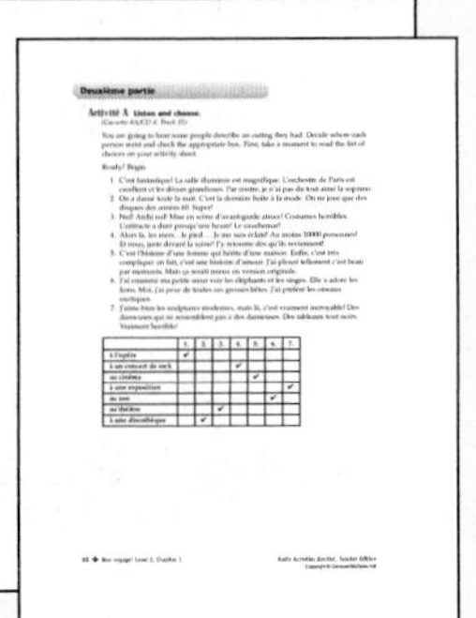

Additional Practice, pages 10–11

Assessment

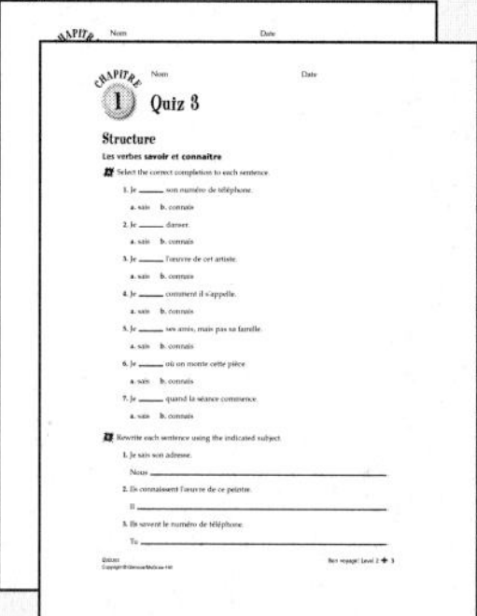

Vocabulary and Structure Quizzes, pages 1–5

Chapter Tests, Chapter 1

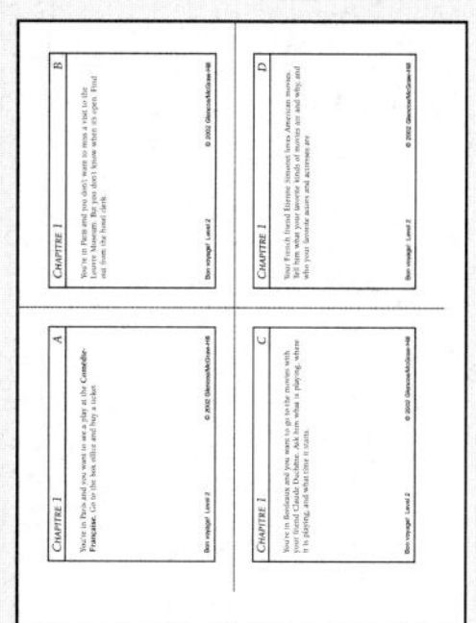

Situation Cards, Chapter 1

Timesaving Teacher Tools

Interactive Teacher Edition

Imagine having your Teacher's Edition and all resources on a CD-ROM. Click on a resource and it appears on your screen, ready to be printed, sorted, or planned.

Interactive Lesson Planner

The Interactive Lesson Planner CD-ROM helps you organize your lesson plans for a week, month, semester, or year. Look at this planning tool for easy access to your Chapter 1 resources.

ExamView Pro®

Test Bank software for Macintosh and Windows makes creating, editing, customizing, and printing tests quick and easy.

Technology Resources

In the Chapter 1 Internet activity, you will have a chance to learn more about cultural activities in the Francophone world. Visit french.glencoe.com.

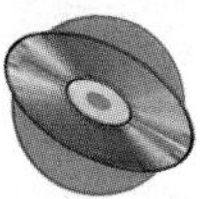

On the Interactive Conversation CD-ROM, students can listen to and take part in a recorded version of the conversation in Chapter 1.

See the National Geographic Teacher's Corner on pages 138–139, 244–245, 372–373, 472–473 for reference to additional technology resources.

Bon Voyage! Video and Video Activities Booklet.

Help your students prepare for the chapter test by playing the **Marathon mental** Videoquiz game show. Teams will compete against each other to review chapter vocabulary and structure and sharpen listening comprehension skills.

Preview

In this chapter, students will learn to discuss cultural events and express their cultural likes and dislikes. In order to do this, they will learn vocabulary associated with films, museums, and the theater. They will also learn to use the verbs **savoir** and **connaître** and the direct object pronouns.

National Standards

Communication

In Chapter 1, students will communicate in spoken and written French on the following topics:

- Going to the movies
- Visiting a museum
- Attending a theater performance

Students will also learn to tell whom and what they know. They will obtain and provide information and engage in conversations about their personal experiences with cultural events. They will also learn to use direct object pronouns.

Communities

After having learned about cultural preferences of the French, have students compare them with those of their own community.

CHAPITRE 1

Les loisirs culturels

Camille Claudel 6,70 F 1,02 € La Valse La Poste 2000 RF

Objectifs

In this chapter you will learn to:

- *discuss movies, plays, and museums*
- *tell what you know and whom you know*
- *tell what happens to you or someone else*
- *refer to people and things already mentioned*
- *talk about some cultural activities in Paris*

Des statues béninoises du seizième siècle

The **Glencoe World Language Web site** (french.glencoe.com) offers several options that enable you and your students to experience the French-speaking world via the Internet:

- The online **Activités** are correlated to the chapters and utilize Francophone Web sites around the world. For the Chapter 1 activity, see student page 31.
- Games and puzzles afford students another opportunity to practice the material learned in a particular chapter.
- The *Enrichment* section offers students an opportunity to visit Web sites related to the theme of the chapter for more information on a particular topic.
- Online *Chapter Quizzes* offer students an opportunity to prepare for a chapter test.
- Visit our virtual **Café** for more opportunities to practice and explore the French-speaking world.

Spotlight on Culture

Photograph The Louvre is the world's largest museum, and at night, as seen here, it is beautifully illuminated by 70,000 lightbulbs. The Louvre as it stands today is the product of centuries of construction. It was originally built by Philippe-Auguste in the thirteenth century as a fortress. Throughout the centuries the palace has served many purposes, from the royal residence to empty apartments that were taken over by artists. Louis XVI and Marie-Antoinette fled from the palace, then called the **Palais des Tuileries,** in 1791, two years after the start of the Revolution. At the end of the eighteenth century, Napoleon made the Louvre into a museum, but three more French kings, Louis XVIII, Charles X, and Louis Philippe, continued to make the Louvre their home.

The Louvre's incredible collections include paintings, drawings, sculpture, furniture, coins, and jewelry. You may wish to see if your school district owns a video copy of the wonderful documentary called *The Louvre,* narrated in English by Charles Boyer. Although the film was made in 1978, it is a fascinating look at the origins, inhabitants, and changing face of the Louvre with amazing facts and stories.

Sculpture For much of its history, Bénin was known as Abomey, and later the kingdom of Dahomey. The cultural history of Bénin is very rich, and the art produced during the Dahomey era attracts international attention. Art served both a functional and spiritual purpose. The bronzes seen here are of leopards, and they date from the sixteenth century.

Une exposition Have groups research different French painters and/or sculptors. Each group can put on an art show, using prints of the artists' most famous works.

Au musée Visit a local museum so that students can see different styles of art and, hopefully, some work by French artists.

Un film You may wish to rent a video of a French film in **version originale** and show it to the class. Your students might enjoy the following movies: *Au revoir les enfants, Les quatre cents coups, L'enfant sauvage, Le ballon rouge, Jean de Florette, La gloire de mon père, Cyrano de Bergerac.*

1 Preparation

Resource Manager

Vocabulary Transparencies 1.2–1.3
Audio Activities Booklet TE, pages 1–2
Audiocassette 2A/CD 2
Workbook, pages 1–2
Quiz 1, page 1
ExamView Pro®

Bellringer Review

Use BRR Transparency 1.1 or write the following on the board.
Make a list of activities you like to do in your free time.

2 Presentation

Step 1 Show Vocabulary Transparencies 1.2–1.3. Point to individual items and have the class repeat the words after you or Audiocassette 2A/CD 2.

Step 2 Call on individual students to point to the corresponding illustration on the transparency as you say the word or expression. **Teaching Tip:** Ask questions about students' personal preferences when practicing the vocabulary. For example: **Jacques, tu préfères les films policiers ou les documentaires? Qui aime les dessins animés?**

Step 3 After presenting the vocabulary orally, have students open their books. Call on individuals to read. Ask questions about the sentences such as: **On joue ce film étranger où? Le film est en V.O. ou on le voit avec des sous-titres?**

Step 4 Call on students to act out the short conversation.

Vocabulaire Mots 1

Au cinéma 

Pierre est devant le guichet.
La prochaine séance est à treize heures.

Qui joue dans ce film?
On joue un film étranger au Rex.
Le film est en V.O. (version originale).
On le voit avec des sous-titres.
Dans un autre cinéma, le film est doublé.
On peut le voir en français.

Qu'est-ce qu'on joue au Rex?
Je ne sais pas. On peut regarder dans *l'Officiel des Spectacles.*
Les places coûtent combien?

Reaching All Students

Total Physical Response
(Student 1), **levez-vous, s'il vous plaît.**
Faites la queue devant le guichet.
Prenez votre billet.
Entrez dans le cinéma.
Choisissez une place.
Prenez votre place. Asseyez-vous.
Regardez le film.
Indiquez que le film est amusant.
Le film est fini. Levez-vous.
Sortez du cinéma.

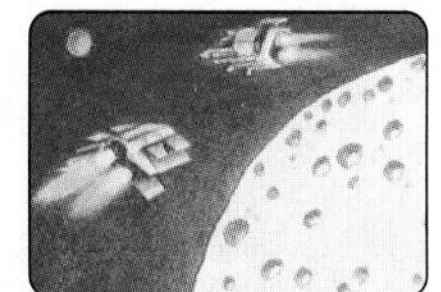
un film de science-fiction

un film d'horreur

un film policier

un documentaire

un film en vidéo

louer une vidéo

un film d'amour

un dessin animé

un film d'aventures

Au théâtre

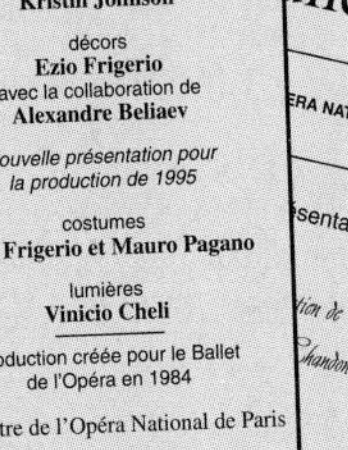

On va monter *Roméo et Juliette.*
C'est une pièce de théâtre en trois actes.
Chaque acte a deux scènes.
Entre deux actes, il y a un entracte.
Roméo et Juliette est aussi un ballet.

Voici d'autres genres de pièces:
- une tragédie
- une comédie
- un drame
- une comédie musicale

Vocabulary Expansion

You may wish to give students the following additional words.

un fauteuil
l'orchestre
le balcon
un rang
le rideau
le lever du rideau
un costume
un décor

Reaching All Students

Additional Practice Have students work in pairs to prepare a skit. One plays the part of a box office clerk at a movie theater; the other plays the part of a ticket buyer.

Class Motivator

Des films Students work in groups of four. Each person writes down the title of a movie he or she has seen recently. They put their titles together and scramble them. Each person in turn picks one and asks: **Qui a vu ce film?** and then makes up as many present-tense questions about it as possible. The student who saw the film answers. If anyone picks his or her own film, he or she tells the others about it.

Variation: Each person in turn picks one and describes the film, the actors, etc., and the others try to name the film.

3 Practice

Commençons
Let's use our new words

Historiette Each time **Historiette** appears, it means that the answers to the activity form a short story. Encourage students to look at the title of the **Historiette,** since it can help them do the activity.

1, **3**, **5** With books closed, ask the questions to these activities and call on individuals to respond.

Note: Answers to these activities can be written at home.

2 and **4** Call on student(s) to retell the information in their own words. Have students open books. Call on individuals to read aloud, completing the sentences with the appropriate words.

Commençons
Let's use our new words

1 Fana de cinéma ou pas?
Donnez des réponses personnelles.

1. Tu vas souvent au cinéma?
2. Qu'est-ce que tu aimes comme films?
3. Quel est ton acteur préféré? Et ton actrice préférée? Il/Elle est très connu(e)?
4. Il y a un cinéma près de chez toi?
5. La première séance est à quelle heure?
6. Où est-ce que tu achètes les billets?
7. Tu fais souvent la queue devant le guichet?
8. Dans la salle de cinéma, tu aimes mieux une place près de l'écran ou loin de l'écran?
9. Si tu vas voir un film étranger, tu aimes mieux voir le film doublé ou en version originale avec des sous-titres?

Le cinéma Champollion, Paris

2 Historiette Au cinéma Complétez.

Ce soir, on __1__ un très bon film au Wepler. C'est un film étranger. Il n'est pas doublé. Il y a des __2__. Le film est en __3__ originale. La prochaine __4__ est à quelle heure? Les __5__ coûtent combien?

3 Tu aimes mieux quels genres de film?
Donnez des réponses personnelles.

1. Tu aimes mieux (préfères) les documentaires ou les westerns?
2. Tu aimes mieux les films policiers ou les films d'horreur?
3. Tu aimes mieux les films comiques ou les films d'amour?
4. Tu aimes mieux les films d'aventures ou les films de science-fiction?
5. Tu vas voir quelquefois des dessins animés?
6. Tu loues quelquefois des films en vidéo? Quels genres de film?

Answers to Commençons

1 *Answers will vary but may include:*

1. Oui, je vais souvent au cinéma.
2. J'aime les films policiers.
3. Mon acteur préféré est ____. Mon actrice préférée est ____. Oui, ils sont très connus.
4. Oui, il y a un cinéma près de chez moi.
5. La première séance est à 19 h.
6. J'achète les billets au guichet.
7. Oui, je fais souvent la queue devant le guichet.
8. Dans la salle de cinéma j'aime mieux une place près de l'écran.
9. Si je vais voir un film étranger, j'aime mieux voir le film en version originale avec des sous-titres.

2

1. joue
2. sous-titres
3. version
4. séance
5. places

3 *Answers will vary but may include:*

1. J'aime mieux les westerns.
2. J'aime mieux les films policiers.
3. J'aime mieux les films comiques.
4. J'aime mieux les films de science-fiction.
5. Oui, je vais voir quelquefois des dessins animés.
6. Oui, je loue quelquefois des films en vidéo. Des films policiers.

4 Des pièces et des films Complétez.

1. Au lycée les élèves ____ une pièce tous les ans.
2. On voit un film au cinéma. On voit une pièce au ____.
3. Une ____ a des actes et les actes sont divisés en ____.
4. Entre deux actes, il y a un ____.
5. Un ____ joue le rôle de Roméo.
6. Une ____ joue le rôle de Juliette.
7. Dans une comédie musicale, les ____ chantent et les ____ dansent.

5 Historiette Au théâtre Donnez des réponses personnelles.

1. Tu aimes le théâtre?
2. Tu vas souvent au théâtre?
3. Il y a un théâtre là où tu habites?
4. Ton école a un club d'art dramatique?
5. Tu es membre de ce club?
6. Le club monte combien de pièces par an?
7. Cette année, le club va monter quelle pièce?
8. C'est quel genre de pièce?
9. Il y a combien d'actes?
10. Il y a combien d'entractes?

6 Mon film préféré Find out what a classmate's favorite movies are and why. Then find out which movies he or she dislikes and why. Take turns.

*For more practice using words from **Mots 1**, do Activity 1 on page H2 at the end of this book.*

Vocabulaire

Writing Development

Have students write the answers to Activities 2–5 in paragraph form.

Cognate Recognition

Have students scan the **Mots 1** words again and then identify and pronounce each cognate.

Reteaching

Show Vocabulary Transparencies 1.2–1.3 and let students say as much as they can about them in their own words.

Learning from Realia

(page 5 middle) You may wish to tell students that Molière was a famous seventeenth-century dramatist whose comedies are still very much appreciated today.

ENCORE PLUS This *infogap* activity will allow students to practice in pairs. The activity should be very manageable for them, since all vocabulary and structures are familiar to them.

Attention!

Note that the activities are color-coded. All the activities in the text are communicative. However, the ones with blue titles are guided communication. The red titles indicate that the answers to the activity are more open-ended and can vary more. You may wish to correct students' mistakes more so in the guided activities than in the activities with a red title, which lend themselves to a freer response.

Answers to Commençons

4

1. montent
2. théâtre
3. pièce, scènes
4. entracte
5. acteur
6. actrice
7. chanteurs, danseurs

5 *Answers will vary but may include:*

1. Oui, j'aime le théâtre.
2. Oui, je vais souvent au théâtre.
3. Oui, il y a un théâtre là où j'habite.
4. Oui, mon école a un club d'art dramatique.
5. Oui, je suis membre de ce club.
6. Le club monte trois pièces par an.
7. Cette année le club va monter ____.
8. C'est ____.
9. Il y a ____ actes.
10. Il y a ____ entractes.

1 Preparation

Resource Manager

Vocabulary Transparencies 1.4–1.5
Audio Activities Booklet TE, page 3
Audiocassette 2A/CD 2
Workbook, pages 3–4
Quiz 2, page 2
ExamView Pro®

Bellringer Review

Use BRR Transparency 1.2 or write the following on the board.
Name your four favorite movies and tell what type of films they are.

2 Presentation

Step 1 Show Vocabulary Transparencies 1.4–1.5. Have students close their books and repeat the new words after you two or three times.

Step 2 Call a student to the front of the room. As you say a new word or phrase, have the student point to the appropriate item on the transparency.

Step 3 After presenting the vocabulary with the transparencies, have students open their books and read the words and sentences.

Vocabulaire Mots 2

Au musée

Une exposition de peinture et sculpture

Reaching All Students

Total Physical Response Before you begin, demonstrate the meaning of **se promener.**

(Student 1), **levez-vous et venez ici, s'il vous plaît.**
Vous êtes devant le musée d'Art Moderne.
Entrez dans le musée.
Promenez-vous dans la grande salle.
Vous voyez un tableau que vous trouvez beau.
Arrêtez-vous.
Regardez le tableau.
Indiquez que vous aimez le tableau, que vous le trouvez beau.
Et voilà un autre tableau. Indiquez que vous n'aimez pas ce tableau. Vous ne le trouvez pas beau.

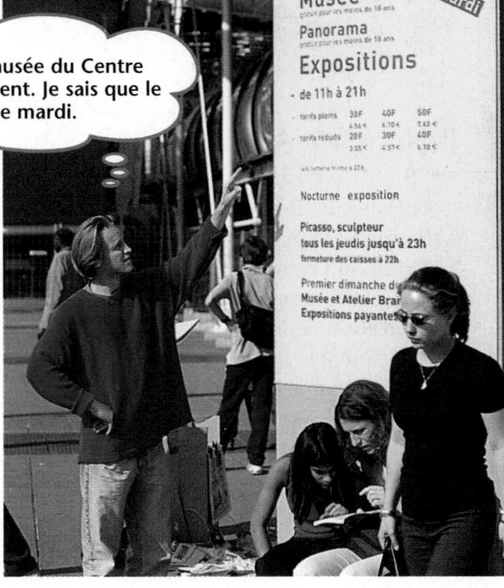

Le musée n'est pas ouvert le mardi.
Il est ouvert tous les jours sauf le mardi.

Vocabulary Expansion

You may wish to give students the following additional vocabulary in order to talk about art.

une gravure
une lithographie
de la poterie
une aquarelle
un portrait
une peinture à l'huile

Cognate Recognition

Ask students to identify as many cognates as they can in **Mots 2.** Pay particular attention to their pronunciation of these cognates.

3 Practice

Commençons
Let's use our new words

8 You may wish to have students write their answers to this activity in paragraph form.

Reaching All Students

Additional Practice Have students quickly write down as many words associated with the movies, theater, or museums as they can. Then have them work in pairs, giving their partner one word at a time from their list. Their partner puts the word into a sentence.

Art Connection

Starting in 1890, Monet had built at his home in Giverny a beautiful garden and a pond, **un jardin d'eau,** which reflected his interest in Japanese art. He did many paintings of his **jardin d'eau.** Many of his paintings of **les nymphéas** *(water lilies)* can be seen today in the Orangerie in Paris.

Vocabulaire

Commençons
Let's use our new words

Un peu de culture Répondez d'après les dessins.

1. C'est un musée ou un théâtre?

2. Le musée est ouvert ou fermé?

3. Elle est peintre ou sculpteur?

4. C'est un tableau ou une statue?

8 Historiette Au musée
Inventez des réponses.

1. Michel sait comment s'appelle le peintre?
2. Il connaît le peintre personnellement?
3. Il connaît l'œuvre du peintre?
4. Annick sait dans quel musée il y a une exposition de Monet?
5. Elle trouve ses tableaux extraordinaires?
6. Elle connaît le musée de l'Orangerie?
7. Elle le visite souvent?
8. Elle sait que le musée est fermé le mardi?
9. Le musée de l'Orangerie est ouvert tous les jours sauf le mardi?

Claude Monet *Le bassin aux nymphéas*

Answers to Commençons

1. C'est un musée.
2. Le musée est ouvert.
3. Elle est sculpteur.
4. C'est un tableau.

8 *Answers will vary but may include:*

1. Non, Michel ne sait pas comment s'appelle le peintre.
2. Non, il ne connaît pas le peintre personnellement.
3. Oui, il connaît l'œuvre du peintre.
4. Oui, elle sait dans quel musée il y a une exposition de Monet.
5. Oui, elle trouve ses tableaux extraordinaires.
6. Oui, elle connaît le musée de l'Orangerie.
7. Oui, elle le visite souvent.
8. Oui, elle sait que le musée est fermé le mardi.
9. Oui, le musée de l'Orangerie est ouvert tous les jours sauf le mardi.

Vocabulaire

L'art français Work with a classmate. Discuss together what you have learned so far about French art and French artists. Find out who appreciates art more and who knows more about art.

Paul Cézanne *Pommes et oranges*

Tours et crypte archéologique
de **Notre-Dame** –12 ans : gratuit

Rue de Cloître, Paris 4e. **M°**: Cité, ou **RER C**: St. Michel. Tours: **tél**: 01 44 32 16 72, groupes: 01 44 32 16 72. **Horaires**: 9h30-19h30 du 1.04 au 30.09; 10h-17h du 1.10 au 31.03. Fermeture des caisses 45mn plus tôt. Crypte: **tél**: 01 43 29 83 51. **Horaires**: 9h30-18h du 1.04 au 30.09; 10h-16h30 du 1.10 au 31.03.
Du haut des tours: une vue exceptionnelle sur la cathédrale et la ville. . . Dans la crypte archéologique: l'histoire de Paris de l'époque gallo-romaine au XIXe s.

Musée de l'**Ordre de la Libération** –12 ans : gratuit

Hôtel national des Invalides, 51 bis, boulevard de Latour-Maubourg, Paris 7e. **Tél**: 01 47 05 35 15. **M°**: Invalides. **Horaires**: 10h-17h.
Musée de la France Libre, de la Résistance et de la Déportation.

Musée d'**Orsay** – 18 ans : gratuit

1, rue de Bellechasse, Paris 7e. **Tél**: 01 40 49 48 14 . **M°**: Solférino, ou **RER C**: Musée d'Orsay. **Horaires**: 10h-18h, nocturne le jeudi jusqu' à 21h45. Le dimanche, et du 20.06 au 20.09: 9h-18h. Fermé le lundi.
Peintures impressionnistes et ensemble de la création artistique de 1848 à 1914.

Renseignements You're in Paris and you'd like to visit one of the museums listed in the brochure on the left. Call the museum and find out from the museum employee (your partner) where it's located, what time it opens and closes, what day it's closed, and how much a ticket costs. Your partner can use the information in the brochure to answer your questions.

*For more practice using words from **Mots 2**, do Activity 2 on page H3 at the end of this book.*

Art Connection

Early in his career, Paul Cézanne (1839–1906) also took part in the first exhibition of the Impressionists. Later studies led him to believe that Impressionist paintings lacked form, solidity, and structure. Cézanne wanted to paint nature, but he was not interested in reproducing exactly the shapes, colors, etc., found in nature. He began to experiment with still-life painting, often painting the same subject over and over until he was completely satisfied with it.

Answers to Commençons

Answers will vary depending upon the painter and/or works of art the students select.

Answers will vary.

1 Preparation

Resource Manager

Audio Activities Booklet TE, pages 4–6
Audiocassette 2A/CD 2
Workbook, pages 5–7
Quizzes 3–5, pages 3–5
ExamView Pro®

Bellringer Review

Use BRR Transparency 1.3 or write the following on the board.
List everything you associate with the following.
le cinéma
le théâtre
un musée

2 Presentation

Les verbes **savoir** et **connaître**

Step 1 Lead students through Items 1–4 and the examples.

Step 2 Make two lists on the board, one of information that follows **connaître** (names of people, cities and other places, artistic and literary works), and the other with facts that follow **savoir** (dates, times, telephone numbers, addresses, infinitives, clauses).

Step 3 Give students the following words or expressions and have them say whether they would use **savoir** or **connaître: André, sa famille, son adresse, son numéro de téléphone, le nom de son école, ses professeurs, sa ville.**

Telling whom and what you know
Les verbes **savoir** et **connaître**

1. Study the following present-tense forms of the verbs **savoir** and **connaître,** both of which mean "to know."

SAVOIR		CONNAÎTRE	
je	sais	je	connais
tu	sais	tu	connais
il/elle/on	sait	il/elle/on	connaît
nous	savons	nous	connaissons
vous	savez	vous	connaissez
ils/elles	savent	ils/elles	connaissent

Note the **passé composé** of these verbs: **j'ai su, j'ai connu.**

2. You use **savoir** to indicate that you know a fact or that you know something by heart.

 Tu sais à quelle heure la séance commence?
 Tu sais le numéro de téléphone de Philippe?

3. You use **savoir** + infinitive to indicate that you know how to do something.

 Tu sais danser le tango?
 Il ne sait pas nager.

4. **Connaître** means "to know" in the sense of "to be acquainted with." You can use **connaître** only with nouns—people, places, and things. Compare the meanings of **connaître** and **savoir** in the sentences below.

 Je sais comment elle s'appelle. Nathalie. **Je connais bien Nathalie.**
 Je sais où elle habite. À Grenoble. **Je connais bien Grenoble.**
 Je sais le nom de l'auteur. Victor Hugo. **Je connais son œuvre.**

Grenoble, France

Learning from Photos

(page 10) Grenoble is the capital of Dauphiné in the Alps. It is a fast growing city with many new skyscrapers. It is home to several universities, and major companies that specialize in electronics, engineering, and nuclear research. Surrounded by mountains, Grenoble is a modern, cosmopolitan city.

24 **Demain** Répondez d'après le modèle.

—Tu as vu ce film?
—Non, mais je vais le voir demain.

1. Tu as vu cette pièce?
2. Tu as vu cette exposition?
3. Tu as vu ces sculptures de Rodin?
4. Tu as vu ces tableaux?
5. Tu as vu l'exposition des tableaux de Gauguin?

Auguste Rodin *Le penseur*

25 **Devinettes** Devinez ce que c'est.

1. On le présente quand on va dans un pays étranger.
2. On le prend pour voyager très loin.
3. On les lave avant de manger.
4. On les lave avec une brosse à dents.
5. On la remplit avant de débarquer.
6. On l'écoute attentivement en classe.

26 **Jeu** **Encore des devinettes** Work in groups and make up riddles similar to those in Activity 25. Ask other groups your riddles. The group that guesses the most riddles wins.

27 **L'artiste** Have some fun. Pretend you are an artist. Draw something. Have a classmate give a critique of your artwork. Take turns.

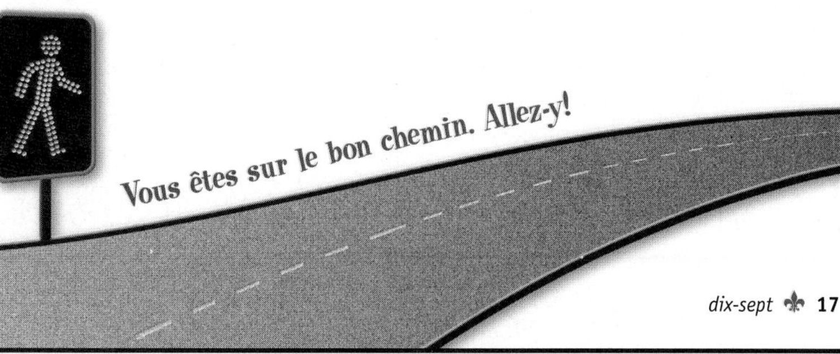

Art Connection

Auguste Rodin (1840–1917) dominated the world of sculpture at the end of the nineteenth century and the beginning of the twentieth century. His technique in sculpture was similar to that of the Impressionists in painting. As he modeled in wax or clay, he added pieces bit by bit to construct his forms, just as the painters added dots and dashes of paint to create their pictures.

This statue, ***Le penseur,*** is one of his most famous. This sculpture, along with others, is located in the garden of **le musée Rodin** in the **7e arrondissement** of Paris. The museum is housed in a beautiful eighteenth-century mansion that was once Rodin's studio.

Allez-y!
At this point in the chapter, students have learned all the vocabulary and structure necessary to complete the chapter. The conversation and cultural readings that follow recycle all the material learned up to this point.

Answers to Continuons

24

1. Non, mais je vais la voir demain.
2. Non, mais je vais la voir demain.
3. Non, mais je vais les voir demain.
4. Non, mais je vais les voir demain.
5. Non, mais je vais la voir demain.

25

1. son passeport
2. l'avion
3. les mains
4. les dents
5. la carte de débarquement
6. le prof, la prof

26 *Answers will vary but may include:*

On le donne à un ami pour son anniversaire. (le cadeau)
On les peigne le matin. (les cheveux)
On l'achète pour voir un film. (le billet)

27 *Answers will vary but may include:*

Je trouve ton dessin très beau. Je le trouve très intéressant.

Conversation

1 Preparation

Resource Manager

Audio Activities Booklet TE, page 7
Audiocassette 2A/CD 2
CD-ROM

Bellringer Review

Use BRR Transparency 1.6 or write the following on the board.
Write the following words under the correct category: **le cinéma** or **le théâtre.**

une pièce, l'écran, les sous-titres, la scène, l'entracte, une séance, une tragédie

2 Presentation

Step 1 Tell students they are going to hear a conversation between Bruno and Léa, who are discussing going to a movie.

Step 2 Have them watch the conversation on the CD-ROM or listen as you read the conversation or play Audiocassette 2A/CD 2.

Step 3 Have students work in pairs to practice the conversation. Then have several pairs present it to the class.

Step 4 You may have a more able student retell the conversation in narrative form in his or her own words.

Glencoe Technology

CD-ROM
On the CD-ROM, students can watch a dramatization of this conversation. They can then play the role of either one of the characters and record themselves in the conversation.

Conversation

On va au cinéma?   

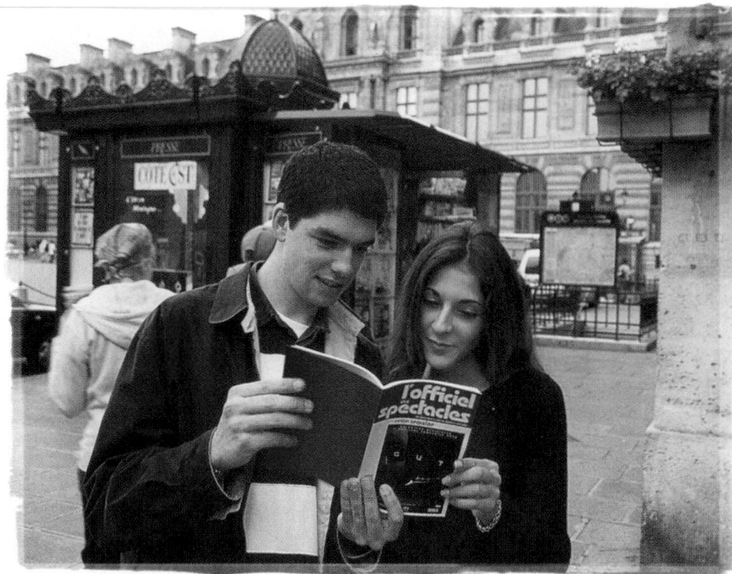

Bruno: Qu'est-ce que tu veux faire?
Léa: Je ne sais pas, moi. Aller au cinéma.
Bruno: Qu'est-ce que tu veux voir?
Léa: Ça m'est égal. Comme tu veux. Qu'est-ce qu'il y a de bien?
Bruno: Attends. Je vais te dire… *(Il prend* l'Officiel des Spectacles, *il l'ouvre et il le lit…)* Il y a un film avec Ricki Dean.
Léa: Ah non, pas Ricki Dean. Je le déteste, ce type. Il est parfaitement ridicule et il ne le sait même pas!
Bruno: Il y a un film espagnol au Ciné-Élysées. Ça t'intéresse?
Léa: Oui, un film espagnol, ça me dit. On va pouvoir travailler notre espagnol.
Bruno: Alors, il faut se dépêcher. La prochaine séance est à seize heures.

Après la conversation

Répondez.

1. Qu'est-ce que Léa veut faire?
2. Qui a *l'Officiel des Spectacles*?
3. Qui le lit?
4. Léa aime Ricki Dean? Pour quelle raison?
5. Bruno et Léa vont voir quel film?
6. Pourquoi est-ce que Léa veut voir un film espagnol?
7. Ils vont aller à quelle séance?

Answers to Après la conversation

1. Elle veut aller au cinéma.
2. Bruno a *l'Officiel des Spectacles.*
3. Bruno le lit.
4. Non, elle n'aime pas Ricki Dean parce qu'il est ridicule.
5. Ils vont voir un film espagnol.
6. Ils vont pouvoir travailler leur espagnol.
7. Ils vont aller à la séance de seize heures.

Parlons un peu plus
Let's talk some more

On va au cinéma? Look at the movie guide. Decide which movie you'd like to see and invite a classmate to see it with you. Tell your partner when and where the movie is playing, whether it is dubbed or in the original language with subtitles. Discuss whether or not you both want to see the movie or figure out an alternative.

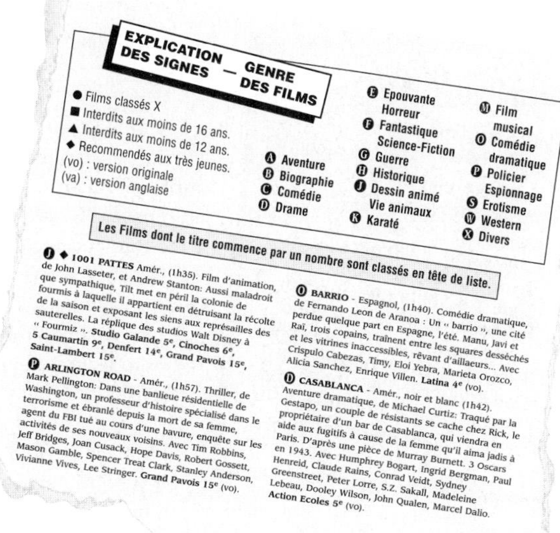

EXPLICATION DES SIGNES — GENRE DES FILMS

● Films classés X
■ Interdits aux moins de 16 ans.
▲ Interdits aux moins de 12 ans.
◆ Recommendés aux très jeunes.
(vo) : version originale
(va) : version anglaise

Ⓐ Aventure
Ⓑ Biographie
Ⓒ Comédie
Ⓓ Drame
Ⓔ Epouvante Horreur
Ⓕ Fantastique Science-Fiction
Ⓖ Guerre
Ⓗ Historique
Ⓙ Dessin animé Vie animaux
Ⓚ Karaté
Ⓜ Film musical
Ⓞ Comédie dramatique
Ⓟ Policier Espionnage
Ⓢ Erotisme
Ⓦ Western
Ⓧ Divers

Les Films dont le titre commence par un nombre sont classés en tête de liste.

Ⓙ ◆ **1001 PATTES** Amér., (1h35). Film d'animation, de John Lasseter, et Andrew Stanton: Aussi maladroit que sympathique, Tilt met en péril la colonie de fourmis à laquelle il appartient en détruisant la récolte de la saison et exposant les siens aux représailles des sauterelles. La réplique des studios Walt Disney à « Fourmiz ». **Studio Galande 5e, Cinoches 6e, 5 Caumartin 9e, Denfert 14e, Grand Pavois 15e, Saint-Lambert 15e.**

Ⓟ **ARLINGTON ROAD** - Amér., (1h57). Thriller, de Mark Pellington: Dans une banlieue résidentielle de Washington, un professeur d'histoire spécialisé dans le terrorisme et ébranlé depuis la mort de sa femme, agent du FBI tué au cours d'une bavure, enquête sur les activités de ses nouveaux voisins. Avec Tim Robbins, Jeff Bridges, Joan Cusack, Hope Davis, Robert Gossett, Mason Gamble, Spencer Treat Clark, Stanley Anderson, Vivianne Vives, Lee Stringer. **Grand Pavois 15e** (vo).

Ⓞ **BARRIO** - Espagnol, (1h40). Comédie dramatique, de Fernando Leon de Aranoa : Un « barrio », une cité perdue quelque part en Espagne, l'été. Manu, Javi et Raï, trois copains, traînent entre les squares desséchés et les vitrines inaccessibles, rêvant d'aillaeurs... Avec Crispulo Cabezas, Timy, Eloi Yebra, Marieta Orozco, Alicia Sanchez, Enrique Villen. **Latina 4e** (vo).

Ⓓ **CASABLANCA** - Amér., noir et blanc (1h42). Aventure dramatique, de Michael Curtiz: Traqué par la Gestapo, un couple de résistants se cache chez Rick, le propriétaire d'un bar de Casablanca, qui viendra en aide aux fugitifs à cause de la femme qu'il aima jadis à Paris. D'après une pièce de Murray Burnett. 3 Oscars en 1943. Avec Humphrey Bogart, Ingrid Bergman, Paul Henreid, Claude Rains, Conrad Veidt, Sydney Greenstreet, Peter Lorre, S.Z. Sakall, Madeleine Lebeau, Dooley Wilson, John Qualen, Marcel Dalio. **Action Ecoles 5e** (vo).

Prononciation

Le son **/ü/** 

1. To say the sound **/ü/**, first say the sound **/i/**, then round your lips. Repeat the following words.

   une statue **une sculpture** **une peinture**
   une voiture **un musée**

2. The sound **/ü/** also occurs in combination with other vowels. Repeat the following words.

   aujourd'hui **depuis** **je suis** **huit**

3. Now repeat the following sentences.

   Tu as vu ces statues?
   C'est une sculpture très connue?
   Le musée est rue Sully depuis huit ans.

une statue

3 Practice

Parlons un peu plus
Let's talk some more

Have students work in pairs. You may wish to choose a pair of students to do these activities for the class.

Prononciation

Step 1 Model the key word **une statue** and have the students repeat in unison.

Step 2 Now lead students through the information on page 19 and model the other words and sentences.

Step 3 You may wish to give the students the following **dictée:**

Le musée n'est pas rue Victor Hugo. Tu as bu du lait?

Answers to Parlons un peu plus

Answers will vary.

Resource Manager

Audio Activities Booklet TE, pages 8–9
Audiocassette 2A/CD 2

National Standards

Cultures

The reading about cultural life in France on pages 20–21 and the related activities on page 21 allow students to find out more about museums, ballet, opera, and theater in France.

Presentation

Pre-reading

Step 1 You may want to have students look at the photos on pages 20–21 now.

Step 2 Read and discuss the Reading Strategy, page 20. Have students identify the main idea of each section of the reading.

Step 3 Have students skim the reading quickly and silently.

Reading

Step 1 Lead students through the Lecture on pages 20–21 by having individuals read two to three sentences at a time. After each one reads, ask others follow-up questions.

Step 2 Ask five or six questions that review the main points. Call on individuals to answer. Answers will give an organized summary of the **Lecture.**

Le Québec

Lectures culturelles

Reading Strategy

Identifying the main idea

When reading, it is important to identify the main idea the author is expressing. Each paragraph usually discusses a different idea. The main idea is often found in the first or second sentence in each paragraph. First, skim the passage. Once you know the main idea of the passage, go back and read it again more carefully.

Les loisirs culturels en France

Les musées

Les musées en France sont toujours très fréquentés par les Français et par les touristes qui visitent la France. Tu connais les impressionnistes? Tu apprécies leurs tableaux? Alors il faut aller au musée d'Orsay. Le musée d'Orsay est une ancienne gare qui a été transformée en musée. C'est le musée du dix-neuvième siècle[1]. On trouve des tableaux, des sculptures, des meubles[2], tout du dix-neuvième siècle. Il y a une exposition permanente de tableaux des impressionnistes.

Si tu es fana d'art moderne, tu vas beaucoup aimer le centre Pompidou. Là, il y a toujours des expositions d'art moderne. Il y a aussi une vue extraordinaire sur Paris.

Mais la perle des musées français, c'est le Louvre. Au Louvre, tu peux admirer des tableaux et des sculptures de grands artistes de tous les siècles.

Le premier dimanche de chaque mois, l'entrée des musées nationaux est gratuite. Les autres dimanches, elle est demi-tarif[3]. C'est pourquoi les musées sont toujours combles le dimanche.

[1] siècle *century*
[2] meubles *furniture*
[3] demi-tarif *half-price*

Centre Pompidou

Musée d'Orsay

Learning from Photos

(page 20 left) The **Centre Pompidou** is named after Georges Pompidou, the French president who launched the project to establish this museum of modern art. Most Parisians simply refer to it as **Beaubourg** because it is located on the plateau **Beaubourg.** The center was opened in 1977, and it soon attracted millions of visitors, five times more than had been estimated. The brightly painted exterior service pipes and the plastic tubing enclosing the escalator were in need of constant repair. In 1996 the government shut down the center for a complete renovation. It reopened in January 2000 and the total complex was greatly expanded.

(page 20 right) The **musée d'Orsay** was once a railroad station. Today it houses the world's most complete and famous collection of Impressionist paintings.

Lectures culturelles

Opéra Garnier

Les ballets et l'opéra

Si tu aimes la danse classique, il faut aller voir un ballet à l'opéra Garnier.

Si tu aimes l'opéra, il faut aller à l'opéra Bastille. On a inauguré le nouvel opéra sur la place de la Bastille en 1989 pour commémorer le bicentenaire de la Révolution française de 1789. Tu préfères l'architecture de quel opéra? De l'ancien opéra Garnier ou du nouvel opéra Bastille? L'architecture, c'est un art aussi, tu sais.

Opéra Bastille

Le théâtre

Tu connais les grands auteurs dramatiques du dix-septième siècle: Racine, Corneille, Molière? Si tu as envie[4] d'aller voir une de leurs pièces, tu peux aller à la Comédie-Française, le plus vieux théâtre national du monde.

[4] as envie *feel like*

Comédie-Française

Après la lecture

A Les musées Répondez.

1. Qui fréquente les musées français?
2. Tu connais quelques peintres impressionnistes?
3. Tu apprécies leurs tableaux?
4. Tu connais leur œuvre?
5. Il y a une exposition permanente des impressionnistes dans quel musée?
6. Quel est le musée d'art moderne?
7. Quel est un autre musée très célèbre à Paris?
8. Qu'est-ce qu'il y a dans ce musée?
9. Les musées sont presque toujours combles le dimanche. Pourquoi?

B D'autres loisirs Répondez.

1. Tu es à Paris et tu veux voir un ballet. Tu vas où?
2. Tu veux voir un opéra. Tu vas où?
3. Tu veux voir une tragédie de Racine ou une comédie de Molière. Tu vas où?

Le Maroc

Le Mali

Post-reading

Have students do the **Après la lecture** activities on page 21 orally after reading the selection in class. Then assign these activities to be written at home. Go over them again the following day.

Après la lecture

A and B Allow students to refer to the story to look up the answers or you may use this activity as a testing device for factual recall.

Learning from Photos

(page 21 top) The **Opéra Garnier** is the original opera house of Paris. Built at the behest of Napoleon III, construction was begun in 1862 but not completed until 1875. It is named after its architect, Charles Garnier. It is a beautiful building with a mélange of many architectural styles. Most operas are now performed at the new **Opéra Bastille,** but there are still occasional performances at the Garnier, which is more often used for ballets.

(page 21 middle) The **Opéra Bastille** on the **place de la Bastille** was designed by the Argentine-born architect Carlos Ott. It opened in 1989 and it seats more than 3,000 people. Many Parisians are not fond of its glass façade that looks like a modern office building.

(page 21 bottom) The **Comédie-Française** theater building dates from 1790. The **Comédie-Française** Acting Company was created by Louis XIV and dates back to 1680. The **Comédie-Française** is the setting for performances of classical French dramas. The comedies of Molière and the tragedies of Racine and Corneille are performed regularly.

Answers to Après la lecture

A

1. Les Français et les touristes qui visitent la France fréquentent les musées français.
2. Oui, je connais quelques peintres impressionnistes.
3. Oui, je les apprécie.
4. Oui, je la connais.
5. Il y a une exposition permanente des impressionnistes au musée d'Orsay.
6. Le musée d'art moderne est le centre Pompidou.
7. Le Louvre est un autre musée très célèbre à Paris.
8. Au Louvre il y a des tableaux et des sculptures de grands artistes de tous les siècles.
9. Les musées sont combles le dimanche parce que l'entrée est gratuite ou demi-tarif.

B

1. Je vais à l'opéra Garnier.
2. Je vais à l'opéra Bastille.
3. Je vais à la Comédie-Française.

National Standards

Cultures
This selection familiarizes students with traditional and popular African music.

Attention!

This reading is optional. You may skip it completely, have the entire class read it, have only several students read it and report to the class, or assign it for extra credit.

Presentation

Step 1 Ask the students if they have heard any African music. You may wish to play a sample of some of the music mentioned in the **Lecture.**

Step 2 Have students read the **Lecture** quickly.

Step 3 Ask what new information they learned about African music.

Lecture supplémentaire

La musique africaine

Quand on parle de musique africaine, on parle de deux sortes de musique—la musique traditionnelle et la musique moderne pop. Il y a une grande différence entre les deux.

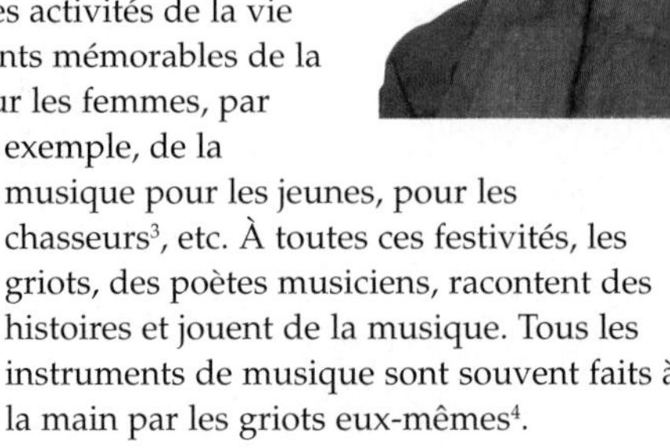

Un griot

La musique traditionnelle

La musique traditionnelle est la musique de la brousse[1], des villages ruraux. Cette musique traditionnelle accompagne toutes les activités de la vie quotidienne ainsi que[2] les événements mémorables de la vie sociale. Il y a de la musique pour les femmes, par exemple, de la musique pour les jeunes, pour les chasseurs[3], etc. À toutes ces festivités, les griots, des poètes musiciens, racontent des histoires et jouent de la musique. Tous les instruments de musique sont souvent faits à la main par les griots eux-mêmes[4].

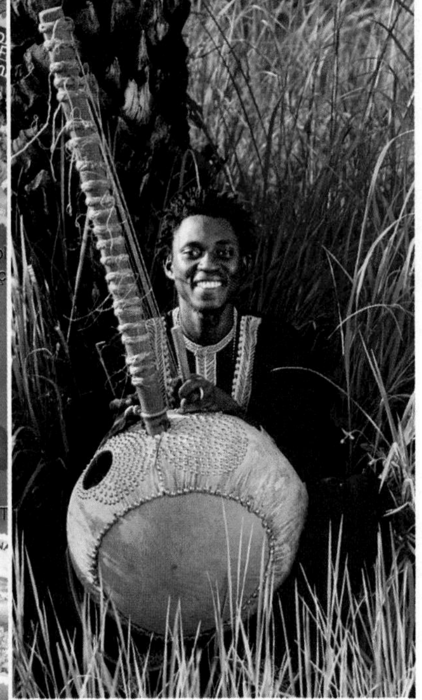

Un musicien joue du kora, Gambie

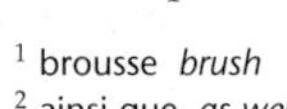

La musique moderne

La musique pop africaine est devenue[5] très populaire au-dehors des pays africains, surtout en Europe. La première fois que vous l'entendez, vous pensez que c'est un mélange de rythmes latins et afro-américains des États-Unis comme le rock et le jazz. C'est vrai. Pourquoi? Parce que la musique africaine est à l'origine de la musique latino-américaine et de la musique afro-américaine d'aujourd'hui.

[1] brousse *brush*
[2] ainsi que *as well as*
[3] chasseurs *hunters*
[4] eux-mêmes *themselves*
[5] est devenue *has become*

Learning from Photos

(page 22 top) The **griot** is a member of a caste responsible for maintaining an oral record of the tribal history in the form of music, poetry, and storytelling. Although the **griots** are the lowest of the castes, they are highly respected. As musicians and songwriters, they used to entertain the royal families. Many musicians who play the **kora,** and quite a few popular singers, are from the **griot** families.

(page 22 bottom) The **kora** is one of the most sophisticated instruments in Sub-Saharan Africa. It has twenty-one strings. The neck is made of rosewood. The neck goes into a somewhat circular gourd covered with cowhide. The **kora** is described as a harp-lute, and it is played most often in Gambia, Guinea, Mali, and Senegal.

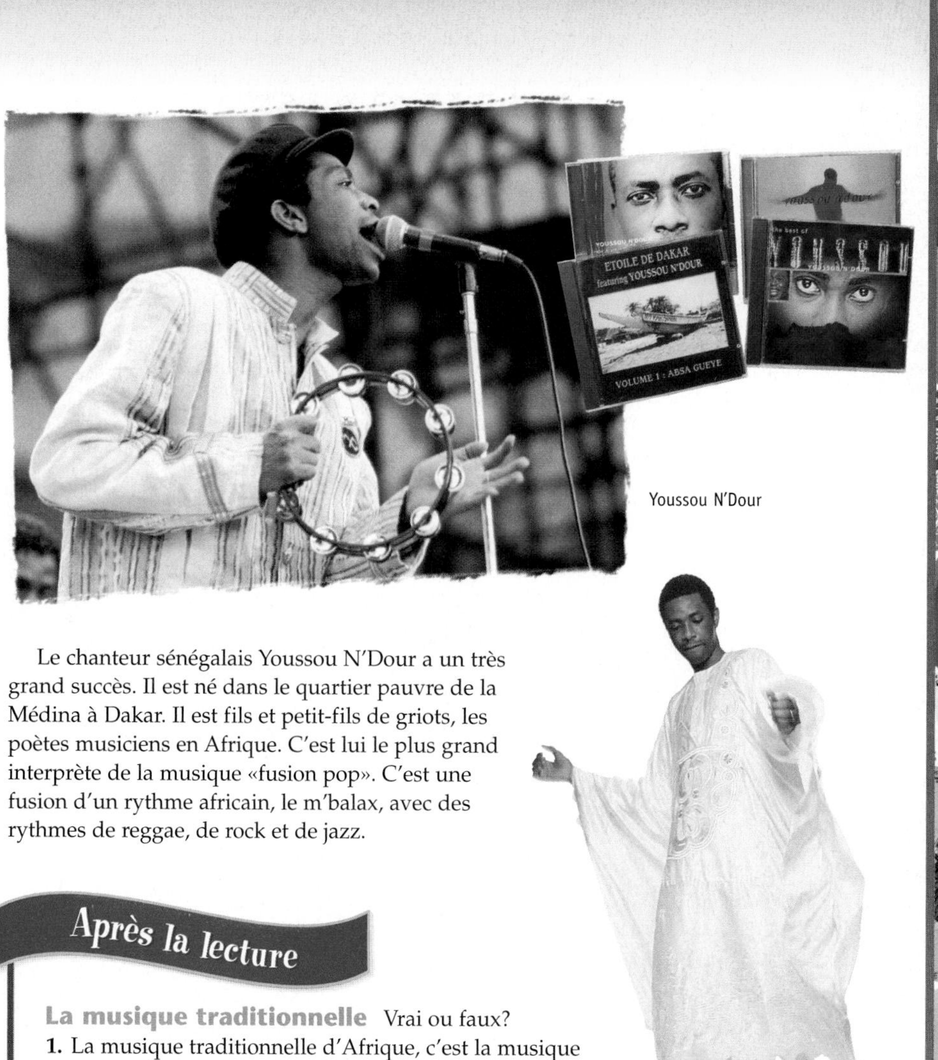

Youssou N'Dour

Le chanteur sénégalais Youssou N'Dour a un très grand succès. Il est né dans le quartier pauvre de la Médina à Dakar. Il est fils et petit-fils de griots, les poètes musiciens en Afrique. C'est lui le plus grand interprète de la musique «fusion pop». C'est une fusion d'un rythme africain, le m'balax, avec des rythmes de reggae, de rock et de jazz.

La Tunisie

Le Maroc

Le Mali

Après la lecture

La musique traditionnelle Vrai ou faux?

1. La musique traditionnelle d'Afrique, c'est la musique des grandes villes cosmopolites.
2. La musique traditionnelle varie selon l'événement.
3. Les griots sont des poètes et des musiciens.
4. Les griots jouent toujours de la guitare électrique.
5. La musique moderne africaine est très populaire aux États-Unis.
6. Le rock et le jazz ont influencé la musique africaine.
7. Youssou N'Dour est un chanteur sénégalais très connu.
8. La musique latino-américaine est une fusion de musique africaine avec du reggae, du rock et du jazz.

Après la lecture

You may wish to have students correct the false statements. You may also wish to have students research some of the types of music and musicians mentioned in the **Lecture.** They can use the Internet to do this or contact their school's music teacher for resources.

Answers to Après la lecture

1. faux
2. vrai
3. vrai
4. faux
5. faux
6. faux
7. vrai
8. faux

CONNEXIONS

National Standards

Connections
This reading about music on pages 24–25 establishes a connection with another discipline, allowing students to reinforce and further their knowledge of music through the study of French.

Attention!

The readings in the **Connexions** section are optional. They focus on some of the major disciplines taught in schools and universities. The vocabulary is useful for discussing such topics as history, literature, art, economics, business, science, etc. You may choose any of the following ways to do the readings in the **Connexions** sections.

Independent reading Have students read the selections and do the post-reading activities as homework, which you collect. This option is least intrusive on class time and requires a minimum of teacher involvement.

Homework with in-class follow-up Assign the readings and post-reading activities as homework. Review and discuss the material in class the next day.

Intensive in-class activity This option includes a pre-reading vocabulary presentation, in-class reading and discussion, assignment of the activities for homework, and a discussion of the assignment in class the following day.

Presentation

Les Beaux-Arts
La musique

Step 1 Have students read the introduction in English on page 24.

CONNEXIONS

Les Beaux-Arts

La musique

Like painting and literature, music is a form of art. Think of all the times you hear music each day. Music has been an integral part of the daily lives of people since the beginning of recorded history.

Before reading some general information about music, let's take a look at some of the many cognates that exist in the language of music.

un ballet

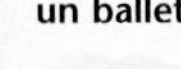

un orchestre symphonique

un opéra

une fanfare

un chœur

The names of many musical instruments are also cognates.

un piano	**un saxophone**	**une trompette**
une guitare	**une flûte**	**une clarinette**
un accordéon	**un violon**	**une harpe**

La musique

Les instruments musicaux

On classifie les instruments musicaux en quatre groupes principaux—les instruments à cordes, les instruments à vent, les instruments à percussion et les instruments à clavier.

Un orchestre ou une fanfare

Quelle est la différence entre un orchestre et une fanfare? Une fanfare n'a pas d'instruments à cordes. Il n'y a pas de violons, par exemple. Et dans une fanfare, il n'y a pas de flûtes ni de hautbois[1]. Les fanfares qui jouent de la musique pendant les événements sportifs et qui participent aux défilés[2] sont plus populaires aux États-Unis qu'en France.

[1] hautbois *oboes* [2] défilés *parades*

Connexions

L'opéra *Carmen*

La chanteuse Céline Dion

L'orchestre symphonique

Un orchestre symphonique est un grand orchestre composé d'instruments de tous les groupes musicaux. Une symphonie est une composition musicale pour orchestre. Une symphonie est en général une composition ambitieuse qui dure de vingt à quarante-cinq minutes.

L'opéra

Un opéra est une composition dramatique sans dialogue parlé. Dans un opéra, les acteurs chantent; ils ne parlent jamais. Ils chantent des airs d'une beauté extraordinaire. L'orchestre les accompagne. L'histoire est en général très tragique. Un opéra comique est un opéra avec des dialogues parlés. Un opéra comique n'est pas nécessairement très amusant. Un opéra bouffe est un opéra dont l'histoire est une comédie. *Carmen* de Georges Bizet et *Dialogue des Carmélites* de Francis Poulenc sont deux opéras français très célèbres.

La musique populaire

Il y a toutes sortes de musique populaire. Il y a des groupes de jazz, de rock et de rap, par exemple. De nos jours, le rap et la musique techno sont très populaires. Les chansons populaires ont souvent des thèmes romantiques. Il y a toujours une relation intime entre la musique populaire et la danse.

Après la lecture

A Des instruments Nommez.

1. un instrument à cordes
2. quelques instruments à vent

B Vous le savez? Répondez.

1. Quelle est la différence entre un orchestre et une fanfare?
2. Qu'est-ce qu'un opéra?
3. Quels sont quelques types de musique populaire?

Step 2 Most students will be familiar with these musical terms in English. Model the terms in French and have students repeat after you.

Step 3 Ask students to scan the readings to get the general information.

Step 4 It is suggested that you play some recordings of the types of music discussed in this section. Ask a music teacher to help you assemble some selections from the Music Department's library.

Après la lecture

A You may wish to ask students if they know how to play these (or other) instruments: **Qui sait jouer de la guitare?**

Music Connection

Georges Bizet, the French composer, wrote the music to the opera *Carmen.* It is based on the short story *Carmen*, by Prosper Mérimée, published in 1845. It is the tragic love story of the bohemian Carmen and the brigadier don José in Seville, Spain. A scene from the opera is shown above.

Learning from Photos

(page 25 middle) This photo of Céline Dion, the popular French-Canadian singer who now resides in the U.S., shows her in concert at the Centre Molson, the home of the Montreal Canadiens.

Answers to Après la lecture

A *Answers will vary but may include:*

1. un violon
2. un saxophone, une flûte, une trompette, une clarinette

B

1. La différence entre un orchestre et une fanfare est qu'une fanfare n'a pas d'instruments à cordes.
2. Un opéra est une composition dramatique sans dialogue parlé, et l'histoire est en général très tragique.
3. Quelques types de musique populaire sont le jazz, le rock, le rap et la musique techno.

C'est à vous

Use what you have learned

Recycling

These activities allow students to use the vocabulary and structure from this chapter in completely open-ended, real-life situations.

Learning from Photos

(page 26 top) The **Maison du Roi** is opposite the town hall (also seen in the photo) in Brussels. In spite of its name, no king ever lived there. The building is a sixteenth-century palace that houses the city museum. It has an excellent collection of ceramics and silverware. Brussels is famous for both ceramics and silverware.

C'est à vous

Use what you have learned

PARLER 1

Pour t'amuser

✔ *Discuss movies, plays, and museums*

Work with a classmate. Pretend you're on vacation in Brussels in Belgium. You meet a Belgian teenager (your partner) who's interested in what you do for fun in your free time. Tell him or her about your leisure activities. Then your partner will tell you about what he or she does.

Maison du Roi, Bruxelles, Belgique

PARLER 2

Une journée au musée

✔ *Ask and answer questions about a museum visit*

Work in groups of three or four. Several of you spent the day at a museum last Saturday. Other friends have some questions. Describe your museum visit and be sure to answer all their questions.

Musée du Louvre

ÉCRIRE 3

Une affiche

✔ *Make a poster for a play*

Prepare a poster in French for your school play. Give all the necessary information to advertise **le spectacle.**

Answers to C'est à vous

1 *Answers will vary depending upon student preferences.*

2 *Answers will vary depending upon whether or not students have been to a museum.*

ÉCRIRE

4 Des renseignements, s'il vous plaît.

✔ *Write for information about cultural events*

You're going to spend a month in the French city of your choice. Write a letter or an e-mail to the tourist office **(le syndicat d'initiative)** asking for information about cultural events during your stay. Be sure to mention your age, what kind of cultural activities you like, and the dates of your stay.

Une colonne Morris, Paris

Les Grandes Heures du Parlement

L'Assemblée nationale présente dans l'aile du Midi du Château de Versailles un musée qui vous permet de découvrir la salle des séances du Congrès du Parlement, troisième hémicycle de la République, dans laquelle vous assisterez à un spectacle audiovisuel sur les grands débats de la Nation.

Sur le pourtour de cette salle, vous revivrez deux cents ans d'histoire parlementaire et vous vous familiariserez avec le travail au quotidien du député. Vous découvrirez l'activité internationale du Parlement français et ses liens avec les différents parlements du monde.

Prix d'entrée

Individuel: visite libre avec audioguide
Tarif normal: 20 F - Tarif réduit 15 F - Gratuit pour les scolaires

Group de 30 personnes au plus: visite commentée
Tarif normal: 200 F - Tarif réduit 150 F - Gratuit pour les scolaires

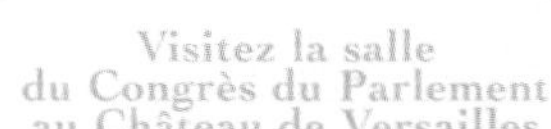

Visitez la salle du Congrès du Parlement au Château de Versailles

Découvrez

l'histoire du Parlement
l'activité parlementaire à l'aube de l'an 2000
le spectacle audiovisuel dans la salle des séances

" Les grandes heures du Parlement "

Musée présenté par l'Assemblée nationale
du mardi au samedi de 9h00 à 17h30

Writing Strategy

Persuasive writing Persuasive writing is writing that encourages a reader to do something or to accept an idea. Newspaper and magazine advertisements, as well as certain articles, are examples of persuasive writing. As you write, present a logical argument to encourage others to follow your line of thinking. Your writing should contain sufficient evidence to persuade readers to "buy into" what you are presenting. Explain how your evidence supports your argument; end by restating your argument.

ÉCRIRE

5 Un reportage

Your local newspaper has asked you to write an article to attract French-speaking readers to a cultural event taking place in your community. You can write about a real or fictitious event. You have seen the event and you really liked it. Tell why as you try to convince or persuade your readers to go see it.

Writing Development

Have students keep a notebook containing their best written work from each chapter. These selected writings can be based on assignments from the Student Textbook and the Writing Activities Workbook. The two activities on page 27 are examples of writing assignments that may be included in each student's portfolio. In the Workbook, students will develop an organized autobiography **(Mon autobiographie).** These workbook pages may also become a part of their portfolio.

Writing Strategy

Taking notes
Have students read the Writing Strategy on page 27. If students have difficulty thinking of related vocabulary, have them use the vocabulary list on page 30.

Reaching All Students

Additional Practice Display Communication Transparency C 1. Have students work in groups to make up as many questions as they can about the illustration. Have groups take turns asking and answering the questions.

Learning from Photos

(page 27) The **colonnes Morris,** such as the one seen in this photo, can be found throughout Paris. Their purpose is to advertise cultural events.

Resource Manager

Communication Transparencies
Quizzes
Test Booklet
ExamView Pro®
Situation Cards
Performance Assessment
Marathon mental Videoquiz

Assessment

This is a pre-test for students to take before you administer the chapter test. Answer sheets for students to do these pages are provided in your transparency binder. Note that each section is cross-referenced so students can easily find the material they have to review in case they made errors. You may wish to collect these assessments and correct them yourself or you may prefer to have the students correct themselves in class. You can go over the answers orally or project them on the overhead, using your Assessment Answers transparencies.

Vocabulaire

To review ***Mots 1****, turn to pages 2–3.*

1 Choisissez.

1. On joue des films où?
   a. dans une séance
   b. dans une salle de cinéma
   c. dans un théâtre
2. Qui joue dans un film?
   a. des acteurs et des actrices
   b. des sous-titres
   c. des joueurs
3. Une pièce de théâtre est divisée en quoi?
   a. en version originale
   b. en entractes
   c. en actes et en scènes
4. Le film est doublé?
   a. Oui, il y a deux films.
   b. Non, il est en V.O.
   c. Oui, il y a des sous-titres.
5. Qu'est-ce que *l'Officiel des Spectacles?*
   a. un magazine
   b. une place
   c. un film

To review ***Mots 2****, turn to pages 6–7.*

2 Identifiez.

6. 

7. 

8. 

9. 

10. 

Answers to Assessment

1	2
1. b	6. un musée
2. a	7. une statue (une sculpture)
3. c	8. une peintre
4. b	9. un sculpteur
5. a	10. un tableau

Structure

3 Récrivez.

11. Je sais le numéro.
    Vous ______.
12. Vous connaissez mon ami?
    Il ______?

4 Complétez avec «savoir» ou «connaître».

13. Je ___ son numéro de téléphone.
14. Vous ___ où il habite, non?
15. Je ___ très bien l'œuvre de cet artiste.
16. Tu ___ Paris?
17. Ils ___ danser le tango.

To review the verbs **savoir** and **connaître**, turn to page 10.

5 Répondez avec un pronom.

18. Il te parle au téléphone? Oui, ___.
19. Tu invites Jean? Oui, ___.
20. Tu vas inviter sa petite amie aussi? Oui, ___.
21. Le prof vous donne beaucoup de devoirs? Oui, ___.
22. Tu vois la petite fille? Oui, ___.
23. Tu connais les pièces de Molière? Oui, ___.

To review the object pronouns, turn to pages 12–14.

Culture

6 Identifiez.

24. un musée à Paris
25. un auteur français dramatique du dix-septième siècle

To review this cultural information, turn to pages 20–21.

Musée du Louvre, Paris

Assessment

Glencoe Technology

MINDJOGGER

You may wish to help your students prepare for the chapter test by playing the MindJogger game show. Teams will compete against each other to review chapter vocabulary and structure and sharpen listening comprehension skills.

Answers to Assessment

11. Vous savez le numéro.
12. Il connaît mon ami?

13. sais
14. savez
15. connais
16. connais
17. savent

5

18. Oui, il me parle au téléphone.
19. Oui, je l'invite.
20. Oui, je vais l'inviter aussi.
21. Oui, le prof nous donne beaucoup de devoirs.
22. Oui, je la vois.
23. Oui, je les connais.

6

24. le musée d'Orsay (le musée du Louvre, le Centre Pompidou)
25. Molière

Vocabulary Review

The words and phrases in the **Vocabulaire** have been taught for productive use in this chapter. They are summarized here as a resource for both student and teacher. This list also serves as a convenient resource for the **C'est à vous** activities on pages 26–27. There are approximately twenty-two cognates in this vocabulary list. Have students find them.

Attention!

You will notice that the vocabulary list here is not translated. This has been done intentionally, since we feel that by the time students have finished the material in the chapter they should be familiar with the meanings of all the words. If there are several words they still do not know, we recommend that they refer to the **Mots 1** and **2** sections in the chapter or go to the dictionaries at the back of this book to find the meanings. However, if you prefer that your students have the English translations, please refer to Vocabulary Transparency 1.1, where you will find all these words listed with their translations.

Vocabulaire

Discussing a movie

un cinéma
une salle de cinéma
un guichet
une place
une séance
un écran

un film comique
  policier
  d'horreur
  de science-fiction
  d'aventures
  d'amour

un documentaire
un dessin animé
étranger
en V.O.
doublé
avec des sous-titres

jouer un film
louer une vidéo

Describing a play

un théâtre
une pièce
un acteur
une actrice
un chanteur
une chanteuse

un danseur
une danseuse
une scène
un acte
un entracte
une tragédie

une comédie
un drame
monter une pièce
chanter
danser

How well do you know your vocabulary?

- Choose the name of a cultural event or artistic profession.
- Have a classmate tell you his or her favorite in the category you chose.

Describing a museum visit

un musée
une exposition
un tableau
une sculpture
une statue

une œuvre
la peinture
la sculpture
une peintre
un sculpteur *(m. et f.)*

Other useful words and expressions

connaître
savoir
ouvert
fermé

célèbre
connu
sauf
ça (m')est égal

Technotour

BON VOYAGE!

VIDÉO • Épisode 1

Avant de visionner

In this video episode, Chloé visits the Musée d'Orsay and puts her artistic skills to work. She later meets up with Vincent, where they experience other cultural wonders.

Chloé visite le musée d'Orsay. Elle trouve les tableaux fabuleux.

Chloé et Vincent sur la place Igor Stravinsky

FRENCH ONLINE

À découvrir

Learn more about the Centre Pompidou online.

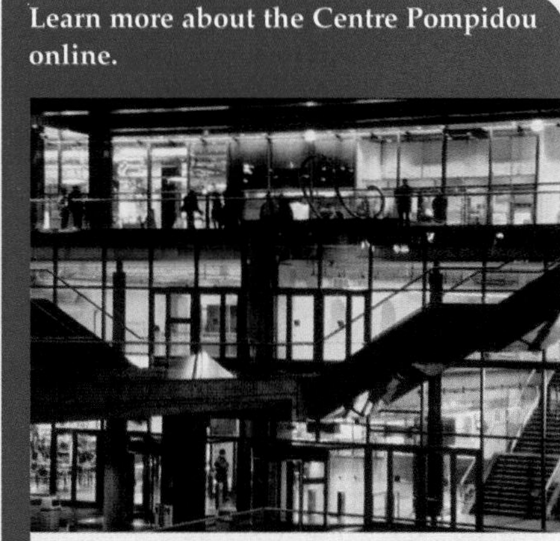

Centre Pompidou, Paris

FRENCH Online

In the Chapter 1 Internet activity, you'll have a chance to learn more about cultural activities in the Francophone world. To begin your virtual adventure, go to the Glencoe French Web site: **french.glencoe.com**

Technotour

Overview

This page previews two key multimedia components of the **Glencoe French** series. Each reinforces the material taught in the chapter in a unique manner.

VIDÉO

The Video Program allows students to see how the chapter vocabulary and structures are used by native speakers. For maximum reinforcement, show the video episode as a final activity for Chapter 1.

The two photos on the left show highlights from the Chapter 1 video episode. Discuss the photos with your students before having them view the episode. See the Video Activities Booklet for detailed suggestions for using this resource.

FRENCH Online

- The **À découvrir** photo on page 31 shows the Centre Pompidou. Students can go online to learn more about this interesting modern art museum.
- Teacher Information and Student Worksheets for this activity can be accessed at the Web site.

Video Synopsis

In this video episode, Chloé explores aspects of cultural life in Paris. As she wanders through the **musée d'Orsay,** we catch glimpses of famous Impressionist paintings. She also talks with some other French teens about the theater and the movies. Finally, the video introduces us to the lively street performers of Paris, demonstrating the wide variety of art forms on display throughout the city.

Planning for Chapter 2

SCOPE AND SEQUENCE, PAGES 32–63

Topics

- Health and medicine
- Prescriptions

Culture

- Doctors make house calls in France
- Discussing the relationship between culture and health
- Medical services in France

Functions

- How to describe an illness
- How to give commands
- How to refer to people, places, and things already mentioned

Structure

- The pronouns **lui, leur**
- The verbs **souffrir** and **ouvrir**
- The imperative
- The pronoun **en**

National Standards

- Communication Standard 1.1 pages 36, 37, 40, 41, 43, 44, 46, 47, 48, 49, 51, 58
- Communication Standard 1.2 pages 36, 37, 40, 41, 43, 44, 47, 49, 50, 53, 54, 57
- Communication Standard 1.3 pages 36, 40, 41, 43, 44, 58, 59
- Cultures Standard 2.1 pages 52–53, 54, 55
- Connections Standard 3.1 pages 56–57
- Connections Standard 3.2 page 54
- Comparisons Standard 4.2 page 54
- Communities Standard 5.1 page 59

PACING AND PRIORITIES

The chapter content is color coded below to assist you in planning.

■ **required** ■ **recommended** ■ **optional**

Vocabulaire *(required)* *Days 1–4*

- ■ Mots 1
  - On est malade.
- ■ Mots 2
  - Chez le médecin
  - À la pharmacie

Structure *(required)* *Days 5–7*

- ■ Les pronoms **lui, leur**
- ■ Les verbes **souffrir** et **ouvrir**
- ■ L'impératif
- ■ Le pronom **en**

Conversation *(required)*

- ■ Chez le médecin

Prononciation *(recommended)*

- ■ Les sons **/u/** et **/ü/**

Lectures culturelles

- ■ Une consultation *(recommended)*
- ■ Culture et santé *(optional)*
- ■ Les services médicaux en France *(optional)*

Connexions *(optional)*

- ■ La diététique

■ **C'est à vous** *(recommended)*

■ **Assessment** *(recommended)*

■ **Technotour** *(optional)*

Section	Pages	Section Resources
Vocabulaire *Mots 1*		
On est malade.	34–37	Vocabulary Transparencies 2.2–2.3 Audiocassette 2B/CD 2 Audio Activities Booklet TE, pages 12–14 Workbook, pages 11–12 Quiz 1, page 6 ExamView Pro®
Vocabulaire *Mots 2*		
Chez le médecin À la pharmacie	38–39 39–41	Vocabulary Transparencies 2.4–2.5 Audiocassette 2B/CD 2 Audio Activities Booklet TE, pages 15–16 Workbook, page 12 Quiz 2, page 7 ExamView Pro®
Structure		
Les pronoms **lui, leur** Les verbes **souffrir** et **ouvrir** L'impératif Le pronom **en**	42–43 44 45–47 48–49	Audiocassette 2B/CD 2 Audio Activities Booklet TE, pages 17–19 Workbook, pages 13–17 Quizzes 3–6, pages 8–11 ExamView Pro®
Conversation		
Chez le médecin	50	Audiocassette 2B/CD 2 Audio Activities Booklet TE, pages 19–20 CD-ROM
Prononciation		
Les sons **/u/** et **/ü/**	51	Audiocassette 2B/CD 2 Audio Activities Booklet TE, page 20
Lectures culturelles		
Une consultation Culture et santé Les services médicaux en France	52–53 54 55	Audiocassette 2B/CD 2 Audio Activities Booklet TE, page 21 Test Booklet, Chapter 2
Connexions		
La diététique	56–57	Test Booklet, Chapter 2
C'est à vous		
	58–59	**Bon voyage!** Video, Episode 2 Video Activities Booklet, Chapter 2 French Online Activities **french.glencoe.com**
Assessment		
	60–61	Communication Transparency C 2 Quizzes 1–6, pages 6–11 Test Booklet, Chapter 2 ExamView Pro® Situation Cards, Chapter 2 **Marathon mental** Videoquiz

Using Your Resources for Chapter 2

Transparencies

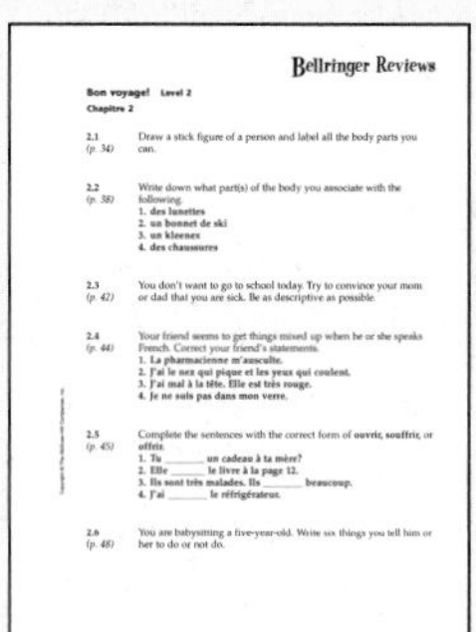
Bellringer Reviews
Bon voyage! Level 2
Chapitre 2

Bellringer 2.1–2.8

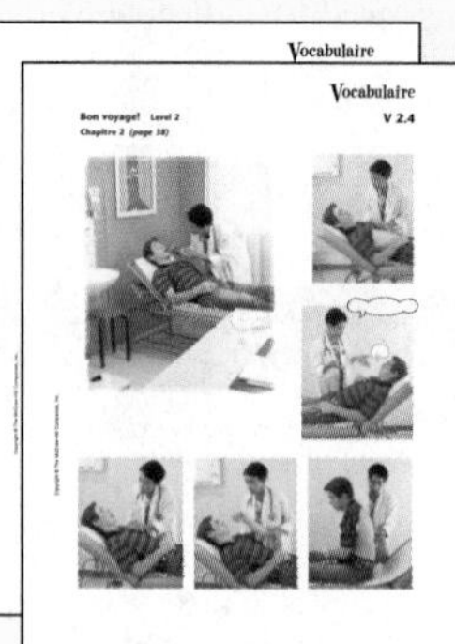
Vocabulaire
V 2.4
Bon voyage! Level 2
Chapitre 2 (page 38)

Vocabulary 2.1–2.5

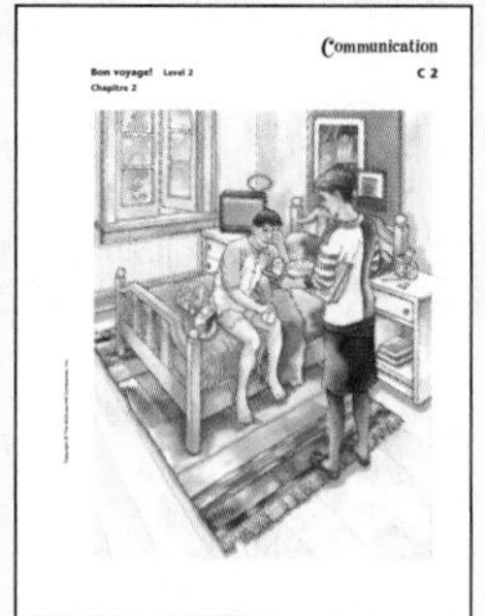
Communication
C 2
Bon voyage! Level 2
Chapitre 2

Communication C 2

Writing Activities Workbook

La santé et la médecine
Vocabulaire

Vocabulary, pages 11–12

Structure

Structure, pages 13–17

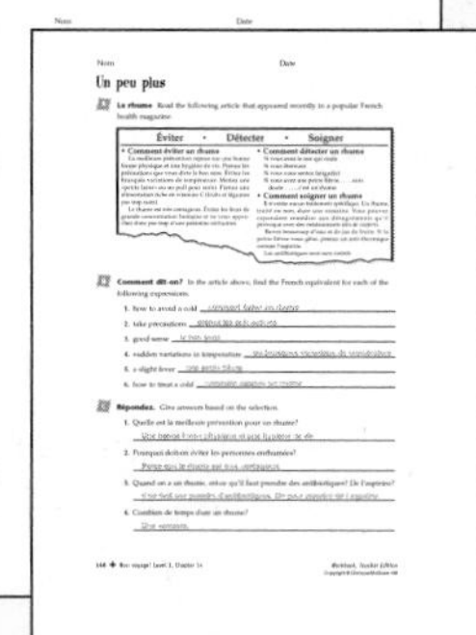
Un peu plus

Enrichment, pages 18–20

Audio Program and Audio Activities Booklet

Vocabulary, pages 12–16

Structure

Structure, pages 17–19

Conversation, pages 19–20

Pronunciation, page 20

Lecture culturelle

Cultural Reading, page 21

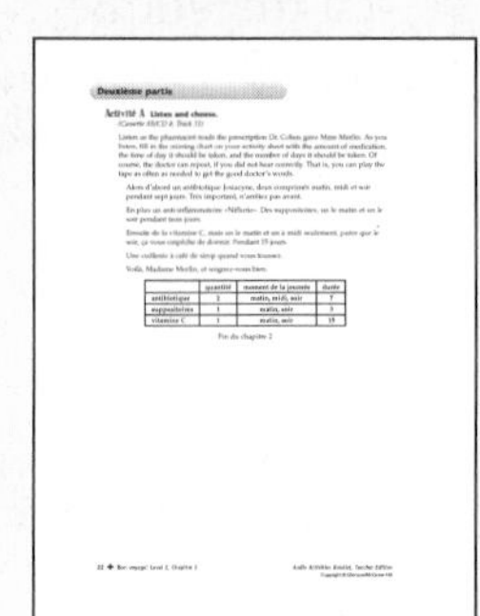
Deuxième partie

Additional Practice, page 22

Assessment

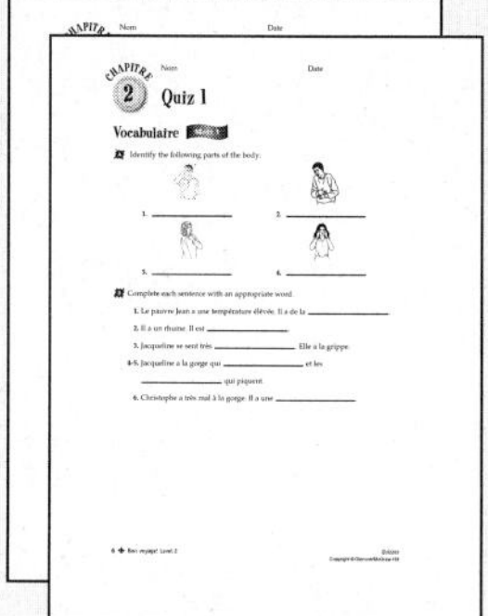

Vocabulary and Structure Quizzes, pages 6–11

Chapter Tests, Chapter 2

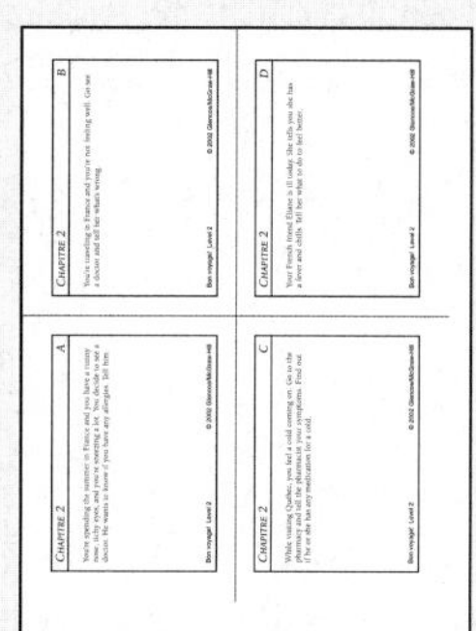

Situation Cards, Chapter 2

Timesaving Teacher Tools

Interactive Teacher Edition

Imagine having your Teacher's Edition and all resources on a CD-ROM. Click on a resource and it appears on your screen, ready to be printed, sorted, or planned.

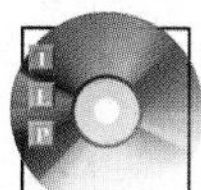

Interactive Lesson Planner

The Interactive Lesson Planner CD-ROM helps you organize your lesson plans for a week, month, semester, or year. Look at this planning tool for easy access to your Chapter 2 resources.

ExamView Pro®

Test Bank software for Macintosh and Windows makes creating, editing, customizing, and printing tests quick and easy.

Technology Resources

In the Chapter 2 Internet activity, you will have a chance to learn more about health and medicine in the Francophone world. Visit french.glencoe.com.

On the Interactive Conversation CD-ROM, students can listen to and take part in a recorded version of the conversation in Chapter 2.

See the National Geographic Teacher's Corner on pages 138–139, 244–245, 372–373, 472–473 for reference to additional technology resources.

Bon voyage! Video and Video Activities Booklet.

Help your students prepare for the chapter test by playing the **Marathon mental** Videoquiz game show. Teams will compete against each other to review chapter vocabulary and structure and sharpen listening comprehension skills.

Preview

In this chapter, students will learn to talk about routine illnesses and to describe their symptoms to a doctor. In order to do this, they will learn vocabulary associated with medical exams, prescriptions, and minor ailments such as colds, the flu, and headaches. Students will learn the indirect object pronouns **lui** and **leur,** the **present** and **passé composé** of verbs like **ouvrir** and **souffrir,** and the imperative forms of verbs.

National Standards

Communication

In Chapter 2, students will communicate in spoken and written French on the following topics:

- Describing symptoms of minor ailments
- Getting a prescription at a pharmacy

Students will obtain and provide information and engage in conversations about their personal health. They will also learn to tell others what to do. Students will also learn to use indirect object pronouns.

CHAPITRE 2

La santé et la médecine

Objectifs

In this chapter you will learn to:

- *explain a minor illness to a doctor*
- *have a prescription filled at a pharmacy*
- *tell for whom something is done*
- *talk about some more activities*
- *give commands*
- *refer to people, places, and things already mentioned*
- *discuss medical services in France*

Édouard Vuillard *Le docteur Viau dans son cabinet*

32

The **Glencoe World Language Web site** (french.glencoe.com) offers several options that enable you and your students to experience the French-speaking world via the Internet:

- The online **Activités** are correlated to the chapters and utilize Francophone Web sites around the world. For the Chapter 2 activity, see student page 63.
- Games and puzzles afford students another opportunity to practice the material learned in a particular chapter.
- The *Enrichment* section offers students an opportunity to visit Web sites related to the theme of the chapter for more information on a particular topic.
- Online *Chapter Quizzes* offer students an opportunity to prepare for a chapter test.
- Visit our virtual **Café** for more opportunities to practice and explore the French-speaking world.

Spotlight on Culture

Photograph This old-style pharmacy is on the lovely **rue des Francs-Bourgeois,** one of the main, though narrow, streets in the Marais section of Paris. The sign with the serpent is called **un caducée.** It is a symbol for pharmacists and physicians.

Painting Édouard Jean Vuillard (1868–1940) was a painter, watercolorist, and engraver. He also became a decorator, and he worked for **le Théâtre-Libre.** He also did some large murals. He was a friend of many symbolist painters, but in his own paintings he preferred intimate scenes with a bourgeois background. He enjoyed doing street scenes and portraits. In this painting we see Doctor Viau in his dental surgical suite.

Chapter Projects

La santé Obtain a video on first aid, health, or nutrition in French or English from the health department in your school or county. Use it as a springboard for discussing health and illnesses with the new vocabulary from this chapter.

Le corps humain Have students create a poster of a human body like the kind in doctors' offices, labeling in French as many external and internal body parts as they can. This poster can be displayed in your classroom.

Vocabulaire *Mots 1*

1 Preparation

Resource Manager

Vocabulary Transparencies 2.2–2.3
Audio Activities Booklet TE, pages 12–14
Audiocassette 2B/CD 2
Workbook, pages 11–12
Quiz 1, page 6
ExamView Pro®

Bellringer Review

Use BRR Transparency 2.1 or write the following on the board.
Draw a stick figure of a person and label all the body parts you can.

2 Presentation

Teaching Tip: You may wish to bring a handkerchief, tissues, and throat lozenges to class to use in the presentation of the **Mots 1** vocabulary.

Step 1 Point to yourself to model the following parts of the body: **la bouche, le nez, la gorge, l'oreille, les yeux, le ventre.**

Step 2 Use gestures to teach the following expressions: **avoir de la fièvre; avoir des frissons; il est très malade; il n'est pas en bonne santé; il a mal au ventre; il tousse; il éternue; il a mal à la tête; il a mal aux oreilles; elle a le nez qui coule; elle a les yeux qui piquent; elle a la gorge qui gratte.**

Step 3 Have students repeat the cognates carefully after you or Audiocassette 2B/CD 2. These are the words they are most likely to anglicize.

Note: Remind students that in French the definite article is usually used when talking about parts of the body. Introduce the plural of **un œil (les yeux).**

Vocabulaire *Mots 1*

On est malade.

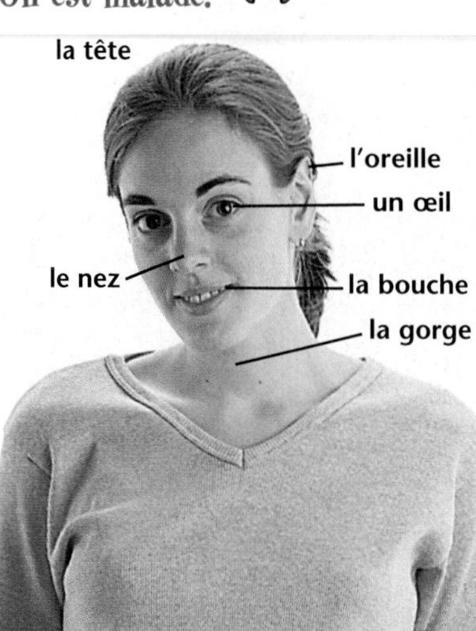

avoir de la fièvre

Paul a un rhume.
Il est enrhumé.
Il éternue.
Il a besoin d'un kleenex ou d'un mouchoir.

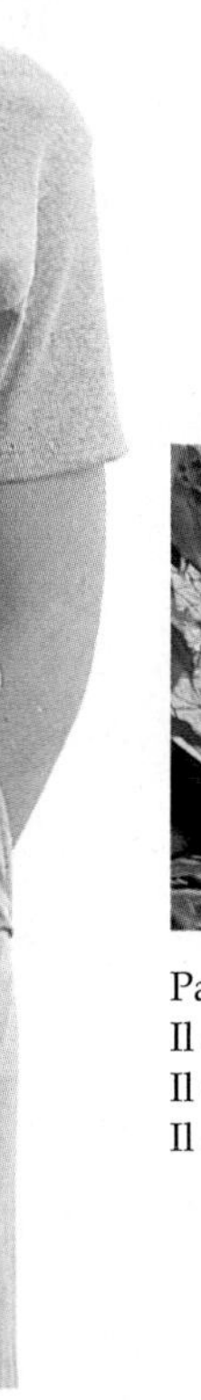

David tousse.

Reaching All Students

Total Physical Response Before you begin, demonstrate the meaning of **toucher.**

(Student 1), **venez ici, s'il vous plaît.**
Montrez-moi votre bouche.
Montrez-moi votre main.
Montrez-moi votre nez.
Montrez-moi votre pied.
Montrez-moi votre ventre.
Montrez-moi votre gorge.
Montrez-moi vos yeux.
Levez la main.
Ouvrez la bouche.
Fermez les yeux.
Mettez la main sur la tête.
Touchez vos pieds avec vos mains.
Merci, *(Student 1).* **Retournez à votre place et asseyez-vous, s'il vous plaît.**

Continuons
Let's put our words together

13 **Historiette** **Une consultation**
Répondez en utilisant un pronom.

1. Le médecin parle à Paul?
2. Il demande à Paul s'il a de la fièvre?
3. Paul explique ses symptômes au médecin?
4. Le médecin dit à Paul qu'il a de la fièvre?
5. Il donne une ordonnance à Paul?
6. Paul téléphone à la pharmacienne?

14 **Un match de foot** Complétez avec **lui** ou **leur.**

1. Il lance le ballon à Marianne? Oui, il ____ lance le ballon.
2. Les joueurs parlent à l'arbitre? Oui, ils ____ parlent.
3. Et l'arbitre parle aux joueurs? Oui, il ____ parle.
4. L'arbitre explique les règles aux joueuses? Oui, il ____ explique les règles.
5. L'employée au guichet parle à un spectateur? Oui, elle ____ parle.

15 **Personnellement** Répondez en utilisant **lui** ou **leur.**

1. Tu parles souvent à tes professeurs?
2. Tu dis toujours bonjour à ton professeur de français?
3. Tu vas téléphoner à ton copain/ta copine ce week-end?
4. Tu aimes parler à tes copains au téléphone?
5. Tu parles souvent à tes copains?
6. Tu vas écrire à tes grands-parents?

16 **Des cadeaux pour tout le monde?** Work with a classmate. Describe your favorite friends or relatives. Then tell what you buy or give to each one as a gift.

ENCORE PLUS *For more practice using using **lui** and **leur**, do Activity 7 on page H8 at the end of this book.*

Step 4 You may wish to give some additional sentences and have students indicate if the object is direct or indirect. For example: **J'écris une lettre. Une lettre? J'écris à mon ami. Mon ami? Je lis un livre. Un livre? Je lis à mon petit frère. Mon petit frère? J'achète un cadeau. Un cadeau? J'offre le cadeau à ma mère. Ma mère?**

3 Practice

Continuons
Let's put our words together

13 and **15** Do these activities first with books closed, calling on individuals to respond to each question. Activities can be done again with books open for additional reinforcement.

14 and **16** These activities have to be done with books open.

ENCORE PLUS This *infogap* activity will allow students to practice in pairs. The activity should be very manageable for them, since all vocabulary and structures are familiar to them.

Answers to Continuons

13
1. Oui, le médecin lui parle.
2. Oui, il lui demande s'il a de la fièvre.
3. Oui, Paul lui explique ses symptômes.
4. Oui, le médecin lui dit qu'il a de la fièvre.
5. Oui, il lui donne une ordonnance.
6. Oui, Paul lui téléphone.

14
1. lui
2. lui
3. leur
4. leur
5. lui

15
1. Oui, je leur parle souvent.
2. Oui, je lui dis toujours bonjour.
3. Oui, je vais lui téléphoner.
4. Oui, j'aime leur parler au téléphone.
5. Oui, je leur parle souvent.
6. Oui, je vais leur écrire.

16 *Answers will vary but may include:*

Papa, il aime le chocolat. Je lui achète une boîte de chocolats.
Maman, elle aime voyager en France. Je lui achète un livre sur la France.
Ma sœur, elle aime la musique. Je lui achète un CD.

1 Preparation

Bellringer Review

Use BRR Transparency 2.4 or write the following on the board.
Your friend seems to get things mixed up when he or she speaks French. Correct your friend's statements.
1. **La pharmacienne m'ausculte.**
2. **J'ai le nez qui pique et les yeux qui coulent.**
3. **J'ai mal à la tête. Elle est très rouge.**
4. **Je ne suis pas dans mon verre.**

2 Presentation

Les verbes **souffrir** et **ouvrir**

Note: This material should be rather easy since students have already had a great deal of practice with the **-er** verbs. Since all of these verbs, except for **ouvrir,** are of fairly low frequency, it is suggested that you go over them quickly.

Step 1 Lead students through Items 1–2. Have them repeat the forms after you.

Step 2 Explain to students that as with any regular **-er** verb the **je, tu, il, ils** forms of these verbs are all pronounced the same.

Expansion: You may wish to explain to students that **couvrir, découvrir,** and **offrir** follow the same pattern as **ouvrir** and **souffrir.**

3 Practice

Continuons
Let's put our words together

17 You may wish to have students retell the activity in their own words.

Describing more activities
Les verbes **souffrir** et **ouvrir**

1. The verbs **souffrir** and **ouvrir** are conjugated the same way as regular **-er** verbs in the present.

SOUFFRIR	OUVRIR
je souffre	j' ouvre
tu souffres	tu ouvres
il/elle/on souffre	il/elle/on ouvre
nous souffrons	nous ouvrons
vous souffrez	vous ouvrez
ils /elles souffrent	ils/elles ouvrent

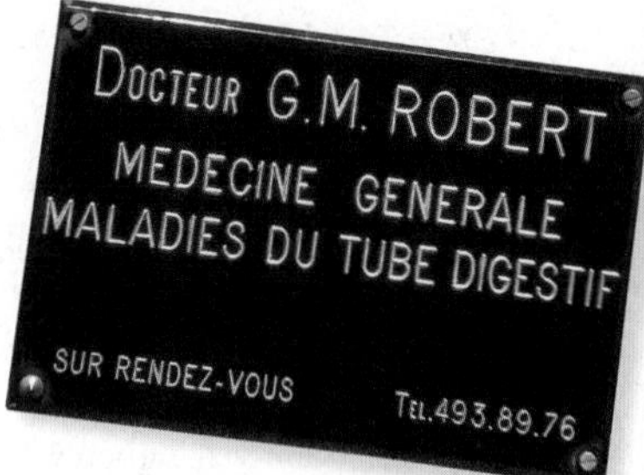

2. Note the past participles.

souffrir → souffert	**Ils ont beaucoup souffert.**
ouvrir → ouvert	**Il a ouvert la bouche.**

Continuons
Let's put our words together

17 Historiette Elle est malade.
Inventez des réponses.

1. Caroline souffre d'une angine?
2. Quand tu souffres d'une angine, tu as mal où?
3. Caroline va chez le médecin?
4. Quand le médecin lui examine la gorge, Caroline ouvre la bouche?
5. Le médecin lui donne une ordonnance?
6. Caroline va à la pharmacie?
7. Elle donne l'ordonnance au pharmacien?
8. Le pharmacien lui donne un paquet de comprimés?
9. Caroline ouvre le paquet?
10. Elle avale un comprimé?
11. Elle ne souffre plus?

À la pharmacie

Answers to Continuons

17 *Answers will vary but may include:*
1. Oui, Caroline souffre d'une angine.
2. Quand je souffre d'une angine j'ai mal à la gorge.
3. Oui, Caroline va chez le médecin.
4. Oui, quand le médecin lui examine la gorge, Caroline ouvre la bouche.
5. Oui, le médecin lui donne une ordonnance.
6. Oui, Caroline va à la pharmacie.
7. Oui, elle lui donne l'ordonnance.
8. Oui, le pharmacien lui donne un paquet de comprimés.
9. Oui, Caroline l'ouvre.
10. Oui, elle l'avale.
11. Non, elle ne souffre plus.

Telling people what to do
L'impératif

1. You use the imperative to give commands and make suggestions. The forms are usually the same as the **tu, vous,** and **nous** forms. Note that the **nous** form means "Let's . . ."

PARLER	FINIR	ATTENDRE
Parle à ton prof!	Finis tes devoirs!	Attends ton ami.
Parlez à votre prof!	Finissez vos devoirs!	Attendez votre ami.
Parlons à notre prof!	Finissons nos devoirs!	Attendons notre ami.

2. Note that with **-er** verbs, you drop the final **s** of the **tu** form. The same is true for **aller** and verbs like **ouvrir.**

Regarde!
Va voir le médecin!
Ouvre la bouche!

3. In negative commands, you put the **ne... pas** or any other negative expression around the verb.

Ne respirez plus!
Ne dis rien.

Structure

1 Preparation

Bellringer Review

Use BRR Transparency 2.5 or write the following on the board.
Complete the sentences with the correct form of **ouvrir, souffrir,** or **offrir.**

1. **Tu _____ un cadeau à ta mère?**
2. **Elle _____ le livre à la page 12.**
3. **Ils sont très malades. Ils _____ beaucoup.**
4. **J'ai _____ le réfrigérateur.**

2 Presentation

L'impératif

Note: Students should have little trouble learning the imperative since they are already familiar with the verb forms. The only thing that will be new to them is the dropping of the **s** in the spelling of the **tu** form of **-er** verbs.

Step 1 Have students open their books to page 45. Lead them through Items 1–3.

Step 2 Illustrate the difference between singular and plural imperatives by giving commands to one student and to groups or pairs of students. For example: **Yvonne, prends ton livre de français. Va au tableau. Ouvre le livre à la page 15. Guillaume et Martine, sortez.**

Step 3 Practice the negative forms by calling out TPR commands and having students change them to the negative. Then reverse the procedure.

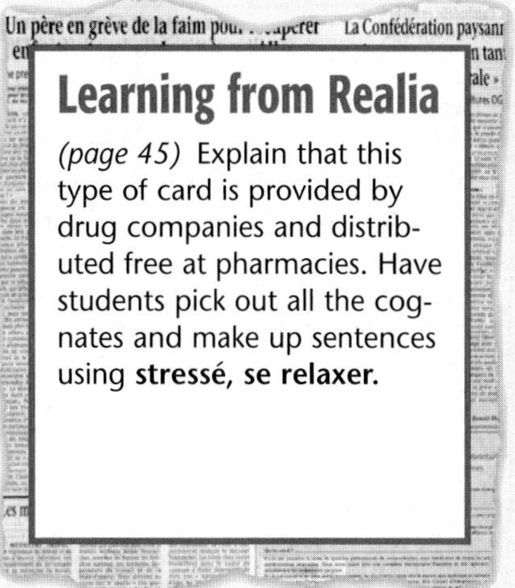

Learning from Realia

(page 45) Explain that this type of card is provided by drug companies and distributed free at pharmacies. Have students pick out all the cognates and make up sentences using **stressé, se relaxer.**

3 Practice

Continuons
Let's put our words together

18 and 19 You may wish to have students work in pairs and then in groups. The recipient(s) of the command should show comprehension by miming the activity suggested in the command.

Reaching All Students

Additional Practice
Students work in groups of three. One student tells another what to do. That student dramatizes the command. The third student describes the scene. Rotate roles.

Student 1: *(Student 2),* **ouvre la bouche.**
(Student 2 dramatizes)
Student 3: *(Student 2)* **ouvre la bouche, mais moi, je n'ouvre pas la bouche.**

Learning from Realia

(page 46) Ask students what the important message is on the cover of this brochure.

Continuons
Let's put our words together

18 La loi, c'est moi! Donnez un ordre à un copain ou à une copine d'après le modèle.

—regarder
—Regarde!

1. téléphoner à Jean
2. passer l'examen
3. parler français
4. travailler plus
5. préparer le dîner
6. ouvrir la porte
7. mettre la table
8. choisir un film
9. faire le travail
10. écrire l'exercice

19 Et vous aussi
Donnez un ordre d'après le modèle.

—regarder
—Regardez.

1. téléphoner à Jean
2. passer l'examen
3. parler français
4. travailler plus
5. préparer le dîner
6. ouvrir la porte
7. mettre la table
8. choisir un film
9. faire le travail
10. écrire l'exercice

Answers to Continuons

18

1. Téléphone à Jean!
2. Passe l'examen!
3. Parle français!
4. Travaille plus!
5. Prépare le dîner!
6. Ouvre la porte!
7. Mets la table!
8. Choisis un film!
9. Fais le travail!
10. Écris l'exercice!

19

1. Téléphonez à Jean!
2. Passez l'examen!
3. Parlez français!
4. Travaillez plus!
5. Préparez le dîner!
6. Ouvrez la porte!
7. Mettez la table!
8. Choisissez un film!
9. Faites le travail!
10. Écrivez l'exercice!

20 **Ne fais pas ça!** Donnez un ordre à un copain ou à une copine d'après le modèle.

—**regarder**
—**Ne regarde pas!**

1. lire le journal
2. écrire une lettre
3. prendre le métro
4. attendre devant la porte
5. descendre
6. aller plus vite
7. faire attention
8. entrer
9. sortir

YEUX ROUGES,
YEUX IRRITES

DÉCOUVREZ CE COLLYRE EN MONODOSES!

Une monodose stérile, pratique, évitant la contamination

Ceci est un médicament. Lire attentivement la notice. Pas en-dessous de 36 mois. Contre-indiqué en cas de glaucome. Demandez conseil à votre pharmacien.

ANTALYRE®
Collyre en monodoses

21 **Ne faites pas ça!**
Refaites l'Activité 20 d'après le modèle.

—**regarder**
—**Ne regardez pas!**

22 **Allons-y!** Répondez d'après le modèle.

1. On va à la plage?
2. On nage?
3. On fait du ski nautique?
4. On prend notre petit déjeuner?
5. On dîne au restaurant?
6. On sort?

23 **Jeu** **Jacques a dit...** This game is called "Simon Says" in English. Play in groups of five people or more. Give orders to your classmates. If you say **Jacques a dit** first, they have to obey the order. If you don't say **Jacques a dit** first, they should not obey your order. If they do, they are eliminated.

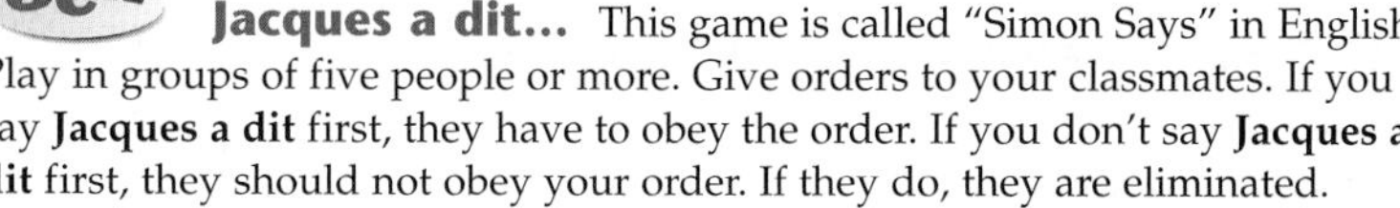

For more practice using the commands, do Activity 8 on page H9 at the end of this book.

Structure

Assessment

As an informal assessment, you may wish to have students quickly make up as many commands as they can. If they can make up logical (and reasonable) commands, you could comply. For example: Students say **Ouvrez la porte.** You open the door.

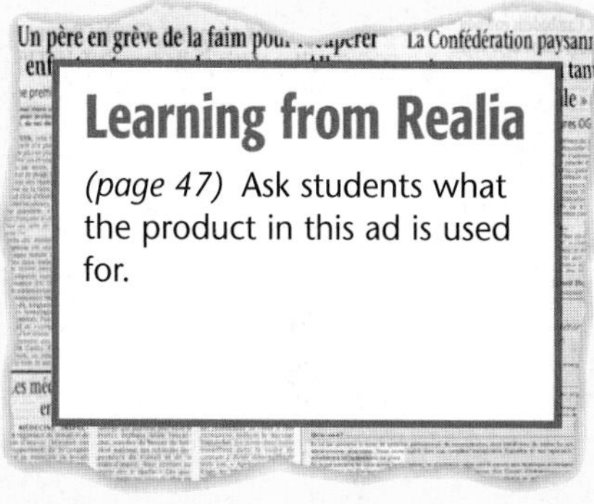

Learning from Realia

(page 47) Ask students what the product in this ad is used for.

ENCORE PLUS This *infogap* activity will allow students to practice in pairs. The activity should be very manageable for them, since all vocabulary and structures are familiar to them.

ANSWERS TO Continuons

20

1. Ne lis pas le journal!
2. N'écris pas de lettre!
3. Ne prends pas le métro!
4. N'attends pas devant la porte!
5. Ne descends pas!
6. Ne va pas plus vite!
7. Ne fais pas attention!
8. N'entre pas!
9. Ne sors pas!

21

1. Ne lisez pas le journal!
2. N'écrivez pas de lettre!
3. Ne prenez pas le métro!
4. N'attendez pas devant la porte!
5. Ne descendez pas!
6. N'allez pas plus vite!
7. Ne faites pas attention!
8. N'entrez pas!
9. Ne sortez pas!

22

1. D'accord, allons à la plage!
2. D'accord, nageons!
3. D'accord, faisons du ski nautique!
4. D'accord, prenons notre petit déjeuner!
5. D'accord, dînons au restaurant!
6. D'accord, sortons!

1 Preparation

Bellringer Review

Use BRR Transparency 2.6 or write the following on the board.
You are babysitting a five-year-old. Write six things you tell him or her to do or not do.

2 Presentation

Le pronom **en**

Step 1 Have students open their books to page 48. Lead them through the explanation.

Step 2 Read the sample sentences with **en** and have students repeat them in unison.

3 Practice

Continuons

Let's put our words together

24 This can be done as a paired activity.

Referring to people, places, and things already mentioned

Le pronom **en**

1. The pronoun **en** is used to replace a noun that is introduced by **de** or any form of **de—du, de la, de l', des. En** refers mostly to things.

Tu as de l'aspirine?	Oui, j' en‿ai.
Il parle de sa santé?	Oui, il en parle.
Vous sortez de l'hôpital?	Oui, j' en sors.
Tu prends des médicaments?	Oui, j' en prends.

2. You also use the pronoun **en** with numbers or expressions of quantity. Note that in this case **en** refers not only to things but also to people.

Tu as des frères?	**Oui, j'en ai deux.**
Il prend combien de comprimés?	**Il en prend trois par jour.**
Il a combien de CD?	**Il en a beaucoup.**

3. Just like other pronouns, **en** comes directly before the verb whose meaning it is linked to.

Il en parle.
Il n'en parle pas.
Il veut en parler.
Il ne veut pas en parler.

Continuons

Let's put our words together

24 **Historiette** **La fête de Laurence** Répondez.

—Laurence sert du coca?
—Oui, elle en sert.

1. Elle sert de l'eau minérale?
2. Elle sert des sandwichs?
3. Elle sert de la pizza?
4. Elle sert de la salade?
5. Elle sert du fromage?
6. Elle sert des chocolats?
7. Elle sert de la glace?
8. Elle sert de la mousse au chocolat?

Answers to Continuons

24

1. Oui, elle en sert.
2. Oui, elle en sert.
3. Oui, elle en sert.
4. Oui, elle en sert.
5. Oui, elle en sert.
6. Oui, elle en sert.
7. Oui, elle en sert.
8. Oui, elle en sert.

Dans le frigo Répondez d'après le modèle.

du coca
—Il y a du coca dans ton frigo?
—Non, il n'y en a pas.

1. de l'eau minérale
2. de la glace
3. des légumes surgelés
4. du jambon
5. des tartes
6. de la viande

Historiette Tu es malade?
Répondez d'après le modèle.

1. Tu prends combien de comprimés? (trois)
2. Tu bois de l'eau? (un litre)
3. Tu manges des fruits? (beaucoup)
4. Tu lis des magazines? (deux ou trois)
5. Tu regardes des vidéos? (trop)

Devinettes Devinez ce que c'est.

1. On en prend quand on est malade.
2. On en boit beaucoup quand on a de la fièvre.
3. On en utilise pour se laver les mains.
4. On en met sur une brosse à dents pour se laver les dents.
5. On en donne au vendeur quand on achète quelque chose.

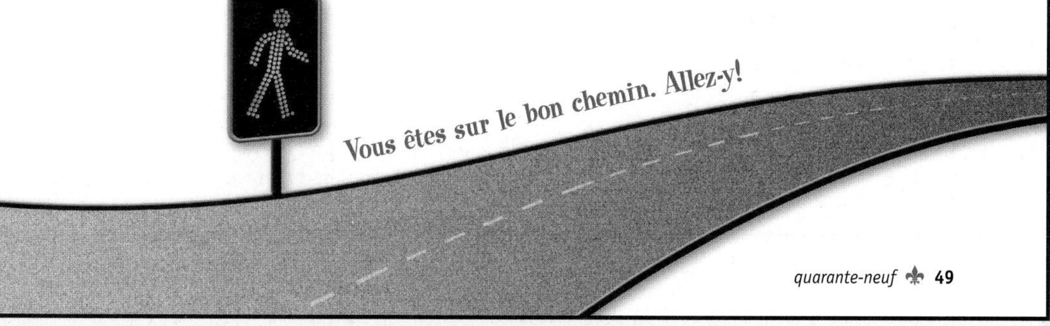

Structure

25 You may wish to remind students to answer questions based on what is or is not in the refrigerator.

Expansion: Ask additional questions about what is or is not in the refrigerator:

Il y a des yaourts?
Oui, il y en a.

Il y a des pommes?
Non, il n'y en a pas.

Allez-y!
At this point in the chapter, students have learned all the vocabulary and structure necessary to complete the chapter. The conversation and cultural readings that follow recycle all the material learned up to this point.

Answers to Continuons

25

1. Oui, il y en a.
2. Non, il n'y en a pas.
3. Non, il n'y en a pas.
4. Non, il n'y en a pas.
5. Non, il n'y en a pas.
6. Oui, il y en a.

26

1. J'en prends trois!
2. Oui, j'en bois un litre!
3. Oui, j'en mange beaucoup!
4. Oui, j'en lis deux ou trois.
5. Oui, j'en regarde trop.

27

1. des comprimés
2. de l'eau
3. du savon
4. du dentifrice
5. de l'argent

Conversation

1 Preparation

Resource Manager

Audio Activities Booklet TE, pages 19–20
Audiocassette 2B/CD 2
CD-ROM

Bellringer Review

Use BRR Transparency 2.7 or write the following on the board.
Rewrite the following sentences with a pronoun.

1. **Le médecin examine *le malade.***
2. **Le malade ouvre *la bouche.***
3. **Le malade lit *l'ordonnance.***
4. **Il donne *l'ordonnance* au pharmacien.**
5. **Le pharmacien donne *les médicaments* au malade.**

2 Presentation

Step 1 Tell students they are going to hear a conversation between Sylvie and her doctor.

Step 2 Have them listen as you read the conversation or play Audiocassette 2B/CD 2.

Step 3 Have students work in pairs to practice the conversation. Then have several pairs present it to the class.

Conversation

Chez le médecin   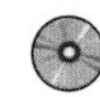

Sylvie: Bonjour, docteur.
Médecin: Bonjour, Sylvie. Alors, qu'est-ce qui ne va pas?
Sylvie: Je ne sais pas… Je ne me sens pas bien du tout.
Médecin: Tu as mal où?
Sylvie: Ben, j'ai mal un peu partout, mais surtout à la gorge.
Médecin: Tu as mal à la tête?
Sylvie: Oui, à la tête aussi. Et j'ai froid, j'ai des frissons…
Médecin: Tu dois avoir de la fièvre. Ouvre la bouche, s'il te plaît. Dis «Aaa… »
Sylvie: Aaa…
Médecin: Tu as la gorge très rouge. C'est certainement une angine.
Sylvie: Une angine!
Médecin: Oui, mais ce n'est pas grave. Je vais te donner des antibiotiques. Tu vas en prendre trois par jour pendant une semaine.

Après la conversation

Répondez.

1. Qui est malade?
2. Quels sont ses symptômes?
3. Elle a mal où?
4. Sylvie ouvre la bouche. Pourquoi?
5. Qu'est-ce que le médecin lui donne?
6. Sylvie doit prendre combien de comprimés par jour?
7. Pendant combien de temps?

Glencoe Technology

CD-ROM
On the CD-ROM, students can watch a dramatization of this conversation. They can then play the role of either one of the characters and record themselves in the conversation.

Answers to Après la conversation

1. Sylvie est malade.
2. Elle a froid et elle a des frissons.
3. Elle a mal partout, mais surtout à la gorge et à la tête.
4. Elle ouvre la bouche parce que le médecin veut examiner sa gorge.
5. Le médecin lui donne des antibiotiques.
6. Elle doit en prendre trois par jour.
7. Pendant une semaine.

Learning from Photos

(page 50) You may wish to ask the following questions about the photo:
Qui examine la malade?
Elle lui parle?
La malade explique ses symptômes au médecin?
Qu'est-ce qu'elle lui dit? Elle a mal où?

Parlons un peu plus
Let's talk some more

A **Tu dois ou tu ne dois pas être médecin.** Work with a classmate. Interview each other and decide who would make a good doctor. Make a list of questions for your interview. One question you may want to ask is: **Tu as beaucoup de patience ou très peu de patience?**

B **Je suis très malade.** Imagine you're sick with a cold, the flu, or a sore throat. Tell the doctor (your partner) what your symptoms are. He or she makes a diagnosis and tells you what to do to get better. Use the model as a guide.

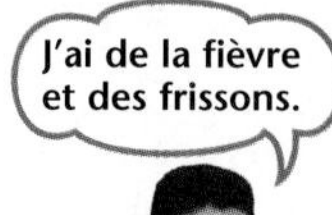

Prononciation

Les sons **/u/** et **/ü/** 

1. It is important to make a distinction between the sounds **/u/** and **/ü/,** since many words differ only in these two sounds. Repeat the following pairs of words.

   vous / vu **dessous / dessus** **roux / rue**
   loue / lu **tout / tu**

2. Now repeat the following sentences.

   Tu as beaucoup de température?
   J'éternue toutes les deux minutes.

3 Practice

Parlons un peu plus
Let's talk some more

Have students work in pairs. You may wish to choose a pair of students to do these activities for the class.

Prononciation

Step 1 Model the key words **souffrir** and **température** and have the students repeat in unison.

Step 2 Now lead students through the information on page 51 and model the other words and sentences.

Step 3 You may wish to give the students the following **dictée:**

Il est descendu à l'avenue Victor-Hugo.
Vous avez vu la rue.
Au-dessous ou au-dessus?

Answers to Parlons un peu plus

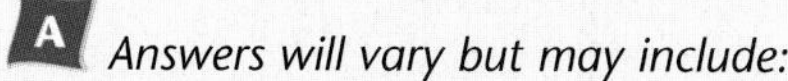

A *Answers will vary but may include:*

—Tu aimes la biologie et la chimie?
—Oui, j'aime beaucoup ces matières.
—Tu es bon étudiant/bonne étudiante?
—Oui, j'aime bien étudier.
—Tu es sociable?
—Oui, je suis très sociable!

B *Answers will vary but may include:*

—J'ai le nez qui coule et la gorge qui gratte.
—Vous êtes enrhumé. Vous avez un virus. Je ne vous donne pas d'antibiotiques parce que vous n'avez pas d'infection bactérienne. Buvez du jus d'orange et beaucoup d'eau. Et vous pouvez prendre un sirop pour la gorge.

Resource Manager

Audio Activities Booklet TE, page 21
Audiocassette 2B/CD 2

Bellringer Review

Use BRR Transparency 2.8 or write the following on the board.
Choose the correct completion.

ouvre **avale**
respire **souffre**
prend

1. **Il_____ la bouche.**
2. **Il est très malade. Il _____ beaucoup.**
3. **Il _____ à fond.**
4. **Il _____ les comprimés avec de l'eau.**
5. **Il _____ ses médicaments.**

National Standards

Cultures
The reading about a visit with the doctor on pages 52–53 and the related activities give students an understanding of health services in France.

Comparisons
The reading will allow students to make comparisons between the French and American medical systems.

Le Québec

Lectures culturelles

Reading Strategy

Identifying important concepts

A quick way to identify the important concepts in a passage is to first read the questions that follow it. This will tell you what ideas the author is emphasizing and what type of information you should look for as you read.

Une consultation

La pauvre Mélanie. Elle est très malade! Elle tousse. Elle éternue. Elle a mal à la tête. Elle a de la température. Elle a des frissons. Elle n'est pas du tout dans son assiette. Elle veut appeler le médecin, mais c'est le week-end et son médecin ne donne pas de consultations le week-end. La seule solution, c'est d'appeler S.O.S. Médecins.

S.O.S. Médecins est un service qui envoie des médecins à domicile[1]. Un médecin arrive chez Mélanie et l'examine. Elle l'ausculte, elle lui prend sa température. Elle lui dit qu'elle a la grippe. Mais ce n'est pas grave. Elle va être vite sur pied. Le médecin lui fait une ordonnance. Elle prescrit des

[1] à domicile *to the home*

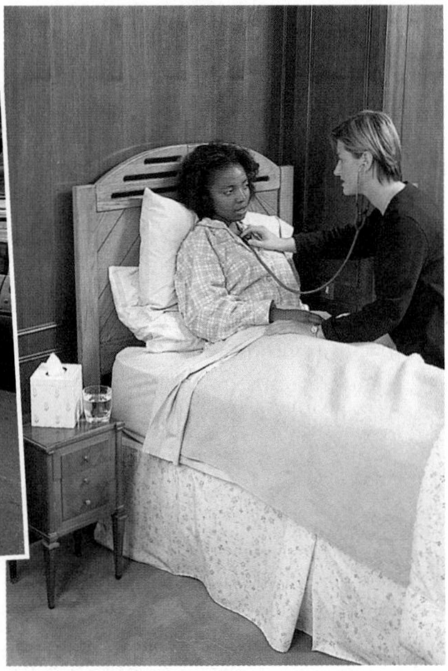

Le médecin ausculte la malade.

Presentation

Pre-reading

Step 1 Read and discuss the Reading Strategy, page 52. Have students skim the questions in the **Après la lecture** activities.

Step 2 Have students skim the reading quickly and silently.

Reading

Step 1 Have individuals read two or three sentences at a time. After each one reads, ask others comprehension questions.

Lectures culturelles

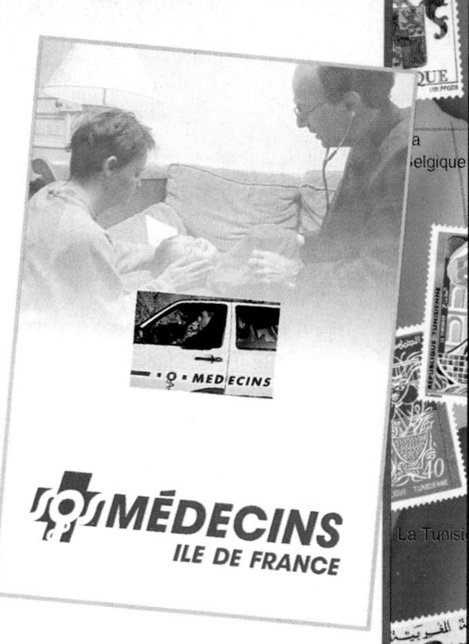

antibiotiques: trois comprimés par jour pendant une semaine. Mélanie va en prendre un à chaque repas.

Mélanie paie le médecin. Mais en France, la Sécurité Sociale rembourse les honoraires des médecins, c'est-à-dire l'argent qu'on donne aux médecins. Les honoraires et tous les frais[2] médicaux sont remboursés de 80 à 100% (pour cent) par la Sécurité Sociale.

[2] frais *expenses*

Après la lecture

A Autrement dit Dites d'une autre manière.
1. Mélanie a *de la fièvre.*
2. Elle *ne se sent pas bien.*
3. Elle veut *téléphoner au* médecin.
4. Le médecin *ne voit pas de malades* le week-end.
5. S.O.S. Médecins envoie des médecins *chez les malades.*
6. Le médecin *écoute la respiration de* Mélanie.
7. La grippe n'est pas une maladie *alarmante.*
8. Mélanie va vite *se sentir mieux.*

B Vous avez compris? Répondez.
1. Mélanie est très malade?
2. Elle a beaucoup de fièvre?
3. Elle a mal au ventre?
4. Elle veut aller chez le médecin?
5. Son médecin donne des consultations tous les jours?
6. Mélanie téléphone à qui?
7. Le médecin lui prescrit de l'aspirine?
8. Les frais médicaux ne sont pas remboursés en France?

C En France Qu'est-ce que vous avez appris sur les médecins et les services médicaux en France?

La Belgique La Tunisie Le Maroc Le Mali

Step 2 Ask five or six questions that review the main points. The answers will give a coherent oral review of the **Lecture.**

Post-reading

Have students do the **Après la lecture** activities on page 53 orally after reading the selection in class. Then assign these activities to be written at home. Go over them again the following day.

Après la lecture

A and B Allow students to refer to the story to look up the answers or you may use this activity as a testing device for factual recall.

About the French Language

Explain to students that **les honoraires** is the term used for the fees of professionals such as doctors and lawyers.

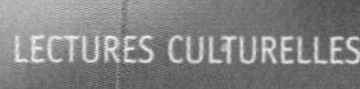

ANSWERS TO Après la lecture

A
1. Mélanie a de la température.
2. Elle n'est pas du tout dans son assiette.
3. Elle veut appeler le médecin.
4. Le médecin ne donne pas de consultations le week-end.
5. S.O.S. Médecins envoie des médecins à domicile.
6. Le médecin ausculte Mélanie.
7. La grippe n'est pas une maladie grave.
8. Mélanie va être vite sur pied.

B
1. Oui, Mélanie est très malade.
2. Non, elle a un peu de fièvre.
3. Non, elle n'a pas mal au ventre.
4. Oui, elle veut aller chez le médecin.
5. Non, son médecin ne donne pas de consultations le week-end.
6. Mélanie téléphone à S.O.S. Médecins.
7. Non, le médecin ne lui prescrit pas d'aspirine.
8. Si, les frais médicaux sont remboursés en France.

C *Answers will vary but may include:*

En France les médecins viennent chez vous. Mais vous devez payer le médecin après la consultation. Les honoraires et les frais médicaux sont remboursés par la Sécurité Sociale.

Lecture supplémentaire 1

National Standards

Cultures
This selection familiarizes students with cultural differences dealing with health matters.

Comparisons
This selection makes a comparison between typical health concerns of Americans and French people.

Attention!

This reading is optional. You may skip it completely, have the entire class read it, have only several students read it and report to the class, or assign it for extra credit.

Learning from Realia

(page 54) Point to the rabbit and say: **C'est un lapin. Qu'est-ce qu'il a, le lapin? Qu'est-ce qu'il a mangé? Il a mangé trop de carottes? Tu aimes les carottes? Tu manges beaucoup de carottes? On dit que les carottes sont bonnes pour les yeux?**

Lecture supplémentaire 1

Culture et santé

LES TROUBLES DIGESTIFS

La culture influence la santé et la médecine? Certainement. Par exemple, en France tout le monde parle de son foie[1]. Les Français disent souvent, «J'ai mal au foie.» Aux États-Unis, on n'entend jamais dire ça. Pourquoi? Parce qu'aux États-Unis, une maladie du foie, c'est grave. Mais quand un Français dit qu'il a mal au foie, il veut dire tout simplement qu'il a un trouble digestif. Rien de grave. Il n'est peut-être pas dans son assiette aujourd'hui, mais il va vite être sur pied!

Aux États-Unis, par contre, on parle beaucoup d'allergies. De nombreux Américains souffrent d'une petite allergie. Les symptômes d'une allergie ressemblent aux symptômes d'un rhume. On éternue et on a souvent mal à la tête. Une allergie, c'est désagréable, mais ce n'est pas grave. En France, on parle moins souvent d'allergies. Pourquoi? Qui sait? Vive la différence!

[1] foie *liver*

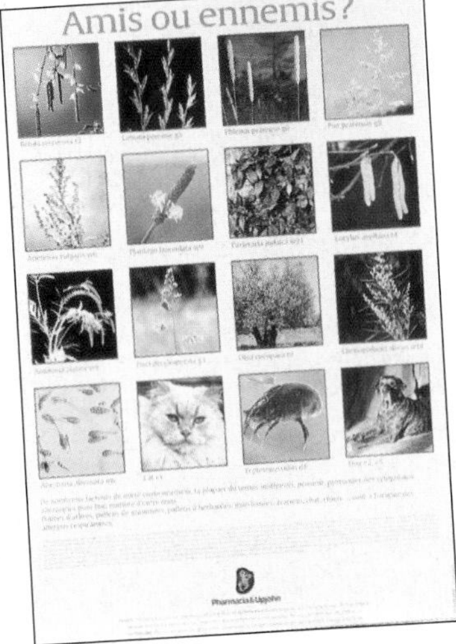

Après la lecture

Des différences Répondez.

1. On dit souvent qu'on a mal au foie dans quel pays?
2. Que veut dire un Français quand il dit qu'il a mal au foie?
3. Et pour un Américain, qu'est-ce que cela veut dire «J'ai mal au foie»?
4. Qui parle souvent d'allergies?
5. Quels sont les symptômes d'une allergie?

Answers to Après la lecture

1. en France
2. qu'il a un trouble digestif
3. que c'est une maladie grave
4. les Américains
5. On éternue, on a les yeux qui piquent et on a mal à la tête.

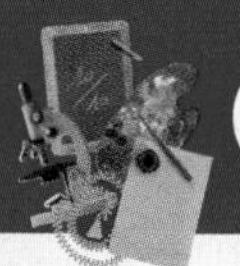

Les glucides (les hydrates de carbone)

Les glucides (les pommes de terre, les pâtes comme les spaghettis, le riz[4]) sont la source d'énergie la plus efficace pour le corps humain.

Les lipides (les graisses)

Les lipides sont aussi une bonne source d'énergie. Mais pour les personnes qui ont un taux de cholestérol élevé[5], les graisses ne sont pas bonnes. Il faut faire un régime sans graisse. Il faut les éliminer.

Les minéraux

Beaucoup de minéraux sont essentiels pour le corps humain. Le calcium est absolument nécessaire pour les os[6] et les dents.

L'eau

L'eau est absolument essentielle au corps humain qui est fait de 65% d'eau.

Les vitamines

Les vitamines sont indispensables au bon fonctionnement du corps humain. Ce tableau indique la source de quelques vitamines importantes.

Vitamines	Sources
A	légumes, lait, quelques fruits
B	viande, œufs, céréales, légumes verts
C	fruits, tomates, salade verte
D	lait, œufs, poisson
E	huiles, légumes, œufs, céréales

[4] riz *rice* [5] élevé *elevated, high* [6] os *bones*

Après la lecture

A La diététique Répondez.

1. Qu'est-ce qu'on doit manger tous les jours?
2. Le nombre de calories pour chaque individu dépend de quoi?
3. Qui a particulièrement besoin de calories? Pourquoi?
4. Quelle est une source importante d'énergie?
5. Pourquoi faut-il contrôler la consommation de graisses?
6. Quel est un minéral important pour les os et les dents?
7. Qu'est-ce qui est indispensable au bon fonctionnement du corps humain?

B Assez de vitamines? Faites une liste de tout ce que vous avez mangé hier. Vous avez eu toutes les vitamines nécessaires?

CONNEXIONS

Presentation

Les sciences naturelles
La diététique

Step 1 Have students read the introduction in English on page 56.

Step 2 Ask students to scan the reading on pages 56–57.

Après la lecture

A Students can refer to the reading to answer these questions if necessary.

Recycling

This reading serves to review and reinforce the names for many foods.

Reaching All Students

Additional Practice Have students write out a balanced menu for **le petit déjeuner, le déjeuner,** and **le dîner.**

Answers to Après la lecture

A

1. Tous les jours on doit manger une variété de légumes et de fruits, des céréales, de la viande ou du poisson.
2. Le nombre de calories pour chaque individu dépend de son métabolisme, de sa taille, de son âge et de son activité physique.
3. Les adolescents ont particulièrement besoin de calories parce qu'ils sont actifs et en période de croissance.
4. Les lipides (les glucides) sont une source importante d'énergie.
5. Il faut contrôler la consommation de graisses pour ne pas avoir un taux de cholestérol élevé.
6. Le calcium est un minéral important pour les os et les dents.
7. Les vitamines sont indispensables au bon fonctionnement du corps humain.

B *Answers will vary depending upon what the students ate.*

C'est à vous

Use what you have learned

 **Recycling**

These activities allow students to use the vocabulary and structure from this chapter in completely open-ended, real-life situations.

Presentation

Encourage students to say as much as possible when they do these activities. Tell them not to be afraid to make mistakes, since the goal of these activities is real-life communication. If someone in the group makes an error, allow the others to politely correct him or her. Let students choose the activities they would like to do.

You may wish to divide students into pairs or groups. Encourage students to elaborate on the basic theme and to be creative. They may use props, pictures, or posters if they wish.

C'est à vous

Use what you have learned

PARLER 1

Tout le monde est malade.

✔ *Describe cold symptoms and minor ailments*

Work with a classmate. Choose one of the people in the illustrations. Describe him or her. Your partner will guess which person you're talking about and say what's the matter with the person. Take turns.

1. 

2. 

3. 

4. 

PARLER 2

Une ordonnance

✔ *Discuss a prescription with a pharmacist*

You are in a pharmacy in Bordeaux. Your classmate will be the pharmacist. Make up a conversation about your prescription. Explain why and how you have to take the medicine.

PARLER 3

Jeu Je suis malade comme un chien!

✔ *Talk about how you are feeling*

Work with a partner. Make gestures to indicate how you're feeling today. Your partner will ask you why you feel that way. Tell him or her. Be as creative and humorous as possible.

ANSWERS TO C'est à vous

1 *Answers will vary but may include:*

—Le pauvre! Il a très mal au ventre. Il a aussi de la fièvre. Sa mère va téléphoner au médecin.
—C'est le dessin numéro 1. Il a la grippe.

2 *Answers will vary but may include:*

—J'ai une angine. Le médecin m'a donné cette ordonnance.
—Ah, oui. C'est un très bon antibiotique.
—Il faut prendre combien de comprimés?
—Trois par jour. Et vous allez être vite sur pied.

3 *Answers will vary but may include:*

Student points to his or her stomach.
—Tu as mal au ventre?
—Oui. Hier je suis allé(e) à une fête et j'ai beaucoup mangé. Je sais que j'ai mangé trop de gâteau au chocolat.

Excusez-moi...

✔ *Write a note describing a minor illness*

You're supposed to take a French test today but you're not feeling well. Write a note to your French teacher explaining why you can't take the test, and mention some symptoms you have.

Une ambulance du SAMU

Des bénévoles

Your French club has a community service requirement. You have decided to work in the emergency room **(le service des urgences)** at your local hospital. You serve as a translator or interpreter for patients who speak only French. Write a flyer for your French club. Tell about your experience with one or more patients. Give your feelings about the work you do and try to encourage other club members to volunteer their services, too.

Writing Strategy

Writing a personal essay In writing a personal essay, a writer has several options: to tell a story, describe something, or encourage readers to think a certain way or to do something. Whatever its purpose, a personal essay allows a writer to express a viewpoint based on his or her own experience. Your essay will be much livelier if you choose interesting details and vivid words to relay your message.

Answers to C'est à vous

4 *Answers will vary.*

5 *Answers will vary.*

C'est à vous

Writing Development

Have students keep a notebook containing their best written work from each chapter. These selected writings can be based on assignments from the Student Textbook and the Writing Activities Workbook. The two activities on page 59 are examples of writing assignments that may be included in each student's portfolio. In the Workbook, students will develop an organized autobiography **(Mon autobiographie).** These workbook pages may also become a part of their portfolio.

Writing Strategy

Taking notes Have students read the Writing Strategy on page 59. If students have difficulty thinking of related vocabulary, have them use the vocabulary list on page 62.

Reaching All Students

Additional Practice Display Communication Transparency C 2. Have students work in groups to make up as many questions as they can about the illustration. Have groups take turns asking and answering the questions.

Reaching All Students

For the Younger Students Have students make colorful get-well cards using some of the expressions they have learned. If someone they know is ill, they can send him or her the cards.

Assessment

Resource Manager

Communication Transparencies
Quizzes
Test Booklet
ExamView Pro®
Situation Cards
Performance Assessment
Marathon mental Videoquiz

Assessment

This is a pre-test for students to take before you administer the chapter test. Answer sheets for students to do these pages are provided in your transparency binder. Note that each section is cross-referenced so students can easily find the material they have to review in case they made errors. You may wish to collect these assessments and correct them yourself or you may prefer to have the students correct themselves in class. You can go over the answers orally or project them on the overhead, using your Assessment Answers transparencies.

Assessment

Vocabulaire

1 Choisissez.

a. 
b. 
c. 
d. 

1. ____ Elle a mal à la tête.
2. ____ Elle a mal au ventre.
3. ____ Elle tousse.
4. ____ Elle est enrhumé.

2 Identifiez.

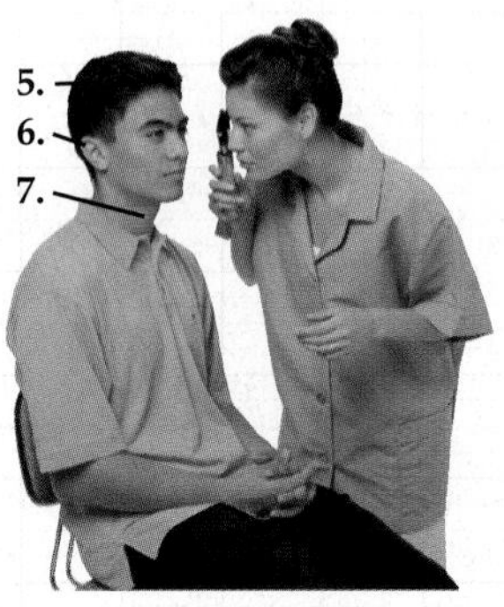

To review **Mots 2**, turn to pages 38–39.

3 Complétez.

8. Le médecin ____ le malade.
9. Le malade ouvre la ____ quand le médecin lui examine la gorge.
10. Le médecin fait un ____. Il dit que Nathalie a une sinusite aiguë.
11. Le médecin lui fait une ____ pour des antibiotiques.
12. Elle va à la ____ pour acheter ses médicaments.

Answers to Assessment

1. c
2. a
3. d
4. b

5. la tête
6. l'oreille
7. la gorge

8. examine
9. bouche
10. diagnostic
11. ordonnance
12. pharmacie

Assessment

Structure

4 Complétez.

13. Le médecin parle au malade?
Oui, il ____ parle.
14. Le médecin donne une ordonnance à ses patients?
Oui, il ____ donne une ordonnance.
15. Paul donne son ordonnance à la pharmacienne?
Oui, il ____ donne son ordonnance.

*To review **lui** and **leur**, turn to page 42.*

5 Complétez.

16. Ils ____ beaucoup, les pauvres. (souffrir)
17. J'____ le livre à la page 100. (ouvrir)
18. Vous ____ la bouche quand le médecin vous examine? (ouvrir)

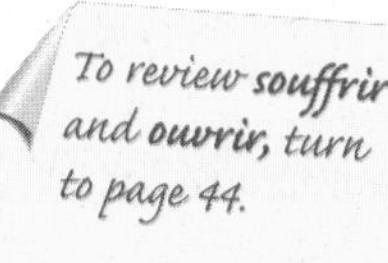

*To review **souffrir** and **ouvrir**, turn to page 44.*

6 Complétez avec l'impératif.

19. (ouvrir) Paul, ____ ton livre.
Luc et Louise, ____ vos livres aussi.
20. (attendre) Carole, ____ un moment.
Sandrine et Maïa, ____ avec Carole.
21. (dire) Luc, ____ au médecin où tu as mal.
Vous deux, ____ au médecin où vous avez mal.

To review commands, turn to page 45.

7 Répondez avec un pronom.

22. Tu as de l'aspirine?
Oui, ________.
23. Tu as douze comprimés?
Oui, ________.
24. Tu peux sortir de l'hôpital demain?
Oui, ________.
25. Il a beaucoup d'argent?
Oui, ________.

*To review the use of **en**, turn to page 48.*

Glencoe Technology

MINDJOGGER

You may wish to help your students prepare for the chapter test by playing the MindJogger game show. Teams will compete against each other to review chapter vocabulary and structure and sharpen listening comprehension skills.

Answers to Assessment

4

13. lui
14. leur
15. lui

5

16. souffrent
17. ouvre
18. ouvrez

6

19. ouvre, ouvrez
20. attends, attendez
21. dis, dites

7

22. Oui, j'en ai.
23. Oui, j'en ai douze.
24. Oui, je peux en sortir.
25. Oui, il en a beaucoup.

Vocabulary Review

The words and phrases in the **Vocabulaire** have been taught for productive use in this chapter. They are summarized here as a resource for both student and teacher. This list also serves as a convenient resource for the **C'est à vous** activities on pages 58–59. There are approximately sixteen cognates in this vocabulary list. Have students find them.

Attention!

You will notice that the vocabulary list here is not translated. This has been done intentionally, since we feel that by the time students have finished the material in the chapter they should be familiar with the meanings of all the words. If there are several words they still do not know, we recommend that they refer to the **Mots 1** and **2** sections in the chapter or go to the dictionaries at the back of this book to find the meanings. However, if you prefer that your students have the English translations, please refer to Vocabulary Transparency 2.1, where you will find all these words listed with their translations.

Vocabulaire

Describing minor health problems

la santé
en bonne santé
en mauvaise santé
une infection
un frisson
la grippe
un rhume
une angine
une sinusite aiguë
une allergie
un mouchoir
un kleenex
se sentir bien
mal
être enrhumé(e)
tousser
éternuer
avoir mal
à la tête
au ventre
aux oreilles
à la gorge
avoir de la fièvre
le nez qui coule
les yeux qui piquent
la gorge qui gratte
malade
viral(e)
bactérien(ne)
allergique

Speaking with the doctor

le médecin
le/la malade
un diagnostic
une ordonnance
souffrir
ouvrir
examiner
ausculter
respirer
prescrire

How well do you know your vocabulary?

- Find as many cognates as you can in the list.
- Use five cognates to write several sentences.

Identifying more parts of the body

la tête
un œil, des yeux
le nez
la bouche
une oreille
la gorge
le ventre

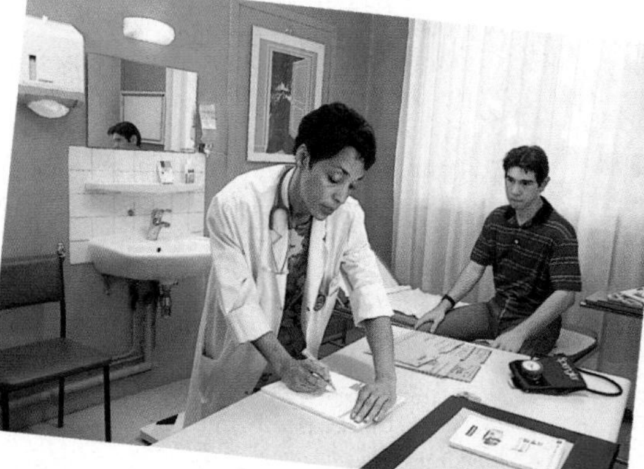

Speaking with a pharmacist

un(e) pharmacien(ne)
une pharmacie
un médicament
un comprimé
un antibiotique
un sirop
de la pénicilline
de l'aspirine *(f.)*
avaler

Other useful words and expressions

À tes souhaits!
Qu'est-ce qu'il a?
le/la pauvre
à fond

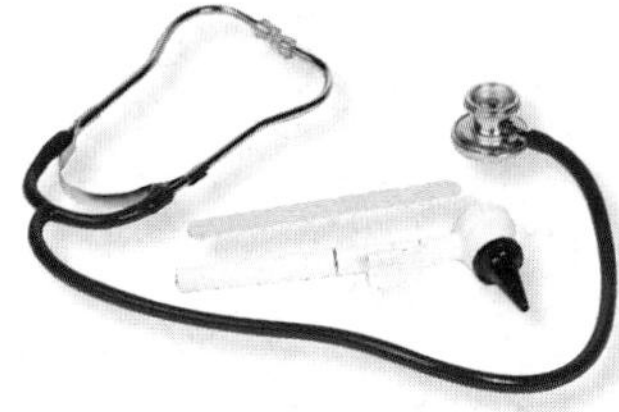

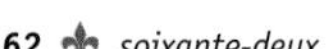

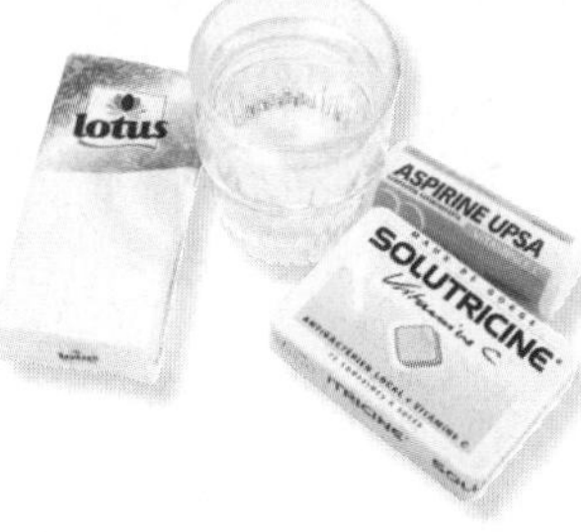

Technotour

BON VOYAGE!

VIDÉO • Épisode 2

Avant de visionner

In this video episode, Vincent experiences a strange nightmare. The next day he pays a visit to his doctor.

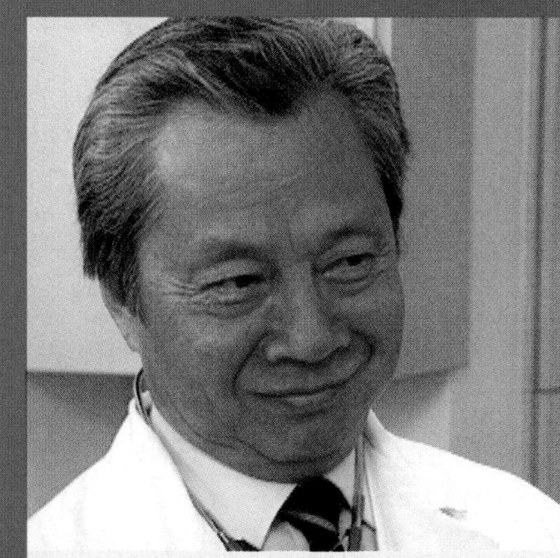

Le docteur Nguyen est très sympa.

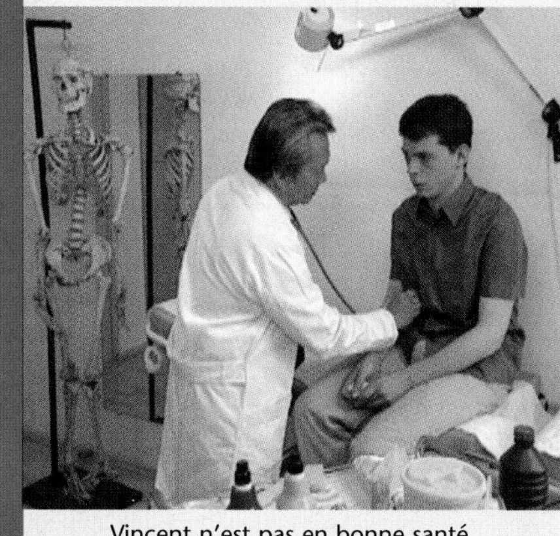

Vincent n'est pas en bonne santé.

FRENCH ONLINE

À découvrir

Learn more about l'Institut Pasteur online.

L'Institut Pasteur

FRENCH Online

In the Chapter 2 Internet activity, you will have a chance to learn more about health and medicine in the Francophone world. To begin your virtual adventure, go to the Glencoe French Web site: **french.glencoe.com**

Technotour

Overview

This page previews two key multimedia components of the **Glencoe French** series. Each reinforces the material taught in the chapter in a unique manner.

VIDÉO

The Video Program allows students to see how the chapter vocabulary and structures are used by native speakers. For maximum reinforcement, show the video episode as a final activity for Chapter 2.

The two photos on the left show highlights from the Chapter 2 video episode. Discuss the photos with your students before having them view the episode. See the Video Activities Booklet for detailed suggestions for using this resource.

FRENCH Online

- The **À découvrir** photo on page 63 shows the **Institut Pasteur.** Students can go online to learn more about this important research institute.
- Teacher Information and Student Worksheets for this activity can be accessed at the Web site.

Video Synopsis

In this video episode, Vincent has a bad dream about the famous Paris catacombs. The video flashes from these ancient skeletons to one in a doctor's office. Vincent explains his symptoms, and the doctor conducts a routine examination. Vincent is relieved to receive a diagnosis of the flu and not something more serious.

Planning for Chapter 3

SCOPE AND SEQUENCE, PAGES 64–95

Topics

- Technology
- Telecommunications

Culture

- The telephone—yesterday and today
- Telephone cards
- Communication advances

Functions

- How to describe habitual and continuous actions in the past
- How to narrate in the past

Structure

- **L'imparfait** of regular verbs
- Uses of **l'imparfait**

National Standards

- Communication Standard 1.1 pages 68, 69, 72, 73, 75, 76, 77, 81, 83, 90
- Communication Standard 1.2 pages 68, 69, 72, 73, 75, 76, 77, 79, 80, 82, 85, 86, 87, 89
- Communication Standard 1.3 pages 68, 69, 72, 73, 76, 77, 80, 81, 83, 90, 91
- Cultures Standard 2.1 pages 71, 83, 84–85, 87
- Cultures Standard 2.2 pages 79, 83, 86
- Connections Standard 3.1 pages 88–89
- Comparisons Standard 4.1 page 89
- Communities Standard 5.1 page 91

PACING AND PRIORITIES

The chapter content is color coded below to assist you in planning.
■ required ■ recommended ■ optional

Vocabulaire *(required)* *Days 1–4*
- ■ Mots 1
  - L'ordinateur
  - Le télécopieur, le fax
- ■ Mots 2
  - Le téléphone

Structure *(required)* *Days 5–7*
- ■ L'imparfait
- ■ Les emplois de l'imparfait

Conversation *(required)*
- ■ Des devoirs difficiles

Lectures culturelles
- ■ Le téléphone d'hier et d'aujourd'hui *(recommended)*
- ■ La télécarte *(optional)*
- ■ Les communications avant et maintenant *(optional)*

Connexions *(optional)*
- ■ L'ordinateur

■ **C'est à vous** *(recommended)*

■ **Assessment** *(recommended)*

■ **Technotour** *(optional)*

RESOURCE GUIDE

SECTION	PAGES	SECTION RESOURCES
Vocabulaire *Mots 1*		
L'ordinateur Le télécopieur, le fax	66–67 67–69	Vocabulary Transparencies 3.2–3.3 Audiocassette 3A/CD 3 Audio Activities Booklet TE, pages 23–25 Workbook, pages 21–22 Quiz 1, page 12 ExamView Pro®
Vocabulaire *Mots 2*		
Le téléphone	70–73	Vocabulary Transparencies 3.4–3.5 Audiocassette 3A/CD 3 Audio Activities Booklet TE, pages 25–27 Workbook, pages 23–24 Quiz 2, page 13 ExamView Pro®
Structure		
L'imparfait Les emplois de l'imparfait	74–77 78–81	Audiocassette 3A/CD 3 Audio Activities Booklet TE, pages 28–29 Workbook, pages 25–28 Quizzes 3–4, pages 14–15 ExamView Pro®
Conversation		
Des devoirs difficiles	82–83	Audiocassette 3A/CD 3 Audio Activities Booklet TE, pages 29–30 CD-ROM
Lectures culturelles		
Le téléphone d'hier et d'aujourd'hui La télécarte Les communications avant et maintenant	84–85 86 87	Audiocassette 3A/CD 3 Audio Activities Booklet TE, pages 30–31 Test Booklet, Chapter 3
Connexions		
L'ordinateur	88–89	Test Booklet, Chapter 3
C'est à vous		
	90–91	**Bon voyage!** Video, Episode 3 Video Activities Booklet, Chapter 3 French Online Activities french.glencoe.com
Assessment		
	92–93	Communication Transparency C 3 Quizzes 1–4, pages 12–15 Test Booklet, Chapter 3 ExamView Pro® Situation Cards, Chapter 3 **Marathon mental** Videoquiz

Using Your Resources for Chapter 3

Transparencies

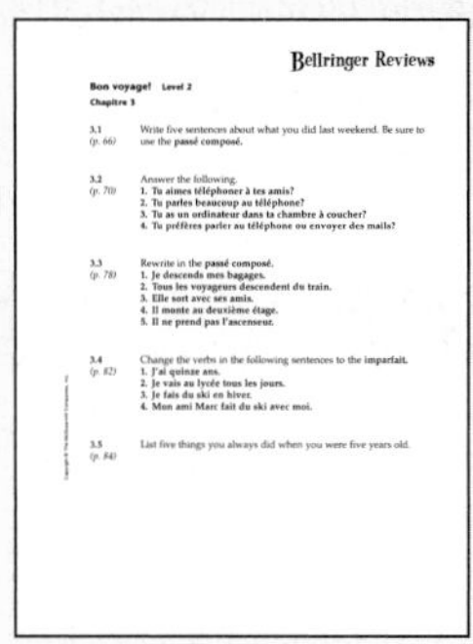
Bellringer 3.1–3.5

Vocabulary 3.1–3.5

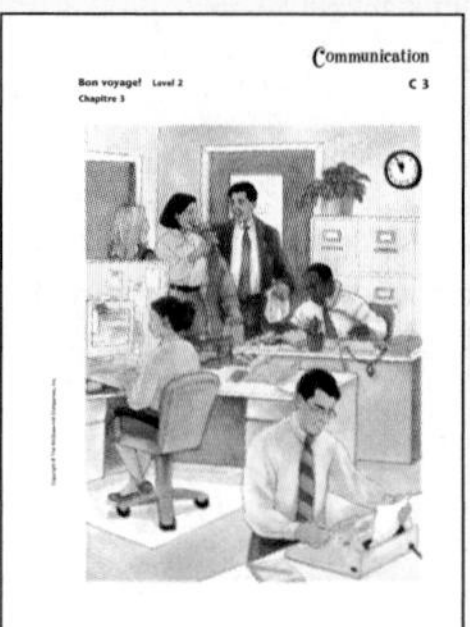
Communication C 3

Writing Activities Workbook

Vocabulary, pages 21–24

Structure, pages 25–28

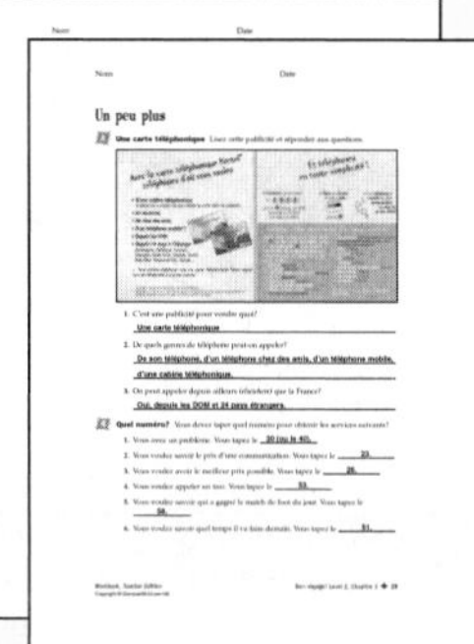
Enrichment, pages 29–32

Audio Program and Audio Activities Booklet

Vocabulary, pages 23–27

Structure, pages 28–29

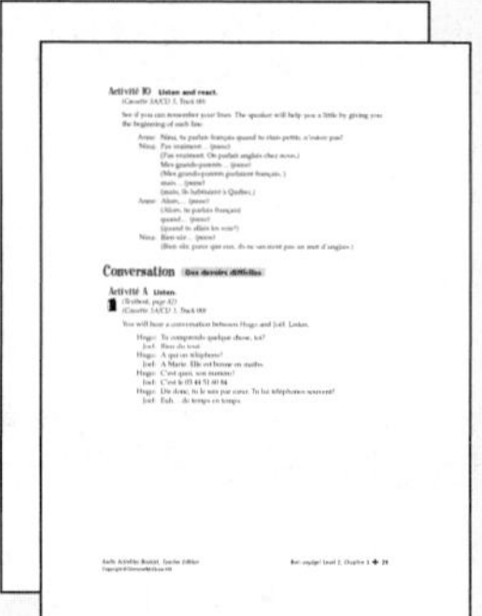
Conversation, pages 29–30

Cultural Reading, pages 30–31

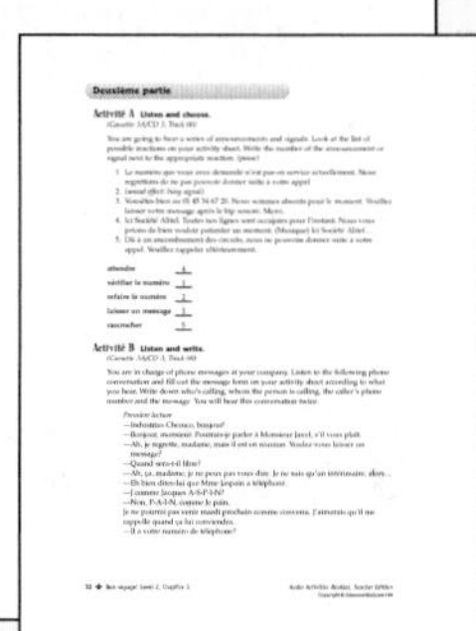
Additional Practice, pages 32–33

Assessment

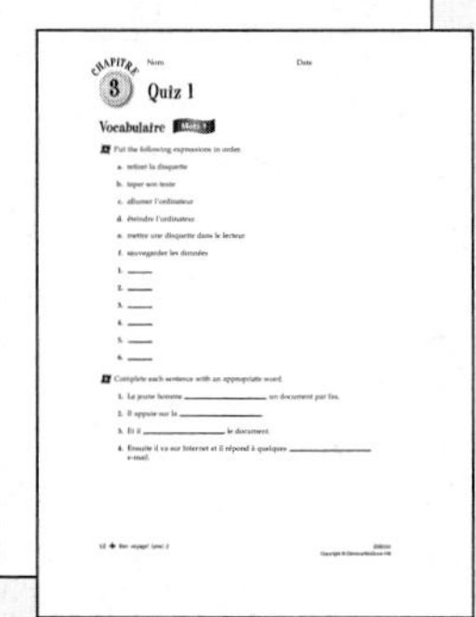

Vocabulary and Structure Quizzes, pages 12–15

Chapter Tests, Chapter 3

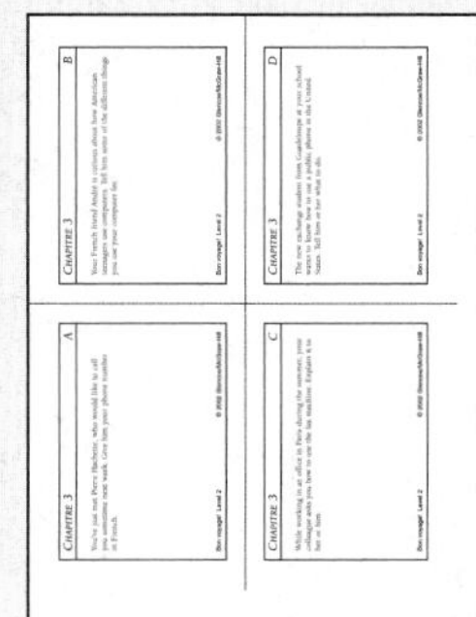

Situation Cards, Chapter 3

Timesaving Teacher Tools

Interactive Teacher Edition

Imagine having your Teacher's Edition and all resources on a CD-ROM. Click on a resource and it appears on your screen, ready to be printed, sorted, or planned.

Interactive Lesson Planner

The Interactive Lesson Planner CD-ROM helps you organize your lesson plans for a week, month, semester, or year. Look at this planning tool for easy access to your Chapter 3 resources.

ExamView Pro®

Test Bank software for Macintosh and Windows makes creating, editing, customizing, and printing tests quick and easy.

Technology Resources

In the Chapter 3 Internet activity, you will have a chance to learn more about the use of computers in the Francophone world. Visit french.glencoe.com.

On the Interactive Conversation CD-ROM, students can listen to and take part in a recorded version of the conversation in Chapter 3.

See the National Geographic Teacher's Corner on pages 138–139, 244–245, 372–373, 472–473 for reference to additional technology resources.

Bon voyage! Video and Video Activities Booklet.

Help your students prepare for the chapter test by playing the **Marathon mental** Videoquiz game show. Teams will compete against each other to review chapter vocabulary and structure and sharpen listening comprehension skills.

CHAPITRE 3

Preview

In this chapter, students will learn to talk about computers, e-mail, and the Internet. They will learn how to send a fax and make a telephone call in France. Students will also learn the formation and uses of the imperfect tense.

National Standards

Communication

In Chapter 3, students will communicate in spoken and written French on the following topics:

- Computers, e-mail, and the Internet
- Using the telephone and fax machine
- Activities that they did frequently

Students will obtain and provide information and engage in conversations dealing with computers and the telephone as they fulfill the chapter objectives listed on this page.

CHAPITRE 3

Les télécommunications

Objectifs

In this chapter you will learn to:

- *talk about computers, e-mail, the Internet, faxes, and telephones*
- *talk about habitual and continuous actions in the past*
- *narrate in the past*
- *discuss today's telecommunications*

Maurice de Vlaminck *La route*

64

FRENCH Online

The **Glencoe Foreign Language Web site** (french.glencoe.com) offers several options that enable you and your students to experience the French-speaking world via the Internet:

- The online **Activités** are correlated to the chapters and utilize Francophone Web sites around the world. For the Chapter 3 activity, see student page 95.
- Games and puzzles afford students another opportunity to practice the material learned in a particular chapter.
- The *Enrichment* section offers students an opportunity to visit Web sites related to the theme of the chapter for more information on a particular topic.
- Online *Chapter Quizzes* offer students an opportunity to prepare for a chapter test.
- Visit our virtual **Café** for more opportunities to practice and explore the French-speaking world.

Spotlight on Culture

Photograph These phone booths are near the Forum des Halles in the 1st arrondissement of Paris.

Painting Maurice de Vlaminck (1876–1958) was a French painter, engraver, and writer. In his early years he was both a bicycle racer and an accomplished violinist. He started to paint for fun. In 1907, he met Henri Matisse. He was much impressed by the works of both Matisse and Van Gogh. He painted landscapes, urban sites, and scenes of streets.

Learning from Photos

(pages 64–65)

- **Recycling:** Have students say as much as they can about the clothing the people are wearing in the photo.
- After presenting **Mots 2** vocabulary, have students identify the following people in the photo on pages 64–65:
  1. **Il fait un appel d'une cabine téléphonique.**
  2. **Il se sert de son portable.**
  3. **Ils font la queue devant une cabine téléphonique.**

Chapter Projects

Bonjour! Your students may enjoy sending electronic postcards and greeting cards from **Café Glencoe** (**french.glencoe.com**).

National Standards

Communities

Have students prepare a pamphlet in French for French-speaking visitors to the United States that explains how to make calls from a public telephone. Send it to your local Chamber of Commerce or the nearest foreign exchange student organization.

1 Preparation

Resource Manager

Vocabulary Transparencies 3.2–3.3
Audio Activities Booklet TE, pages 23–25
Audiocassette 3A/CD 3
Workbook, pages 21–22
Quiz 1, page 12
ExamView Pro®

Bellringer Review

Use BRR Transparency 3.1 or write the following on the board.
Write five sentences about what you did last weekend. Be sure to use the **passé composé.**

2 Presentation

Step 1 Have students close their books. Introduce the **Mots 1** vocabulary using Vocabulary Transparencies 3.2–3.3. Have students repeat each word after you or the recording on Audiocassette 3A/CD 3 two or three times as you point to the appropriate illustration on the transparencies.

Step 2 When presenting the sentences, intersperse questions to enable students to use the new words immediately. Build from simple to more complex questions. **Teaching Tip:** When introducing material, proceed from the easiest to the most difficult type of question. Begin with *yes/no* or *either/or* questions. **(C'est un écran?)** Save information questions **(Qu'est-ce que c'est?)** until students have had a chance to produce or at least hear the new vocabulary several times.

Vocabulaire Mots 1

L'ordinateur

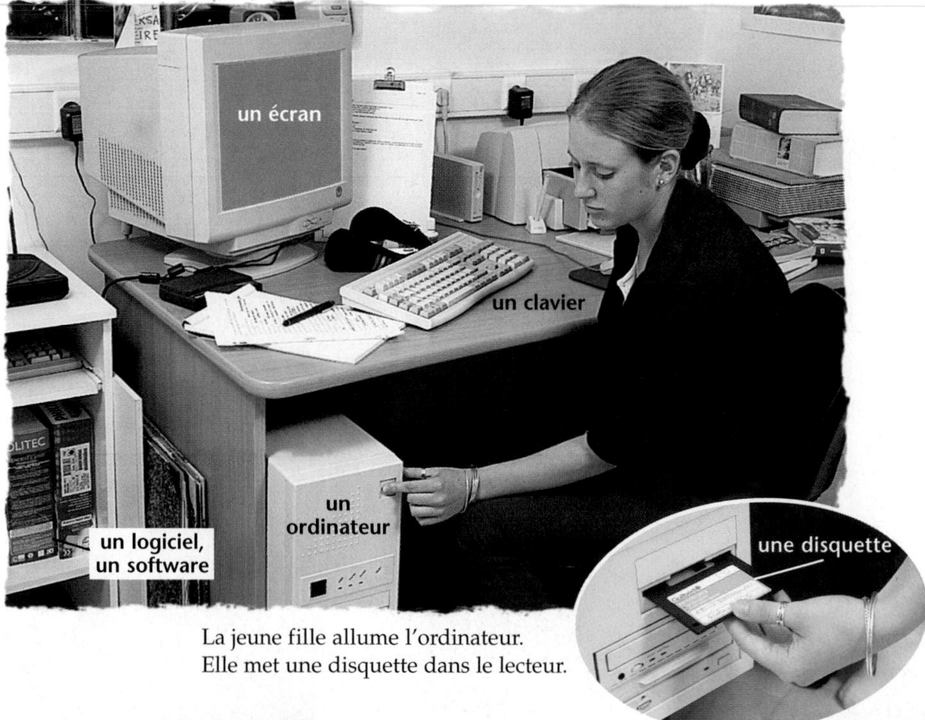

La jeune fille allume l'ordinateur.
Elle met une disquette dans le lecteur.

Elle utilise l'ordinateur pour faire ses devoirs.
Elle tape son texte (ses données).

Elle ne perd pas son texte.
Elle le sauvegarde.

Elle retire la disquette.

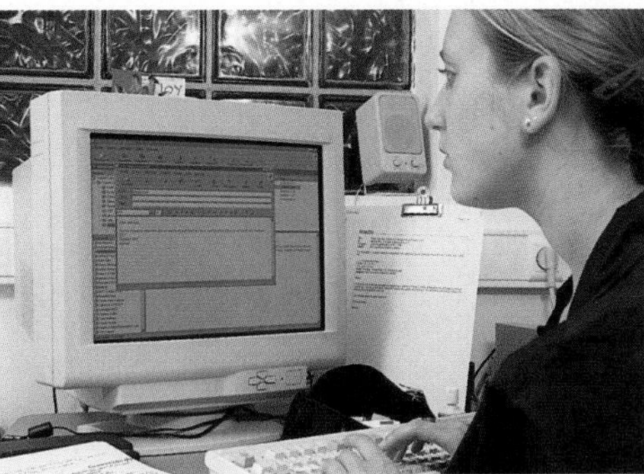
Ensuite, elle va sur Internet.
Elle clique sur ses messages.
Elle répond à quelques messages.
Elle envoie quelques (e-)mails.

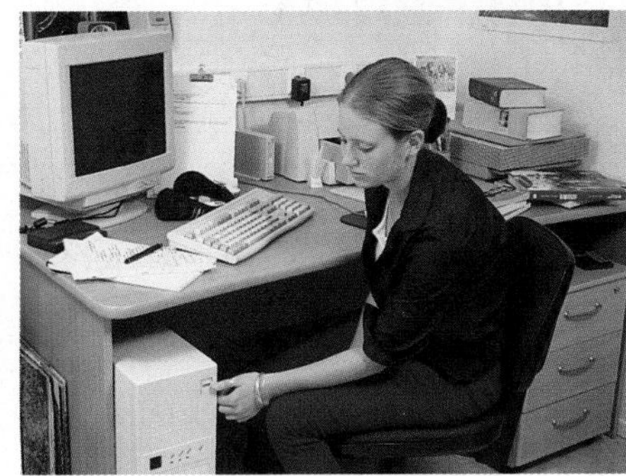
Enfin, elle éteint son ordinateur.

Le télécopieur, le fax

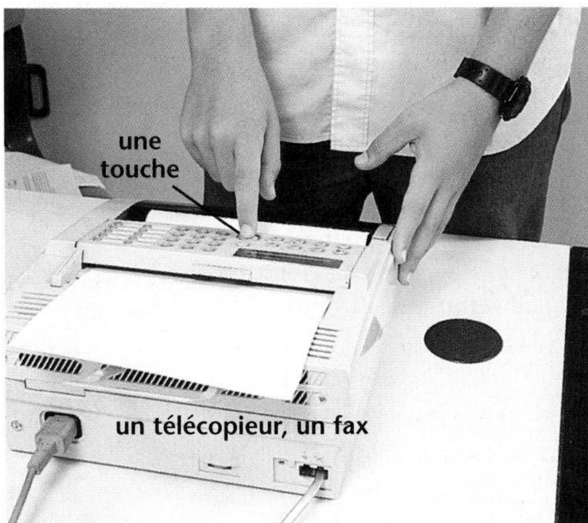

Le jeune homme envoie un document par télécopieur (fax).
Il met le document face écrite non visible.
Il ne le met pas face écrite visible.
Il appuie sur la touche.

Il transmet (envoie) le document.

Step 3 Have students open their books and read the new words and sentences aloud.

Teaching Tips: If you have a computer in class, you can use it to teach much of this vocabulary. When presenting the fax vocabulary on page 67, use a sheet of paper to show **face écrite visible** vs. **face écrite non visible.**

About the French Language

Both **mail** and **e-mail** are used in French, but **mail** is actually more common.

Learning from Photos

(pages 66–67) All photos for the vocabulary section were taken in Brunoy, France.

Teacher note: We have varied the **tu** and **vous** forms with the TPR activities so students hear both forms. If you prefer to use **tu** with an individual student, change the commands in later activities to **tu.**

Reaching All Students

Total Physical Response

(Student 1), **lève-toi et viens ici, s'il te plaît.**
On va imaginer que c'est un ordinateur.
Allume l'ordinateur.
Mets une disquette.
Tape ton texte.
Retire la disquette.
Éteins l'ordinateur.

(Student 2), **lève-toi et viens ici, s'il te plaît.**
Tu vas envoyer un fax.
Mets le document dans le télécopieur.
Tu l'as mis face écrite visible.
Retire le document.
Remets le document face écrite non visible.
Appuie sur la touche pour envoyer le document.

3 Practice

Commençons
Let's use our new words

Attention!

When students are doing the **Commençons** activities, accept any answer that makes sense. The purpose of these activities is to have students use the new vocabulary. They are not factual recall activities. Thus, it is not necessary for students to remember specific factual information from the vocabulary presentation when answering.

Historiette Each time **Historiette** appears, it means that the answers to the activity form a short story. Encourage students to look at the title of the **Historiette,** since it can help them do the activity.

1 It is suggested that you go over this activity orally in class with books closed. Then have students write the answers for homework and go over the activity once again the following day.

2 Students can do this activity on their own and then read their answers.

3 This activity can also be done as a paired activity. One student asks the question and another responds.

Commençons
Let's use our new words

1 L'ordinateur Donnez des réponses personnelles.

1. Tu as un ordinateur chez toi ou tu utilises un ordinateur à l'école?
2. Tu utilises un ordinateur pour faire tes devoirs?
3. Tu as un dictionnaire ou une encyclopédie sur CD-ROM?
4. Quand tu tapes ton texte, tu regardes l'écran ou le clavier?
5. Quand tu commences à travailler, tu allumes ou tu éteins l'ordinateur?
6. Tu mets ta disquette où?
7. Tu vas quelquefois sur Internet?
8. Tu envoies des e-mails à tes amis?
9. Tu retires la disquette quand tu as fini tes devoirs?
10. Tu as une imprimante? Tu imprimes tes devoirs?

2 Les instructions à suivre Mettez les phrases suivantes en ordre.

1. On met une disquette dans le lecteur.
2. On tape les données.
3. On allume l'ordinateur.
4. On retire la disquette.
5. On éteint l'ordinateur.
6. On sauvegarde les données.
7. On clique sur l'icône du logiciel avec la souris.

3 Historiette Au bureau
Inventez une histoire.

1. La femme veut envoyer un fax?
2. Elle utilise un ordinateur ou un télécopieur?
3. Le télécopieur est allumé?
4. La femme met le document face écrite visible ou non visible?
5. Elle appuie sur quoi?
6. Qu'est-ce qu'elle fait de son document?

Answers to Commençons

1 *Answers will vary but may include:*

1. Oui, j'ai un ordinateur chez moi et j'utilise un ordinateur à l'école.
2. Oui, j'utilise un ordinateur pour faire mes devoirs.
3. Oui, j'ai une encyclopédie sur CD-ROM.
4. Quand je tape mon texte, je regarde l'écran.
5. Quand je commence à travailler, j'allume l'ordinateur.
6. Je mets ma disquette dans le lecteur.
7. Oui, je vais quelquefois sur Internet.
8. Oui, j'envoie des (e-)mails à mes amis.
9. Oui, je retire la disquette quand j'ai fini mes devoirs.
10. Oui, j'ai une imprimante. J'imprime mes devoirs.

2 *Answers may vary slightly in order:*

1. On allume l'ordinateur.
2. On met une disquette dans le lecteur.
3. On clique sur l'icône du logiciel avec la souris.
4. On tape les données.
5. On sauvegarde les données.
6. On retire la disquette.
7. On éteint l'ordinateur.

3 *Answers will vary but may include:*

1. Oui, la femme veut envoyer un fax.
2. Elle utilise un télécopieur.
3. Oui, le télécopieur est allumé.
4. La femme met le document face écrite non visible.
5. Elle appuie sur la touche.
6. Elle transmet le document.

4 **Comment utiliser un ordinateur** Un(e) élève du Québec passe un an dans votre école. Il/Elle veut savoir comment utiliser votre ordinateur. Vous lui expliquez ce qu'il faut faire.

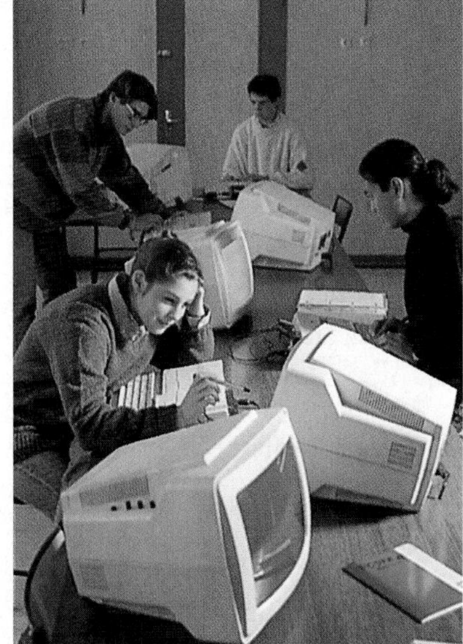

Un cours d'informatique

5 **Comment envoyer un fax** Vous travaillez quelques heures par semaine dans un bureau. Un copain y travaille aussi. Pour travailler votre français, vous discutez en français de tout ce qu'il faut faire pour envoyer un fax (une télécopie).

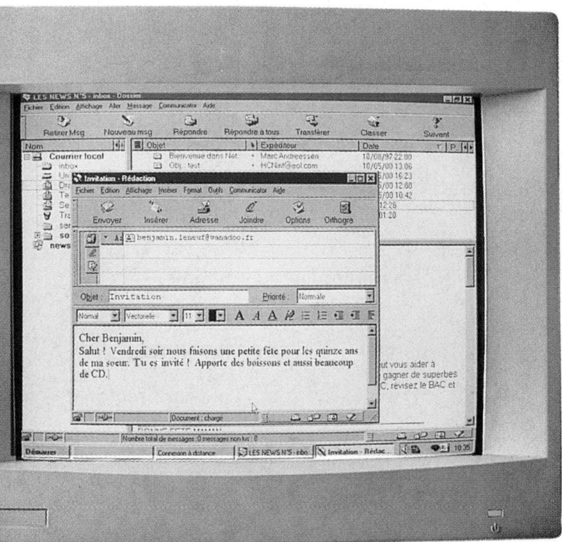

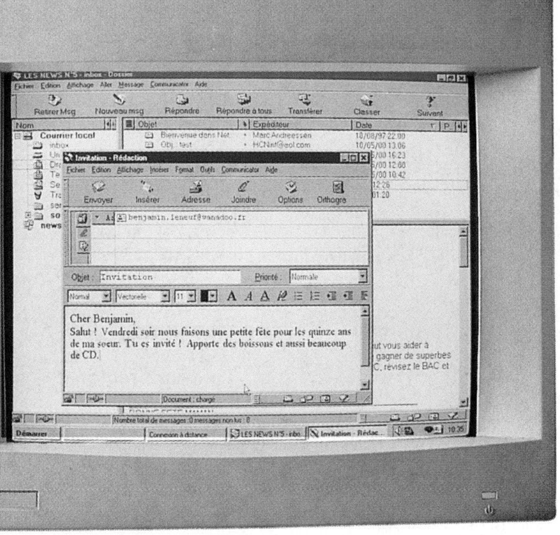

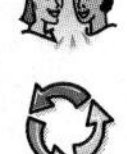

6 **Logiciels** Avec un copain, parlez de tout ce que vous faites sur votre ordinateur. Vous faites vos devoirs? Vous jouez à des jeux? Vous envoyez des e-mails à vos amis? Quels sont les logiciels que vous utilisez? Ensuite, regardez l'écran à gauche. Décrivez ce que vous voyez sur l'écran.

For more practice using words from ***Mots 1****, do Activity 9 on page H10 at the end of this book.*

Vocabulaire

4 You may wish to briefly review **tu** form commands, which were presented in **Bon voyage! Level 1,** Chapter 14, and **Bon voyage! Level 2,** Chapter 1. Write the **tu** forms of the computer-related verbs on the board: **tu allumes, tu mets, tu tapes, tu retires, tu éteins, tu sauvegardes, tu cliques.** Remind students to drop the **s** from **-er** verbs.

Writing Development

Have students write the answers to Activity 3 in paragraph form.

Cognate Recognition

Have students scan the **Mots 1** words again and then identify and pronounce each cognate.

Reteaching

Show Vocabulary Transparencies 3.2–3.3 and let students say as much as they can about them in their own words.

ENCORE PLUS This *infogap* activity will allow students to practice in pairs. The activity should be very manageable for them, since all vocabulary and structures are familiar to them.

Answers to Commençons

4 *Answers will vary but may include:*

Allume l'ordinateur. Puis, mets une disquette dans le lecteur. Clique sur l'icône du logiciel «Word» avec la souris. Tape ton texte et sauvegarde ton texte. Retire la disquette et éteins l'ordinateur.

5 *Answers will vary but may include:*

—Pour envoyer une télécopie il faut allumer le télécopieur.
—Oui, et puis il faut mettre le document face écrite non visible dans le télécopieur.
—Puis il faut appuyer sur la touche.
—Et voilà, le fax transmet le document.

6 *Answers will vary but may include:*

—Moi, j'aime beaucoup utiliser mon ordinateur. Je fais tous mes devoirs sur mon ordinateur.
—Moi, je préfère jouer à des jeux. J'ai beaucoup de jeux sur CD-ROM.
—J'envoie aussi des mails à mes amis qui habitent loin d'ici.
—Oui, j'adore répondre à mes mails.
—J'utilise beaucoup de logiciels différents.

—À gauche sur l'écran je vois un mail. Un copain de Benjamin lui écrit une lettre. Je vois des icônes.

1 Preparation

Resource Manager

Vocabulary Transparencies 3.4–3.5
Audio Activities Booklet TE, pages 25–27
Audiocassette 3A/CD 3
Workbook, pages 23–24
Quiz 2, page 13
ExamView Pro®

Bellringer Review

Use BRR Transparency 3.2 or write the following on the board.
Answer the following.

1. **Tu aimes téléphoner à tes amis?**
2. **Tu parles beaucoup au téléphone?**
3. **Tu as un ordinateur dans ta chambre à coucher?**
4. **Tu préfères parler au téléphone ou envoyer des mails?**

2 Presentation

Step 1 Show Vocabulary Transparencies 3.4–3.5. Have students close their books and repeat the words after you or Audiocassette 3A/CD 3 as you point to the appropriate illustration on the transparency.

Step 2 If possible, use props such as a telephone, a telephone book, coins, a telephone card, etc., to help teach the new vocabulary.

Step 3 Ask *yes/no* or *either/or* questions to elicit the new vocabulary. For example: **Je décroche ou je raccroche? C'est un annuaire ou une télécarte?**

Point out to students that they must dial 33 when making a call to France. This is the country code for France.

Vocabulaire

Mots 2

Le téléphone 

un téléphone (à touches)

décrocher

attendre la tonalité

un répondeur automatique

un numéro de téléphone

l'indicatif régional

l'indicatif du pays (France)

(33) 01 44 20 60 98

le bon numéro

01 44 20 60 98

01 44 20 60 18

le mauvais numéro, une erreur

composer (faire) le numéro

raccrocher

Reaching All Students

Total Physical Response You may wish to bring in a play telephone and a phone book to use as props.

(Student 1), **venez ici, s'il vous plaît.**
Prenez l'annuaire.
Ouvrez l'annuaire.
Regardez dedans.
Cherchez un numéro.
Allez au téléphone.
Ouvrez la porte de la cabine téléphonique.
Entrez.
Mettez votre télécarte dans la fente du téléphone.
Décrochez.
Attendez la tonalité.
Faites le numéro que vous voulez.
Parlez.
Raccrochez.
Merci, *(Student 1).* **Retournez à votre place et asseyez-vous.**

Les communications avant et maintenant

Depuis toujours, les hommes essaient de communiquer. Les Romains envoyaient des messagers à pied ou à cheval[1]. Les Indiens utilisaient des signaux de fumée[2]. Les Africains, eux, jouaient du tam-tam. Au dix-neuvième siècle[3], on utilisait le morse—inventé par l'Américain Samuel Morse. Puis c'est le télégraphe et enfin… le téléphone. Au début[4], la qualité des communications n'était pas très bonne, mais avec l'invention du microphone, elle s'est beaucoup améliorée[5].

Aujourd'hui, on utilise encore très souvent le téléphone. Mais de plus en plus, c'est l'ordinateur qu'on utilise pour communiquer. Non seulement on peut envoyer des messages à ses amis sur Internet, mais on peut aussi chercher des renseignements, réserver des places de cinéma ou de théâtre, ou acheter toutes sortes de produits. L'Internet offre des possibilités immenses de communication.

Comment donner une adresse e-mail en français? Voici comment on doit dire l'adresse suivante: veronique.perse@wanadoo.fr = Véronique (point) Perse (arrobase) wanadoo (point) fr. Et vous, vous avez une adresse e-mail?

[1] à cheval *on horseback*
[2] fumée *smoke*
[3] siècle *century*
[4] Au début *In the beginning*
[5] s'est… améliorée *got better*

Après la lecture

A Devinez. D'après le contexte, quelle est la signification des mots suivants?
1. des messages de fumée
2. au dix-neuvième siècle
3. le morse

B Votre adresse e-mail Donnez votre adresse e-mail (ou celle de votre école) à votre ami(e) français(e)—votre camarade.

Lecture supplémentaire 2

National Standards

Cultures
This selection familiarizes students with the history of communication in the world and in France.

Attention!

This reading is optional. You may skip it completely, have the entire class read it, have only several students read it and report to the class, or assign it for extra credit.

Presentation

Step 1 Have students read the **Lecture** quickly.

Step 2 Ask what new information they learned about **les communications** in France and throughout history.

Après la lecture

Go over the **Après la lecture** activities on page 87.

Answers to Après la lecture

A
1. smoke signals
2. in the nineteenth century
3. Morse Code

B *Answers will vary.*

Learning from Photos

(page 87) Have students identify everything they can in the photo of the office.

CONNEXIONS

National Standards

Connections
This reading about changes in computer technology and the prevalence of English in the field of computer science establishes a connection with another discipline, allowing students to reinforce and further their knowledge of technology through the study of French.

Comparisons
This reading points out how much of the computer vocabulary in French has been derived from English and gives students a better understanding of the interrelatedness of the two languages.

Attention!

The readings in the **Connexions** section are optional. They focus on some of the major disciplines taught in schools and universities. The vocabulary is useful for discussing such topics as history, literature, art, economics, business, science, etc. You may choose any of the following ways to do the readings in the **Connexions** sections.

Independent reading Have students read the selections and do the post-reading activities as homework, which you collect. This option is least intrusive on class time and requires a minimum of teacher involvement.

Homework with in-class follow-up Assign the readings and post-reading activities as homework. Review and discuss the material in class the next day.

Intensive in-class activity This option includes a pre-reading vocabulary presentation, in-class reading and discussion, assignment of the activities for homework, and a discussion of the assignment in class the following day.

CONNEXIONS

La technologie

L'ordinateur

It's hard to imagine life before the computer. The computer has revolutionized many fields, including travel, medicine, architecture, the military, banking, and commerce. Even agriculture and the arts make extensive use of the new technology. The changes have been tremendous. Because the United States has led the way in computer science, much of the vocabulary used worldwide is in English or derived from English. Let's read about some of these changes in technology and the prevalence of English in this domain.

L'ordinateur ENIAC, 1946

Les progrès des télécommunications

Les ordinateurs d'il y a trente ans étaient énormes. Un ancien ordinateur comme le premier ENIAC exécutait moins d'instructions qu'une calculatrice actuelle[1] et occupait toute une salle! Aujourd'hui, il y a des ordinateurs portables qui pèsent moins de deux kilos. Ce qui a facilité le progrès en informatique, c'est la miniaturisation. Une seule micropuce[2] peut emmagasiner[3] des centaines de millions d'informations. Les premiers télécopieurs aussi étaient très grands et les télécopies qu'on recevait étaient souvent illisibles[4].

Marianne Silberfeld travaille pour un ministère du gouvernement français. Le bâtiment[5] est du dix-neuvième siècle, mais les appareils[6]

1 actuelle *of today*
2 micropuce *microchip*
3 emmagasiner *store*
4 illisibles *illegible*
5 bâtiment *building*
6 appareils *machines*

Learning from Photos

(page 88) ENIAC stood for *Electronic Numerical Integrator and Computer.* ENIAC, with its thousands of tubes, was the first electronic digital computer.

que Marianne utilise sont très modernes. Elle a un ordinateur et un fax. À l'université, Marianne a fait des études d'anglais. Une bonne idée, parce qu'il y a beaucoup de mots anglais en informatique. Par exemple, il faut «cliquer» sur une «icône» pour accéder au «software». Un «virus» peut infecter les programmes. Voici d'autres exemples de la prédominance de l'anglais dans le monde de l'informatique: une disquette, la mémoire, un format, le hardware, un processeur, un bogue, un mail. Vous savez comment on dit tout ça en anglais?

Un ordinateur aujourd'hui

Un portable

Après la lecture

A En français Donnez le mot en français.

1. e-mail
2. fax
3. software
4. virus
5. hardware
6. format
7. memory
8. to access
9. to click
10. icon

B Définitions Dites d'une autre façon.

1. un petit ordinateur qu'on peut transporter facilement
2. qu'on ne peut pas lire
3. des machines
4. accumuler, mettre en réserve
5. un télécopieur ou une télécopie

Presentation

La technologie
L'ordinateur

Step 1 Have students read the introduction in English on page 88.

Step 2 Have students scan the reading for cognates. Then have them do the reading again, this time for comprehension.

Note: Since many students are interested in computers, you may wish to have all students scan or read this selection quickly to get some general information and acquaint themselves with some vocabulary for receptive purposes.

Answers to Après la lecture

A

1. un (e-)mail
2. un télécopieur, un fax
3. un logiciel, un software
4. un virus
5. un hardware
6. un format
7. la mémoire
8. accéder
9. cliquer
10. une icône

B

1. un portable
2. illisible
3. des appareils
4. emmagasiner
5. un fax

C'est à vous

Recycling

These activities allow students to use the vocabulary and structure from this chapter in completely open-ended, real-life situations.

Presentation

Encourage students to say as much as possible when they do these activities. Tell them not to be afraid of making mistakes since the goal of these activities is real-life communication. If someone in the group makes an error, allow the others to politely correct him or her. Let students choose the activities they would like to do.

You may wish to divide students into pairs or groups. Encourage students to elaborate on the basic theme and to be creative. They may use props, pictures, or posters if they wish.

Writing Development

Have students keep a notebook containing their best written work from each chapter. These selected writings can be based on assignments from the Student Textbook and the Writing Activities Workbook. The three activities on page 91 are examples of writing assignments that may be included in each student's portfolio. In the Workbook, students will develop an organized autobiography **(Mon autobiographie).** These workbook pages may also become a part of their portfolio.

C'est à vous

Use what you have learned

PARLER 1

Qu'est-ce qu'on fait?

✔ *Talk about computers, e-mail, the Internet, faxes, and telephones*

Choisissez une photo et décrivez-la à votre camarade.

PARLER 2

Les étés de mon enfance

✔ *Talk about past habitual actions*

Demandez à un(e) camarade ce qu'il/elle faisait d'habitude en été quand il/elle était petit(e). Demandez-lui où il/elle allait, avec qui, ce qu'il/elle faisait, etc. Changez ensuite de rôle.

PARLER 3

Vos amis et vous

✔ *Talk about today's telecommunications and how you keep in touch with your friends*

Expliquez à un(e) camarade comment vous restez en contact avec vos amis. Dites-lui si vous avez un portable, un répondeur ou une adresse e-mail. Dites-lui aussi si vous téléphonez à vos amis tous les jours ou si vous leur envoyez des e-mails. Ensuite demandez-lui comment il/elle reste en contact avec ses amis.

PARLER 4

Jeu Le jeu du téléphone

✔ *Describe routine actions*

Divide into teams by row. Using the imperfect, the last person in each row whispers to the person in front of him or her one sentence about what he or she used to do in the past. Each person whispers the sentence to the next person until the message reaches the front of the row. The first person in each row says the sentence to the class. The team whose final sentence most closely resembles the original wins!

Answers to C'est à vous

1 *Answers will vary but may include:*

(photo on far right) L'homme vérifie un numéro de téléphone dans l'annuaire. Il a un téléphone dans la main. Il veut téléphoner à un restaurant.

2 *Answers will vary but may include:*

—Tu allais où quand tu étais petit(e)?
—J'allais à la plage avec ma famille.
—Qu'est-ce que vous faisiez à la plage?
—Nous prenions de bains de soleil, nous nagions, et nous nous amusions.

3 *Answers will vary but may include:*

Je téléphone souvent à mes amis parce que j'ai un portable. Quand je ne suis pas chez moi, mes amis me laissent un message sur mon répondeur. J'envoie aussi des (e-)mails à mes amis. J'aime recevoir des (e-)mails!

4 *Students will play the game.*

Assessment

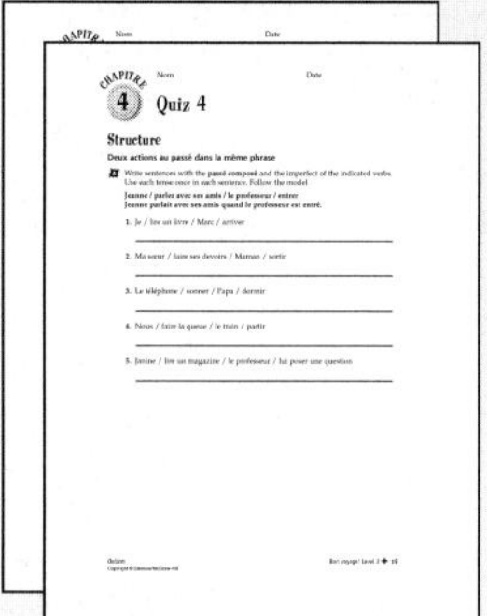

Vocabulary and Structure Quizzes, pages 16–19

Chapter Tests, Chapter 4

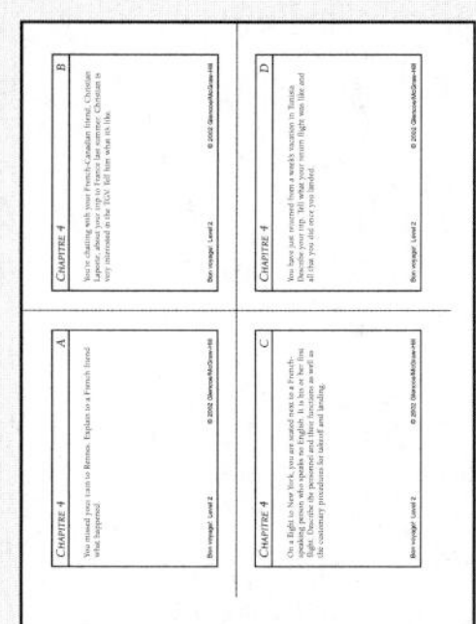

Situation Cards, Chapter 4

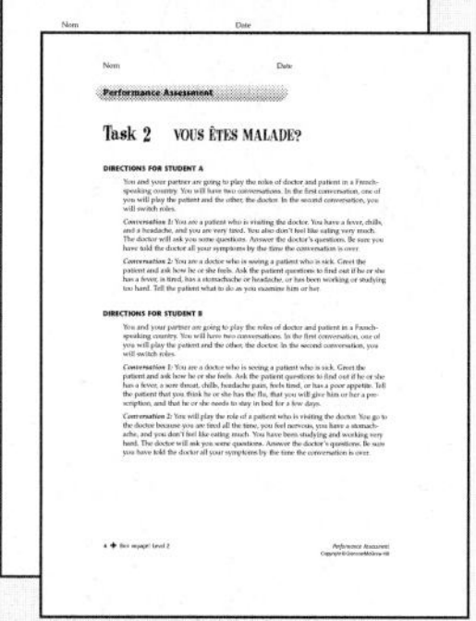

Performance Assessment, pages 1–8

Timesaving Teacher Tools

Interactive Teacher Edition

Imagine having your Teacher's Edition and all resources on a CD-ROM. Click on a resource and it appears on your screen, ready to be printed, sorted, or planned.

Interactive Lesson Planner

The Interactive Lesson Planner CD-ROM helps you organize your lesson plans for a week, month, semester, or year. Look at this planning tool for easy access to your Chapter 4 resources.

ExamView Pro®

Test Bank software for Macintosh and Windows makes creating, editing, customizing, and printing tests quick and easy.

Technology Resources

In the Chapter 4 Internet activity, you will have a chance to learn more about train travel in France. Visit french.glencoe.com.

On the Interactive Conversation CD-ROM, students can listen to and take part in a recorded version of the conversation in Chapter 4.

See the National Geographic Teacher's Corner on pages 138–139, 244–245, 372–373, 472–473 for reference to additional technology resources.

Bon Voyage! Video and Video Activities Booklet.

Help your students prepare for the chapter test by playing the **Marathon mental** Videoquiz game show. Teams will compete against each other to review chapter vocabulary and structure and sharpen listening comprehension skills.

Preview

In this chapter, students will increase their ability to communicate in situations involving travel by train and plane. They will be able to distinguish between local and long-distance trains, modern and old-fashioned trains, services onboard the train, boarding planes, in-flight services, and disembarking at the airport. They will learn the difference between the imperfect and the **passé composé.** They will also learn the verb **venir** and the prepositions used with geographic names.

National Standards

Communication

In Chapter 4, students will communicate in spoken and written French on the following topics:

- Traveling on board a train
- Services on board an airplane
- Arriving at an airport
- Geography

Students will obtain and provide information and engage in conversations dealing with train and plane travel as they fulfill the chapter objectives listed on this page.

CHAPITRE 4

Des voyages intéressants

RF
Alexandra David-Néel
1868-1969
3,00F+0,60F 0,55€

Objectifs

In this chapter you will learn to:

- *talk about train travel*
- *talk about air travel*
- *describe past events*
- *identify cities, countries, and continents*
- *discuss old and modern trains in France*

Claude Monet *La gare Saint-Lazare*

96

The **Glencoe Foreign Language Web site** (french.glencoe.com) offers several options that enable you and your students to experience the French-speaking world via the Internet:

- The online **Activités** are correlated to the chapters and utilize Francophone Web sites around the world. For the Chapter 4 activity, see student page 129.
- Games and puzzles afford students another opportunity to practice the material learned in a particular chapter.
- The *Enrichment* section offers students an opportunity to visit Web sites related to the theme of the chapter for more information on a particular topic.
- Online *Chapter Quizzes* offer students an opportunity to prepare for a chapter test.
- Visit our virtual **Café** for more opportunities to practice and explore the French-speaking world.

Spotlight on Culture

Photograph The photo shows the **TGV (le train à grande vitesse)** roaring past a field of sunflowers. The **TGV,** a train designed and manufactured in France, is one of the fastest trains in the world.

Painting Claude Monet (1840–1926) is one of the most famous French Impressionists. He loved to paint outdoors. He is very well known for both his landscapes and portraits. In 1877, Monet decided to undertake the task of painting the interior of the gare Saint-Lazare, a building that symbolized both the industrialization and the glass and metal architectural style of the era. In the painting seen here, Monet is interested in both the building and the locomotive. He shows the puffs of smoke that escape from the engine forming clouds that dance in the light.

National Standards

Communities
Have students create a huge poster of a cutaway train or plane filled with passengers (self-portraits). All parts of the train or plane should be labeled in French. Hang the poster in the main hallway of the school for National Foreign Language Week (the first full week in March).

Comparaisons Bring brochures from a local travel agency about American and French rail service to class. Ask students to compare and contrast the rail service available in the two countries.

Le train If passenger train travel is nonexistent in your area, have students find out in which areas passenger service is available.

Un voyage Have groups plan a rail trip through France using a guide such as the one from Eurail (available at many travel agencies). Give them a time limit and have them include at least one overnight stay. They should plan arrival and departure times and the length of each stop on the itinerary. Groups can describe their trip to the class.

1 Preparation

Resource Manager

Vocabulary Transparencies 4.2–4.3
Audio Activities Booklet TE, pages 34–35
Audiocassette 3B/CD 3
Workbook, pages 33–34
Quiz 1, page 16
ExamView Pro®

Bellringer Review

Use BRR Transparency 4.1 or write the following on the board.
List all telecommunication equipment you have in your home or in your school.

2 Presentation

Recycling Some of the vocabulary dealing with rail travel was taught in **Bon voyage! Level 1,** Chapter 9. In this chapter it is recycled, expanded upon, and used in the imperfect and **passé composé.**

Step 1 Have students close their books. Introduce the **Mots 1** vocabulary using Vocabulary Transparencies 4.2–4.3. Have students repeat each word after you or the recording on Audiocassette 3B/CD 3 two or three times as you point to the appropriate illustration on the transparencies.

Step 2 Now ask **Qu'est-ce que c'est?** as you point to the item on the transparency and have students come up with the new words themselves.

Step 3 Have students open their books and read the new words and sentences aloud.

Vocabulaire Mots 1

Les trains d'hier et d'aujourd'hui 

Les lignes de banlieue sont les trains qui desservent les villages et les petites villes autour d'une grande ville.

Les grandes lignes sont les trains qui desservent les grandes villes en France et dans les autres pays.

La voiture d'un train moderne a un couloir central.
Il y a deux sièges de chaque côté.
Le contrôleur est entré dans la voiture.
Il a contrôlé les billets.

Reaching All Students

Additional Practice Using props, pictures, and various areas of the classroom, guide students with TPR techniques in acting out as many of the vocabulary phrases as possible. For example: **Indiquez un passager assis. Indiquez un passager debout. Indiquez une place libre. Vous êtes le contrôleur: Entrez dans la voiture. Vérifiez les billets,** etc.

Les vieux trains avaient des compartiments.
De temps en temps, il n'y avait pas de places disponibles.
Tous les compartiments étaient complets.
Il y avait des voyageurs debout dans le couloir.

Le TGV est un train à grande vitesse.
Il roule très vite.
Le paysage est splendide.

Step 4 Have students close their books again. Ask someone in the classroom to stand up. Point to the person and say **debout.** Now point to a student who is seated and say **assis(e).**

Step 5 Ask for individual repetitions of the words and phrases. Intersperse the repetitions with *yes/no, either/or,* or interrogative-word questions. For example: **Tous les compartiments étaient complets? Il y avait des places libres? Tous les passagers étaient assis ou debout? Les passagers étaient debout où?**

Step 6 After you have introduced the **Mots 1** vocabulary using the Vocabulary Transparencies, have students open their books and read the words and sentences on these pages.

Assessment

As an informal assessment, you may wish to show the Vocabulary Transparencies for **Mots 1** again and let students identify items at random. Now have students make up questions about what they see on the transparencies. You may answer the questions or have them call on other students to answer.

3 Practice

Commençons
Let's use our new words

Attention!

When students are doing the **Commençons** activities, accept any answer that makes sense. The purpose of these activities is to have students use the new vocabulary. They are not factual recall activities. Thus, it is not necessary for students to remember specific factual information from the vocabulary presentation when answering. If you wish, have students use the photos on this page as a stimulus, when possible.

1 and **2** It is suggested that you go over these activities orally in class with books closed. Then have students write the answers for homework and go over the activities once again the following day.

2 The information on the departure board in the photo on page 100 gives students the answer to number 2 of this activity.

Learning from Photos

(page 100 top) The train in which the conductor is checking the tickets is on the Paris to Dijon route. Have students imagine a dialogue between the people in the photo.

(page 100 bottom) This departure board is at the gare Montparnasse. In addition to serving destinations to the west of Paris, the gare Montparnasse has become the major terminus for trains to Southwest France with the introduction of the **TGV–Atlantique** service.

Commençons
Let's use our new words

1 Historiette Le voyage du père de Sylvain

Inventez une histoire.

1. Le père de Sylvain a fait un voyage en train quand il était jeune?
2. Il est allé de Paris à Dijon?
3. Le train avait des compartiments?
4. Tous les voyageurs étaient assis?
5. Il y avait des places disponibles?
6. Le père de Sylvain a trouvé une place?
7. Le contrôleur est entré dans le compartiment?
8. Il a contrôlé les billets?
9. Le train est arrivé à Dijon à l'heure?

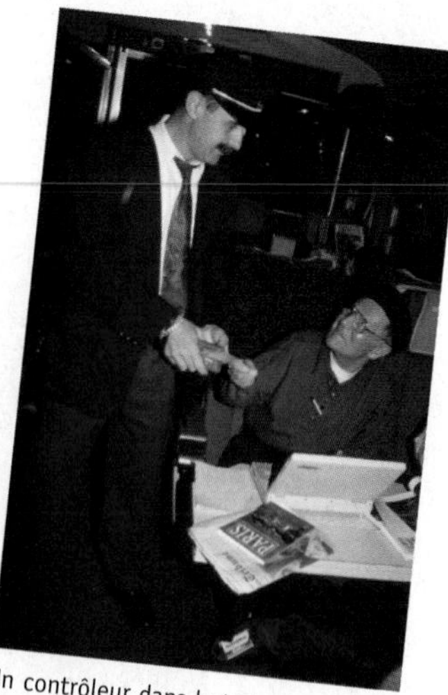

Un contrôleur dans le train de Paris à Dijon

2 Historiette À la gare Répondez.

1. Charlotte va voyager en train. Elle est à la gare ou à l'aéroport?
2. Elle va de Paris à Chartres. Elle va consulter le tableau des grandes lignes ou le tableau des lignes de banlieue?
3. Elle va partir. Elle regarde le tableau des arrivées ou le tableau des départs?
4. Charlotte est montée dans le train sur le quai ou dans la salle d'attente?
5. Elle est arrivée à la gare à l'heure. Elle a raté son train ou pas?

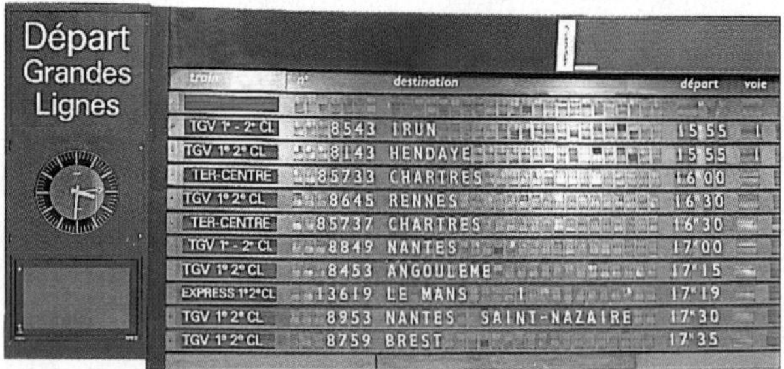

Tableau des départs à la gare Montparnasse à Paris

Answers to Commençons

1 *Answers will vary but may include:*

1. Oui, le père de Sylvain a fait un voyage en train quand il était jeune.
2. Oui, il est allé de Paris à Dijon.
3. Oui, le train avait des compartiments.
4. Non, tous les voyageurs n'étaient pas assis.
5. Oui, il y avait des places disponibles.
6. Oui, le père de Sylvain a trouvé une place.
7. Oui, le contrôleur est entré dans le compartiment.
8. Oui, il a contrôlé les billets.
9. Oui, le train est arrivé à Dijon à l'heure.

2

1. Elle est à la gare.
2. Elle va consulter le tableau des grandes lignes.
3. Elle regarde le tableau des départs.
4. Elle est montée dans le train sur le quai.
5. Elle n'a pas raté son train.

Vocabulaire

Les trains Vrai ou faux?

1. Les vieux trains avaient un couloir avec deux sièges de chaque côté.
2. Il y a beaucoup de places disponibles quand le train est complet.
3. Il y a des voyageurs debout quand il n'y a plus de places disponibles.
4. Les voyageurs aiment avoir un siège réglable s'ils veulent dormir un peu.
5. Les lignes de banlieue desservent toutes les grandes villes.
6. Les voyageurs prennent la correspondance quand ils doivent changer de train.
7. Le TGV est un petit train qui dessert les villages de banlieue.
8. Quand on voyage en train, on peut regarder le paysage.
9. Le TGV roule très vite.

À la gare Travaillez avec un copain ou une copine. Vous êtes à la gare. Vous allez prendre le train de Nice à Grenoble. Décrivez ce que vous faites à la gare. Vous pouvez utiliser les expressions suivantes.

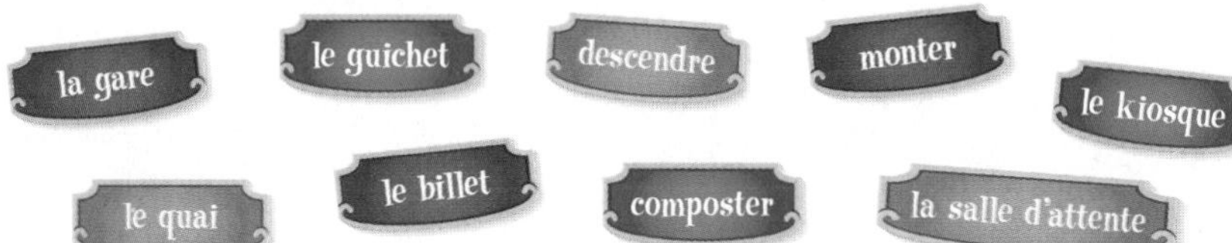

Mon train! Travaillez avec un(e) camarade. Regardez le dessin et décrivez tout ce que vous y voyez.

*For more practice using words from **Mots 1**, do Activity 10 on page H11 at the end of this book.*

3 You may wish to ask students to correct the false statements in this activity.

4 You may wish to have groups of students compete to see which group can make the most (correct and logical) sentences for this activity within a time limit.

Note: The words indicated in Activity 4 reintroduce vocabulary taught in **Bon voyage! Level 1.**

Writing Development

Have students write the answers to Activities 1 and 2 in paragraph form.

Reteaching

Show Vocabulary Transparencies 4.2–4.3 and let students say as much as they can about them in their own words.

This *infogap* activity will allow students to practice in pairs. The activity should be very manageable for them, since all vocabulary and structures are familiar to them.

Answers to Commençons

3

1. faux
2. faux
3. vrai
4. vrai
5. faux
6. vrai
7. faux
8. vrai
9. vrai

4 *Answers will vary but may include:*

À la gare j'achète un billet aller-retour au guichet. J'achète un magazine au kiosque. J'attends un peu dans la salle d'attente. Je composte mon billet et puis je cherche le quai numéro 3. Je monte dans le train et je trouve ma place.

5 *Answers will vary but may include:*

Il est dix heures et quart. Le train pour Lyon part de la voie numéro cinq. Le train part à l'heure. Le jeune homme est en retard. Il rate son train. Il perd des choses sur le quai.

Vocabulaire Mots 2

1 Preparation

Resource Manager

Vocabulary Transparencies 4.4–4.5
Audio Activities Booklet TE, pages 36–38
Audiocassette 3B/CD 3
Workbook, pages 35–36
Quiz 2, page 17
ExamView Pro®

Bellringer Review

Use BRR Transparency 4.2 or write the following on the board.
Complete with the **passé composé.**

1. **Hier je _____ à Versailles. (aller)**
2. **J'_____ le train. (prendre)**
3. **Le train _____ à l'heure. (arriver)**
4. **Mes amis et moi, nous _____ le château. (visiter)**
5. **Nous _____ une promenade dans les jardins. (faire)**

2 Presentation

Note: The vocabulary in this section emphasizes words needed on board the plane and at the airport upon arrival. The vocabulary needed for the departure airport was presented in **Bon voyage! Level 1,** Chapter 8.

Step 1 Show Vocabulary Transparencies 4.4–4.5. Have students close their books and repeat the words after you or Audiocassette 3B/CD 3 as you point to the appropriate illustration on the transparency.

Step 2 Call on students to point out the correct item on the transparency as you say the new word or expression.

Vocabulaire Mots 2

À l'aéroport

À bord de l'avion

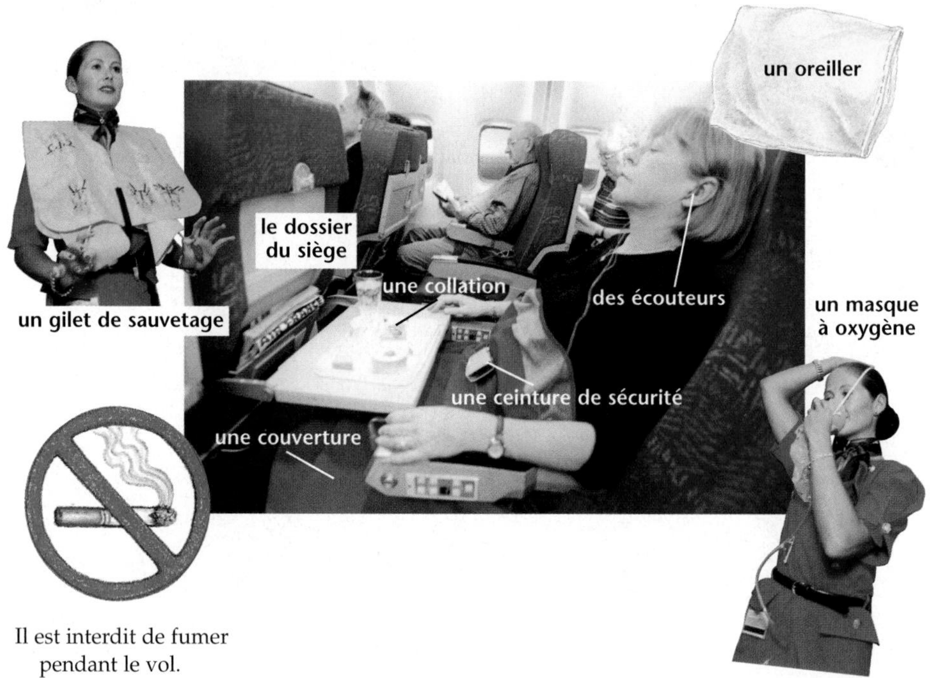

Il est interdit de fumer pendant le vol.

Reaching All Students

Total Physical Response

(Student 1), **venez ici, s'il vous plaît.**
On va imaginer que votre vol vient d'arriver à Paris.
Détachez votre ceinture de sécurité.
Levez-vous.
Débarquez de l'avion.
Dites «au revoir» à l'hôtesse de l'air.
Vous êtes au contrôle des passeports. Montrez votre passeport.
Vous allez récupérer vos bagages. Cherchez un chariot.
Mettez vos bagages sur le chariot.
Poussez le chariot.
Vous passez par la douane sans aucun problème.
Vous êtes maintenant devant l'aérogare. Enlevez vos bagages du chariot.
Attendez votre ami(e) qui vient vous chercher à l'aéroport.

Lectures culturelles

La gare Saint-Lazare

Madame Carrigan voyageait toujours en seconde. Elle trouvait ça beaucoup plus sympa. Pourquoi? Parce que tout le monde montait en voiture muni de provisions[1]: un filet ou deux pleins de fromage, de jambon, de pâté, de fruits et un litre de vin[2] rouge. Tous les voyageurs du même compartiment se parlaient et faisaient connaissance[3]. Si quelqu'un n'avait rien à manger, on partageait[4]. De temps en temps, on sortait dans le couloir pour se dégourdir les jambes[5] et bavarder avec les voyageurs des autres compartiments.

Ces vieux trains existent toujours? Oui, il y en a encore quelques-uns. Mais ils commencent à disparaître. Les TGV deviennent de plus en plus nombreux et ils desservent de plus en plus de villes. Tout le monde adore la vitesse.

[1] muni de provisions *loaded with food*
[2] vin *wine*
[3] faisaient connaissance *got to know one another*
[4] partageait *shared*
[5] se dégourdir les jambes *to stretch one's legs*

Un TGV en Bourgogne

La Belgique · Tunisie · Le Maroc · Le Mali

Après la lecture

A Le voyage d'Ashley Répondez.

1. Quand est-ce qu'Ashley est allée en France?
2. Elle y est allée avec qui?
3. Ils y ont passé combien de temps?
4. Ils ont pris quel train pour aller de Bordeaux à Paris?
5. C'est un train qui roule très vite?
6. Il roule à combien de kilomètres à l'heure?
7. Que faisait Madame Carrigan quand elle était étudiante?
8. Comment étaient les vieux trains?
9. Madame Carrigan voyageait en quelle classe? Pourquoi?
10. Tous les voyageurs montaient en voiture munis de quoi?
11. Qu'est-ce qu'on partageait?
12. Comment est-ce que les passagers faisaient connaissance?

B Le TGV Décrivez le TGV. Dites tout ce que vous savez sur ce train.

Reading

Step 1 To vary the presentation, you may wish to read the **Lecture** to students. Use as much expression as you can.

Step 2 Call on an individual to read several sentences. Then ask other students about the sentences the student has just read.

Step 3 You may wish to select several paragraphs that students will read silently.

Post-reading

Have students do the **Après la lecture** activities on page 119 orally after reading the selection in class. Then assign these activities to be written at home. Go over them again the following day.

Learning from Photos

(page 119 top) As students can see in this photo of one of the older trains, people often lined up in the corridor and looked out the window. It was not uncommon to see people load their luggage on to the train through the windows.

Answers to Après la lecture

A

1. Ashley est allée en France l'été dernier.
2. Elle y est allée avec son professeur de français et ses copains.
3. Ils y ont passé trois semaines.
4. Ils ont pris le TGV pour aller de Bordeaux à Paris.
5. Oui, c'est un train qui roule très vite.
6. Ce train roule à plus de 300 kilomètres à l'heure.
7. Quand Mme Carrigan était étudiante elle voyageait en France.
8. Les vieux trains étaient bien différents du TGV. Ils avaient des compartiments.
9. Mme Carrigan voyageait en seconde parce qu'elle trouvait ça beaucoup plus sympa.
10. Tous les voyageurs montaient en voiture munis de provisions.
11. On partageait ses provisions.
12. Les passagers faisaient connaissance dans le compartiment. Ils se parlaient et partageaient leurs provisions.

B *Answers will vary but may include:*

Le TGV est un train très rapide. Il roule très vite: à plus de 300 kilomètres à l'heure. Pour réserver une place à l'avance, il faut payer un supplément. Ce train n'a pas de compartiments. Il y a un couloir central.

National Standards

Cultures
This selection about Switzerland allows students to develop an appreciation for this unique French-speaking country.

Attention!

This reading is optional. You may skip it completely, have the entire class read it, have only several students read it and report to the class, or assign it for extra credit.

Learning from Photos

(page 120 top) The Bernina is an extension of the Rhaetian Alps on the border between Switzerland and Italy.

(page 120 middle) Zermatt is at an altitude of 1,616 meters, or 5,300 feet. It is a car-free resort in a rugged valley at the eastern end of the Alpine canton of Valais. The mountainous scenery is spectacular, and Zermatt offers a wide variety of upscale accommodations. Tourists have been flocking to Zermatt since the first cog railway between Visp and Zermatt opened in 1891.

(page 120 bottom) Zermatt is also known for the Matterhorn, **le Cervin** in French. The Matterhorn is 4,477 meters, or 14,690 feet high, and it attracts tourists, as well as mountain climbers, from all over the world.

Lecture supplémentaire 1

Un voyage en Suisse

Thomas a fait un voyage en Suisse. Il a pris l'avion de Paris à Genève. Il a trouvé que c'était une expérience super. L'avion a survolé les Alpes et Thomas a eu des vues superbes des sommets des montagnes couvertes de neige.

Après une courte visite de Genève, il a pris le train pour Lausanne. Pendant le voyage, les vues du lac Léman étaient très belles.

Un train dans le massif de la Bernina en Suisse

De Lausanne, Thomas est passé par la région du Valais. Le paysage alpin de cette région est d'une extrême beauté. Avant, le Valais était un canton (une région) difficilement accessible. Mais maintenant, il y a un très bon réseau[1] de routes, de chemins de fer et de funiculaires.

À Visp, Thomas a pris un autre train pour aller à Zermatt. C'est un chemin de fer à voie étroite[2]. Le train monte les pentes[3] jusqu'à Zermatt, une station de sports d'hiver fabuleuse. Les voitures privées sont interdites dans ce petit village pittoresque.

Thomas a remarqué à Visp que les gens ne parlaient plus français. Ils parlaient allemand. En Suisse, il y a quatre langues officielles: le français, l'allemand, l'italien et le romanche.

Zermatt en Suisse

[1] réseau *network*
[2] à voie étroite *narrow gauge*
[3] pentes *slopes*

Après la lecture

Des renseignements Trouvez les informations suivantes dans la lecture.

1. deux villes suisses francophones
2. quatre langues parlées en Suisse
3. une station de sports d'hiver très connue
4. un canton suisse
5. un lac en Suisse

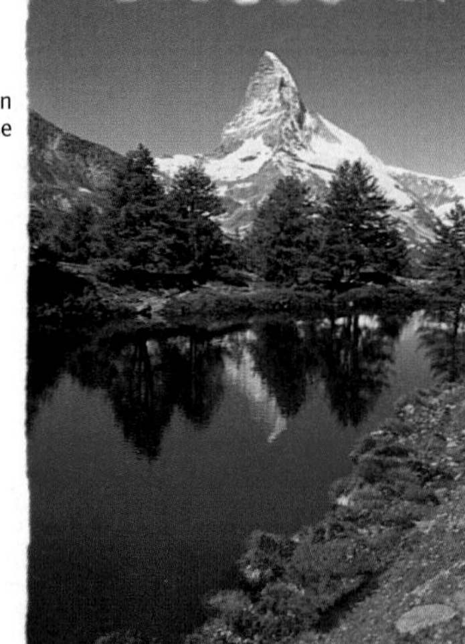

Le Cervin en Suisse

Answers to Après la lecture

1. Genève, Lausanne
2. le français, l'allemand, l'italien, le romanche
3. Zermatt
4. Valais
5. le lac Léman

Lecture supplémentaire 2

Un voyage au Bénin

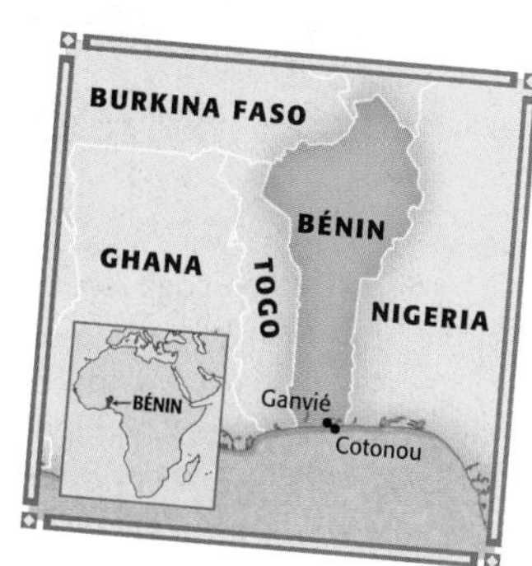

Regardez une carte d'Afrique. Cherchez le Bénin. Ensuite, cherchez Cotonou, la ville principale du pays. Tout près de Cotonou, sur une jolie lagune, il y a un petit village de 12 000 habitants qui s'appelle Ganvié. Pour aller à Ganvié, on ne prend pas le train. On y va en pirogue—un genre de long canoë en bois. Tous les habitants du village habitent dans des huttes de bambou sur pilotis. Les habitants vivent[1] presque exclusivement de la pêche[2].

Une maison sur pilotis à Ganvié

Que font les femmes du village? Elles vendent les poissons que les hommes attrapent. Elles vendent aussi des légumes, des fruits et des épices[3]. Le matin, il y a un marché, un marché où il y a des pirogues, pas des étals[4]. Les femmes vendent leurs produits dans des pirogues.

Ganvié est très pittoresque et beaucoup de touristes européens qui visitent le Bénin passent par ce village.

[1] vivent *live*
[2] la pêche *fishing*
[3] épices *spices*
[4] étals *stalls*

Après la lecture

Le Bénin Vrai ou faux?

1. Le Bénin est un pays africain.
2. Le Bénin est en Afrique occidentale, sur la côte de l'océan Atlantique.
3. Ganvié est la ville principale du Bénin.
4. Les maisons à Ganvié sont construites sur pilotis.
5. Les femmes de Ganvié vont à la pêche.
6. Une pirogue est un petit train en bois.

Une pirogue à Ganvié

FUN-FACTS

Ganvié, a village on stilts, is a very interesting place. The main industry is fishing. The men do the fishing and the women are entrepreneurs. It is they who do the selling. **Ganvié** has two hotels on stilts and quite a modern-looking school.

Attention!

This reading is optional. You may skip it completely, have the entire class read it, have only several students read it and report to the class, or assign it for extra credit.

Presentation

Step 1 Have students read the **Lecture** quickly.

Step 2 Ask what information they learned about **le Bénin.**

Après la lecture

Go over the **Après la lecture** activities on page 121. You may wish to have the students correct the false statements.

National Standards

Cultures

This selection about **Bénin** allows students to develop an appreciation for this French-speaking country in Africa.

Answers to Après la lecture

1. vrai
2. vrai
3. faux
4. vrai
5. faux
6. faux

National Standards

Connections
This reading about archaeology establishes a connection with another discipline, allowing students to reinforce and further their knowledge of the social sciences through the study of French.

Comparisons
This reading allows students to make comparisons between the ancient history of France and North Africa.

Attention!

The readings in the **Connexions** section are optional. They focus on some of the major disciplines taught in schools and universities. The vocabulary is useful for discussing such topics as history, literature, art, economics, business, science, etc. You may choose any of the following ways to do the readings in the **Connexions** sections.

Independent reading Have students read the selections and do the post-reading activities as homework, which you collect. This option is least intrusive on class time and requires a minimum of teacher involvement.

Homework with in-class follow-up Assign the readings and post-reading activities as homework. Review and discuss the material in class the next day.

Intensive in-class activity This option includes a pre-reading vocabulary presentation, in-class reading and discussion, assignment of the activities for homework, and a discussion of the assignment in class the following day.

CONNEXIONS

Les sciences sociales

L'archéologie

Archaeology is a fascinating field. Many interesting trips that tourists take include visits to famous ruins discovered by archaeologists. Archaeologists travel to every corner of the globe to excavate and study the ruins of ancient civilizations. The French-speaking world is no exception. There have been excellent finds of Roman ruins, particularly in France and in some of the French-speaking areas of North Africa.

L'archéologie

L'archéologie est la science qui étudie et analyse les vestiges[1] des civilisations anciennes découvertes par les archéologues. Les archéologues font des fouilles[2] pour déterrer[3] des ruines et des objets anciens faits par des êtres humains. En France et en Afrique du Nord, beaucoup de touristes visitent des sites où il y a des ruines magnifiques de l'Empire romain.

En France

Il y a un amphithéâtre à Arles et un autre à Nîmes. Ces amphithéâtres, appelés aussi des arènes, pouvaient recevoir entre vingt mille et vingt-cinq mille spectateurs. C'est là où avaient lieu des combats de gladiateurs. De nos jours on y donne des concerts, des manifestations sportives et des corridas[4].

C'est l'empereur Auguste qui a fait construire le théâtre à Arles. Les deux colonnes qui survivent sont très impressionnantes. Même aujourd'hui on continue à y présenter des spectacles et en été le théâtre accueille des

[1] vestiges *remains*
[2] fouilles *digs*
[3] déterrer *unearth*
[4] corridas *bullfights*

Le théâtre romain à Arles

Learning from Photos

(page 122) The two beautiful columns seen here in the **théâtre romain** in Arles are affectionately called **les deux veuves** *(the two widows)*.

festivals de musique, de photographie et de film.

La Maison Carrée à Nîmes est un temple construit par Agrippa, un général romain.

Le pont du Gard est un aqueduc romain construit en 19 avant J.-C. pour apporter de l'eau à Nîmes.

La Maison Carrée à Nîmes

En Tunisie

En Tunisie on peut voir beaucoup de vestiges de la civilisation romaine. C'est à Carthage où les Romains ont battu[5] les Carthaginois après la troisième guerre punique en 146 avant J.-C.

À Dougga, il y a les ruines de toute une ville romaine. On peut voir des temples, des bains, des maisons privées et le forum—le marché romain.

[5] ont battu *beat*

Les ruines romaines à Carthage

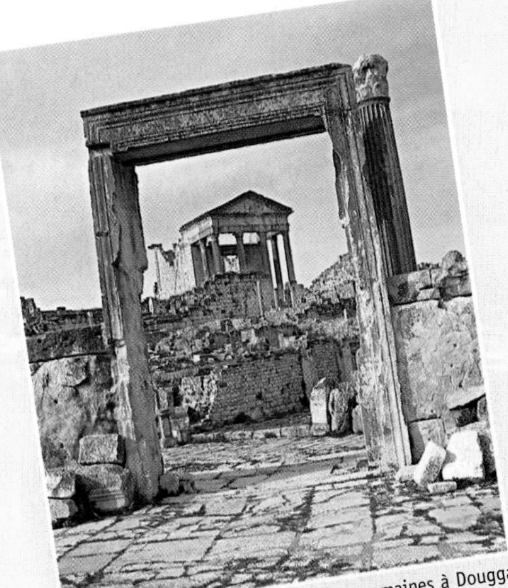

Les ruines romaines à Dougga

Après la lecture

Un peu d'histoire Discutez.

There is some interesting historical information in this selection about the Roman influence on both France and North Africa. Discuss some of these interesting facts. You can have your discussion in English.

CONNEXIONS

Presentation

Les sciences sociales
L'archéologie

Step 1 Have students read the introduction in English on page 122.

Step 2 Have students scan the reading for cognates. Then have them do the reading again, this time for comprehension.

Learning from Photos

(page 123 top) The locals refer to Nîmes as the "Rome of France." The **Maison Carrée** is the rather prosaic name given to this Roman temple that was built between the second and third centuries A.D. The **Maison Carrée** is considered one of the best-conserved antiquities in the world. Today it is used as a museum of Gallo-Roman art.

(page 123 middle left) The ruins at Carthage, some better preserved than others, cover many acres along the Mediterranean coast. Carthage today is a lovely upscale residential area of Tunis, the capital of Tunisia.

(page 123 middle right) The ancient town of Dougga is beautifully situated on a hill. One can still get the feel of being in a Roman town when visiting Dougga since the Forum, theater, baths, temples, and streets are quite well preserved.

Career Connection

Many important archaeological sites and digs are located in the French-speaking world. Students interested in a career in this area would need a reading knowledge of French for research purposes and good verbal skills to communicate with native speakers in the field.

Use what you have learned

Recycling

These activities allow students to use the vocabulary and structure from this chapter in completely open-ended, real-life situations.

Presentation

Encourage students to say as much as possible when they do these activities. Tell them not to be afraid to make mistakes, since the goal of these activities is real-life communication. If someone in the group makes an error, allow the others to politely correct him or her. Let students choose the activities they would like to do.

You may wish to divide students into pairs or groups. Encourage students to elaborate on the basic theme and to be creative. They may use props, pictures, or posters if they wish.

Learning from Photos

(page 124) Québec City is perched on a cliff above a narrow point in the St. Lawrence River. There is both the lower town and the upper town. The Château Frontenac is one of the city's most celebrated landmarks. Several buildings stood on this site before the present château was constructed beginning in 1893. It was built as a hotel and still functions as such. It owes its name to the Comte de Frontenac, governor of the French colony between 1672 and 1698.

UNESCO has designated **le Vieux-Québec** a World Heritage Site.

C'est à vous

Use what you have learned

PARLER 1

Un voyage super

✔ Talk about air or train travel

Vous parlez à des amis d'un voyage que vous avez fait en avion ou en train. Expliquez à vos camarades où vous étiez, avec qui, ce que vous avez fait, etc.

PARLER 2

Un pays francophone

✔ Talk about a French-speaking country you'd like to visit

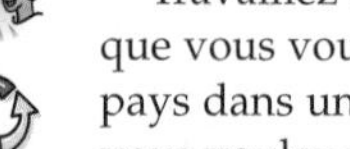

Travaillez avec un(e) camarade. Choisissez un pays francophone que vous voulez visiter un jour. Trouvez des renseignements sur ce pays dans une encyclopédie, sur Internet, etc. Ensuite, dites pourquoi vous voulez visiter ce pays, comment vous l'imaginez…

Le château Frontenac à Québec

PARLER 3

Un peu de géographie

✔ Identify French-speaking countries and cities

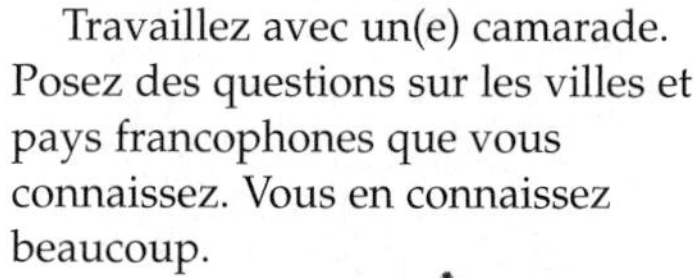

Travaillez avec un(e) camarade. Posez des questions sur les villes et pays francophones que vous connaissez. Vous en connaissez beaucoup.

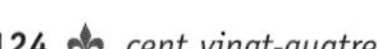

Answers to C'est à vous

1 *Answers will vary but may include:*

J'ai fait un voyage en train avec mon copain Jacques. Nous sommes allés à New York parce que nous voulions visiter le musée d'art moderne. Nous étions très contents et il faisait très beau. Nous lisions quand le contrôleur est venu nous demander nos billets. Jacques dormait quand le train est arrivé à New York. Je l'ai réveillé quand nous sommes arrivés. Nous nous sommes bien amusés.

2 *Answers will vary.*

Students can pick any destination they wish.

3 *Answers will vary.*

Students can recall information about the many areas of the French-speaking world they are now familiar with from their study of French.

C'est à vous

ÉCRIRE

4 **Préparons notre voyage**

✔ *Write for information on a French-speaking country you'd like to visit*

Reprenez le pays que vous avez choisi dans l'Activité 2, page 124. Écrivez un e-mail à une agence de voyage pour demander tous les renseignements nécessaires: quelles villes visiter, en quelle saison, quels vêtements prendre, etc.

Writing Strategy

Identifying sources for a research paper
To write a research paper, you must plan, set goals, and gather information. When you find a source, skim it to see whether it has any useful information. If it does, record the publication information on an index card so you can find the source easily when you begin your research. Be sure to use all resources available to you—both in print and nonprint. Your school library will be an excellent place to begin looking for sources for your research paper.

ÉCRIRE

5 **Mon état**

You have to write a brief description of the interesting sites in your state for a French-speaking audience. Your school librarian will help you select the most appropriate print resources—encyclopedias, almanacs, geography books. The Internet is also an excellent resource. Your state's Web sites are a good place to start. Once you have assembled your resources, scan them for the information you need. Remember to include references at the end of your report. Prepare a draft of your report in French and ask your French teacher to review it for you. After you have seen your teacher's comments, prepare the final version of your report.

Answers to C'est à vous

4 *Answers will vary.*

5 *Answers will vary.*

Writing Strategy

Identifying sources for a research paper
Have students read the Writing Strategy on page 125. Have students refer to the vocabulary list on page 128 if they need more ideas to write this selection.

Reaching All Students

Additional Practice
Display Communication Transparency C 4. Have students work in groups to make up as many questions as they can about the illustration. Have groups take turns asking and answering the questions.

Writing Development

Have students keep a notebook containing their best written work from each chapter. These selected writings can be based on assignments from the Student Textbook and the Writing Activities Workbook. The two activities on page 125 are examples of writing assignments that may be included in each student's portfolio. In the Workbook, students will develop an organized autobiography **(Mon autobiographie).** These workbook pages may also become a part of their portfolio.

Resource Manager

Communication Transparencies
Quizzes
Test Booklet
ExamView Pro®
Situation Cards
Performance Assessment
Marathon mental Videoquiz

Assessment

This is a pre-test for students to take before you administer the chapter test. Answer sheets for students to do these pages are provided in your transparency binder. Note that each section is cross-referenced so students can easily find the material they have to review in case they made errors. You may wish to collect these assessments and correct them yourself or you may prefer to have the students correct themselves in class. You can go over the answers orally or project them on the overhead, using your Assessment Answers transparencies.

Assessment

Vocabulaire

To review ***Mots 1****, turn to pages 98–99.*

1 Complétez.

1. Les lignes ____ desservent les petites villes autour d'une grande ville.
2. Il a ____ son train. Le train est parti une minute avant son arrivée.
3. ____ vérifie ou contrôle les billets dans le train.
4. Toutes les places sont occupées. Il n'y a plus de places ____.
5. Dans une gare il y a ____ qui indique les arrivées et un autre qui indique les départs.

To review ***Mots 2****, turn to pages 102–103.*

2 Identifiez.

6. 
7. 
8. 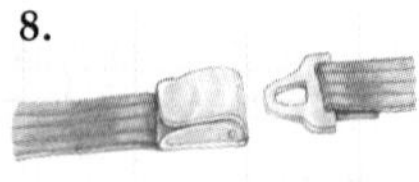
9. 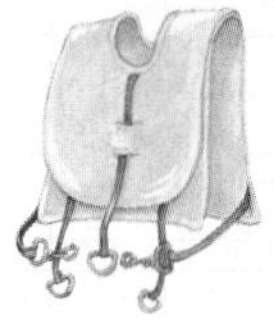
10. 

Structure

To review the imperfect and the ***passé composé****, turn to pages 106, 109–110.*

3 Choisissez la bonne réponse.

11–12. Quand ____ petit, les trains ____ des compartiments.
   a. j'étais, avaient
   b. j'ai été, ont eu

13–14. Hier nous ____ dans le train et il ____.
   a. montions, partait
   b. sommes montés, est parti

15. Hier vous ____ le train quand je vous ai vu à la gare?
   a. preniez
   b. avez pris

Answers to Assessment

 1

1. de banlieue
2. raté
3. Le contrôleur
4. disponibles
5. un tableau

 2

6. un oreiller
7. une couverture
8. une ceinture de sécurité
9. un gilet de sauvetage
10. un masque à oxygène

 3

11–12. a. j'étais, avaient
13–14. b. sommes montés, est parti
15. a. preniez

Assessment

4 Complétez avec «venir».

16. Tes copains ____ à quelle heure?
17. Et vous, vous ____ avec eux?
18. Il est ____ hier.

*To review the verb **venir**, turn to page 112.*

5 Complétez.

19–20. Je suis allé(e) ____ France et ____ Israël.
21. Mais, mes amis sont allés ____ Maroc.
22. Leur vol arrive ____ Canada.
23. Elle vient ____ Espagne.

To review use of prepositions with country names, turn to page 113.

Culture

6 Choisissez.

24. Le TGV est ____.
    - **a.** un avion supersonique
    - **b.** un train français qui roule très vite
    - **c.** un compartiment dans un train
25. Tout le monde montait en voiture muni de provisions, c'est-à-dire qu'ils montaient ____.
    - **a.** avec tous leur bagages
    - **b.** avec beaucoup de munitions
    - **c.** avec des choses à manger

To review this cultural information, turn to pages 118–119.

La gare TGV Lyon-Satolas

Learning from Photos

(page 127) The train station seen here is quite new. It was built to accommodate the TGV. The first route of the TGV was Paris-Lyon.

Glencoe Technology

MINDJOGGER

You may wish to help your students prepare for the chapter test by playing the MindJogger game show. Teams will compete against each other to review chapter vocabulary and structure and sharpen listening comprehension skills.

Answers to Assessment

 4

16. viennent
17. venez
18. venu

 5

19. en
20. en
21. au
22. du
23. d'

 6

24. b
25. c

Vocabulaire

Vocabulary Review

The words and phrases in the **Vocabulaire** have been taught for productive use in this chapter. They are summarized here as a resource for both student and teacher. This list also serves as a convenient resource for the **C'est à vous** activities on pages 124–125. There are approximately eight cognates in this vocabulary list. Have students find them.

Attention!

You will notice that the vocabulary list here is not translated. This has been done intentionally, since we feel that by the time students have finished the material in the chapter they should be familiar with the meanings of all the words. If there are several words they still do not know, we recommend that they refer to the **Mots 1** and **2** sections in the chapter or go to the dictionaries at the back of this book to find the meanings. However, if you prefer that your students have the English translations, please refer to Vocabulary Transparency 4.1, where you will find all these words listed with their translations.

Vocabulaire

Getting around a train station

un tableau
une ligne de banlieue
une grande ligne
un TGV (train à grande vitesse)

On board the train

un compartiment
le couloir
un contrôleur
un siège réglable
une place
disponible
complet, complète
assis(e)
debout

Getting around an airport

embarquer
débarquer
récupérer les bagages
le contrôle des passeports
un décollage
un atterrissage
un chariot
la douane

How well do you know your vocabulary?

- Choose words to describe a train trip.
- Write a brief description for someone who is traveling by train for the first time.

On board the plane

un oreiller
une couverture
des écouteurs *(m. pl.)*
une collation
le dossier du siège
un masque à oxygène
un gilet de sauvetage
une ceinture de sécurité

Other useful words and expressions

desservir
rouler
rater
faire escale
venir
Il est interdit de fumer
un paysage
splendide
de chaque côté
annulé(e)
sans escale

Technotour

BON VOYAGE!

VIDÉO • Épisode 4

Avant de visionner

In this video episode, Amadou takes the train to Chartres. He's doing a report on the town's famous Gothic cathedral.

Amadou arrive à Chartres.
Il a pris le train de Paris.

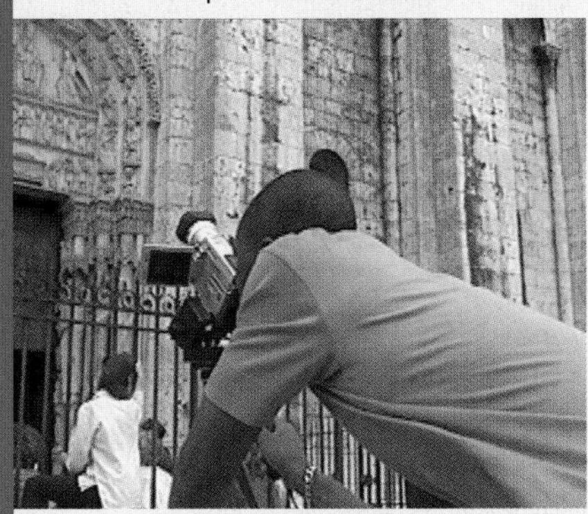

Amadou filme la cathédrale de Chartres.

FRENCH ONLINE

À découvrir

Learn more about the history of the Chartres cathedral online.

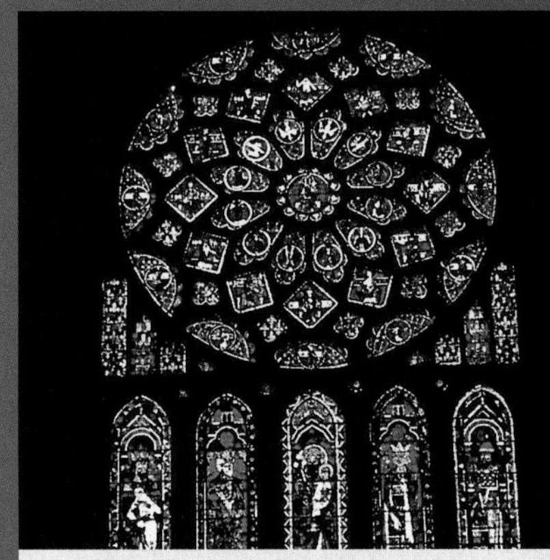

De beaux vitraux de la cathédrale

FRENCH *Online*

In the Chapter 4 Internet activity, you will have a chance to learn more about train travel in France. To begin your virtual adventure, go to the Glencoe French Web site: **french.glencoe.com**

Overview

This page previews two key multimedia components of the Glencoe French series. Each reinforces the material taught in the chapter in a unique manner.

VIDÉO

The Video Program allows students to see how the chapter vocabulary and structures are used by native speakers. For maximum reinforcement, show the video episode as a final activity for Chapter 4. The two photos on the left show highlights from the Chapter 4 video episode. Discuss the photos with your students before having them view the episode. See the Video Activities Booklet for detailed suggestions for using this resource.

FRENCH *Online*

- The **À découvrir** photo on page 129 shows the beautiful Chartres cathedral. Students can go online to learn more about the history of this cathedral.
- Teacher Information and Student Worksheets for this activity can be accessed at the Web site.

Video Synopsis

In this video episode, Amadou sets off on a day-trip to Chartres to work on a report about the town's cathedral. He hurries to catch a train from the gare Montparnasse, nearly leaving some of his camera equipment behind. Fortunately, a fellow passenger finds it, and Amadou is able to film the cathedral. The video introduces us to some of the cathedral's architectural highlights, including the beautiful stained-glass windows.

Révision

Preview

This section reviews the salient points from Chapters 1–4. In the **Conversation,** students will review health, cultural, telecommunication and travel vocabulary, as well as the **imparfait.** In the **Structure** sections, they will review pronouns and the imperfect and **passé composé.**

Resource Manager

Workbook, Self-Test pages 45–50
Test Booklet

Presentation

Conversation

Step 1 Have students open their books to page 130. Call on two students to read this short conversation aloud.

Step 2 Have one student summarize the conversation in his or her own words.

Révision

Conversation

Une sortie

Emma: Allô, Julie? Salut, c'est Emma.
Julie: Ah, bonjour, ça va?
Emma: Ça va. On va toujours au concert ce soir?
Julie: Oui, mais Cyril ne peut pas venir avec nous.
Emma: Pourquoi?
Julie: Il m'a envoyé un mail ce matin. Son train arrive à minuit.
Emma: Son train? Où est-ce qu'il est allé?
Julie: Voir sa grand-mère. Et pendant qu'il était chez elle, elle est tombée malade.
Emma: Rien de grave, j'espère.
Julie: Non, elle va mieux maintenant.

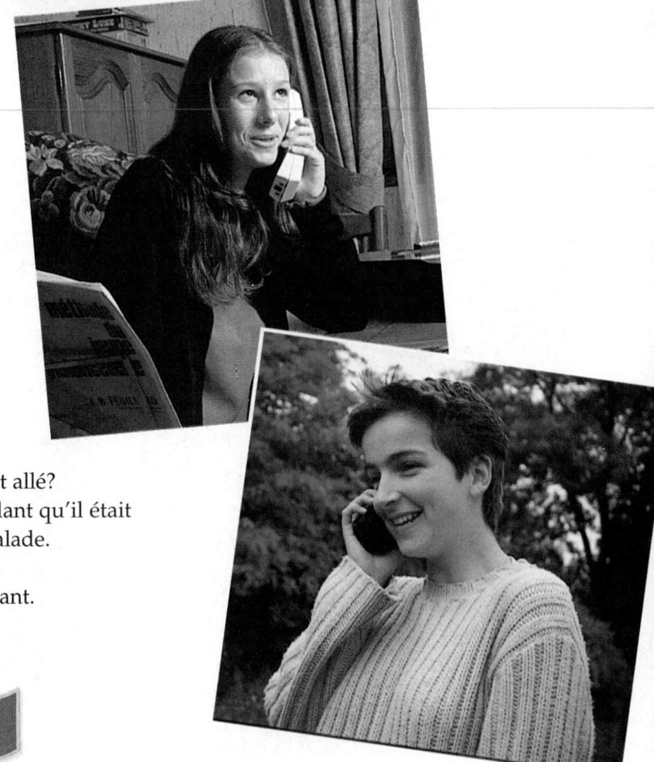

Après la conversation

Emma et Julie Choisissez la bonne réponse.

1. Emma ____ à Julie.
   a. envoie un mail
   b. donne un coup de fil
   c. envoie un fax
2. Emma va aller ____ ce soir.
   a. à un concert
   b. au théâtre
   c. chez sa grand-mère
3. Julie a reçu ____ de Cyril.
   a. un mail
   b. une carte postale
   c. un fax
4. Cyril ne peut pas aller au concert parce qu'il ____.
   a. va rester chez sa grand-mère qui est malade
   b. va s'occuper de sa grand-mère
   c. ne va pas arriver à l'heure
5. Le train va arriver ____.
   a. avec du retard
   b. trop tard
   c. à l'heure
6. Quand Cyril était chez sa grand-mère, elle ____.
   a. est tombée malade
   b. est allée à l'hôpital
   c. a eu un accident grave

Answers to Après la conversation

1. b
2. a
3. a
4. c
5. b
6. a

Structure

Les pronoms

1. **Le, la, (l'), les** are direct object pronouns. A direct object receives the action of the verb. Remember that **le, la, l', les** can replace people or things.

Marie regarde l'horaire.	**Elle le regarde.**
Elle regarde l'ordonnance.	**Elle la regarde.**
Elle regarde les magazines.	**Elle les regarde.**
Elle regarde les cartes postales.	**Elle les regarde.**
Marie regarde Ludovic.	**Elle le regarde.**
Ludovic regarde Marie.	**Il la regarde.**

2. **Lui, leur** are indirect objects. An indirect object is the indirect receiver of the action of the verb. Remember that **lui** and **leur** replace **à** + a person.

Je donne un cadeau à Éric.	**Je lui donne un cadeau.**
Je donne un cadeau à Emma.	**Je lui donne un cadeau.**
Je donne un cadeau aux garçons.	**Je leur donne un cadeau.**
Je donne un cadeau aux filles.	**Je leur donne un cadeau.**

3. The pronouns **me (m'), te (t'), nous,** and **vous** can be either direct or indirect objects.

Cyril te regarde?	**Oui, il me regarde, mais il ne me parle pas.**
Cyril vous regarde?	**Oui, il nous regarde, mais il ne nous parle pas.**

4. An object pronoun always comes right before the verb it is linked to.

Je	lui parle.
Je ne	te parle pas.
Je veux	les voir.
Je ne veux pas	leur parler.

CHAPITRES 1–4

Presentation

Les pronoms

Step 1 Write the examples on the board. Circle the nouns and draw a box around the object pronouns. Draw a line from the noun to the corresponding pronoun.

Step 2 Read each sentence on the left and have the students answer you with the sentences on the right.

Art Connection

Pierre Auguste Renoir (1841–1919), one of the famous French Impressionist painters, loved to paint portraits and scenes. He delighted in showing the happiest sides of nature. He once said, "For me, a picture must be an amiable thing, joyous and pretty, yes, pretty! There are enough troublesome things in life without inventing them."

Renoir loved to paint. He did so up to the day he died, even though he was crippled with arthritis and sometimes had to have his brushes tied to his wrists.

Learning from Photos

(page 132) Have students say everything they can about the photo.

1 **Super!** Répondez d'après le modèle.

—Tu vois le tableau?
—Oui, je le vois. Il est très beau.

1. Tu vois la statue?
2. Tu entends le concert?
3. Tu lis le poème?
4. Tu vois l'actrice?
5. Tu regardes les tableaux?
6. Tu regardes le ballet?

Pierre Auguste Renoir *Portrait de Margot*

Un cinéma à Aix-en-Provence

2 **Historiette En version originale**
Répondez d'après le modèle.

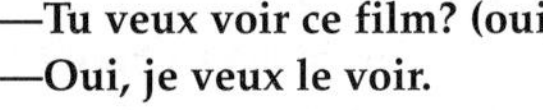

—Tu veux voir ce film? (oui)
—Oui, je veux le voir.

1. Tu vas voir ce film? (oui)
2. Tu vas voir ce film en version originale? (oui)
3. Tu comprends le français? (oui, un peu)
4. Tu comprends le français assez bien pour comprendre le film? (non)
5. Tu lis les sous-titres? (oui)

3 **Qu'est-ce que tu fais?**
Répondez en utilisant **lui** ou **leur.**

1. Tu parles souvent à ton meilleur ami au téléphone?
2. Tu parles souvent à ta meilleure amie aussi?
3. Tu téléphones à tes cousins?
4. Tu donnes un cadeau à ta mère pour son anniversaire?
5. Tu achètes un chemisier à ta mère?

Answers to Révision

1. Oui, je la vois. Elle est très belle.
2. Oui, je l'entends. Il est très beau.
3. Oui, je le lis. Il est très beau.
4. Oui, je la vois. Elle est très belle.
5. Oui, je les regarde. Ils sont très beaux.
6. Oui, je le regarde. Il est très beau.

1. Oui, je vais le voir.
2. Oui, je vais le voir en version originale.
3. Oui, je le comprends un peu.
4. Non, je ne le comprends pas assez bien pour le comprendre.
5. Oui, je les lis.

1. Oui, je lui parle souvent au téléphone.
2. Oui, je lui parle souvent aussi.
3. Oui, je leur téléphone.
4. Oui, je lui donne un cadeau pour son anniversaire.
5. Oui, je lui achète un chemisier.

Vraiment? Complétez en utilisant un pronom.

Charles: Mélanie, Guillaume __1__ cherche.
Mélanie: Guillaume __2__ cherche? Qu'est-ce qu'il veut?
Charles: Il veut __3__ dire quelque chose.
Mélanie: Qu'est-ce qu'il veut __4__ dire? Il sait bien que je ne veux plus __5__ voir.
Charles: Oui, mais il __6__ adore!
Mélanie: Et moi, je ne __7__ adore pas!
Charles: Et moi, je ne __8__ crois pas!

L'imparfait et le passé composé

1. The use of the imperfect or **passé composé** depends on whether the speaker sees the past action as an event or an action with a beginning and an end; or as an action in progress, a state, a situation with no real beginning or end. Compare the following sentences.

   Jean lisait quand il a entendu l'explosion.
   Jean est allé à la fenêtre quand il a entendu l'explosion.

   The first sentence states what happened **(passé composé)** and describes what was going on (imperfect) when the event occurred. The second sentence tells what the person did **(passé composé)** when the event occurred.

2. The following time expressions are often used with the indicated tenses.

Passé composé	Imparfait
hier	souvent
lundi (l'an) dernier	tous les jours (mois, ans)
pendant une heure (un mois)	de temps en temps
à trois heures	toujours

3. The difference between the imperfect and the **passé composé** is best shown in context. The more you are exposed to examples in context, the more you will get a feel for when to use one tense or the other.

Presentation

L'imparfait et le passé composé

Step 1 As you go through Items 1–3, remind students to think of a play (or movie), as suggested on page 109 of the Student Edition.

Step 2 In Item 2, use an abrupt, chopping motion of the hand to indicate **passé composé** constructions and a sweeping horizontal motion for the imperfect.

Answers to Révision

1. te
2. me
3. te
4. me
5. le
6. t'
7. l'
8. te

5 In this activity, you may wish to discuss with students why the first verb is in the **passé composé** and the second in the imperfect. One way to demonstrate the difference is to ask students which activity began first and continued for some time, and which was more sudden, with a clear start and finish.

6 In this activity, emphasize that both actions were short, separate, and independent, with clear starting and ending points. They are cause and effect actions.

7 Allow students time to prepare this activity before working together on it. Then have each student read two or three sentences as you write the verb forms on the board.
Expansion: Assign the roles to individuals and have them read the finished activity.
Note: Tell students **avoir raison** means **donner la bonne réponse, répondre correctement.**

5 **Que faisait-il?** Complétez d'après le modèle.

lire
Quand il a entendu l'explosion, il ____.
Quand il a entendu l'explosion, il lisait.

1. faire une promenade à vélo
2. travailler
3. être au téléphone
4. regarder la télévision
5. écrire un mail
6. prendre un bain
7. mettre le couvert
8. dormir

Qu'avez-vous fait? Répondez d'après le modèle.

aller à la fenêtre
Quand j'ai entendu l'explosion, je ____.
Quand j'ai entendu l'explosion, je suis allé(e) à la fenêtre.

1. se lever
2. téléphoner à la police
3. sortir dehors
4. regarder par la fenêtre
5. se réveiller

Historiette Une rencontre à Paris Complétez en utilisant le passé composé ou l'imparfait.

Steffi __1__ (rencontrer) Mark à Paris. Quand elle l'__2__ (rencontrer), il __3__ (porter) une chemise bleue. C'est Steffi qui __4__ (parler) la première. Elle __5__: (dire)

Steffi: Je crois que je vous __6__ déjà __7__ (voir) quelque part *(somewhere)*.
Mark: Ah non, je ne crois pas, je ne __8__ jamais __9__ (venir) ici avant. Vous __10__ (voir) quelqu'un qui me ressemble, peut-être.
Steffi: Non, je crois bien que je vous __11__ (voir) quelque part. Mais ce n'est peut-être pas ici que je vous __12__ (voir) la première fois. Voyons, vous __13__ déjà __14__ (aller) à la tour Eiffel?
Mark: Oui, nous y __15__ (aller), ma sœur et moi, hier.
Steffi: Alors, vous voyez, j' __16__ (avoir) raison! Je vous __17__ déjà __18__! (voir) Moi aussi, j'__19__ (être) à la tour Eiffel hier avec mon frère. Nous __20__ (passer) toute la matinée à regarder Paris du haut du deuxième étage. Le temps __21__ (être) magnifique. Il ne __22__ (faire) pas trop froid… Mais vous le savez, vous y __23__ (être) aussi. Vous êtes américain?

ANSWERS TO Révision

1. Quand il a entendu l'explosion, il faisait une promenade à vélo.
2. Quand il a entendu l'explosion, il travaillait.
3. Quand il a entendu l'explosion, il était au téléphone.
4. Quand il a entendu l'explosion, il regardait la télévision.
5. Quand il a entendu l'explosion, il écrivait un mail.
6. Quand il a entendu l'explosion, il prenait un bain.
7. Quand il a entendu l'explosion, il mettait le couvert.
8. Quand il a entendu l'explosion, il dormait.

1. Quand j'ai entendu l'explosion, je me suis levé(e).
2. Quand j'ai entendu l'explosion, j'ai téléphoné à la police.
3. Quand j'ai entendu l'explosion, je suis sorti(e) dehors.
4. Quand j'ai entendu l'explosion, j'ai regardé par la fenêtre.
5. Quand j'ai entendu l'explosion, je me suis réveillé(e).

7

1. a rencontré
2. a rencontré
3. portait
4. a parlé
5. a dit
6. ai
7. vu
8. suis
9. venu
10. avez vu
11. ai vu
12. ai vu
13. êtes
14. allé
15. sommes allés
16. avais
17. ai
18. vu
19. étais
20. avons passé
21. était
22. faisait
23. étiez

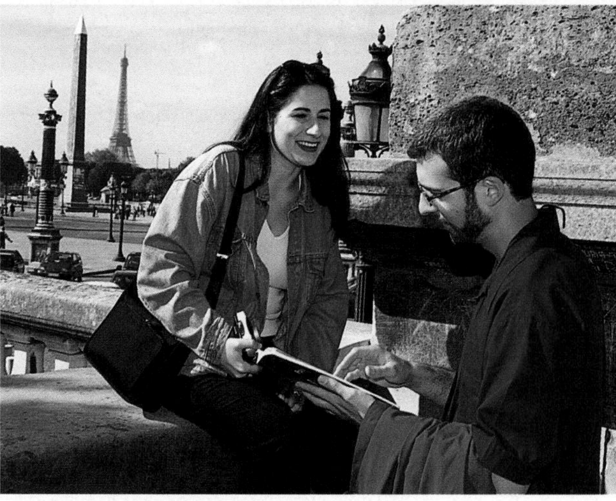

Des touristes près de la place de la Concorde à Paris

Mark: Oui. Et vous, allemande?
Steffi: Non, suisse.
Mark: Ah, vraiment? Quelle coïncidence! Nous __24__ (passer) la semaine dernière en Suisse.
Steffi: Et vous __25__ (aimer) la Suisse?
Mark: Beaucoup. Nous __26__ (aller) à Genève, Lausanne, Neuchâtel et aussi à Zermatt. C'est splendide.
Steffi: Oui, mais il faut venir en hiver. C'est là où c'est bien. Vous faites du ski?
Mark: Oui, j'adore le ski. Quand j'__27__ (être) petit, nous __28__ (habiter) dans le Vermont et je __29__ (faire) du ski tout le temps.

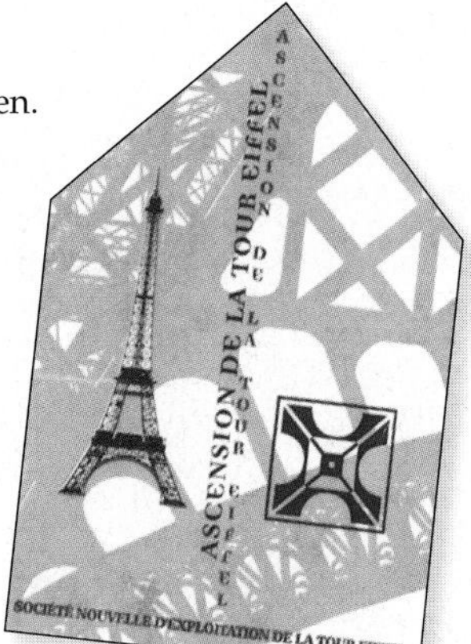

8 **Chez le médecin** Travaillez avec un(e) camarade. Parlez de votre dernière visite chez le médecin. Dites comment vous vous sentiez, ce que vous avez dit au médecin et ce qu'il/elle a fait.

9 **Une critique** Vous parlez à des amis d'un film que vous avez vu. Expliquez à vos copains qui jouait dans le film et ce qui s'est passé.

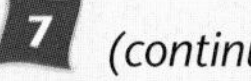

Literary Companion *You may wish to read the excerpt about train travel from* **Le livre de mon père,** *written by Émile Henriot. You will find this literary selection on page 476.*

Learning from Photos

(page 135) Have students say everything they can about the photo.

Reaching All Students

Additional Practice Have students work in groups. Each student writes five sentences beginning with **Quand j'étais petit(e)...** + an imperfect verb, and five beginning with **L'autre jour...** + the **passé composé.** Students take turns reading one sentence at a time, to which the others in the group respond with their own statements.

Literary Companion

When you finish this **Révision,** if you wish, have students read the excerpt from ***Le Livre de mon père,*** on pages 476–479.

Answers to Révision

7 *(continued)*
24. avons passé
25. avez aimé
26. sommes allés
27. étais
28. habitions
29. faisais

8 *Answers will vary.*
Students will use the medical and health-related vocabulary they learned in Chapter 2.

9 *Answers will vary.*
Students will reincorporate vocabulary learned in Chapter 1 with the imperfect and **passé composé** structure points learned in Chapters 3 and 4.

Preview

The section **Reflets de la France** was prepared by National Geographic Society. Its purpose is to give students greater insight, through these visual images, into the culture and people of France. Have students look at the photographs on pages 136–139 for enjoyment. If they would like to talk about them, let them say anything they can, using the vocabulary they have learned to this point.

National Standards

Cultures

The **Reflets de la France** photos and the accompanying captions allow students to gain insights into the people and culture of France.

About the Photos

1. Champs de lavande en Provence When one thinks of Provence, beauty and color are what most frequently come to mind—the Mediterranean landscapes with their bright colors, red roofed **mas** *(country homes)* surrounded by cypress trees, and beautifully scented lavender fields, which inspired the famous paintings of Cézanne and Van Gogh.

2. Le célèbre toit de l'hôtel-Dieu à Beaune en Bourgogne Beaune is the capital of the Côte de Beaune region, home of many famous vineyards.The **hôtel-Dieu** was built in 1450 and served as a hospital until 1971. During this time, nurses in the hospital continued to wear the medieval dresses they wore in the fifteenth century. There is a museum in the **hôtel-Dieu** that displays medical instruments used a century ago.

3. Les remparts d'Antibes sur la Côte d'Azur Antibes is a picturesque old town half-way between Nice and Cannes on the Côte

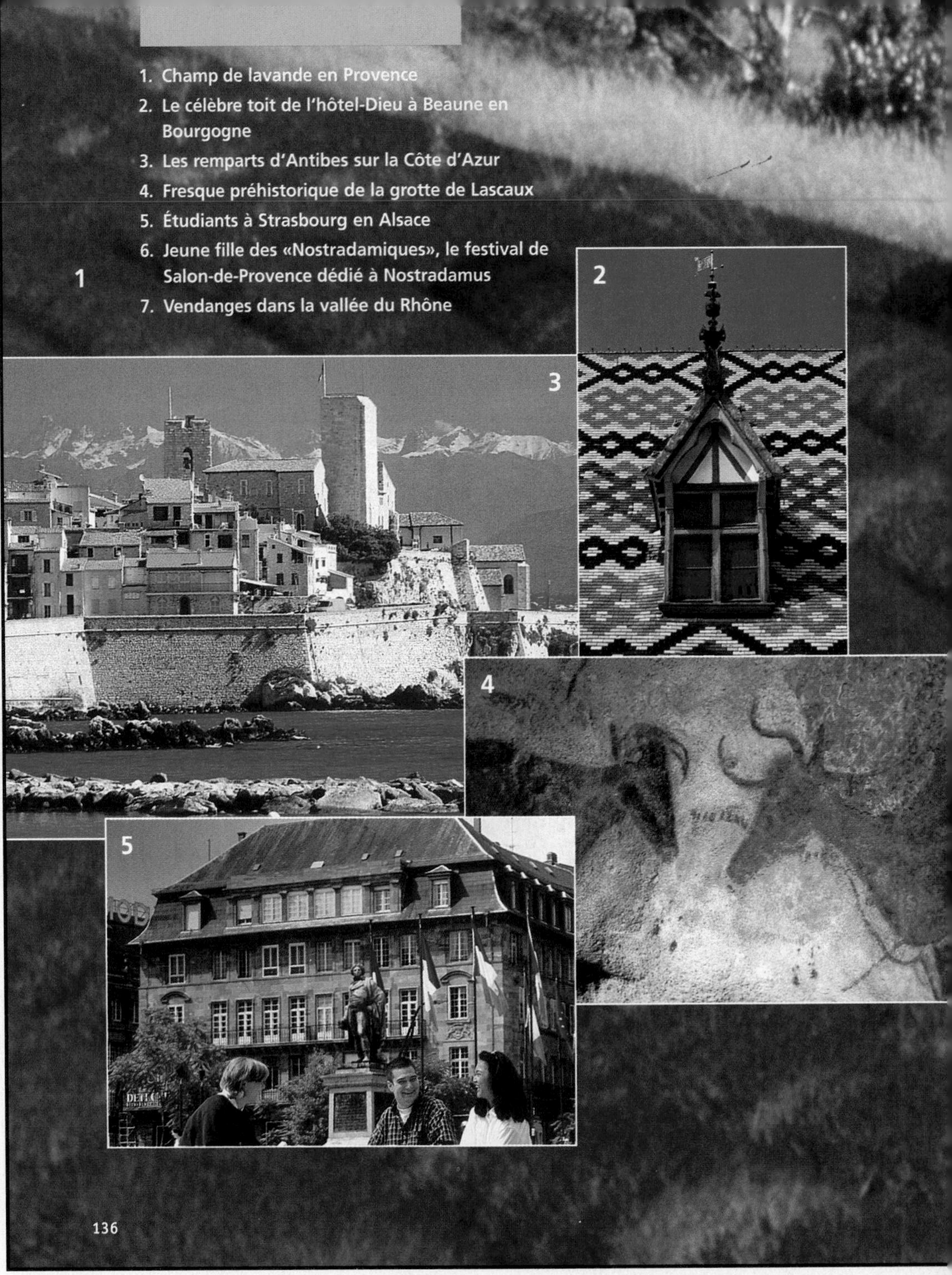

1. Champ de lavande en Provence
2. Le célèbre toit de l'hôtel-Dieu à Beaune en Bourgogne
3. Les remparts d'Antibes sur la Côte d'Azur
4. Fresque préhistorique de la grotte de Lascaux
5. Étudiants à Strasbourg en Alsace
6. Jeune fille des «Nostradamiques», le festival de Salon-de-Provence dédié à Nostradamus
7. Vendanges dans la vallée du Rhône

1

2

3

4

5

136

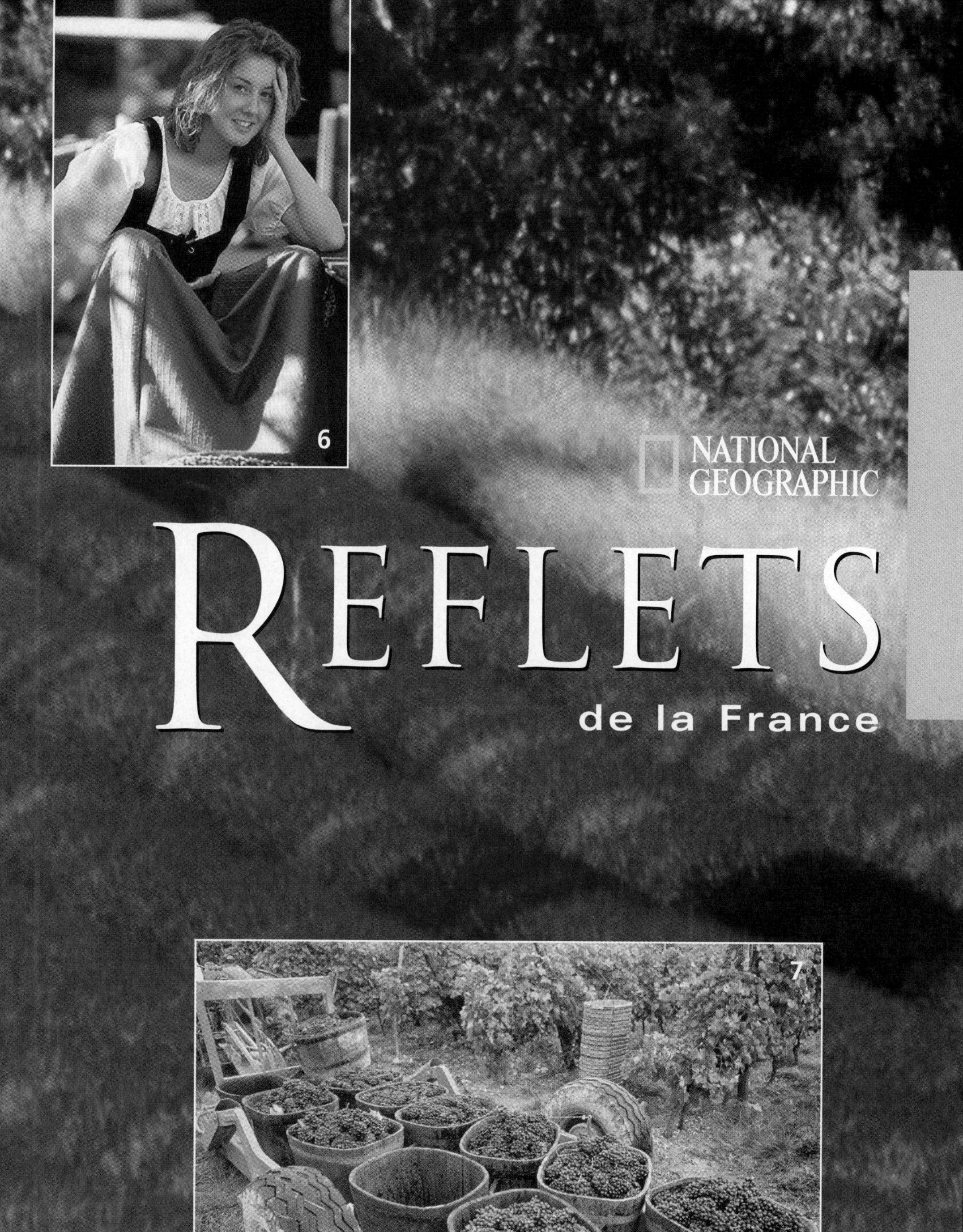

d'Azur. In its early days, Antibes was a strategic military place as evidenced by these ramparts.

4. Fresque préhistorique de la grotte de Lascaux Lascaux, in the Périgord region, is known for its prehistoric art. In the area there are many caves and caverns in which archaeologists have uncovered bones, utensils, and paintings of Cro-Magnon people. The caves of Lascaux were discovered in 1940. They contain the finest prehistoric paintings in Europe. It is believed that some are 30,000 years old. In 1963 it was discovered that in spite of precautions, some of the paintings had begun to deteriorate. The caves were closed, and an exact replica of the caves was constructed.

5. Étudiants à Strasbourg en Alsace Strasbourg is the capital of Alsace. Strasbourg is a charming city with many medieval streets with timbered houses, reminiscent of the architecture of many areas of Germany. It was in Strasbourg that Rouget de Lisle composed the words and music for ***La Marseillaise,*** the French national anthem.

6. Jeune fille des «Nostradamiques», le festival de Salon-de-Provence dédié à Nostradamus Salon-de-Provence is a market town near Aix-en-Provence. This small town was the home of the famous astrologer Nostradamus. The house where he lived is now a museum devoted to him. He is buried in the fourteenth century church of St. Laurent in Salon-de-Provence.

7. Vendanges dans la vallée du Rhône The Rhône valley has a recorded history that dates back to the time of the Romans. It is an area known for its excellent restaurants and fine wines. The northern part of the Rhône valley produces the light tasting Beaujolais wine.

8. Menton sur la Côte d'Azur Menton is just a very short distance from the Italian border at the tip of the Côte d'Azur. Part of Menton is still a sleepy fishing village. Another part has wide avenues, upscale hotels, and a lovely beach. Many well-to-do retired people live in Menton.

9. Un «nez» testant un parfum à Paris France is famous for its perfume industry. The perfumes are made from flowers that grow in Provence.

10. Fortifications de la haute-ville et le port de Bonifacio, en Corse The island of Corsica is known for its natural beauty. It is now a **département** of France, and has a population of some 220,000. Bonifacio is an ancient fortress town situated on high chalk cliffs. It still has an active garrison. Napoleon was born in Ajaccio, the major town of the island.

11. Les jardins décoratifs du château d'Angers, dans la vallée de la Loire The Loire Valley is famous for its beautiful **châteaux** with their magnificent geometrical French gardens. The Château d'Angers has the appearance of a fortress, but it also has an elegant hibiscus-filled garden. The Château was originally built by one of the Comtes d'Anjou, but it was rebuilt by Louis IX, in the thirteenth century. It is an excellent example of feudal architecture.

12. Source naturelle à Contrexéville, une station thermale des Vosges Contrexéville is a thermal bath resort in the Vosges mountains, in Lorraine.

8. Menton sur la Côte d'Azur
9. Un «nez» testant un parfum à Paris
10. Fortifications de la haute-ville et le port de Bonifacio, en Corse
11. Les jardins décoratifs du château d'Angers, dans la vallée de la Loire
12. Source naturelle à Contrexéville, une station thermale des Vosges
13. La plage de Deauville, en Normandie
14. Le pont du Gard à Nîmes

NATIONAL GEOGRAPHIC Teacher's Corner

Index to the NATIONAL GEOGRAPHIC MAGAZINE

The following related articles may be of interest:

- "Art Treasures from the Ice Age: Lascaux Cave," by Jean-Philippe Rigaud, October 1998.
- "Essence of Provence," by Bill Bryson, September 1995.
- "Europe Faces an Immigrant Tide," by Peter Range, May 1993.
- "Darcey: A Village That Refuses to Die," by William S. Ellis, July 1989.
- "Tour de France—An Annual Madness," by Gilbert Duclos-Lassalle, July 1989.
- "The Great Revolution," by Merle Severy, July 1989.
- "Paris: *La Belle Époque*," by Eugen Weber, July 1989.
- "The Civilizing Seine," by Charles McCarry, April 1982.

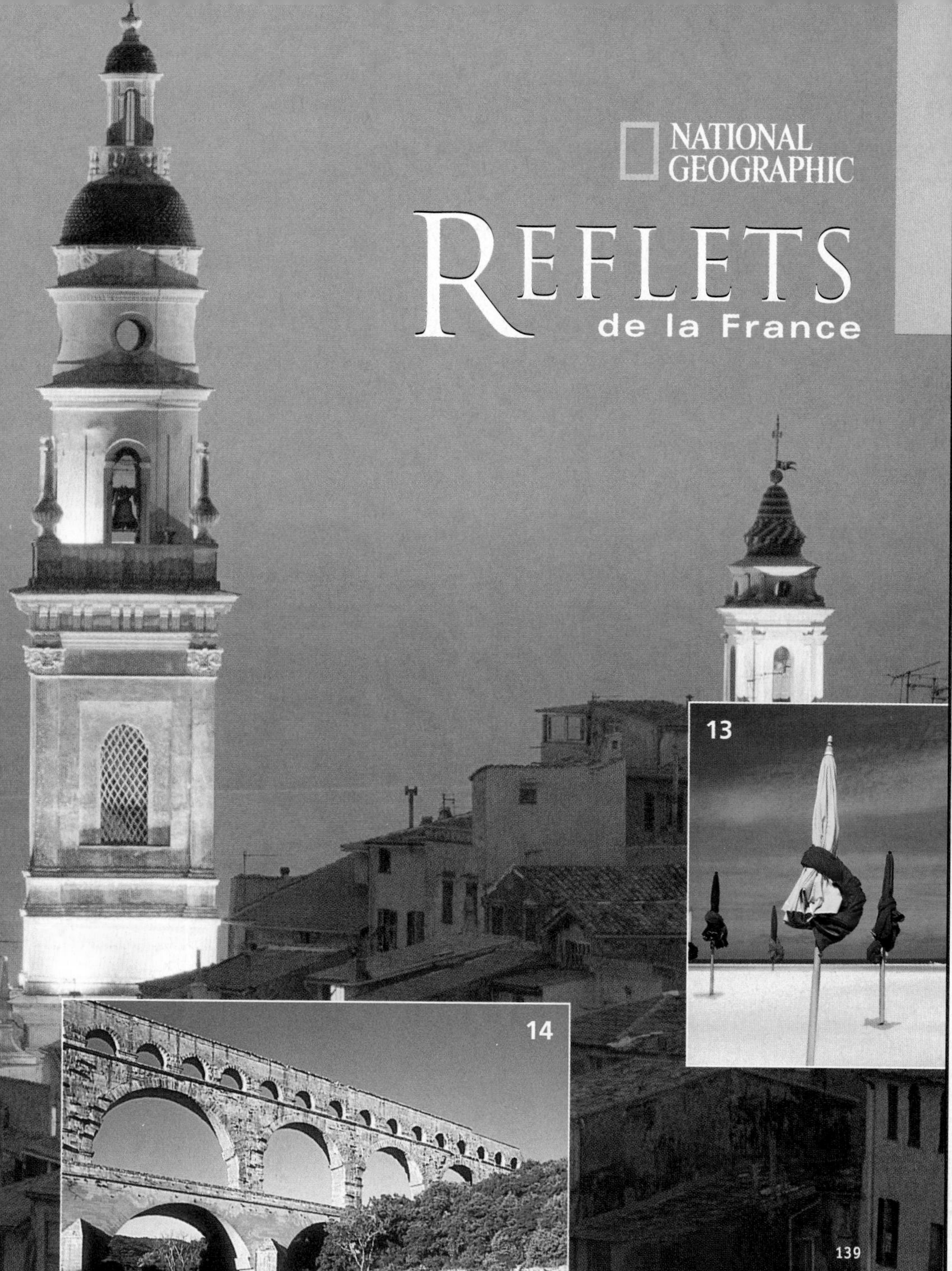

13. La plage de Deauville, en Normandie Deauville is famous for its sandy beach dotted with brightly colored tents and sun umbrellas. Along the beach there are **planches,** wooden walkways for parading up and down to see and be seen. Deauville has a rather aristocratic ambiance.

14. Le pont du Gard à Nîmes Le pont du Gard was built by the Romans some two thousand years ago as an aqueduct. It is 49 meters high, and for almost five centuries it carried water from Uzès to the city of Nîmes.

Products available from Glencoe/McGraw-Hill

To order the following products, call Glencoe/McGraw-Hill at 1-800-334-7344.

CD-ROMs
- Picture Atlas of the World
- The Complete National Geographic: 112 Years of National Geographic Magazine

Transparency Set
- NGS PicturePack: Geography of Europe

Products available from National Geographic Society

To order the following products, call National Geographic Society at 1-800-368-2728.

Books
- National Geographic World Atlas for Young Explorers
- National Geographic Satellite Atlas of the World

Software
- ZingoLingo: French Diskette

Video
- France
- Europe

Planning for Chapter 5

SCOPE AND SEQUENCE, PAGES 140–171

Topics

- Bank and postal services

Culture

- Mélanie and her weekly allowance
- Foreign currencies
- Discussing differences between postal services in the United States and France

Functions

- How to use expressions related to bank and postal services
- How to refer to people and things already mentioned
- How to express what you and others do for one another
- How to make negative statements

Structure

- The relative pronouns **qui** and **que**
- Agreement of the past participle
- Reciprocal actions
- Negative expressions: **personne ne** and **rien ne**

National Standards

- Communication Standard 1.1 pages 144, 145, 148, 149, 151, 152, 154, 156, 157, 159, 166
- Communication Standard 1.2 pages 144, 145, 148, 149, 151, 152, 154, 156, 157, 158, 161, 162, 163, 165, 166
- Communication Standard 1.3 pages 154, 166, 167
- Cultures Standard 2.1 pages 142, 143, 158, 160–161, 162, 163
- Connections Standard 3.1 pages 164–165
- Comparisons Standard 4.2 pages 163, 167
- Communities Standard 5.1 page 167

PACING AND PRIORITIES

The chapter content is color coded below to assist you in planning.

■ required ■ recommended ■ optional

Vocabulaire *(required)* *Days 1–4*

- ■ Mots 1
  - À la banque
  - Au bureau de change
  - Sandrine et Luc
- ■ Mots 2
  - À la poste

Structure *(required)* *Days 5–7*

- ■ Les pronoms relatifs **qui** et **que**
- ■ L'accord du participe passé
- ■ Les actions réciproques
- ■ **Personne ne…** et **rien ne…**

Conversation *(required)*

- ■ Au bureau de change

Lectures culturelles

- ■ La semaine des jeunes Français *(recommended)*
- ■ Les devises étrangères *(optional)*
- ■ La Poste *(optional)*

Connexions *(optional)*

- ■ Les finances

■ **C'est à vous** *(recommended)*

■ **Assessment** *(recommended)*

■ **Technotour** *(optional)*

RESOURCE GUIDE

Section	Pages	Section Resources
Vocabulaire *Mots 1*		
À la banque Au bureau de change Sandrine et Luc	142 143 143–145	Vocabulary Transparencies 5.2–5.3 Audiocassette 4A/CD 4 Audio Activities Booklet TE, pages 48–50 Workbook, page 51 Quiz 1, page 20 ExamView Pro®
Vocabulaire *Mots 2*		
À la poste	146–149	Vocabulary Transparencies 5.4–5.5 Audiocassette 4A/CD 4 Audio Activities Booklet TE, pages 50–52 Workbook, pages 52–54 Quiz 2, page 21 ExamView Pro®
Structure		
Les pronoms relatifs **qui** et **que** L'accord du participe passé Les actions réciproques **Personne ne…** et **rien ne…**	150–152 153–154 155–156 157	Audiocassette 4A/CD 4 Audio Activities Booklet TE, pages 52–53 Workbook, pages 55–58 Quizzes 3–6, pages 22–25 ExamView Pro®
Conversation		
Au bureau de change	158–159	Audiocassette 4A/CD 4 Audio Activities Booklet TE, page 54 CD-ROM
Lectures culturelles		
La semaine des jeunes Français Les devises étrangères La Poste	160–161 162 163	Audiocassette 4A/CD 4 Audio Activities Booklet TE, page 55 Test Booklet, Chapter 5
Connexions		
Les finances	164–165	Test Booklet, Chapter 5
C'est à vous		
	166–167	**Bon voyage!** Video, Episode 5 Video Activities Booklet, Chapter 5 French Online Activities french.glencoe.com
Assessment		
	168–169	Communication Transparency C 5 Quizzes 1–6, pages 20–25 Test Booklet, Chapter 5 ExamView Pro® Situation Cards, Chapter 5 **Marathon mental** Videoquiz

Using Your Resources for Chapter 5

Transparencies

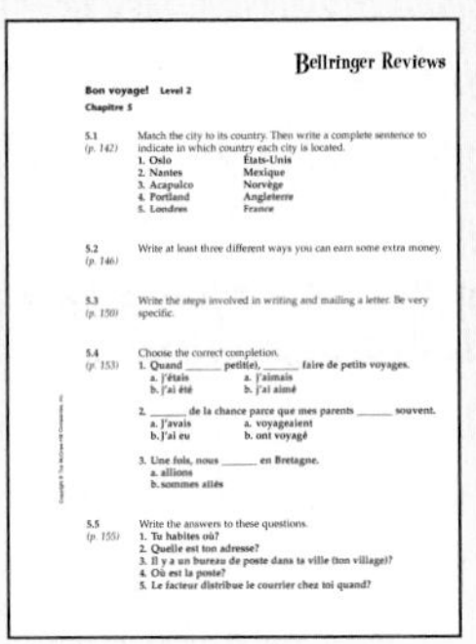

Bellringer 5.1–5.8

Vocabulary 5.1–5.5

Communication C 5

Writing Activities Workbook

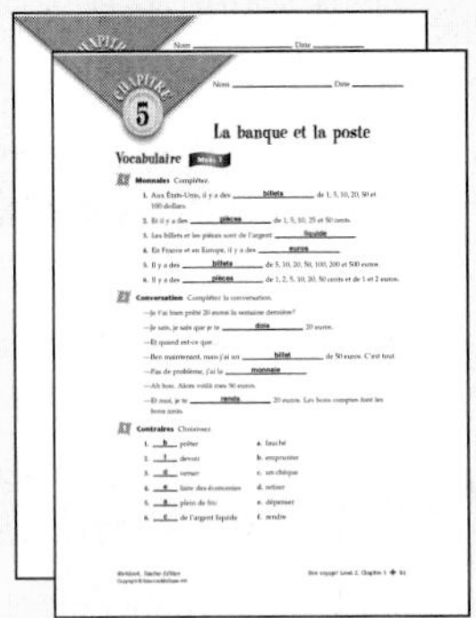

Vocabulary, pages 51–54

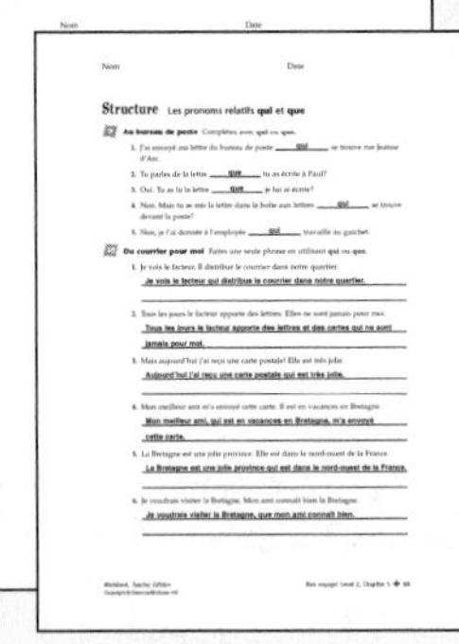

Structure, pages 55–58

Enrichment, pages 59–62

Audio Program and Audio Activities Booklet

Vocabulary, pages 48–52

Structure, pages 52–53

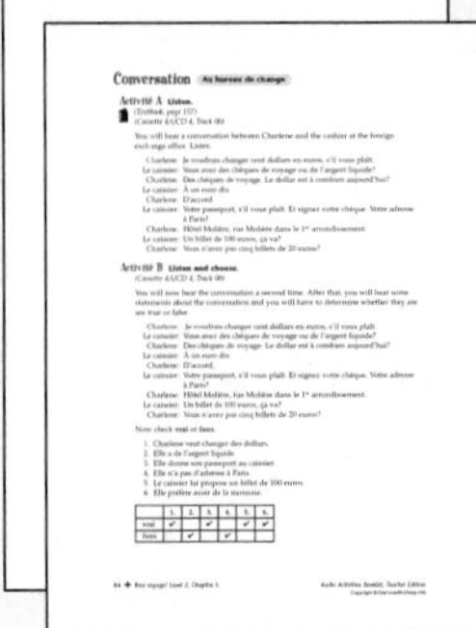

Conversation, page 54

Cultural Reading, page 55

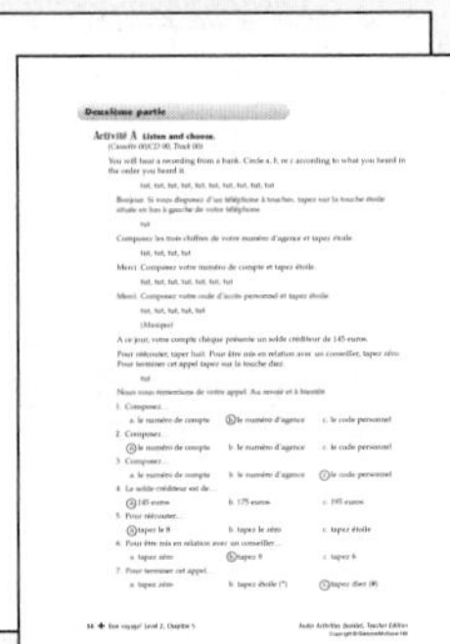

Additional Practice, pages 56–57

Assessment

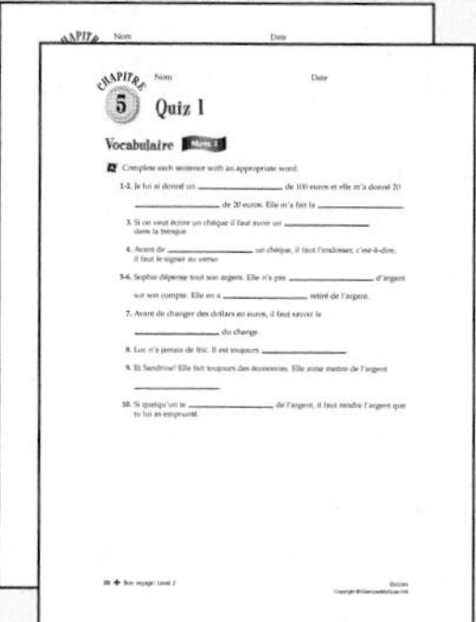
Vocabulary and Structure Quizzes, pages 20–25

Chapter Tests, Chapter 5

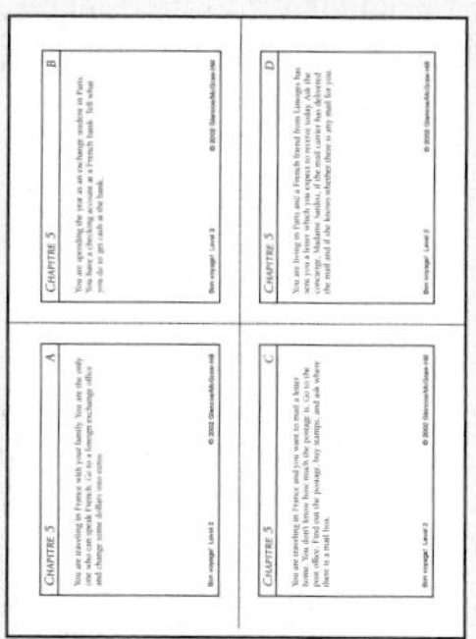
Situation Cards, Chapter 5

Timesaving Teacher Tools

Interactive Teacher Edition

Imagine having your Teacher's Edition and all resources on a CD-ROM. Click on a resource and it appears on your screen, ready to be printed, sorted, or planned.

Interactive Lesson Planner

The Interactive Lesson Planner CD-ROM helps you organize your lesson plans for a week, month, semester, or year. Look at this planning tool for easy access to your Chapter 5 resources.

ExamView Pro®

Test Bank software for Macintosh and Windows makes creating, editing, customizing, and printing tests quick and easy.

Technology Resources

In the Chapter 5 Internet activity, you will have a chance to learn more about banking and postal services in France. Visit french.glencoe.com.

On the Interactive Conversation CD-ROM, students can listen to and take part in a recorded version of the conversation in Chapter 5.

See the National Geographic Teacher's Corner on pages 138–139, 244–245, 372–373, 472–473 for reference to additional technology resources.

Bon voyage! Video and Video Activities Booklet.

Help your students prepare for the chapter test by playing the **Marathon mental** Videoquiz game show. Teams will compete against each other to review chapter vocabulary and structure and sharpen listening comprehension skills.

CHAPITRE 5

Preview

In this chapter, students will learn to communicate with postal and bank clerks, write letters, address an envelope in French, exchange money, and carry out simple banking transactions. Structure points presented are the pronouns **qui** and **que,** the agreement of the past participle, reciprocal actions, and negative statements.

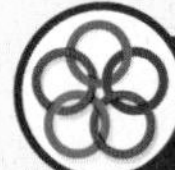

National Standards

Communication

In Chapter 5, students will communicate in spoken and written French on the following topics:

- Personal banking
- Using the postal service

Students will obtain and provide information and engage in conversations dealing with money, banking, correspondence, and the post office as they fulfill the chapter objectives listed on this page.

Communities

If you live in an area where foreign language materials are available, have students look for French greeting cards. Prepare a bulletin board using these cards.

CHAPITRE 5

La banque et la poste

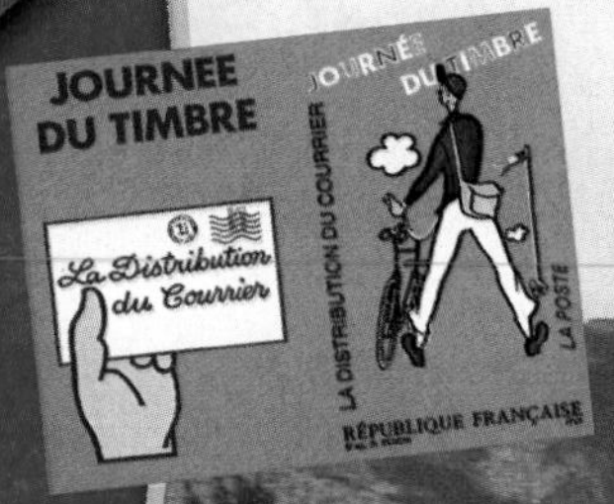

JOURNEE DU TIMBRE
La Distribution du Courrier
LA DISTRIBUTION DU COURRIER
LA POSTE
RÉPUBLIQUE FRANÇAISE

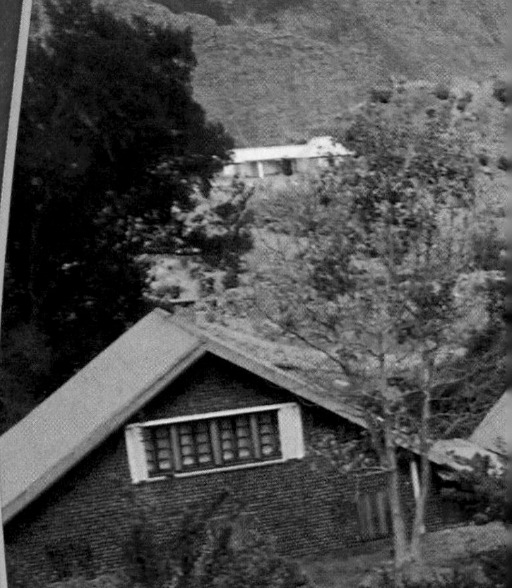

Objectifs

In this chapter you will learn to:

- *talk about using the services of the bank*
- *use words and expressions related to postal services*
- *give more information in one sentence*
- *refer to people and things already mentioned*
- *tell what you and others do for one another*
- *make negative statements*
- *talk about teen spending habits*

PRIORITAIRE
PRIORITY
PAR AVION/AIR MAIL

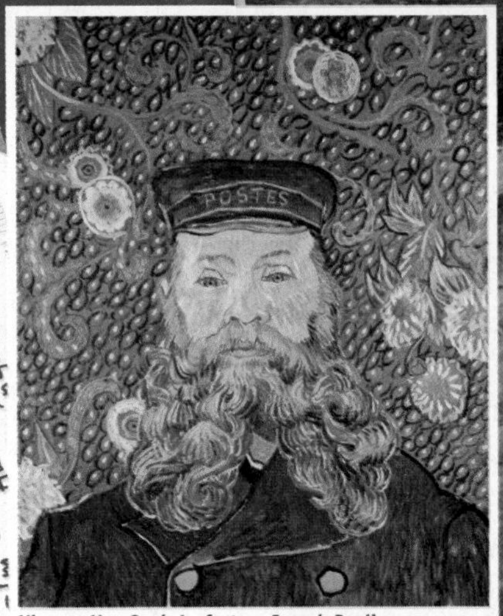

POSTES

Vincent Van Gogh *Le facteur Joseph Roulin*

140

FRENCH Online

The Glencoe Foreign Language Web site (french.glencoe.com) offers several options that enable you and your students to experience the French-speaking world via the Internet:

- The online **Activités** are correlated to the chapters and utilize Francophone Web sites around the world. For the Chapter 5 activity, see student page 171.
- Games and puzzles afford students another opportunity to practice the material learned in a particular chapter.
- The *Enrichment* section offers students an opportunity to visit Web sites related to the theme of the chapter for more information on a particular topic.
- Online *Chapter Quizzes* offer students an opportunity to prepare for a chapter test.
- Visit our virtual **Café** for more opportunities to practice and explore the French-speaking world.

cent quarante et un 141

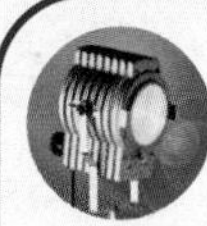

Spotlight on Culture

Photograph In this photo, we see a letter carrier delivering mail in the interior mountainous town of Cirque de Mafate on the island of la Réunion in the Indian Ocean. The town has two letter carriers who make their rounds delivering mail completely on foot.

Painting As a young man, Van Gogh worked as a lay missionary in a poor mining village in Belgium. He became quite an introvert and turned to his true love of art. His early paintings, done in drab hues, showed peasants going about their daily routines.

In 1866 Van Gogh went to live in Paris to be with his brother, Theo, an art dealer. Theo immediately recognized his brother's artistic talents and provided him with an allowance so he could continue painting. Van Gogh's paintings became less somber and he began to use brighter colors. In 1888 he went to Arles, where he developed his own painting style marked by bright colors, bold brushstrokes, and twisting lines.

Van Gogh was an unstable individual who suffered from epilepsy and depression. He worried about the burden he placed on his brother who now had a young son. In July of 1890, Van Gogh shot himself in a wheatfield where he had been painting. The wound was not immediately fatal. Van Gogh returned to his room, and his brother rushed to be with him. He died two days later at the age of 37. His brother was so overcome by grief that he died six months later.

Van Gogh sold only one painting in his lifetime, but his work inspired many future artists. Today his paintings are among the most acclaimed in art history.

Chapter Projects

À la poste Have students make a list of services offered by the U.S. Postal Service and ask them to explain them in French.

Des économies Have students draw up a personal budget and keep a diary of their expenditures as you do this chapter. At the chapter's end, have them tell or write what they learned about themselves by doing this.

Note: You may also have them check the Internet or newspaper for the exchange rates for the euro and ask them to convert their expenses into this currency. If they are available, pass around some real euros or refer students to the photos on pages 142, 144.

Vocabulaire *Mots 1*

1 Preparation

Resource Manager

Vocabulary Transparencies 5.2–5.3
Audio Activities Booklet TE, pages 48–50
Audiocassette 4A/CD 4
Workbook, page 51
Quiz 1, page 20
ExamView Pro®

Bellringer Review

Use BRR Transparency 5.1 or write the following on the board.
Match the city to its country. Then write a complete sentence to indicate in which country each city is located.

1. Oslo	**États-Unis**
2. Nantes	**Mexique**
3. Acapulco	**Norvège**
4. Portland	**Angleterre**
5. Londres	**France**

2 Presentation

Step 1 Have students close their books. Introduce the **Mots 1** vocabulary using Vocabulary Transparencies 5.2–5.3. Have students repeat each word after you or the recording on Audiocassette 4A/CD 4 two or three times as you point to the appropriate illustration on the transparencies.

Step 2 Now ask **Qu'est-ce que c'est?** as you point to the item on the transparency and have students come up with the new words themselves.

Step 3 Have students open their books and read the new words and sentences aloud. Ask questions such as: **Jean est allé où? Qu'est-ce qu'il a donné à la caissière?**

Step 4 Show students some euros or refer them to the photos on pages 142, 144.

Vocabulaire *Mots 1*

À la banque

des euros

Pour écrire un chèque, il faut avoir un compte courant.
Jean donne le chèque à la caissière et elle lui donne de l'argent liquide.
Il touche le chèque.

Jean parle à la caissière.

Magali a ouvert un compte d'épargne.
Elle a versé de l'argent sur son compte.

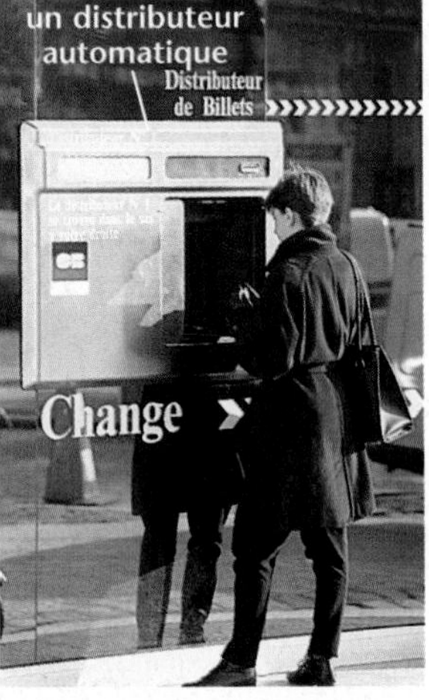

Sophie a retiré de l'argent au distributeur automatique.

Reaching All Students

Total Physical Response Have students dramatize the following:
(Student 1), **venez ici, s'il vous plaît.**
Vous avez de l'argent?
Montrez-moi un billet.
Montrez-moi une pièce.
Imaginez que vous avez un chèque. Signez votre chèque.
Et maintenant, imaginez que vous êtes fauché(e).
Indiquez-moi que vous n'avez pas de fric.

RESOURCE GUIDE

Section	Pages	Section Resources
Vocabulaire *Mots 1*		
Dans la cuisine Des aliments	174 174–177	Vocabulary Transparencies 6.2–6.3 Audiocassette 4B/CD 4 Audio Activities Booklet TE, pages 58–59 Workbook, page 63 Quiz 1, page 26 ExamView Pro®
Vocabulaire *Mots 2*		
Faisons la cuisine! D'autres aliments	178 179–181	Vocabulary Transparencies 6.4–6.5 Audiocassette 4B/CD 4 Audio Activities Booklet TE, pages 60–61 Workbook, pages 64–65 Quiz 2, page 27 ExamView Pro®
Structure		
Le futur simple Deux pronoms dans la même phrase **Faire** + infinitif	182–184 185–186 187–189	Audiocassette 4B/CD 4 Audio Activities Booklet TE, pages 62–64 Workbook, pages 66–69 Quizzes 3–5, pages 28–30 ExamView Pro®
Conversation		
La cuisine et moi, ça fait deux!	190–191	Audiocassette 4B/CD 4 Audio Activities Booklet TE, pages 64–65 CD-ROM
Lectures culturelles		
Un voyage gastronomique Un dîner chez une famille maghrébine Navarin d'agneau	192–193 194 195	Audiocassette 4B/CD 4 Audio Activities Booklet TE, pages 66–67 Test Booklet, Chapter 6
Connexions		
La littérature	196–197	Test Booklet, Chapter 6
C'est à vous		
	198–199	**Bon voyage!** Video, Episode 6 Video Activities Booklet, Chapter 6 French Online Activities french.glencoe.com
Assessment		
	200–201	Communication Transparency C 6 Quizzes 1–5, pages 26–30 Test Booklet, Chapter 6 ExamView Pro® Situation Cards, Chapter 6 **Marathon mental** Videoquiz

Using Your Resources for Chapter 6

Transparencies

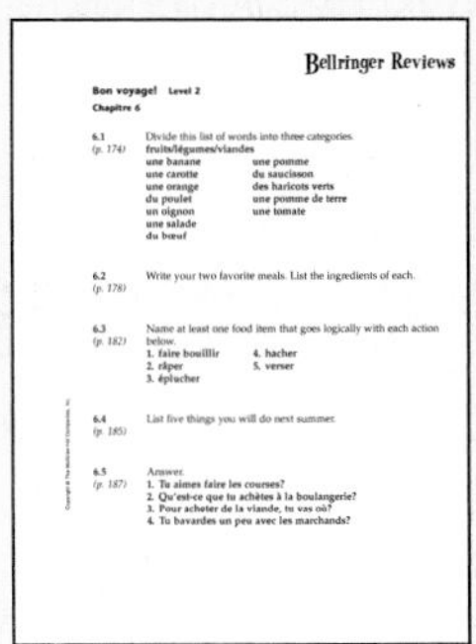
Bellringer Reviews

Vocabulaire
V 6.5

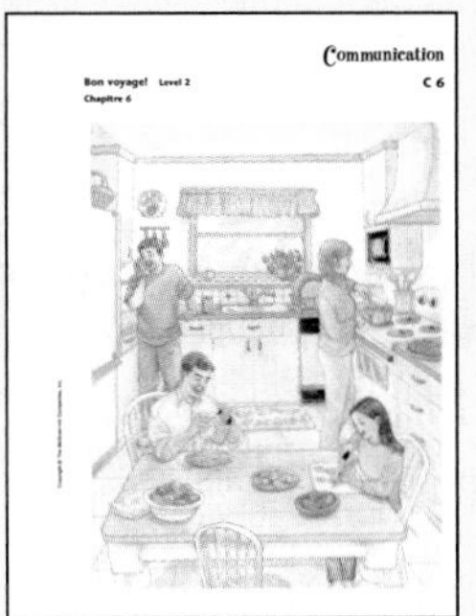
Communication
C 6

Bellringer 6.1–6.7

Vocabulary 6.1–6.5

Communication C 6

Writing Activities Workbook

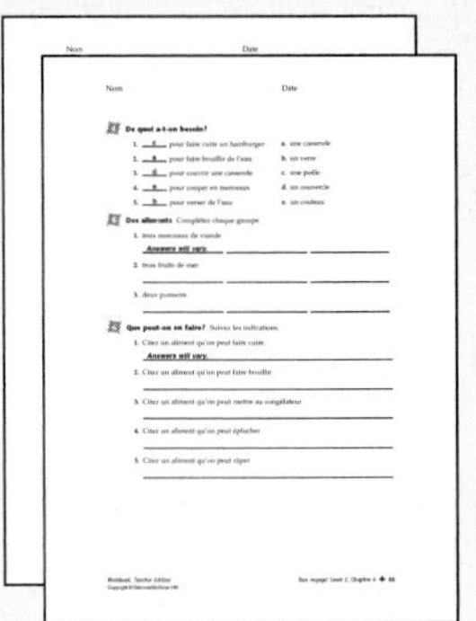

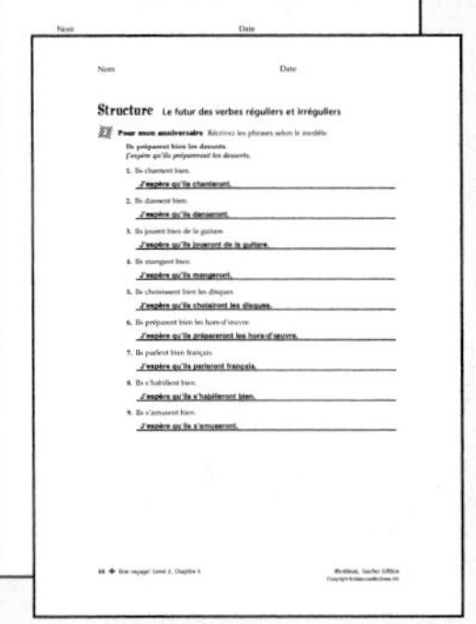

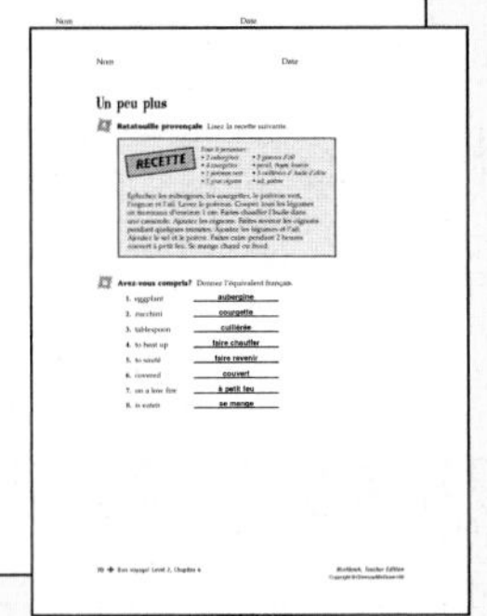

Vocabulary, pages 63–65

Structure, pages 66–69

Enrichment, pages 70–72

Audio Program and Audio Activities Booklet

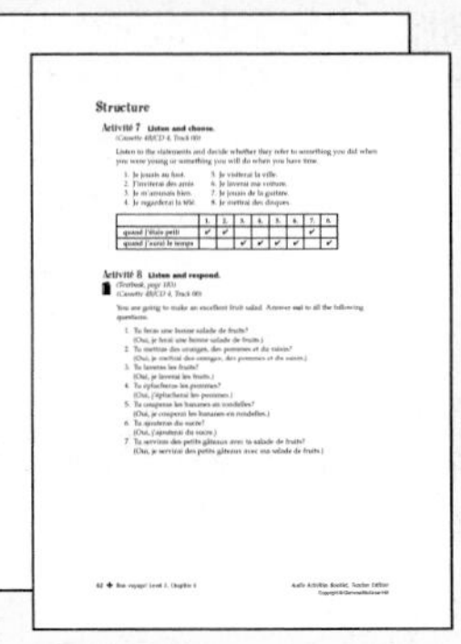

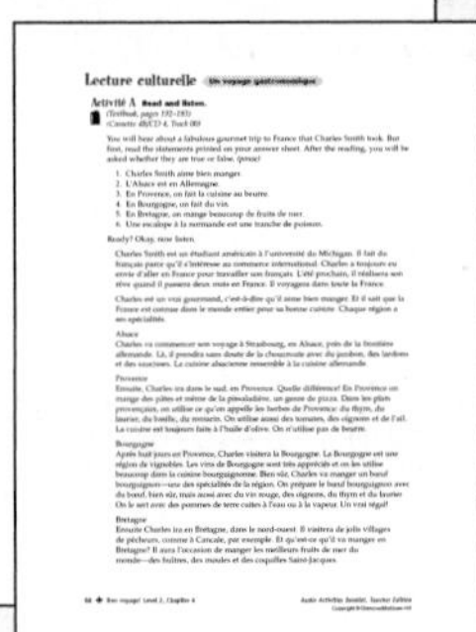

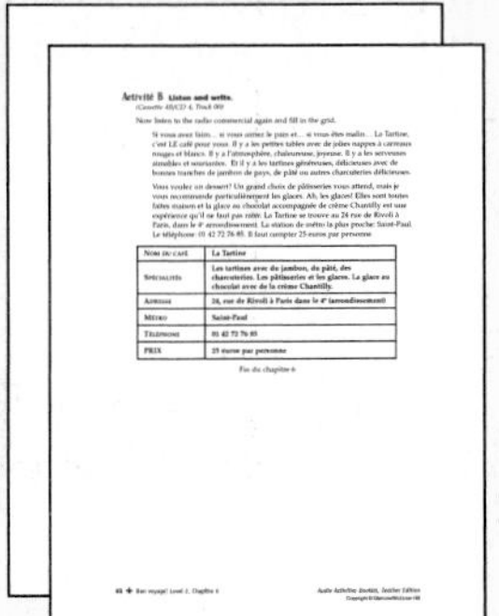

Vocabulary, pages 58–61

Structure, pages 62–64

Conversation, pages 64–65

Cultural Reading, pages 66–67

Additional Practice, pages 67–68

Assessment

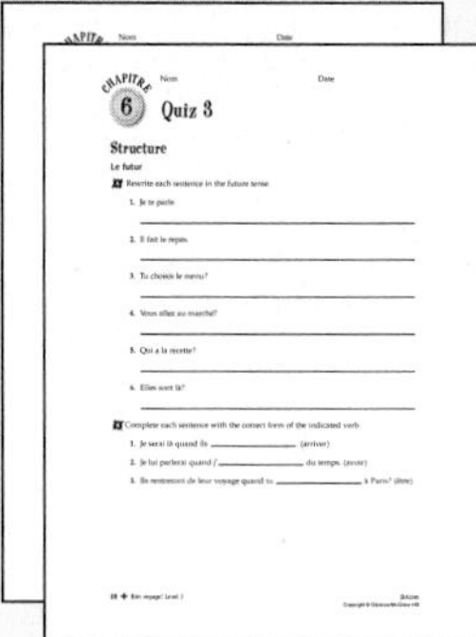

Vocabulary and Structure Quizzes, pages 26–30

Chapter Tests, Chapter 6

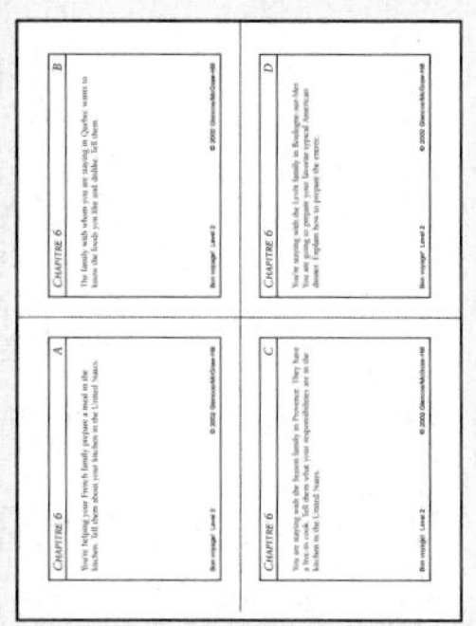

Situation Cards, Chapter 6

Timesaving Teacher Tools

Interactive Teacher Edition

Imagine having your Teacher's Edition and all resources on a CD-ROM. Click on a resource and it appears on your screen, ready to be printed, sorted, or planned.

Interactive Lesson Planner

The Interactive Lesson Planner CD-ROM helps you organize your lesson plans for a week, month, semester, or year. Look at this planning tool for easy access to your Chapter 6 resources.

ExamView Pro®

Test Bank software for Macintosh and Windows makes creating, editing, customizing, and printing tests quick and easy.

Technology Resources

In the Chapter 6 Internet activity, you will have a chance to learn more about food in the Francophone world. Visit french.glencoe.com.

On the Interactive Conversation CD-ROM, students can listen to and take part in a recorded version of the conversation in Chapter 6.

See the National Geographic Teacher's Corner on pages 138–139, 244–245, 372–373, 472–473 for reference to additional technology resources.

Bon voyage! Video and Video Activities Booklet.

Help your students prepare for the chapter test by playing the **Marathon mental** Videoquiz game show. Teams will compete against each other to review chapter vocabulary and structure and sharpen listening comprehension skills.

CHAPITRE 6

Preview

In this chapter, students will learn to talk about food and its preparation. Students will also increase their communication skills by learning the future tense, the placement of two object pronouns in the same sentence, and the construction **faire** + infinitive.

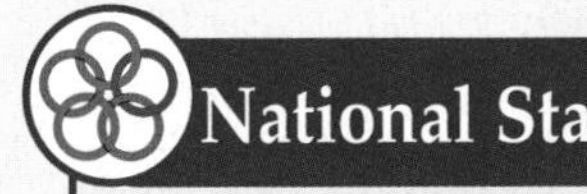

National Standards

Communication

In Chapter 6, students will communicate in spoken and written French on the following topics:

- Foods
- Food preparation

Students will obtain and provide information about these topics and engage in conversations that would typically take place in a kitchen as they fulfill the chapter objectives listed on this page.

CHAPITRE 6

La gastronomie

Objectifs

In this chapter you will learn to:

- *talk about foods and food preparation*
- *describe future events*
- *refer to people and things already mentioned*
- *tell what you have others do*
- *discuss the cuisine of various French provinces*

Henri Matisse *L'harmonie en rouge*

172

The **Glencoe Foreign Language Web site** (french.glencoe.com) offers options that enable you and your students to experience the French-speaking world via the Internet:

- The online **Activités** are correlated to the chapters and utilize Francophone Web sites around the world. For the Chapter 6 activity, see student page 203.
- Games and puzzles afford students another opportunity to practice the material learned in a particular chapter.
- The *Enrichment* section offers students an opportunity to visit Web sites related to the theme of the chapter for more information on a particular topic.
- Online *Chapter Quizzes* offer students an opportunity to prepare for a chapter test.
- Visit our virtual **Café** for more opportunities to practice and explore the French-speaking world.

Photograph This photo shows the French chef Philippe Jousse at the culinary school in Paris. After completing the vocabulary sections, have students say everything they can about the photo.

Painting The turn of the century saw a new series of art movements in Europe. The first movement started in 1905, when a group of young painters under the tutelage of Henri Matisse (1869–1954) exhibited in Paris. The paintings were very simple in design and brightly colored. They were also very loose in brushwork. An enraged critic called the artists **fauves** or "wild beasts."

Henri Matisse was the leader of the Fauves. He was born to a middle-class couple from northern France. Matisse convinced his family to allow him to study art rather than law. Early on, Matisse developed a style that made use of broad areas of color, as seen here in ***L'harmonie en rouge,*** that were not meant to look like the shapes or colors found in nature.

Chapter Projects

Un repas français Have students select a French recipe to prepare at home. You may assign or have them select a region of France from which a dish is representative. Groups could work together at home to make the recipe, bring it to class, and present information about the region and the ingredients.

Qu'est-ce qu'on mange? Have students work in small groups. Each group will determine their favorite fruits, vegetables, meats, and fish. Each group will complete its lists and determine their favorite foods. Are they healthy foods or not?

Mon repas favori Have students prepare a menu for their favorite American meal. If a student is from another ethnic background, he or she may choose to prepare the menu for a meal from his or her ethnic group.

Au restaurant If there is a French restaurant in your area, you may wish to plan a field trip to allow students to experience eating at a French restaurant.

1 Preparation

Resource Manager

Vocabulary Transparencies 6.2–6.3
Audio Activities Booklet TE, pages 58–59
Audiocassette 4B/CD 4
Workbook, pages 63
Quiz 1, page 26
ExamView Pro®

Bellringer Review

Use BRR Transparency 6.1 or write the following on the board.
Divide this list of words into three categories:
fruits/légumes/viandes

une banane	**une pomme**
une carotte	**du saucisson**
une orange	**des haricots verts**
du poulet	**une pomme de terre**
un oignon	**une tomate**
une salade	
du bœuf	

2 Presentation

Step 1 Have students close their books. Introduce the **Mots 1** vocabulary using Vocabulary Transparencies 6.2–6.3. Have students repeat each word after you or the recording on Audiocassette 4B/CD 4 two or three times as you point to the appropriate illustration on the transparencies. You may wish to use your own props, such as photos of kitchens or items from your own kitchen.

Step 2 Intersperse the presentation with questions which elicit the new vocabulary.

Vocabulaire Mots 1

Dans la cuisine 

Des aliments 

des fruits

une orange
un pamplemousse
un citron
du raisin

des légumes

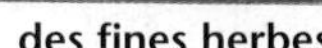

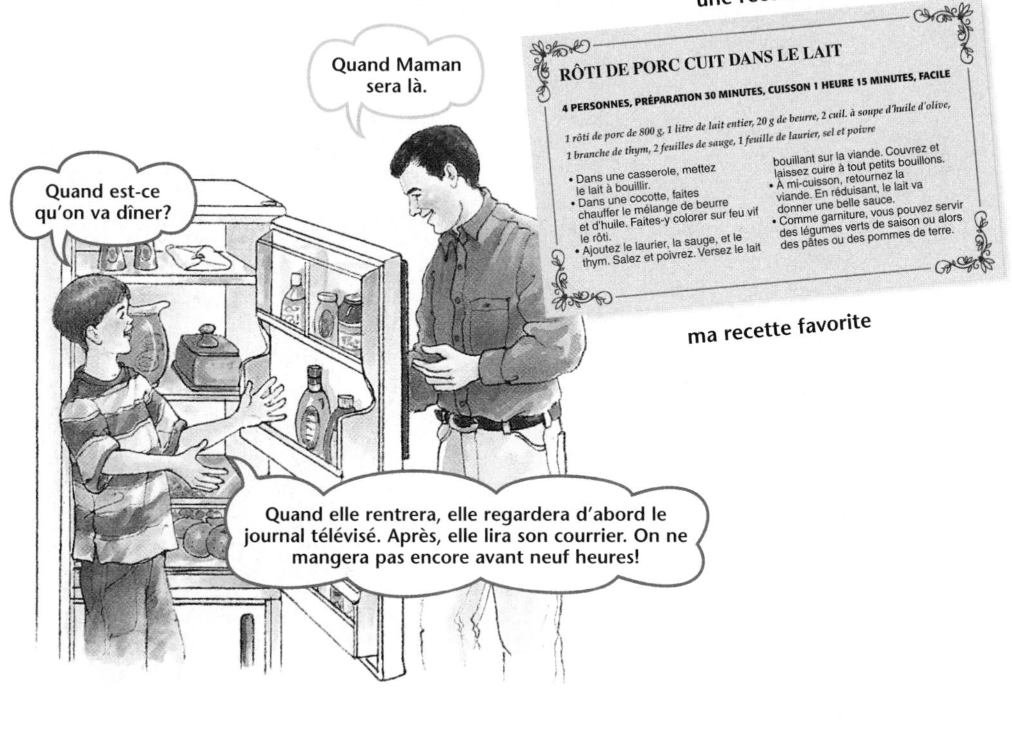

Step 3 After students have produced the new vocabulary several times, have them open their books to pages 174–175. Call on volunteers to read the new words, phrases, and sentences.

Step 4 When presenting the conversation between the father and son, introduce it by saying: **Il est maintenant cinq heures. Maman rentrera vers sept heures, c'est-à-dire dans deux heures.**

Assessment

As an informal assessment after the vocabulary presentation, you may wish to call on students to look at the illustrations and say as much as they can about them.

Reaching All Students

Total Physical Response **Note:** The following reviews some of the foods students have learned to identify so far in French.

You will hear the names of foods. If the food is a vegetable, raise your right hand. If it is a fruit, raise your left hand. If it is a meat, stand up. If it is seafood, do nothing.

un crabe
un champignon
des haricots verts
une banane
une poire
une pomme de terre
une pomme
du veau
un pamplemousse
des carottes
du porc
des moules

3 Practice

Commençons
Let's use our new words

Attention!

When students are doing the **Commençons** activities, accept any answer that makes sense. The purpose of these activities is to have students use the new vocabulary. They are not factual recall activities. Thus, it is not necessary for students to remember specific factual information from the vocabulary presentation when answering. If you wish, have students use the photos on this page as a stimulus, when possible.

Historiette Each time **Historiette** appears, it means that the answers to the activity form a short story. Encourage students to look at the title of the **Historiette**, since it can help them do the activity.

ENCORE PLUS This *infogap* activity will allow students to practice in pairs. The activity should be very manageable for them, since all vocabulary and structures are familiar to them.

Recycling

Have students say as much as they can about the photo of the market stall on page 177. Have them create a dialogue with the **marchand.**

Reteaching

Show Vocabulary Transparencies 6.2–6.3 and let students say as much as they can about them in their own words.

Vocabulaire

Commençons
Let's use our new words

Au magasin d'électroménager Travaillez avec un(e) camarade. Quels sont les appareils que vous pouvez trouver sur cette photo?

Le magasin Electro Star à Bonneuil-sur-Marne

2 Historiette Dans la cuisine
Répondez d'après la photo.

1. Il y a quelqu'un dans la cuisine?
2. C'est une cuisine moderne?
3. C'est une cuisinière électrique ou à gaz?
4. Il y a aussi un four?
5. Le réfrigérateur a combien de portes?
6. Il y a un congélateur dans le réfrigérateur?

*For more practice using words from **Mots 1**, do Activity 12 on page H13 at the end of this book.*

ANSWERS TO Commençons

Il y a des réfrigérateurs (des frigos, des frigidaires), des congélateurs, (des congés), des fours à micro-ondes, des fours, et des cuisinières.

1. Non, il n'y a personne dans la cuisine.
2. Oui, c'est une cuisine moderne.
3. C'est une cuisinière électrique.
4. Oui, il y a aussi un four.
5. Le réfrigérateur a deux portes.
6. Oui, il y a un congélateur dans le réfrigérateur.

Quelle catégorie? Choisissez.

un légume un fruit une herbe aromatique

1. une pomme de terre
2. un citron
3. un champignon
4. un poivron vert ou rouge
5. du thym
6. du laurier
7. du raisin
8. des haricots verts
9. un pamplemousse
10. des oignons

Le marché d'Arpajon

4 Ce que j'aime Donnez des réponses personnelles.

1. Tu aimes la salade de fruits avec des bananes et des pamplemousses?
2. Tu aimes les pâtes avec de la sauce tomate?
3. Tu aimes l'ail dans la sauce tomate? Tu y mets combien de gousses d'ail?
4. Tu aimes la salade avec de l'huile et du vinaigre?
5. Tu aimes les pommes de terre avec du beurre et du persil?
6. Tu aimes la choucroute avec des saucisses?
7. Tu prépares un repas de temps en temps?
8. Tu as une recette favorite? Quelle est cette recette?
9. Tu as un plat favori? Quel est ce plat?

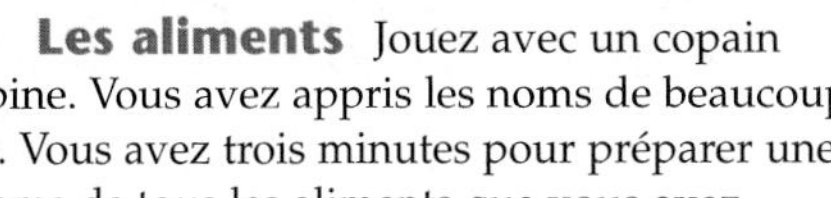

Les aliments Jouez avec un copain ou une copine. Vous avez appris les noms de beaucoup d'aliments. Vous avez trois minutes pour préparer une liste des noms de tous les aliments que vous avez appris. Celui qui a la plus longue liste gagne.

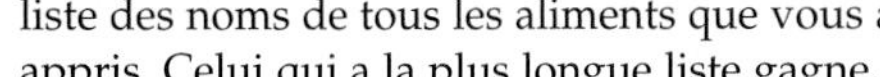

Learning from Photos

(*page 177*) Arpajon is a small town about 50 km south of Paris. It is an area known for truck-farming—**des cultures maraîchères.**

Learning from Realia

(*page 177*) Have students look at the realia. Have them identify the fruits they see and, when possible, tell where they are from.

Writing Development

Have students write the answers to Activities 2 and 4 in paragraph form.

4 Have students form other questions like the ones in Activity 4, and use them as a classwide survey. Tabulate the results on the board to see which foods are class favorites.

5 You could divide the class into small groups to do this activity as a classwide competition.

Answers to Commençons

1. un légume
2. un fruit
3. un légume
4. un légume
5. une herbe aromatique
6. une herbe aromatique
7. un fruit
8. des légumes
9. un fruit
10. des légumes

4 *Answers will vary but may include:*

1. Oui, j'aime la salade de fruits avec des bananes et des pamplemousses.
2. Oui, j'aime les pâtes avec de la sauce tomate.
3. Oui, j'aime l'ail dans la sauce tomate. J'y mets une gousse d'ail.
4. Oui, j'aime la salade avec de l'huile et du vinaigre.
5. Oui, j'aime les pommes de terre avec du beurre et du persil.
6. Oui, j'aime la choucroute avec des saucisses.
7. Oui, je prépare un repas de temps en temps.
8. Oui, j'ai une recette favorite. C'est ____.
9. Oui, j'ai un plat favori. C'est ____.

5 *Answers will vary.*

1 Preparation

Resource Manager

Vocabulary Transparencies 6.4–6.5
Audio Activities Booklet TE, pages 60–61
Audiocassette 4B/CD 4
Workbook, pages 64–65
Quiz 2, page 27
ExamView Pro®

Bellringer Review

Use BRR Transparency 6.2 or write the following on the board.
Write your two favorite meals.
List the ingredients of each.

2 Presentation

Step 1 Show Vocabulary Transparencies 6.4–6.5. Have students close their books and repeat the words after you or Audiocassette 4B/CD 4 as you point to the appropriate illustration on the transparency.

Step 2 Dramatize the meaning of these words: **éplucher, couper, hacher, râper, verser, remuer.**

Step 3 When students have produced the new vocabulary several times, have them open their books to pages 178–179 and call on volunteers to read the words, phrases, and sentences. Model pronunciation as necessary.

Faisons la cuisine! 

éplucher des pommes de terre

couper en morceaux

un morceau

couper en rondelles

une rondelle

verser du lait

remuer une sauce

un couvercle

une poêle

une casserole

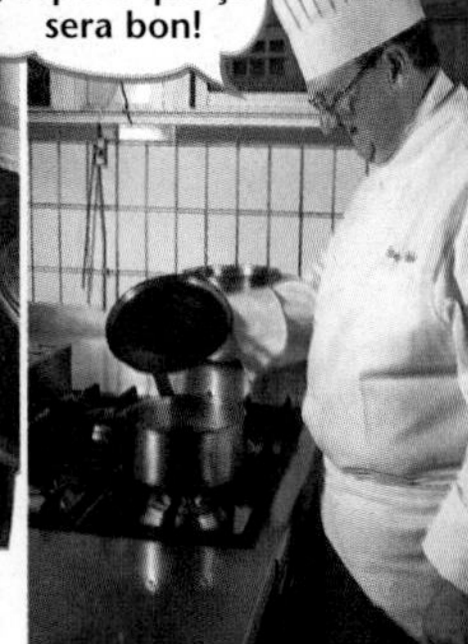

M. Arnaud est bon cuisinier.
Il va faire cuire les carottes.
Il fait bouillir l'eau à feu vif.
Il met les carottes dans l'eau bouillante.

Il laisse bouillir les carottes à feu doux.

D'autres aliments 

la viande

les poissons et les fruits de mer

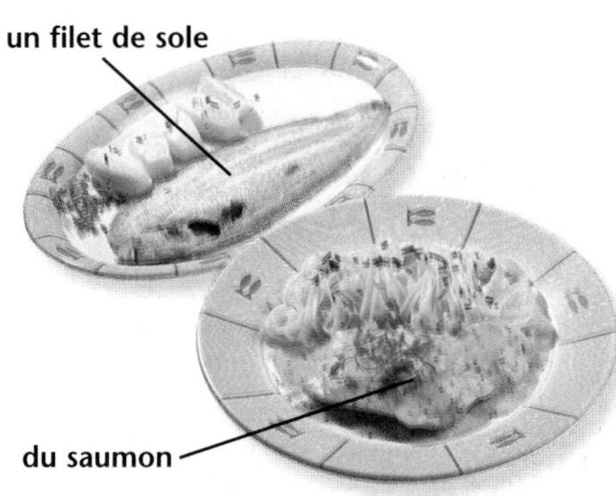

une moule
un homard
une huître
un crabe

Reaching All Students

Total Physical Response You may wish to bring some kitchen items to use for this activity.

(Student 1), **venez ici, s'il vous plaît. C'est une pomme de terre.**
Lavez la pomme de terre.
Épluchez la pomme de terre.
Et maintenant, coupez la pomme de terre. Coupez-la en tranches.
Mettez les tranches dans une casserole.
Ajoutez de l'eau.
Allumez le feu.
Merci, *(Student 1)*, **C'est très bien. Vous pouvez retourner à votre place.**
(Student 2), **venez ici, s'il vous plaît. C'est du fromage.**
Coupez le fromage. Faites des gros morceaux.
Prenez une casserole.
Mettez un peu de lait dans le casserole.
Ajoutez le fromage.
Mettez la casserole sur le feu.
Remuez la sauce.
Remuez-la vite.
Versez un peu plus de lait.
Merci, *(Student 2)*.

3 Practice

Commençons
Let's use our new words

6 You may wish to have students correct any false statements.

Writing Development
Have students write the answers to questions in Activity 7 in paragraph form.

Learning from Photos
(pages 180–181) Have students identify everything they can in the photos.

(page 180 top) Saint-Paul-de-Vence is a beautiful small town in the hills to the north of Nice. Have students note how beautifully produce is displayed in many French markets.

Commençons
Let's use our new words

6 En cuisine
Indiquez si ça se fait ou si ça ne se fait pas.

1. On coupe un concombre en rondelles.
2. On coupe l'eau en petits morceaux.
3. On met de l'eau dans une casserole pour faire bouillir quelque chose.
4. On fait les frites dans de l'eau.
5. On râpe le fromage avant de le mettre sur les pâtes.
6. On fait les hamburgers avec de la viande hachée.
7. On fait bouillir l'eau dans une poêle.
8. On verse du lait dans un couvercle.
9. On remue une sauce.
10. On épluche les pommes de terre et les carottes avant de les faire cuire.

Un marché de fruits et légumes à Saint-Paul-de-Vence

7 Historiette Un bon cuisinier
Inventez une histoire.

1. Luc aime faire la cuisine?
2. Il est bon cuisinier?
3. C'est lui qui va préparer le repas pour l'anniversaire de sa copine?
4. Qu'est-ce qu'il va préparer, de la viande ou du poisson?
5. Qu'est-ce qu'il préfère, la viande ou le poisson? Et sa copine?
6. Qu'est-ce qu'il va servir comme légumes?
7. Qu'est-ce qu'il va servir comme dessert?

Cuisine in France varies from region to region. To learn more about the differences of some of these regions, go to the Glencoe French Web site: french.glencoe.com

Answers to Commençons

6

1. Oui, on coupe un concombre en rondelles.
2. Non, on ne coupe pas l'eau en petits morceaux.
3. Oui, on met de l'eau dans une casserole pour faire bouillir quelque chose.
4. Non, on ne fait pas les frites dans de l'eau.
5. Oui, on râpe le fromage avant de le mettre sur les pâtes.
6. Oui, on fait les hamburgers avec de la viande hachée.
7. Non, on ne fait pas bouillir l'eau dans une poêle.
8. Non, on ne verse pas de lait dans un couvercle.
9. Oui, on remue une sauce.
10. Oui, on épluche les pommes de terre et les carottes avant de les faire cuire.

7 *Answers will vary but may include:*

1. Oui, Luc aime faire la cuisine.
2. Oui, il est bon cuisinier.
3. Oui, c'est lui qui va préparer le repas pour l'anniversaire de sa copine.
4. Il va préparer du poisson.
5. Il préfère la viande. Sa copine préfère le poisson.
6. Il va servir des haricots verts.
7. Il va servir un gâteau au chocolat.

8 J'aime ça.

Donnez des réponses personnelles.

1. Quels sont les poissons que tu aimes?
2. Quels sont les fruits de mer que tu aimes?
3. Quelles sont les viandes que tu aimes?
4. Quels sont tes fruits favoris?
5. Quels sont tes légumes favoris?

Le marché d'Arpajon

le bar à huîtres
PARIS
SEA FOOD
RESTAURANT DE POISSONS
SAINT-GERMAIN DES PRÉS • BASTILLE • MONTPARNASSE

9 Nos repas favoris

Avec un copain ou une copine, parlez de vos repas favoris. Ensuite, décidez si vous mangez des aliments qui sont bons pour la santé.

Carcassonne dans le sud-ouest de la France

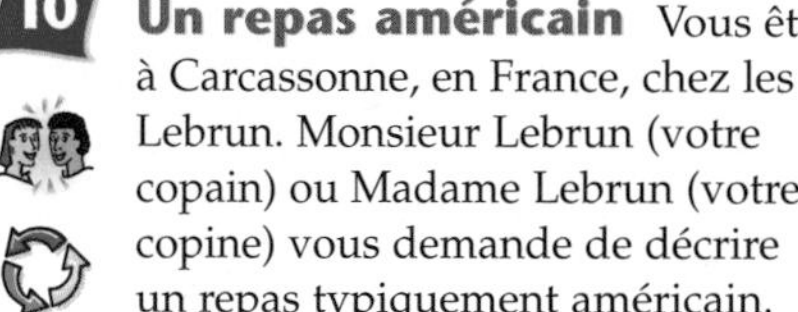

10 Un repas américain

Vous êtes à Carcassonne, en France, chez les Lebrun. Monsieur Lebrun (votre copain) ou Madame Lebrun (votre copine) vous demande de décrire un repas typiquement américain. Faites-le et expliquez-lui, si possible, comment on le prépare. Ensuite changez de rôle.

Learning from Realia

(page 181) Have students look at the realia. Have them guess the meaning of the following terms:

livré à domicile
livraison gratuite

Learning from Photos

(page 181 bottom)
Carcassonne is probably the largest and one of the most complete of Europe's medieval fortresses. The view seen in this photo is magnificent at night when the towers and battlements are floodlit.

Answers to Commençons

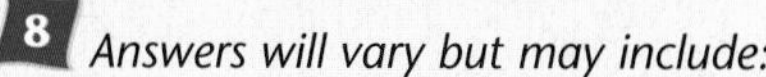

8 *Answers will vary but may include:*

1. J'aime le saumon et la sole.
2. J'aime le crabe et le homard.
3. J'aime le bœuf et le poulet.
4. Mes fruits favoris sont les bananes, les pêches et les fraises.
5. Mes légumes favoris sont les haricots verts et les tomates.

9 and **10** *Answers will vary.*
Students can use all the vocabulary related to food they have learned in this and previous chapters.

1 Preparation

Resource Manager

Audio Activities Booklet TE, pages 62–64
Audiocassette 4B/CD 4
Workbook, pages 66–69
Quizzes 3–5, pages 28–30
ExamView Pro®

Bellringer Review

Use BRR Transparency 6.3 or write the following on the board.
Name at least one food item that goes logically with each action below.

1. faire bouillir
2. râper
3. éplucher
4. hacher
5. verser

2 Presentation

Le futur simple

Step 1 Review **aller** + infinitive as discussed in the **Rappelez-vous que...** section. Remind students that these actions will take place in the near future. Write some examples on the board.

Step 2 Go over Item 1. Stress that the **e** is dropped from **-re** verbs.

Step 3 Have students repeat the verb forms after you.

Step 4 Ask students what the future endings remind them of. Write the forms of **avoir** on the board and point out the similarity.

Expressing future events
Le futur simple

Rappelez-vous que...

You already learned that the future can be expressed in French by using **aller** + infinitive.
Vendredi, je vais sortir avec Émilie.

1. To form the future tense in French, you add the future endings to the entire infinitive of verbs that end in **-er** or **-ir.** You drop the **e** before adding the endings to **-re** verbs. Study the following.

	PARLER	FINIR	ATTENDRE
Infinitive	parler	finir	attendre
Stem	parler-	finir-	attendr-
	je parlerai tu parleras il/elle/on parlera nous parlerons vous parlerez ils/elles parleront	je finirai tu finiras il/elle/on finira nous finirons vous finirez ils/elles finiront	j' attendrai tu attendras il/elle/on attendra nous attendrons vous attendrez ils/elles attendront

2. The verbs **être, faire, aller,** and **avoir** have an irregular stem in the future tense.

ÊTRE **je serai, tu seras, il sera, nous serons, vous serez, ils seront**
FAIRE **je ferai, tu feras, il fera, nous ferons, vous ferez, ils feront**
ALLER **j'irai, tu iras, il ira, nous irons, vous irez, ils iront**
AVOIR **j'aurai, tu auras, il aura, nous aurons, vous aurez, ils auront**

3. The future tense is not commonly used in spoken French. You use **aller** + the infinitive more often to express the future. However, you must use the future tense after **quand** when the main verb in the sentence is in the future tense.

Je te ferai un bon repas quand tu seras à Paris.
Quand tout le monde sera là, je mettrai la viande au four.

About the French Language

You may wish to explain to students that the present tense of **aller** is frequently used to express the future.

J'y vais demain mais Robert y va la semaine prochaine. ⚜

Writing Development

Have students write Activities 11 and 12 in paragraph form.

Continuons

Let's put our words together

11 Historiette Un de ces jours... Répondez que oui.

1. Un de ces jours, Sandra voyagera en France?
2. Elle prendra l'avion pour y aller?
3. Elle passera quelques semaines à Paris?
4. Elle visitera les monuments?
5. Elle s'amusera?
6. Sa copine Liz l'accompagnera?
7. Elles sortiront souvent?
8. Elles dîneront dans de bons restaurants?

Une fondue au fromage

12 Historiette Une bonne cuisinière

Inventez des réponses.

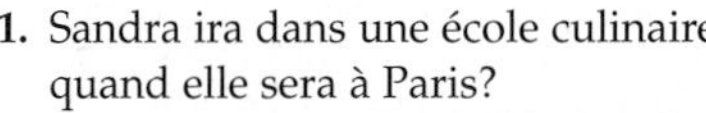

1. Sandra ira dans une école culinaire quand elle sera à Paris?
2. Elle apprendra à faire des plats français quand elle sera à Paris?
3. Elle préparera des repas exquis quand elle rentrera aux États-Unis?
4. Elle invitera ses amis à dîner?
5. Elle leur fera de la cuisine française quand elle les invitera?

Un marché à Aix-en-Provence

13 Une salade de fruits Répondez que oui.

1. Tu feras une bonne salade de fruits?
2. Tu mettras des oranges, des pommes et du raisin?
3. Tu laveras les fruits?
4. Tu éplucheras les pommes?
5. Tu couperas les bananes en rondelles?
6. Tu ajouteras du sucre?
7. Tu serviras des petits gâteaux avec ta salade de fruits?

3 Practice

Continuons

Let's put our words together

11 You may wish to ask the questions or have students do this activity in pairs, once with books closed and then again with books open.

Learning from Realia

(page 183) This postcard shows the Egyptian Obelisk in the Place de la Concorde in Paris.

Learning from Photos

(page 183 middle) Fondue is a dish of Swiss origin. Cheese fondue is a saucelike dish with melted cheese and seasonings mixed with dry white wine. It is served as a hot dip for pieces of bread.

(page 183 bottom) Have students identify some of the items in this outdoor market in Aix-en-Provence.

Answers to Continuons

11

1. Oui, un de ces jours, Sandra voyagera en France.
2. Oui, elle prendra l'avion pour y aller.
3. Oui, elle passera quelques semaines à Paris.
4. Oui, elle visitera les monuments.
5. Oui, elle s'amusera.
6. Oui, sa copine Liz l'accompagnera.
7. Oui, elles sortiront souvent.
8. Oui, elles dîneront dans de bons restaurants.

12 *Answers will vary but may include:*

1. Oui, Sandra ira dans une école culinaire quand elle sera à Paris.
2. Oui, elle apprendra à faire des plats français quand elle sera à Paris.
3. Oui, elle préparera des repas exquis quand elle rentrera aux États-Unis.
4. Oui, elle invitera ses amis à dîner.
5. Oui, elle leur fera de la cuisine française quand elle les invitera.

13 *Answers will vary but may include:*

1. Oui, je ferai une bonne salade de fruits.
2. Oui, je mettrai des oranges, des pommes et du raisin.
3. Oui, je laverai les fruits.
4. Oui, j'éplucherai les pommes.
5. Oui, je couperai les bananes en rondelles.
6. Oui, j'ajouterai du sucre.
7. Oui, je servirai des petits gâteaux avec ma salade de fruits.

3 Practice *(continued)*

14 **Expansion:** Have students work in pairs. One asks the questions, the other answers each question.

16 **Expansion:** Have students invent original sentences telling what they will do at the beach. For example: **J'irai à la plage où je prendrai un bain de soleil.**

14 **Pour ton anniversaire?** Posez des questions à Laurent d'après le modèle.

donner une fête
Laurent, tu donneras une fête?

1. inviter des amis
2. préparer des hors-d'œuvre
3. jouer de la guitare
4. chanter
5. mettre des disques
6. danser

Le restaurant Julien à Paris

15 **Historiette** **Au restaurant**
Répondez d'après les indications.

1. Tu iras au restaurant à quelle heure demain soir? (à neuf heures)
2. C'est toi qui choisiras le restaurant? (oui)
3. Tu y dîneras seul? (non, avec Julie)
4. Vous prendrez une table avant l'arrivée de vos amis? (oui)
5. Vous demanderez la carte aussi? (non)
6. Vous attendrez vos amis? (absolument)

16 **Un voyage à la Martinique** Répondez que oui.

1. L'hiver prochain Émilie aura des vacances?
2. Elle fera un voyage?
3. Elle ira à la Martinique?
4. Elle fera le voyage en avion?
5. Elle sera fatiguée après le vol?
6. Tu feras ce voyage avec Émilie?
7. Vous irez ensemble à la Martinique?
8. Vous y ferez des excursions ensemble?
9. Vous irez à la plage?
10. Vous prendrez des bains de soleil?
11. Vous serez bronzé(e)s?

17 **De bonnes résolutions** Vous avez décidé de prendre de bonnes résolutions pour le nouvel an. Par exemple: **Je serai gentil(le) avec ma sœur.** Faites une liste et comparez-la avec la liste d'un(e) camarade. Quelles sont les résolutions qui sont les mêmes?

18 **J'espère...** Travaillez avec un(e) camarade. Dites ce que vous espérez pour l'avenir. Par exemple: **J'espère que je n'aurai plus de devoirs l'année prochaine.**

Answers to Continuons

14
1. Laurent, tu inviteras des amis?
2. Laurent, tu prépareras des hors-d'œuvre?
3. Laurent, tu joueras de la guitare?
4. Laurent, tu chanteras?
5. Laurent, tu mettras des disques?
6. Laurent, tu danseras?

15
1. J'irai au restaurant à neuf heures.
2. Oui, c'est moi qui choisirai le restaurant.
3. Non, j'y dînerai avec Julie.
4. Oui, nous prendrons une table avant l'arrivée de nos amis.
5. Non, nous ne demanderons pas la carte.
6. Absolument, nous attendrons nos amis.

16
1. Oui, elle aura des vacances l'hiver prochain.
2. Oui, elle fera un voyage.
3. Oui, elle ira à la Martinique.
4. Oui, elle fera le voyage en avion.
5. Oui, elle sera fatiguée après le vol.
6. Oui, je ferai ce voyage avec Émilie.
7. Oui, nous irons ensemble à la Martinique.
8. Oui, nous y ferons des excursions ensemble.
9. Oui, nous irons à la plage.
10. Oui, nous prendrons des bains de soleil.
11. Oui, nous serons bronzé(e)s.

17 *Answers will vary.*

18 *Answers will vary.*

Structure

24 **Un prof exigeant** Votre professeur de français vous fait faire beaucoup de choses. Avec un(e) camarade, parlez de tout ce qu'il/elle vous fait faire en classe. Vous pouvez utiliser les mots et expressions suivantes.

beaucoup parler	**faire des devoirs**
écrire des paragraphes	**bien prononcer**
passer des examens	**répéter les phrases**
répondre à trop de questions	**lire des lectures**
écrire au tableau noir	

MOIS Janvier Février
Absences 9 Retards 0
NOM
CLASSE 2nde A Nombre d'Élèves 16

	DEVOIRS	LEÇONS	OBSERVATIONS DU PROFESSEUR
Philosophie			
Français (grammaire et orthographe)	12 10		
Français (composition et dissertation)			Élève souvent absente. Mr Malagiao
Récitation			
Anglais (grammaire et composition)		13 10	
Anglais (littérature)	B+	B+	Devrait pouvoir mieux faire. Mme Krause
Espagnol	11		Making good progress. Mr Rhodes
Version Anglaise			Assez bien. Mlle Becanbeau
Histoire Américaine			
Algèbre / Géométrie	abs. 20		Beaucoup d'absences. Des difficultés en géométrie. Mr De Sablet
Chimie / Physique	abs. 14,5		
Sciences Naturelles	17		Des progrès en Physique. Mr Smolya
Histoire / Géographie	13 abs. 20	A	Très bons résultats. Élève intéressée. Mlle Nauris
Thème Latin			Bien. En progrès. Mme Cohen-Jagell
Version Latine			
Économie	16		
Civics	B+	B+	Très bien. Mr Aldebert
Écriture			
Dessin			
Éducation Physique	A-		

Bon ensemble

Conduite: Excellente — Application:
INSCRIT / ~~NON INSCRIT~~ au TABLEAU D'HONNEUR
Signature du professeur — Signature des parents

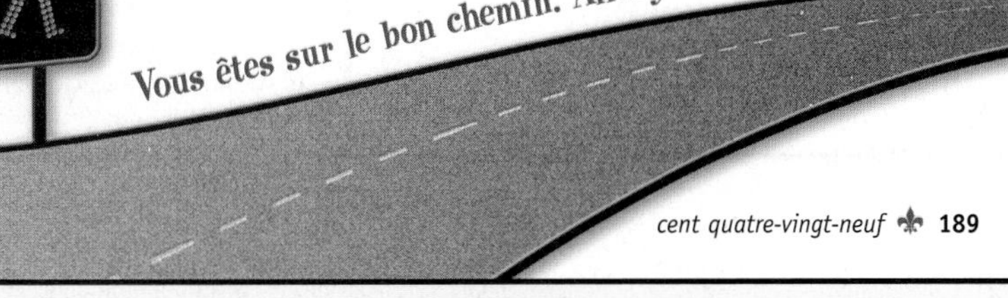

Learning from Realia

(page 189) This is a report card from a French lycée in the United States. You may wish to explain to students that in France, all of the grades would be given in numbers rather than letters, usually on a scale of 1 to 20.

Have students look at the report card and read the teacher's comments. What seems to be the problem the student is having?

Assessment

As an informal assessment, you may wish to ask students if the subject is acting alone or having someone else perform the action: (Tell them that **repasser** means *to iron.*)

1. **Je lave ma chemise.**
2. **Je fais laver ma chemise.**
3. **Je repasse ma chemise.**
4. **Je fais repasser ma chemise.**
5. **Je lave ma voiture.**
6. **Je fais laver ma voiture.**

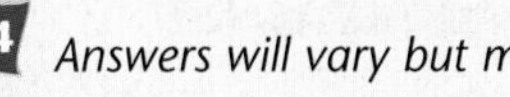

Answers to Continuons

24 *Answers will vary but may include:*

Il/Elle nous fait faire beaucoup de devoirs.
Il/Elle nous fait répondre à trop de questions.
Il/Elle nous fait passer des examens difficiles.

Allez-y!

At this point in the chapter, students have learned all the vocabulary and structure necessary to complete the chapter. The conversation and cultural readings that follow recycle all the material learned up to this point.

1 Preparation

Resource Manager

Audio Activities Booklet TE, pages 64–65
Audiocassette 4B/CD 4
CD-ROM

Bellringer Review

Use BRR Transparency 6.6 or write the following on the board.
Imagine you won the lottery. Give five things you will do as a result.

2 Presentation

Step 1 Tell students they will hear a conversation between Serge and Peter. Have students close their books and listen as you read the conversation aloud or play Audiocassette 4B/CD 4. Have students listen carefully to the recorded version and pay particular attention to the intonation.

Step 2 Have pairs of students role-play Serge and Peter, repeating their lines after you.

Step 3 Have two students read the conversation to the class.

Conversation

La cuisine et moi, ça fait deux!   

Serge: Tu aimes faire la cuisine, toi, Peter, non?
Peter: Moi? Faire la cuisine! Tu rigoles! Jamais de la vie!
Serge: Moi, j'aime bien de temps en temps.
Peter: Qu'est-ce que tu sais faire comme plats?
Serge: Ben, le couscous, la bouillabaisse…
Peter: La bouillabaisse? Qu'est-ce que c'est?
Serge: C'est la spécialité de Marseille. C'est une soupe de poissons avec des tomates, des oignons, de l'ail et du pain.
Peter: Alors quand est-ce qu'on la mange, cette bouillabaisse?
Serge: Ben si tu veux, j'en ferai une la semaine prochaine.

Après la conversation

Répondez.

1. Est-ce que Peter aime faire la cuisine?
2. Quels plats est-ce que Serge sait faire?
3. Qu'est-ce que la bouillabaisse?
4. Qu'est-ce qu'on met dans la bouillabaisse?
5. Marseille est sur la mer Méditerranée ou sur l'océan Atlantique?
6. Quand est-ce que Serge fera une bouillabaisse?

Reaching All Students

Additional Practice
After completing the **Conversation** activity, ask a student to retell the conversation in his or her own words.

Glencoe Technology

CD-ROM
On the CD-ROM, students can watch a dramatization of this conversation. They can then play the role of either one of the characters and record themselves in the conversation.

Answers to Après la conversation

1. Non, Peter n'aime pas faire la cuisine.
2. Serge sait faire le couscous et la bouillabaisse.
3. C'est la spécialité de Marseille.
4. On met du poisson, des tomates, des oignons, de l'ail et du pain.
5. Marseille est sur la mer Méditerranée.
6. Serge fera une bouillabaisse la semaine prochaine.

ÉCRIRE

4 Un repas délicieux

✔ ***Describe the cuisine of one of the French provinces***

Vous faites un voyage en Normandie. Vous passez quelques jours à Dieppe. Vous avez dîné dans un très bon restaurant qu'un ami français vous a recommandé. Vous lui écrivez un petit mot pour le remercier. Vous lui décrivez ce que vous avez mangé et vous lui dites combien vous avez aimé le restaurant et pourquoi.

FORMULE BUFFET

1 Entrée + 1 Plat 79,00 F 12,04 €

La soupe de poisson du pêcheur

Les 6 huîtres de Normandie

Au choix *Servies sur glace pillée*

La salade cocktail

Crevettes roses - Saumon fumé

Le jambon à l'os à la Normande

Pommes frites - Champignons à la crème

L'entrecôte grillée

Pommes frites - Salade

Sauce beurre maître d'hôtel, ou aux deux poivres, ou roquefort, ou barbecue.

Le port de plaisance de Dieppe en Normandie

Writing Strategy

Writing about a process When you write an explanation of a process, keep in mind that your readers should be able to follow your explanation from start to finish. Present the steps of the process in a logical order and include as many details as possible. Remember to define any terms that may be unfamiliar to your readers.

ÉCRIRE

5 Un(e) Américain(e) à Colmar

You are living with a French family in Colmar, in Alsace. One day last week you prepared your favorite American dish for them. They loved it! They want you to write down the recipe for them before you return to the United States. Since they don't know much English, you'll have to write the recipe in French. Be sure to explain all the steps as clearly as possible so that they can prepare something delicious rather than a disaster!

C'est à vous

Learning from Photos

(page 199) The coast east of Le Havre, near the mouth of the Seine, is known for its spectacular white cliffs from which it gets its name, Alabaster Coast. The biggest town along this coast is Dieppe, which is a busy fishing port. The **port de plaisance** seen here is the marina for pleasure craft.

Writing Development

Have students keep a notebook containing their best written work from each chapter. These selected writings can be based on assignments from the Student Textbook and the Writing Activities Workbook. The two activities on page 199 are examples of writing assignments that may be included in each student's portfolio. In the Workbook, students will develop an organized autobiography **(Mon autobiographie).** These workbook pages may also become a part of their portfolio.

Writing Strategy

Writing about a process
Have students read the Writing Strategy on page 199. Have students refer to the vocabulary list on page 202 if they need more ideas to write this selection.

Answers to C'est à vous

4 *Answers will vary but may include:*

Cher François,

J'ai beaucoup aimé le restaurant que tu m'as recommandé. Le serveur était très aimable, et le restaurant était charmant. J'y ai mangé une escalope à la normande. C'était formidable! J'ai pris aussi une bonne tarte aux pommes comme dessert. Merci beaucoup!

5 *Answers will vary, depending upon the recipe the student selects.*

Reaching All Students

Additional Practice
Display Communication Transparency C 6. Have students work in groups to make up as many questions as they can about the illustration. Have groups take turns asking and answering the questions.

Resource Manager

Communication Transparencies
Quizzes
Test Booklet
ExamView Pro®
Situation Cards
Performance Assessment
Marathon mental Videoquiz

Assessment

This is a pre-test for students to take before you administer the chapter test. Answer sheets for students to do these pages are provided in your transparency binder. Note that each section is cross-referenced so students can easily find the material they have to review in case they made errors. You may wish to collect these assessments and correct them yourself or you may prefer to have the students correct themselves in class. You can go over the answers orally or project them on the overhead, using your Assessment Answers transparencies.

Vocabulaire

To review **Mots 1**, turn to pages 174–175.

1 Complétez.

1–2. ____ et ____ sont des légumes.
3–4. ____ et ____ sont des fruits.
5. ____ est une fine herbe.

2 Choisissez.

a. 

b. 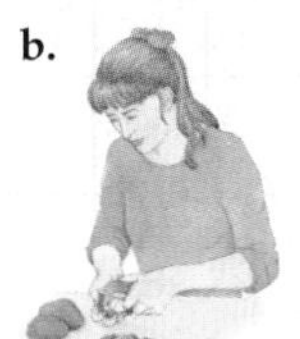

c. 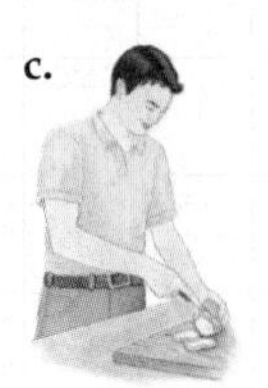

d. 

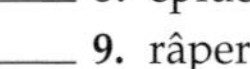

To review **Mots 2**, turn to pages 178–179.

____ 6. remuer
____ 7. couper
____ 8. éplucher
____ 9. râper

3 Identifiez.

10. 11. 

12. 

13. 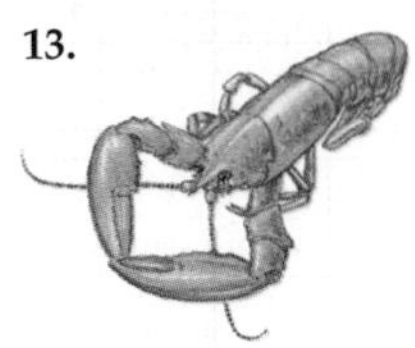

14. 

Answers to Assessment

1 *Answers will vary but may include:*
1. un poivron rouge
2. un champignon
3. un pamplemousse
4. un citron
5. Le thym

2
6. d
7. c
8. b
9. a

3
10. un couvercle
11. une casserole
12. un rôti
13. un homard
14. des huîtres

Structure

4 Complétez avec le futur.

15. Je ___ au chef. (parler)
16. Il me ___ la recette. (lire)
17. Vous ___ à faire le plat? (apprendre)
18. On ___ un plat pas trop compliqué. (choisir)

To review the future tense, turn to page 182.

5 Répondez avec des pronoms.

19. Il te donnera la recette?
20. Elle va me préparer les champignons?

To review using pronouns, turn to page 185.

6 Complétez.

21. Moi, je ne répare pas l'évier. Je ___ l'évier.
22. Elle ne prépare pas le dîner. Elle ___ le dîner.

To review *faire* + an infinitive, turn to page 187.

Culture

7 Choisissez la région.

l'Alsace la Provence la Bourgogne la Normandie

23. Sa cuisine utilise beaucoup de fines herbes et d'épices.
24. La choucroute y est un plat très apprécié.
25. Beaucoup de ses recettes sont à base de crème et de beurre.

To review this cultural information, turn to pages 192–193.

Le marais vernier en Normandie

Glencoe Technology

MINDJOGGER

You may wish to help your students prepare for the chapter test by playing the MindJogger game show. Teams will compete against each other to review chapter vocabulary and structure and sharpen listening comprehension skills.

Answers to Assessment

4

15. parlerai
16. lira
17. apprendrez
18. choisira

5

19. Oui, il me la donnera.
20. Oui, elle va me les préparer.

6

21. fais réparer
22. fait préparer

7

23. la Provence
24. l'Alsace
25. la Normandie

Vocabulary Review

The words and phrases in the **Vocabulaire** have been taught for productive use in this chapter. They are summarized here as a resource for both student and teacher. This list also serves as a convenient resource for the **C'est à vous** activities on pages 198–199. There are approximately sixteen cognates in this vocabulary list. Have students find them.

Attention!

You will notice that the vocabulary list here is not translated. This has been done intentionally, since we feel that by the time students have finished the material in the chapter they should be familiar with the meanings of all the words. If there are several words they still do not know, we recommend that they refer to the **Mots 1** and **2** sections in the chapter or go to the dictionaries at the back of this book to find the meanings. However, if you prefer that your students have the English translations, please refer to Vocabulary Transparency 6.1, where you will find these words listed with their translations.

Vocabulaire

Identifying some kitchen appliances and utensils

la cuisine
une cuisinière
un congé(lateur)
un réfrigérateur
un frigidaire, un frigo
un four
(à micro-ondes)
une poêle
une casserole
un couvercle

Talking about some cooking procedures

faire la cuisine
faire cuire
faire bouillir
éplucher
hacher
couper
râper
ajouter
remuer
verser
une rondelle
un morceau
une recette
un plat

How well do you know your vocabulary?

- Choose words from the list and describe a meal you would like to serve.
- Describe as many steps in the preparation of the meal as you can.

Identifying more foods

un aliment
un légume
un poivron rouge
un oignon
une gousse d'ail
un champignon
une pomme de terre
un haricot vert
un fruit
un citron
une orange
un pamplemousse
du raisin
une herbe
des fines herbes
du persil
du laurier
du thym
de l'huile *(f.)* d'olive
des pâtes *(f. pl.)*
de la choucroute
une sauce
la viande
une saucisse
le bœuf
le veau
le porc
l'agneau *(m.)*
une côtelette
un rôti
un gigot
un poisson
un filet de sole
du saumon
des fruits *(m. pl.)* de mer
un homard
une moule
un crabe
une huître

Other useful words and expressions

à feu vif
à feu doux
bouillant(e)

Technotour

BON VOYAGE!

VIDÉO • Épisode 6

Avant de visionner

In this video episode, Manu reveals his cooking secrets to a surprised Vincent.

Vincent et Manu parlent dans la cuisine.

Vincent croit qu'il va être malade.

FRENCH ONLINE

À découvrir

Learn more about French cuisine online.

Le chef Patrick Terrieu au Cordon Bleu à Paris

In the Chapter 6 Internet activity, you will have a chance to learn more about food in the Francophone world. To begin your virtual adventure, go to the Glencoe French Web site: **french.glencoe.com**

Overview

This page previews two key multimedia components of the **Glencoe French** series. Each reinforces the material taught in the chapter in a unique manner.

VIDÉO

The Video Program allows students to see how the chapter vocabulary and structures are used by native speakers. For maximum reinforcement, show the video episode as a final activity for Chapter 6.

The two photos on the left show highlights from the Chapter 6 video episode. Discuss the photos with your students before having them view the episode. See the Video Activities Booklet for detailed suggestions for using this resource.

- The **À découvrir** photo on page 203 shows the **Cordon Bleu** cooking school. Students can go online to learn more about French cuisine.
- Teacher Information and Student Worksheets for this activity can be accessed at the Web site.

Video Synopsis

In this video episode, Manu has prepared a special dinner for Mme Chentouf's birthday. Vincent is impressed until Manu reveals some of his cooking shortcuts. Like many French people today, he prepares frozen and canned foods and relies on the microwave rather than the stove. For a look at more traditional French cooking, the video takes us to the **Cordon Bleu** cooking school.

Planning for Chapter 7

SCOPE AND SEQUENCE, PAGES 204–235

Topics

- Cars and driving
- Giving directions

Culture

- Driving in France
- Tunisian adventure
- **Reflets du Maghreb**

Functions

- How to talk about what would happen
- How to describe future events
- How to refer to something already mentioned

Structure

- The conditional tense
- The future and conditional of irregular verbs
- Clauses with **si**
- Two pronouns in the same sentence

National Standards

- Communication Standard 1.1 pages 208, 209, 213, 215, 218, 219, 220, 221, 223, 230
- Communication Standard 1.2 pages 208, 209, 212, 213, 215, 217, 218, 219, 220, 221, 222, 225, 227, 229
- Communication Standard 1.3 pages 208, 209, 213, 215, 219, 223, 230, 231
- Cultures Standard 2.1 pages 206, 213, 217, 224–225, 226–227, 228–229
- Cultures Standard 2.2 pages 206, 224–225, 226–227
- Connections Standard 3.1 pages 226–227, 228–229
- Comparisons Standard 4.2 page 206
- Communities Standard 5.1 page 231

PACING AND PRIORITIES

The chapter content is color coded below to assist you in planning.

■ **required** ■ **recommended** ■ **optional**

Vocabulaire *(required)* *Days 1–4*

- ■ Mots 1
  - La voiture
  - À la station-service
- ■ Mots 2
  - En ville
  - Sur la route

Structure *(required)* *Days 5–7*

- ■ Le conditionnel
- ■ Le futur et le conditionnel des verbes irréguliers
- ■ Les propositions introduites par **si**
- ■ Deux pronoms dans la même phrase

Conversation *(required)*

- ■ À la station-service

Lectures culturelles

- ■ La conduite en France *(recommended)*
- ■ Partez à l'aventure en Tunisie! *(optional)*

Connexions *(optional)*

- ■ L'écologie

■ **C'est à vous** *(recommended)*

■ **Assessment** *(recommended)*

■ **Technotour** *(optional)*

RESOURCE GUIDE

Section	Pages	Section Resources
Vocabulaire *Mots 1*		
La voiture	206–207	Vocabulary Transparencies 7.2–7.3
À la station-service	207–209	Audiocassette 5A/CD 5
		Audio Activities Booklet TE, pages 69–71
		Workbook, pages 73–74
		Quiz 1, page 31
		ExamView Pro®
Vocabulaire *Mots 2*		
En ville	210	Vocabulary Transparencies 7.4–7.5
Sur la route	211–213	Audiocassette 5A/CD 5
		Audio Activities Booklet TE, pages 72–73
		Workbook, pages 75–76
		Quiz 2, page 32
		ExamView Pro®
Structure		
Le conditionnel	214–215	Audiocassette 5A/CD 5
Le futur et le conditionnel des verbes irréguliers	216–218	Audio Activities Booklet TE, pages 74–75
		Workbook, pages 77–79
Les propositions introduites par **si**	218–219	Quizzes 3–6, pages 33–36
Deux pronoms dans la même phrase	220–221	ExamView Pro®
Conversation		
À la station-service	222–223	Audiocassette 5A/CD 5
		Audio Activities Booklet TE, pages 76–77
		CD-ROM
Lectures culturelles		
La conduite en France	224–225	Audiocassette 5A/CD 5
Partez à l'aventure en Tunisie!	226–227	Audio Activities Booklet TE, pages 77–78
		Test Booklet, Chapter 7
Connexions		
L'écologie	228–229	Test Booklet, Chapter 7
C'est à vous		
	230–231	**Bon voyage!** Video, Episode 7
		Video Activities Booklet, Chapter 7
		French Online Activities french.glencoe.com
Assessment		
	232–233	Communication Transparency C 7
		Quizzes 1–6, pages 31–36
		Test Booklet, Chapter 7
		ExamView Pro®
		Situation Cards, Chapter 7
		Performance Assessment, pages 9–14
		Marathon mental Videoquiz

Using Your Resources for Chapter 7

Transparencies

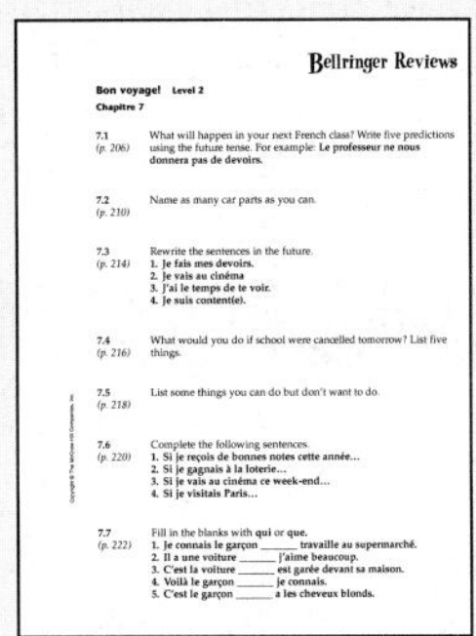

Bellringer Reviews

Bon voyage! Level 2
Chapitre 7

7.1 *(p. 206)* What will happen in your next French class? Write five predictions using the future tense. For example: **Le professeur ne nous donnera pas de devoirs.**

7.2 *(p. 210)* Name as many car parts as you can.

7.3 *(p. 214)* Rewrite the sentences in the future.
1. **Je fais mes devoirs.**
2. **Je vais au cinéma**
3. **J'ai le temps de te voir.**
4. **Je suis content(e).**

7.4 *(p. 216)* What would you do if school were cancelled tomorrow? List five things.

7.5 *(p. 218)* List some things you can do but don't want to do.

7.6 *(p. 220)* Complete the following sentences.
1. **Si je reçois de bonnes notes cette année...**
2. **Si je gagnais à la loterie...**
3. **Si je vais au cinéma ce week-end...**
4. **Si je visitais Paris...**

7.7 *(p. 222)* Fill in the blanks with **qui** or **que.**
1. **Je connais le garçon ______ travaille au supermarché.**
2. **Il a une voiture ______ j'aime beaucoup.**
3. **C'est la voiture ______ est garée devant sa maison.**
4. **Voilà le garçon ______ je connais.**
5. **C'est le garçon ______ a les cheveux blonds.**

Bellringer 7.1–7.9

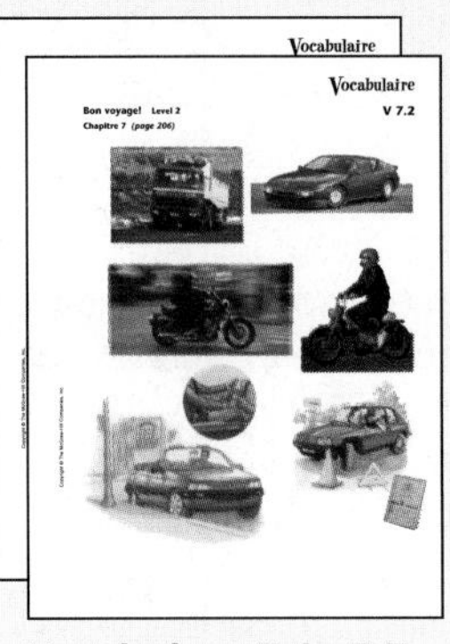

Vocabulaire V 7.2

Bon voyage! Level 2
Chapitre 7 (page 206)

Vocabulary 7.1–7.5

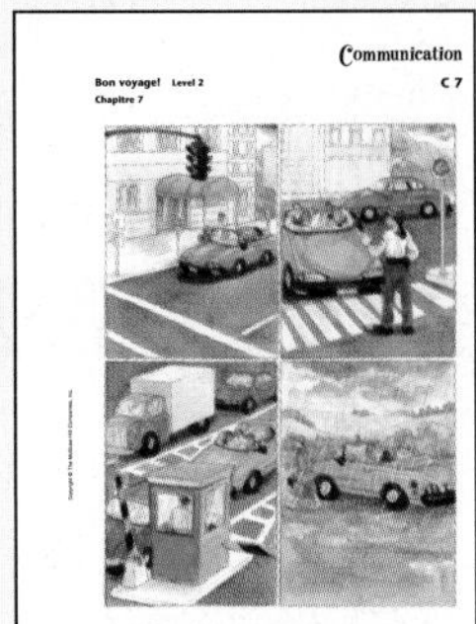

Communication C 7

Bon voyage! Level 2
Chapitre 7

Communication C 7

Writing Activities Workbook

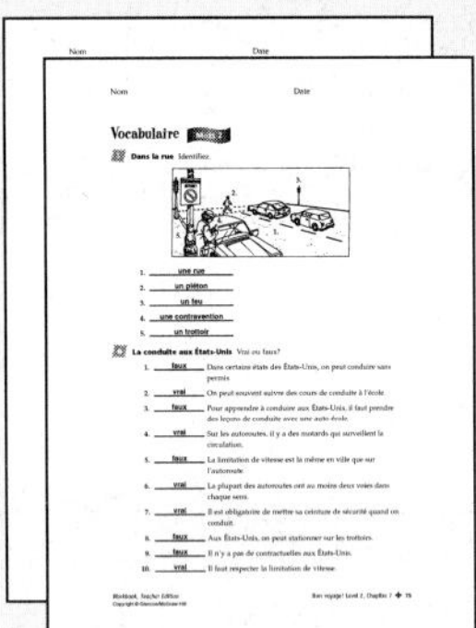

Vocabulary, pages 73–76

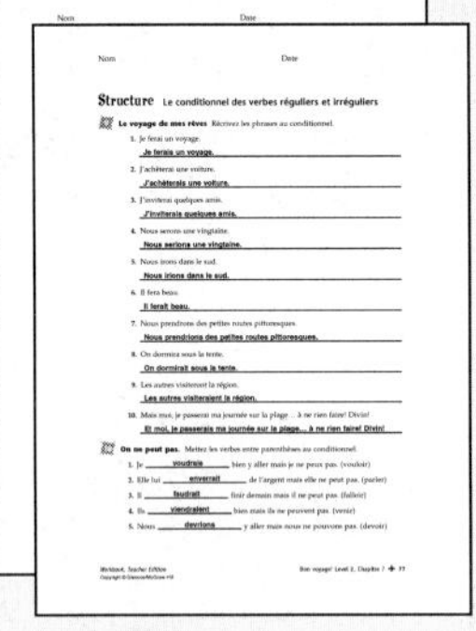

Structure, pages 77–79

Enrichment, pages 80–82

Audio Program and Audio Activities Booklet

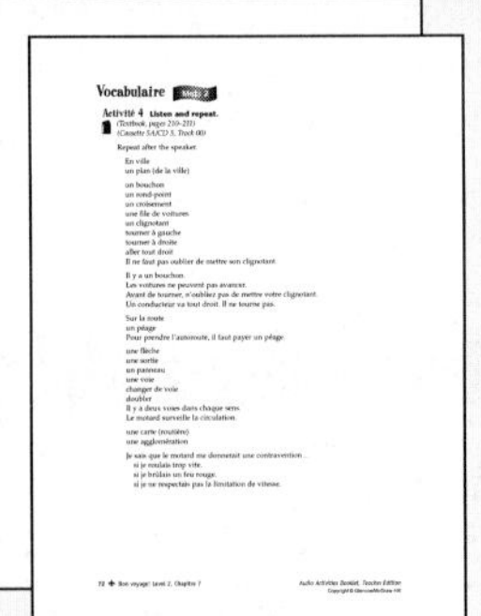

Vocabulary, pages 69–73

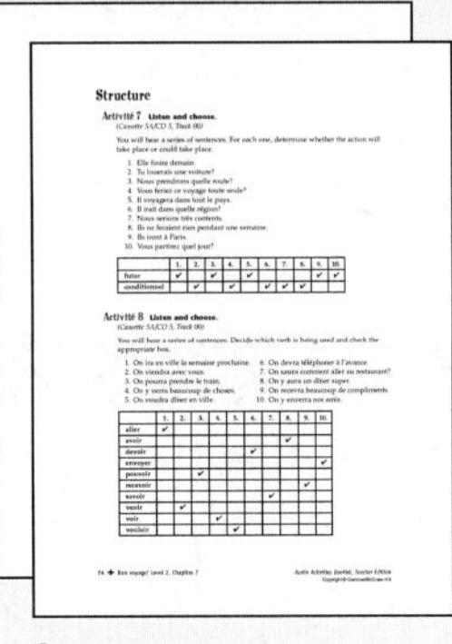

Structure, pages 74–75

Conversation, pages 76–77

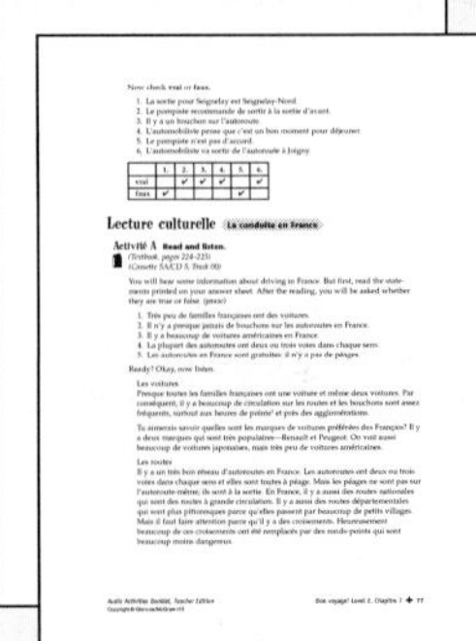

Cultural Reading, pages 77–78

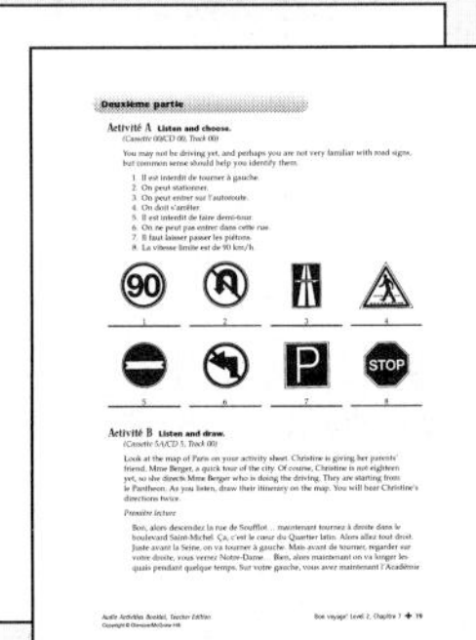

Additional Practice, pages 79–80

Assessment

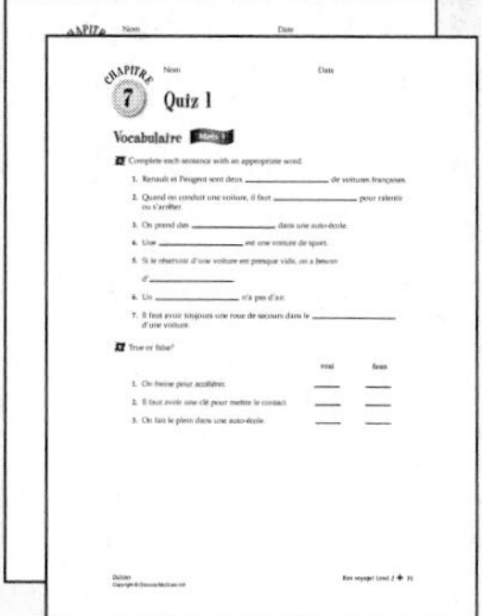

Vocabulary and Structure Quizzes, pages 31–36

Chapter Tests, Chapter 7

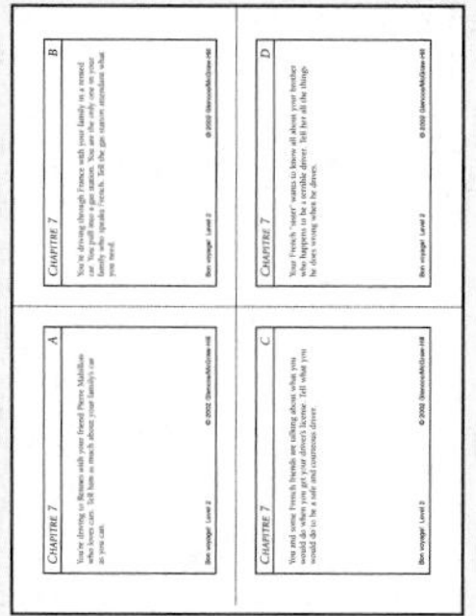

Situation Cards, Chapter 7

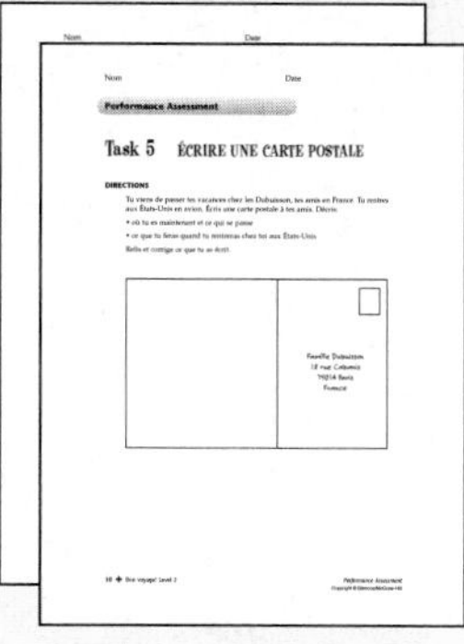

Performance Assessment, pages 9–14

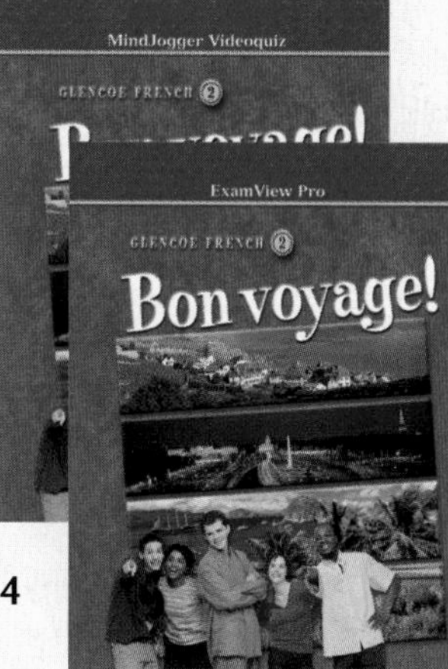

Timesaving Teacher Tools

Interactive Teacher Edition

Imagine having your Teacher's Edition and all resources on a CD-ROM. Click on a resource and it appears on your screen, ready to be printed, sorted, or planned.

Interactive Lesson Planner

The Interactive Lesson Planner CD-ROM helps you organize your lesson plans for a week, month, semester, or year. Look at this planning tool for easy access to your Chapter 7 resources.

ExamView Pro®

Test Bank software for Macintosh and Windows makes creating, editing, customizing, and printing tests quick and easy.

Technology Resources

In the Chapter 7 Internet activity, you will have a chance to learn more about traveling by car in France. Visit french.glencoe.com.

On the Interactive Conversation CD-ROM, students can listen to and take part in a recorded version of the conversation in Chapter 7.

See the National Geographic Teacher's Corner on pages 138–139, 244–245, 372–373, 472–473 for reference to additional technology resources.

Bon voyage! Video and Video Activities Booklet.

Help your students prepare for the chapter test by playing the **Marathon mental** Videoquiz game show. Teams will compete against each other to review chapter vocabulary and structure and sharpen listening comprehension skills.

CHAPITRE 7

Preview

In this chapter, students will learn to talk about cars, roads, and driving. They will learn vocabulary associated with different types of cars, gas station services, and city and highway driving. Students will also increase their communication skills by learning the conditional, the future forms of irregular verbs, how to form sentences with direct object pronouns and **lui** or **leur,** and clauses with **si.**

National Standards

Communication
In Chapter 7, students will communicate in spoken and written French on the following topics:

- Cars and driving
- Giving directions
- Road travel in France

Students will obtain and provide information about these topics and engage in conversations that would typically take place when driving as they fulfill the chapter objectives listed on this page.

Spotlight on Culture

Photograph In this photo we see le château d'Ussé, which is on the banks of the Indre River, about 1 kilometer south of the Loire. The château was built in the fifteenth and sixteenth centuries on the site of an old medieval fortress.

In 1807 the château was bought by the Duc et Duchesse de Duras. The Duchesse was a friend of the novelist Chateaubriand, who wrote most of the novel ***Les mémoires d'outre tombe*** at this château.

CHAPITRE 7

La voiture et la route

Objectifs
In this chapter you will learn to:

- *talk about cars and driving*
- *give directions on the road*
- *talk about what would happen under certain conditions*
- *describe future events*
- *refer to something already mentioned*
- *talk about driving and highways in France*

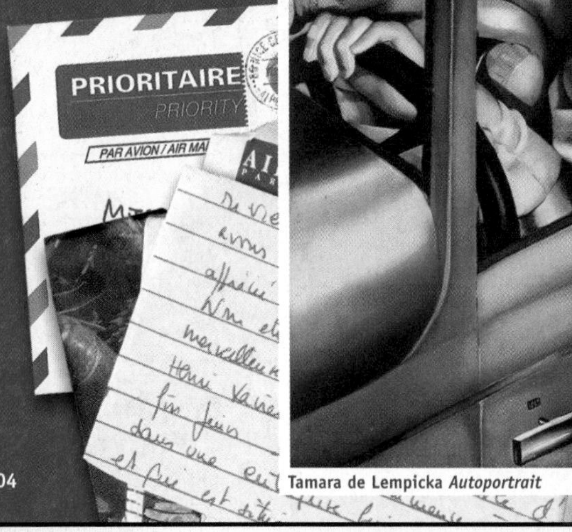

Tamara de Lempicka *Autoportrait*

204

The **Glencoe Foreign Language Web site** (french.glencoe.com) offers several options that enable you and your students to experience the French-speaking world via the Internet:

- The online **Activités** are correlated to the chapters and utilize Francophone Web sites around the world. For the Chapter 7 activity, see student page 235.
- Games and puzzles afford students another opportunity to practice the material learned in a particular chapter.
- The *Enrichment* section offers students an opportunity to visit Web sites related to the theme of the chapter for more information on a particular topic.
- Online *Chapter Quizzes* offer students an opportunity to prepare for a chapter test.
- Visit our virtual **Café** for more opportunities to practice and explore the French-speaking world.

Parlons un peu plus
Let's talk some more

A **En voyage** Travaillez avec un(e) camarade. Vous êtes sur la route. L'un(e) de vous conduit, l'autre regarde la carte ci-dessous et donne des instructions. Choisissez d'abord un itinéraire. Ensuite choisissez un deuxième itinéraire et changez de rôle.

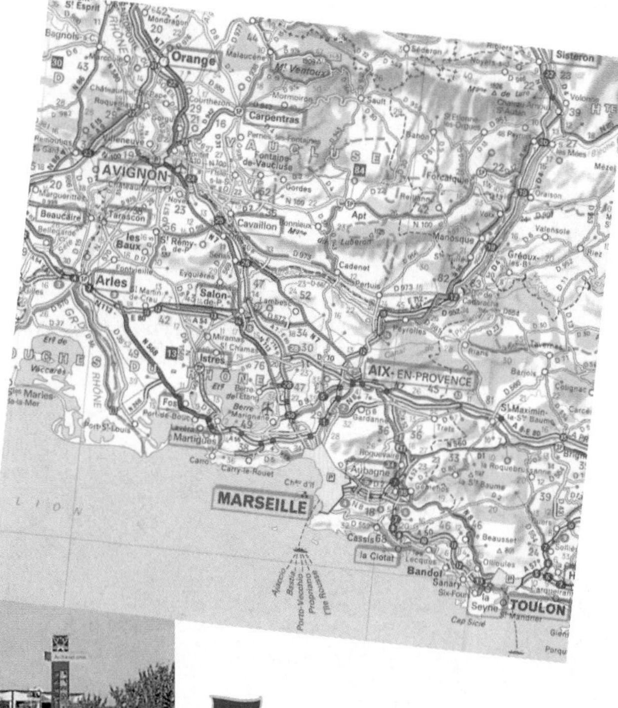

Un restoroute près de Beaune

B **Au restaurant** Travaillez avec un(e) camarade. Vous êtes sur l'autoroute en France. Vous décidez de vous arrêter pour faire le plein et prendre quelque chose au restoroute. Ensemble, parlez de tout ce que vous allez faire.

3 Practice

Parlons un peu plus
Let's talk some more

These activities enable students to use the vocabulary and structures learned in the chapter in open-ended exchanges. You may wish to assign different activities to different groups or allow the students to choose the activities they wish to do.

A **Expansion:** You may wish to also use local area maps to do this activity a second time.

Learning from Photos

(page 223) French autoroutes have rest stops with gas stations, restrooms, and restaurants or snack bars, just like U.S. expressways and turnpikes.

Answers to Parlons un peu plus

A and B *Answers will vary.*

Students will do these activities expressing their own ideas using vocabulary that for the most part comes from this chapter.

Resource Manager

Audio Activities Booklet TE, pages 77–78
Audiocassette 5A/CD 5

Bellringer Review

Use BRR Transparency 7.8 or write the following on the board.
Make two lists: one of good driving habits, the other of bad ones.

Presentation

Pre-reading

Step 1 Ask how many students have their license.

Step 2 Discuss the highways and secondary roads in your area. Are there toll roads? Do you have traffic circles?

Reading

Step 1 Have students read the **Lecture** silently. Allow five minutes. Encourage them to read for the main ideas and important details only. Tell them they will have a chance to reread.

Step 2 Call on an individual to read several sentences. Then ask other students questions about the sentences the student has just read.

Geography Connection

Beaune is the capital of the region known as the **Côte de Beaune** where one finds the famous vineyards of Burgundy.

Le Québec

Lectures culturelles

Reading Strategy

Summarizing
When you read passages, you may want to develop a strategy for remembering the material, especially if the topic is new to you. Summarizing will help you retain what you read. Take notes as you read. From your notes, write a sentence about each section of the reading. These sentences will help you recall the information in each section. Then write one sentence that summarizes the main idea of the selection.

La conduite en France  

Les voitures

Presque toutes les familles françaises ont une voiture et même deux voitures. Par conséquent, il y a beaucoup de circulation sur les routes et les bouchons sont assez fréquents, surtout aux heures de pointe[1] et près des agglomérations.

Tu aimerais savoir quelles sont les marques de voitures préférées des Français? Il y a deux marques qui sont très populaires—Renault et Peugeot. On voit aussi beaucoup de voitures japonaises, mais très peu de voitures américaines.

Les routes

Il y a un très bon réseau[2] d'autoroutes en France. Les autoroutes ont deux ou trois voies dans chaque sens et elles sont toutes à péage. Mais les péages ne sont pas sur l'autoroute même; ils sont à la sortie. En France, il y a aussi des routes nationales qui sont des routes à grande circulation. Il y a aussi des routes départementales qui sont plus pittoresques parce qu'elles passent par beaucoup de petits villages. Mais il faut faire attention parce qu'il y a des croisements. Heureusement beaucoup de ces croisements ont été remplacés par des ronds-points qui sont beaucoup moins dangereux.

L'autoroute A 31 près de Beaune

[1] heures de pointe *rush hours*
[2] réseau *network*

National Standards

Cultures
This reading familiarizes students with driving in France.

Comparisons
Students learn that French teenagers must be 18 before they can get a license to drive a car, but that many teenagers drive mopeds at 16.

Learning from Photos

(page 225) Tell students that the beautiful tree-lined road in the photo is very typical of France. Plane trees **(les platanes)** often form an arch over the road. The trees grow in temperate regions of the northern hemisphere, particularly in Europe. A species that grows in North America is called the buttonwood or sycamore tree.

En France, comme partout[3], il faut respecter la limitation de vitesse. Sur les routes, il y a beaucoup de motards. Si tu roules trop vite, ils te donneront une contravention.

Le permis de conduire

En France, pour passer son permis de conduire, il faut avoir dix-huit ans. Si tu habitais en France, tu pourrais avoir un permis de conduire? Beaucoup de jeunes Français ont un vélomoteur. Mais leur rêve[4], c'est d'avoir une moto. On peut conduire une moto à partir de seize ans avec un permis spécial moto. Et le casque est obligatoire. Si tu habitais en France, tu aimerais avoir une moto?

[3] partout *everywhere else*
[4] rêve *dream*

Une route pittoresque à Melun en France

Après la lecture

A Les voitures Vrai ou faux?

1. Très peu de familles françaises ont des voitures.
2. Il n'y a presque jamais de bouchons sur les autoroutes en France.
3. Il y a beaucoup de voitures américaines en France.
4. La plupart des autoroutes ont deux ou trois voies dans chaque sens.
5. Les autoroutes en France sont gratuites; il n'y a pas de péages.

B La conduite Répondez.

1. Les bouchons sont fréquents où et quand?
2. Les routes départementales sont plus pittoresques que les autoroutes. Pourquoi?
3. Qui surveille la circulation sur les autoroutes?
4. Qu'est-ce que les motards donnent aux automobilistes qui ne respectent pas la limitation de vitesse?
5. Il faut avoir quel âge pour passer son permis de conduire en France? Et là où tu habites?
6. Tu pourrais avoir une moto si tu habitais en France? Et là où tu habites?

ANSWERS TO  Après la lecture

A

1. faux
2. faux
3. faux
4. vrai
5. faux

B *Answers will vary but may include:*

1. Les bouchons sont fréquents aux heures de pointe et près des agglomérations.
2. Parce qu'elles passent par beaucoup de petits villages.
3. Les motards surveillent la circulation sur les autoroutes.
4. Ils leur donnent une contravention.
5. Il faut avoir 18 ans pour passer son permis de conduire en France. Où j'habite il faut avoir ____ ans pour passer son permis de conduire.
6. Oui, je pourrais avoir une moto si j'habitais en France. Où j'habite je (ne) pourrais (pas) avoir une moto.

Lectures culturelles

Cross-Cultural Comparison

In France, the minimum age requirement for driving various types of vehicles is the same throughout the entire country. In the United States, it varies from state to state.

- **Un cyclomoteur (une sorte de bicyclette avec un petit moteur): 14 ans**
- **Un vélomoteur: 16 ans**
- **Une moto: 16 ans**
- **Une voiture: 18 ans**

Student drivers must learn many things besides driving: the names of engine parts, how to change a flat tire, etc. All of this is part of the very difficult test to get a driver's license.

You may wish to give students the following information about the French police.

Le gendarme est toujours sur la route.

L'agent de police règle la circulation dans les villes. Il aide les gens à trouver leur chemin. Et il oblige tout le monde à respecter la loi.

Un C.R.S. (Compagnie républicaine de sécurité) porte un uniforme de combat. S'il y a une manifestation, le C.R.S. défend l'ordre public.

La police nationale dépend du ministère de l'Intérieur. La gendarmerie nationale est une force militaire et dépend du ministère de la Défense.

Most drivers fear the **motards,** motorcycle police officers. The **motards** mean business when they stop speeding motorists. They ride powerful motorcycles and dress to allow a minimum of friction while on a speed chase. Some **motards** wear egg-shaped helmets to reduce air drag.

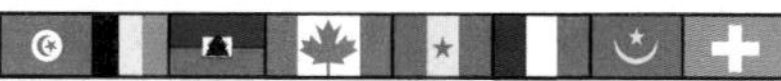

National Standards

Cultures
This reading familiarizes students with two desert villages in Tunisia.

Attention!

This reading is optional. You may skip it completely, have the entire class read it, have only several students read it and report to the class, or assign it for extra credit.

Presentation

Step 1 Have students read the passage quickly as they look at the photos that accompany it.

History Connection

The oasis at Tozeur is watered by six thermal springs that were originally tapped by the Romans. Nefta, with its 220,000 palms, is an artificial oasis, made possible by the boring of 2,100-foot wells in the 1960s. The oasis at Nefta is shown in the photo on this page.

Lecture supplémentaire

Partez à l'aventure en Tunisie!

Dans le désert saharien du sud de la Tunisie, il y a deux villages très intéressants—Nefta et Tozeur. Là où on ne voit que les dunes et le sable du désert, se trouvent ces deux villages, pleins de végétation et de verdure[1]. À l'entrée de Nefta, une large avenue bordée d'eucalyptus vous souhaite la bienvenue. Ici, le désert cède la place à des oasis où des sources[2] d'eau sortent du sable. Nefta compte 150 sources d'eau chaude et plus de 300 000 palmiers. C'est à Nefta qu'on cultive les deglas—les dattes réputées être les plus délicieuses du monde.

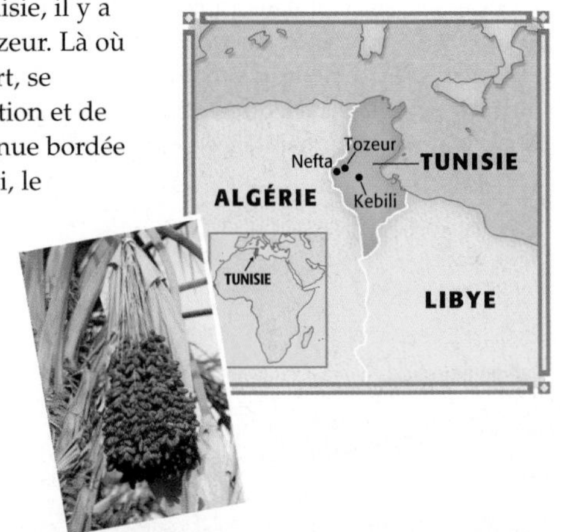

[1] verdure *greenery*
[2] sources *springs*

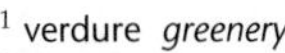

L'oasis de Nefta en Tunisie

Pas loin de Nefta, on trouve Tozeur—un village de 15 000 habitants et 250 000 palmiers. Les maisons de Tozeur sont d'une jolie couleur marron-rouge. On fait les briques de ces maisons avec le sable du désert. Les briques de la façade des maisons forment de très jolis dessins géométriques.

Si tu es courageux, et si tu veux faire un voyage extraordinaire, tu dois traverser le chott el-Djerid de Tozeur à Kebili—une distance de 90 kilomètres. Un chott, c'est un ancien lac salé[3], mais l'eau du lac s'est évaporée et il reste seulement une croûte de sel sèche et dure[4]. L'après-midi, l'air est chauffé[5] par le soleil et le sel brûlant[6]. Il déforme alors le paysage. On croit voir des îles, des palmiers et des villages où rien n'existe. Quelle sensation extraordinaire que de voir un mirage! Ces mirages ont égaré[7] beaucoup de caravanes de Bédouins[8] qui circulaient dans le désert. Alors, allez-y! Partez à l'aventure!

[3] salé *salt*
[4] sèche et dure *dry and hard*
[5] chauffé *heated*
[6] brûlant *burning*
[7] ont égaré *led astray*
[8] Bédouins *Bedouins (nomadic Arab tribes)*

Une rue à Tozeur

Des Bédouins dans le Sahara en Tunisie

Après la lecture

A Descriptions Décrivez.

1. Nefta
2. Tozeur
3. le chott el-Djerid

B Qu'est-ce que c'est?
Expliquez les mots suivants.

1. une oasis
2. un désert
3. une deglas
4. un chott

Learning from Photos

(page 227 top) Both Nefta and Tozeur, which are quite close to one another, appear to spring out of nowhere in the undulating desert. The people of Nefta and Tozeur take the sand of the desert to make bricks, which they mold into geometric patterns when building their homes.

Geography Connection

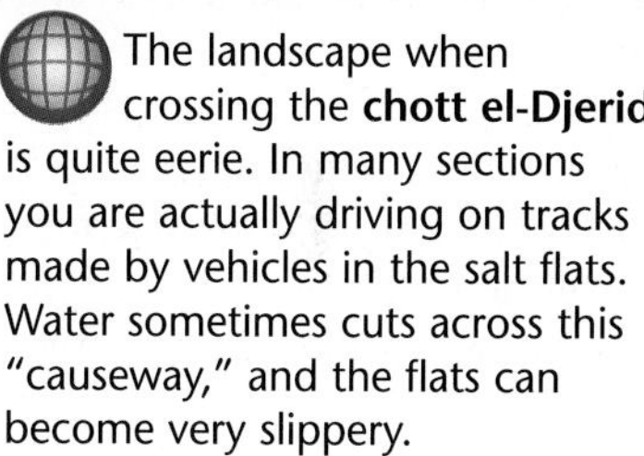

The landscape when crossing the **chott el-Djerid** is quite eerie. In many sections you are actually driving on tracks made by vehicles in the salt flats. Water sometimes cuts across this "causeway," and the flats can become very slippery.

Après la lecture

Go over the **Après la lecture** activities on page 227.

Answers to Après la lecture

A *Answers will vary but may include:*

1. Nefta est un village du Sahara. Ce village a 150 sources d'eau chaude et plus de 300 000 palmiers. On cultive des dattes à Nefta.
2. Tozeur est un village du Sahara. Ce village a 250 000 palmiers et 15 000 habitants. À Tozeur on fait les maisons avec des briques de sable.
3. Le chott el-Djerid est un ancien lac salé où l'eau s'est évaporée.

B *Answers will vary but may include:*

1. Une oasis est un lieu dans le désert où on trouve de l'eau et beaucoup de végétation.
2. Un désert est une région où il y a des dunes et du sable.
3. Une deglas est une datte.
4. Un chott est un ancien lac salé où l'eau s'est évaporée.

National Standards

Connections
This reading about air pollution establishes a connection with another discipline, allowing students to reinforce and further their knowledge of ecology through the study of French.

Attention!

The readings in the **Connexions** section are optional. They focus on some of the major disciplines taught in schools and universities. The vocabulary is useful for discussing such topics as history, literature, art, economics, business, science, etc. You may choose any of the following ways to do the readings in the **Connexions** sections.

Independent reading Have students read the selections and do the post-reading activities as homework, which you collect. This option is least intrusive on class time and requires a minimum of teacher involvement.

Homework with in-class follow-up Assign the readings and post-reading activities as homework. Review and discuss the material in class the next day.

Intensive in-class activity This option includes a pre-reading vocabulary presentation, in-class reading and discussion, assignment of the activities for homework, and a discussion of the assignment in class the following day.

CONNEXIONS

Les sciences

L'écologie

Ecology is a subject of great interest and concern to people around the world. People are increasingly aware of how pollution damages the environment. The automobile is a primary cause of air pollution. Recently, the French teen magazine *Phosphore* interviewed some students from different areas of France. They were asked whether cars should be banned. Let's see what they had to say.

Faut-il interdire les voitures?

Sylvain: 24 ans, étudiant en informatique à Paris, circule à vélo

Claire: 18 ans, étudiante à Marseille, circule à pied et en transports en commun

Nicolas: 21 ans, étudiant en économie à Nice, circule à pied et en voiture

Trouvez-vous qu'il y a trop de voitures dans votre ville? Est-ce que vous souffrez de la pollution automobile?

Sylvain: Oui, je trouve que les voitures sont dangereuses à Paris. Je vois souvent des automobilistes énervés qui ne respectent pas les limitations de vitesse, les feux… De plus, je ressens[1] la pollution dans ma chair[2], elle m'irrite comme la fumée[3], je sens que l'air n'est pas pur. Je ne ressens pas ça en province et à la campagne.

[1] ressens *feel*
[2] chair *flesh*
[3] fumée *smoke*

Nicolas: Moi, je prends la voiture assez souvent pour aller dans le centre ou pour sortir. Mais pour trouver des places de parking, c'est toujours la galère[4]! Je n'ai jamais vraiment souffert de la pollution, même si je suis asthmatique. Sauf une fois, quand j'étais à Paris sur les Champs-Élysées. Je n'arrivais plus à respirer. Paris, c'est

[4] c'est la galère *it's a real hassle*

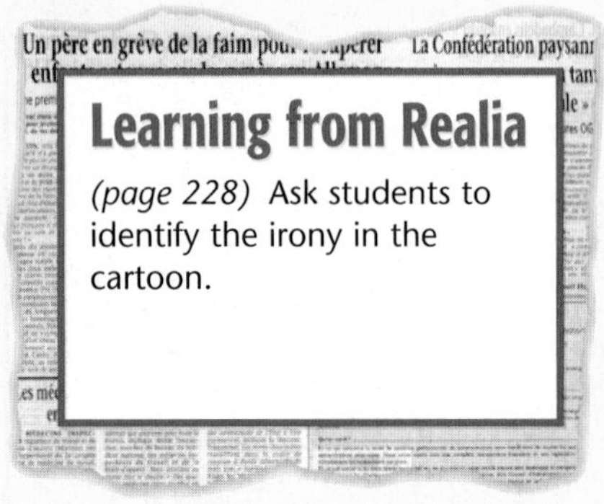

Learning from Realia

(page 228) Ask students to identify the irony in the cartoon.

vraiment pollué. À Nice, la situation est en progrès. La municipalité a mis en place des bus au gaz naturel. C'est vraiment agréable.

Claire: Non, à Marseille, le mistral[5] chasse vite la pollution. Mais la situation est catastrophique dans des villes comme Mexico, par exemple.

Si vous aviez le choix entre la voiture et un mode de transport moins polluant, est-ce que vous adopteriez ce dernier par civisme[6]?

[5] mistral *mistral, strong cold wind*
[6] civisme *civic duty*

Sylvain: Il est normal que, si j'ai une opinion, je l'applique à moi-même. Mais je ne le fais pas par civisme. Un mode de transport moins polluant serait aussi plus agréable.

Claire: Je ne sais pas. Je vais au lycée en bus ou à pied. Mais la voiture, c'est important pour sortir et aller travailler. Ça dépend où on habite.

Nicolas: Il faut améliorer[7] les transports en commun[8]. Dans ce cas, je serais prêt[9].

[7] améliorer *to improve*
[8] transports en commun *mass transit*
[9] prêt *ready*

Après la lecture

A Un résumé Préparez un résumé des réponses des jeunes Français à la première question de l'interview.

B Recherches Faites des recherches sur les nouveaux moyens de propulsion des voitures (voitures électriques et voitures au gaz GPL).

Presentation

Les sciences
L'écologie

Note: You may wish to have all students scan this selection quickly. The topic is of great interest today and the reading selection is quite easy.

Step 1 Have students read the introduction in English on page 228.

Step 2 Have students scan the reading for cognates. Then have them do the reading again, this time for comprehension.

About the French Language

You may wish to point out to students that the inverted question format is almost always used in interview questions: **Faut-il interdire les voitures?**

Answers to Après la lecture

A *Answers will vary but may include:*

Sylvain trouve qu'il y a trop de voitures à Paris. Il y a beaucoup de pollution.

Nicolas ne dit pas qu'il y a trop de voitures à Nice. Mais il n'y a pas assez de places de parking. Il n'a pas souffert de la pollution.

Claire dit qu'il n'y a pas de pollution à Marseille à cause du mistral.

B *Students will research the topic.*

C'est à vous

Use what you have learned

Bellringer Review

Use BRR Transparency 7.9 or write the following on the board.
Write the opposite of each term.
accélérer
stationner
tourner à gauche
brûler un feu rouge
prudemment
plein

Recycling

These activities allow students to use the vocabulary and structure from this chapter in completely open-ended, real-life situations.

Presentation

Encourage students to say as much as possible when they do these activities. Tell them not to be afraid to make mistakes, since the goal of these activities is real-life communication. If someone in the group makes an error, allow the others to politely correct him or her. Let students choose the activities they would like to do.

You may wish to divide students into pairs or groups. Encourage students to elaborate on the basic theme and to be creative. They may use props, pictures, or posters if they wish.

1 Tell students that **mener** means *to lead.*

C'est à vous

Use what you have learned

PARLER **1**

Près de chez vous

✔ *Talk about cars and driving*

Avec un(e) camarade, choisissez une ville près de chez vous. Décrivez les routes qui mènent à cette ville. Discutez s'il y a beaucoup de circulation. Quand? Pourquoi?

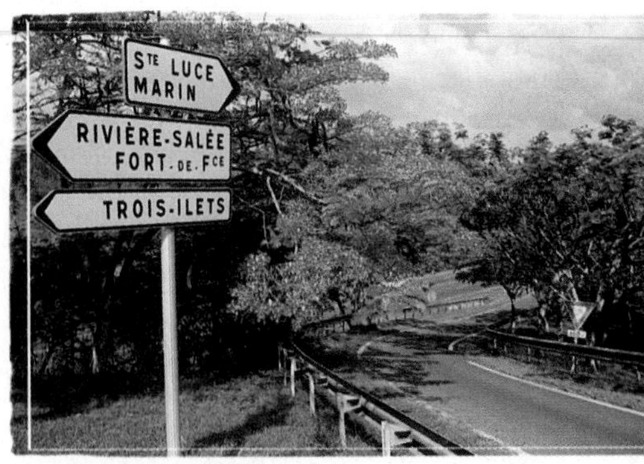

Des panneaux à la Martinique

PARLER **2**

Jeu Attention aux contraventions!

✔ *Talk about driving in France*

Regardez le dessin ci-dessous. Vous êtes un motard et vous donnez une contravention à un(e) des automobilistes (votre camarade) qui ne respecte pas les panneaux.

Answers to C'est à vous

1 *Answers will vary depending on the town or city students choose to describe. They will, however, be able to use the vocabulary presented in this chapter.*

2 *Answers will vary but may include the following problems:*
Vous avez brûlé un feu rouge.
Il est interdit de tourner à droite.
Vous n'avez pas respecté la limitation de vitesse.
Il est interdit de doubler.

BON VOYAGE!

VIDÉO • Épisode 7

Avant de visionner

In this video episode, Christine learns that driving with Mme Séguin can be quite an adventure.

Mme Séguin fait le plein à la station-service.

Elle reçoit une contravention.

FRENCH ONLINE

À découvrir

Learn more about the Paris-Dakar road race online.

Une voiture du rallye Paris-Dakar

In the Chapter 7 Internet activity, you will have a chance to learn more about traveling by car in France. To begin your virtual adventure, go to the Glencoe French Web site: **french.glencoe.com**

Technotour

Overview

This page previews two key multimedia components of the **Glencoe French** series. Each reinforces the material taught in the chapter in a unique manner.

VIDÉO

The Video Program allows students to see how the chapter vocabulary and structures are used by native speakers. For maximum reinforcement, show the video episode as a final activity for Chapter 7.

The two photos on the left show highlights from the Chapter 7 video episode. Discuss the photos with your students before having them view the episode. See the Video Activities Booklet for detailed suggestions for using this resource.

- The **À découvrir** photo on page 235 shows the Paris-Dakar race. Students can go online to learn more about this famous road race.
- Teacher Information and Student Worksheets for this activity can be accessed at the Web site.

Video Synopsis

In this video episode, Mme Séguin is behind the wheel as she and Christine drive to Fontainebleau for a picnic. Mme Séguin's haphazard driving style makes for an eventful trip: they miss the exit for the autoroute, nearly run out of gas, and finally Mme Séguin receives a speeding ticket! We then witness the speed of the Paris-Dakar road race as the video highlights some stages of this difficult course.

Preview

This section reviews the salient points from Chapters 5–7. In the **Conversation,** students will review car and bank vocabulary, as well as the future and conditional. In the **Structure** sections, they will review the future, the conditional, and object pronouns.

Resource Manager

Workbook, Self-Test pages 83–88
Test Booklet

Presentation

Conversation

Step 1 Have students open their books to page 236. Call on two students to read this short conversation aloud.

Step 2 Go over the activity in the **Après la conversation** section.

History Connection

The **banque de France** was created in 1800 and nationalized in 1945. It is the central bank of the country and the bank of the State Treasury.

FUN FACTS

The **Twingo** is a popular, rather inexpensive car. As one can see in this photo, it has the shape of a small station wagon or van. It is manufactured by Renault, and it is available in many vivid colors.

Révision

Conversation

Une voiture

Aurore: On va prendre quelque chose au Sélect?
Jérôme: Désolé, mais j'ai rendez-vous à la banque.
Aurore: Pour quoi faire?
Jérôme: Pour demander un prêt.
Aurore: Tu as besoin d'argent?
Jérôme: Oui, pour acheter une voiture.
Aurore: Ah oui? Qu'est-ce que tu vas acheter?
Jérôme: La vieille Twingo de mon cousin.
Aurore: Tu ne vas pas te ruiner!
Jérôme: Ben si, justement. Je n'ai pas le fric que tu as, moi! Si je l'avais, je n'achèterais pas une vieille Twingo! Ça, tu peux en être sûre!

Après la conversation

Une nouvelle voiture Répondez.

1. Pourquoi est-ce que Jérôme ne peut pas aller au café avec Aurore?
2. Qu'est-ce qu'il va y faire?
3. Pour quoi faire?
4. Il va acheter quelle voiture?
5. D'après Aurore, c'est une voiture chère?
6. Si Jérôme avait de l'argent, il achèterait une vieille Twingo?

Answers to Après la conversation

1. Il a rendez-vous à la banque.
2. Il va demander un prêt.
3. Il va acheter une voiture.
4. Il va acheter la vieille Twingo de son cousin.
5. Non, ce n'est pas une voiture chère.
6. Non, si Jérôme avait de l'argent, il n'achèterait pas une vieille Twingo.

Structure

Le futur et le conditionnel

1. The infinitive of **-er** and **-ir** verbs serves as the stem for the formation of the future and the conditional. Note that with **-re** verbs you drop the final **-e** of the infinitive. As in English, you use the future to express what will happen and the conditional to express what would or could happen under certain circumstances.

LE FUTUR

	PARLER	FINIR	ATTENDRE
Infinitive	parler	finir	attendre
Stem	parler-	finir-	attendr-
	je parlerai tu parleras il/elle/on parlera nous parlerons vous parlerez ils/elles parleront	je finirai tu finiras il/elle/on finira nous finirons vous finirez ils/elles finiront	j' attendrai tu attendras il/elle/on attendra nous attendrons vous attendrez ils/elles attendront

LE CONDITIONNEL

	PARLER	FINIR	ATTENDRE
Infinitive	parler	finir	attendre
Stem	parler-	finir-	attendr-
	je parlerais tu parlerais il/elle/on parlerait nous parlerions vous parleriez ils/elles parleraient	je finirais tu finirais il/elle/on finirait nous finirions vous finiriez ils/elles finiraient	j' attendrais tu attendrais il/elle/on attendrait nous attendrions vous attendriez ils/elles attendraient

CHAPITRES 5–7

Presentation

Le futur et le conditionnel

Step 1 Quickly go over the verb forms that appear here.

Step 2 Have individuals read the verb forms aloud.

Learning from Photos

(page 238) The tropical island of Tahiti in French Polynesia is known for its beautiful, secluded bays.

Have students say three things they would do if they were in Tahiti right now.

Révision

2. The following verbs have an irregular future and conditional stem.

ÊTRE	je serai	je serais
FAIRE	je ferai	je ferais
ALLER	j'irai	j'irais
AVOIR	j'aurai	j'aurais
SAVOIR	je saurai	je saurais
VOIR	je verrai	je verrais
ENVOYER	j'enverrai	j'enverrais
POUVOIR	je pourrai	je pourrais
DEVOIR	je devrai	je devrais
RECEVOIR	je recevrai	je recevrais
VOULOIR	je voudrai	je voudrais
VENIR	je viendrai	je viendrais
FALLOIR	il faudra	il faudrait

3. Review the sequence of tenses with **si** clauses.

Si + Présent → Futur	Si + Imparfait → Conditionnel
Si j'ai assez d'argent, je ferai un voyage.	Si j'avais assez d'argent, je ferais un voyage.

Une baie à Tahiti

1 Un jour!

Répondez d'après le modèle.

voyager beaucoup
Un jour, je voyagerai beaucoup.
Et vous, vous voyagerez beaucoup aussi?

1. gagner beaucoup d'argent
2. aller à Tahiti
3. faire un voyage au Maroc
4. voir les sept merveilles du monde
5. savoir beaucoup de choses
6. pouvoir parler dix langues
7. recevoir le prix Nobel

Answers to Révision

1. Un jour, je gagnerai beaucoup d'argent. Et vous, vous gagnerez beaucoup d'argent aussi?
2. Un jour, j'irai à Tahiti. Et vous, vous irez à Tahiti aussi?
3. Un jour je ferai un voyage au Maroc. Et vous, vous ferez un voyage au Maroc aussi?
4. Un jour, je verrai les sept merveilles du monde. Et vous, vous verrez les sept merveilles du monde aussi?
5. Un jour, je saurai beaucoup de choses. Et vous, vous saurez beaucoup de choses aussi?
6. Un jour, je pourrai parler dix langues. Et vous, vous pourrez parler dix langues?
7. Un jour, je recevrai le prix Nobel. Et vous, vous recevrez le prix Nobel aussi?

Révision

2 Mes amis et moi

Mes amis et moi Répondez en utilisant **Mes amis et moi, on...**

1. Vous aimeriez aller à Washington?
2. Vous iriez en hiver ou au printemps?
3. Vous prendriez l'avion ou le train pour y aller?
4. Vous visiteriez la Maison Blanche?
5. Vous visiteriez les autres monuments de la capitale? Quels monuments?

Washington

PRÉSENTATION
Capitale des États-Unis, Washington est le siège du gouvernement fédéral et d'organisations nationales et internationales.

UN PEU D'HISTOIRE
Dessinée par un ingénieur français: Pierre-Charles L'enfant, la ville a été créée en 1791 dans l'unique but de devenir capitale politique.

QUE VOIR ET QUE FAIRE?
Le Capitole, la Maison Blanche, le cimetière d'Arlington, Lincoln Memorial, Washington Monument et son obélisque, Le Mall et les musées Smithsonian (gratuits).

Petit déjeuner américain. Visite guidée de Washington. Vous passez devant la Maison Blanche, l'édifice de la Cour Suprême, l'obélisque du Washington Monument, le mémorial de Jefferson. Déjeuner dans un restaurant typique. Après-midi libre pour la visite des musées du Smithsonian. Dîner libre.

3 Si on avait 10 000 dollars!

Dites ce que chaque personne ferait.

1. moi
2. mon père
3. mes grands-parents
4. ma sœur
5. toi
6. mes copains et moi
7. vous deux

National Standards

Communities

If any students in the class have been to Washington, D.C., you may wish to have them tell in French what they did or saw.

History Connection

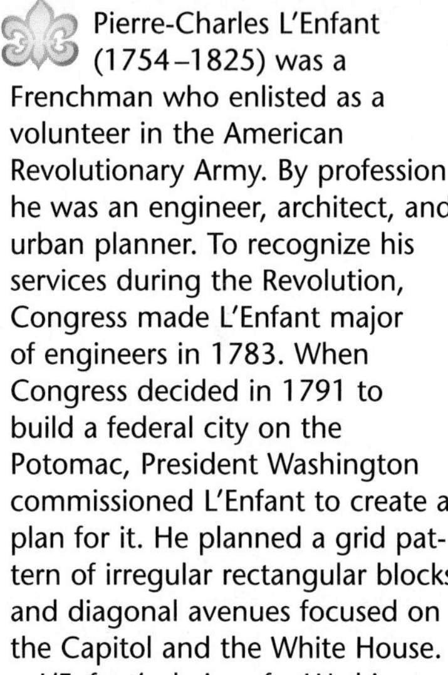

Pierre-Charles L'Enfant (1754–1825) was a Frenchman who enlisted as a volunteer in the American Revolutionary Army. By profession he was an engineer, architect, and urban planner. To recognize his services during the Revolution, Congress made L'Enfant major of engineers in 1783. When Congress decided in 1791 to build a federal city on the Potomac, President Washington commissioned L'Enfant to create a plan for it. He planned a grid pattern of irregular rectangular blocks and diagonal avenues focused on the Capitol and the White House.

L'Enfant's designs for Washington were influenced by the architecture of Paris. The Mall, which goes from the Capitol to the Lincoln Memorial, was intended to be a broad tree-lined avenue similar to the Champs-Élysées.

Answers to Révision

2

1. Mes amis et moi, on aimerait aller à Washington.
2. Mes amis et moi, on irait au printemps.
3. Mes amis et moi, on prendrait l'avion pour y aller.
4. Mes amis et moi, on visiterait la Maison Blanche.
5. Mes amis et moi, on visiterait les autres monuments de la capitale; ____.

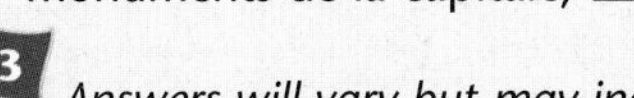

3 *Answers will vary but may include:*

1. J'irais en France avec ma famille.
2. Mon père achèterait une nouvelle voiture.
3. Mes grands-parents voyageraient.
4. Ma sœur achèterait des vêtements très chers.
5. Tu inviterais toute la classe au restaurant français.
6. Mes copains et moi prendrions le train pour aller faire du ski au Canada.
7. Vous deux, vous iriez en vacances.

Presentation

Deux pronoms dans la même phrase

Step 1 Read the questions in Item 2 and have students read the responses.

Reaching All Students

Additional Practice
Replace the words in italics with pronouns.

1. **Marc va apporter *le cadeau à Marie.***
2. **Serge te prête *les cassettes.***
3. **Catherine nous a donné *les livres.***
4. **Ma mère m'a prêté *la voiture.***
5. **Mon père m'a donné *les clés.***

Learning from Photos

(page 240) Bouillabaisse is a fish stew from the Marseille area. An authentic bouillabaisse has about six different types of fish, including rascasse (scorpion fish) and eel, as well as langoustines, crabs, and lobster. They are all cooked together with olive oil, tomato, garlic, fennel, saffron, and a touch of anise. It is served with garlic toast and **rouille**—a type of mayonnaise flavored with garlic and red chili pepper.

Deux pronoms dans la même phrase

1. When two pronouns are used in the same sentence, the order is as follows.

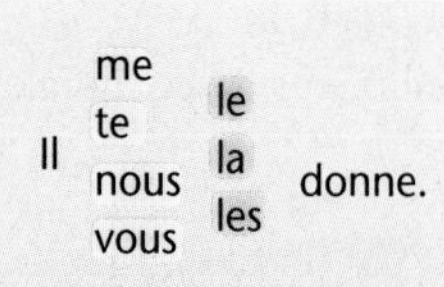

Il	me te nous vous	le la les	donne.

Elle	le la les	lui leur	donne.

Il me le dit toujours.
Il ne le lui dit jamais.

2. Remember that the past participle must agree with a preceding direct object.

La recette? Je la lui ai donnée.
Les 100 dollars? Elle me les a rendus.

Une bouillabaisse

4 Une promesse Répondez d'après le modèle.

la bouillabaisse de Grand-Maman
Moi, je te la prépare.

1. le bœuf bourguignon de Grand-Maman
2. la choucroute de Grand-Maman
3. les haricots verts de Grand-Maman
4. le couscous de Grand-Maman
5. la pizza de Grand-Maman

Literary Companion *You may wish to read the poems by Camara Laye and René Philombe. You will find the* **Deux poèmes africains** *on page 480.*

Answers to Révision

4

1. Moi, je te le prépare.
2. Moi, je te la prépare.
3. Moi, je te les prépare.
4. Moi, je te le prépare.
5. Moi, je te la prépare.

Literary Companion

When you finish this review section, if you wish, have students read the ***Deux poèmes africains*** on pages 480–485.

FUN FACTS

The cars in the photo on page 241 are **deux chevaux.** They were extremely popular in the late 50s and 60s. They were quite small and economical. They are no longer manufactured, but they are today considered collector's items.

5 Une carte Répondez en utilisant des pronoms.

1. Tu voulais envoyer une carte et un cadeau d'anniversaire à ton ami(e). Tu as écrit la carte à ton ami(e)?
2. Tu lui as envoyé la carte?
3. Tu as donné la carte au facteur?
4. Tu as envoyé le cadeau?
5. Ton ami(e) a reçu la carte?
6. Il/Elle a reçu le cadeau?
7. Il/Elle a aimé la carte et le cadeau?
8. Ton ami(e) a montré la carte et le cadeau à ses autres amis?

6 L'avenir Travaillez avec un(e) camarade. Parlez chacun de ce que sera votre avenir.

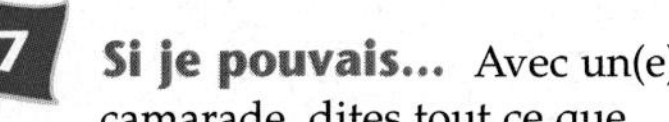

7 Si je pouvais... Avec un(e) camarade, dites tout ce que vous aimeriez faire si vous pouviez le faire.

8 Quand j'aurai mon permis de conduire... Quand est-ce que vous aurez votre permis de conduire? Quelle sorte de conducteur/conductrice est-ce que vous serez? Qu'est-ce que vous ferez (ou ne ferez pas) quand vous aurez votre permis? Quand vous achèterez une voiture, quelle marque est-ce que vous choisirez? Pourquoi?

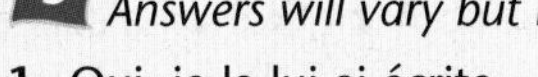

ANSWERS TO Révision

5 *Answers will vary but may include:*

1. Oui, je la lui ai écrite.
2. Oui, je la lui ai envoyée.
3. Oui, je la lui ai donnée.
4. Oui, je l'ai envoyé.
5. Oui, il l'a reçue.
6. Oui, il l'a reçu.
7. Oui, il les a aimés.
8. Oui, il les leur a montrés.

6 *Answers will vary.*

Students can use any vocabulary they have learned up to this point and put the verbs in the future.

7 *Answers will vary.*

Students will use the conditional with the imperfect after **si.**

8 *Answers will vary.*

Students can use the following types of expressions with the verbs in the future: **conduire prudemment, ne rouler pas trop vite, respecter la limitation de vitesse, acheter.**

NATIONAL GEOGRAPHIC

Preview

This section, **Reflets du Maghreb,** was prepared by National Geographic Society. Its purpose is to give students greater insight, through these visual images, into the culture and people of North Africa. Have students look at the photographs on pages 242–245 for enjoyment. If they would like to talk about them, let them say anything they can, using the vocabulary they have learned up to this point.

National Standards

Culture

The **Reflets du Maghreb** photos and the accompanying captions allow students to gain insights into the people and culture of North Africa.

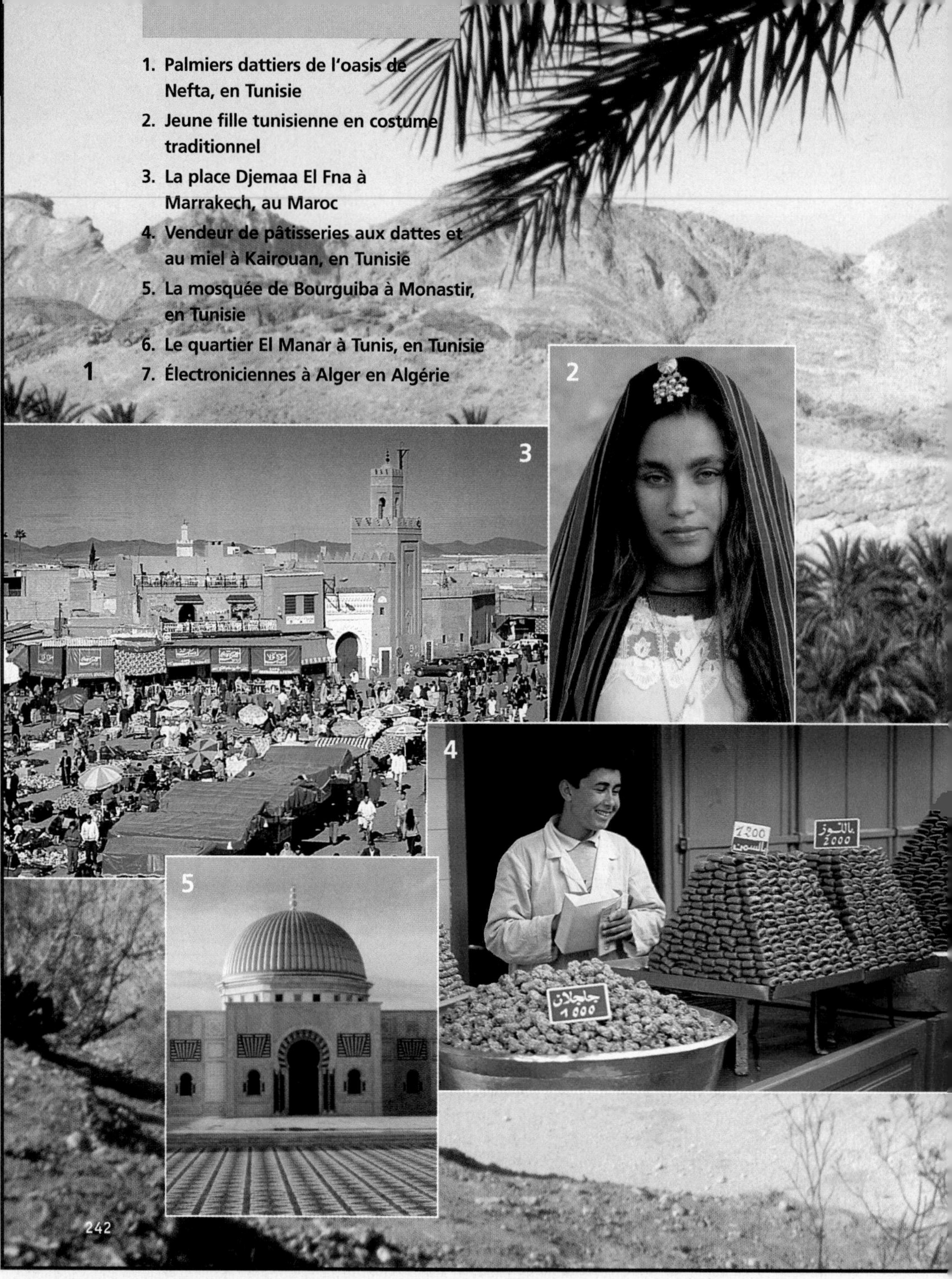

About the Photos

1. Palmiers dattiers de l'oasis de Nefta, en Tunisie Nefta is surrounded by undulating desert. When one approaches Nefta, it appears to be a stretch of green beside the chott (see below). Nefta is an artificial oasis, made possible by the boring of 2,100-foot wells during the 1960s. The oasis has some 300,000 palm trees, including 70,000 deglas, that are reputed to be among the world's best date palms. The original oasis of Roman days had 152 warm springs, dominated by a hilltop called the Corbeille. A **chott** is a salt flat. The Tunisian chotts are a distinctive geological feature on the northern fringe of the Sahara, and they stretch for about 200 miles from the Gulf of Gabes into Algeria. Some of them are lower than sea level.

1. Palmiers dattiers de l'oasis de Nefta, en Tunisie
2. Jeune fille tunisienne en costume traditionnel
3. La place Djemaa El Fna à Marrakech, au Maroc
4. Vendeur de pâtisseries aux dattes et au miel à Kairouan, en Tunisie
5. La mosquée de Bourguiba à Monastir, en Tunisie
6. Le quartier El Manar à Tunis, en Tunisie
7. Électroniciennes à Alger en Algérie

1

2

3

4

5

242

2. Jeune fille tunisienne en costume traditionnel The young woman seen here is in a somewhat traditional Bedouin dress. Today it is not common to see Tunisian women go about their daily routine in such traditional dress, with the exception of some Berber women. The terms Bedouin (Beduin, in English) and Berber are often confused. Tunisia's aborigines were the Berbers. It is believed that around 10,000 B.C., dark-haired, brown-skinned Berbers settled in and around Tunisia. They subsequently interbred with the Blacks from the Sahara and blue-eyed, blond immigrants from the north. The offspring called themselves **Imazighen,** meaning "noble ones," but the Romans called them **Barbari** ("uncouth ones"). Beduin is the plural of the Arabic bedui, meaning "belonging to the desert." "Beduin" has come to be synonymous with "nomad," since many Berber groups were, and still are, nomadic herders. These two terms are loosely used as one, even in Tunisia itself.

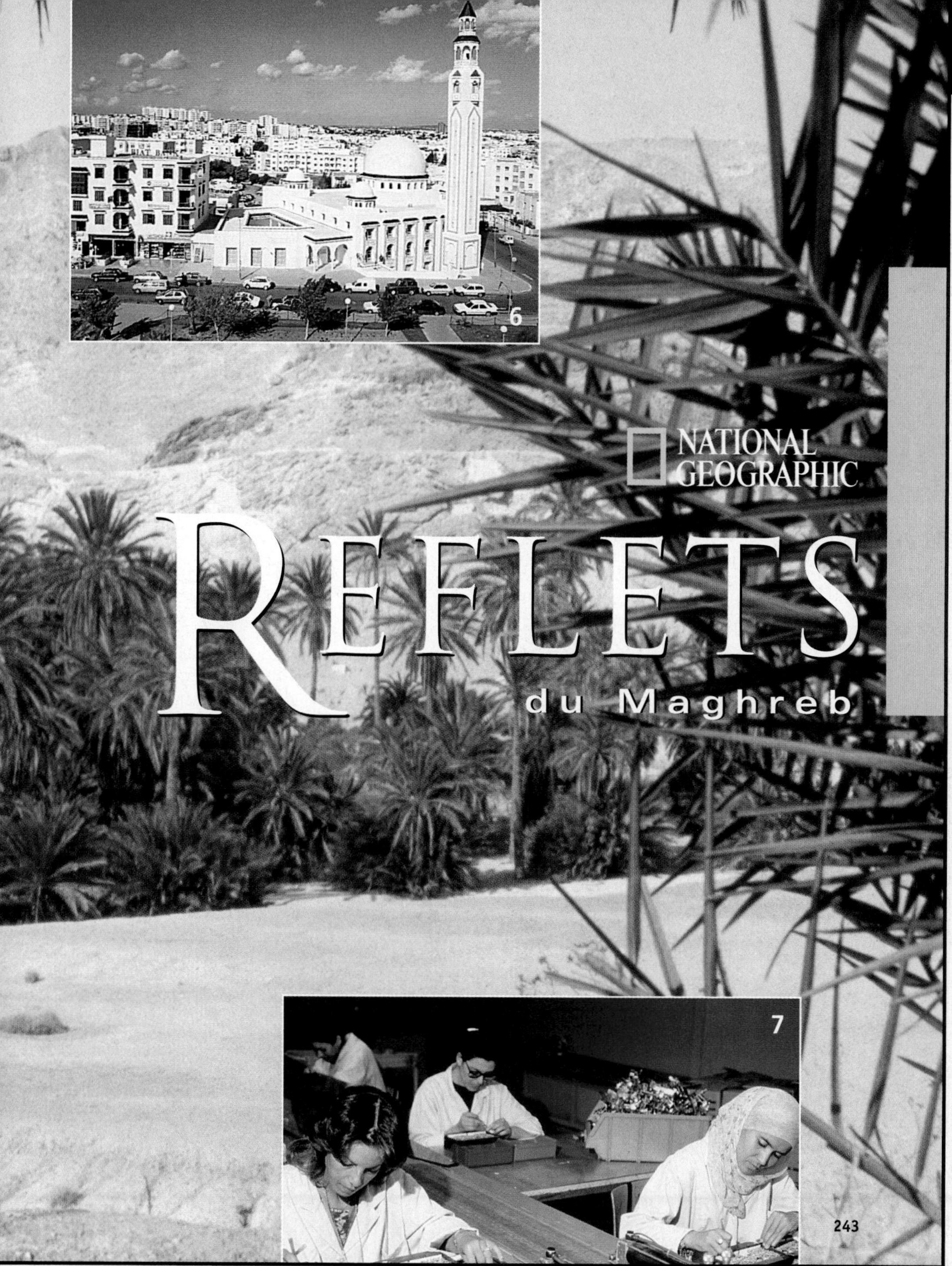

3. La place Djemaa El Fna à Marrakech, au Maroc The famous Djemaa El Fna square in Marrakech (often Marrakesh in English) is one of the liveliest and most colorful spots in Morocco. There are many little wooden-shuttered shops and stalls that belong to traveling merchants, in addition to dozens of little charcoal stoves that are kept burning all day to make couscous, brochettes, and boiling water for mint tea. In the afternoon the **Djemaa El Fna** becomes a gigantic sideshow of entertainers and storytellers.

4. Vendeur de pâtisseries aux dattes et au miel à Kairouan, en Tunisie Dates are well-known in Tunisia. Tunisians are also famous for their pastries, some of which are sweet. The city of Kairouan is a holy Islamic city with the Great Mosque and the shrines of several Moslem saints.

5. La mosquée de Bourguiba à Monastir, en Tunisie Monastir is a lovely coastal city with a university campus, film studios, and a stadium seating 20,000. A wide coastal boulevard skirts the beaches. There are several mosques in Monastir, including the **Mosquée de Bourguiba.** Adjoining this mosque is the Bourguiba family mausoleum, the final resting-place of Habib Bourguiba, who was born in Monastir. Bourguiba is considered the "Father of the Nation." He fought for and negotiated Tunisia's independence, which was recognized by France on March 20, 1956. On July 25, 1957, he declared himself president of the Republic. Bourguiba adapted Moslem traditions to modern life. He was overthrown in a bloodless coup in 1987, because of his advanced age and reports of senility.

6. Le quartier El Manar à Tunis, en Tunisie The El Manar area is a chic residential section of metropolitan Tunis.

7. Électroniciennes à Alger en Algérie Algeria has had a turbulent history in comparison to other countries of the Maghreb. Algeria was not a French protectorate, but rather a part of metropolitan France. Prior to independence, some 3 million French settlers lived in Algeria, along with 7 million Moslems of great diversity. After a bloody civil war that lasted 7 years and cost 1 million lives, President DeGaulle considered the drain on France too great, and in March, 1962, Algerian independence was recognized. After independence, only 40,000 French remained, and many Algerians migrated to France. The political situation in Algeria is still unstable with much fighting between divergent groups of moderates, Islamic fundamentalists, and Berbers.

8. Un village dans la vallée du Dadès, au Maroc The Dadès Valley in the deep south of Morocco is a narrow band of cultivated land dotted with Ksour, or fortified villages, such as the one seen in this photo. The Dadès Valley also has many gorges.

9. Vendeur de pain sur l'île de Djerba, en Tunisie The island of Djerba today is a popular tourist destination. The island is covered with palm trees, orange and lemon orchards, and beautiful gardens.

10. Plage de Monastir en Tunisie For information on Monastir see number 5 on page 243.

11. Détail de la façade du Palais Royal à Fès, au Maroc Fez (**Fès,** in French) was founded as the first political capital of Morocco in 809. Although the capital has been moved several times, Fez continues to be a very important intellectual, cultural, and religious center. The beautiful Royal Palace, the Dar el Makhzen, is on a large square in the center of town. The medina of Fez was declared a World Patrimony by UNESCO in 1980.

12. Femme berbère filant la laine à Tínerhir, au Maroc At the beginning of the historical era, the Berbers were inhabitants of North Africa. There is not much known about their origin. Their language today is mostly a spoken language, but the Saharan Touarego still write it. The town of Tinerhir is near the Todra gorges explained in number 8.

8. Un village dans la vallée du Dadès, au Maroc
9. Vendeur de pain sur l'île de Djerba, en Tunisie
10. Plage de Monastir en Tunisie
11. Détail de la façade du Palais Royal à Fès, au Maroc
12. Femme berbère filant la laine à Tinerhir, au Maroc
13. Jeunes Tunisiens lisant le journal
14. Ruines romaines de Dougga, en Tunisie

8

9

10

11

12

244

Teacher's Corner

Index to the NATIONAL GEOGRAPHIC MAGAZINE

The following related articles may be of interest:

- "In Focus: Central Africa's Cycle of Violence," by Mike Edwards, June 1997.
- "Hunting the Mighty Python," by Karen Lange, May 1997.
- "Morocco: North Africa's Timeless Mosaic," by Erla Zwingle, October 1996.
- "Below the Cliff of Tombs: Mali's Dogon," by David Roberts, October 1990.
- "Africa's Sahel: The Stricken Land," by William S. Ellis, August 1987.
- "Oasis of Art in the Sahara," by Henri Lhote, August 1987.
- "Senegambia: A Now and Future Nation," by Aubine Kirtley and Michael Kirtley, August 1985.
- "Finding West Africa's Oldest City," by Roderick McIntosh and Susan McIntosh, September 1982.
- "The Ivory Coast—African Success Story," by Aubine Kirtley and Michael Kirtley, July 1982.
- "Tunisia: Sea, Sand, Success," by Mike W. Edwards, February 1980.

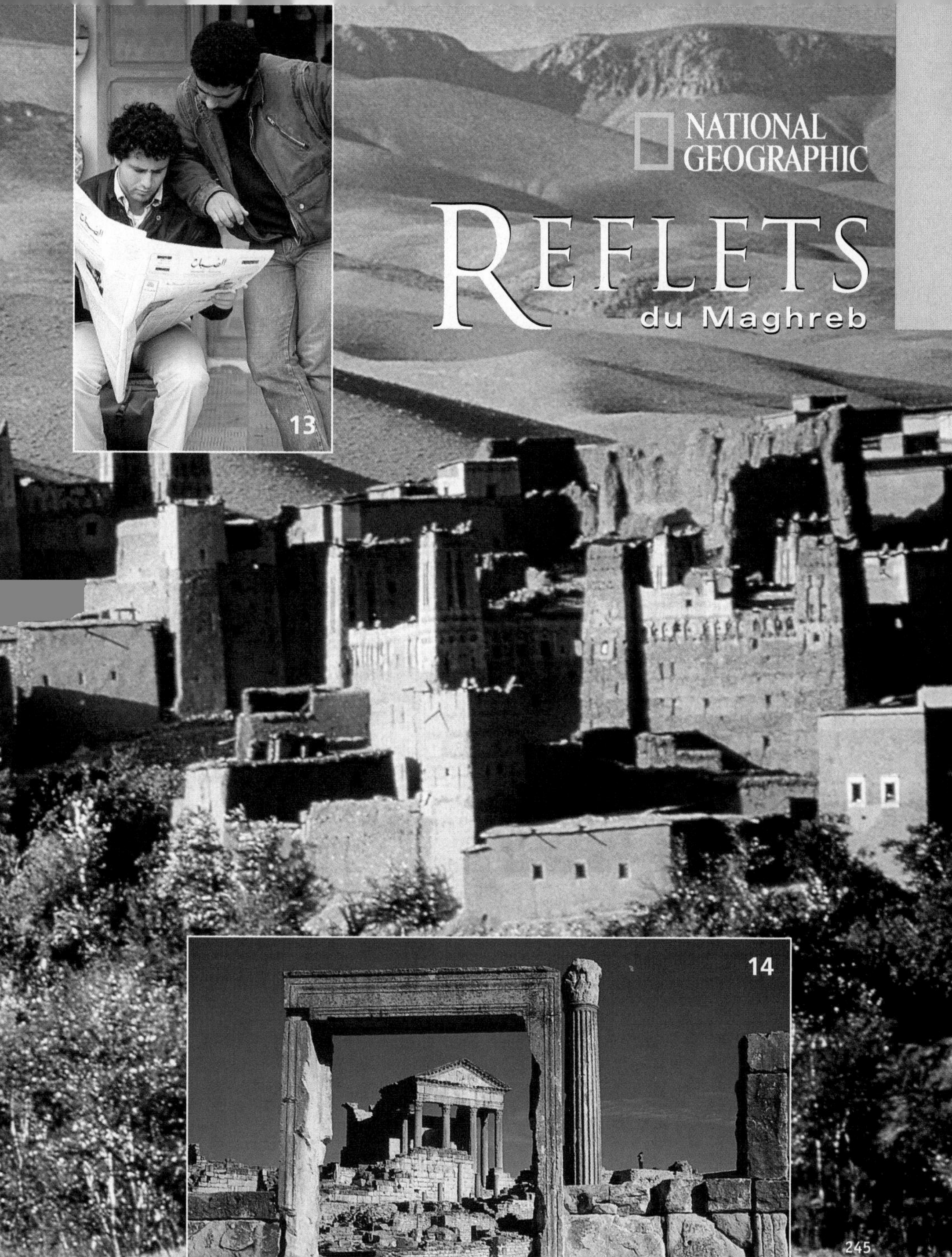

REFLETS du Maghreb

13. Jeunes Tunisiens lisant le journal As is the case with many young Tunisians, both male and female, these men are dressed in Western dress.

14. Ruines romaines de Dougga, en Tunisie Dougga, ancient name Thugga, was already an important town in the Punic era. Like all Roman towns in North Africa developed during the second and third centuries, it was densely populated. The remains date from that period. The principal remains are the theater, the Forum, and the temple of Caelestis. There are other temples, tombs, baths, and cisterns.

Products available from GLENCOE/MCGRAW-HILL

To order the following products, call Glencoe/McGraw-Hill at 1-800-334-7344.

CD-ROMs
- Picture Atlas of the World
- The Complete National Geographic: 112 Years of National Geographic Magazine

Transparency Set
- NGS PicturePack: Geography of Africa

Products available from NATIONAL GEOGRAPHIC SOCIETY

To order the following products, call National Geographic Society at 1-800-368-2728.

Books
- National Geographic World Atlas for Young Explorers
- National Geographic Satellite Atlas of the World

Software
- ZingoLingo: French Diskette

Video
- Africa

Planning for Chapter 8

SCOPE AND SEQUENCE, PAGES 246–277

Topics

- Medical care
- Emergency room procedures

Culture

- Hugo goes to the emergency room
- Doctors Without Borders

Functions

- How to describe accidents and medical problems
- How to ask different types of questions
- How to tell people what to do
- How to compare people and things

Structure

- Interrogative and relative pronouns
- Pronouns and commands
- Superlative adjectives
- Expressing **meilleur** and **mieux**

National Standards

- Communication Standard 1.1 pages 251, 254, 255, 257, 259, 260, 261, 263, 265, 272
- Communication Standard 1.2 pages 250, 251, 254, 255, 257, 259, 260, 261, 263, 264, 267, 269, 271
- Communication Standard 1.3 pages 251, 261, 263, 272, 273
- Cultures Standard 2.1 pages 266–267, 268–269, 271
- Connections Standard 3.1 pages 270–271
- Comparisons Standard 4.2 pages 266–267
- Communities Standard 5.1 page 273

PACING AND PRIORITIES

The chapter content is color coded below to assist you in planning.

■ **required** ■ **recommended** ■ **optional**

Vocabulaire *(required)* *Days 1–4*

- ■ Mots 1
  - Un accident
  - Au service des urgences
  - Le corps
- ■ Mots 2
  - À l'hôpital
  - Une salle d'opération

Structure *(required)* *Days 5–7*

- ■ Les pronoms interrogatifs et relatifs
- ■ Les pronoms et l'impératif
- ■ Le superlatif des adjectifs
- ■ Meilleur/mieux

Conversation *(required)*

- ■ Au service des urgences

Lectures culturelles

- ■ À l'Hôtel-Dieu, à toute vitesse! *(recommended)*
- ■ Médecins Sans Frontières *(optional)*

Connexions *(optional)*

- ■ Louis Pasteur et l'Institut Pasteur

■ **C'est à vous** *(recommended)*

■ **Assessment** *(recommended)*

■ **Technotour** *(optional)*

RESOURCE GUIDE

SECTION	PAGES	SECTION RESOURCES
Vocabulaire *Mots 1*		
Un accident Au service des urgences Le corps	248 248 249–251	Vocabulary Transparencies 8.2–8.3 Audiocassette 5B/CD 5 Audio Activities Booklet TE, pages 81–83 Workbook, pages 89–91 Quiz 1, page 37 ExamView Pro®
Vocabulaire *Mots 2*		
À l'hôpital Une salle d'opération	252 253–255	Vocabulary Transparencies 8.4–8.5 Audiocassette 5B/CD 5 Audio Activities Booklet TE, pages 84–86 Workbook, page 91 Quiz 2, page 38 ExamView Pro®
Structure		
Les pronoms interrogatifs et relatifs Les pronoms et l'impératif Le superlatif des adjectifs Meilleur/mieux	256–257 258–260 261 262–263	Audiocassette 5B/CD 5 Audio Activities Booklet TE, pages 86–89 Workbook, pages 92–96 Quizzes 3–5, pages 39–41 ExamView Pro®
Conversation		
Au service des urgences	264–265	Audiocassette 5B/CD 5 Audio Activities Booklet TE, pages 89–90 CD-ROM
Lectures culturelles		
À l'Hôtel-Dieu, à toute vitesse! Médecins Sans Frontières	266–267 268–269	Audiocassette 5B/CD 5 Audio Activities Booklet TE, pages 91–92 Test Booklet, Chapter 8
Connexions		
Louis Pasteur et l'Institut Pasteur	270–271	Test Booklet, Chapter 8
C'est à vous		
	272–273	**Bon voyage!** Video, Episode 8 Video Activities Booklet, Chapter 8 French Online Activities french.glencoe.com
Assessment		
	274–275	Communication Transparency C 8 Quizzes 1–5, pages 37–41 Test Booklet, Chapter 8 ExamView Pro® Situation Cards, Chapter 8 **Marathon mental** Videoquiz

Using Your Resources for Chapter 8

Transparencies

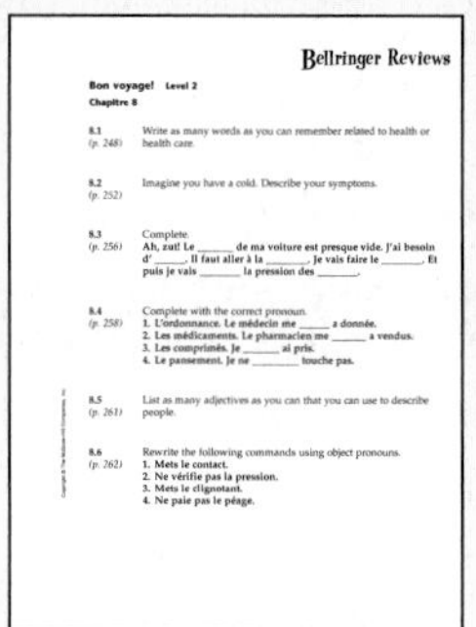

Bellringer 8.1–8.9

Vocabulary 8.1–8.5

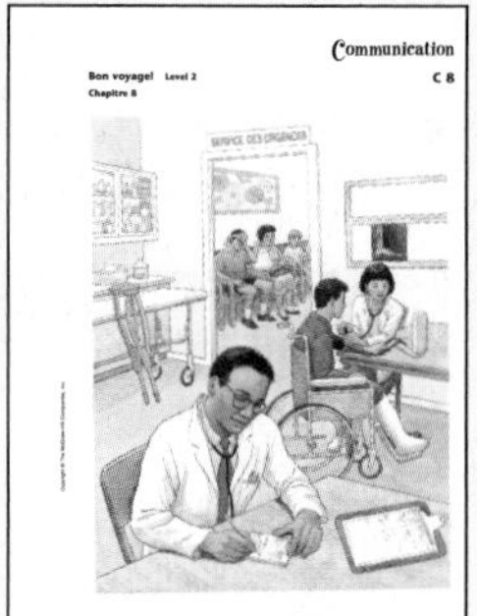

Communication C 8

Writing Activities Workbook

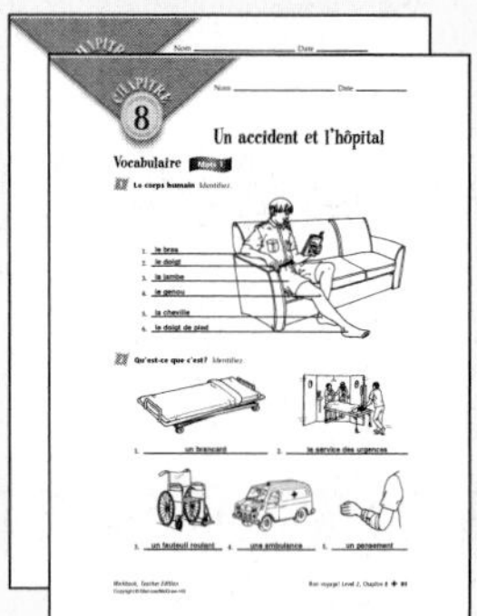

Vocabulary, pages 89–91

Structure, pages 92–96

Enrichment, pages 97–100

Audio Program and Audio Activities Booklet

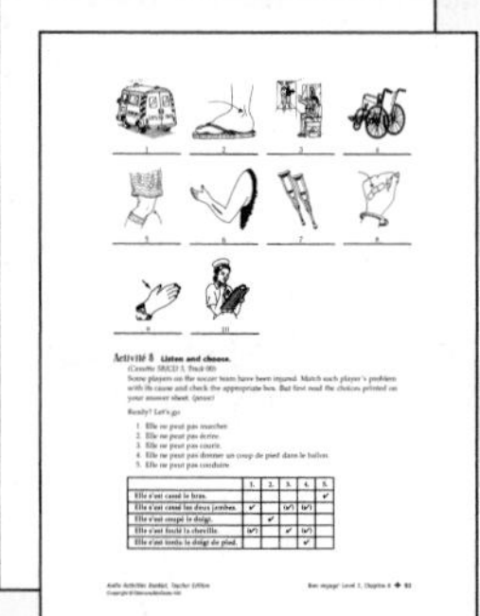

Vocabulary, pages 81–86

Structure, pages 86–89

Conversation, pages 89–90

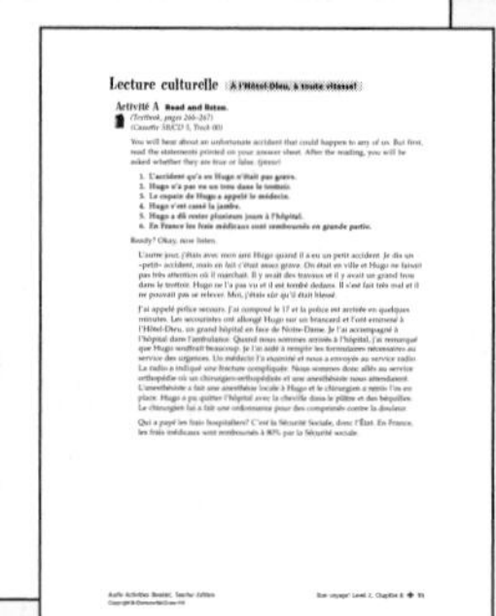

Cultural Reading, pages 91–92

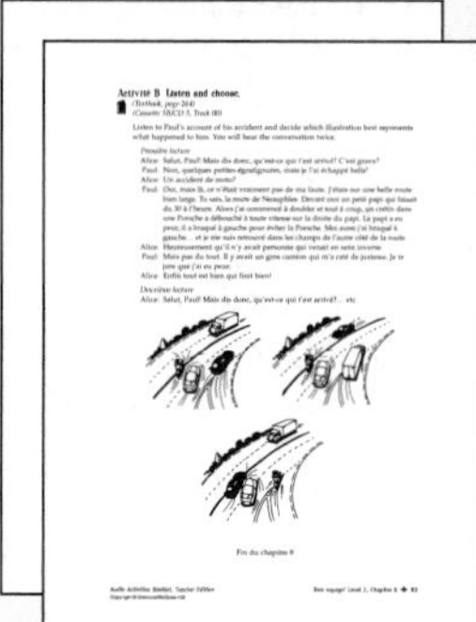

Additional Practice, pages 92–93

Assessment

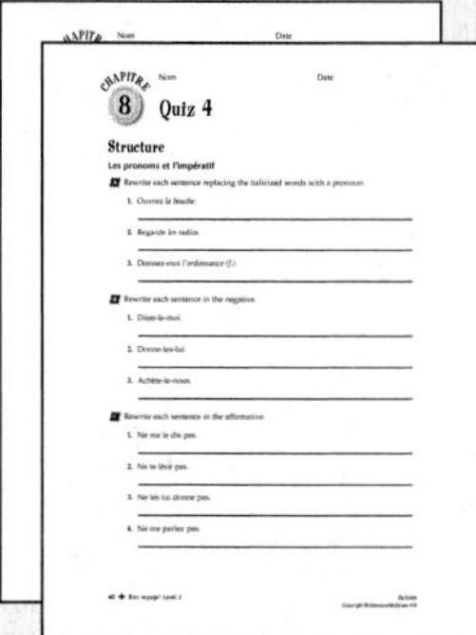

Vocabulary and Structure Quizzes, pages 37–41

Chapter Tests, Chapter 8

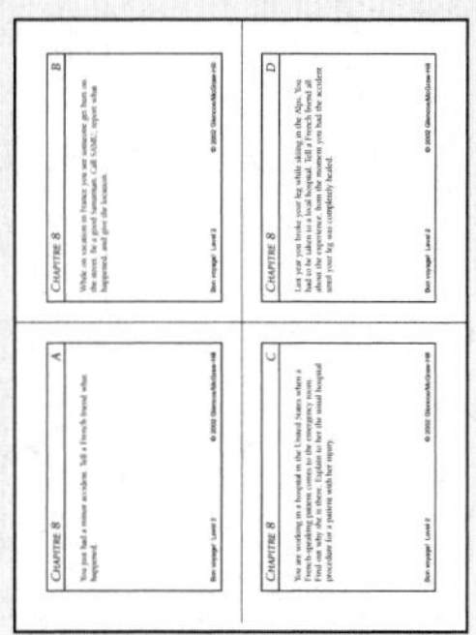

Situation Cards, Chapter 8

Timesaving Teacher Tools

Interactive Teacher Edition

Imagine having your Teacher's Edition and all resources on a CD-ROM. Click on a resource and it appears on your screen, ready to be printed, sorted, or planned.

Interactive Lesson Planner

The Interactive Lesson Planner CD-ROM helps you organize your lesson plans for a week, month, semester, or year. Look at this planning tool for easy access to your Chapter 8 resources.

ExamView Pro®

Test Bank software for Macintosh and Windows makes creating, editing, customizing, and printing tests quick and easy.

Technology Resources

In the Chapter 8 Internet activity, you will have a chance to learn more about medical care in the Francophone world. Visit french.glencoe.com.

On the Interactive Conversation CD-ROM, students can listen to and take part in a recorded version of the conversation in Chapter 8.

See the National Geographic Teacher's Corner on pages 138–139, 244–245, 372–373, 472–473 for reference to additional technology resources.

Bon voyage! Video and Video Activities Booklet.

Help your students prepare for the chapter test by playing the **Marathon mental** Videoquiz game show. Teams will compete against each other to review chapter vocabulary and structure and sharpen listening comprehension skills.

Preview

In this chapter, students will learn to report and describe certain accidents and talk about minor injuries. They will learn vocabulary associated with emergency hospital treatment. Students will learn to form questions using **qu'est-ce que** and **qu'est-ce qui.** They will also learn to use **ce qui** and **ce que,** express opinions using superlative statements about people and things, use the expressions **meilleur** and **mieux,** and use the imperative form of the verb with an object pronoun.

National Standards

Communication

In Chapter 8, students will communicate in spoken and written French on the following topics:

- Accidents and injuries
- Emergency room treatment

Students will obtain and provide information about these topics and engage in conversations that would typically take place at the scene of an accident or in a hospital emergency room as they fulfill the chapter objectives listed on this page.

CHAPITRE 8

Un accident et l'hôpital

NOUVELLE-CALEDONIE 95F RF

Objectifs

In this chapter you will learn to:

- *talk about accidents and medical problems*
- *talk about emergency room procedures*
- *ask different types of questions*
- *tell people what to do*
- *compare people and things*
- *talk about a medical emergency in France*

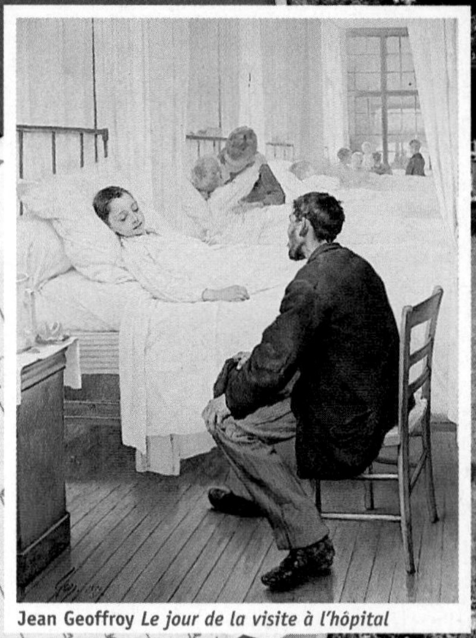

Jean Geoffroy *Le jour de la visite à l'hôpital*

246

The Glencoe Foreign Language Web site (french.glencoe.com) offers several options that enable you and your students to experience the French-speaking world via the Internet:

- The online **Activités** are correlated to the chapters and utilize Francophone Web sites around the world. For the Chapter 8 activity, see student page 277.
- Games and puzzles afford students another opportunity to practice the material learned in a particular chapter.
- The *Enrichment* section offers students an opportunity to visit Web sites related to the theme of the chapter for more information on a particular topic.
- Online *Chapter Quizzes* offer students an opportunity to prepare for a chapter test.
- Visit our virtual **Café** for more opportunities to practice and explore the French-speaking world.

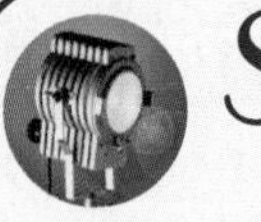

Spotlight on Culture

Photograph **L'hôpital la Salpêtrière,** today called **l'hôpital de la Pitié-Salpêtrière,** is situated on a site that once housed a powder factory, from which it gets its name (saltpeter). The hospital was conceived by Louis XIV in 1656, as a general hospital for the poor of Paris. In 1796, it became a mental hospital, and later served as an old-age home for women, to which a surgical wing was added. Today it serves as a large general hospital with several areas of specialization. It was to this hospital that Lady Diana was brought after the horrible automobile accident in which she was killed.

The large buildings were constructed by the famous architects, Levau and Le Muet (1660). They are built around interior courtyards with classic French gardens and a central chapel, the dome of which can be seen in this photograph.

Painting ***Le jour de la visite à l'hôpital*** was painted in 1889 by the French painter Jean Geoffroy (1853–1924). The painting presently hangs in the **Hôtel de Ville** in Vichy. Geoffroy was very well known as an illustrator.

Chapter Projects

Louis Pasteur You may wish to have students who are interested in science or medicine prepare a report on Louis Pasteur and the Pasteur Institute.

MSF Have students find out information about **les Médecins Sans Frontières.**

Ça fait mal! Have students select a health problem or injury they learn about in this chapter and write a paragraph about it in French.

National Standards

Communities
Have students write a short article in French about healthcare where they live. They can write about their local hospital and first aid squad.

1 Preparation

Resource Manager

Vocabulary Transparencies 8.2–8.3
Audio Activities Booklet TE, pages 81–83
Audiocassette 5B/CD 5
Workbook, pages 89–91
Quiz 1, page 37
ExamView Pro®

Bellringer Review

Use BRR Transparency 8.1 or write the following on the board.
Write as many words as you can remember related to health or health care.

2 Presentation

Step 1 Have students close their books. In addition to using Vocabulary Transparencies 8.2–8.3, you may wish to use gestures or dramatizations to introduce many of these terms. Those which lend themselves to easy dramatization are: **glisser, tomber, se couper le doigt, se fouler la cheville, se tordre le genou, se casser la jambe,** and **marcher avec des béquilles.**

Step 2 Refer to yourself or a student model to demonstrate **le bras, le genou, la jambe, le doigt, la cheville,** and **le doigt de pied.**

Vocabulaire

Mots 1

Un accident 

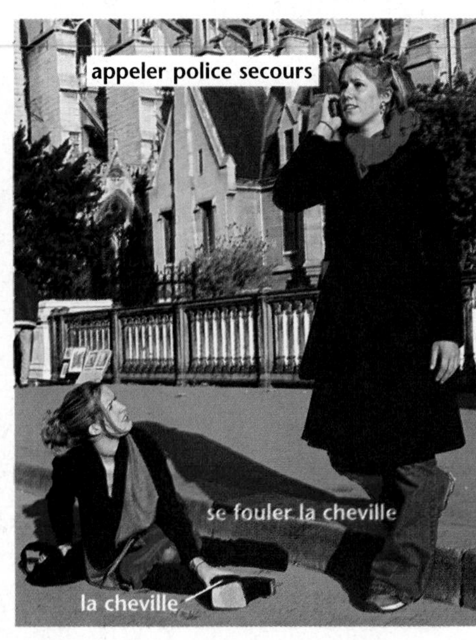

La pauvre Anne s'est foulé la cheville.

Au service des urgences 

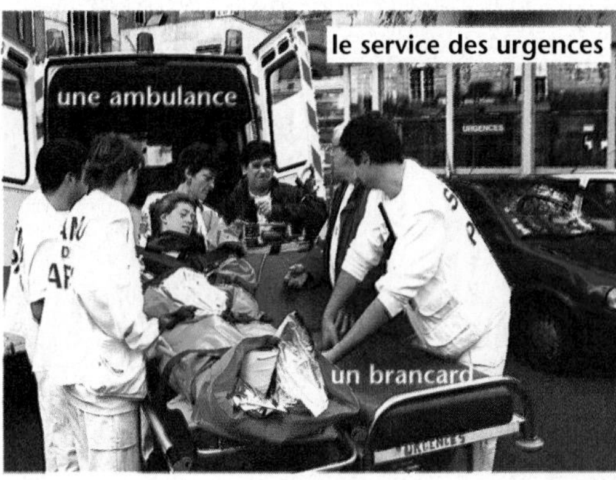

Les secouristes sont arrivés.
Ils ont emmené Anne à l'hôpital en ambulance.

Reaching All Students

Total Physical Response

(Student 1), **venez ici, s'il vous plaît.**
Montrez-moi votre bras.
Montrez-moi votre doigt.
Montrez-moi votre pied.
Montrez-moi votre genou.
Montrez-moi votre cheville.
Montrez-moi votre jambe.
Montrez-moi votre ventre.
Montrez-moi vos lèvres.
Montrez-moi vos yeux.
Merci, *(Student 1).*

(Student 2), **venez ici, s'il vous plaît.**
Vous allez appeler police secours.
Prenez votre portable.
Décrochez.
Composez le numéro.
Parlez. Dites ce qui est arrivé.
Merci, *(Student 2).*

Et maintenant *(Student 3),* **venez ici, s'il vous plaît.**
Mimez ce qui vous est arrivé.
Vous avez glissé.
Vous êtes tombé(e).
Vous vous êtes foulé la cheville.
Vous marchez avec des béquilles.
Merci, *(Student 3).*

Continuons
Let's put our words together

Je n'ai pas entendu. Répondez en utilisant **qu'est-ce que** ou **qu'est-ce qui.** Suivez le modèle.

L'infirmier a mis *un pansement* sur la blessure.
Qu'est-ce que l'infirmier a mis sur la blessure?

1. *Ton livre de biologie* est sur la table.
2. Le malade a eu *un accident.*
3. Il s'est cassé *le bras.*
4. *La science-fiction* intéresse Paul.
5. La mère de Romain s'est coupé *le doigt.*
6. *La médecine* intéresse beaucoup ma sœur.

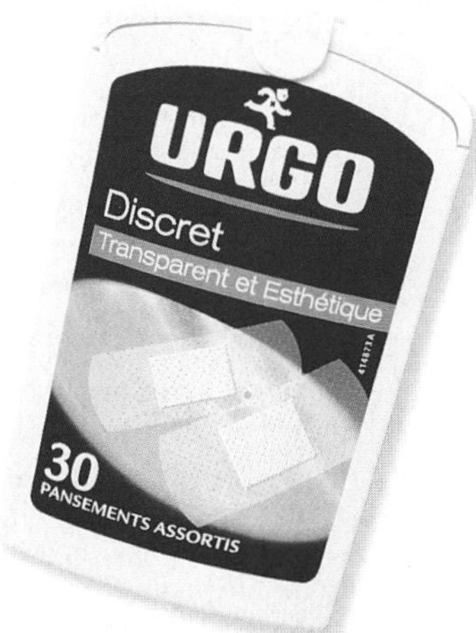

Docteur Henri ANSART
50, résidence du Bois du Four
78640 NEAUPHLE-LE-CHÂTEAU
(Yvelines)
Tél. 36.89.00.07 36.89.08.95

DUROSEL Charlotte

Hyconcil :

2 gélules matin et soir pendant 5 jours.

Locabiotal :

3 pulvérisations par jour.

Dis donc! Tu sais ce qui est arrivé? Répondez que oui.

1. Tu sais ce qui est arrivé?
2. Tu sais ce qui se passe maintenant?
3. Tu sais ce que le médecin a dit à Charlotte?
4. Tu sais ce qu'il a fait?
5. Tu sais ce que le médecin a prescrit?
6. Tu sais ce qu'il a écrit sur l'ordonnance?
7. Tu as compris ce que le pharmacien a dit?

Je ne suis pas content(e)! Complétez avec **ce qui** ou **ce que.**

1. Je sais bien ___ se passe.
2. Je ne comprends pas ___ tu dis.
3. Je ne veux pas savoir ___ est arrivé.
4. Je veux te dire ___ il a fait.
5. Je crois ___ je vois, c'est tout.
6. Je ne crois jamais ___ elle dit.

3 Practice

Continuons
Let's put our words together

11 It is recommended that you let students prepare this activity before going over it in class.

Learning from Realia

(page 257) Note the use of the word **gelules** on the prescription. **Une gelule** is a capsule. **Un comprimé,** the term which students have already learned, is the general term for a pill.

You may wish to ask questions about the prescription: **Qu'est-ce que c'est? Comment s'appelle le médecin? Quelle est son adresse? Quel est le nom de la malade? L'ordonnance est pour quels médicaments? La malade va prendre l'Hyconcil quand? Combien de fois par jour? Et pendant combien de jours?**

Have students look at the prescription again and determine how to say *two capsules* and *three sprays.*

Answers to Continuons

1. Qu'est-ce qui est sur la table?
2. Qu'est-ce que le malade a eu?
3. Qu'est-ce qu'il s'est cassé?
4. Qu'est-ce qui intéresse Paul?
5. Qu'est-ce que la mère de Romain s'est coupé?
6. Qu'est-ce qui intéresse beaucoup ta sœur?

12

1. Oui, je sais ce qui est arrivé.
2. Oui, je sais ce qui se passe maintenant.
3. Oui, je sais ce que le médecin a dit à Charlotte.
4. Oui, je sais ce qu'il a fait.
5. Oui, je sais ce que le médecin a prescrit.
6. Oui, je sais ce qu'il a écrit sur l'ordonnance.
7. Oui, j'ai compris ce que le pharmacien a dit.

13

1. ce qui
2. ce que
3. ce qui
4. ce qu'
5. ce que
6. ce qu'

1 Preparation

Bellringer Review

Use BRR Transparency 8.4 or write the following on the board.

Complete with the correct pronoun.

1. **L'ordonnance. Le médecin me _____ a donnée.**
2. **Les médicaments. Le pharmacien me _____ a vendus.**
3. **Les comprimés. Je _____ ai pris.**
4. **Le pansement. Je ne _____ touche pas.**

2 Presentation

Les pronoms et l'impératif

Step 1 Guide the students through Items 1–3.

Step 2 Provide students with this summary of pronoun use.

1. The pronoun always precedes the verb except in the affirmative command. There it follows the verb.
2. **Me** and **te** become **moi** and **toi** when they follow the verb.

Step 3 You may wish to have students do the following easy exercises before beginning the activities in the text. Tell them to follow the model: **Ne le regardez pas. Regardez-le.**

Ne le touchez pas.
Ne le dites pas.
Ne le faites pas.

Now tell them to follow this model: **Regardez-le. Non, ne le regardez pas.**

Touchez-le.
Dites-le.
Faites-le.

Finally, have them follow this model: **Ne me regarde pas. Regarde-moi.**

Ne m'écoute pas.
Ne me parle pas.
Ne me donne pas ça.

Telling people what to do

Les pronoms et l'impératif

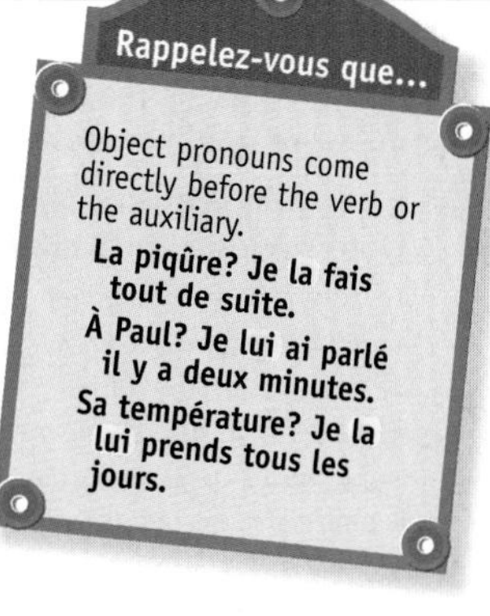

1. In the affirmative command, object pronouns follow the verb. They are attached to the verb by a hyphen.

   La piqûre? Faites-la tout de suite!
   Les radios? Regarde-les maintenant!
   À Paul? Prends-lui sa température!

   Note that in the negative command, the pronouns precede the verb in the usual way.

   La piqûre? Ne la fais pas tout de suite!

2. In the affirmative command, **me** becomes **moi** and **te** becomes **toi.** Study the following.

Négatif	Affirmatif
Ne me dites pas ça!	Dites-moi ça!
Ne me donne pas ça!	Donne-moi ça!
Ne te couche pas!	Couche-toi!
Ne te lève pas!	Lève-toi!

3. In the affirmative command, the pronouns **le, la, les** always precede the other object pronouns—**lui, leur, moi, toi, nous, vous.** Note that in the negative command the order is the usual one.

Négatif	Affirmatif
Ne me le donnez pas!	Donnez-le-moi!
Ne les leur achète pas!	Achète-les-leur!

Learning from Realia

(page 258) Students should be able to guess the meaning of many of the diseases on this poster. The following, however, are more difficult.

la coqueluche	*whooping cough*
la rougeole	*measles*
la rage	*rabies*

Continuons
Let's put our words together

 **Bon! Fais-le si tu veux.** Répondez d'après le modèle.

1. Je vais regarder ce film.
2. Je vais écouter ta cassette.
3. Je vais lire mon magazine.
4. Je vais écrire ma lettre.
5. Je vais acheter les billets.
6. Je vais mettre le couvert.
7. Je vais faire la vaisselle.
8. Je vais aider Maman.

 **Ne le fais pas maintenant.** Refaites l'Activité 14 d'après le modèle.

—Je vais regarder la télé.
—S'il te plaît, ne la regarde pas maintenant.

 **D'accord, vas-y!** Répondez d'après le modèle.

1. Je voudrais téléphoner à mes grands-parents.
2. Je voudrais parler à Simone.
3. Je voudrais écrire à mon copain.
4. Je voudrais acheter quelque chose à mes parents.
5. Je voudrais dire bonjour au professeur de français.

Structure

3 Practice

Continuons
Let's put our words together

14 to **16** You may do these activities with books open or closed.

Answers to Continuons

14

1. Bon! Regarde-le, si tu veux.
2. Bon! Écoute-la, si tu veux.
3. Bon! Lis-le, si tu veux.
4. Bon! Écris-la, si tu veux.
5. Bon! Achète-les, si tu veux.
6. Bon! Mets-le, si tu veux.
7. Bon! Fais-la, si tu veux.
8. Bon! Aide-la, si tu veux.

15

1. S'il te plaît, ne le regarde pas maintenant.
2. S'il te plaît, ne l'écoute pas maintenant.
3. S'il te plaît, ne le lis pas maintenant.
4. S'il te plaît, ne l'écris pas maintenant.
5. S'il te plaît, ne les achète pas maintenant.
6. S'il te plaît, ne le mets pas maintenant.
7. S'il te plaît, ne la fais pas maintenant.
8. S'il te plaît, ne l'aide pas maintenant.

16

1. D'accord, téléphone-leur.
2. D'accord, parle-lui.
3. D'accord, écris-lui.
4. D'accord, achète-leur quelque chose.
5. D'accord, dis-lui bonjour.

3 Practice *(continued)*

17 Expansion: Have students redo the activity making negative commands.

18 Expansion: Have students redo the activity making positive commands.

19 Expansion: Have students redo the activity making negative commands.

Learning from Realia

(page 260 top) Have students find the commands in this little song.

Prête-moi
Ouvre-moi

Explain to students that **une plume** is **un stylo.** Have them look at the illustrations of the candle and the moon to figure out the meaning of the song.

(page 260 bottom) Have students identify all commands in the poster.

17 Alors, fais-le! Répondez d'après le modèle.

—Je vais me maquiller.
—Alors, maquille-toi!

1. Je vais me lever.
2. Je vais me laver.
3. Je vais me brosser.
4. Je vais me raser.
5. Je vais me peigner.
6. Je vais m'habiller.
7. Je vais me coucher.

Au clair de la lune
Au clair de la lu-ne, Mon a-mi Pier-ro
Prête-moi ta plu-me Pour écrire un mot.
Ma chandelle est mor-te, je n'ai plus de feu
Ouvre-moi ta por-te Pour l'amour de Dieu.

18 Ce n'est pas nécessaire.

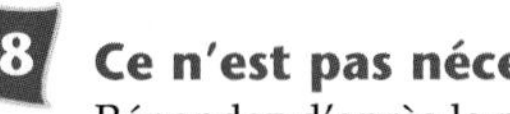

Répondez d'après le modèle.

1. Je me lave?
2. Je me peigne?
3. Je me rase?
4. Je m'habille bien?

À LA MAISON, LES DANGERS, APPRENONS À LES ÉVITER.

Attention: manipuler un **appareil électrique** en marche avec les mains ou les pieds mouillés, ou même humides, vous expose au risque grave d'électrocution. Débranchez toujours un appareil électrique avant de le nettoyer et rangez-le après usage.

Ne vous approchez pas d'une **flamme**, en particulier si vous portez des vêtements synthétiques. Ne laissez pas de torchons ou de papiers près d'une flamme. N'allumez pas un barbecue avec de l'alcool ou de l'essence.

PRÉVENTION DES ACCIDENTS DOMESTIQUES

19 Maintenant ou plus tard?

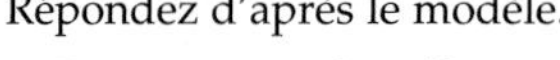

Répondez d'après le modèle.

—Je vous passe le sel?
—Oui, passez-le moi, s'il vous plaît.

1. Je vous passe le beurre?
2. Je vous passe le lait?
3. Je vous passe le poivre?
4. Je vous passe le sucre?
5. Je vous passe le pain?
6. Je vous passe la crème?
7. Je vous passe les olives?

20 Attention à l'accident!

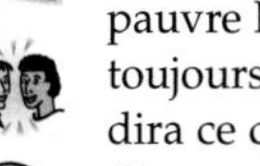

Le pauvre Marc (votre camarade)! Il a toujours des petits accidents. Marc vous dira ce qui lui est arrivé et vous lui direz ce qu'il faut faire ou ne pas faire.

Answers to Continuons

17
1. Alors, lève-toi.
2. Alors, lave-toi.
3. Alors, brosse-toi.
4. Alors, rase-toi.
5. Alors, peigne-toi.
6. Alors, habille-toi.
7. Alors, couche-toi.

18
1. Non, ne te lave pas.
2. Non, ne te peigne pas.
3. Non, ne te rase pas.
4. Non, ne t'habille pas bien.

19
1. Oui, passez-le moi, s'il vous plaît.
2. Oui, passez-le moi, s'il vous plaît.
3. Oui, passez-le moi, s'il vous plaît.
4. Oui, passez-le moi, s'il vous plaît.
5. Oui, passez-le moi, s'il vous plaît.
6. Oui, passez-la moi, s'il vous plaît.
7. Oui, passez-les moi, s'il vous plaît.

20 *Answers will vary.*
Students can use the vocabulary from this chapter.

Comparing people and things
Le superlatif des adjectifs

The superlative expresses "the most" or "the least." To form the superlative in French you use the definite article **le, la, les** with **plus** or **moins.** The superlative is followed by **de.** Study the following chart.

Pierre est le plus sérieux de la classe. Marie est la moins sérieuse de la classe.
Marc et Sophie sont les plus sérieux de la classe. Anne et Virginie sont les moins sérieuses de la classe.

21 Dans une boutique Conversez selon le modèle.

—La robe rose est très jolie.
—Oui, c'est la plus jolie de la boutique.

1. Le pantalon noir est très élégant.
2. Le pull rouge est très joli.
3. Les chaussures marron sont très chères.
4. Le manteau bleu marine est très beau.
5. La jupe bleue est très belle.
6. La robe noire est très habillée.

22 Historiette Ma famille Donnez des réponses personnelles.

1. Qui est le plus jeune ou la plus jeune de ta famille?
2. Qui est le plus âgé ou la plus âgée de ta famille?
3. Qui est le plus amusant ou la plus amusante de ta famille?
4. Qui est le plus beau ou la plus belle de ta famille?
5. Qui est le plus intelligent ou la plus intelligente de ta famille?
6. Qui est le plus timide ou la plus timide de ta famille?
7. Qui est le plus sérieux ou la plus sérieuse de ta famille?

23 Comparaisons Travaillez avec un(e) camarade. Comparez des personnes que vous connaissez ou que vous ne connaissez pas: une star de cinéma, un champion de basket-ball, par exemple.

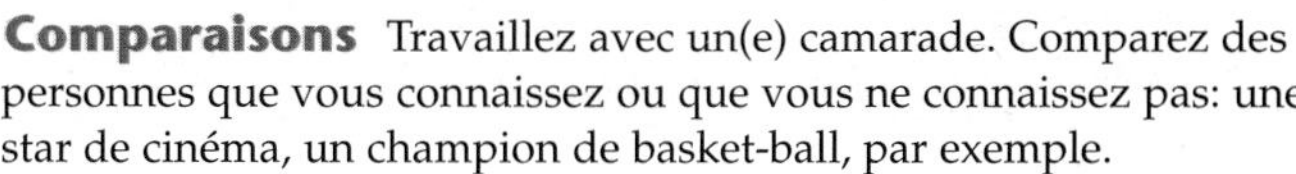

Structure

1 Preparation

Bellringer Review

Use BRR Transparency 8.5 or write the following on the board.
List as many adjectives as you can that you can use to describe people.

2 Presentation

Le superlatif des adjectifs

Step 1 Lead students through the explanation on page 261.

Step 2 Have students share their word lists from the Bellringer Review activity.

Step 3 Draw three stick figures on the board and name them. Using their list of adjectives, have students make up sentences comparing one of the stick figures to the other two.

Step 4 Provide additional examples by comparing objects or students in the room. For example: **Regardez. Roland est le plus grand de la classe.**

Step 5 Tell students that the superlative is followed by **de** in French. Do not explain that it is **de** in French and "in" in English. When this comparison is not made, students tend not to use **dans.**

Answers to Continuons

21

1. Oui, c'est le plus élégant de la boutique.
2. Oui, c'est le plus joli de la boutique.
3. Oui, ce sont les plus chères de la boutique.
4. Oui, c'est le plus beau de la boutique.
5. Oui, c'est la plus belle de la boutique.
6. Oui, c'est la plus habillée de la boutique.

22 *Answers will vary.*
Students can use words such as **mon cousin, ma cousine, mon oncle, ma tante,** etc. Agreement will depend upon the relative selected.

23 *Answers will vary.*

1 Preparation

Bellringer Review

Use BRR Transparency 8.6 or write the following on the board.
Rewrite the following commands using object pronouns.

1. **Mets le contact.**
2. **Ne vérifie pas la pression.**
3. **Mets le clignotant.**
4. **Ne paie pas le péage.**

2 Presentation

Meilleur/mieux

Step 1 Lead students through Items 1 and 2 on page 262.

Learning from Photos

(page 262) Have students create a dialogue between the students.

Expressing "better"
Meilleur/mieux

1. The adjective **bon(ne)** has irregular forms in the comparative and superlative—**meilleur(e)(s)** and **le (la, les) meilleur(e)(s).**

   Charles est bon en maths.
   Mais Vincent est meilleur en maths que Charles.
   Caroline est la meilleure en maths de la classe.
   Caroline et son frère sont les meilleurs en maths de toute l'école!

2. The adverb **bien** also has an irregular comparative and superlative: **mieux, le mieux.**

   Luc chante bien. Mais moi, je chante mieux.
   Mais c'est Virginie qui chante le mieux.

   Note that **mieux,** just like **bien,** is an adverb and therefore is invariable.

Magali est meilleure en maths que Thomas.

Continuons

Let's put our words together

Toi ou quelqu'un d'autre?

Donnez des réponses personnelles.

1. Tu skies bien?
2. Qui skie mieux que toi?
3. Qui est un meilleur skieur ou une meilleure skieuse que toi?
4. De tous tes amis, qui skie le mieux?
5. Qui est le meilleur skieur ou la meilleure skieuse?
6. Tu nages bien?
7. Qui nage mieux que toi?
8. Qui est un meilleur nageur ou une meilleure nageuse que toi?
9. De tous tes amis, qui nage le mieux?
10. Qui est le meilleur nageur ou la meilleure nageuse?

To learn more about skiing and other winter sports in the Francophone world, go to the Glencoe French Web site: french.glencoe.com

Des skieurs dans les Alpes

Vous êtes sur le bon chemin. Allez-y!

3 Practice

Continuons

Let's put our words together

Reaching All Students

Additional Practice

You may wish to ask the following questions.

1. **Qui est le meilleur danseur de la classe? Qui danse le mieux?**
2. **Qui est le meilleur joueur de foot de la classe? Qui joue le mieux au foot?**
3. **Qui est la meilleure danseuse de la classe? Qui danse le mieux?**
4. **Qui est la meilleure joueuse de foot? Qui joue le mieux au foot?**

Learning from Photos

(page 263) Have students recall as much as they can about skiing. Call on students to give random sentences about this topic.

Allez-y!

At this point in the chapter, students have learned all the vocabulary and grammar necessary to complete the chapter. The conversation and cultural readings that follow recycle all the material learned up to this point.

Answers to Continuons

24 *Answers will vary.*

Note: Agreement will vary depending upon the subject the student gives.

1. Oui, je skie bien.
2. _____ skie mieux que moi.
3. _____ est un meilleur skieur que moi.
4. _____ skie le mieux de tous mes amis.
5. _____ est la meilleure skieuse.
6. Oui, je nage bien.
7. _____ nage mieux que moi.
8. _____ est une meilleure nageuse que moi.
9. _____ nage le mieux de tous mes amis.
10. _____ est la meilleure nageuse.

1 Preparation

Resource Manager

Audio Activities Booklet TE, pages 89–90
Audiocassette 5B/CD 5
CD-ROM

Bellringer Review

Use BRR Transparency 8.7 or write the following on the board.
Identify the following people.
Il distribue le courrier.
Elle travaille à la banque.
Il fait le plein.
Il donne des contraventions.
Elle sert une collation à bord d'un avion.
Elle fait un pansement.

2 Presentation

Step 1 Tell students they will hear a conversation in an emergency room. Have students close their books and listen as you read the conversation aloud or play Audiocassette 5B/CD 5. Have students listen carefully to the recorded version and pay particular attention to the intonation.

Step 2 Have pairs of students practice reading the conversation with as much expression as possible.

Step 3 Have two students read the conversation to the class.

Step 4 After going over the conversation, have students say as much as they can about the photograph.

Learning from Photos

(page 264) This photo was taken at the **Hôtel-Dieu** in the **4^e^ arrondissment** of Paris.

Conversation

Au service des urgences   

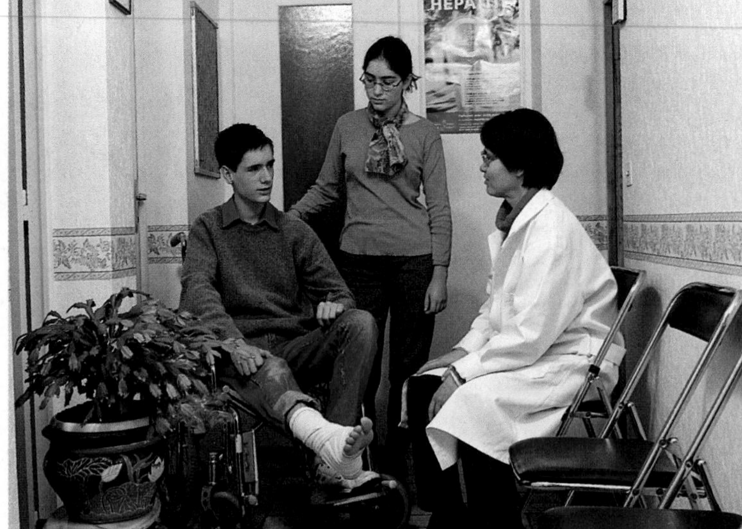

Juliette: Ben, mon pauvre vieux, qu'est-ce qui t'arrive?
Fabien: Oh, je suis tombé et je me suis fait mal à la cheville.
Juliette: Qu'est-ce que tu attends?
Fabien: Le résultat de mes radios.
Médecin: Fabien Morel, c'est vous?
Fabien: Oui, c'est moi.
Médecin: Alors, c'est bien une fracture.
Fabien: Je me suis cassé la cheville?
Médecin: Oui. Mais je vais vous arranger ça. Je vais vous plâtrer et vous pourrez rentrer tranquillement chez vous.
Fabien: Euh… ça va faire mal?
Médecin: Non, ne vous en faites pas! On va vous faire une petite anesthésie locale.
Fabien: Juliette, tu restes avec moi, hein?

Après la conversation

Répondez.

1. Fabien a mal où?
2. Comment est-ce qu'il s'est blessé?
3. Qu'est-ce qu'il attend?
4. Quel est le résultat des radios?
5. Qu'est-ce que le médecin va faire?
6. Pourquoi est-ce que ça ne va pas faire mal?
7. Est-ce que Fabien va passer la nuit à l'hôpital?

Reaching All Students

Additional Practice After completing the **Conversation** activity, ask a student to retell the situation of the conversation in his or her own words.

Answers to Après la conversation

1. Il a mal à la cheville.
2. Il est tombé.
3. Il attend le résultat de ses radios.
4. C'est une fracture.
5. Elle va plâtrer la cheville.
6. On va lui faire une petite anesthésie locale.
7. Non, il va pouvoir rentrer chez lui.

Parlons un peu plus

Let's talk some more

Ne vous en faites pas! Votre meilleur(e) ami(e) a eu un petit accident. Vous étiez ensemble quand ça s'est passé. C'est vous qui téléphonez aux parents de votre ami(e) pour leur dire ce qui est arrivé. Le père ou la mère de votre amie (votre camarade) répond au téléphone et vous pose beaucoup de questions. Rassurez-le/la!

Il téléphone de l'Hôtel-Dieu à Paris.

Une visite médicale

Une visite médicale Vous avez obtenu une bourse *(scholarship)* pour aller en France. Mais avant de partir, il faut passer une visite médicale. Votre camarade est l'assistant(e) du médecin. Il/Elle vous pose des questions sur votre état de santé. Répondez à ses questions. Ensuite changez de rôle.

Glencoe Technology

CD-ROM

On the CD-ROM, students can watch a dramatization of this conversation. They can then play the role of either one of the characters and record themselves in the conversation.

3 Practice

Parlons un peu plus

Let's talk some more

These activities enable students to use the vocabulary and structures learned in the chapter in open-ended exchanges. You may wish to assign different activities to different groups or allow the students to choose the activities they wish to do.

Answers to Parlons un peu plus

 and B

Answers to these open-ended activities will vary depending on the accident the student wishes to speak about and, in Activity B, the questions the students ask each other. Students can use the vocabulary presented in this chapter and also reincorporate vocabulary from Chapter 2.

Resource Manager

Audio Activities Booklet TE, pages 91–92
Audiocassette 5B/CD 5

Bellringer Review

Use BRR Transparency 8.8 or write the following on the board.
Write that the following people are the most or best of the following categories.

1. **Jeanne / intelligente / classe**
2. **Marc / bon / en maths / classe**
3. **Julie et Colette / sympathiques / toutes les filles**

National Standards

Cultures
This reading about an emergency hospital visit in France familiarizes students with aspects of the health care system in France.

Comparisons
Students learn that, unlike in the United States, the majority of medical costs of French people are paid by the French social security system.

Presentation

Note: This **Lecture** provides many examples of the contrast between the **passé composé** and the imperfect.

Pre-reading

Step 1 Find out if any students in the class have ever had a broken bone. Ask how the injury was treated.

Step 2 Have students look at a map of Paris or use the Map Transparency M 3. Say: **L'Hôtel-Dieu se trouve à Paris sur l'Île de la Cité tout près de Notre-Dame.**

Lectures culturelles

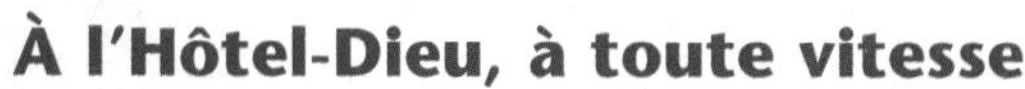

À l'Hôtel-Dieu, à toute vitesse!

Reading Strategy

Visualizing

Visualizing can help you to better understand a passage. As you read, use the details that the writer gives you to form mental pictures. Pause and really try to "see" the scene. If the passage includes characters, observe how they interact with each other. This attention to detail will help you clarify what you read.

L'autre jour, j'étais avec mon ami Hugo quand il a eu un petit accident. Je dis un «petit» accident, mais en fait c'était assez grave. On était en ville et Hugo ne faisait pas très attention où il marchait. Il y avait des travaux[1] et il y avait un grand trou[2] dans le trottoir[3]. Hugo ne l'a pas vu et il est tombé dedans. Il s'est fait très mal et il ne pouvait pas se relever. Moi, j'étais sûr qu'il était blessé.

J'ai appelé police secours. J'ai composé le 17 et la police est arrivée en quelques minutes. Les secouristes ont allongé Hugo sur un brancard et l'ont emmené à l'Hôtel-Dieu, un grand hôpital en face de Notre-Dame. Je l'ai accompagné à l'hôpital dans l'ambulance. Quand nous sommes arrivés à l'hôpital, j'ai remarqué que Hugo souffrait beaucoup. Je l'ai aidé à remplir les formulaires nécessaires au service des urgences. Un médecin l'a examiné et nous a envoyés au service radio. La radio a indiqué une fracture compliquée. Nous sommes

[1] travaux *construction work*
[2] trou *hole*
[3] trottoir *sidewalk*

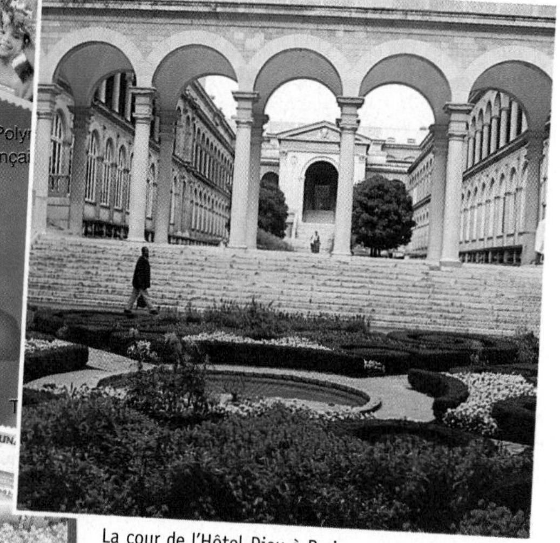

La cour de l'Hôtel-Dieu à Paris

L'Hôtel-Dieu à Paris

Learning from Photos

Recycling

(page 266 right) Have students look at the sign **hôpitaux de Paris.** Have them give the singular and then quickly review words such as:

le journal	**les journaux**
le général	**les généraux**
le canal	**les canaux**

Cross-Cultural Comparison

Ask students if they are surprised by the appearance of some French hospitals. Many of the older hospitals in France look like beautiful châteaux. However, many of them have the same modern equipment as newer ones. The newer medical centers look more like the hospitals in the United States.

donc allés au service orthopédie où un chirurgien-orthopédiste et une anesthésiste nous attendaient. L'anesthésiste a fait une anesthésie locale à Hugo et le chirurgien a remis l'os en place. Hugo a pu quitter l'hôpital avec la cheville dans le plâtre et des béquilles. Le chirurgien lui a fait une ordonnance pour des comprimés contre la douleur[4].

Qui paie les frais[5] hospitaliers? C'est la Sécurité sociale, donc l'État[6]. En France, les frais médicaux sont remboursés à 80% par la Sécurité sociale.

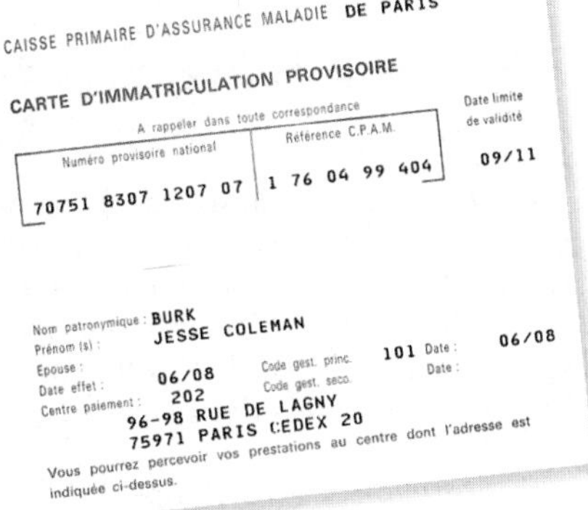
CAISSE PRIMAIRE D'ASSURANCE MALADIE DE PARIS

CARTE D'IMMATRICULATION PROVISOIRE

A rappeler dans toute correspondance

Numéro provisoire national	Référence C.P.A.M.	Date limite de validité
70751 8307 1207 07	1 76 04 99 404	09/11

Nom patronymique : BURK
Prénom (s) : JESSE COLEMAN
Epouse :
Date effet : 06/08 Code gest. princ. 101 Date : 06/08
Centre paiement : 202 Code gest. seco. Date :
96-98 RUE DE LAGNY
75971 PARIS CEDEX 20
Vous pourrez percevoir vos prestations au centre dont l'adresse est indiquée ci-dessus.

[4] contre la douleur *for pain*
[5] frais *expenses*
[6] État *government*

Après la lecture

Un accident Répondez.

1. Qui a eu un accident?
2. Comment est arrivé cet accident?
3. Qu'est-ce que Hugo n'a pas vu?
4. L'ami de Hugo a appelé police secours. Pourquoi?
5. Comment est-ce que Hugo est allé à l'hôpital?
6. Qui l'a accompagné?
7. Où est-ce que les deux copains ont rempli des formulaires?
8. Qui s'est occupé de Hugo?
9. Qu'est-ce que la radio a indiqué?
10. Qui a mis la cheville de Hugo dans le plâtre?
11. Le chirurgien a fait une ordonnance pour quels médicaments?
12. Quel service rembourse les frais hospitaliers en France?

Reading

Step 1 You may wish to divide the **Lecture** into two or three segments.

Step 2 Call on an individual to read several sentences. Then ask other students about the sentences the student has just read.

Step 3 Have students scan the reading and make a list of things that were done to Hugo before his leg was set.

Après la lecture

Allow students to refer to the story to look up the answers or you may use this activity as a testing device for factual recall.

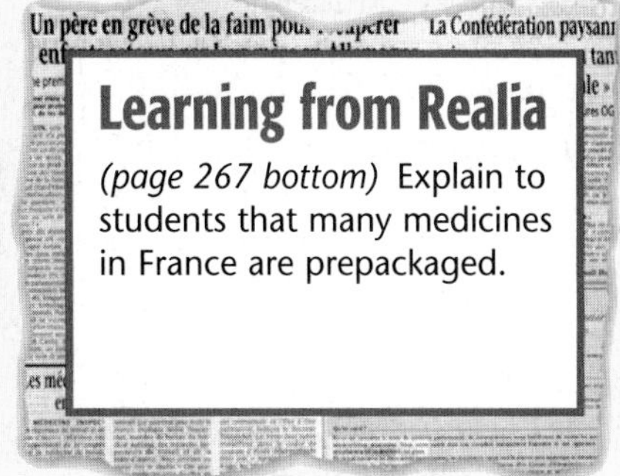

Learning from Realia

(page 267 bottom) Explain to students that many medicines in France are prepackaged.

Answers to Après la lecture

1. Hugo a eu un accident.
2. Hugo ne faisait pas attention et il est tombé.
3. Il n'a pas vu un grand trou dans le trottoir.
4. L'ami de Hugo a appelé police secours parce que Hugo ne pouvait pas se relever.
5. Hugo est allé à l'hôpital dans une ambulance.
6. Son ami l'a accompagné.
7. Ils ont rempli des formulaires au service des urgences.
8. Un médecin a examiné Hugo.
9. La radio a indiqué une fracture compliquée.
10. Le chirurgien-orthopédiste a mis la cheville de Hugo dans le plâtre.
11. Il a fait une ordonnance pour des comprimés contre la douleur.
12. La Sécurité sociale rembourse les frais hospitaliers en France.

History Connection

The first **Hôtel-Dieu (18e arrondissement)** was built in 660 by Saint Landry, Bishop of Paris. He opened the doors to all, without regard to the patient's sex, race, creed, age, nationality, or ability to pay—a philosophy way ahead of its time. The hospital grew and expanded into two buildings spanning across a bridge. The bridge itself housed a 100-bed annex. By the eighteenth century, the hospital had expanded to 9,000 beds. The hospital only lost about one-fifth of its patients, a low rate considering the state of medicine at that time. The original hospital was demolished in 1878, and the present hospital near Notre-Dame Cathedral was constructed.

National Standards

Cultures

This reading familiarizes students with the organization Doctors Without Borders.

Attention!

This reading is optional. You may skip it completely, have the entire class read it, have only several students read it and report to the class, or assign it for extra credit.

Presentation

Step 1 Have students read the passage quickly as they look at the photos that accompany it.

Polynésie française

Tahiti

Lecture supplémentaire

Médecins Sans Frontières

C'est qui? C'est quoi?

L'organisation Médecins Sans Frontières (MSF) est née en 1971. Un groupe de médecins français invente l'aide médicale d'urgence. Ces médecins sont allés au Biafra en Afrique avec la Croix-Rouge[1]. En trente mois, ils ont vu mourir un million de Biafrais! Ils ont fait tout leur possible pour soigner les victimes des combats et de la famine. Mais la situation était désespérée. À leur retour en France, ils créent Médecins Sans Frontières.

Qui sont les Médecins Sans Frontières?

Au début, les Médecins Sans Frontières—les *French Doctors* comme on les appelle souvent maintenant—étaient peu nombreux. De nos jours, environ trois mille volontaires partent en mission avec Médecins Sans Frontières. Parmi eux, il y a des médecins, des chirurgiens, des infirmiers et infirmières. Mais les volontaires n'appartiennent[2] pas tous au corps médical. Il y a aussi des personnes responsables des questions de matériel et d'administration. Pour leur travail, les membres de Médecins Sans Frontières sont très peu payés.

[1] Croix-Rouge *Red Cross*
[2] appartiennent *belong*

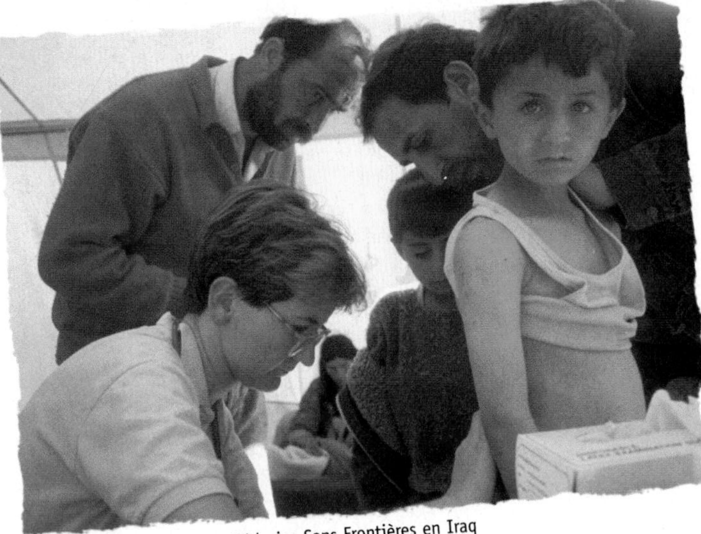

Médecins Sans Frontières en Iraq

Où intervient Médecins Sans Frontières?

Médecins Sans Frontières est présent actuellement[3] dans plus de soixante pays. Chaque année, de nouvelles missions ouvrent et d'autres ferment. Médecins Sans Frontières est la plus grande organisation médicale d'urgence. Elle se retrouve dans des zones de conflits, dans des camps de réfugiés et dans des régions qui ont été ravagées par une catastrophe naturelle comme un tremblement de terre[4], par exemple.

Le rôle de Médecins Sans Frontières est aussi d'alerter l'opinion publique. Tous les ans, l'organisation publie un rapport sur les populations en danger.

En 1999, Médecins Sans Frontières a reçu le prestigieux Prix Nobel de la Paix.

[3] actuellement *nowadays*
[4] tremblement de terre *earthquake*

Après la lecture

Une organisation non-gouvernementale (une O.N.G.)

Expliquez.

1. comment l'organisation Médecins Sans Frontières est née
2. qui sont les volontaires
3. où travaillent les volontaires
4. un deuxième rôle de Médecins Sans Frontières
5. le prix que l'organisation a reçu

Après la lecture

Go over the **Après la lecture** activity on page 269.

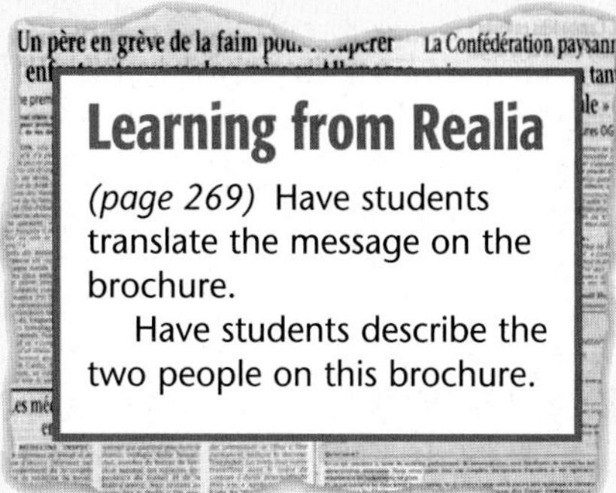

Learning from Realia

(page 269) Have students translate the message on the brochure.

Have students describe the two people on this brochure.

About the French Language

Another term used for volunteers in French is **les bénévoles.**

Answers to Après la lecture

1. En 1971 un groupe de médecins français invente l'aide médicale d'urgence. Ils sont allés au Biafra pour soigner les victimes des combats et de la famine.
2. Les volontaires sont des médecins, des chirurgiens, des infirmiers et infirmières, et des personnes responsables des questions de matériel et d'administration.
3. Les volontaires travaillent dans plus de soixante pays: dans des zones de conflits, dans des camps de réfugiés et dans des régions qui ont été ravagées par une catastrophe naturelle.
4. Un deuxième rôle de Médecins Sans Frontières est d'alerter l'opinion publique.
5. L'organisation a reçu le Prix Nobel de la Paix.

National Standards

Connections
This reading about Louis Pasteur and the Pasteur Institute establishes a connection with another discipline, allowing students to reinforce and further their knowledge of microbiology through the study of French.

Attention!

The readings in the **Connexions** section are optional. They focus on some of the major disciplines taught in schools and universities. The vocabulary is useful for discussing such topics as history, literature, art, economics, business, science, etc. You may choose any of the following ways to do the readings in the **Connexions** sections.

Independent reading Have students read the selections and do the post-reading activities as homework, which you collect. This option is least intrusive on class time and requires a minimum of teacher involvement.

Homework with in-class follow-up Assign the readings and post-reading activities as homework. Review and discuss the material in class the next day.

Intensive in-class activity This option includes a pre-reading vocabulary presentation, in-class reading and discussion, assignment of the activities for homework, and a discussion of the assignment in class the following day.

Connexions

Les sciences

Louis Pasteur et l'Institut Pasteur

The Pasteur Institute in Paris is one of the world's renowned institutions for medical and pharmaceutical research. The Institute is named after a famous French scientist—Louis Pasteur. You may recognize his name from the word *pasteurized* (as in pasteurized milk). Pasteur is considered the founder of the science of microbiology—the study of germs. The young Frenchman, who thought he wanted to be an artist, was the first to develop a vaccine against rabies which would save millions of lives.

L'Institut Pasteur à Paris

Louis Pasteur (1822–1895)

Louis Pasteur est né en 1822 dans le Jura, près de la Suisse. Au collège, il n'était pas très bon élève. Ses cours ne l'intéressaient pas beaucoup, mais il aimait le dessin. On l'appelait «l'artiste». Après le lycée, Louis Pasteur pense devenir professeur et entre à l'École Normale, un institut qui forme les professeurs. À l'École Normale, il se passionne pour les sciences et passe son temps à faire de la recherche. Il se spécialise en chimie.

En 1854, il commence à étudier ce que nous appelons aujourd'hui des microbes. Pasteur, lui, appelait ces microbes des «germes». Une nouvelle science est née: la microbiologie!

En 1873, Pasteur présente à l'Académie de Médecine un rapport qui révolutionne la médecine. Avant ce rapport, on croyait que c'était le corps humain qui créait des maladies comme la typhoïde et le choléra. Mais au cours de ses recherches, Pasteur a découvert que toutes les maladies étaient causées par des micro-organismes. On leur a donné le nom de «microbes». Pour Pasteur, ces microbes sont partout. C'est pourquoi il dit aux chirurgiens de l'époque de se laver les mains avant d'opérer leurs patients et de laver soigneusement[1] tous leurs instruments, c'est-à-dire, de pratiquer l'asepsie. Malheureusement on ne l'écoute pas beaucoup. Pourquoi? Parce que Pasteur n'est pas médecin. Il est chimiste et biologiste.

Louis Pasteur

[1] soigneusement *carefully*

Pasteur ne s'arrête pas là. Il continue ses recherches. Il veut lutter[2] contre les microbes. Ses recherches sur les maladies infectieuses des animaux le conduisent[3] à découvrir la vaccination. En 1885, il réalise le vaccin contre la rage[4]. Il vaccine alors pour la première fois un être humain, un petit garçon de neuf ans—Joseph Meister. Le petit Joseph a été mordu[5] par un chien enragé. Pasteur lui sauve la vie[6]. C'est la victoire, après quarante ans de recherches.

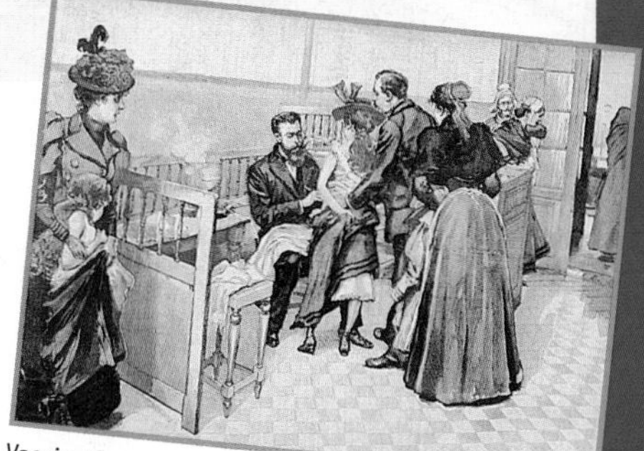
Vaccination contre la rage à l'Institut Pasteur

L'Institut Pasteur (1888)

L'enthousiasme est grand, non seulement en France, mais dans le monde entier. L'Académie des Sciences reçoit de l'argent de nombreux pays pour la construction d'un centre de recherches en microbiologie. L'Institut Pasteur est inauguré en 1888. Et qui est son concierge? C'est… Joseph Meister.

De nos jours, il y a des instituts Pasteur un peu partout dans le monde. À l'Institut Pasteur de Paris, il y a un centre de recherches et un centre d'enseignement[7]. En 1983, c'est à l'Institut Pasteur que le docteur Montagnier a isolé le virus du sida (syndrome immunodéficitaire acquis). Aujourd'hui, on continue à faire des recherches pour trouver une cure à cette terrible maladie.

[2] lutter *fight*
[3] conduisent *lead*
[4] rage *rabies*
[5] mordu *bitten*
[6] vie *life*
[7] enseignement *teaching*

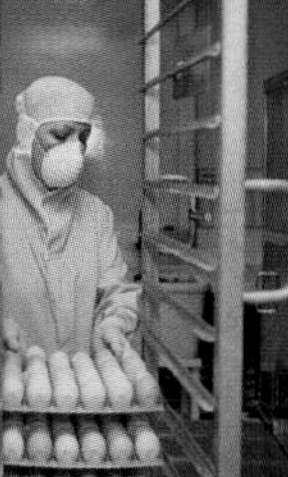
La fabrication de vaccins à l'Institut Pasteur

Après la lecture

Des informations Trouvez les informations suivantes dans la lecture.

1. ce qui intéressait beaucoup Pasteur quand il était jeune
2. les deux sciences qu'il a étudiées
3. la science qu'il a fondée ou découverte
4. où il disait que les microbes se trouvaient
5. ce qu'est l'asepsie
6. le vaccin qu'il a réalisé
7. la découverte du professeur Montagnier

Presentation

Les sciences
Louis Pasteur et l'Institut Pasteur

Step 1 Have students read the introduction in English on page 270.

Step 2 Have students scan the reading for cognates. Then have them do the reading again, this time for comprehension.

Answers to 

1. Le dessin.
2. La chimie et la biologie.
3. La science des microbes: la microbiologie.
4. Partout.
5. C'est de faire attention à se laver les mains et à laver les instruments avant d'opérer un patient.
6. Le vaccin contre la rage.
7. Le virus du sida.

C'est à vous

Use what you have learned

Bellringer Review

Use BRR Transparency 8.9 or write the following on the board.
List as many things as you can that are found in a kitchen.

Recycling

These activities allow students to use the vocabulary and structure from this chapter in completely open-ended, real-life situations.

Presentation

Encourage students to say as much as possible when they do these activities. Tell them not to be afraid to make mistakes, since the goal of these activities is real-life communication. If someone in the group makes an error, allow the others to politely correct him or her. Let students choose the activities they would like to do.

You may wish to divide students into pairs or groups. Encourage students to elaborate on the basic theme and to be creative. They may use props, pictures, or posters if they wish.

C'est à vous

Use what you have learned

PARLER 1

Les services médicaux de la municipalité

✔ *Describe medical services*

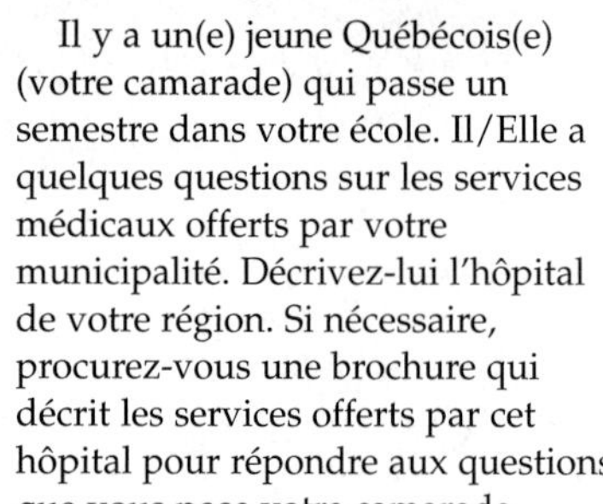

Il y a un(e) jeune Québécois(e) (votre camarade) qui passe un semestre dans votre école. Il/Elle a quelques questions sur les services médicaux offerts par votre municipalité. Décrivez-lui l'hôpital de votre région. Si nécessaire, procurez-vous une brochure qui décrit les services offerts par cet hôpital pour répondre aux questions que vous pose votre camarade.

L'hôpital Royal Victoria à Montréal

PARLER 2

Je vais être interprète.

✔ *Ask questions about medical problems*

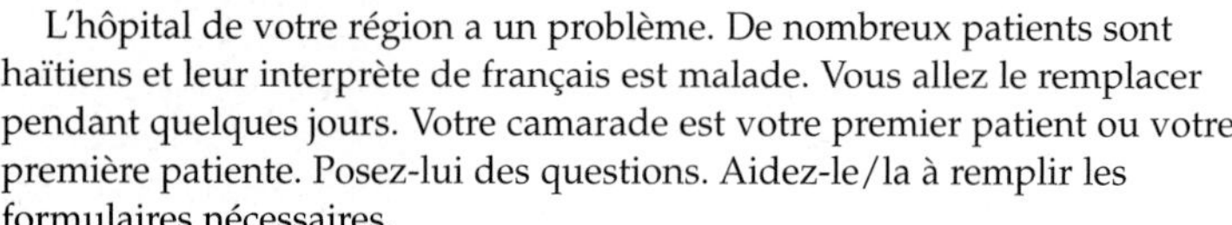

L'hôpital de votre région a un problème. De nombreux patients sont haïtiens et leur interprète de français est malade. Vous allez le remplacer pendant quelques jours. Votre camarade est votre premier patient ou votre première patiente. Posez-lui des questions. Aidez-le/la à remplir les formulaires nécessaires.

PARLER ÉCRIRE 3

Un sketch *(skit)* comique

✔ *Talk about emergency room procedures and accidents*

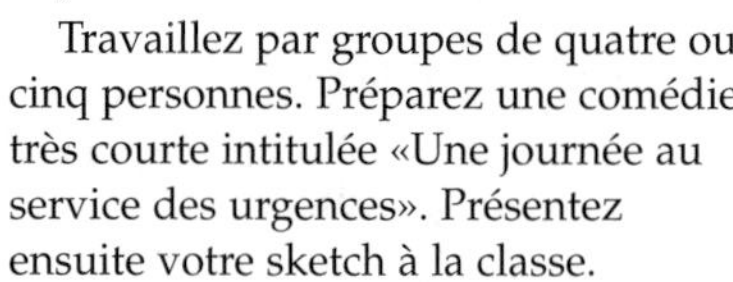

Travaillez par groupes de quatre ou cinq personnes. Préparez une comédie très courte intitulée «Une journée au service des urgences». Présentez ensuite votre sketch à la classe.

Answers to C'est à vous

1 *Answers will vary.*

Students can use the vocabulary from this chapter to discuss the local medical services.

2 *Conversations will vary but may include the following questions:*

Comment vous appelez-vous?
Votre âge?
Votre adresse?
Qu'est-ce que vous avez?
Quels sont vos symptômes?
Qui est votre médecin?
Vous avez des allergies?

3 *Answers will vary.*

RESOURCE GUIDE

SECTION	PAGES	SECTION RESOURCES
Vocabulaire *Mots 1*		
L'arrivée à l'hôtel	280–283	Vocabulary Transparencies 9.2–9.3 Audiocassette 6A/CD 6 Audio Activities Booklet TE, pages 94–96 Workbook, pages 101–102 Quiz 1, page 42 ExamView Pro®
Vocabulaire *Mots 2*		
Dans la chambre d'hôtel Dans la salle de bains	284 284–287	Vocabulary Transparencies 9.4–9.5 Audiocassette 6A/CD 6 Audio Activities Booklet TE, pages 96–98 Workbook, page 103 Quiz 2, page 43 ExamView Pro®
Structure		
Le passé composé: **être** ou **avoir** Le pronom **y** Un pronom + **en** La formation des adverbes	288–289 289–291 291–292 292–293	Audiocassette 6A/CD 6 Audio Activities Booklet TE, pages 98–100 Workbook, pages 104–106 Quizzes 3–6, pages 44–47 ExamView Pro®
Conversation		
À la réception de l'hôtel	294–295	Audiocassette 6A/CD 6 Audio Activities Booklet TE, pages 100–101 CD-ROM
Lectures culturelles		
L'Hôtel de la Gare Les auberges de jeunesse Le Club Med	296–297 298 299	Audiocassette 6A/CD 6 Audio Activities Booklet TE, pages 102–103 Test Booklet, Chapter 9
Connexions		
Le langage	300–301	Test Booklet, Chapter 9
C'est à vous		
	302–303	**Bon voyage!** Video, Episode 9 Video Activities Booklet, Chapter 9 French Online Activities **french.glencoe.com**
Assessment		
	304–305	Communication Transparency C 9 Quizzes 1–6, pages 42–47 Test Booklet, Chapter 9 ExamView Pro® Situation Cards, Chapter 9 **Marathon mental** Videoquiz

Using Your Resources for Chapter 9

Transparencies

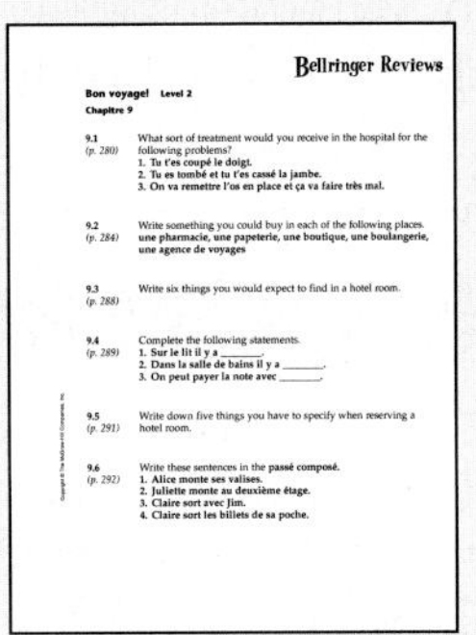
Bellringer 9.1–9.8

Vocabulary 9.1–9.5

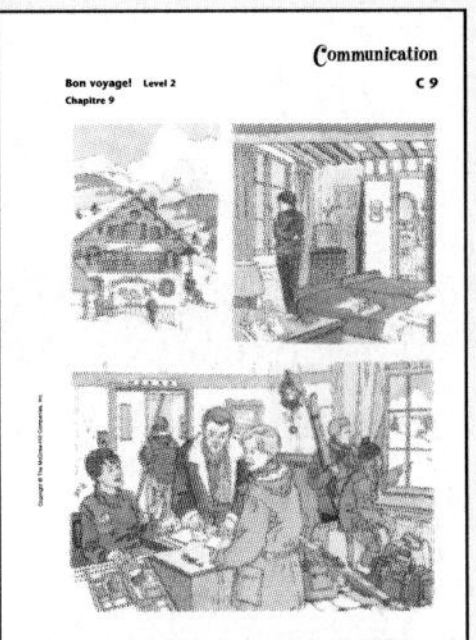
Communication C 9

Writing Activities Workbook

Vocabulary, pages 101–103

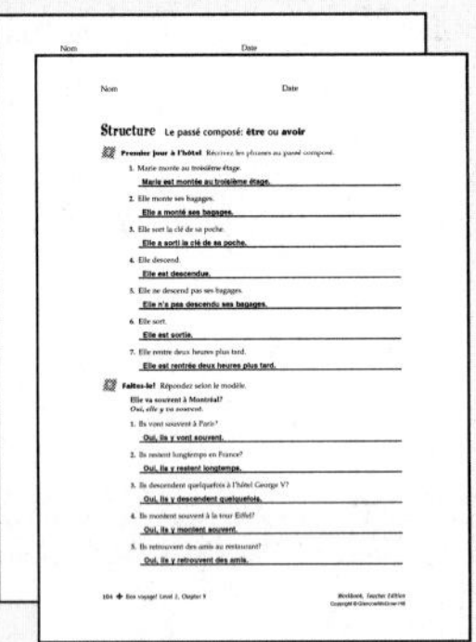
Structure, pages 104–106

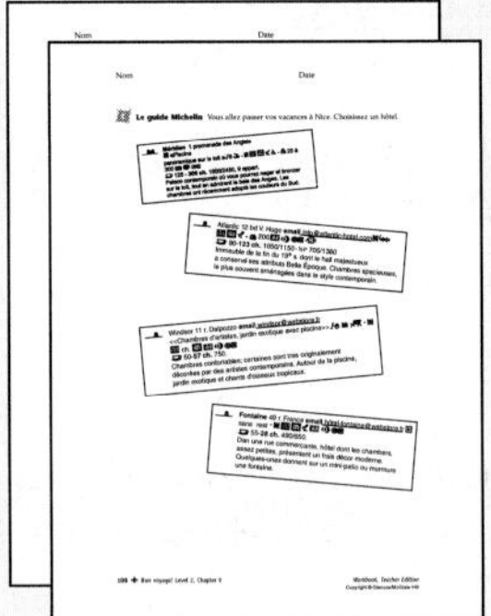
Enrichment, pages 107–110

Audio Program and Audio Activities Booklet

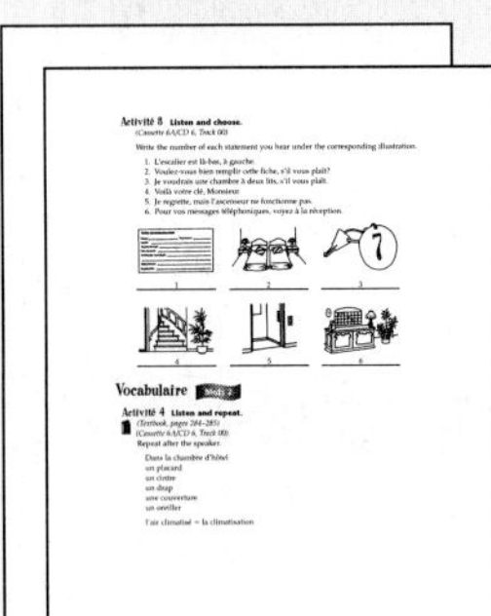
Vocabulary, pages 94–98

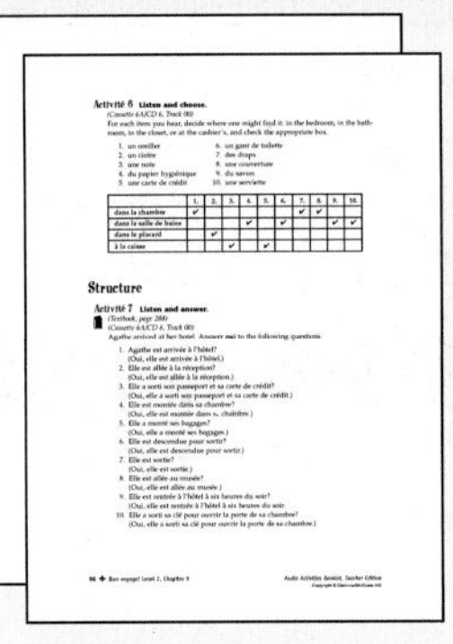
Structure, pages 98–100

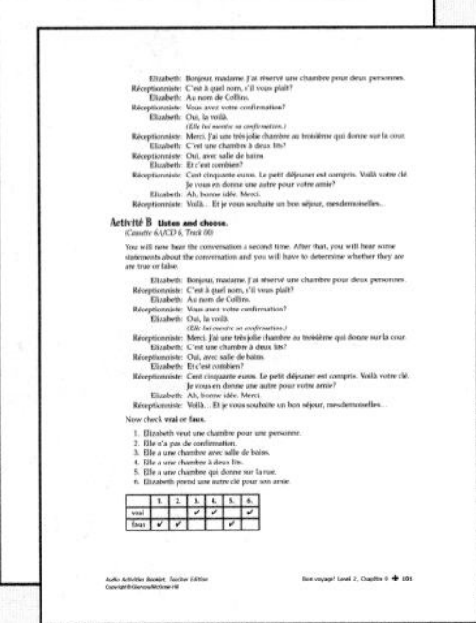
Conversation, pages 100–101

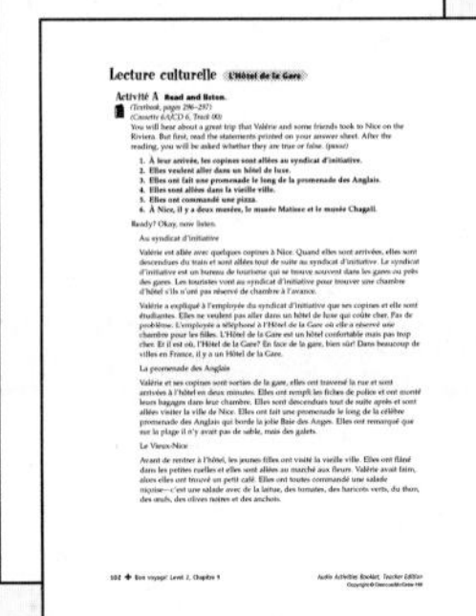
Cultural Reading, pages 102–103

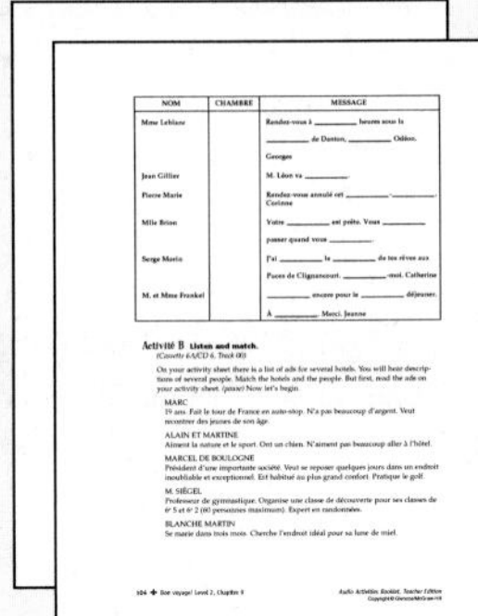
Additional Practice, pages 103–105

Elle a défait son sac.

Ensuite elle est sortie de sa chambre.
Elle a fermé sa porte à clé.

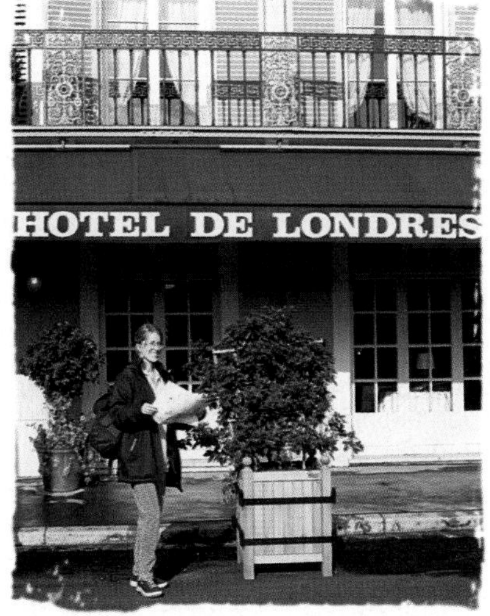

Elle est descendue.
Elle a sorti un plan de la ville de son sac à dos.

Elle est allée visiter la ville.
Il y avait beaucoup de monde.

Vocabulaire

Mots 1

Teaching Tip: You can also use *either/or* questions to introduce the new vocabulary by contrasting a new item with one known to students. For example: **C'est un ascenseur ou un escalier? (C'est un escalier.)**

Step 2 Now have students open their books and repeat chorally as you model the entire **Mots 1** vocabulary or play Audiocassette 6A/CD 6.

Step 3 While showing the Vocabulary Transparencies, call on students to read the vocabulary words and sentences.

Step 4 Ask **vrai ou faux** questions such as the following: **Le hall est dans le jardin de l'hôtel? La réception est dans le hall? La réceptionniste remplit une fiche de police? On peut monter plus vite dans l'ascenseur?**

Assessment

After completing the vocabulary presentation, as an informal assessment you may wish to call on students to look at the illustrations and say as much as they can about them.

About the French Language

In the bottom left photo on page 281, point out that the word **Hôtel** on the awning does not have the **circonflex** over the **o.** Accents are usually dropped when words are written in all capital letters.

Vocabulary Expansion

You may wish to give students the following useful expressions they may need at a hotel.
Il y a des messages pour moi?
Il y a des lettres pour moi?

Reaching All Students

Spatial and Bodily Kinesthetic Intelligence Call on individuals to dramatize or pantomime the following:

remplir une fiche
monter l'escalier
monter les bagages
ouvrir un sac
défaire le sac
fermer la porte à clé
descendre l'escalier
sortir quelque chose d'un sac

Learning from Photos

(page 280 top left) The photos that appear in this vocabulary section were taken at the small **Hôtel de Londres** in Fontainebleau. The proprietor seen here is Madame Ginette Columbier.

Have students look at the photo and say all they can about it.

3 Practice

Commençons
Let's use our new words

Historiette Each time **Historiette** appears, it means that the answers to the activity form a short story. Encourage students to look at the title of the **Historiette,** since it can help them do the activity.

1 After completing the activity, have students take turns describing one of the illustrations to the class.

2 Focus on the listening skill by having students work in pairs. One partner reads the questions in random order while the other answers with his or her book closed.

Assessment

As an informal assessment, you may wish to check comprehension by mixing true and false statements about the illustrations on pages 280–281. Students respond with **«C'est vrai.»** or **«C'est faux.»**

Art Connection

The small village of Barbizon is close to Fontainebleau on the outskirts of Paris. In the mid-nineteenth century, Barbizon was a favorite haunt of painters such as Corot, Théodore Rousseau, and Jean-Francois Millet. Rousseau and Millet both had studios in Barbizon. There is now a museum in the barn that once served as Rousseau's studio.

Commençons
Let's use our new words

1 Qu'est-ce que c'est? Identifiez.

1. C'est le hall ou la réception?
2. C'est une clé ou une fiche de police?
3. C'est une porte ou une chambre?
4. C'est une chambre à un lit ou à deux lits?
5. La jeune fille fait ou défait ses bagages?

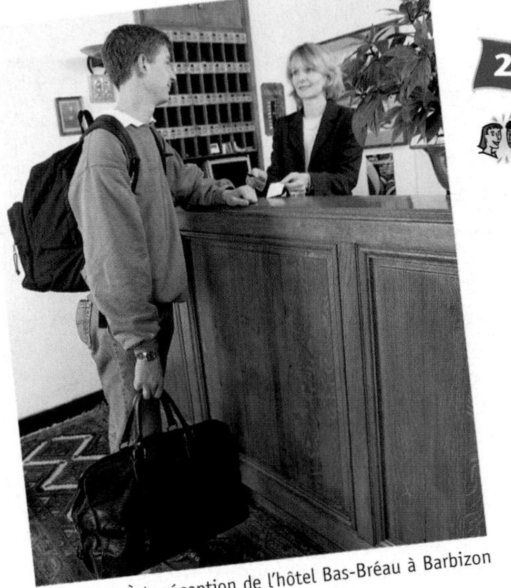

À la réception de l'hôtel Bas-Bréau à Barbizon

2 Historiette L'arrivée
Inventez une histoire.

1. Stéphane est arrivé à l'hôtel?
2. Il est entré dans le hall?
3. Il a trouvé la réception?
4. Il a demandé une chambre pour une personne?
5. Il a demandé le prix de la chambre? Le petit déjeuner est compris?
6. La réceptionniste lui a donné sa clé?
7. Elle lui a souhaité un bon séjour?
8. Stéphane est monté dans sa chambre?
9. Il a monté ses bagages?
10. Il a défait ses bagages?
11. Il a sorti un plan de la ville de sa valise?
12. Quand il est sorti, il a fermé la porte à clé?

Answers to Commençons

1

1. C'est la réception.
2. C'est une clé.
3. C'est une porte.
4. C'est une chambre à un lit.
5. La jeune fille défait ses bagages.

2 *Answers will vary but may include:*

1. Oui, il est arrivé à l'hôtel.
2. Oui, il est entré dans le hall.
3. Oui, il a trouvé la réception.
4. Oui, il a demandé une chambre pour une personne.
5. Oui, il a demandé le prix de la chambre. Oui, le petit déjeuner est compris.
6. Oui, la réceptionniste lui a donné sa clé.
7. Oui, elle lui a souhaité un bon séjour.
8. Oui, il est monté dans sa chambre.
9. Oui, il a monté ses bagages.
10. Oui, il a défait ses bagages.
11. Oui, il a sorti un plan de la ville de sa valise.
12. Oui, quand il est sorti, il a fermé la porte à clé.

3 Le touriste Choisissez.

1. À l'hôtel, le touriste remplit ____.
   a. une fiche b. une chambre c. une clé
2. Pour monter dans sa chambre, il prend ____.
   a. la clé b. l'ascenseur c. la porte
3. Il ouvre la porte de sa chambre avec ____.
   a. sa fiche b. son lit c. sa clé
4. Il prend une douche dans ____.
   a. la salle de bains b. le hall c. l'escalier
5. Il dort dans ____.
   a. son lit b. sa salle de bains c. sa rue
6. Le matin, il se lève et prend ____.
   a. son petit déjeuner b. son lit c. sa fiche
7. Le petit déjeuner est ____ dans le prix de la chambre.
   a. servi b. compris c. rempli
8. Il faut verser ____ pour réserver une chambre.
   a. une carte de crédit b. des arrhes c. des taxes

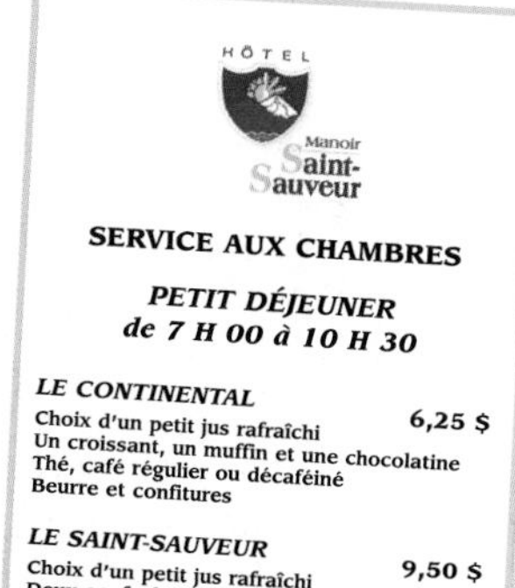
HÔTEL
Manoir Saint-Sauveur

SERVICE AUX CHAMBRES

PETIT DÉJEUNER
de 7 H 00 à 10 H 30

LE CONTINENTAL — 6,25 $
Choix d'un petit jus rafraîchi
Un croissant, un muffin et une chocolatine
Thé, café régulier ou décaféiné
Beurre et confitures

LE SAINT-SAUVEUR — 9,50 $
Choix d'un petit jus rafraîchi
Deux oeufs, bacon ou saucisses ou jambon
Rôties de pain de ménage
Pommes de terres rissolées
Thé, café régulier ou décaféiné

4 Une réservation

Votre classe de français pense faire un voyage en France. Chaque élève a quelque chose à faire pour aider à organiser le séjour. Votre camarade et vous, vous êtes chargés de réserver les chambres. Vous téléphonez à l'hôtel. Vous, vous êtes l'élève et votre camarade est le/la réceptionniste de l'hôtel. Mentionnez les dates d'arrivée et de départ, le nombre de chambres, le nombre d'élèves par chambre, les repas, le prix, et demandez s'il faut verser des arrhes, etc.

5 Dans le hall

Travaillez avec un(e) camarade. Décrivez tout ce que vous voyez sur le dessin.

Vocabulaire

Reteaching

Show Vocabulary Transparencies 9.2–9.3 and let students say as much as they can about them in their own words.

Writing Development

Have students write the answers to Activity 2 in paragraph form.

Learning from Photos

(page 282) Have students create a dialogue between the people in the photo.

Learning from Realia

(page 283) Ask the following questions about the realia: **Quel est le nom de l'hôtel? Le petit déjeuner est servi à quelle heure? Il est servi où? D'après vous, c'est un hôtel français ou canadien?**

Answers to Commençons

3

1. a
2. b
3. c
4. a
5. a
6. a
7. b
8. b

4 *Answers will vary but may include:*

—Bonjour, madame. Je voudrais réserver des chambres, s'il vous plaît.
—Oui, c'est pour quelle date? Et combien de chambres?
—On va arriver le 4 juin. On est 10 élèves et 2 professeurs, alors 6 chambres à deux lits.
—Oui, ça va. C'est pour combien de nuits?
—Sept. Le petit déjeuner est compris?
—Absolument.
—C'est combien, la chambre?
—Une chambre à deux lits, 85 euros tout compris.
—Il faut verser des arrhes?
—Non, vous pouvez me donner le numéro de votre carte de crédit.
—Merci.

 *Answers will vary.*

1 Preparation

Resource Manager

Vocabulary Transparencies 9.4–9.5
Audio Activities Booklet TE, pages 96–98
Audiocassette 6A/CD 6
Workbook, page 103
Quiz 2, page 43
ExamView Pro®

Bellringer Review

Use BRR Transparency 9.2 or write the following on the board.
Write something you could buy in each of the following places.
une pharmacie, une papeterie, une boutique, une boulangerie, une agence de voyages

2 Presentation

Step 1 Show Vocabulary Transparencies 9.4–9.5. Have students close their books and repeat the words after you or Audiocassette 6A/CD 6 as you point to the appropriate illustration on the transparency.

Step 2 Point to the appropriate illustration and ask questions such as: **Qu'est-ce que la cliente demande? Qu'est-ce qu'elle vérifie? Elle paie avec quoi?**

Vocabulaire Mots 2

Dans la chambre d'hôtel

Dans la salle de bains

Camille a demandé poliment une serviette propre.
La femme de chambre lui en a donné une.

Reaching All Students

Total Physical Response Before you begin, demonstrate the word **expliquer.**

(Student 1), **venez ici, s'il vous plaît.**
Vous allez quitter l'hôtel.
Allez à la caisse.
Demandez votre note.
Prenez votre note.
Regardez et vérifiez les frais.
Il y a quelque chose sur la note que vous ne comprenez pas. Indiquez le problème au/à la réceptionniste.
Le/La réceptionniste vous l'explique. Vous comprenez. Sortez votre carte de crédit.
Donnez votre carte de crédit au/à la réceptionniste.
Merci, *(Student 1).* **Retournez à votre place.**
(Student 2), **venez ici, s'il vous plaît.**
Vous êtes dans un hôtel.
Vous êtes dans votre chambre.
Ouvrez la porte du placard.
Prenez un cintre.
Accrochez votre veste.
Mettez-la dans le placard.
Fermez la porte du placard.
Allez dans la salle de bains.
Prenez le gant de toilette.
Prenez le savon. Lavez-vous la figure.
Regardez-vous dans la glace.
Prenez une serviette.
Séchez-vous la figure avec la serviette.
Merci, *(Student 2).*
Maintenant retournez à votre place, s'il vous plaît.

Camille a libéré sa chambre.

HOTEL DE LONDRES
FONTAINEBLEAU

les frais de téléphone

Camille a demandé la note.
La caissière la lui a donnée.
Camille a vérifié les frais de téléphone.
Elle a payé avec une carte de crédit.
Elle n'a pas payé en espèces (en liquide).

Vocabulaire

Mots 2

Step 3 Using props as cues (a pillow, a wash mitt, soap, a towel, money, etc.), ask students what one needs in order to do various things. For example: **On va prendre une douche. On va prendre un bain. On va se laver la figure. On va se sécher. On va dormir. On va mettre nos vêtements dans le placard.**

Step 4 When presenting the sentences on page 285, ask questions in order to give students the opportunity to use the words. For example: **Camille est allée à l'hôtel. Qui est allé à l'hôtel? Elle est allée où? Elle est restée une semaine à l'hôtel? Elle est restée combien de temps à l'hôtel? Elle a libéré sa chambre? Elle est descendue où? C'est une note d'hôtel? Qu'est-ce que c'est? Qui a demandé la note? Elle a demandé la note à la réception? Elle a demandé la note où?**

Teaching Tip: When asking the questions above, direct the easier questions to the less able students and the more difficult questions to the more able students.

Vocabulary Expansion

You may wish to give students the following useful expressions.

Je voudrais plus de cintres, s'il vous plaît.
J'ai besoin d'une autre couverture.
Un autre oreiller, s'il vous plaît.
Il n'y a pas de savon.
Il n'y a pas de papier hygiénique.

3 Practice

Commençons
Let's use our new words

7 Have a student retell the story in his or her own words.

Writing Development
Have students write the answers to the questions in Activity 7 in paragraph form.

Learning from Photos
(page 286) Have students describe the photo. Have them create a dialogue between the two people in the photo.

Vocabulaire

Commençons
Let's use our new words

 **Qu'est-ce que c'est?** Identifiez.

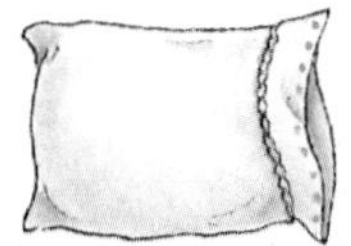

1. C'est un oreiller ou une couverture?

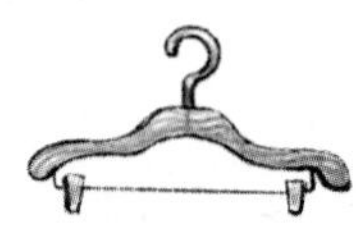

2. C'est un cintre ou un gant de toilette?

3. C'est du savon ou du shampooing?

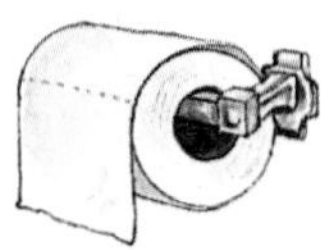

4. C'est un gant de toilette ou du papier hygiénique?

5. C'est une note d'hôtel ou une serviette?

6. C'est une carte de crédit ou de l'argent liquide?

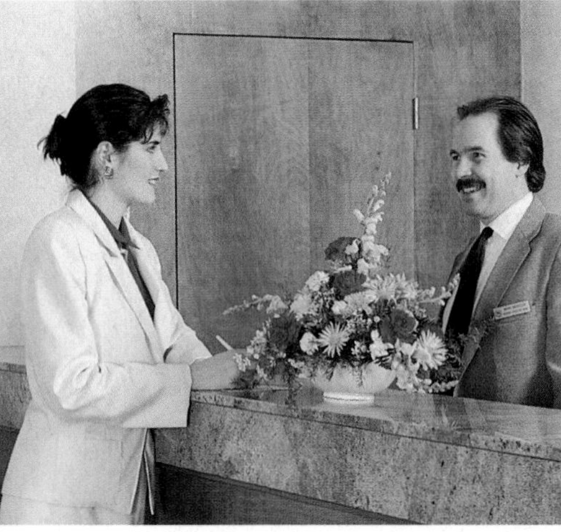

Mme Legrand paie sa note d'hôtel.

 **Historiette Elle a libéré la chambre.** Inventez une histoire.

1. Mme Legrand a libéré la chambre?
2. Elle est descendue à la réception?
3. Elle a demandé ses frais de téléphone?
4. Elle a parlé au caissier?
5. Elle a vérifié sa note?
6. Elle a payé avec une carte de crédit ou en espèces?

Answers to Commençons

1. C'est un oreiller.
2. C'est un cintre.
3. C'est du savon.
4. C'est du papier hygiénique.
5. C'est une note d'hôtel.
6. C'est une carte de crédit.

7 *Answers will vary but may include:*

1. Oui, Mme Legrand a libéré la chambre.
2. Oui, elle est descendue à la réception.
3. Oui, elle a demandé ses frais de téléphone.
4. Oui, elle a parlé au caissier.
5. Oui, elle a vérifié sa note.
6. Elle a payé avec une carte de crédit.

Parlons un peu plus
Let's talk some more

A **Un hôtel à Québec** Cet été vous allez passer vos vacances à Québec avec votre famille. Vous montrez à votre camarade des brochures sur les hôtels de Québec. Expliquez à votre camarade quel hôtel vous avez choisi et pour quelles raisons. Ensuite, votre camarade vous dira s'il/si elle est d'accord avec vous ou pas, et pour quelles raisons.

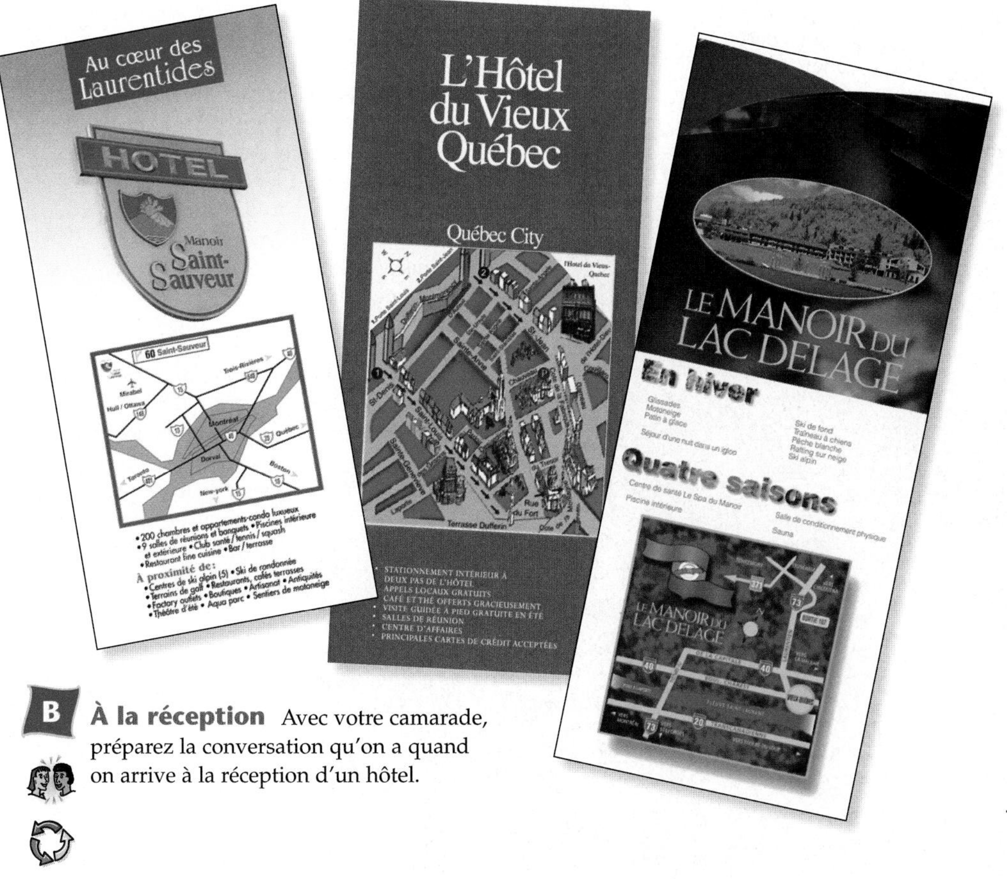

B **À la réception** Avec votre camarade, préparez la conversation qu'on a quand on arrive à la réception d'un hôtel.

3 Practice

Parlons un peu plus
Let's talk some more

These activities enable students to use the vocabulary and structures learned in the chapter in open-ended exchanges. You may wish to assign different activities to different groups or allow the students to choose the activities they wish to do.

A Have students look carefully at the three hotel brochures before they begin this activity. If necessary, help them identify the activities listed in each brochure.

FUN FACTS

Usually, breakfast is included in the price of a room in a French hotel. It is a continental breakfast with a choice of hot tea, coffee, or hot chocolate, a croissant, and bread. Breakfast is served in a small room on the ground floor or in the dining room. Breakfast can also be served in one's room.

Reaching All Students

Additional Practice After completing the **Conversation** on page 294, ask a student to retell the situation of the conversation in his or her own words.

Answers to Parlons un peu plus

A *Answers will vary.*

B *Answers will vary.*
Students may refer to the **Conversation** on page 294 as a guide. All of the necessary vocabulary has been presented in this chapter.

Resource Manager

Audio Activities Booklet TE, pages 102–103
Audiocassette 6A/CD 6

Bellringer Review

Use BRR Transparency 9.8 or write the following on the board.
Rewrite the following sentences replacing the words in italics with pronouns.

1. **Notre prof de français nous donne *des devoirs* tous les jours.**
2. **La fille met *du lait* dans le frigo.**
3. **J'ai beaucoup *d'argent*.**

National Standards

Cultures
This reading about a visit to Nice familiarizes students with the French tourist bureau and this popular city on the Riviera.

Presentation

Pre-reading

Step 1 Ask students what resources they would use to plan a trip to France. If you have access to a Michelin Guide, share its rating system with the students.

Step 2 Have students look at the map of France on page xxxi (French 1A, 1B: page xxiv) or use Map Transparency M 2. Have them locate Nice.

Reading

Step 1 You may wish to divide the **Lecture** into two or three segments.

Step 2 Call on an individual to read several sentences. Then ask other students about the sentences the student has just read.

Lectures culturelles

Reading Strategy

Previewing
Often you can learn about the topic of a passage simply by looking at the titles and pictures before you begin to read. Previewing a reading selection will give you an overview of its purpose, organization, and content.

L'Hôtel de la Gare  

Au syndicat d'initiative

Valérie est allée avec quelques copines à Nice. Quand elles sont arrivées, elles sont descendues du train et sont allées tout de suite au syndicat d'initiative. Le syndicat d'initiative est un bureau de tourisme qui se trouve souvent dans les gares ou près des gares. Les touristes vont au syndicat d'initiative pour trouver une chambre d'hôtel s'ils n'ont pas réservé de chambre à l'avance.

Valérie a expliqué à l'employée du syndicat d'initiative que ses copines et elle sont étudiantes. Elles ne veulent pas aller dans un hôtel de luxe qui coûte cher. Pas de problème. L'employée a téléphoné à l'Hôtel de la Gare où elle a réservé une chambre pour les filles. L'Hôtel de la Gare est un hôtel confortable mais pas trop cher. Et il est où, l'Hôtel de la Gare? En face de la gare, bien sûr! Dans beaucoup de villes en France, il y a un Hôtel de la Gare.

La gare de Nice

La promenade des Anglais

Valérie et ses copines sont sorties de la gare, elles ont traversé la rue et sont arrivées à l'hôtel en deux minutes. Elles ont rempli les fiches de police et ont monté leurs bagages dans leur chambre. Elles sont descendues tout de suite après et sont allées visiter la ville de Nice. Elles ont fait une promenade le long de la célèbre promenade des Anglais qui borde la jolie baie des Anges. Elles ont remarqué que sur la plage il n'y avait pas de sable, mais des galets[1].

[1] galets *pebbles, stones*

La promenade des Anglais à Nice

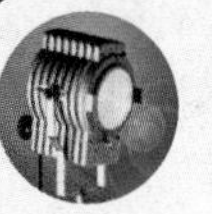

Spotlight on Culture

Photograph In this photo we see a public bus in Abidjan, the capital of Côte d'Ivoire. The public municipal buses are all yellow and green. The woman on the street is wearing a typical West African dress called a **boubou.**

Painting This painting was done by the twentieth-century Haitian folk artist G.E. Ducasse. This painting shows some buses or **camionnettes** known as **tap taps** in Haiti. They are on avenue Dessalines, a main street in the capital, Port-au-Prince. The street is named after Jean-Jacques Dessalines, (1758–1806), a former slave who revolted against colonial domination. He fought the French and proclaimed Haitian independence on January 1, 1804. He was then crowned emperor of Haiti with the name Jacques I.

National Standards

Communities
If you live in an area with a public transportation system, have students prepare a brochure for French-speaking visitors on how to use it. Then send it to the local Chamber of Commerce or the nearest foreign student exchange organization.

Chapter Projects

On prend le métro! Have students study the Paris **métro** map on page 310. They should choose a starting point and destination and write out the directions necessary to get from one to the other.

Je suis touriste. Have groups prepare questions they feel would be most useful when making their way about an unfamiliar French city.

Des comparaisons Have groups research and compare various aspects of French and American cities and suburbs. Possible topics might include: public transportation, populations of city centers vs. suburbs, etc.

Vocabulaire *Mots 1*

1 Preparation

Resource Manager

Vocabulary Transparencies 10.2–10.3
Audio Activities Booklet TE, pages 106–108
Audiocassette 6B/CD 6
Workbook, pages 111–112
Quiz 1, page 48
ExamView Pro®

Bellringer Review

Use BRR Transparency 10.1 or write the following on the board.
List all the words and expressions you can remember that have to do with train travel.

2 Presentation

Step 1 Have students close their books. Use Vocabulary Transparencies 10.2–10.3 to present **Mots 1.** Have students repeat the words, phrases, and sentences after you or Audiocassette 6B/CD 6.

Step 2 Ask *either/or* and *yes/no* questions to elicit the vocabulary. Then point in random order to illustrations on the Vocabulary Transparencies and ask **Qu'est-ce que c'est?**

Step 3 Have students open their books and read pages 310–311. Model the correct pronunciation as necessary.

Step 4 Have students repeat the miniconversation with as much expression as possible.

Vocabulaire *Mots 1*

Le métro

la station (de métro)

METROPOLITAIN

Pardon, monsieur, la station de métro Les Halles, s'il vous plaît?

C'est Châtelet-Les Halles, et c'est là-bas, au coin de la rue.

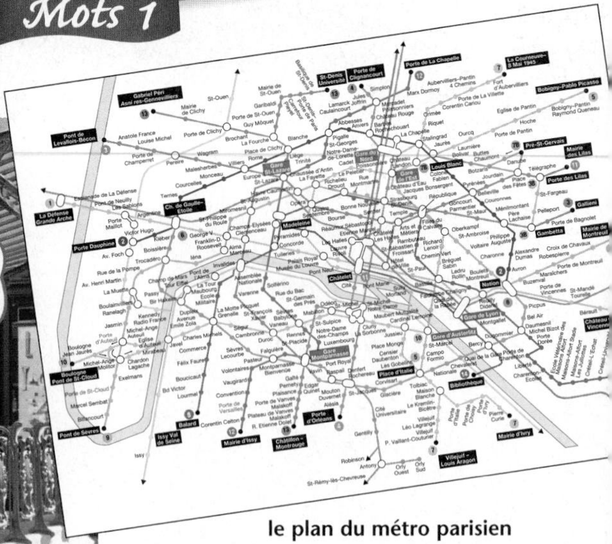

le plan du métro parisien

un carnet

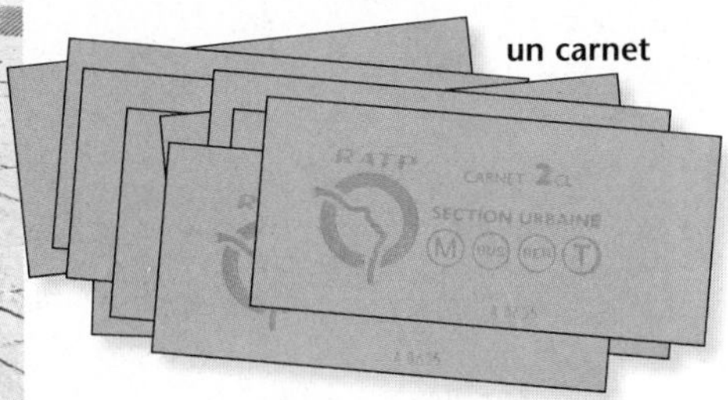

un guichet

un tourniquet

un distributeur automatique

un ticket

Il faut valider son ticket.
Il faut le glisser dans le tourniquet.

Reaching All Students

Total Physical Response Call on individuals to mimic the following.

Regardez le plan du métro.
Prenez un ticket au distributeur automatique.
Glissez le ticket dans le tourniquet.
Attendez le métro sur le quai.
Montez en voiture.
Cherchez une place.
Prenez votre place.
Levez-vous.
Descendez du métro.

Étienne Marcel
Arts et Métiers
Filles du Calvaire
Rambuteau
Oberkampf
St-Sébastien Froissart
Richard Lenoir
← La Défense
Chemin Vert
Hôtel de Ville
Châtelet
Ledru Rollin
Cité
Pont Marie
St-Paul
Bastille
Sully-Morland
Château de Vincennes ↘
Maubert-Mutualité
Cardinal Lemoine
Quai de la Rapée
Jussieu

Pour aller à Bastille, il faut prendre la ligne N° 1, direction Vincennes.
Plusieurs lignes se croisent à Bastille.
Quand on prend la correspondance, on change de ligne.
On peut prendre la correspondance à Bastille.

un escalier mécanique

Les voyageurs descendent l'escalier mécanique.
Ils viennent d'acheter leurs tickets.

le quai
le métro

Les voyageurs attendent le métro.
Ils n'attendent pas longtemps.
Il y a un métro toutes les quatre minutes.

Il y a beaucoup de gens dans le métro.
Aux heures de pointe, les métros sont bondés.

Step 5 You may wish to ask the following questions about the illustrations: **Les voyageurs attendent le métro sur le quai? On peut acheter un ticket au guichet et au distributeur automatique? Les voyageurs prennent la correspondance là où les deux lignes se croisent? On peut descendre sur le quai par l'escalier mécanique? Le métro vient de partir? Les voyageurs l'ont raté?**

Step 6 Have students repeat the sentences on the top of page 311, substituting different place names. They can refer to the metro map on page 310.

Learning from Photos

(page 310) The typical older **métro** entrance shown on page 310 shows the entrance to the **Châtelet** station in central Paris.

(page 311 right) The escalator is in the **gare Montparnasse.**

(page 311 left) The subway platform is at the **Concorde** station.

Assessment

As an informal assessment after completing the vocabulary presentation, you may wish to call on students to look at the illustrations and say as much as they can about them.

Reaching All Students

Additional Practice Have pairs or groups of students write and present short skits in which they must refer to a map, buy a ticket, ask for directions, etc.

3 Practice

Commençons
Let's use our new words

Attention!

When students are doing the **Commençons** activities, accept any answer that makes sense. The purpose of these activities is to have students use the new vocabulary. They are not factual recall activities. Thus, it is not necessary for students to remember specific factual information from the vocabulary presentation when answering. If you wish, have students use the photos on this page as a stimulus, when possible.

Historiette Each time **Historiette** appears, it means that the answers to the activity form a short story. Encourage students to look at the title of the **Historiette,** since it can help them do the activity.

 First ask the questions with books closed and call on individuals to answer. Activity 2 can be done a second time as a reading activity with books open.

Commençons
Let's use our new words

 **Qu'est-ce que c'est?** Identifiez.

1. C'est un guichet ou un distributeur automatique?

2. C'est une station de métro ou le coin d'une rue?

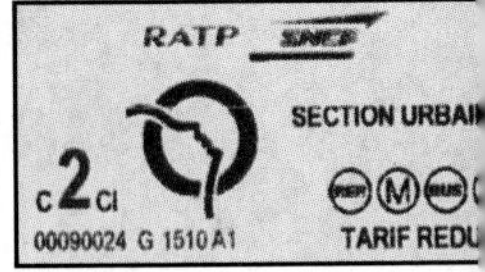

3. C'est un ticket ou un carnet?

4. C'est un métro ou un autobus?

5. C'est un tourniquet ou un escalier mécanique?

2 Historiette Le métro Répondez que oui.

1. Il y a un escalier mécanique pour descendre sur le quai?
2. Il y a un guichet où on peut acheter des tickets de métro?
3. Il y a des distributeurs automatiques?
4. Il faut valider son ticket avant d'aller sur le quai?
5. Il faut passer par un tourniquet avant d'arriver sur le quai?
6. Les voyageurs attendent le métro sur le quai?
7. Le métro vient de partir?
8. Il y a un métro toutes les quatre minutes?
9. De temps en temps, il faut changer de ligne?
10. On peut prendre la correspondance dans une station où deux lignes se croisent?

Answers to Commençons

1

1. C'est un guichet.
2. C'est une station de métro.
3. C'est un ticket.
4. C'est un métro.
5. C'est un tourniquet.

2

1. Oui, il y a un escalier mécanique pour descendre sur le quai.
2. Oui, il y a un guichet où on peut acheter des tickets de métro.
3. Oui, il y a des distributeurs automatiques.
4. Oui, il faut valider son ticket avant d'aller sur le quai.
5. Oui, il faut passer par un tourniquet avant d'arriver sur le quai.
6. Oui, les voyageurs attendent le métro sur le quai.
7. Oui, le métro vient de partir.
8. Oui, il y a un métro toutes les quatre minutes.
9. Oui, de temps en temps, il faut changer de ligne.
10. Oui, on peut prendre la correspondance dans une station où deux lignes se croisent.

Vocabulaire

3 Historiette **Dans la station de métro** Complétez.

1. Quand je ne sais pas où se trouve une ____ de métro, je demande à quelqu'un.
2. Je vais prendre le métro. Je descends sur le ____.
3. Je peux acheter un ticket au ____ ou au ____.
4. Je peux acheter un seul ticket ou un ____ de dix tickets.
5. Je prends l'____ pour descendre sur le quai de la station.
6. Si je ne sais pas quelle direction prendre, je regarde le ____.
7. On peut prendre la ____ dans une station où deux lignes se croisent.
8. Les métros sont souvent ____ aux heures de pointe.

4 Pardon...

Vous êtes à Montréal. Votre camarade est canadien(ne). Vous voulez prendre le métro et vous demandez les renseignements suivants à votre camarade: **où prendre le métro; où acheter des tickets; comment aller sur le quai.**

5 Quelle station?

Vous êtes un(e) touriste à Paris. Choisissez un monument ou un musée que vous voulez visiter. Demandez à quelqu'un dans le métro (votre camarade) à quelle station vous devez descendre. Ensuite changez de rôle.

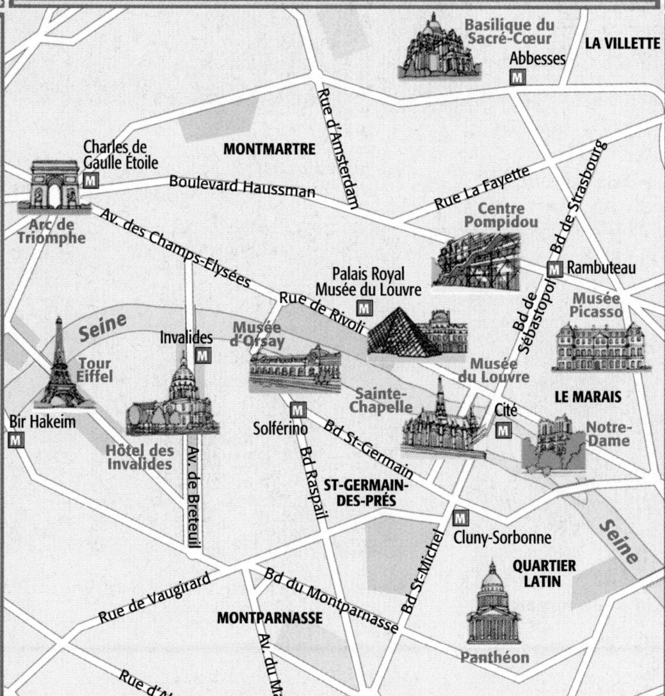

3 After completing this activity, have one student read the entire activity as a story.

Writing Development

Have students write the answers to Activities 2–3 in paragraph form.

Learning from Photos

(page 312) The photos in Activity 1 are as follows:

1. Metro entrance, **Place des Abbesses** in Paris
2. Paris metro station **Bastille**
3. A metro ticket
4. Metro at the **gare de Lyon** station
5. Turnstiles at the **gare de Lyon** station

Reteaching

Show Vocabulary Transparencies 10.2–10.3 and let students say as much as they can about them in their own words.

Answers to Commençons

3

1. station
2. quai
3. guichet, distributeur automatique
4. carnet
5. escalier mécanique
6. plan du métro
7. correspondance
8. bondés

4 *Conversations will vary but will include much of the metro vocabulary presented in* ***Mots 1.***

5 *Answers will vary depending upon the Paris monument the student selects.*

1 Preparation

Resource Manager

Vocabulary Transparencies 10.4–10.5
Audio Activities Booklet TE, pages 108–110
Audiocassette 6B/CD 6
Workbook, pages 112–113
Quiz 2, page 49
ExamView Pro®

Bellringer Review

Use BRR Transparency 10.2 or write the following on the board.
Write words and expressions associated with an airport.

2 Presentation

Step 1 Show Vocabulary Transparencies 10.4–10.5. Have students close their books and repeat the words after you or Audiocassette 6B/CD 6 as you point to the appropriate illustration on the transparency.

Step 2 Ask students questions such as: **On attend l'autobus où? On attend le 48 à cet arrêt d'autobus? On met son ticket dans la machine ou le conducteur prend le ticket? On met le ticket dans l'appareil pour le valider? Pour demander un arrêt, on appuie sur le bouton ou s'appuie contre la porte? Il est interdit de s'appuyer contre la porte?**

Step 3 To elicit the new vocabulary on these pages, ask questions such as: **On descend de l'autobus par où? On monte par le milieu ou l'avant? Le jeune homme a poussé un homme? Qu'est-ce qu'il dit pour s'excuser? Quels sont les deux terminus de la ligne 61?**

Vocabulaire
Mots 2

L'autobus

un arrêt d'autobus

Pour demander un arrêt, on appuie sur le bouton.
Il n'est pas prudent de s'appuyer contre la porte.

Assessment

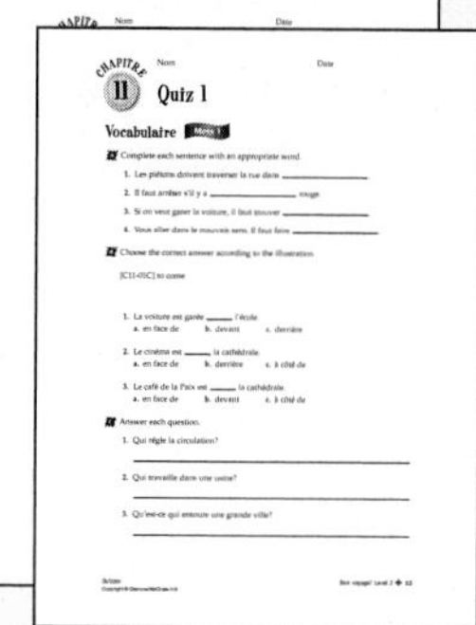

Vocabulary and Structure Quizzes, pages 53–57

Chapter Tests, Chapter 11

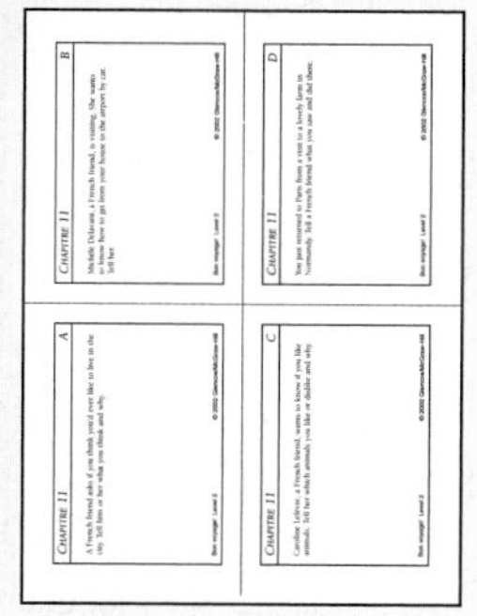

Situation Cards, Chapter 11

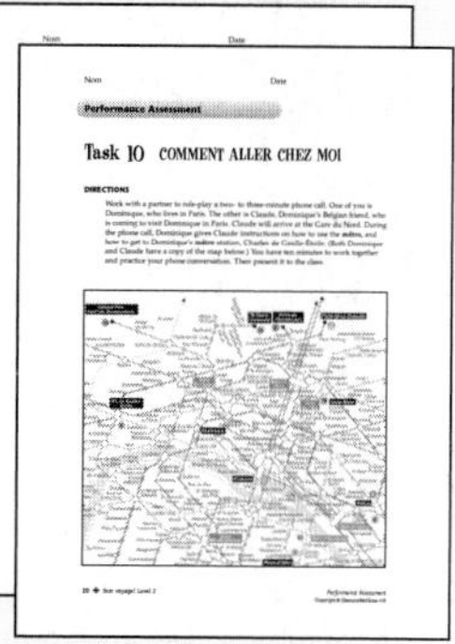

Performance Assessment, pages 15–22

Timesaving Teacher Tools

Interactive Teacher Edition

Imagine having your Teacher's Edition and all resources on a CD-ROM. Click on a resource and it appears on your screen, ready to be printed, sorted, or planned.

Interactive Lesson Planner

The Interactive Lesson Planner CD-ROM helps you organize your lesson plans for a week, month, semester, or year. Look at this planning tool for easy access to your Chapter 11 resources.

ExamView Pro®

Test Bank software for Macintosh and Windows makes creating, editing, customizing, and printing tests quick and easy.

Technology Resources

In the Chapter 11 Internet activity, you will have a chance to visit other cities in the Francophone world. Visit french.glencoe.com.

On the Interactive Conversation CD-ROM, students can listen to and take part in a recorded version of the conversation in Chapter 11.

See the National Geographic Teacher's Corner on pages 138–139, 244–245, 372–373, 472–473 for reference to additional technology resources.

Bon voyage! Video and Video Activities Booklet.

Help your students prepare for the chapter test by playing the **Marathon mental** Videoquiz game show. Teams will compete against each other to review chapter vocabulary and structure and sharpen listening comprehension skills.

Preview

In this chapter, students will learn to compare and contrast city and country life. Students will also learn the pronouns **celui** and **lequel,** the verbs **suivre, vivre,** and **conduire,** and the infinitive after a preposition.

National Standards

Communication

In Chapter 11, students will communicate in spoken and written French on the following topics:

- City life
- Country life

Students will obtain and provide information about these topics and engage in conversations that would typically take place in urban or rural environments as they fulfill the chapter objectives listed on this page.

CHAPITRE 11

À la ville et à la campagne

Objectifs

In this chapter you will learn to:

- *talk about life in the city and give directions*
- *talk about life in the country*
- *ask questions to distinguish between two or more people or things*
- *describe some more activities*
- *talk about life on a farm in France*

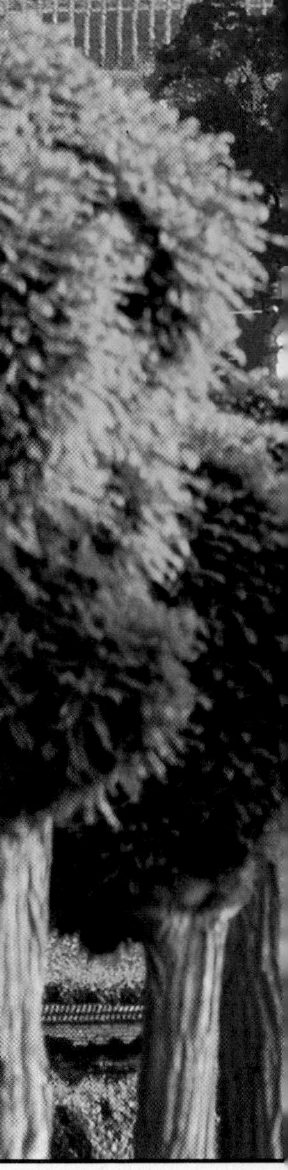

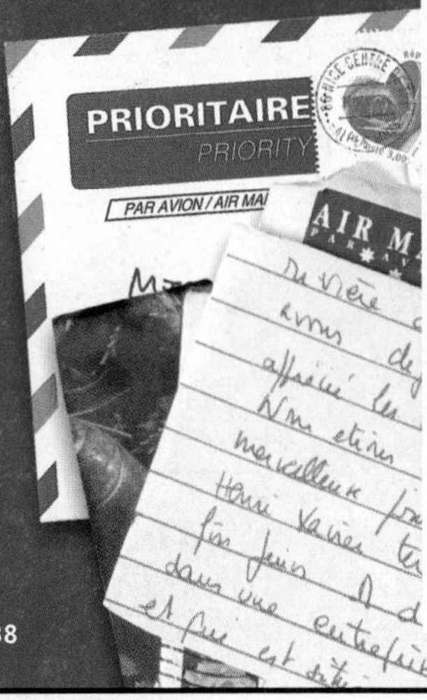

Ornement traditionnel du Mali

338

FRENCH Online

The **Glencoe Foreign Language Web site** (french.glencoe.com) offers several options that enable you and your students to experience the French-speaking world via the Internet:

- The online **Activités** are correlated to the chapters and utilize Francophone Web sites around the world. For the Chapter 11 activity, see student page 365.
- Games and puzzles afford students another opportunity to practice the material learned in a particular chapter.
- The *Enrichment* section offers students an opportunity to visit Web sites related to the theme of the chapter for more information on a particular topic.
- Online *Chapter Quizzes* offer students an opportunity to prepare for a chapter test.
- Visit our virtual **Café** for more opportunities to practice and explore the French-speaking world.

Spotlight on Culture

Photograph This photo of a tractor on a tree-lined street in front of the village church was taken in the Côte d'Or area of Burgundy. This rural area is famous for its vineyards and superb Burgundy wines.

Headdress To appreciate African art, it is necessary to know the context in which an object is used. Almost all traditional African art has a practical purpose. It can involve religion, daily life, health, or successful crops. The piece seen here is a traditional harvest headdress from Mali. It is in the art museum in Bamako, the capital of Mali.

trois cent trente-neuf 339

Chapter Projects

J'aimerais habiter... Have students choose a French-speaking city or town that they would like to live in, according to whether they prefer urban or rural life. Have them prepare a report on their city or town and ask them to explain why they selected it. Students should include photos and maps of the city or town in their report, if possible. The Internet is a good source for this information.

La cuisine régionale Have students make a large map of France. Ask students to bring in pictures of French food products from magazines and have them glue them in the appropriate region on the map.

Vocabulaire Mots 1

1 Preparation

Resource Manager

Vocabulary Transparencies 11.2–11.3
Audio Activities Booklet TE, pages 118–120
Audiocassette 7A/CD 7
Workbook, pages 121–122
Quiz 1, page 53
ExamView Pro®

Bellringer Review

Use BRR Transparency 11.1 or write the following on the board.
List all the words and expressions you can remember that have to do with taking the metro.

2 Presentation

Step 1 Have students close their books. Use Vocabulary Transparencies 11.2–11.3 to present **Mots 1.** Have students repeat the words, phrases, and sentences after you or Audiocassette 7A/CD 7.

Step 2 Ask *either/or* and *yes/no* questions to elicit the vocabulary. Then point in random order to illustrations on the Vocabulary Transparencies and ask **Qu'est-ce que c'est?**

Step 3 Use gestures and dramatizations to convey the meaning of **à gauche, à droite, devant, derrière, tout droit, en face de, tourner,** and **faire demi-tour.**

Step 4 Have students repeat the miniconversation with as much expression as possible.

Vocabulaire Mots 1

La ville

La banlieue est l'ensemble des agglomérations qui entourent une grande ville.

une usine

un bureau

Au centre-ville / En ville

L'agent de police règle la circulation.

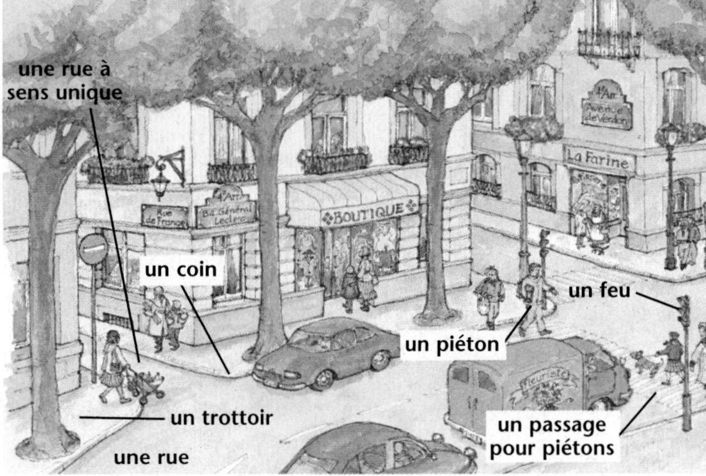

Avant de traverser la rue, il faut regarder à gauche et à droite.
Le feu va changer.
Les piétons traversent la rue dans un passage pour piétons.

Learning from Photos

(page 340 top left) The photo shows **la Défense,** the relatively new commercial business area beyond Neuilly.

Les voitures circulent dans la ville.
La voiture rouge roule derrière la voiture jaune: elle la suit.
Mais elle ne la suit pas de trop près.
Le conducteur conduit bien.
Il respecte le code de la route.

derrière l'église
à côté de l'église
devant l'église
en face de l'église

Reaching All Students

Spatial Intelligence Have students draw diagrams of the following either on paper or on the board:

devant l'école
derrière l'école
à côté de l'école
en face de l'école
à gauche de l'école
à droite de l'école
un carrefour
un rond-point

Assessment

As an informal assessment after completing the vocabulary presentation, you may wish to call on students to look at the illustrations and say as much as they can about them.

Reaching All Students

Total Physical Response Have students mimic the following:

Vous allez traverser la rue. Regardez à droite.
Regardez à gauche.

Mettez une pièce dans l'horodateur.
Prenez votre ticket.
Mettez le ticket sur le pare-brise de votre voiture.
Tournez à gauche.
Tournez à droite.
Faites demi-tour.

3 Practice

Commençons
Let's use our new words

Attention!

When students are doing the **Commençons** activities, accept any answer that makes sense. The purpose of these activities is to have students use the new vocabulary. They are not factual recall activities. Thus, it is not necessary for students to remember specific factual information from the vocabulary presentation when answering. If you wish, have students use the photos on pages 342–343 as a stimulus, when possible.

Historiette Each time **Historiette** appears, it means that the answers to the activity form a short story. Encourage students to look at the title of the **Historiette,** since it can help them do the activity.

1 and 2 After completing these activities, have one student read each activity as a story.

Writing Development

Have students write the answers to Activities 1 and 2 in paragraph form.

Commençons
Let's use our new words

1 Historiette En ville, à pied

Répondez.

1. Avant de traverser, les piétons attendent sur le trottoir?
2. Ils attendent au coin, où il y a un feu?
3. Ils traversent la rue quand le feu est rouge?
4. Il faut regarder à gauche et à droite avant de traverser?
5. Les piétons traversent dans un passage pour piétons?
6. Est-ce qu'un agent de police règle la circulation?
7. Il donne une contravention aux automobilistes qui ne respectent pas le code de la route?

Le boulevard du Montparnasse à Paris

2 Historiette Le mauvais sens

Répondez d'après les indications.

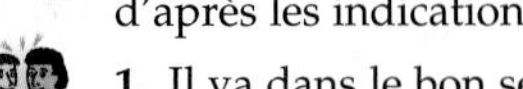

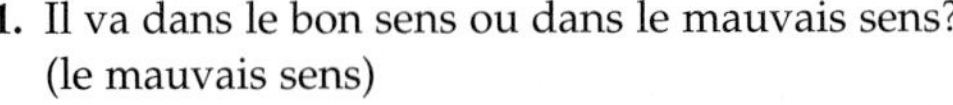

1. Il va dans le bon sens ou dans le mauvais sens? (le mauvais sens)
2. C'est une rue à sens unique? (oui)
3. Il doit aller tout droit ou faire demi-tour? (faire demi-tour)
4. Il doit aller jusqu'où? (au troisième carrefour)
5. Qu'est-ce qu'il y a là? (un feu)
6. Il doit continuer tout droit jusqu'où? (au rond-point)
7. S'il suit une autre voiture de trop près, il risque d'avoir un accident? (oui)
8. Il est interdit de stationner sur le rond-point? (oui)
9. Il peut se garer où? (au parking)

3 Où est le café?

Répondez d'après le dessin.

1. Le café est à droite ou à gauche du théâtre?
2. Le cinéma est à côté du restaurant ou derrière le restaurant?
3. Le parc est à côté du restaurant ou en face du café?
4. La voiture est garée devant l'école ou derrière l'école?
5. Le cinéma est derrière le théâtre ou en face du théâtre?

Answers to Commençons

1 *Answers will vary but may include:*

1. Oui, avant de traverser, les piétons attendent sur le trottoir.
2. Oui, ils attendent au coin, où il y a un feu.
3. Non, ils ne traversent pas la rue quand le feu est rouge. Ils la traversent quand le feu est vert.
4. Oui, il faut regarder à gauche et à droite avant de traverser.
5. Oui, les piétons traversent dans un passage pour piétons.
6. Oui, un agent de police règle la circulation.
7. Oui, il donne une contravention aux automobilistes qui ne respectent pas le code de la route.

2

1. Il va dans le mauvais sens.
2. Oui, c'est une rue à sens unique.
3. Il doit faire demi-tour.
4. Il doit aller jusqu'au troisième carrefour.
5. Là, il y a un feu.
6. Il doit continuer tout droit jusqu'au rond-point.
7. Oui, s'il suit une autre voiture de trop près, il risque d'avoir un accident.
8. Oui, il est interdit de stationner sur le rond-point.
9. Il peut se garer au parking.

3

1. Le café est à droite du théâtre.
2. Le cinéma est à côté du restaurant.
3. Le parc est en face du café.
4. La voiture est garée derrière l'école.
5. Le cinéma est en face du théâtre.

Des champs dans le sud-ouest de la France

En 1960, 25% de la population active en France—c'est-à-dire la population qui travaille—était dans l'agriculture. Aujourd'hui, c'est moins de 6%. Mais il y a aussi des paysans[3] qui adorent la campagne. Ceux qui l'adorent ne changeraient leur vie pour rien au monde.

[3] paysans *peasants*

Après la lecture

A Qui est-ce? Identifiez.

1. celui qui se consacre à l'agriculture
2. celui qui a une propriété
3. celui qui a une ferme
4. celui qui vit à la campagne

B Les Fauvet

Répondez d'après la lecture.

1. Où est la ferme des Fauvet?
2. Où est Soual?
3. Que fait M. Fauvet?
4. Les Fauvet ont une maison en bois?
5. Qu'est-ce qu'il y a à côté de leur maison?
6. Où M. Fauvet entrepose-t-il son matériel?
7. Les Fauvet ont combien d'enfants?
8. Après leurs études, les enfants resteront à la ferme?

On cultive des fraises dans le sud-ouest.

Post-reading

Have the students discuss the last paragraph of the reading. Does a similar situation exist in the United States?

Après la lecture

A and B Allow students to refer to the story to look up the answers or you may use these activities as a testing device for factual recall.

Geography Connection

Although the southwest of France has some industrial areas such as Toulouse, the region is mostly known for its agriculture. One of the favorite dishes of the area is a **cassoulet** made from goose, pork, sausage, and beans. It is a very hearty dish and best eaten at midday.

Critical Thinking Activity

Drawing conclusions, making inferences

Read the following to the class or write it on the board or on a transparency:

1. **Le lever et le coucher du soleil sont très importants pour les fermiers. Pourquoi?**
2. **Qu'est-ce qui se passe si le fermier a une mauvaise récolte? Quelles en sont les conséquences?**

Answers to Après la lecture

A

1. un agriculteur
2. un propriétaire
3. un fermier
4. un paysan

B

1. La ferme des Fauvet est à quelques kilomètres de Soual.
2. Soual est dans le sud-ouest de la France.
3. M. Fauvet est fermier.
4. Non, ils ont une maison en pierre.
5. À côté de leur maison il y a une étable, une grange et un hangar.
6. M. Fauvet entrepose son matériel dans le hangar.
7. Les Fauvet ont deux enfants.
8. Non, les enfants ne resteront pas à la ferme après leurs études.

National Standards

Cultures
This reading familiarizes students with the city of Abidjan.

Attention!

This reading is optional. You may skip it completely, have the entire class read it, have only several students read it and report to the class, or assign it for extra credit.

Presentation

Step 1 Have students look carefully at the photos on page 356. Have them describe the photos.

Step 2 Have students quickly read the selection.

Après la lecture

Go over the **Après la lecture** activity and have students correct any false statements.

History Connection

Houphouet-Boigny became the first president of the Côte d'Ivoire after the country gained independence in 1960. Houphouet-Boigny ruled with an iron hand. He became increasingly unpopular throughout his reign and he died in 1993 at age 88.

Abidjan was the capital of the Côte d'Ivoire until 1983 when Yamoussoukro was proclaimed the capital. Yamoussoukro is still the capital, but Abidjan remains the most important city of the country. Yamoussoukro is the native village of Houphouet-Boigny, and it was he who invested a great deal of money in the village and proclaimed it the capital.

Lecture supplémentaire 1

Abidjan

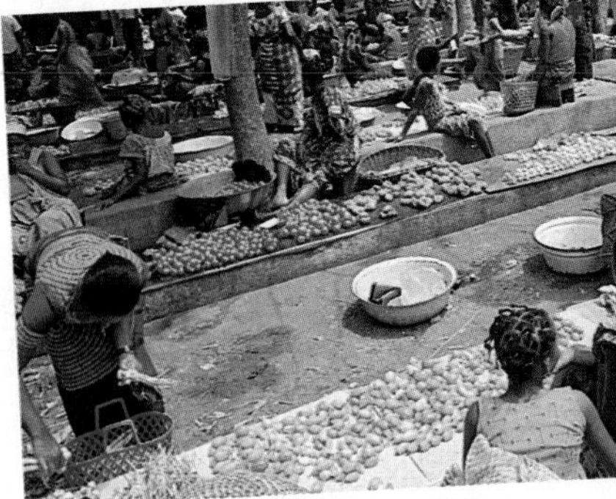

Un marché dans la rue à Abidjan

En 1951 Abidjan était une petite ville de moins de 100 000 habitants. Aujourd'hui, c'est une grande ville cosmopolite de plus de 2,5 millions d'habitants et la ville principale de la Côte d'Ivoire. On appelle Abidjan le Paris de l'Afrique occidentale. Cette ville tout proche de l'équateur a même une patinoire couverte.

Le Plateau

Abidjan est construite autour d'une jolie lagune. La zone commerciale du centre-ville s'appelle Le Plateau. Là, il y a des tours modernes. Près du Plateau se trouve Cocody, un quartier résidentiel très chic.

Le Plateau à Abidjan

Treichville et Adjamé

Treichville et Adjamé sont deux quartiers très intéressants du point de vue du tourisme. Il y a deux grands ponts[1] qui relient ces deux quartiers au Plateau. On peut aussi prendre le bateau-bus. Treichville a le plus grand marché de la ville. Au marché, il vaut mieux[2] savoir quelques mots de dioula. Le dioula, c'est une langue spéciale qu'on parle uniquement sur les marchés africains. Adjamé a aussi un marché et une immense gare routière.

[1] ponts *bridges* [2] il vaut mieux *you'd better*

Après la lecture

Une ville cosmopolite Vrai ou faux?

1. Abidjan a toujours été une grande ville.
2. On n'est jamais loin de l'eau à Abidjan.
3. Il y a beaucoup de tours modernes au centre-ville.
4. Adjamé est le nom du centre-ville.
5. Le plus grand marché d'Abidjan se trouve à Treichville.
6. Le dioula est la langue qu'on parle dans tous les quartiers d'Abidjan.

Answers to Après la lecture

1. faux
2. vrai
3. vrai
4. faux
5. vrai
6. faux

Fun Facts

Street markets such as the one seen here in Abidjan are extremely common in West Africa.

Dioula, pronounced *Jou-lah,* is the major language spoken in the markets of several West African countries. The following are some expressions in **Dioula:**

Good morning	**e-nee-sott-goh-mah**
How are you?	**E-kah-kay-nay-WAH?**
I'm fine	**ah-HON-kah-kay-nay**
Thank you	**e-nee-chay**
Good-bye	**AM-bay-soh-goh-mah**

Montréal

Montréal est la ville francophone la plus importante après Paris. La ville de Montréal est située sur une île du même nom—l'île de Montréal. Elle est née de la confluence de la rivière des Outaouais et du fleuve Saint-Laurent. Une quinzaine de ponts[1] relient l'île au continent. Montréal est un important centre industriel, commercial et financier.

Une ville souterraine à Montréal

Une patinoire à Montréal

Montréal en hiver

À Montréal, la température varie beaucoup d'une saison à l'autre. En hiver, il fait très froid et il neige beaucoup. Grâce à une «ville sous la ville», on peut flâner[2] dans un immense centre commercial sans souffrir des rigueurs du climat. La ville souterraine a des passages piétons qui permettent d'avoir accès aux principaux hôtels, aux bureaux, aux grands magasins, à des centaines de boutiques, à de nombreux cinémas et restaurants et à deux gares.

Une calèche devant l'hôtel de ville de Montréal

Le vieux Montréal

Le vieux Montréal est aujourd'hui un quartier très agréable. Les demeures[3] anciennes ont été rénovées et les vieux entrepôts[4] ont été convertis en appartements et en bureaux. Des calèches permettent aux touristes de visiter ces beaux quartiers du temps passé.

[1] ponts *bridges*
[2] flâner *wander around*
[3] demeures *abodes, dwellings*
[4] entrepôts *warehouses*

La Tunisie

Le Maroc

Le Mali

Après la lecture

Une ville importante Décrivez.

1. où est située la ville de Montréal
2. le temps qu'il y fait en hiver
3. la ville souterraine
4. le vieux Montréal

National Standards

Cultures
This reading familiarizes students with the city of Montreal.

Attention!

This reading is optional. You may skip it completely, have the entire class read it, have only several students read it and report to the class, or assign it for extra credit.

Presentation

Step 1 Have students look carefully at the photos on page 357. Have them describe the photos.

Step 2 Have students quickly read the selection.

Après la lecture

Go over the **Après la lecture** activity.

Answers to Après la lecture

1. La ville de Montréal est située sur une île. Il y a beaucoup de ponts qui relient l'île au continent.
2. En hiver il fait très froid et il neige beaucoup.
3. La ville souterraine est un centre commercial sous la ville de Montréal. Il y a des passages piétons qui permettent d'avoir accès à beaucoup de boutiques, cinémas, restaurants, etc.
4. Le vieux Montréal est très joli avec de vieilles maisons et de vieux bâtiments. On peut visiter la ville en calèche.

Fun Facts

Today Montreal is the second-largest French-speaking city in the world after Paris. It was founded by French settlers some 365 years ago. In the mid-seventeenth century, Montreal was a mere handful of woodhouses around a few stone buildings, all of which were fortified by a wood stockade.

The construction of the **Cité souterraine** began in 1966 when the Montreal metro opened.

CONNEXIONS

National Standards

Connections
This reading about demographics in France establishes a connection with another discipline, allowing students to reinforce and further their knowledge of the social sciences through the study of French.

Comparisons
This reading contrasts certain demographic statistics of the United States with those of France, affording students a better understanding of the nature of both the size and age of the two populations.

Attention!

The readings in the **Connexions** section are optional. They focus on some of the major disciplines taught in schools and universities. The vocabulary is useful for discussing such topics as history, literature, art, economics, business, science, etc. You may choose any of the following ways to do the readings in the **Connexions** sections.

Independent reading Have students read the selections and do the post-reading activities as homework, which you collect. This option is least intrusive on class time and requires a minimum of teacher involvement.

Homework with in-class follow-up Assign the readings and post-reading activities as homework. Review and discuss the material in class the next day.

Intensive in-class activity This option includes a pre-reading vocabulary presentation, in-class reading and discussion, assignment of the activities for homework, and a discussion of the assignment in class the following day.

CONNEXIONS

La sociologie

La démographie

Demography is the study of human populations, of their distribution, density, and vital statistics. Demographics explain where people choose to live and why. They also explain population shifts—why people move from place to place.

The demography of France is quite similar to that of most industrialized nations. The urban areas are becoming more populated because people are migrating from rural areas to the cities. Newly arrived immigrants from foreign countries also settle in the cities where employment is often more available.

La démographie

La démographie est l'étude des populations humaines. La démographie étudie où vivent les gens et les raisons pour lesquelles ils y vivent. La démographie explique quand et pourquoi les gens décident de déménager[1] et de s'installer ailleurs.

Déplacements de population

De nombreux agriculteurs se trouvent actuellement dans une situation économique précaire. Le matériel agricole qui est indispensable à une bonne exploitation de la terre coûte cher. Il faut souvent s'endetter pour acheter des machines, des tracteurs, etc., et le revenu que leur rapporte[2] leur petite propriété—surtout les années où la récolte n'est pas bonne—n'est pas suffisant pour couvrir les frais. Pour cette raison, de nombreux paysans[3] quittent les régions rurales pour aller chercher du travail dans les agglomérations urbaines. Au milieu du dix-neuvième siècle, les ruraux représentaient les 2/3 (les deux tiers) de la population totale de la France. Aujourd'hui, leur part est tombée à 6% (six pour cent).

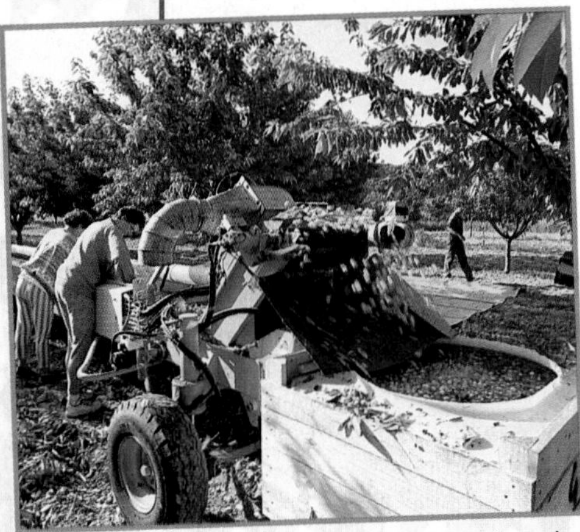

La cueillette des cerises

[1] déménager *to move*
[2] rapporte *brings*
[3] paysans *peasants*

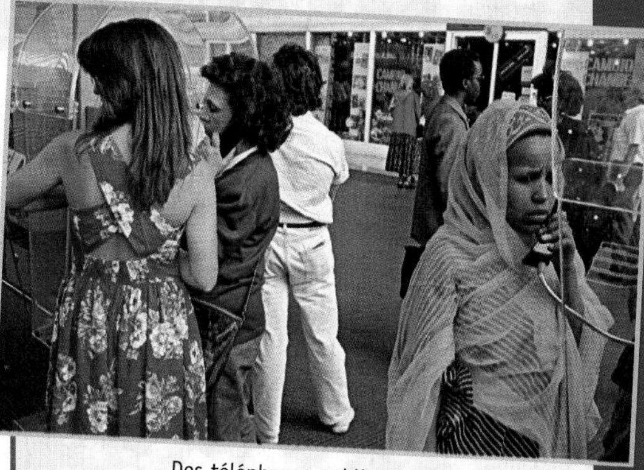
Des téléphones publics à Paris

L'immigration

La France n'a jamais été un grand pays d'émigration. En revanche (au contraire), la France a fait appel à l'immigration pour se procurer la main-d'œuvre[4] nécessaire au développement de son économie. Pendant les années 80, la hausse du chômage[5] a provoqué l'arrêt de l'immigration. Récemment, l'immigration a repris[6], mais le nombre des immigrés de pays européens est en baisse[7]. La plupart des nouveaux arrivés sont du Maghreb, d'Afrique occidentale et d'Asie. Estimée à 3,6 millions (trois millions six) de personnes, la population étrangère représente 6,3% (six virgule trois pour cent) de la population totale. De ces 3,6 millions, un million sont des jeunes de moins de 16 ans.

[4] main-d'œuvre *work force*
[5] hausse du chômage *rise in unemployment*
[6] a repris *started up again*
[7] en baisse *lower*

Pays d'origine des étrangers résidant en France

Pays	Nombre
Portugal	606 000
Algérie	572 000
Italie	523 000
Maroc	447 000
Espagne	413 000
Tunisie	182 000
Afrique occidentale	182 000
Turquie	159 000
Pays d'Asie	158 000
Yougoslavie	60 000
Pologne	40 000

Après la lecture

Discussion Discutez en anglais.

1. What is demography?
2. What migratory patterns exist within France?
3. Why did France call upon immigrants?

CONNEXIONS

Presentation

La sociologie
La démographie

Step 1 Have students read the introduction in English on page 358.

Step 2 Have students read the selection independently.
Note: The figures given here for **étrangers** living in France are the latest available (1997).

Most of the Asians residing in France are from Vietnam and Cambodia.

ANSWERS TO Après la lecture

Students will discuss the topics.

Use what you have learned

Presentation

Encourage students to say as much as possible when they do these activities. Tell them not to be afraid to make mistakes, since the goal of these activities is real-life communication. If someone in the group makes an error, allow the others to politely correct him or her. Let students choose the activities they would like to do.

You may wish to divide students into pairs or groups. Encourage students to elaborate on the basic theme and to be creative. They may use props, pictures, or posters if they wish.

C'est à vous

Use what you have learned

Le Quartier latin à Paris

PARLER 1

La ville

✓Talk about life in the city

Avec un(e) camarade, parlez de tout ce que vous savez de Paris. Dites si vous aimeriez habiter à Paris et pourquoi.

PARLER 2

Une ville francophone

✓Talk about life in an interesting Francophone city

Depuis que vous faites du français, vous avez «visité» plusieurs villes francophones. Choisissez une ville qui vous intéresse et décrivez-la à votre camarade. Ensuite, il/elle fera de même.

PARLER 3

Jeu Comparaisons

✓Talk about animals—an aspect of country life

Travaillez avec un(e) camarade. Essayez de deviner ce que les expressions suivantes veulent dire. (Vous en connaissez déjà quelques-unes.) Essayez ensuite de trouver leur équivalent en anglais.

avoir une faim de loup
avoir une fièvre de cheval
compter les moutons
être malade comme un chien
être mère poule
manger comme un cochon
jouer au chat et à la souris

Quand le chat n'est pas là, les souris dansent.
Il fait un temps de chien.

Answers to C'est à vous

1 *Answers will vary.*

Students can tell about the many monuments they have learned about, different areas of the city, museums, public transport, etc.

2 *Answers will vary depending upon the city students choose.*

3 *Answers will vary but may include:*

To be as hungry as a wolf
To be burning up with fever
To count sheep
To be as sick as a dog
To be a mother hen
To eat like a pig
To play cat and mouse
When the cat's away, the mice will play.
It's raining cats and dogs.

C'est à vous

4 Je ne pourrais jamais vivre...

✔Give your opinion about city life vs. country life

Écrivez une rédaction intitulée «Je ne pourrais jamais vivre à la campagne (à la ville)». Donnez vos raisons.

Writing Strategy

Comparing and contrasting
Comparing and contrasting involves writing about similarities and differences between two or more related things. A Venn diagram will help you do this. First draw two intersecting circles; title the circles with the subjects to be compared. List unique features of each subject. Then list the similarities of the two subjects in the area where the circles intersect. This tool, or any other similar one you can think of, will help you organize your thoughts so you can clearly and effectively write your comparison.

5 Deux villes

Think of two cities you have visited. Write a paper comparing the two places. If you are not familiar with two different cities, compare the town where you live with a nearby city or other town. Be sure to organize your thoughts with a list or a graph, showing the similarities and differences.

La ville de Luxembourg

Fort-de-France à la Martinique

Recycling

These activities allow students to use the vocabulary and structure from this chapter in completely open-ended, real-life situations.

Writing Development

Have students keep a notebook containing their best written work from each chapter. These selected writings can be based on assignments from the Student Textbook and the Writing Activities Workbook. The two activities on page 361 are examples of writing assignments that may be included in each student's portfolio. In the Workbook, students will develop an organized autobiography **(Mon autobiographie).** These workbook pages may also become a part of their portfolio.

Writing Strategy

Comparing and contrasting
Have students read the Writing Strategy on page 361. Have students refer to the vocabulary list on page 364 if they need more ideas to write this selection.

Learning from Photos

(page 361 left) Fort-de-France is the main city of Martinique—**un département français d'outre-mer (un D.O.M.).** It is a colorful city on the Caribbean coast.

(page 361 right) Luxembourg is a small principality that serves as one of the financial capitals of Europe. Its residents speak three languages: Luxembourgish, German, and French. Luxembourg City is the capital.

Reaching All Students

Additional Practice
Display Communication Transparency C 11. Have students work in groups to make up as many questions as they can about the illustration. Have groups take turns asking and answering the questions.

Answers to C'est à vous

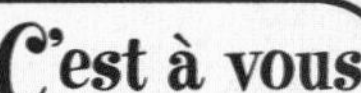

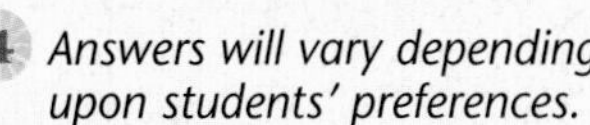

4 *Answers will vary depending upon students' preferences.*

5 *Answers will vary depending upon the cities selected.*

Resource Manager

Communication Transparencies
Quizzes
Test Booklet
ExamView Pro®
Situation Cards
Performance Assessment
Marathon mental Videoquiz

Assessment

This is a pre-test for students to take before you administer the chapter test. Answer sheets for students to do these pages are provided in your transparency binder. Note that each section is cross-referenced so students can easily find the material they have to review in case they made errors. You may wish to collect these assessments and correct them yourself or you may prefer to have the students correct themselves in class. You can go over the answers orally or project them on the overhead, using your Assessment Answers transparencies.

Vocabulaire

1 Identifiez.

To review **Mots 1**, *turn to pages 340–341.*

2 Complétez.

6. Vous allez dans le mauvais sens. Il faut faire _____.
7. Les piétons _____ la rue dans un passage pour piétons.
8. L'école n'est pas devant l'église. Elle est _____ l'église.

To review **Mots 2**, *turn to pages 344–345.*

3 Répondez.

9. Qui cultive la terre?
10. Donnez les noms de deux animaux.
11. Les fermiers mettent les animaux où?
12. Ils mettent leur récolte où?
13. Quel animal donne du lait.

Answers to Assessment

 1

1. une piétonne
2. le coin
3. le trottoir
4. un agent de police
5. un feu rouge

 2

6. demi-tour
7. traversent
8. derrière

3 *Answers will vary but may include:*

9. un agriculteur (un fermier)
10. une vache, un mouton
11. dans une étable
12. dans une grange
13. une vache

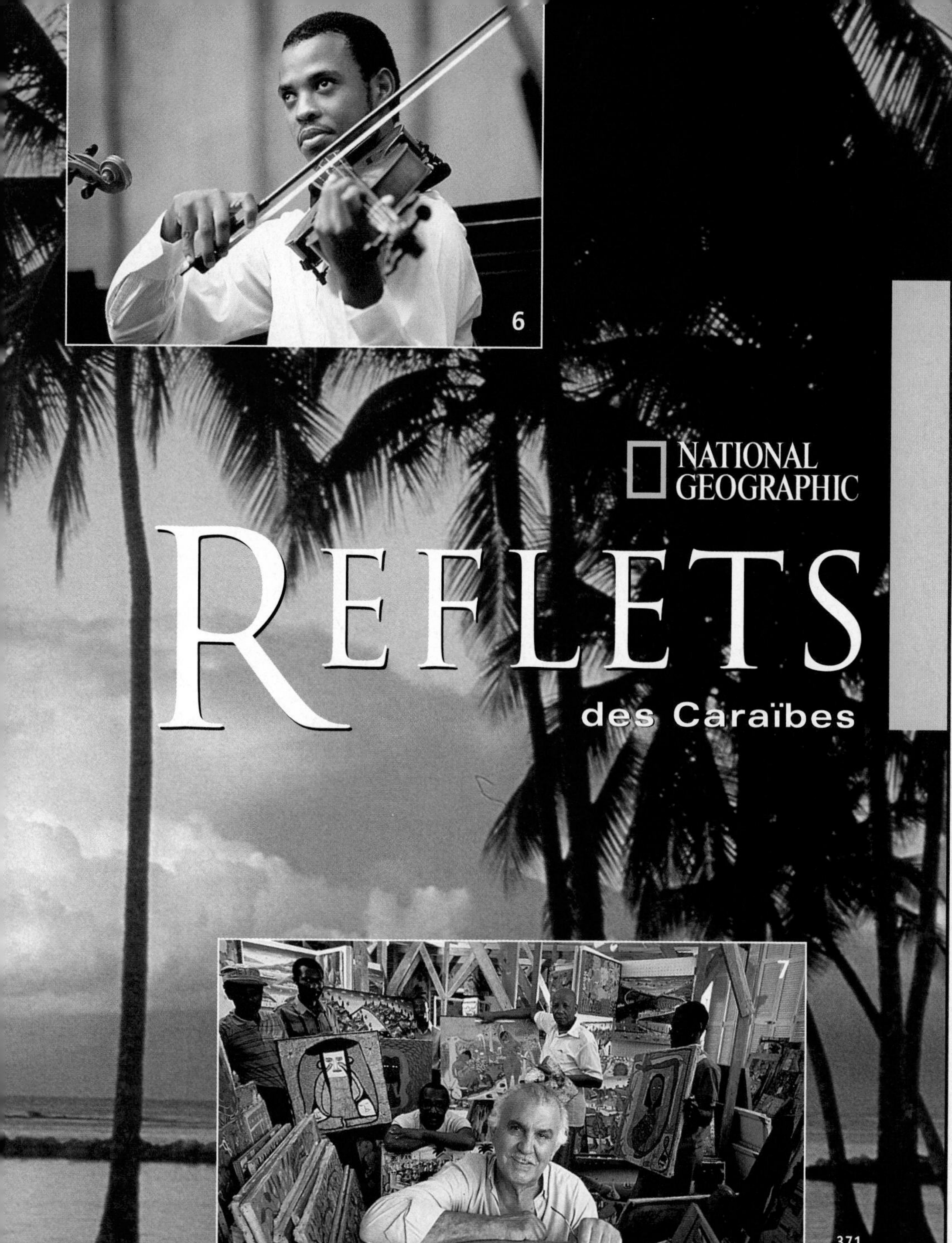

REFLETS
des Caraïbes

3. Homme portant des anthuriums et autres fleurs exotiques à Fond-Saint-Denis, à la Martinique Martinique is known for its exotic flora. In the capital, Fort-de-France, there is the **Parc Floral et Culturel** where one can learn about the many varieties of flowers that grow around the island.

4. La place de la Victoire à Pointe-à-Pitre, à la Guadeloupe Pointe-à-Pitre is a city of some 100,000 people on **Grande-Terre.** It is the island's commercial and industrial hub. The heart of the old city is the **place de la Victoire.** The square is surrounded by wood buildings, which have balconies and shutters. In the center of the square there is a palm-shaded park that is a popular gathering place.

5. Jeune Haïtienne Haiti occupies the western part of the island of Hispaniola, which it shares with the Dominican Republic. Its population of more than six million people speak French and Creole. The people are extremely industrious, but Haiti has suffered from one political crisis after another. It is the poorest country in the Western Hemisphere.

6. Jeune violoniste de l'Orchestre Philharmonique Sainte Trinité, en Haïti In spite of the poverty in Haiti, its people find ways to express their talents, particularly in the fields of music and art. **Sainte Trinité** is the name of Port-au-Prince's cathedral. The major religions of Haiti are Roman Catholic and voodoo.

7. Artistes peintres exposant leurs tableaux à Port-au-Prince, en Haïti Many Haitians excel in art, and their paintings are popular in art galleries around the world. Many of the artists are self-taught, and their paintings depict scenes of everyday life or Biblical scenes. In Port-au-Prince, the **Centre d'art** is run by charitable groups, and it helps to promote Haitian art. Some of the artists are too poor to get canvas, and they paint on cardboard.

8. Ouvriers agricoles dans un champ de canne à sucre dans la région du Moule, à la Guadeloupe Although tourism is very popular in Guadeloupe, sugar is still Guadeloupe's principal source of income. Sugar harvest time is in February, and the fields are filled with workers cutting cane. The roads are clogged with trucks taking cane to factories and distilleries.

9. L'héliconia, une fleur exotique des Antilles There are many varieties of Heliconia. The one pictured is commonly known as "lobster claw." These beautiful flowers grow throughout the Caribbean.

10. Fresque décorant le mur d'une pharmacie de Fort-de-France, à la Martinique Here we see a painting done by a local resident on the wall of a pharmacy in Fort-de-France.

11. Courses de gommiers au large des côtes de la Martinique The boats seen in this race are **gommiers. Gommiers** are actually fishing boats that are made from the wood of a gum tree.

12. La bibliothèque Schœlcher à Fort-de-France, à la Martinique The **bibliothèque Schœlcher** is a rather elaborate building, incorporating several architectural styles. It is a public library, and it was named after Victor Schœlcher. Schœlcher was an Alsatian who led the fight for the abolition of slavery in the West Indies during the nineteenth century. The Fort-de-France suburb of Schœlcher is also named after him. It is a pleasant area, home to the University of the French West Indies and Guyana.

8. Ouvriers agricoles dans un champ de canne à sucre dans la région du Moule, à la Guadeloupe
9. L'héliconia, une fleur exotique des Antilles
10. Fresque décorant le mur d'une pharmacie de Fort-de-France, à la Martinique
11. Courses de gommiers au large des côtes de la Martinique
12. La bibliothèque Schœlcher à Fort-de-France, à la Martinique
13. Jeunes gens jouant aux dames au Cap-Haïtien, en Haïti
14. Un des fameux taps taps bigarrés de Port-au-Prince, en Haïti

Teacher's Corner

Index to the NATIONAL GEOGRAPHIC MAGAZINE

The following related articles may be of interest:

- "Haiti—Against All Odds," by Charles E. Cobb, November 1987.
- "Searching for Columbus's Lost Colony: La Navidad," by Kathleen A. Deagan, November 1987.
- "The Caribbean: Sun, Sea, and Seething," by Noel Grove, February 1981.

13. Jeunes gens jouant aux dames au Cap-Haïtien, en Haïti Cap-Haïtien is the second-largest city in Haiti, with a population of some 90,000. It was destroyed several times by fires and earthquakes. Above the city sits an old **Citadelle** reachable by donkey.

14. Un des fameux taps taps bigarrés de Port-au-Prince, en Haïti **Taps taps** are the major means of public transportation in Haiti. The brightly painted trucks of a wide variety of sizes are given creative names, many of which are religious in nature. Many of the **taps taps** are privately owned, and their owners are proud of them and maintain them very well.

Products available from GLENCOE/MCGRAW-HILL

To order the following products, call Glencoe/McGraw-Hill at 1-800-334-7344.

CD-ROMs
- Picture Atlas of the World
- The Complete National Geographic: 112 Years of National Geographic Magazine

Transparency Set
- NGS PicturePack: Geography of North America

Products available from NATIONAL GEOGRAPHIC SOCIETY

To order the following products, call National Geographic Society at 1-800-368-2728.

Books
- National Geographic World Atlas for Young Explorers
- National Geographic Satellite Atlas of the World

Software
- ZingoLingo: French Diskette

Planning for Chapter 12

SCOPE AND SEQUENCE, PAGES 374–403

Topics

- Holidays and celebrations

Culture

- Celebrations and holidays in France
- **Carnaval** in France, the Caribbean, the United States, and Canada

Functions

- How to talk about things that may or may not happen
- How to express what you wish, hope, or would like others to do

Structure

- The subjunctive
- The subjunctive with expressions of wish or desire

National Standards

- Communication Standard 1.1 pages 378, 379, 382, 383, 386, 387, 388, 389, 391, 398
- Communication Standard 1.2 pages 378, 379, 382, 383, 386, 387, 388, 389, 390, 393, 395, 397
- Communication Standard 1.3 pages 378, 379, 383, 387, 389, 391, 398, 399
- Cultures Standard 2.1 pages 376, 377, 380, 381, 385, 386, 392–393, 394–395
- Connections Standard 3.1 pages 396–397
- Comparisons Standard 4.2 pages 379, 383, 391
- Communities Standard 5.1 page 399

PACING AND PRIORITIES

The chapter content is color coded below to assist you in planning.

■ required ■ recommended ■ optional

Vocabulaire *(required)* *Days 1–4*

- ■ Mots 1
  - Le 14 juillet
  - Le carnaval
- ■ Mots 2
  - Noël
  - Hanouka
  - Le jour de l'An
  - Le mariage

Structure *(required)* *Days 5–7*

- ■ Le subjonctif
- ■ Le subjonctif après les expressions de souhait ou de volonté

Conversation *(required)*

- ■ C'est bientôt le 14 juillet

Lectures culturelles

- ■ Des fêtes en France *(recommended)*
- ■ Carnaval *(optional)*

Connexions *(optional)*

- ■ Histoire et Littérature

■ **C'est à vous** *(recommended)*

■ **Assessment** *(recommended)*

■ **Technotour** *(optional)*

Spotlight on Culture

Photograph The young women in the photo are marching in a parade during the Flower Festival in Digne, Provence.

Painting André Lhote (1885–1962) was both a painter and an art critic. Influenced by fauvists and cubists, he liked to paint realistic human figures using vivid colors.

Students can send electronic greeting cards in French for various holidays from Café Glencoe (french.glencoe.com).

trois cent soixante-quinze ⚜ 375

Chapter Projects

Une fête Have students select a holiday that is celebrated in the French-speaking world and the United States. Ask them to prepare a report comparing and contrasting the ways in which the holiday is celebrated in the two different cultures.

Vous êtes invités! Have students prepare a wedding invitation or a wedding announcement in French.

La fête nationale Have the students prepare a report on **le 14 juillet**.

1 Preparation

Resource Manager

Vocabulary Transparencies 12.2–12.3
Audio Activities Booklet TE, pages 128–130
Audiocassette 7B/CD 7
Workbook, pages 137–138
Quiz 1, page 58
ExamView Pro®

Bellringer Review

Use BRR Transparency 12.1 or write the following on the board.
Complete.

1. **Aujourd'hui Marie a quinze ans. C'est son ____.**
2. **Marie donne une ____ et elle ____ ses amis.**
3. **Ses amis lui donnent des ____.**
4. **Il y a un ____ avec quinze bougies.**

2 Presentation

Step 1 Have students close their books. Use Vocabulary Transparencies 12.2–12.3 to present **Mots 1.** Have students repeat the words, phrases, and sentences after you or Audiocassette 7B/ CD 7.

Vocabulaire

Mots 1

Le 14 juillet 

C'est la fête nationale française.
La fête a lieu le 14 juillet.

une fanfare

La fanfare joue l'hymne national.
C'est «La Marseillaise».

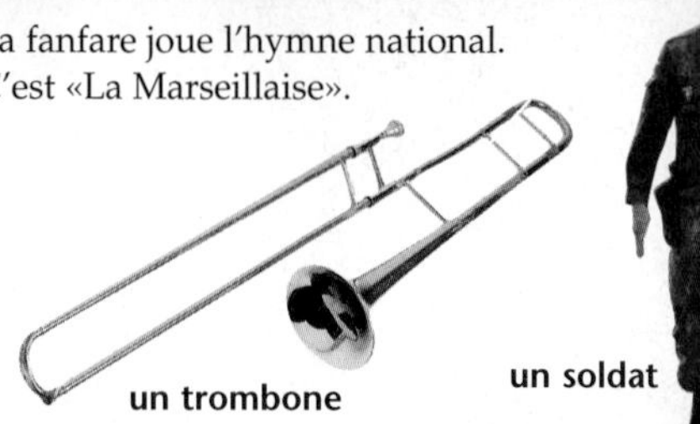

un soldat

des feux d'artifice

une tribune

Les soldats défilent.
Ils passent devant les tribunes.

Learning from Photos

(page 376 top left) The photo is of a military band participating in the July 14th parade on the **Champs-Élysées.**

(page 376 top right) The marching band is playing at the Bastille Day celebrations in Beaune.

Fun Facts

The **Garde républicaine de Paris,** pictured in the illustration on page 376, is an arm of the national police force under the Department of Defense. Their appearance, with gleaming sabers, shining helmets with plumes, varnished boots, and flashing breastplates, is impressive at state functions like the Bastille Day parade. The **Garde** provides color and pageantry, but they are also honored for their service as a riot squad and in battle.

Reaching All Students

Bodily Kinesthetic Intelligence

Pantomime Game Write these expressions on cards. Distribute them to students to mime. The others guess what instrument is being played.

jouer de la guitare
jouer du piano
jouer de l'accordéon
jouer du trombone
jouer du tambour
jouer des cymbales
jouer du violon

Le carnaval

un char

lancer des confettis

des serpentins

Un défilé de chars traverse la ville.

Dans la rue, il y a des groupes masqués.

Step 2 As you are presenting the vocabulary, you may wish to ask the following types of questions: **La fête nationale française est le 4 ou le 14 juillet? Le 14 juillet, il y a un grand défilé? Les soldats défilent? Il y a beaucoup de monde dans les tribunes? Le maire et les notables regardent le défilé? Quels instruments y a-t-il dans une fanfare? Comment s'appelle l'hymne national français? Quand est-ce qu'il y a des feux d'artifice? Qu'est-ce qu'on lance pendant le carnaval?**

Step 3 Have students open their books and read the new words and expressions.

About the French Language

Tell students that **jouer de** is used to express the meaning *to play a musical instrument.*

On joue du piano.
On joue du violon.

Review **jouer à** with a sport.

On joue au foot.

Learning from Photos

(page 377) All of these photos were taken during the **carnaval** celebrations in Nice.

Reaching All Students

Additional Practice You may wish to ask students the following additional questions about the **Mots 1** vocabulary: **Il faut que tout le monde applaudisse après «La Marseillaise»? Qui joue l'hymne national, la fanfare ou l'orchestre? Il y a des tambours dans une fanfare? On tire des feux d'artifice le 14 ou le 4 juillet en France? Et aux États-Unis?**

Vocabulary Expansion

You may wish to give students the names of these musical instruments:

un violon	**une clarinette**
un piano	**un saxophone**
une harpe	**un cornet**
un orgue	**un tuba**
une flûte	**un triangle**
un hautbois	**une grosse caisse**
un piccolo	

Assessment

As an informal assessment after completing the vocabulary presentation, you may wish to call on students to look at the illustrations and say as much as they can about them.

3 Practice

Commençons
Let's use our new words

Historiette Each time **Historiette** appears, it means that the answers to the activity form a short story. Encourage students to look at the title of the **Historiette,** since it can help them do the activity.

2 and **3** After completing these activities, have one student read each one as a story.

Learning from Photos

(page 378) The photos are as follows:

1. a float at the Mardi Gras Festival in New Orleans, Louisiana
2. fireworks in Paris for Bastille Day
3. French Foreign Legion marching band on Bastille Day in Paris

Writing Development

Have students write the answers to Activities 2 and 3 in paragraph form.

Commençons
Let's use our new words

1 Qu'est-ce que c'est? Identifiez.

1. C'est un char ou des confettis?

2. C'est un drapeau ou un feu d'artifice?

3. C'est une tribune ou une fanfare?

4. C'est un tambour ou un drapeau?

5. C'est un soldat ou le maire?

2 Historiette Le quatorze juillet Répondez.

1. La fête nationale française, c'est le 14 juillet?
2. Pour célébrer la fête nationale, il y a des défilés?
3. Est-ce que les soldats défilent?
4. Ils défilent au son d'une fanfare?
5. Les tribunes sont pleines de spectateurs?
6. Le défilé passe devant les tribunes?
7. Le maire est au premier rang?
8. Est-ce qu'il y a d'autres notables dans les tribunes?
9. La fanfare joue l'hymne national?
10. «La Marseillaise», c'est l'hymne national français?

3 Historiette Une grande fête
Inventez une histoire.

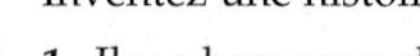

1. Il y a beaucoup de monde dans la rue?
2. Un défilé de chars passe dans la rue?
3. Des gens masqués chantent et dansent dans la rue?
4. Il y a un orchestre qui joue dans la rue?
5. Il y a des feux d'artifice?

*For more practice using words from **Mots 1**, do Activity 18 on page H19 at the end of this book.*

Answers to Commençons

1

1. C'est un char.
2. C'est un feu d'artifice.
3. C'est une fanfare.
4. C'est un drapeau.
5. C'est un soldat.

2

1. Oui, la fête nationale française, c'est le 14 juillet.
2. Oui, il y a des défilés.
3. Oui, les soldats défilent.
4. Oui, ils défilent au son d'une fanfare.
5. Oui, les tribunes sont pleines de spectateurs.
6. Oui, le défilé passe devant les tribunes.
7. Oui, le maire est au premier rang.
8. Oui, il y a d'autres notables dans les tribunes.
9. Oui, la fanfare joue l'hymne national.
10. Oui, «La Marseillaise» est l'hymne national français.

3

1. Oui, il y a beaucoup de monde dans la rue.
2. Oui, un défilé de chars passe dans la rue.
3. Oui, des gens masqués chantent et dansent dans la rue.
4. Oui, il y a un orchestre qui joue dans la rue.
5. Oui, il y a des feux d'artifice.

Vocabulaire

4 **Deux fêtes nationales** Vrai ou faux?

1. La fête nationale française a lieu le 14 juillet.
2. La fête nationale française est le même jour que la fête nationale américaine.
3. L'hymne national français s'appelle «La Marseillaise» et l'hymne national américain s'appelle «The Star-Spangled Banner».
4. Aux États-Unis le 4 juillet, il y a des feux d'artifice.
5. À Paris le 14 juillet, il y a un grand défilé militaire le matin et des feux d'artifice le soir.
6. Dans une fanfare, les musiciens jouent de la trompette, du trombone, du tambour, des cymbales.
7. Les soldats passent devant le maire et les notables.
8. Le 4 juillet, aux États-Unis, on joue «La Marseillaise».

Le 14 juillet aux Champs-Élysées

Le carnaval à Fort-de France

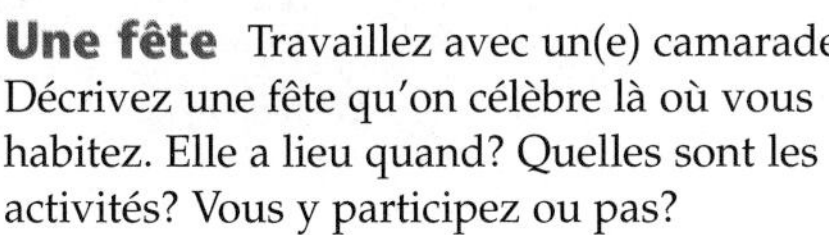

5 **Une fête** Travaillez avec un(e) camarade. Décrivez une fête qu'on célèbre là où vous habitez. Elle a lieu quand? Quelles sont les activités? Vous y participez ou pas?

6 **La fanfare de votre école** Votre camarade est un(e) jeune Français(e) qui visite votre école. Décrivez-lui la fanfare de votre école. Dites-lui si elle est grande ou petite, quand elle joue et où. Dites-lui comment les musiciens sont habillés (ce qu'ils portent) et s'ils ont gagné des trophées. Ensuite changez de rôle.

4 Have students correct each false statement.

Reteaching

Show Vocabulary Transparencies 12.2–12.3 and let students say as much as they can about them in their own words.

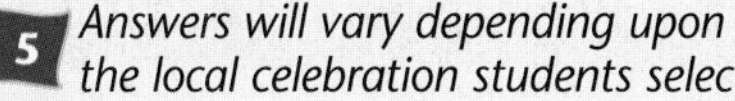

Answers to Commençons

4

1. vrai
2. faux
3. vrai
4. vrai
5. vrai
6. vrai
7. vrai
8. faux

5 *Answers will vary depending upon the local celebration students select.*

6 *Answers will vary but may include:*

La fanfare de notre école est très grande. Elle joue aux matchs de football et dans des défilés en ville. Les musiciens portent des pantalons noirs et des vestes rouges. Ils portent des bérets noirs. Ils ont gagné quelques trophées.

1 Preparation

Resource Manager

Vocabulary Transparencies 12.4–12.5
Audio Activities Booklet TE, pages 131–133
Audiocassette 7B/CD 7
Workbook, page 139
Quiz 2, page 59
ExamView Pro®

Bellringer Review

Use BRR Transparency 12.2 or write the following on the board.
Look at the Paris metro map on page xxxiii. Find the Cité station, located on the Île de la Cité island in the Seine River. Write directions from that stop to the Opéra station.

2 Presentation

Step 1 Show Vocabulary Transparencies 12.4–12.5. Have students close their books and repeat the words after you or Audiocassette 7B/CD 7 as you point to the appropriate illustration on the transparency.

Step 2 You may wish to ask the following questions during your presentation: **Qui apporte les cadeaux de Noël? Qui reçoit les cadeaux de Noël? Il faut qu'ils soient sages? Où sont les souliers? Les cadeaux de Noël sont dans les souliers et sous l'arbre de Noël? Quel est votre chant de Noël préféré? Quel est un autre nom pour la fête des Lumières? C'est une fête juive ou chrétienne? Qui allume les bougies de la menorah?**

Vocabulaire Mots 2

Noël

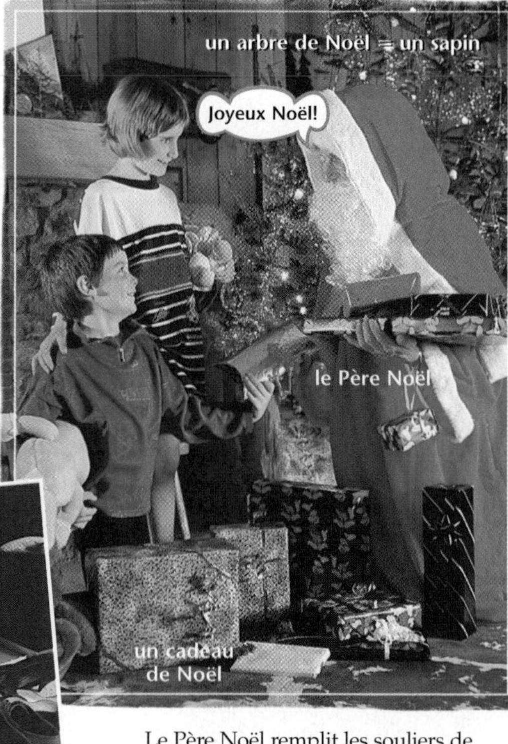

une cheminée
un soulier

Le Père Noël remplit les souliers de cadeaux la veille de Noël.
Il faut que les enfants soient sages s'ils veulent recevoir des cadeaux de Noël.

Le réveillon est le repas qu'on fait la veille de Noël.
Ils réveillonnent.

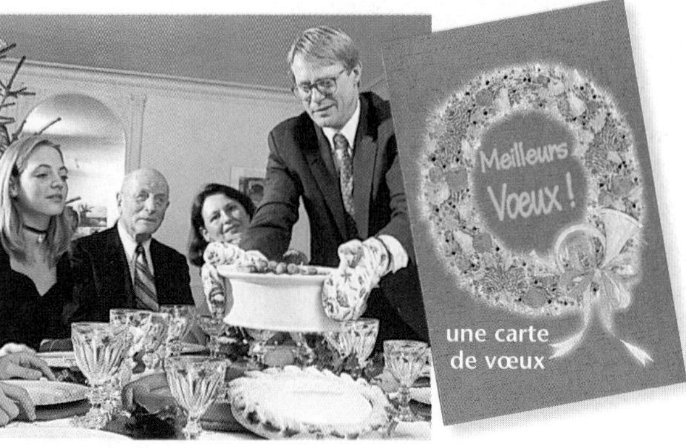

Reaching All Students

Bodily Kinesthetic Intelligence

Pantomime Have students mime the following actions:

Ouvrez votre cadeau de Noël.
Chantez un chant de Noël.
Allumez une bougie.
Signez une carte de vœux.
Souhaitez «Bonne Année» à quelqu'un.

Learning from Photos

(page 380 top left) The Midnight Mass is taking place at the church in Kayersberg in Alsace.

Assessment

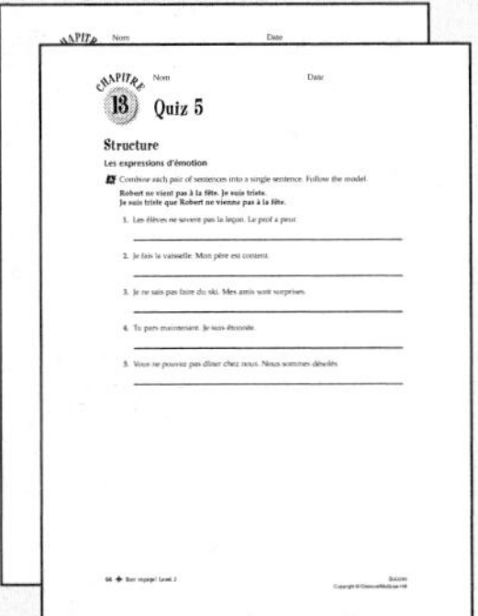
Vocabulary and Structure Quizzes, pages 62–66

Chapter Tests, Chapter 13

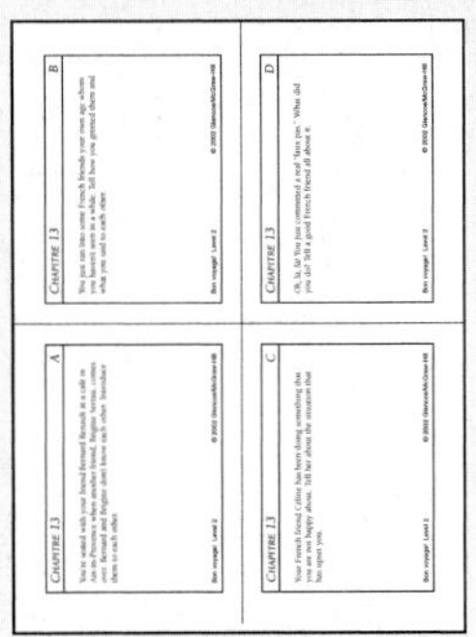
Situation Cards, Chapter 13

Timesaving Teacher Tools

Interactive Teacher Edition

Imagine having your Teacher's Edition and all resources on a CD-ROM. Click on a resource and it appears on your screen, ready to be printed, sorted, or planned.

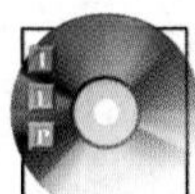

Interactive Lesson Planner

The Interactive Lesson Planner CD-ROM helps you organize your lesson plans for a week, month, semester, or year. Look at this planning tool for easy access to your Chapter 13 resources.

ExamView Pro®

Test Bank software for Macintosh and Windows makes creating, editing, customizing, and printing tests quick and easy.

Technology Resources

In the Chapter 13 Internet activity, you will have a chance to learn more about etiquette in France. Visit french.glencoe.com.

On the Interactive Conversation CD-ROM, students can listen to and take part in a recorded version of the conversation in Chapter 13.

See the National Geographic Teacher's Corner on pages 138–139, 244–245, 372–373, 472–473 for reference to additional technology resources.

Bon voyage! Video and Video Activities Booklet.

Help your students prepare for the chapter test by playing the **Marathon mental** Videoquiz game show. Teams will compete against each other to review chapter vocabulary and structure and sharpen listening comprehension skills.

CHAPITRE 13

Preview

In this chapter, students will learn vocabulary associated with good manners and some French social customs. They will learn the subjunctive forms of some irregular verbs and the use of the subjunctive with expressions of necessity and possibility and with expressions of emotion.

National Standards

Communication

In Chapter 13, students will communicate in spoken and written French on the following topics:

- Good manners
- Social customs
- Emotions

Students will obtain and provide information about these topics, express feelings, and engage in conversations that would typically take place in social settings as they fulfill the chapter objectives listed on this page.

CHAPITRE 13

Le savoir-vivre

Objectifs

In this chapter you will learn to:

- *talk about social etiquette*
- *introduce people to each other*
- *describe some feelings*
- *express opinions*
- *talk about more things that may or may not happen*
- *express emotional reactions to what others do*
- *compare etiquette in France and the United States*

Anton Van DYCK 1599-1641 6,70F 1,02€ RF

Berthe Morisot *Au Bal*

The **Glencoe Foreign Language Web site** (french.glencoe.com) offers several options that enable you and your students to experience the French-speaking world via the Internet:

- The online **Activités** are correlated to the chapters and utilize Francophone Web sites around the world. For the Chapter 13 activity, see student page 433.
- Games and puzzles afford students another opportunity to practice the material learned in a particular chapter.
- The *Enrichment* section offers students an opportunity to visit Web sites related to the theme of the chapter for more information on a particular topic.
- Online *Chapter Quizzes* offer students an opportunity to prepare for a chapter test.
- Visit our virtual **Café** for more opportunities to practice and explore the French-speaking world.

Spotlight on Culture

Photograph In this photo we see families visiting one another at the home of one of the couples in Brunoy, a residential suburb of Paris.

Painting Berthe Morisot (1841–1895), a granddaughter of Jean-Honoré Fragonard, was born into a family with a rich artistic tradition. From a very early age she was certain she would become a painter. At age fifteen she started to copy paintings in the Louvre. At this time, this was a common way to learn to paint. At the Louvre she met Édouard Manet. They became good friends, and several years later she married his brother Eugène.

Like Manet, Morisot concentrated on portraits and interior scenes. Her figures are attractive and properly reserved. Note how the woman in the painting ***Au Bal*** would not be so bold as to stare directly at you. She shyly lowers her gaze.

Morisot posed her models for short periods of time and then painted them from memory. She was thus able to avoid the somewhat stiff expressions displayed when poses were held over long periods of time.

Chapter Projects

À table Have students prepare in French a list of do's and don'ts concerning table manners in the United States.

Des comparaisons Have students prepare a report that contrasts French and American table manners.

Salut! Have students prepare a list of formal and informal greetings and farewells in French.

Bien élevé(e)? Have students make some simple drawings that depict good and bad manners. Have them write captions for their drawings. You may wish to use them for a bulletin board display.

Savoir-vivre Have the students write an article for a book entitled ***Savoir-vivre.***

Vocabulaire
Mots 1

1 Preparation

Resource Manager

Vocabulary Transparencies 13.2–13.3
Audio Activities Booklet TE, pages 142–144
Audiocassette 8A/CD 8
Workbook, page 147
Quiz 1, page 62
ExamView Pro®

Bellringer Review

Use BRR Transparency 13.1 or write the following on the board.
List all the parts of the body that you remember in French.

2 Presentation

Step 1 Have students close their books. Use Vocabulary Transparencies 13.2–13.3 to present **Mots 1.** Have students repeat the words, phrases, and sentences after you or Audiocassette 8A/CD 8.

Step 2 Point to the parts of the body **(un doigt, la main, le poignet, l'avant-bras, le coude, le pouce, la joue, la bouche, la lèvre).**

Step 3 Dramatize the meaning of **bousculer, resquiller, se serrer la main, s'embrasser, manger la bouche fermée, manger la bouche ouverte, s'essuyer les lèvres.**

Step 4 Have students open their books and read the new words and expressions.

Vocabulaire
Mots 1

D'autres parties du corps

Bien ou mal élevé(e)?

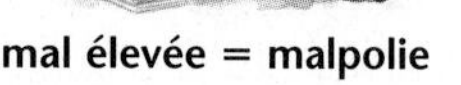

mal élevée = malpolie

bien élevé = poli

bousculer

resquiller

Reaching All Students

Bodily Kinesthetic Intelligence
Pantomime Game
Have students do the following:
Montrez-moi votre bouche.
Montrez-moi votre pouce.
Montrez-moi votre coude.
Montrez-moi votre main.
Montrez-moi vos lèvres.

Write the following words or phrases on index cards. Have students pick a card and mime the action. The class will guess what the person is doing.
bousculer
resquiller
se serrer la main
s'embrasser
manger la bouche fermée
manger la bouche ouverte
s'essuyer les lèvres

Le savoir-vivre en France

✔ *Describe French customs*

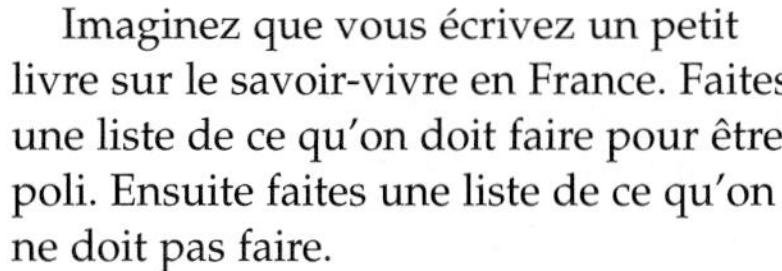

Imaginez que vous écrivez un petit livre sur le savoir-vivre en France. Faites une liste de ce qu'on doit faire pour être poli. Ensuite faites une liste de ce qu'on ne doit pas faire.

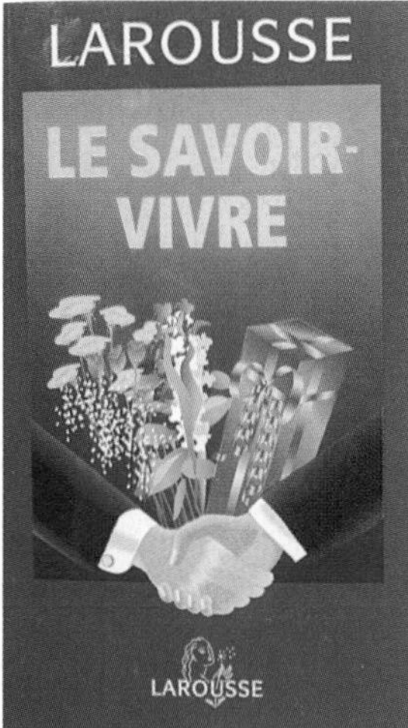

Writing Strategy

Writing an anecdote An anecdote is a story about a lesson learned through experience. Good anecdotes are short, grab the reader's interest, and make a valid point about life. They include the following narrative elements: characters, setting, problem or conflict, and resolution.

À Rome il faut vivre comme les Romains.

Social customs vary from country to country. Sometimes while visiting another country you inadvertently do something humorous or embarrassing because you aren't familiar with the culture. Imagine that you are in a French-speaking country and such a situation occurs. Describe the characters and setting, what happened, and what you learned from the situation. Remember that anecdotes are short and interesting.

C'est à vous

5 Have students give the English equivalent of the title to the activity. *(When in Rome do as the Romans do.)*

Writing Development

Have students keep a notebook containing their best written work from each chapter. These selected writings can be based on assignments from the Student Textbook and the Writing Activities Workbook. The three activities on pages 428–429 are examples of writing assignments that may be included in each student's portfolio. In the Workbook, students will develop an organized autobiography **(Mon autobiographie).** These workbook pages may also become a part of their portfolio.

Writing Strategy

Writing an anecdote

Have students read the Writing Strategy on page 429. Have students refer to the vocabulary list on page 432 if they need more ideas to write this selection.

Answers to C'est à vous

4 *Answers will vary.*

5 *Answers will vary.*

Reaching All Students

Additional Practice

Display Communication Transparency C 13. Have students work in groups to make up as many questions as they can about the illustration. Have groups take turns asking and answering the questions.

Resource Manager

Communication Transparencies
Quizzes
Test Booklet
ExamView Pro®
Situation Cards
Performance Assessment
Marathon mental Videoquiz

Assessment

This is a pre-test for students to take before you administer the chapter test. Answer sheets for students to do these pages are provided in your transparency binder. Note that each section is cross-referenced so students can easily find the material they have to review in case they made errors. You may wish to collect these assessments and correct them yourself or you may prefer to have the students correct themselves in class. You can go over the answers orally or project them on the overhead, using your Assessment Answers transparencies.

Vocabulaire

1 Identifiez.

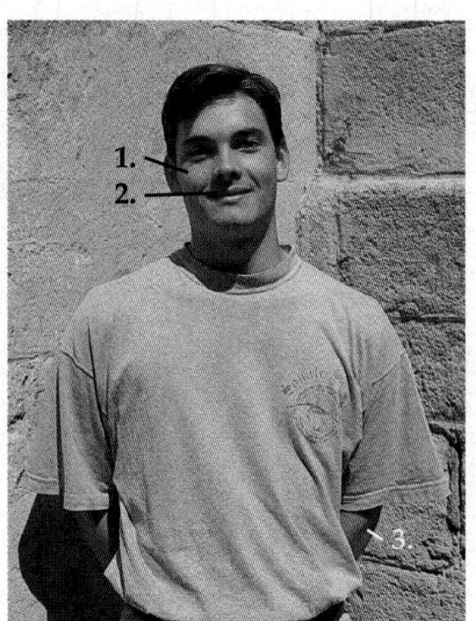

To review **Mots 1**, *turn to pages 406–407.*

2 Donnez un synonyme.

4. poli
5. dire «tu» à quelqu'un

3 Donnez quatre émotions.

6. être ____
7. être ____
8. être ____
9. être ____

To review **Mots 2**, *turn to pages 410–411.*

4 Complétez.

10–11. —Je suis ____ de faire votre connaissance.
—Moi ____.

Answers to Assessment

1

1. la joue
2. la lèvre (la bouche)
3. le coude

2

4. bien élevé
5. tutoyer

3 *Answers will vary but may include:*

6. triste
7. content
8. furieux
9. étonné

4

10. enchanté(e)
11. de même

Structure

5 Complétez.

12. Il est rare qu'elle ____ désagréable. (être)
13. Il vaut mieux que tu le ____ toi-même. (faire)
14. Il est important que vous leur ____. (écrire)
15. Il est possible qu'il te le ____. (dire)
16. Il est nécessaire que vous le ____. (trouver)
17. Il est impossible que nous ____ à l'heure. (arriver)

To review expressing opinions, turn to page 414.

6 Complétez.

18. Je suis triste qu'ils ne ____ pas. (venir)
19. Il ne veut pas que vous le ____. (savoir)
20. J'ai peur qu'il ne ____ pas. (comprendre)
21. Ils regrettent que tu ne ____ pas y assister. (pouvoir)
22. Je suis content qu'il ____. (payer)

To review these verbs in the subjunctive, turn to page 416.

Culture

7 C'est qui? Les Français ou les Américains?

23. Ils s'embrassent souvent sur les joues pour se dire bonjour.
24. Les jeunes ne se serrent presque jamais la main quand ils se rencontrent.
25. On appelle une personne par son prénom uniquement si on connaît bien cette personne.

To review this cultural information, turn to pages 422–423.

Ils se disent «au revoir».

Assessment

Learning from Photos

(page 431) Have students say everything they can about the photo.

Glencoe Technology

MINDJOGGER

You may wish to help your students prepare for the chapter test by playing the MindJogger game show. Teams will compete against each other to review chapter vocabulary and structure and sharpen listening comprehension skills.

Answers to Assessment

 5

12. soit
13. fasses
14. écriviez
15. dise
16. trouviez
17. arrivions

 6

18. viennent
19. sachiez
20. comprenne
21. puisses
22. paie

 7

23. les Français
24. les Américains
25. les Français

Vocabulaire

Vocabulary Review

The words and phrases in the **Vocabulaire** have been taught for productive use in this chapter. They are summarized here as a resource for both student and teacher. This list also serves as a convenient resource for the **C'est à vous** activities on pages 428–429. There are approximately four cognates in this vocabulary list. Have students find them.

Attention!

You will notice that the vocabulary list here is not translated. This has been done intentionally, since we feel that by the time students have finished the material in the chapter they should be familiar with the meanings of all the words. If there are several words they still do not know, we recommend that they refer to the **Mots 1** and **2** sections in the chapter or go to the dictionaries at the back of this book to find the meanings. However, if you prefer that your students have the English translations, please refer to Vocabulary Transparency 13.1, where you will find all these words listed with their translations.

Vocabulaire

Identifying more parts of the body

la joue
la bouche
la lèvre
le doigt
le pouce
la main
le poignet
l'avant-bras *(m.)*
le coude

Talking about polite and rude behavior

mal élevé(e), malpoli(e)
bien élevé(e), poli(e)
bruyant(e)
le bruit
bousculer
resquiller

Talking about table manners

la bouche
fermée
ouverte
pleine
une serviette
se tenir à table
manger
s'essuyer
faire du bruit

How well do you know your vocabulary?

Choose five emotions from the list. Write a sentence for each one, describing your reaction to an event or situation—for example, meeting someone new, an evening out with friends, or a situation where someone behaved rudely.

Talking about going out with friends

le tutoiement
se tutoyer
avoir rendez-vous
se retrouver
se serrer la main
s'embrasser
partager les frais

Describing some emotions

une émotion
étonné(e)
content(e)
furieux(se)
triste
désolé(e)
regretter
avoir peur
avoir l'air

Introducing people to each other

présenter
faire la connaissance de
Je suis enchanté(e)
Moi de même.

Other useful words and expressions

il vaut mieux

Technotour

BON VOYAGE!

VIDÉO • Épisode 13

Avant de visionner

In this video episode, Manu and "Emmanuel" claim to be experts on etiquette.

Est-ce que Manu est bien élevé?

«Emmanuel» sait comment se tenir à table.

FRENCH ONLINE

À découvrir

Learn more about French social customs online.

Il est important de bien se tenir à table.

FRENCH Online

In the Chapter 13 Internet activity, you will have a chance to learn more about etiquette in France. To begin your virtual adventure, go to the Glencoe French Web site: **french.glencoe.com**

Overview

This page previews two key multimedia components of the **Glencoe French** series. Each reinforces the material taught in the chapter in a unique manner.

VIDÉO

The Video Program allows students to see how the chapter vocabulary and structures are used by native speakers. For maximum reinforcement, show the video episode as a final activity for Chapter 13.

The two photos on the left show highlights from the Chapter 13 video episode. Discuss the photos with your students before having them view the episode. See the Video Activities Booklet for detailed suggestions for using this resource.

FRENCH Online

- The **À découvrir** photo on page 433 shows the French method of eating. Students can go online to learn more about French social customs.
- Teacher Information and Student Worksheets for this activity can be accessed at the Web site.

Video Synopsis

In this video episode, Manu and his counterpart, "Emmanuel," each demonstrate their version of good manners. They discuss greeting friends, being on time, eating quietly, and other table manners. Manu doesn't always follow his own guidelines, much to the annoyance of "Emmanuel," who takes the rules of etiquette to heart.

Planning for Chapter 14

SCOPE AND SEQUENCE, PAGES 434–463

Topics

- Careers and professions
- Applying for a job

Culture

- A young man named Bobby
- French and your career
- Job announcements
- **Reflets de l'Europe francophone**

Functions

- How to express doubt
- How to express wishes about yourself and others
- How to express certainty and uncertainty

Structure

- The subjunctive with expressions of doubt
- The infinitive or the subjunctive
- The subjunctive in relative clauses

National Standards

- Communication Standard 1.1 pages 438, 439, 442, 443, 445, 446, 447, 448, 451, 458
- Communication Standard 1.2 pages 438, 439, 442, 443, 445, 446, 447, 448, 449, 450, 453, 454, 455, 457
- Communication Standard 1.3 pages 443, 446, 447, 448, 451, 458, 459
- Connections Standard 3.1 pages 456–457
- Communities Standard 5.1 pages 452–453, 454

PACING AND PRIORITIES

The chapter content is color coded below to assist you in planning.

■ **required** ■ **recommended** ■ **optional**

Vocabulaire *(required)* *Days 1–4*

- ■ Mots 1
  - Un lieu de travail
  - Des professions
  - Des métiers
- ■ Mots 2
  - Au bureau de placement
  - On travaille.

Structure *(required)* *Days 5–7*

- ■ Le subjonctif après les expressions de doute
- ■ L'infinitif ou le subjonctif
- ■ Le subjonctif dans les propositions relatives

Conversation *(required)*

- ■ Au bureau de placement

Lectures culturelles

- ■ Un jeune homme appelé Bobby *(recommended)*
- ■ Le français et votre carrière *(optional)*
- ■ Petites annonces *(optional)*

Connexions *(optional)*

- ■ L'économie

■ **C'est à vous** *(recommended)*

■ **Assessment** *(recommended)*

■ **Technotour** *(optional)*

RESOURCE GUIDE

Section	Pages	Section Resources
Vocabulaire *Mots 1*		
Un lieu de travail Des professions Des métiers	436 436–437 437–439	Vocabulary Transparencies 14.2–14.3 Audiocassette 8B/CD 8 Audio Activities Booklet TE, pages 154–156 Workbook, pages 155–156 Quiz 1, page 67 ExamView Pro®
Vocabulaire *Mots 2*		
Au bureau de placement On travaille.	440 441–443	Vocabulary Transparencies 14.4–14.5 Audiocassette 8B/CD 8 Audio Activities Booklet TE, pages 156–158 Workbook, pages 156–157 Quiz 2, page 68 ExamView Pro®
Structure		
Le subjonctif après les expressions de doute L'infinitif ou le subjonctif Le subjonctif dans les propositions relatives	444–446 447–448 448–449	Audiocassette 8B/CD 8 Audio Activities Booklet TE, pages 158–159 Workbook, pages 158–160 Quizzes 3–5, pages 69–71 ExamView Pro®
Conversation		
Au bureau de placement	450–451	Audiocassette 8B/CD 8 Audio Activities Booklet TE, pages 160–161 CD-ROM
Lectures culturelles		
Un jeune homme appelé Bobby Le français et votre carrière Petites annonces	452–453 454 455	Audiocassette 8B/CD 8 Audio Activities Booklet TE, pages 161–162 Test Booklet, Chapter 14
Connexions		
L'économie	456–457	Test Booklet, Chapter 14
C'est à vous		
	458–459	**Bon voyage!** Video, Episode 14 Video Activities Booklet, Chapter 14 French Online Activities **french.glencoe.com**
Assessment		
	460–461	Communication Transparency C 14 Quizzes 1–5, pages 67–71 Test Booklet, Chapter 14 ExamView Pro® Situation Cards, Chapter 14 Performance Assessment, pages 23–28 **Marathon mental** Videoquiz

Using Your Resources for Chapter 14

Transparencies

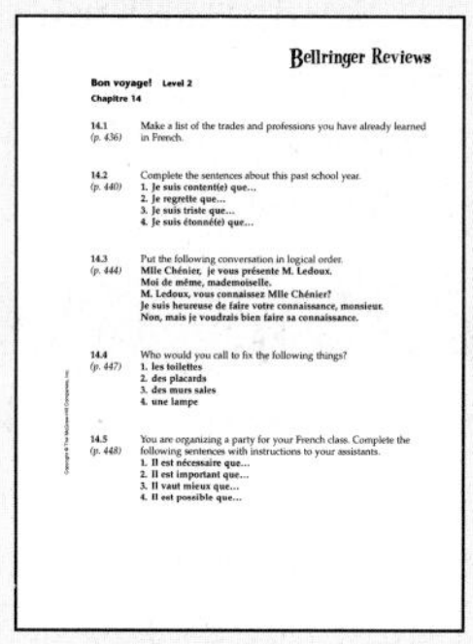
Bellringer 14.1–14.7

Vocabulary 14.1–14.5

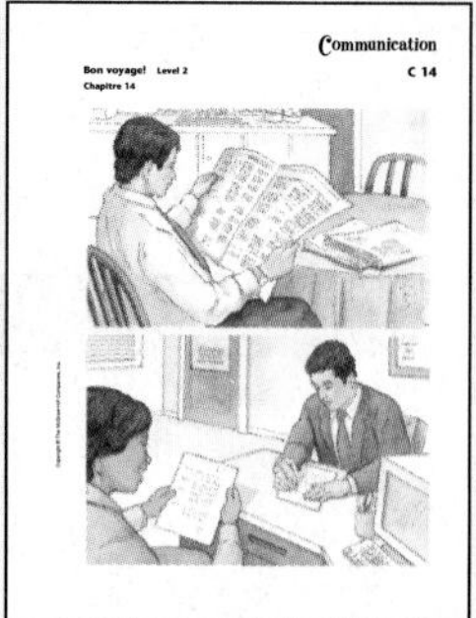
Communication C 14

Writing Activities Workbook

Vocabulary, pages 155–157

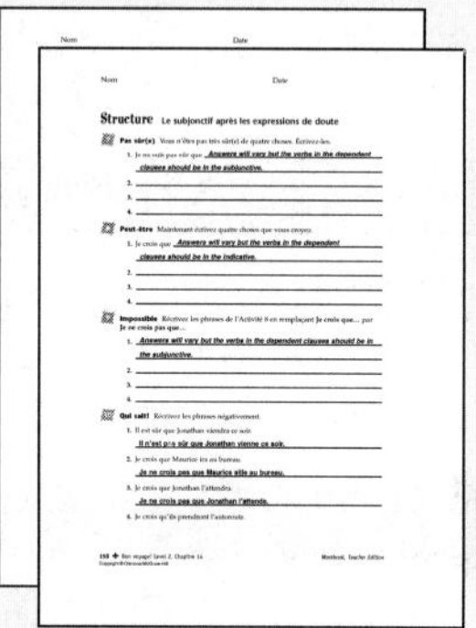
Structure, pages 158–160

Enrichment, pages 161–164

Audio Program and Audio Activities Booklet

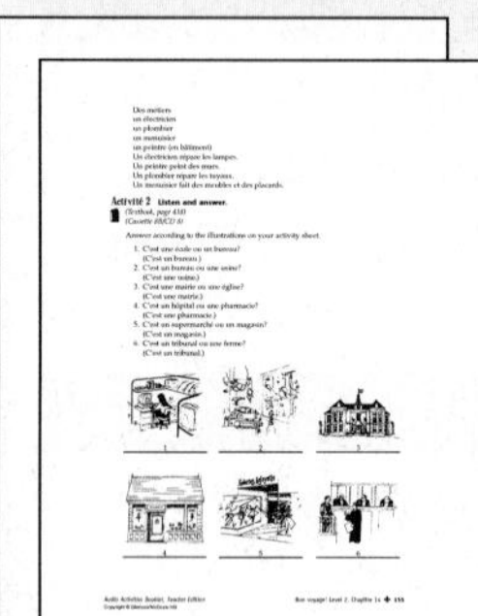
Vocabulary, pages 154–158

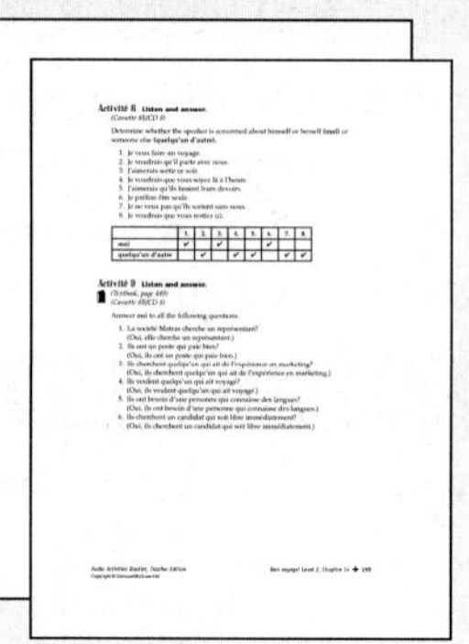
Structure, pages 158–159

Conversation, pages 160–161

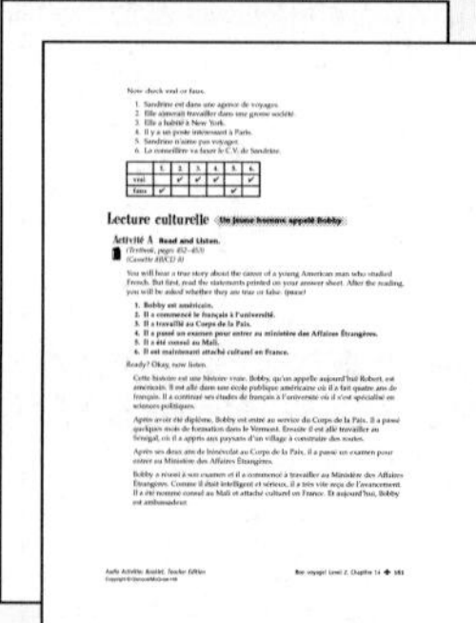
Cultural Reading, pages 161–162

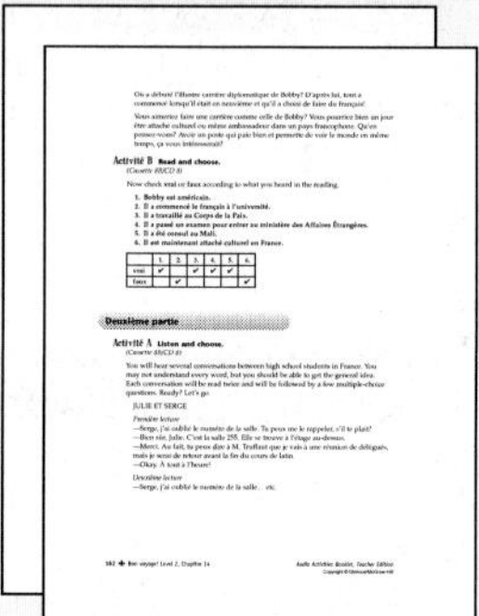
Additional Practice, pages 162–165

Assessment

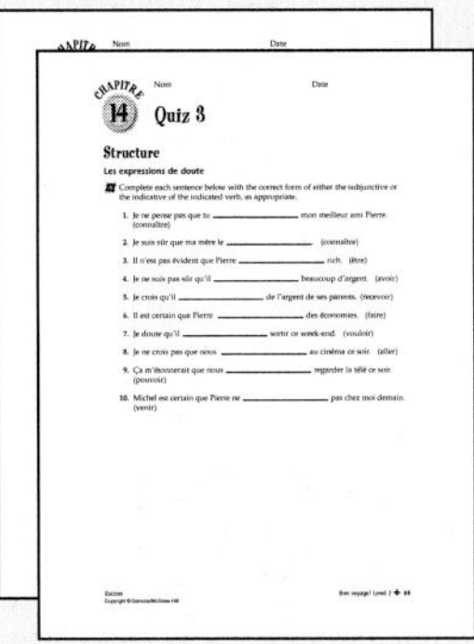

Vocabulary and Structure Quizzes, pages 67–71

Chapter Tests, Chapter 14

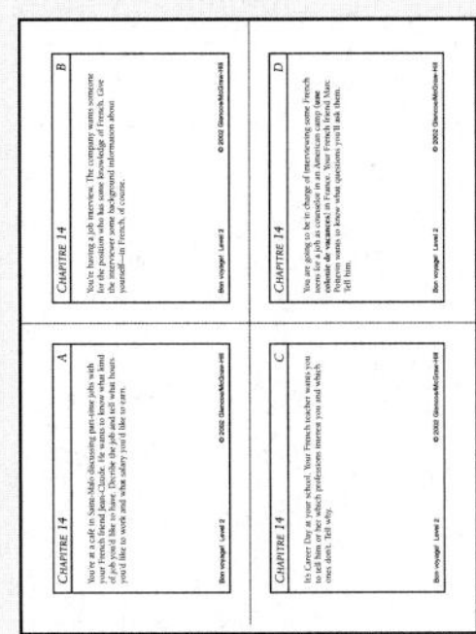

Situation Cards, Chapter 14

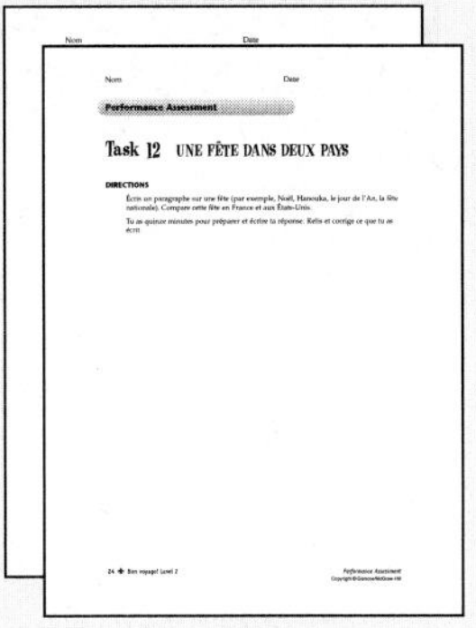

Performance Assessment, pages 23–28

Timesaving Teacher Tools

Interactive Teacher Edition

Imagine having your Teacher's Edition and all resources on a CD-ROM. Click on a resource and it appears on your screen, ready to be printed, sorted, or planned.

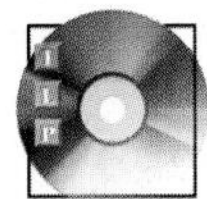

Interactive Lesson Planner

The Interactive Lesson Planner CD-ROM helps you organize your lesson plans for a week, month, semester, or year. Look at this planning tool for easy access to your Chapter 14 resources.

ExamView Pro®

Test Bank software for Macintosh and Windows makes creating, editing, customizing, and printing tests quick and easy.

Technology Resources

In the Chapter 14 Internet activity, you will have a chance to learn more about career opportunities in the Francophone world. Visit french.glencoe.com.

On the Interactive Conversation CD-ROM, students can listen to and take part in a recorded version of the conversation in Chapter 14.

See the National Geographic Teacher's Corner on pages 138–139, 244–245, 372–373, 472–473 for reference to additional technology resources.

Bon voyage! Video and Video Activities Booklet.

Help your students prepare for the chapter test by playing the **Marathon mental** Videoquiz game show. Teams will compete against each other to review chapter vocabulary and structure and sharpen listening comprehension skills.

Preview

In this chapter, students will learn to talk about professions, occupations, and looking for work, including interviewing for a position. They will also learn to use the subjunctive after expressions of doubt and in relative clauses.

National Standards

Communication

In Chapter 14, students will communicate in spoken and written French on the following topics:

- Professions and occupations
- Looking for work
- Interviewing for a job

Students will obtain and provide information about these topics, express doubt, and engage in conversations that would typically take place when discussing their future plans as they fulfill the chapter objectives listed on this page.

CHAPITRE 14

Les professions et les métiers

Objectifs

In this chapter you will learn to:

- *talk about professions*
- *apply for a job*
- *express doubt*
- *express wishes about yourself and others*
- *express certainty and uncertainty*
- *discuss the advantages of learning French for future employment*

Jacques-Yves Cousteau 1910-1997 3,00F +0,60F 0,55€

Fernand Léger *Les constructeurs*

434

FRENCH Online

The **Glencoe Foreign Language Web site** (french.glencoe.com) offers several options that enable you and your students to experience the French-speaking world via the Internet:

- The online **Activités** are correlated to the chapters and utilize Francophone Web sites around the world. For the Chapter 14 activity, see student page 463.
- Games and puzzles afford students another opportunity to practice the material learned in a particular chapter.
- The *Enrichment* section offers students an opportunity to visit Web sites related to the theme of the chapter for more information on a particular topic.
- Online *Chapter Quizzes* offer students an opportunity to prepare for a chapter test.
- Visit our virtual **Café** for more opportunities to practice and explore the French-speaking world.

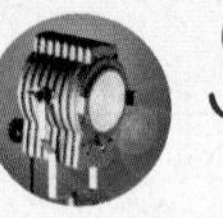

Spotlight on Culture

Photograph This photo of the escalator from the **métro** was taken in the **quartier de La Défense,** the modern business district just west of Paris. The avenue leading to it is a continuation of the Champs-Élysées.

Painting Fernand Léger (1881–1955) worked as a draftsman in an architectural firm in Caen before dedicating himself to art. In the very early part of the twentieth century, he met Modigliani, Delaunay, Apollinaire, and Max Jacob, and he took part in the expositions of the Cubists. After World War I, he began to paint mechanical motifs. The Fernand-Léger museum was opened in 1960 in Biot, France. It is this museum that houses the painting seen here, ***Les constructeurs.***

Recycling

Have students describe the photo to recycle city and metro vocabulary.

Chapter Projects

Ma carrière Have students prepare a report on what they think they would like to do when they complete their education and how French will possibly help them in their career.

National Standards

Communities
Have students prepare their **curriculum vitæ** in French to pursue summer or future employment with an American company that does business in the French-speaking world. They might like to use the French C.V. on page 440 as a model.

Vocabulaire Mots 1

1 Preparation

Resource Manager

Vocabulary Transparencies 14.2–14.3
Audio Activities Booklet TE, pages 154–156
Audiocassette 8B/CD 8
Workbook, pages 155–156
Quiz 1, page 67
ExamView Pro®

Bellringer Review

Use BRR Transparency 14.1 or write the following on the board.
Make a list of the trades and professions you have already learned in French.

2 Presentation

Step 1 Have students close their books. Use Vocabulary Transparencies 14.2–14.3 to present **Mots 1.** Have students repeat the words, phrases, and sentences after you or Audiocassette 8B/CD 8.

Step 2 Have the students open their books and read pages 436–437.

Step 3 Call on students to point to items on the transparencies and name the professions.

Note: To clarify the meaning of **cadre,** explain that it is a salaried employee at the managerial level—from lower management to upper management: **un cadre inférieur, un cadre moyen, un cadre supérieur.** A feminine form for the word does not exist: one would say **une femme cadre.**

Chef de service also does not have a feminine form.

Vocabulaire Mots 1

Un lieu de travail

Elle est cadre. Elle dirige des employés. C'est une femme d'affaires.

Des professions

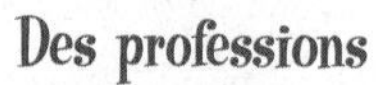

Reaching All Students

Bodily Kinesthetic Intelligence
Have students pantomime the following.

Vous êtes informaticien(ne). Tapez sur votre ordinateur.
Vous êtes cinéaste. Tournez un film.
Vous êtes écrivain. Écrivez quelque chose.
Vous êtes électricien(ne). Réparez une lampe.
Vous êtes menuisier. Faites un placard.

une assistante sociale

un fonctionnaire

Un fonctionnaire travaille pour l'État (le gouvernement).
Une assistante sociale s'occupe des gens qui ont besoin d'aide.

Des métiers 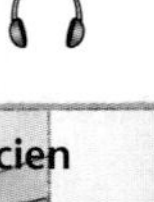

Un électricien répare les lampes.
Un peintre peint des murs.
Un plombier répare les tuyaux.
Un menuisier fait des meubles et des placards.

Step 4 You may wish to ask the following questions about the vocabulary: **Où travaille une assistante sociale? Et un fonctionnaire? Une avocate et un juge travaillent au tribunal? Qui répare les lampes? Qu'est-ce qu'un plombier répare? Que fait un menuisier?**

Vocabulary Expansion

It is possible that a student will want to know the name of a profession or trade not presented in this chapter. Since it would be impossible to list every profession in this Teacher's Wraparound Edition, have the student look up the word in a bilingual dictionary.

 Assessment

As an informal assessment after completing the vocabulary presentation, you may wish to call on students to look at the illustrations and say as much as they can about them.

Reaching All Students

Additional Practice
Have students work in groups. Each person chooses a profession from **Mots 1**. The group works together to draw up a list of courses that students would need to take to pursue the profession they chose. Groups can compare lists for the same professions and see if they agree.

3 Practice

Commençons
Let's use our new words

Attention!

When students are doing the **Commençons** activities, accept any answer that makes sense. The purpose of these activities is to have students use the new vocabulary. They are not factual recall activities. Thus, it is not necessary for students to remember specific factual information from the vocabulary presentation when answering. If you wish, have students use the photos on this page as a stimulus, when possible.

Historiette Each time **Historiette** appears, it means that the answers to the activity form a short story. Encourage students to look at the title of the **Historiette,** since it can help them do the activity.

1 This activity must be done with books open.

2 **and** 3 These activities include vocabulary related to work and professions that was taught in earlier chapters of **Bon voyage! Levels 1** and **2.**

Commençons
Let's use our new words

1 Les lieux de travail Identifiez d'après les dessins.

1. C'est une école ou un bureau?

2. C'est un bureau ou une usine?

3. C'est une mairie ou une église?

4. C'est un hôpital ou une pharmacie?

5. C'est un supermarché ou un magasin?

6. C'est un tribunal ou une ferme?

2 Qui fait ce travail? Trouvez les mots qui correspondent.

1. celui/celle qui aide un chirurgien
2. celui/celle qui répare les lampes
3. celui/celle qui fait le programme d'un ordinateur
4. celui/celle qui défend les criminels au tribunal
5. celui/celle qui vend des marchandises
6. celui/celle qui tient les livres de comptes
7. celui qui répare les éviers, les lavabos, les toilettes
8. celui qui fait des placards, des tables, des chaises
9. celui qui dirige des employés
10. celui qui crée des routes, des bâtiments, etc.

a. un(e) comptable
b. un ingénieur
c. un(e) vendeur(se)
d. un cadre
e. un(e) avocat(e)
f. un(e) informaticien(ne)
g. un(e) infirmier(ère)
h. un(e) électricien(ne)
i. un plombier
j. un menuisier

Answers to Commençons

1

1. C'est un bureau.
2. C'est une usine.
3. C'est une mairie.
4. C'est une pharmacie.
5. C'est un magasin.
6. C'est un tribunal.

2

1. g
2. h
3. f
4. e
5. c
6. a
7. i
8. j
9. d
10. b

Reaching All Students

Additional Practice
Have students work in pairs. Students take turns describing one of the illustrations in Activity 1 without saying which one it is and guessing which place of employment is being described.

Vocabulaire

3 **Qui travaille où?** Répondez. Utilisez toutes les professions ou métiers que vous connaissez.

1. Qui écrit des livres?
2. Qui fait des films?
3. Qui écrit des articles pour un journal?
4. Qui dessine les bâtiments?
5. Qui peint les bâtiments?
6. Qui travaille dans une mairie?
7. Qui travaille dans un hôpital?
8. Qui travaille dans un bureau?
9. Qui travaille dans un tribunal?
10. Qui travaille dans une pharmacie?
11. Qui travaille dans un hôtel?
12. Qui travaille dans un théâtre?
13. Qui travaille dans un magasin?
14. Qui travaille dans une station-service?

Des architectes

4 **Une profession** Travaillez avec un(e) camarade. Parlez des métiers ou professions qui vous intéressent. Expliquez pourquoi.

Des avocats

5 **Jeu** **Je pense à...**
Pensez à une profession ou à un métier. Votre camarade doit vous poser au maximum cinq questions pour essayer de deviner la profession à laquelle vous pensez. Ensuite changez de rôle.

ENCORE PLUS *For more practice using words from **Mots 1**, do Activity 20 on page H21 at the end of this book.*

Reteaching

Show Vocabulary Transparencies 14.2–14.3 and let students say as much as they can about them in their own words.

ENCORE PLUS This *infogap* activity will allow students to practice in pairs. The activity should be very manageable for them, since all vocabulary and structures are familiar to them.

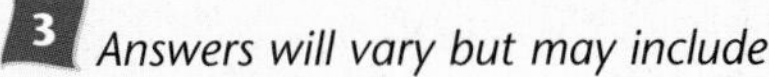

Answers to Commençons

3 *Answers will vary but may include:*

1. des écrivains
2. des cinéastes
3. des journalistes
4. des architectes
5. des peintres en bâtiment
6. des fonctionnaires et des assistantes sociales
7. des infirmiers, des médecins, des chirurgiens
8. des secrétaires, des chefs de service, des assistantes administratives
9. des juges, des avocats
10. des pharmaciens
11. des réceptionnistes
12. des acteurs
13. des vendeurs et des commerçants
14. des pompistes

4 *Answers will vary depending upon the profession the students select.*

Vocabulaire

Mots 2

1 Preparation

Resource Manager

Vocabulary Transparencies 14.4–14.5
Audio Activities Booklet TE, pages 156–158
Audiocassette 8B/CD 8
Workbook, pages 156–157
Quiz 2, page 68
ExamView Pro®

Bellringer Review

Use BRR Transparency 14.2 or write the following on the board.
Complete the sentences about this past school year.

1. **Je suis content(e) que...**
2. **Je regrette que...**
3. **Je suis triste que...**
4. **Je suis étonné(e) que...**

2 Presentation

Step 1 Show Vocabulary Transparencies 14.4–14.5. Have students close their books and repeat the words after you or Audiocassette 8B/CD 8 as you point to the appropriate illustration on the transparency.

Step 2 Ask questions such as: **La femme cherche du travail? Elle a donné son curriculum vitæ au D.R.H.? Elle a vu une petite annonce dans le journal? C'était pour quel poste?**, etc.

Step 3 You may wish to ask the following questions about the illustrations on page 441: **C'est une grosse société ou une petite entreprise? Les employés reçoivent un salaire ou paient un salaire? Qui paie les salaires? Monsieur Moreau travaille chez lui. Il travaille pour une grosse**

Vocabulaire

Mots 2

Au bureau de placement 

une carrière — **COMPTABILITÉ**

⇨ SOCIÉTÉ MONÉGASQUE recherche comptable connaissant salaires, déclarations sociales, expérience souhaitée. Envoyer lettre + CV + photo : à l'attention du service du Personnel, MERCURE INTERNATIONAL, 9 rue du Gabian, 98000 Monaco.

une petite annonce

CURRICULUM VITÆ

Jean Desjardins
25, avenue de l'Université
Outremont (Québec) H3T 1T3
Téléphone : (514) 652.3530
Courrier électronique : jeandesj@ere.umont.ca

FORMATION
1993–1996 **Baccalauréat spécialisé en biochimie**
Université cle Montréal
1991–1993 **Diplôme d'études collégiales et baccalauréat international**
Concentration sciences naturelles
Collège Jean-de-Brébeuf
1986–1991 **Diplôme d'études secondaires**
Collège Jean-de-Brébeuf

BOURSES
1994 • Bourse d'excellence de la fondation Rose-Daoust-Duquette
1993–1994–1995 • Bourse Canada

RÉALISATIONS
1991–1996 • **Implication active pour la promotion des sciences au collège Jean-de-Brébeuf**
Juge au concours scientifique annuel du collège Brébeuf
Membre fondateur d'un club sciences au collégial
1992 • **Projet d'innovation scientifique « Cholestérol en excès : une solution? »**
Médaille d'or à l'Expo-Sciences pancanadienne (niveau national), catégorie « sciences de la vie »
1990 • **Projet d'expérimentation scientifique : « Déplacement linéaire par magnétisme »**
1er prix de l'Expo-Sciences de Montréal
Médaille de l'Association canadienne-française pour l'avancement des sciences (ACFAS)

EXPÉRIENCE PROFESSIONNELLE
été 1995
été 1994 • **Stages d'été à temps plein au laboratoire de neuroendocrinologie de l'hôpital Notre-Dame**
Synthèse de peptides en phase solide à la main et à la machine
été 1993 • **Stage d'été à temps plein au laboratoire de génie biomédical de l'Institut de recherches cliniques de Montréal**
Aide à la mise au point d'un stéthoscope électronique
été 1992 • **Préposé aux bénéficiaires au Centre d'accueil Marcelle-Ferron**

LOISIRS
Sports : cyclisme, badminton, plongée sous-marine, ski de fond, musculation
Voyages, lecture, cinéma, musique

RÉFÉRENCES SUR DEMANDE

un curriculum vitæ (un C.V.)

un entretien

Mlle Leblanc est candidate à un poste.
Elle pose sa candidature.
Elle a un entretien avec le D.R.H.

Elle est libre immédiatement.
Elle peut commencer à travailler demain.

About the French Language

In the ad on this page, **déclarations sociales** refers to documents dealing with insurance, social security, pension, etc. ⚜

On travaillé.

Philippe fait un stage.
Un stagiaire est une personne qui travaille pour avoir de l'expérience.

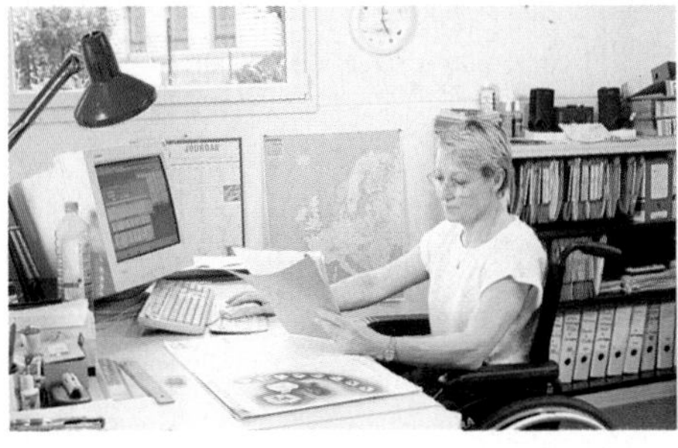

Elle travaille à plein temps (35 heures par semaine).
Elle travaille pour une grosse société.
Une grosse société a beaucoup d'employés.

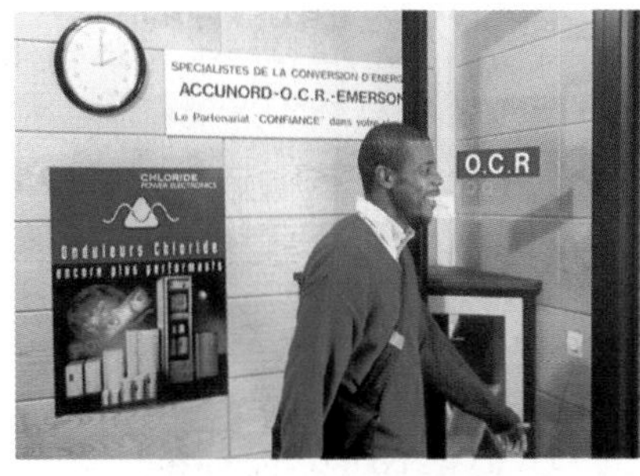

Il travaille à mi-temps (20 heures par semaine).

Elle ne travaille pas pour une entreprise.
Elle est à son compte.

Il est au chômage. Il est chômeur. Il n'a pas de travail.
Il y a chômage quand il n'y a pas d'emplois.

société ou il est à son compte? Monsieur Pelletier est au chômage. Pourquoi? Madame Legendre travaille à plein temps. Elle travaille combien d'heures par semaine?, etc.

Step 4 Have the students open their books and read the new words and expressions.

Cross-Cultural Comparison

Explain to students that the official full-time workweek in France is 35 hours, not 40 hours.

Vocabulary Expansion

You may wish to teach students the following words and expressions:
une intérimaire
faire de l'intérim
Elle est intérimaire. Elle ne travaille ici que pour un mois.

You may also wish to give students the names of these French employment agencies:
ANPE (Agence Nationale Pour l'Emploi) is a public organization.
APEC (Agence Pour l'Emploi des Cadres) is private.

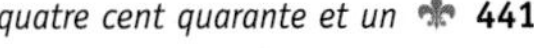

Assessment

As an informal assessment, you may wish to show Vocabulary Transparencies 14.4–14.5. Call on students to point to and identify various items at random.

National Standards

Communities
Have students write to international organizations that offer students jobs in French-speaking countries and request information about summer job possibilities.

3 Practice

Commençons
Let's use our new words

6 You may wish to have a student retell the story in his or her own words

7 This activity is to be done with books open. **Expansion:** You may wish to have students use the words in the first column in original sentences.

Class Motivator

Jeu Use Activity 2, page 438, Activity 3, page 439, and Activity 7, page 442 to play a game. Divide the class into two teams. Read the definitions and have two players at a time compete to give the word first. Keep score and award a prize to the winning team!

Commençons
Let's use our new words

Une femme d'affaires

6 Historiette Elle cherche du travail.
Répondez d'après les indications.

1. Mme Robert cherche du travail? (oui)
2. Qu'est-ce qu'elle lit? (une annonce dans le journal)
3. Quelle compagnie cherche des candidats? (France Télécom)
4. C'est une grosse société ou une multinationale? (une grosse société)
5. Que fait Mme Robert? (poser sa candidature)
6. Qu'est-ce qu'elle donne à la directrice des ressources humaines? (son curriculum vitæ)
7. Elle a des références? (bien sûr)
8. Mme Robert est diplômée en quoi? (informatique)
9. Qu'est-ce qu'elle va avoir? (un entretien)
10. Quand est-ce qu'elle peut commencer à travailler? (tout de suite)

7 Définitions Trouvez les mots qui correspondent.

1. les petites annonces
2. un poste
3. être à son compte
4. être libre immédiatement
5. travailler à plein temps
6. être au chômage
7. travailler à mi-temps
8. un bureau de placement
9. une entreprise
10. un(e) employé(e)
11. une carrière

a. travailler environ 20 heures par semaine
b. un emploi
c. être sans travail
d. ce qu'on lit dans le journal quand on cherche du travail
e. une société
f. le lieu où on va quand on cherche du travail
g. pouvoir commencer à travailler tout de suite
h. travailler pour soi
i. quelqu'un qui travaille pour un employeur
j. travailler 35 heures par semaine
k. la profession qu'on choisit pour la vie

Answers to Commençons

6
1. Oui, elle cherche du travail.
2. Elle lit une annonce dans le journal.
3. France Télécom cherche des candidats.
4. C'est une grosse société.
5. Mme Robert pose sa candidature.
6. Elle lui donne son curriculum vitæ.
7. Bien sûr qu'elle a des références.
8. Mme Robert est diplômée en informatique.
9. Elle va avoir un entretien.
10. Elle peut commencer à travailler tout de suite.

7
1. d
2. b
3. h
4. g
5. j
6. c
7. a
8. f
9. e
10. i
11. k

Vocabulaire

8 **Mon travail** Donnez des réponses personnelles.

1. Tu travailles ou tu aimerais travailler? Où?
2. À plein temps ou à mi-temps?
3. Tu as ou tu aimerais avoir un bon salaire?
4. Qu'est-ce que tu fais ou ferais de ton argent?
5. Tu aimerais faire un stage pour avoir de l'expérience?

Au bureau

Un entretien Vous êtes le/la D.R.H. d'une grosse société. Votre camarade veut faire un stage dans votre société. Il/Elle vient pour un entretien. Vous lui posez des questions sur ses études, son expérience, ses intérêts, ses talents. Ensuite changez de rôle.

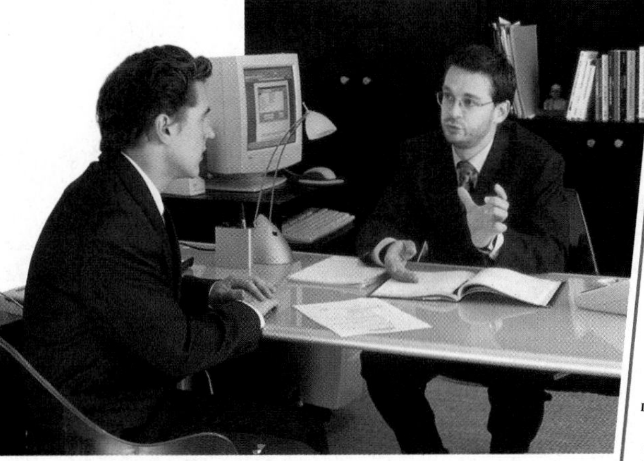

Un entretien

Netgem

Netgem, premier fournisseur mondial de solutions et technologies dans le secteur de la convergence de l'Internet et du téléviseur, recherche:

Un(e) Responsable Communication Interne

De Langue Maternelle Anglaise ou parfaitement bilingue

- Mise en place des outils (journal interne, guide, formation)
- Accueil des nouveaux collaborateurs
- Animation de l'Intranet
- Organisation d'événements internes et externes

De formation supérieure Communication ou RH, vous bénéficiez d'une expérience similaire d'au moins 5 ans en environnement international.

Merci d'adresser votre CV et prétentions à:
Netgem, Sarah DUPONT
27 rue d'Orléans - 92 200 NEUILLY
sdt@netgem.com

Learning from Photos

(pages 442–443) Have students describe the photos and recycle vocabulary from Chapter 3.

Answers to Commençons

Answers will vary but may include:

1. Je travaille dans une boutique de vêtements.
2. Je travaille à mi-temps.
3. J'ai un bon salaire.
4. Je dépense un peu de l'argent que je gagne, mais je fais des économies pour aller à l'université.
5. Oui, j'aimerais faire un stage dans un hôpital. J'aimerais être médecin.

1 Preparation

Resource Manager

Audio Activities Booklet TE, pages 158–159
Audiocassette 8B/CD 8
Workbook, pages 158–160
Quizzes 3–5, pages 69–71
ExamView Pro®

Bellringer Review

Use BRR Transparency 14.3 or write the following on the board.
Put the following conversation in logical order.

Mlle Chénier, je vous présente M. Ledoux.
Moi de même, mademoiselle.
M. Ledoux, vous connaissez Mlle Chénier?
Je suis heureuse de faire votre connaissance, monsieur.
Non, mais je voudrais bien faire sa connaissance.

2 Presentation

Le subjonctif après les expressions de doute

Step 1 Have the students read the model sentences aloud.

Step 2 You may wish to explain to students that the future indicative is often used after expressions of belief or certainty.

Structure

Expressing doubt
Le subjonctif après les expressions de doute

1. In French, any verb or expression that implies doubt, uncertainty, or disbelief about present and future actions is followed by the present subjunctive.

Je doute Je ne pense pas Je ne crois pas Je ne suis pas sûr(e) Je ne suis pas certain(e) Ça m'étonnerait Il n'est pas évident Il n'est pas sûr Il n'est pas certain Il est peu probable	qu'ils soient là.

L'université McGill à Montréal

2. Note that many expressions of uncertainty or disbelief are actually expressions of certainty or belief in the negative. You use the indicative with expressions of certainty or belief. Compare the following pairs of sentences.

Certainty → Indicative	Uncertainty → Subjunctive
Elle est sûre qu'il aura un travail.	Elle n'est pas sûre qu'il ait un travail.
Elles croient qu'il est ingénieur.	Elles ne croient pas qu'il soit ingénieur.
Il est certain qu'il fera beau.	Il n'est pas certain qu'il fasse beau.

Learning from Photos

(page 444) McGill University in Montreal is considered to be the finest English-language university in Canada. A wealthy Scottish fur trader named James McGill gave the money and the land to establish the university, which opened its doors in 1828. Today there are approximately 15,000 students.

Continuons
Let's put our words together

10 Historiette **Ça m'étonnerait.** Répondez selon le modèle.

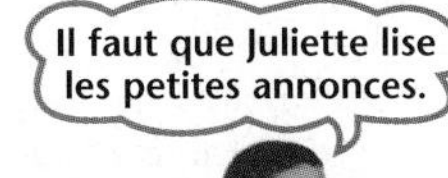

1. Il faut que Juliette fasse un stage.
2. Il faut que Juliette envoie son C.V.
3. Il faut que Juliette écrive une lettre.
4. Il faut que Juliette ait un entretien.
5. Il faut que Juliette ait un travail.
6. Il faut que Juliette veuille travailler.

11 Tu crois? Suivez le modèle.

—Finir ses études! Nathalie?
—Oui, je crois qu'elle finira ses études. J'en suis certain(e).

1. Aller à l'université! Paul?
2. Recevoir un diplôme! Annette?
3. Travailler dans une grosse société! Julie?
4. Gagner beaucoup d'argent! Alexandre?
5. Bien réussir! Stéphane?
6. Voyager! Mélanie?

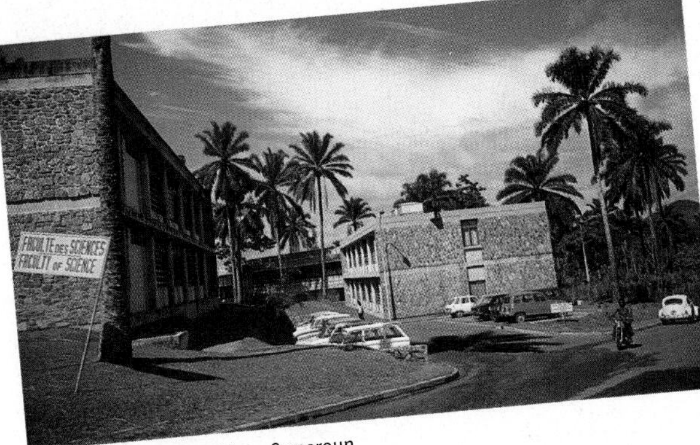

L'université de Yaoundé au Cameroun

Un amphithéâtre à la Sorbonne

3 Practice

Continuons
Let's put our words together

10 Have students practice in pairs and then present their dialogues to the class.

Learning from Photos

(page 445 right) Many of the lecture halls at the Sorbonne are like the amphitheater shown in this photo.

Answers to Continuons

10

1. Ça m'étonnerait que Juliette fasse un stage.
2. Ça m'étonnerait que Juliette envoie son C.V.
3. Ça m'étonnerait que Juliette écrive une lettre.
4. Ça m'étonnerait que Juliette ait un entretien.
5. Ça m'étonnerait que Juliette ait un travail.
6. Ça m'étonnerait que Juliette veuille travailler.

11

1. Oui, je crois qu'il ira à l'université. J'en suis certain(e).
2. Oui, je crois qu'elle recevra un diplôme. J'en suis certain(e).
3. Oui, je crois qu'elle travaillera dans une grosse société. J'en suis certain(e).
4. Oui, je crois qu'il gagnera beaucoup d'argent. J'en suis certain(e).
5. Oui, je crois qu'il réussira bien. J'en suis certain(e).
6. Oui, je crois qu'elle voyagera. J'en suis certain(e).

3 Practice *(continued)*

Continuons
Let's put our words together

14 You may wish to use this activity as the basis for a classwide survey. Have students compile this sort of information about their classmates and share the results with the class.

Recycling

Have students say everything they can about the marriage announcement on page 446.

mariages

M. et Mme
Romain KOSINSKI
M. et Mme
Hubert de LATAILLADE

sont heureux de vous faire part
du mariage de leurs enfants

Hélène et Jean

qui sera célébré le samedi
3 juin, à 16 h 30, en l'église de
Saint-Lons-les-Mines (Landes).

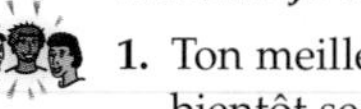

12 Historiette Un mariage Répondez en utilisant **Je crois que** ou **Je ne crois pas que.**

1. Ton meilleur ami ou ta meilleure amie va bientôt se marier?
2. Il/Elle aura deux cérémonies de mariage?
3. Tu seras son garçon d'honneur/sa demoiselle d'honneur?
4. La réception aura lieu dans un grand hôtel?
5. Tu lui feras un très beau cadeau?

Un ingénieur

13 Certain ou pas certain?
Répondez d'après les indications.

1. Paul va aller à l'université? (Je crois)
2. Il finira ses études? (Il est probable)
3. Il aimera tous ses cours? (Je ne suis pas sûr)
4. Il sera avocat? (Ça m'étonnerait)
5. Il deviendra médecin? (Il est peu probable)
6. Il sera ingénieur? (Je crois)

14 Mon avenir Travaillez avec un(e) camarade. Parlez de ce qui vous arrivera probablement plus tard—votre profession, votre famille, etc. Parlez aussi de ce qui ne vous arrivera certainement pas. Vous pouvez utiliser les mots suivants.

je crois que	**il est probable que**
je ne crois pas que	**ça m'étonnerait que**

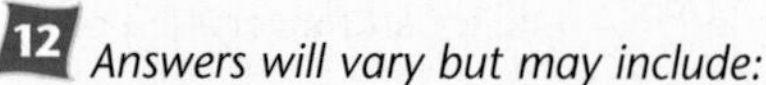

Answers to Continuons

12 *Answers will vary but may include:*

1. Je ne crois pas que mon meilleur ami se marie bientôt.
2. Je ne crois pas qu'il ait deux cérémonies de mariage.
3. Je ne crois pas que je sois son garçon d'honneur.
4. Je ne crois pas que la réception ait lieu dans un grand hôtel.
5. Je ne crois pas que je lui fasse un très beau cadeau.

If students answer with je crois que, *the verb in the dependent clause will be in the future:* Je crois que mon meilleur ami se mariera bientôt.

13

1. Je crois que Paul va aller à l'université.
2. Il est probable qu'il finira ses études.
3. Je ne suis pas sûr(e) qu'il aime tous ses cours.
4. Ça m'étonnerait qu'il soit avocat.
5. Il est peu probable qu'il devienne médecin.
6. Je crois qu'il sera ingénieur.

Expressing wishes about oneself and others

L'infinitif ou le subjonctif

You use the subjunctive when the subject of the second clause and the subject of the main clause are not the same. You use the infinitive when there is only one subject. Compare the following.

Different subjects	Same subject
J'aimerais que tu sois informaticien.	J'aimerais être informaticien.
Il voudrait que vous réussissiez dans la vie.	Il voudrait réussir dans la vie.

Continuons

Let's put our words together

15 La même personne ou quelqu'un d'autre?
Inventez des réponses.

1. Maman veut dormir un peu?
2. Elle veut que tu dormes?
3. Ton frère aime mieux sortir seul?
4. Ton frère aime mieux que tu sortes avec lui?
5. Thomas veut faire ses devoirs?
6. Il veut que tu lui fasses ses devoirs?
7. Florence veut acheter un dictionnaire ou elle veut que tu l'achètes?
8. Tu veux venir avec nous ou tu veux que Christine vienne à ta place?

Le rallye Paris-Dakar

16 Ils le veulent.
Répondez d'après le modèle.

—Ils veulent que tu y ailles.
—Oui, je sais. Et je veux y aller.

1. Ils veulent que tu fasses le voyage.
2. Ils veulent que tu viennes avec eux.
3. Ils veulent que tu conduises.
4. Ils veulent que tu prennes ta voiture.
5. Ils veulent que tu achètes une carte.
6. Ils veulent que tu partes immédiatement.

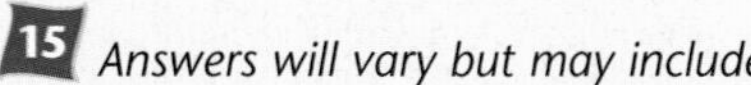

Answers to Continuons

15 *Answers will vary but may include:*

1. Oui, Maman veut dormir un peu.
2. Oui, elle veut que je dorme.
3. Oui, mon frère aime mieux sortir seul.
4. Non, mon frère n'aime pas que je sorte avec lui.
5. Non, Thomas ne veut pas faire ses devoirs.
6. Oui, il veut que je lui fasse ses devoirs.
7. Florence veut que j'achète un dictionnaire.
8. Je veux venir avec vous.

16

1. Oui, je sais. Et je veux faire le voyage.
2. Oui, je sais. Et je veux venir avec eux.
3. Oui, je sais. Et je veux conduire.
4. Oui, je sais. Et je veux prendre ma voiture.
5. Oui, je sais. Et je veux acheter une carte.
6. Oui, je sais. Et je veux partir immédiatement.

Structure

1 Preparation

Bellringer Review

Use BRR Transparency 14.4 or write the following on the board.
Who would you call to fix the following things?

1. **les toilettes**
2. **des placards**
3. **des murs sales**
4. **une lampe**

2 Presentation

L'infinitif ou le subjonctif

Step 1 Go over the explanation with the students. Have them read the model sentences aloud.

3 Practice

Continuons

Let's put our words together

15 This activity contrasts the use of the subjunctive with the use of the infinitive.

Learning from Photos

(page 447) **Le rallye Paris-Dakar** is a race that takes place each year. The exact route, however, is not always the same.

3 Practice *(continued)*

Continuons
Let's put our words together

17 Expansion: Have students work in pairs and interview each other. Then have each partner choose what they think would be the best occupation for the other, based on the answers they gave.

Recycling
Have students imagine a telephone conversation for the photo on page 448.

1 Preparation

Bellringer Review

Use BRR Transparency 14.5 or write the following on the board.
You are organizing a party for your French class. Complete the following sentences with instructions to your assistants.
1. **Il est nécessaire que...**
2. **Il est important que...**
3. **Il vaut mieux que...**
4. **Il est possible que...**

2 Presentation

Le subjonctif dans les propositions relatives

Step 1 Have the students read the model sentences aloud.

17 Vous préférez... ? Dites si vous préférez...
1. avoir un entretien ou envoyer votre C.V.
2. travailler pour une grosse société ou être à votre compte
3. travailler à mi-temps ou à plein temps
4. être stagiaire ou être employé(e)
5. être informaticien(ne) ou avocat(e)
6. travailler ou être au chômage
7. rester tout le temps au bureau ou faire des voyages d'affaires de temps en temps

Un homme d'affaires

18 Mon week-end Travaillez avec un(e) camarade. Parlez de ce que vous voulez faire ce week-end. Ensuite, parlez de ce que vos parents respectifs veulent que vous fassiez.

Expressing certainty and uncertainty
Le subjonctif dans les propositions relatives

1. You know that clauses introduced by the relative pronouns **qui** and **que** describe people or things.

   Nous avons un secrétaire qui parle très bien le français.
   Nous avons un chef que nous aimons beaucoup.

2. You will sometimes use the subjunctive in a relative clause. The subjunctive indicates uncertainty—it is not certain that you will be able to find the person or thing in question. However, if there is no doubt, you use the indicative in the relative clause. Compare the following.

Certainty → Indicative	Uncertainty → Subjunctive
Elle a un ami qui sait conduire. J'ai un métier qui est intéressant.	Elle cherche quelqu'un qui sache conduire. Je voudrais un métier qui soit intéressant.

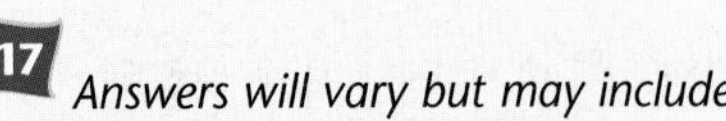

Answers to Continuons

17 *Answers will vary but may include:*
1. Je préfère avoir un entretien.
2. Je préfère être à mon compte.
3. Je préfère travailler à mi-temps.
4. Je préfère être employé(e).
5. Je préfère être informaticien(ne).
6. Je préfère travailler.
7. Je préfère faire des voyages d'affaires de temps en temps.

18 *Answers will vary depending upon what individual students want to do this weekend.*

Structure

Continuons
Let's put our words together

19 **Historiette** **On cherche un représentant.** Répondez que oui.

1. La société Matras cherche un représentant?
2. Ils ont un poste qui paie bien?
3. Ils cherchent quelqu'un qui ait de l'expérience en marketing?
4. Ils veulent quelqu'un qui ait voyagé?
5. Ils ont besoin d'une personne qui connaisse des langues?
6. Ils cherchent un candidat qui soit libre immédiatement?

20 **Historiette** **Certaines qualifications** Complétez.

La société Calmant cherche quelqu'un qui __1__ (avoir) de l'expérience, qui __2__ (parler) bien le français et l'anglais et qui __3__ (pouvoir) voyager. Le directeur des ressources humaines m'a dit qu'ils avaient besoin de quelqu'un qui __4__ (être) libre immédiatement. Ils ont eu beaucoup de candidats. Finalement, ils ont trouvé une candidate qui __5__ (avoir) de l'expérience, qui __6__ (vouloir) et qui __7__ (pouvoir) commencer à travailler immédiatement. Malheureusement, elle parle seulement le français et la société continue à chercher quelqu'un qui __8__ (savoir) parler anglais et qui __9__ (connaître) le marché américain.

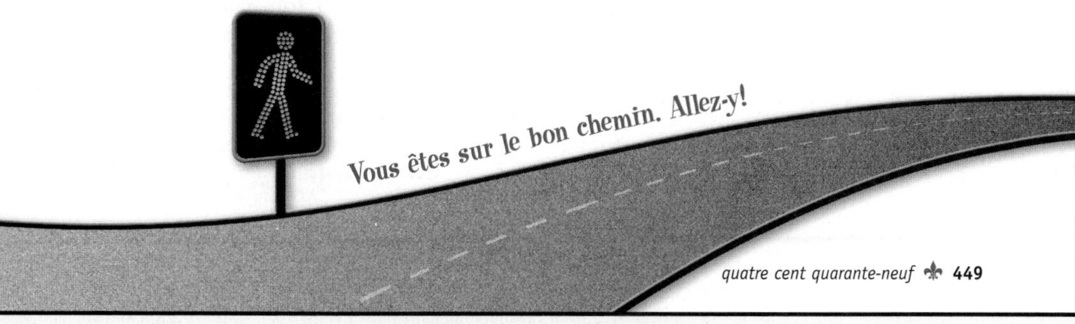

3 Practice

Continuons
Let's put our words together

Note: When you are going over these activities, you may wish to ask students why they did or did not use the subjunctive.

Allez-y! At this point in the chapter, students have learned all the vocabulary and structure necessary to complete the chapter. The conversation and cultural readings that follow recycle all the material learned up to this point.

Answers to Continuons

19

1. Oui, la société Matras cherche un représentant.
2. Oui, ils ont un poste qui paie bien.
3. Oui, ils cherchent quelqu'un qui ait de l'expérience en marketing.
4. Oui, ils veulent quelqu'un qui ait voyagé.
5. Oui, ils ont besoin d'une personne qui connaisse des langues.
6. Oui, ils cherchent un candidat qui soit libre immédiatement.

20

1. ait
2. parle
3. puisse
4. soit
5. a
6. veut
7. peut
8. sache
9. connaisse

Conversation

1 Preparation

Resource Manager

Audio Activities Booklet TE, pages 160–161
Audiocassette 8B/CD 8
CD-ROM

Bellringer Review

Use BRR Transparency 14.6 or write the following on the board.
Complete the sentences with the indicative or subjunctive of the verbs in parentheses.

1. **Je ne crois pas que nous _____ au Maghreb cette année. (aller)**
2. **Il est certain que vous y _____ l'année prochaine. (voyager)**
3. **Je suis sûr(e) que cette région _____ très belle. (être)**
4. **Ça m'étonnerait que mes parents ne _____ pas la visiter. (vouloir)**
5. **Mais il n'est pas certain qu'ils _____ assez d'argent. (avoir)**

2 Presentation

Step 1 Have students close their books and listen as you read the conversation aloud or play Audiocassette 8B/CD 8. Have students listen carefully to the recorded version and pay particular attention to the intonation.

Step 2 Have students open their books and read along with you or the Audiocassette 8B/CD 8.

Step 3 Call on a pair of volunteers to read the conversation to the class with as much expression as possible.

Conversation

Au bureau de placement   

Conseillère: Je trouve votre C.V. très intéressant. Vous cherchez quel genre de travail?
Sandrine: J'aimerais travailler dans une grosse société. Mais… j'aimerais tout de même qu'il y ait des possibilités d'avancement.
Conseillère: Je crois que j'ai un poste qui pourrait vous intéresser. Mais il faut quelqu'un qui sache parler anglais.
Sandrine: Pas de problème. J'ai vécu deux ans à New York.
Conseillère: Parfait. C'est avec une société multinationale américaine, ici à Paris. Mais il faut pouvoir voyager.
Sandrine: Voyager? Pas de problème. J'aime beaucoup ça.
Conseillère: Alors, je vais leur faxer votre C.V. et arranger un entretien.
Sandrine: Merci beaucoup, madame.
Conseillère: Je vous en prie. Et ne vous en faites pas, je suis sûre que tout se passera très bien.

Après la conversation

Répondez d'après la conversation.

1. Où est Sandrine?
2. Qu'est-ce qu'elle aimerait faire?
3. Pourquoi Sandrine parle-t-elle anglais?
4. Quel genre de société cherche un(e) candidat(e)?
5. Est-ce qu'il faut voyager?
6. C'est un problème pour Sandrine?
7. Qu'est-ce que la conseillère va faire du C.V. de Sandrine?

Glencoe Technology

CD-ROM
On the CD-ROM, students can watch a dramatization of this conversation. They can then play the role of either one of the characters and record themselves in the conversation.

Answers to Après la conversation

1. Sandrine est au bureau de placement.
2. Elle aimerait travailler dans une grosse société.
3. Elle parle anglais parce qu'elle a vécu deux ans à New York.
4. Une société multinationale américaine cherche un(e) candidat(e).
5. Oui, il faut pouvoir voyager.
6. Non, elle aime beaucoup voyager.
7. Elle va le faxer à la société.

Parlons un peu plus
Let's talk some more

A **Un poste idéal** Travaillez avec un(e) camarade. Décrivez-lui ce qui serait pour vous un poste idéal. Ensuite changez de rôle.

Ils tournent un film.

B **Possibilités de carrières** Travaillez avec un(e) camarade. Préparez chacun une liste des choses qui vous intéressent et une liste des cours que vous aimez. Comparez vos listes et voyez si vous avez des intérêts communs. Parlez ensuite des carrières qui vous intéresseraient.

C **Un entretien** Lisez les petites annonces et choisissez-en une qui vous intéresse. Votre camarade vous accordera un entretien pour ce poste. Préparez ensemble votre conversation et présentez-la à la classe.

RESTAURANT, Nice, 120 couverts, cuisine locale et traditionnelle, recherche chef de cuisine à l'année, libre début août, références exigées. Envoyer CV + prétentions : 38 Bd Victor Hugo, 06000 Nice.

ÉCOLE DE LANGUES recherche professeur anglais / américain, langue maternelle, large expérience adultes et anglais des affaires. CV : EUROSUD, 208 route de Grenoble, 06200 Nice, 00335799 qui transmettra.

3 Practice

Parlons un peu plus
Let's talk some more

These activities enable students to use the vocabulary and structures learned in the chapter in open-ended exchanges. You may wish to assign different activities to different groups or allow the students to choose the activities they wish to do.

Answers to Parlons un peu plus

A *Answers will vary depending upon what each individual thinks an ideal job would be. Students will use the vocabulary introduced in this chapter that relates to the job of their choice.*

B *Answers will vary but the following gives an indication as to the way in which students can organize their responses.*

Les choses qui m'intéressent: les animaux, la médecine, aider les gens, la campagne

Les cours que j'aime: la biologie, les mathématiques, la physique

Je crois que j'aimerais être infirmier (infirmière), ou médecin, peut-être. Ou même vétérinaire ou agriculteur!

Lectures culturelles

Resource Manager

Audio Activities Booklet TE, pages 161–162
Audiocassette 8B/CD 8

Bellringer Review

Use BRR Transparency 14.7 or write the following on the board.
List the people you would find working in the following places.
une école, un tribunal, un hôpital, une mairie, une grosse société

National Standards

Cultures
This reading allows students to see how, by combining French with his college major, one young man was able to pursue a successful career in diplomacy.

Presentation

Pre-reading

Step 1 Ask students what they know about the Peace Corps.

Step 2 Go over the Reading Strategy on page 452.

Reading

Step 1 Have students first read the questions in the **Après la lecture** activity. Then have them read the selection once silently.

Step 2 Now go over the **Lecture** again, having individuals read four or five sentences aloud.

Post-reading

Call on volunteers to summarize in their own words what they have learned about the young man named Bobby.

Lectures culturelles

Reading Strategy

Scanning for specific information

Before reading a passage, read the questions that follow it. Skim the text and look for the answers to the questions. This will help you focus on the important information in the selection.

Un jeune homme appelé Bobby

Cette histoire est une histoire vraie. Bobby, qu'on appelle aujourd'hui Robert, est américain. Il est allé dans une école publique américaine où il a fait quatre ans de français. Il a continué ses études de français à l'université où il s'est spécialisé en sciences politiques.

Après avoir été diplômé, Bobby est entré au service du Corps de la Paix[1]. Il a passé quelques mois de formation[2] dans le Vermont. Ensuite il est allé travailler au Sénégal, où il a appris aux paysans d'un village à construire des routes.

Après ses deux ans de bénévolat[3] au Corps de la Paix, il a passé un examen pour entrer au Ministère des Affaires Étrangères[4].

Bobby a réussi à son examen et il a commencé à travailler au Ministère des Affaires Étrangères. Comme il était intelligent et sérieux, il a très vite reçu de l'avancement[5]. Il a été nommé consul au Mali et attaché culturel en France. Et aujourd'hui, Bobby est ambassadeur.

[1] Corps de la Paix *Peace Corps*
[2] formation *training*
[3] bénévolat *volunteer work*
[4] Ministère des Affaires Étrangères *State Department*
[5] avancement *promotion*

L'ambassade des États-Unis à Bamako au Mali

Un jeune Américain du Corps de la Paix au Mali

Un bénévole du Corps de la Paix au Mali

Où a débuté l'illustre carrière diplomatique de Bobby? D'après lui, tout a commencé lorsqu'il était en neuvième et qu'il a choisi de faire du français!

Vous aimeriez faire une carrière comme celle de Bobby? Vous pourriez bien un jour être attaché culturel ou même ambassadeur dans un pays francophone. Qu'en pensez-vous? Avoir un poste qui paie bien et permet de voir le monde en même temps, ça vous intéresserait?

Après la lecture

Bobby est devenu Robert. Répondez.

1. Bobby est de quelle nationalité?
2. Il a étudié où?
3. Il a fait combien d'années de français?
4. Quelles études a-t-il faites à l'université?
5. Il a continué à faire du français?
6. Il a travaillé dans quelle organisation humanitaire?
7. Il est entré à quel ministère?
8. Quels postes a-t-il eus?
9. D'après lui, sa carrière a débuté où?
10. Aimeriez-vous faire la même carrière que Bobby?

Après la lecture

Allow students to refer to the story to look up the answers, or you may use this activity as a testing device for factual recall.

FUN-FACTS

The Peace Corps was founded in 1961 by executive order of President Kennedy. Volunteers serve for two-year periods. Volunteers serve in many developing nations, working in areas such as agriculture; the teaching of languages, mathemetics, and science; vocational training; business and public administration; and natural resource development.

CAREER CONNECTION

In this reading, students learned about some careers in foreign service and the Peace Corps in which a knowledge of French is a great asset. You may wish to have students write to the State Department and Peace Corps for more information about these jobs, or have the school guidance counselor talk to your class about these careers.

ANSWERS TO Après la lecture

1. Bobby est américain.
2. Il a étudié dans une école publique américaine.
3. Il a fait quatre ans de français.
4. À l'université il a fait des études en sciences politiques.
5. Oui, il a continué à faire du français.
6. Il a travaillé dans le Corps de la Paix.
7. Il est entré au Ministère des Affaires Étrangères.
8. Il a été consul au Mali, attaché culturel en France, et ambassadeur.
9. Tout a commencé quand il a choisi de faire du français en neuvième.
10. *Answers will vary.*

National Standards

Cultures
This reading familiarizes students with the importance of knowing foreign languages in international business.

Attention!

This reading is optional. You may skip it completely, have the entire class read it, have only several students read it and report to the class, or assign it for extra credit.

Presentation

Step 1 Ask students to list any French companies they know of.

Step 2 Have students quickly read the selection.

Après la lecture

Go over the **Après la lecture** activity.

Learning from Photos

(page 454 bottom) Some of the modern construction in the **Défense** area is quite spectacular.

Lecture supplémentaire 1

Le français et votre carrière

Une agence immobilière à Auxerre

Vous ne savez pas si le français vous sera utile dans votre carrière parce qu'il est possible que vous n'ayez pas encore décidé ce que vous ferez ni où vous travaillerez quand vous aurez votre diplôme. Mais il n'y a pas de doute que la connaissance d'une langue étrangère comme le français sera un atout[1].

De nos jours, le commerce international est d'importance majeure. Ainsi, de nombreuses grosses sociétés américaines sont devenues multinationales. C'est-à-dire qu'elles se sont implantées à l'étranger[2]. Pour cette raison, il est possible que vous soyez engagé(e)[3] par une compagnie ou société américaine et que votre bureau se trouve dans un pays francophone.

Souvenez-vous bien que le français en soi[4] n'est pas forcément une carrière. Mais le français avec une autre spécialisation peut vous être très utile. Si vous connaissez la médecine, la comptabilité, le commerce, l'informatique, etc. et qu'en plus vous parlez français, vous pourrez faire un travail intéressant, voyager à l'étranger et gagner beaucoup d'argent. Vive le français!

[1] atout *advantage*
[2] à l'étranger *abroad*
[3] engagé(e) *hired*
[4] en soi *in itself*

Une tour à la Défense

Après la lecture

Votre carrière Répondez.

1. Croyez-vous que le français vous sera utile dans votre carrière?
2. Vous avez choisi une carrière? Si oui, quelle carrière avez-vous choisie?
3. De nos jours qu'est-ce qui est très important?
4. Que sont devenues de nombreuses grosses sociétés américaines?
5. Qu'est-ce qui est un outil très utile?

Answers to Après la lecture

Answers will vary but may include:

1. Oui, je crois que le français me sera utile dans ma carrière.
2. Non, je n'ai pas choisi de carrière.
3. De nos jours, le commerce international est très important.
4. De nombreuses grosses sociétés américaines sont devenues multinationales.
5. Le français avec une autre spécialisation est un outil très utile.

Lecture supplémentaire 2

Petites annonces

Lisez les petites annonces suivantes:

➩ GROUPE international de travail temporaire recrute son assistant(e) d'agence sur Paris, jeune, motivé(e), Bac à Bac + 2, 2 ans d'expérience minimum dans fonction similaire. Envoyer CV + lettre de motivation à Michelle Breton, 90 Bd Raspail, 75006 Paris.

Société de presse recherche
2 jeunes journalistes
bilingues (fr./ang.)
connaissant le secteur des
technologies avec cinq ans
d'expérience dans la
profession.
Adresser lettre de motivation,
CV et photo, sous réf. 103 à :
Le Monde Publicité,
21 bis, rue Claude-Bernard,
BP 218, 75226 Paris Cedex 05.

Après la lecture

A Groupe international Répondez.

1. C'est un groupe de quoi?
2. Qu'est-ce qu'il recrute?
3. Où est l'agence?
4. Il faut avoir combien d'années d'expérience?
5. Qu'est-ce qu'il faut envoyer? À quelle adresse?

B Société de presse Répondez.

1. Qu'est-ce que la société recherche?
2. Il faut parler quelles langues?
3. Il faut combien d'années d'expérience?
4. Où faut-il envoyer la lettre de motivation?

La Belgique
La Tunisie
Le Maroc
Le Mali

National Standards

Cultures
This reading familiarizes students with want ads that might be found in a typical newspaper in France.

Attention!

This reading is optional. You may skip it completely, have the entire class read it, have only several students read it and report to the class, or assign it for extra credit.

Presentation

Step 1 Have students quickly read the selection.

Go over the **Après la lecture** activities.

Answers to Après la lecture

A

1. C'est un groupe international de travail temporaire.
2. Il recrute un(e) assistant(e) d'agence.
3. L'agence est à Paris.
4. Il faut avoir deux ans d'expérience minimum.
5. Il faut envoyer un CV et une lettre de motivation au 90 Bd Raspail, 75006 Paris.

B

1. La société recherche deux jeunes journalistes bilingues.
2. Il faut parler français et anglais.
3. Il faut cinq ans d'expérience.
4. Il faut envoyer la lettre de motivation au Monde Publicité, 21 bis, rue Claude-Bernard, BP 218, 75226 Paris Cedex 05.

National Standards

Connections
This reading about basic concepts in economics such as opportunity cost establishes a connection with another discipline, allowing students to reinforce and further their knowledge of the social sciences through the study of French.

Attention!

The readings in the **Connexions** section are optional. They focus on some of the major disciplines taught in schools and universities. The vocabulary is useful for discussing such topics as history, literature, art, economics, business, science, etc. You may choose any of the following ways to do the readings in the **Connexions** sections.

Independent reading Have students read the selections and do the post-reading activities as homework, which you collect. This option is least intrusive on class time and requires a minimum of teacher involvement.

Homework with in-class follow-up Assign the readings and post-reading activities as homework. Review and discuss the material in class the next day.

Intensive in-class activity This option includes a pre-reading vocabulary presentation, in-class reading and discussion, assignment of the activities for homework, and a discussion of the assignment in class the following day.

CONNEXIONS

Les sciences sociales

Hédiard, une épicerie fine à Paris

L'économie

Economics is the science that deals with the production, distribution, and consumption of goods and services for the welfare of humankind. It is an interesting and complex science because people need or desire all kinds of goods and services. However, we do not have at our disposal the resources we need to produce all that society would like to have. For this reason, economists provide the information necessary to those who must make decisions as to what will and will not be produced.

Qu'est-ce que l'économie?

Qu'est-ce que l'économie? On peut définir l'économie de plusieurs manières. L'économie, c'est l'étude des décisions que l'on prend en matière de production, de distribution et de consommation de biens[1] et services. C'est l'étude des décisions que prend la société quand elle détermine ce qui va être produit et pour qui. L'économie traite aussi de l'utilisation et du contrôle des ressources pour satisfaire les nécessités et les désirs des êtres humains. C'est un aspect important de l'économie parce que nos ressources sont limitées mais les besoins et les désirs des êtres humains n'ont pas de limite.

Les besoins des êtres humains peuvent être de première nécessité comme la nourriture, le logement et les vêtements. Il y a d'autres besoins qui ne sont pas de première nécessité, comme les voyages ou les châteaux, mais ces besoins sont importants pour certains individus. Les besoins et les désirs humains n'ont pas de limite, mais les ressources, elles, sont limitées. En réalité, il y a une rareté[2] de ressources.

[1] biens *goods* [2] rareté *scarcity*

Une bijouterie à Paris

Critical Thinking Activity

Have pairs of students work together to consider other examples of **manque à gagner** either from their own lives or on a wider scale. They can present their examples to the class.

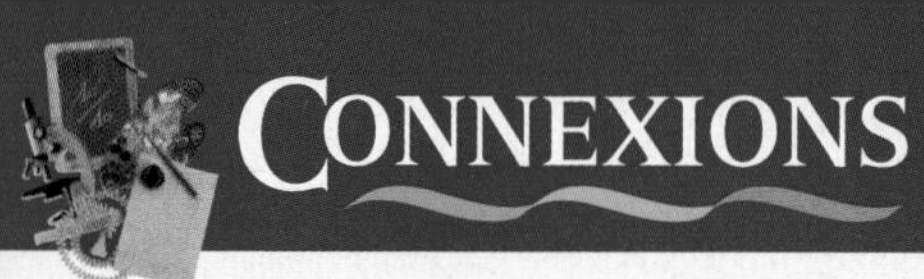

Les sciences sociales
L'économie

Note: You may wish to have only students interested in economics do this reading, along with the accompanying activities.

Step 1 Have students read the introduction in English on page 456.

Step 2 Have students read the selection independently.

Une usine de camions à Anger

Les ressources économiques

Les ressources économiques représentent l'ensemble des ressources naturelles, des ressources financières (le capital), des ressources humaines (la main-d'œuvre[3]) et des ressources manufacturées (fabriquées) qu'on utilise pour la production de biens et la création et la distribution de services. Les ressources naturelles sont les matières premières[4], ce qui vient de la terre. Les ressources manufacturées ou fabriquées incluent les usines, les édifices commerciaux et tout l'équipement mécanique et technique. Les ressources humaines sont la main-d'œuvre—professionnelle, technique, administrative et ouvrière. Les ressources financières, c'est-à-dire le capital, c'est tout simplement l'argent disponible[5].

Le manque à gagner[6]

Puisque[7] toutes les ressources sont limitées, il est impossible de donner à la société tous les biens et services qu'elle désire. La rareté de matériels et de ressources nous oblige à choisir ce qu'on va produire. Si on décide de produire un bien avec les ressources disponibles, on perd l'occasion de produire un autre bien. Cette occasion manquée[8] s'appelle «le manque à gagner». Par exemple, si toute une usine produit des téléviseurs, cette usine ne peut pas fabriquer de réfrigérateurs. C'est le manque à gagner. Il faut toujours considérer le manque à gagner quand on prend une décision économique.

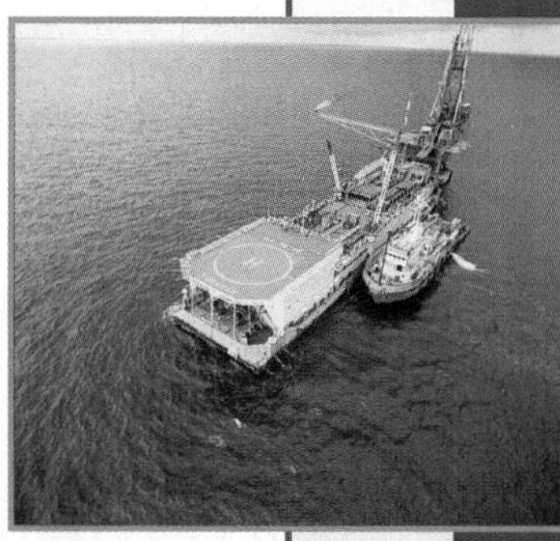
Une plate-forme pétrolière

[3] main-d'œuvre *workforce*
[4] matières premières *raw materials*
[5] disponible *available*
[6] manque à gagner *opportunity cost*
[7] Puisque *Since*
[8] occasion manquée *missed opportunity*

Après la lecture

A L'économie Donnez des exemples:

1. des besoins essentiels
2. des besoins pas essentiels
3. des ressources économiques
4. de la main-d'œuvre

B Le manque à gagner Expliquez ce qu'est le manque à gagner.

Answers to Après la lecture

A

1. la nourriture, le logement, les vêtements
2. les voyages, les châteaux
3. des ressources naturelles, des ressources financières, des ressources humaines, des ressources manufacturées
4. professionnelle, technique, administrative et ouvrière

B

Quand on produit un bien avec les ressources disponibles, on perd l'occasion de produire un autre bien.

Use what you have learned

Recycling

These activities allow students to use the vocabulary and structure from this chapter in completely open-ended, real-life situations.

Presentation

Encourage students to say as much as possible when they do these activities. Tell them not to be afraid to make mistakes, since the goal of these activities is real-life communication. If someone in the group makes an error, allow the others to politely correct him or her. Let students choose the activities they would like to do.

You may wish to divide students into pairs or groups. Encourage students to elaborate on the basic theme and to be creative. They may use props, pictures, or posters if they wish.

Use what you have learned

PARLER 1

Career Day

✔ *Talk about the advantages of learning French for your future employment*

C'est *Career Day* dans votre école. Votre professeur vous a demandé de préparer un petit discours sur l'importance des langues étrangères. Dans votre discours, dites pourquoi le français peut vous être utile plus tard. Présentez votre discours à une autre classe de français.

PARLER 2

Voulez-vous travailler à l'étranger?

✔ *Talk about professions*

Travaillez avec un(e) camarade. Demandez-lui s'il/si elle aimerait travailler pour une société multinationale et pourquoi. Si votre camarade dit oui, demandez-lui s'il/si elle aimerait travailler à l'étranger ou aux États-Unis et pour quelles raisons.

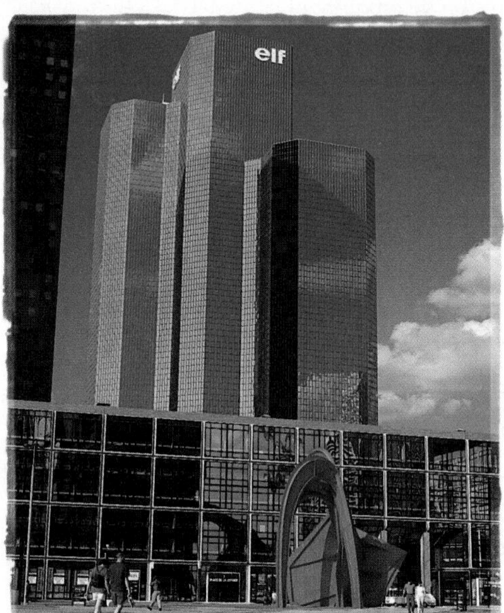

La tour Elf à la Défense

ANSWERS TO C'est à vous

1 *Answers will vary but may include the following ideas:*

La connaissance d'une langue étrangère est très importante.
Le monde devient de plus en plus petit.
Les gens voyagent beaucoup.
Les hommes d'affaires (et femmes d'affaires) voyagent beaucoup à l'étranger.
Beaucoup de grosses sociétés vendent leurs produits à l'étranger.
Il y a beaucoup de commerce international.

2 *Conversations will vary depending upon students' preferences.*

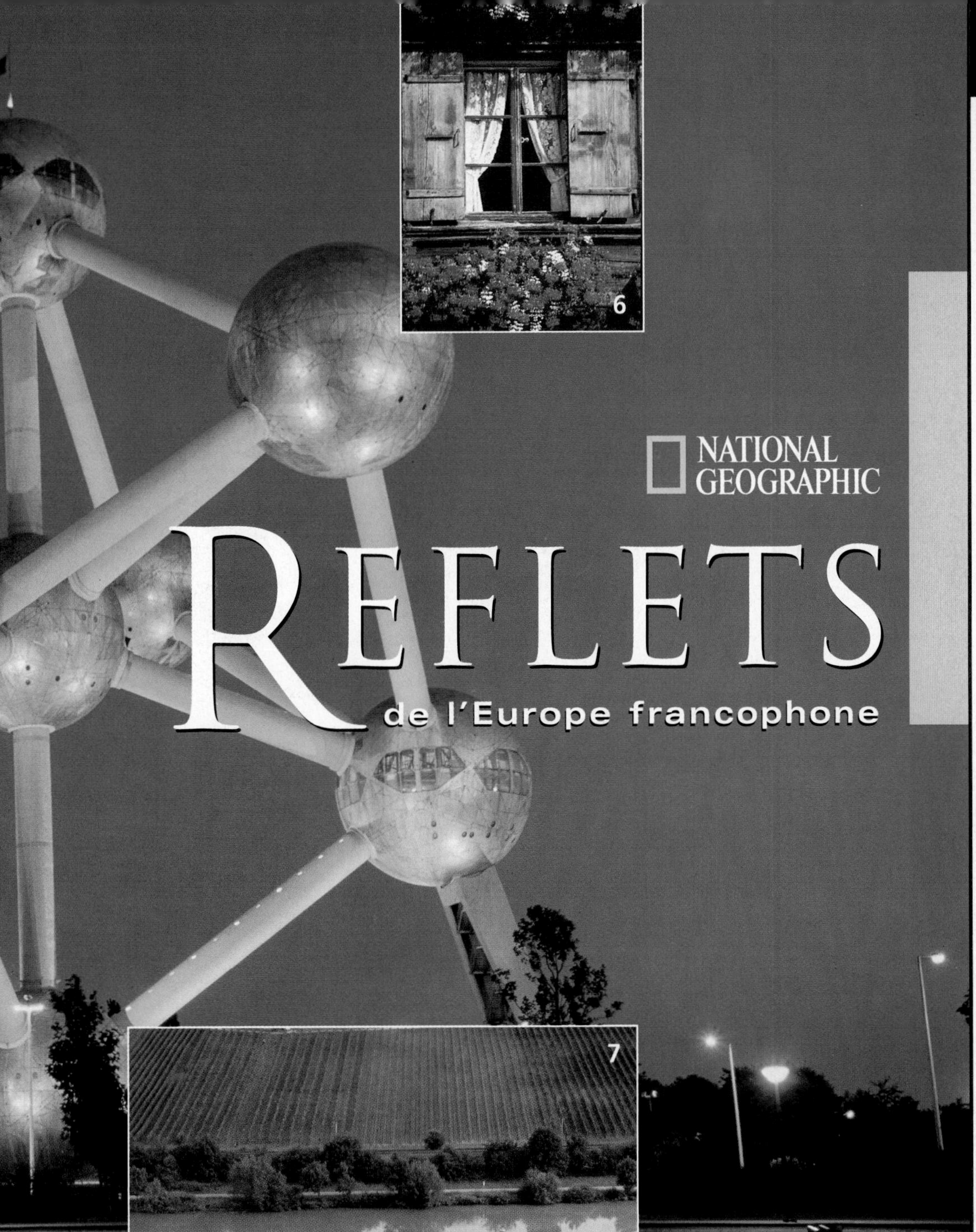

REFLETS
de l'Europe francophone

3. Le port de Monte-Carlo à Monaco The principality of Monaco is one of the smallest countries in the world. It has the shape of a horseshoe, with the Mediterranean Sea on one side and the beginning of the Maritime Alps on the other. The principality has been ruled by members of the Grimaldi family since the Middle Ages. The natives of Monaco are called **Monégasques,** but actual citizens number only about 20% of the population. There are five immigrant residents for every citizen.

4. Appartements donnant sur l'Alzette au Luxembourg Luxembourg is another small country, smaller than Rhode Island. Luxembourg rivals Switzerland as the capital of international banking. The Alzette River flows south to north through the middle of the country.

5. La cueillette des abricots dans le Valais, en Suisse Le Valais is a canton in the southwest of Switzerland. Two-thirds of its population is French-speaking, one-third speaks German. A fair portion of the economy in the area is based on agriculture, particularly the cultivation of peaches and apricots, as well as grains and tobacco. Agriculture, however, has been surpassed by industry. Hydroelectric plants in Le Valais provide 25% of the energy for the country.

6. Fenêtre de châlet fleurie en Suisse This photo shows a window of a charming Swiss **châlet.** The white curtain and the geraniums are quite typical.

7. Péniche sur la Moselle, au Luxembourg The barge seen here on the Moselle is typical of many barges that ply the rivers of Europe, transporting goods from one place to another.

NATIONAL GEOGRAPHIC

8. Les Alpes dans le Valais, en Suisse For information on Le Valais see #5, page 471.

9. Caves de l'Etivaz, fromage des Alpes Vaudoises en Suisse Etivaz is a town in Switzerland that is well-known for its production of cheese.

10. Le jet d'eau de Genève, en Suisse Geneva is one of the most cosmopolitan cities of Switzerland. It is situated at the foot of the Jura Mountains and the Alps, on the West Bank of beautiful Lake Geneva **(le lac Léman).** It is a very short distance from the French border. The **jet d'eau** seen in this photo is the highest fountain in Europe, sending the water 145 meters, or 475 feet, into the air.

11. Ballons à air chaud à Château-d'Œx, en Suisse Hot air ballooning is popular in many areas of both France and Switzerland.

12. Horloger suisse The Swiss have long been known for their production of precision instruments, particularly clocks and watches.

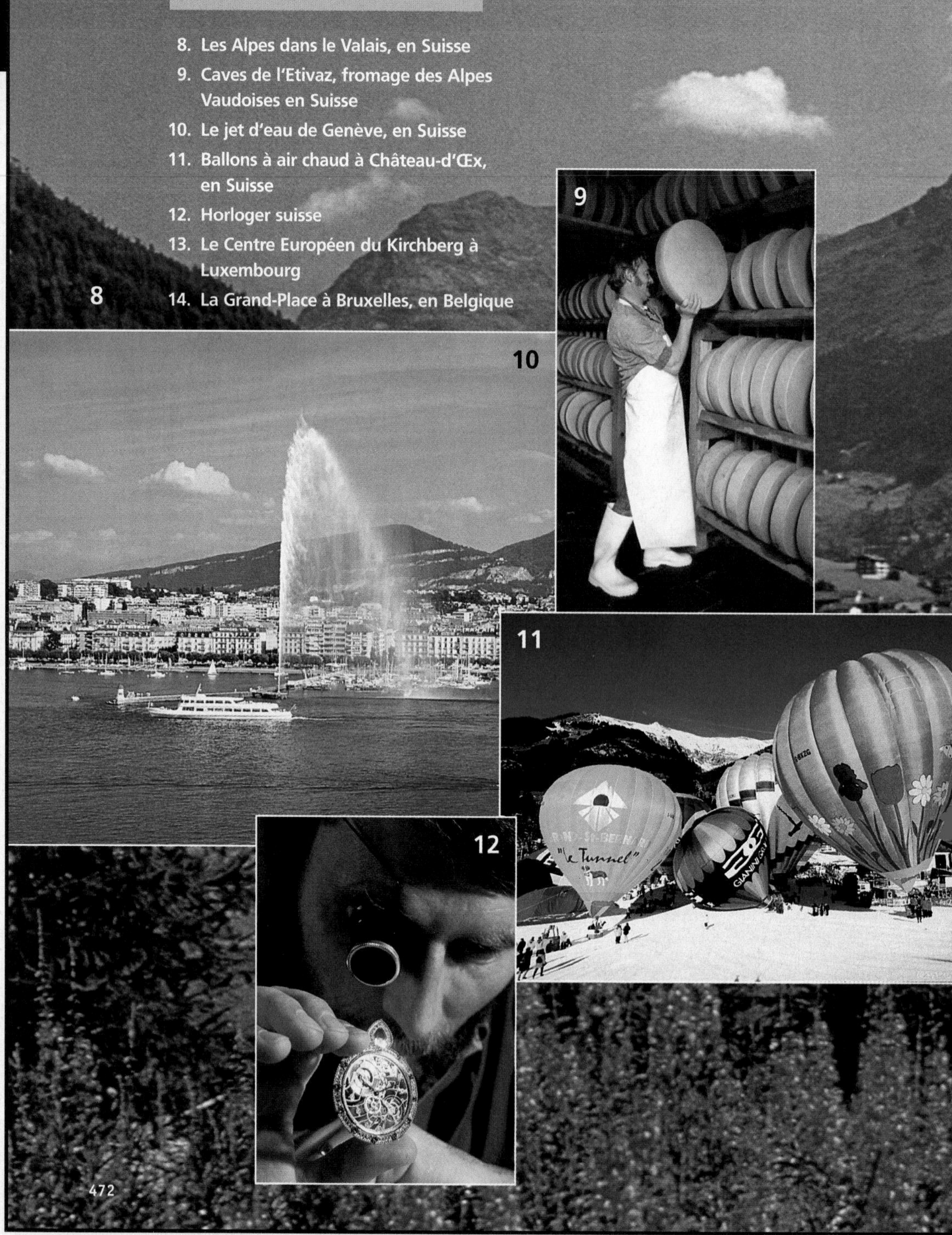

NATIONAL GEOGRAPHIC Teacher's Corner

Index to the NATIONAL GEOGRAPHIC MAGAZINE

The following related articles may be of interest:

- "Monaco," by Richard Conniff, May 1996.
- "Are the Swiss Forests in Peril?" by Christian Mehr, May 1989.
- "Switzerland: The Clockwork Country," by John J. Putman, January 1986.
- "Chocolate: Food of the Gods," by Gordon Young, November 1984.

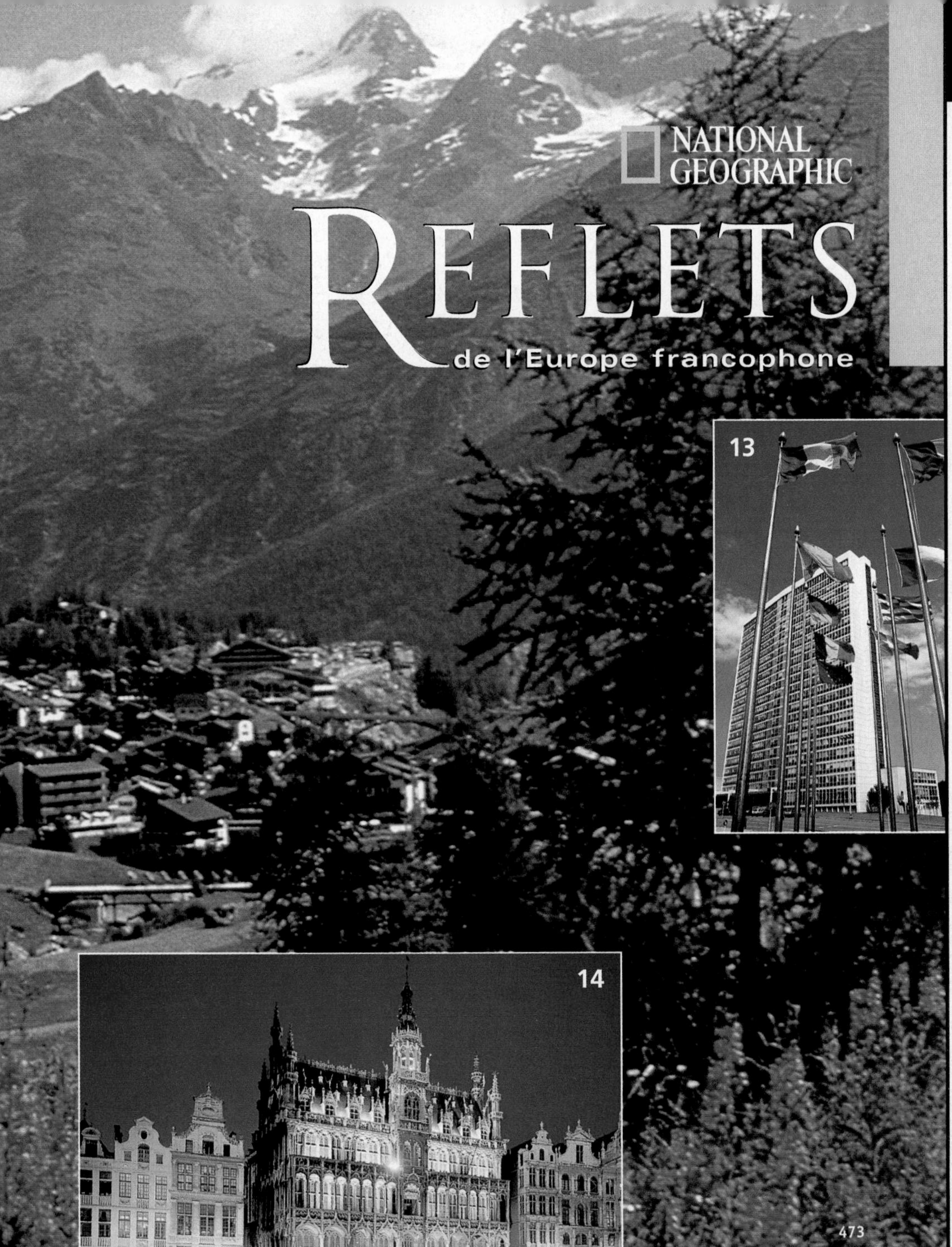

13. Le Centre Européen du Kirchberg à Luxembourg Luxembourg is the seat of all judicial and financial institutions of the European Union, many of which are housed in the **Centre Européen du Kirchberg,** as well as the secretariat of the European Parliament.

14. La Grand-Place à Bruxelles, en Belgique The Grand-Place in Brussels is a very ornate market square. There is a daily flower market, and on Sunday mornings there is even a bird market. The Grand-Place is also the venue for many local pageants.

Products available from GLENCOE/MCGRAW-HILL

To order the following products, call Glencoe/McGraw-Hill at 1-800-334-7344.

CD-ROMs
- Picture Atlas of the World
- The Complete National Geographic: 112 Years of National Geographic Magazine

Transparency Set
- NGS PicturePack: Geography of Europe

Products available from NATIONAL GEOGRAPHIC SOCIETY

To order the following products, call National Geographic Society at 1-800-368-2728.

Books
- National Geographic World Atlas for Young Explorers
- National Geographic Satellite Atlas of the World

Software
- ZingoLingo: French Diskette

Video
- Europe

Preview

All literary selections are optional. You may wish to skip them or present them very thoroughly. In some cases you may have students read the selection quickly just to get a general idea of the selection.

Attention!

The exposure to literature early in one's study of a foreign language should be a pleasant experience. As students read these selections, it is not necessary for them to understand every word. Explain to them that they should try to enjoy the experience of reading literature in a new language. As they read they should look for the following:

- Who the main characters are
- What they are like
- What they are doing—the plot
- What happens to them—the outcome of the story

Literary Companion

These literary selections develop reading and cultural skills and introduce students to French literature.

Learning from Photos

(pages 474–475) Victor Schœlcher was a French politician who served as Undersecretary of State for the provisional government after the Revolution of February 1848. He had fought since 1840 for the abolition of slavery in the French colonies, and through his efforts, a decree was signed to abolish slavery. He served as deputy to Guadeloupe and Martinique from 1848–1851. During the Second Empire, he lived in exile in England, and in 1871, after the abdication of Napoleon III (1870), he was re-elected deputy from Martinique to the National Assembly. In 1875 he was named senator for life.

Today the town of Schœlcher, a residential beach area near Fort-de-France, carries his name. The campus of the **Université des Antilles** is in Schœlcher.

Le Livre de mon père Émile Henriot

National Standards

Cultures

Students experience, discuss, and analyze an expressive product of the culture: an excerpt from the novel, ***Le Livre de mon père,*** by Émile Henriot.

Attention!

This reading is optional. You may wish to present it after students have completed Chapters 1–4, as they will have acquired the vocabulary and structures necessary to read the selection by this point.

You may present the piece thoroughly as a class activity or you may have some or all students merely read it on their own. If you present it as a class activity, you may wish to vary presentation procedures from section to section. Some options are:

- Students read silently.
- Students read after you in unison.
- Call on individuals to read aloud.
- When dialogue appears in the story, call on students to take parts.

With any of the above procedures, intersperse some comprehension questions. Call on a student or students to give a brief synopsis of a section in French.

Vocabulaire

Le jeune homme est amoureux de la jeune fille.
Et elle est amoureuse de lui.

Le train a sifflé.
Le train a dépassé la gare à toute allure.

L'homme règle sa montre.

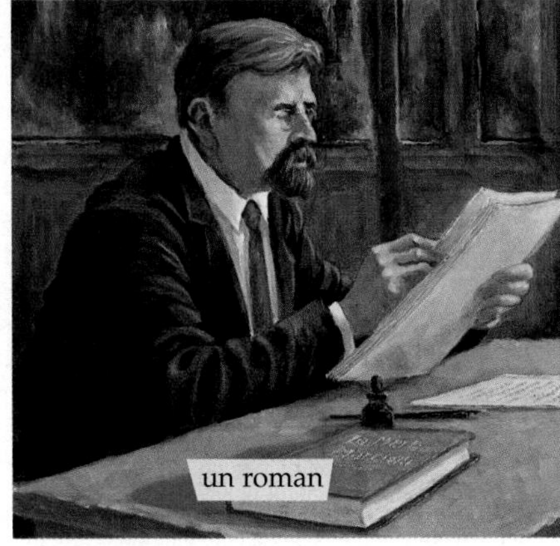

L'auteur d'un roman est un romancier.
Un romancier écrit un roman.

saluer dire bonjour

Activités

Le train Répondez d'après les indications.

1. Est-ce que le train siffle avant d'arriver à la gare? (oui)
2. Le train a fait un arrêt à la gare? (non)
3. Le train a dépassé la gare à toute allure? (oui)
4. Dans le train, qui salue les voyageurs? (le contrôleur)
5. Un voyageur lit le journal? (oui)
6. Il lit *le Temps*, un journal français? (oui)
7. Qu'est-ce que le voyageur regarde? (sa montre)
8. Sa montre indique l'heure exacte? (non)
9. Qu'est-ce que l'homme fait? (régler sa montre)

Un train français vers 1900

Un couple amoureux Dites d'une autre façon.

1. Le jeune homme *dit bonjour à* sa fiancée.
2. La jeune fille *dit bonjour à* son fiancé.
3. La jeune fille *aime* son fiancé.
4. Et le jeune homme *aime* sa fiancée.
5. Le jeune homme a dépassé la maison *très, très vite.*
6. *L'auteur de ce roman* est très connu.

Note: The following teaching suggestions are for a thorough presentation of ***Le Livre de mon père.***

Teaching Vocabulary

Step 1 Have students look at the illustrations as they repeat the new vocabulary. As they repeat the vocabulary, you may wish to ask the following questions:

Est-ce que Roméo était amoureux de Juliette?
Et Juliette était amoureuse de lui?
Le train s'est arrêté ou il a dépassé la gare?
Le train a sifflé avant de dépasser la gare?
Qui écrit un roman?
Nommez deux romanciers américains.
Vous avez lu leurs romans en cours d'anglais?

Step 2 Quickly go over Activities A and B with the class.

Answers to Activités

1. Oui, le train siffle avant d'arriver à la gare.
2. Non, le train n'a pas fait d'arrêt à la gare.
3. Oui, le train a dépassé la gare à toute allure.
4. Dans le train le contrôleur salue les voyageurs.
5. Oui, un voyageur lit le journal.
6. Oui, il lit *le Temps*, un journal français.
7. Le voyageur regarde sa montre.
8. Non, sa montre n'indique pas l'heure exacte.
9. L'homme règle sa montre.

1. Le jeune homme salue sa fiancée.
2. La jeune fille salue son fiancé.
3. La jeune fille est amoureuse de son fiancé.
4. Et le jeune homme est amoureux de sa fiancée.
5. Le jeune homme a dépassé la maison à toute allure.
6. Le romancier est très connu.

Discussing Literature

Introduction

Step 1 You may go over the Introduction with students or you may omit it and just have the students read the story.

Step 2 You can ask the following questions about the Introduction:

Qu'est-ce que l'Académie Française?
Combien de membres y a-t-il?
On les appelle comment?

Step 3 Ask students the following questions in English: Is there an equivalent in America to the **Académie Française?** Do you think there should be? What are the advantages or disadvantages of such a regulatory body?

Le Livre de mon père

Le petit train

Step 1 Have students read several paragraphs silently. Then ask several general questions to ascertain if students got the main idea. Sample questions are:

Qu'est-ce qui indiquait l'arrivée du soir à Nesles?
Le jeune garçon allait où à bicyclette?
Il allait à la gare parce qu'il attendait quelqu'un?
Il attendait un colis-postal?
Les voyageurs venaient d'où?

Step 2 If students can answer the questions, move on to the next section. If they cannot, you may want to have them read selections or parts thereof aloud.

INTRODUCTION Émile Henriot (1889–1961) a d'abord été poète, puis romancier et critique littéraire. En 1945, il a été élu membre de la prestigieuse Académie Française.

L'Académie Française a été créée par Richelieu, ministre de Louis XIV, en 1634. Elle est composée de quarante membres, les «immortels». Ce sont en majorité des écrivains, mais aussi des diplomates, des avocats[1] et des médecins. Les «immortels» sont chargés de la rédaction[2] d'un «Dictionnaire de la langue française». Leur mission est essentiellement de «travailler à épurer et fixer la langue française».

L'extrait qui suit est tiré du *Livre de mon père,* publié en 1938. Dans ce roman Henriot évoque des souvenirs de son enfance et décrit comment la vie a changé depuis son enfance.

[1] avocats *lawyers* [2] rédaction *editing*

Le petit train

Autrefois°, nous connaissions l'heure en écoutant siffler le petit train
qui va de Valmondois à Marines et vice versa,
pour transporter les betteraves° et quelquefois aussi les gens.
C'était un événement que l'arrivée du soir à la gare de Nesles.
Même quand je n'attendais personne, et pas le moindre° colis-postal,
j'allais à bicyclette assister au débarquement des voyageurs qui venaient de Paris,
le notaire, ou Mademoiselle Durand, la fille du pharmacien, qui donne à Pontoise des leçons de musique,
Monsieur de Vigneron qui était allé à la Bourse° et le jeune Henri Delarue qui rapportait *le Temps* à mon père.
Quelquefois encore, je voyais, ô bonheur, descendre du train
une jolie fille, ma voisine, dont j'étais éperdument amoureux.
Je la saluais d'un air indifférent et je rougissais°,
et pour me faire bien venir d'elle°,
je la dépassais à toute allure sur ma bicyclette,
et le soir, au lieu de dormir, j'exhalais° mon amour en vers désespérés et détestables.
Maintenant, les temps ont changé, il n'y a plus de jolie voisine
et, d'ailleurs°, je n'écris plus de vers.
Le petit train passe toujours aux mêmes heures,
mais ce n'est plus à lui que nous faisons attention.

Autrefois *In the past*
betteraves *sugar beets*
pas le moindre *not the littlest*
Bourse *Stock Exchange*
je rougissais *I blushed*
me faire bien venir d'elle *make her like me*
j'exhalais *I expressed*
d'ailleurs *besides*

Ce n'est plus lui qui nous fait dire: «Le petit train a passé depuis un moment, on va déjeuner.»
Maintenant, c'est sur l'avion de Londres que nous réglons nos montres.
Il passe quatre fois par jour, juste au-dessus de mon jardin,
tantôt° comme un pigeon noir, tantôt comme un beau navire d'argent°,
suspendu à rien dans le ciel où il glisse°.
Chaque fois, je lève la tête et le regarde. Et Jean-Claude, que plus rien n'étonne°,
Lui aussi, cependant°, lève la tête et dit, à peu près comme moi autrefois:
—«Voilà l'avion de Londres. On va déjeuner»— ou «on va dîner.»

tantôt *sometimes*
navire d'argent *silver ship*
glisse *glides*
étonne *surprises*
cependant *nevertheless*

Après la lecture

Have students prepare the **Après la lecture** activities at home. Go over them the next day in class.

Autrefois Répondez.

1. Autrefois, comment savait-on l'heure?
2. Qu'est-ce que le train transportait?
3. Il arrivait à quelle gare? À quel moment de la journée?
4. Le narrateur allait à la gare comment?
5. Il y allait pour attendre quelqu'un?
6. D'où venaient les voyageurs?
7. Qui donnait des leçons de musique? Dans quelle ville?
8. Qui rapportait le journal pour le père du narrateur?
9. Qui descendait du train quelquefois?
10. Le narrateur était amoureux d'elle?
11. Il la saluait comment?
12. Le soir, qu'est-ce qu'il écrivait?

Les temps ont changé. Vrai ou faux?

1. La jolie voisine descend toujours du train.
2. Le narrateur continue à écrire des vers.
3. Le train passe toujours aux mêmes heures.
4. Maintenant quand le train passe, on va déjeuner.
5. Maintenant on règle sa montre d'après le passage du train.
6. On règle sa montre sur l'avion de Londres.
7. L'avion passe deux fois par jour.
8. L'avion atterrit dans le jardin.

La vie change. Décrivez comment l'auteur indique que la vie a changé.

Answers to Après la lecture

1. Autrefois, on savait l'heure en écoutant siffler le train.
2. Le train transportait les betteraves et les gens.
3. Il arrivait à la gare de Nesles le soir.
4. Il allait à la gare à bicyclette.
5. Il y allait pour assister au débarquement des voyageurs.
6. Les voyageurs venaient de Paris.
7. La fille du pharmacien donnait des leçons de musique à Pontoise.
8. Henri Delarue rapportait le journal pour le père du narrateur.
9. Quelquefois sa jolie voisine descendait du train.
10. Oui, il était amoureux d'elle.
11. Il la saluait d'un air indifférent.
12. Le soir il écrivait des vers désespérés.

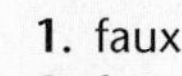

1. faux
2. faux
3. vrai
4. faux
5. faux
6. vrai
7. faux
8. faux

Il dit qu'il n'y a plus de jolie voisine, qu'il n'écrit plus de vers. Il parle de son fils qui fait attention à l'avion de Londres comme il faisait attention au train quand il était petit.

National Standards

Cultures
Students experience, discuss, and analyze an expressive product of the culture: the poems, *«À ma mère»*, by Camara Laye and *«L'homme qui te ressemble»*, by René Philombe.

Attention!

This reading is optional. You may wish to present it after students have completed Chapters 5–7, as they will have acquired the vocabulary and structures necessary to read the selection by this point.

You may present the poems thoroughly as a class activity or you may have some or all students merely read them on their own. If you present them as a class activity, you may wish to vary presentation procedures from section to section. Some options are:

- Students read silently.
- Students read after you in unison.
- Call on individuals to read aloud.
- When dialogue appears in the story, call on students to take parts.

With any of the above procedures, intersperse some comprehension questions. Call on a student or students to give a brief synopsis of a section in French.

Littérature 2

Deux poèmes africains

«À ma mère» Camara Laye
«L'homme qui te ressemble» René Philombe

Vocabulaire

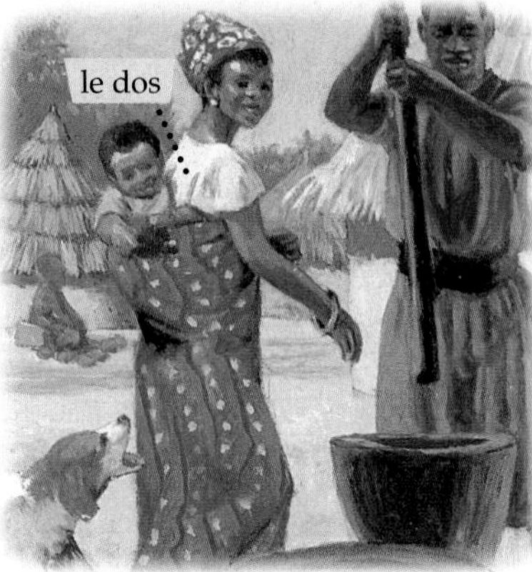

La mère porte son enfant sur le dos.

Elle essuie ses larmes.

Le bébé a fait un pas.
C'est son premier pas.

Activités

Une famille Répondez que oui.

1. Est-ce que la famille est dans les champs?
2. Il y a une rivière près des champs?
3. Il y a une enceinte de résidences?
4. Une mère porte son bébé sur le dos?
5. Le petit bébé a fait un pas? C'est son premier pas?
6. Il a commencé à pleurer?
7. Sa mère essuie ses larmes?
8. Le père est forgeron?

Quel est le mot? Complétez.

1. On dort dans un ____.
2. Quand on va chez quelqu'un, on ____ à la porte avant d'entrer.
3. En hiver quand il fait froid, il y a souvent un ____ dans la cheminée.

Note: The following teaching suggestions are for a thorough presentation of ***«À ma mère»*** and ***«L'homme qui te ressemble»***.

Teaching Vocabulary

Step 1 The vocabulary from these two poems is quite easy, so you may wish to have students look at the illustrations and read the new words.

Step 2 Go over the activities. Activity A can be done orally.

Answers to Activités

1. Oui, la famille est dans les champs.
2. Oui, il y a une rivière près des champs.
3. Oui, il y a une enceinte de résidences.
4. Oui, une mère porte son bébé sur le dos.
5. Oui, le bébé a fait son premier pas.
6. Oui, il a commencé à pleurer.
7. Oui, sa mère essuie ses larmes.
8. Oui, le père est forgeron.

B

1. lit
2. frappe
3. feu

Discussing Literature

Introduction

Step 1 You may wish to ask the following questions about the life of Camara Laye.

Camara Laye est né où? Quand?
Il est allé dans quel genre d'école?
Camara Laye était un très bon élève?
Pourquoi est-il allé en France pour étudier?
De quoi souffrait-il en France?
À quoi pensait-il?
Quel est le titre de son premier roman?

Note: It is recommended that you let students look at the **passé composé** forms of each verb and just familiarize themselves with the **passé simple** forms. It is not suggested that you teach the **passé simple.** The **passé simple** is taught in **Bon voyage! Level 3.**

Learning from Photos

(page 482) Although houses vary from region to region throughout the rural areas of the West African countries, round houses with walls made from mud and thatched roofs such as we see here are quite common in many different areas.

INTRODUCTION Camara Laye est né à Kouroussa en Guinée en 1928. Il est allé dans une école technique à Conakry, la capitale. Il a toujours excellé dans ses études et il a reçu une bourse[1] pour étudier en France. En France, il souffrait beaucoup du mal du pays[2] et pensait souvent à l'enceinte familiale dans son petit village de Kouroussa.

Pendant ses moments de nostalgie, il a décidé d'écrire un roman—*L'Enfant noir*. C'était son premier roman. Le poème qui suit est la préface à ce roman autobiographique qui a eu un très grand succès dès sa publication.

[1] bourse *scholarship*
[2] mal du pays *homesickness*

Dans ce joli poème tendre, certains verbes sont au passé simple. Le passé simple est un temps littéraire qui décrit des actions passées. Dans la conversation, on utilise le passé composé. Voici les verbes qui sont au passé simple dans le poème «*À ma mère*».

portas as porté
m'allaitas m'as allaité
gouvernas as gouverné
ouvris as ouvert
fis as fait

Un village de la brousse en Guinée

«À ma mère»

Femme noire, femme africaine, ô toi, ma mère, je pense à toi…

Ô Dâman, ô ma mère, toi qui me portas sur le dos, toi qui m'allaitas°, toi qui gouvernas mes premiers pas, toi qui la première m'ouvris les yeux aux prodiges° de la terre, je pense à toi…

Femme des champs, femme des rivières, femme du grand fleuve, ô toi, ma mère, je pense à toi…

Ô toi Dâman, ô ma mère, toi qui essuyais mes larmes, toi qui me réjouissais le cœur°, toi qui, patiemment, supportais mes caprices°, comme j'aimerais encore être près de toi, être enfant près de toi!

Femme simple, femme de la résignation, ô toi, ma mère, je pense à toi…

Ô Dâman, Dâman de la grande famille des forgerons, ma pensée toujours se tourne vers toi, la tienne° à chaque pas m'accompagne, ô Dâman, ma mère, comme j'aimerais encore être dans ta chaleur°, être enfant près de toi…

Femme noire, femme africaine, ô toi, ma mère, merci; merci pour tout ce que tu fis pour moi, ton fils, si loin, si près de toi!

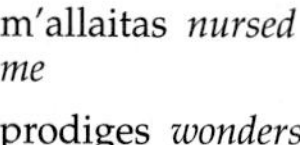

m'allaitas *nursed me*
prodiges *wonders*
me réjouissais le cœur *brought me joy*
caprices *whims*
la tienne *yours*
chaleur *warmth*

Après la lecture

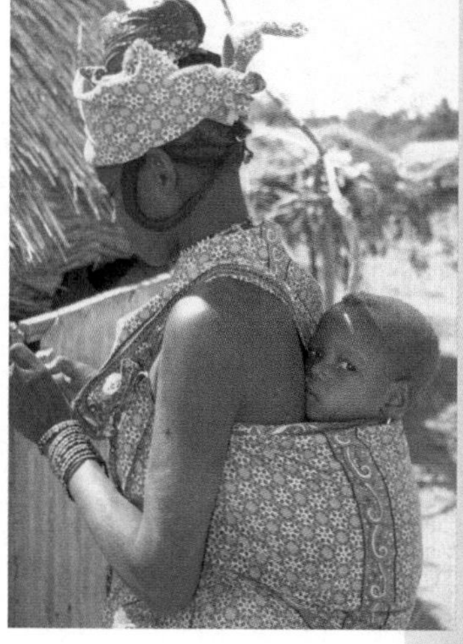

Une mère avec son enfant au Niger

Ô Dâman Répondez.

1. À qui pense l'auteur?
2. Quand il était petit, sa mère le portait sur le dos?
3. Elle l'allaitait?
4. Elle l'a aidé à faire ses premiers pas?
5. Elle essuyait ses larmes quand il pleurait?
6. Qu'est-ce qu'elle supportait?
7. Quels sont les désirs de l'auteur?
8. L'auteur dit merci à sa mère. Pourquoi?

Description Discutez.

1. Quels sont les adjectifs que l'auteur utilise pour décrire sa mère?
2. Comment sait-on que l'auteur habitait à la campagne, c'est-à-dire dans une région rurale?

«À ma mère»

Step 1 Tell students the author is going to talk to his mother in the poem. Tell them to listen and look for the things the young man tells his beloved mother.

Step 2 Give students a few minutes to read the sidenotes.

Step 3 Read the entire poem aloud to the class or have them listen to the recording.

Step 4 Many phrases in the poem can be easily dramatized.

Toi qui me portas sur le dos.
Toi qui gouvernas mes premiers pas.
Toi qui essuyais mes larmes.

Step 5 You may wish to paraphrase some of the more difficult lines.

toi qui gouvernas mes premiers pas = toi qui m'as aidé à marcher
toi qui me réjouissais le cœur = toi qui m'apportais tellement de joie
toi qui patiemment supportais mes caprices = toi qui supportais avec patience les choses stupides que je faisais
ma pensée toujours se tourne vers toi = je pense souvent à toi

Answers to Après la lecture

1. Il pense à sa mère.
2. Oui, quand il était petit, sa mère le portait sur le dos.
3. Oui, elle l'allaitait.
4. Oui, elle l'a aidé à faire ses premiers pas.
5. Oui, elle essuyait ses larmes quand il pleurait.
6. Elle supportait ses caprices.
7. Il aimerait être enfant près d'elle.
8. Il lui dit merci pour tout ce qu'elle a fait pour lui.

B *Answers will vary but may include:*

1. femme noire, femme africaine, femme des champs, femme des rivières, femme du grand fleuve, femme simple…
2. Il parle des champs, des rivières.

Après la lecture

After going over these activities, have students discuss the feeling they got from this poem.

Discussing Literature

Introduction

Step 1 You may wish to ask the following questions about the Introduction:

Il est né où, René Philombe?
Qu'est-ce qu'il a eu à l'âge de vingt-sept ans?
Quel mouvement l'a influencé?
Quel est son désir?

«L'homme qui te ressemble»

Step 1 This beautiful poem is quite easy. It is suggested that you have students listen to you read it as they follow along in their books.

Step 2 Then have the entire class recite the poem aloud in unison with as much expression as possible.

Un tissu du Cameroun

INTRODUCTION René Philombe est né au Cameroun en 1930. À l'âge de vingt-sept ans, il a eu la poliomyélite, mais il a continué sa carrière d'écrivain. Il est poète, romancier[1], journaliste et dramaturge[2].

Philombe a été influencé par le mouvement de la négritude. Sa poésie exprime son désir de voir un monde libre d'oppression. Pour lui, tous les hommes ont les mêmes droits[3]. Dans son poème, «L'homme qui te ressemble», René Philombe parle d'une fraternité entre les êtres humains qui transcende tout.

[1] romancier *novelist*
[2] dramaturge *playwright*
[3] droits *rights*

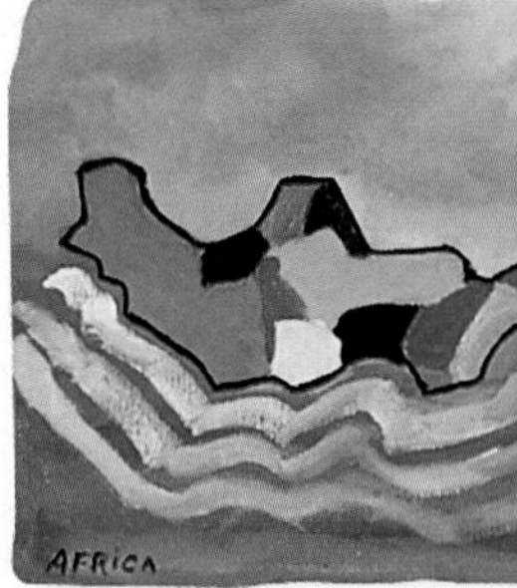

«L'homme qui te ressemble»

J'ai frappé à ta porte
J'ai frappé à ton cœur°
pour avoir bon lit
pour avoir bon feu
pourquoi me repousser°?
Ouvre-moi mon frère... !

Pourquoi me demander
si je suis d'Afrique
si je suis d'Amérique
si je suis d'Asie
si je suis d'Europe?
Ouvre-moi mon frère... !

cœur *heart*
repousser *reject*

Après la lecture

Au téléphone Répondez.

1. Qui téléphone à l'aéroport?
2. Qu'est-ce qu'elle veut savoir?
3. Qui répond au téléphone?
4. Qu'est-ce qu'il dit à la femme de Fabien?
5. À qui est-ce qu'il passe l'écouteur?
6. Qu'est-ce qu'il dit à la femme de Fabien?
7. D'après vous, est-ce que le chef de bureau sait à quelle heure l'avion de Fabien va atterrir?

Un vol retardé Complétez.

1. Fabien a décollé de Commodoro pour aller à ____.
2. Il est retardé par ____.
3. Normalement il faut deux heures pour aller de ____ à ____.
4. Et il vole depuis ____.
5. On ne peut pas entendre les messages à cause du ____.
6. Le chef de bureau ne sait ____.
7. La femme de Fabien veut parler au ____.
8. Le directeur est en ____.

Discussion Pourquoi le secrétaire et le chef de bureau ne veulent-ils pas répondre aux questions de la femme de Fabien?

For more information about Saint-Exupéry and other French authors, go to the Glencoe French Web site: french.glencoe.com

Après la lecture

After reading the selection, have students prepare the **Après la lecture** activities. Go over them in class.

Answers to Après la lecture

A

1. La femme de Fabien téléphone à l'aéroport.
2. Elle veut savoir si Fabien a atterri.
3. Le secrétaire répond au téléphone.
4. Il dit, «une minute...».
5. Il passe l'écouteur au chef de bureau.
6. Il dit à la femme de Fabien que son mari n'a pas encore atterri, qu'il a du retard.
7. Non, le chef de bureau ne sait pas à quelle heure l'avion de Fabien va atterrir.

B

1. Trelew
2. le mauvais temps
3. Commodoro, Trelew
4. six heures
5. mauvais temps
6. rien
7. directeur
8. conférence

C *Answers will vary but may include:*

Parce qu'ils ne peuvent pas trouver Fabien.

National Standards

Cultures
Students experience, discuss, and analyze an expressive product of the culture: an excerpt from the play, ***Le Malade imaginaire,*** by Molière.

Attention!

This reading is optional. You may wish to present it after students have completed Chapters 12–14, as they will have acquired the vocabulary and structures necessary to read the selection by this point.

You may present the piece thoroughly as a class activity or you may have some or all students merely read it on their own. If you present it as a class activity, you may wish to vary presentation procedures from section to section. Some options are:

- Students read silently.
- Students read after you in unison.
- Call on individuals to read aloud.
- When dialogue appears in the story, call on students to take parts.

With any of the above procedures, intersperse some comprehension questions. Call on a student or students to give a brief synopsis of a section in French.

Le Malade imaginaire Molière

Vocabulaire

Le médecin soigne le malade.
Il prend soin du malade.
Le médecin veut guérir sa maladie.

une marque un signe
le soin l'attention
un siècle une période de cent ans
un apothicaire un pharmacien
guérir rendre la santé à quelqu'un
se porter bien être en bonne santé
se servir de utiliser, employer
crever mourir
demeurer d'accord être d'accord

Activités

La médecine Vrai ou faux?

1. Quand on a de la fièvre, on est malade.
2. Un médecin soigne ses patients.
3. Au temps de Molière, on appelait un pharmacien «un apothicaire».
4. Les malades se portent bien.
5. Les médecins se servent des médicaments pour soigner et guérir les malades.
6. Les soins médicaux coûtent cher aux États-Unis.
7. Nous vivons au dix-huitième siècle.
8. «Crever» veut dire «guérir».

Note: The following teaching suggestions are for a thorough presentation of *Le Malade imaginaire.*

Teaching Vocabulary

Step 1 As you present the new vocabulary, you may wish to have students express each of the following in a different way.

Le médecin *prend soin du* malade. (soigne le)
Il veut *lui rendre la santé.* (guérir sa maladie)
La faiblesse et la fatigue sont *des signes* de maladie. (des marques)
Le médecin *utilise* des instruments modernes. (se sert)
Le patient *n'est pas en bonne santé.* (est malade)
Il va *chez l'apothicaire.* (chez le pharmacien, à la pharmacie)

Answers to Activités

1. vrai
2. vrai
3. vrai
4. faux
5. vrai
6. vrai
7. faux
8. faux

Discussing Literature

Introduction

Step 1 It is recommended that you go over the Introduction with the class, since it will help them understand the reading selection.

Step 2 You may wish to ask the following questions about Molière.

Quel est le vrai nom de Molière?
Il est né où?
Comment était son enfance?
Il a reçu quel genre d'éducation?
Quelle était sa vocation?
Il a écrit quels genres de pièces?
Quelle est sa dernière pièce?
Comment Molière meurt-il?

INTRODUCTION Jean-Baptiste Poquelin, dit Molière, est né à Paris en 1622. Il a passé sa jeunesse dans un milieu aisé. Il a reçu une très bonne éducation. Il a étudié les mathématiques, la physique, le latin, la philosophie et la danse. Mais il avait la vocation du théâtre et il a donc décidé de devenir acteur. Il a commencé par écrire des farces. Puis très vite, il a écrit des comédies de mœurs[1]. Molière est un des auteurs français les plus connus. Ses comédies sont jouées dans le monde entier.

Dans *Le Malade imaginaire,* Molière exprime son scepticisme envers la médecine. Comme on le verra dans l'extrait qui suit, Molière n'aimait pas les médecins. *Le Malade imaginaire* est la dernière pièce de Molière. Il présente cette pièce-ballet pour la première fois le 10 février 1673. Molière est malade déjà depuis plusieurs années, mais il joue tout de même le rôle principal d'Argan. Pendant la quatrième représentation, Molière se sent très mal, mais il refuse de quitter la scène. Il meurt quelques heures après la représentation.

Argan est un malade imaginaire, c'est-à-dire, un hypochondriaque. Il est tellement obsédé par sa santé qu'il veut à tout prix marier sa fille au fils d'un médecin alors qu'elle aime quelqu'un d'autre. Il n'hésiterait pas à sacrifier le bonheur[2] de sa fille pour avoir un médecin dans la famille. Dans cette scène Béralde reproche à son frère Argan d'être obsédé par les médecins.

[1] comédies de mœurs *comedy of manners*
[2] bonheur *happiness*

Acte III, Scène 3

BÉRALDE: Est-il possible que vous serez toujours embéguiné° de vos apothicaires et de vos médecins, et que vous vouliez être malade en dépit° des gens et de la nature!

ARGAN: Comment l'entendez-vous°, mon frère?

BÉRALDE: J'entends, mon frère, que je ne vois point° d'homme qui soit moins malade que vous, et que je ne demanderais point une meilleure constitution que la vôtre. Une grande marque que vous vous portez bien, et que vous avez un corps parfaitement composé, c'est qu'avec tous les soins que vous avez pris, vous n'avez pu parvenir encore à gâter la bonté° de votre tempérament, et que vous n'êtes point crevé de toutes les médecines qu'on vous a fait prendre.

ARGAN: Mais savez-vous, mon frère, que c'est cela qui me conserve; et que monsieur Purgon dit que je succomberais, s'il était seulement trois jours sans prendre soin de moi?

BÉRALDE: Si vous n'y prenez garde°, il prendra tant de soin de vous, qu'il vous enverra en l'autre monde.

embéguiné *infatuated*

en dépit *in spite*

Comment l'entendez-vous? *What do you mean by that?*

ne… point *not*

parvenir à gâter la bonté *succeed in spoiling the goodness*

Si vous n'y prenez garde *If you don't watch out*

Le Malade imaginaire

Acte III, Scène 3

Step 1 Give students a few minutes to look at the sidenotes just to become acquainted with them.

Step 2 Read the selection to the students using the paraphrases in Activity A on page 497.

Step 3 Have students read the selection silently and do the **Après la lecture** activities on page 497.

ARGAN: Mais raisonnons un peu, mon frère. Vous ne croyez donc point à la médecine?

BÉRALDE: Non, mon frère, et je ne vois pas que, pour son salut°, il soit nécessaire d'y croire.

ARGAN: Quoi! vous ne tenez° pas véritable une chose établie° par tout le monde, et que tous les siècles ont révérée?

BÉRALDE: Bien loin de la tenir véritable, je la trouve, entre nous, une des grandes folies qui soit parmi les hommes; et, à regarder les choses en philosophe, je ne vois point de plus plaisante momerie°, je ne vois rien de plus ridicule qu'un homme qui se veut mêler° d'en guérir un autre.

ARGAN: Pourquoi ne voulez-vous pas, mon frère, qu'un homme en puisse guérir un autre?

BÉRALDE: Par la raison, mon frère, que les ressorts de notre machine° sont des mystères, jusques ici, où les hommes ne voient goutte°; et que la nature nous a mis au-devant des yeux des voiles trop épais° pour y connaître quelque chose.

ARGAN: Les médecins ne savent donc rien, à votre compte?

BÉRALDE: Si fait°, mon frère. Ils savent la plupart de fort belles humanités, savent parler en beau latin, savent nommer en grec toutes les maladies, les définir et les diviser; mais pour ce qui est de les guérir, c'est ce qu'ils ne savent point du tout.

ARGAN: Mais toujours faut-il demeurer d'accord que, sur cette matière, les médecins en savent plus que les autres. [...] Il faut bien que les médecins croient leur art véritable, puisqu'ils° s'en servent eux-mêmes.

salut *salvation*
tenez *consider*
établie *taken for granted*
plaisante momerie *masquerade*
se veut mêler *wants to get mixed up*
ressorts de notre machine *our body's mechanism*
ne... goutte *nothing*
voiles trop épais *veils too thick*
Si fait *Of course*
puisqu'ils *since they*

ANSWERS TO **Après la lecture**

A

1. Vous serez toujours embéguiné de vos apothicaires.
2. Comment l'entendez-vous, mon frère?
3. Je ne vois point d'homme...
4. Une grande marque que vous vous portez bien...
5. Vous n'avez pu parvenir encore à gâter la bonté de votre tempérament.
6. Si vous n'y prenez garde...
7. Il vous enverra en l'autre monde.
8. Vous ne tenez pas véritable une chose établie par tout le monde...
9. Je ne vois rien de plus ridicule qu'un homme qui se veut mêler d'en guérir un autre.
10. Les ressorts de notre machine sont des mystères, jusques ici, où les hommes ne voient goutte.
11. Les médecins ne savent donc rien à votre compte.
12. Si fait, mon frère.

Après la lecture

D'une autre façon Comment Molière exprime-t-il les phrases suivantes?

1. Vous serez toujours fasciné par vos pharmaciens.
2. Que voulez-vous dire, mon frère?
3. Je ne vois pas d'homme…
4. Une grande marque que vous allez bien…
5. Vous n'avez pas réussi à gâter la bonté de votre tempérament.
6. Si vous ne faites pas attention…
7. Il vous tuera.
8. Vous ne considérez pas véritable quelque chose que tout le monde accepte.
9. Je ne vois rien de plus stupide qu'un homme qui veut essayer de guérir un autre homme.
10. Les moyens de notre corps sont des mystères que les hommes ne comprennent pas.
11. Les médecins ne savent donc rien, à votre avis.
12. Bien sûr, mon frère.

Pas du même avis Répondez.

1. Est-ce que Béralde croit que son frère est vraiment malade?
2. Est-ce qu'il croit que le médecin donne trop de médicaments à son frère?
3. D'après Argan, qu'est-ce qui le conserve?
4. Comment s'appelle le médecin d'Argan?
5. D'après ce médecin, qu'est-ce qui se passerait s'il ne prenait pas soin d'Argan?
6. D'après Béralde, où le médecin va-t-il envoyer Argan?
7. D'après Béralde, qu'est-ce que la médecine?
8. Béralde croit qu'un homme peut guérir un autre homme?
9. Qui dit que notre corps est une machine mystérieuse?
10. D'après Béralde, que savent les médecins?

C **Discussion** Vous êtes d'accord avec les idées de Béralde ou avec celles d'Argan? Expliquez pourquoi.

ANSWERS TO

B

1. Béralde ne croit pas que son frère soit malade.
2. Oui, il croit que le médecin lui donne trop de médicaments.
3. Ce qui le conserve, c'est les médicaments.
4. Le médecin d'Argan s'appelle Purgon.
5. Argan mourrait.
6. Il va envoyer Argan en (dans) l'autre monde.
7. La médecine est une des grandes folies qui soit parmi les hommes.
8. Non, il ne croit pas qu'un homme puisse guérir un autre homme.
9. Béralde dit que notre corps est une machine mystérieuse.
10. Ils savent parler latin et grec. Ils savent nommer, définir et diviser les maladies.

C *Answers will vary.*

Activity 1

CHAPITRE 1, Mots 1, pages 2–3

Élève A Ask your partner the following questions. Correct answers are in parentheses.

1. Qu'est-ce que tu aimes comme film?
   (J'aime les documentaires.)
2. Qu'est-ce qu'on monte?
   (On monte Roméo et Juliette.)
3. Tu aimes mieux aller au cinéma ou louer des vidéos?
   (J'aime mieux louer des vidéos.)

Élève A Answer your partner's questions according to the illustrations.

1.

2.

3.

Élève B Answer your partner's questions according to the illustrations.

1.

2.

Roméo et Juliette
ballet en trois actes
d'après William Shakespeare
musique
Sergueï Prokofiev
chorégraphie et mise en scène
Rudolf Noureev
réglées par
Patricia Ruanne
Frederick Jahn
choréologue
Kristin Johnson
décors
Ezio Frigerio
avec la collaboration de
Alexandre Beliaev
nouvelle présentation pour la production de 1995
costumes
Ezio Frigerio et Mauro Pagano
lumières
Vinicio Cheli
production créée pour le Ballet de l'Opéra en 1984
Orchestre de l'Opéra National de Paris
direction
Vello Pähn
fin du spectacle vers 22 h 40

3.

PONETTE

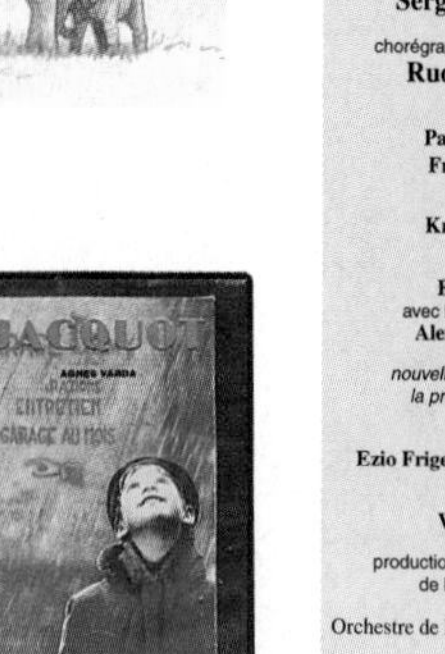

Élève B Ask your partner the following questions. Correct answers are in parentheses.

1. Qu'est-ce que tu aimes comme film?
   (J'aime les dessins animés.)
2. Tu as déjà vu le chanteur?
   (Non, mais j'ai déjà vu la danseuse.)
3. Tu vas voir une pièce de théâtre?
   (Non, je vais voir un film au cinéma.)

Activity 8

CHAPITRE 2, Structure, pages 45–47

Élève A Ask your partner the following questions. Correct answers are in parentheses.

1. Finir les devoirs?
   (Finis tes devoirs!)
2. Préparer le dîner?
   (Prépare le dîner!)
3. Choisir un film?
   (Choisissons un film!)
4. Travailler plus?
   (Travaille plus!)
5. Dîner au restaurant?
   (Dînons au restaurant!)

Élève A Answer your partner's questions based on the information in the chart below.

Personne(s)	**Activité**
tu	prendre le métro
vous	attendre devant la porte
tu	faire du ski
tu	sortir ce soir
vous	regarder le film

Élève B Answer your partner's questions based on the information in the chart below.

Personne(s)	**Activité**
tu	finir les devoirs
tu	préparer le dîner
nous	choisir un film
tu	travailler plus
nous	dîner au restaurant

Élève B Ask your partner the following questions. Correct answers are in parentheses.

1. Prendre le métro?
   (Prends le métro!)
2. Attendre devant la porte?
   (Attendez devant la porte!)
3. Faire du ski?
   (Fais du ski!)
4. Sortir ce soir?
   (Sors ce soir!)
5. Regardez le film?
   (Regardez le film!)

Activity 9

CHAPITRE 3, Mots 1, pages 66–67

Élève A Ask your partner the following questions. Correct answers are in parentheses.

1. Tu mets le document face écrite non visible?
   (Oui, je mets le document face écrite non visible.)
2. Quand tu tapes ton texte, tu regardes l'écran ou le clavier?
   (Je regarde l'écran.)
3. Qu'est-ce que tu mets dans le lecteur?
   (Je mets une disquette.)

Élève A Answer your partner's questions based on the pictures below.

1. 

2. 

3. 

Élève B Answer your partner's questions based on the pictures below.

1. 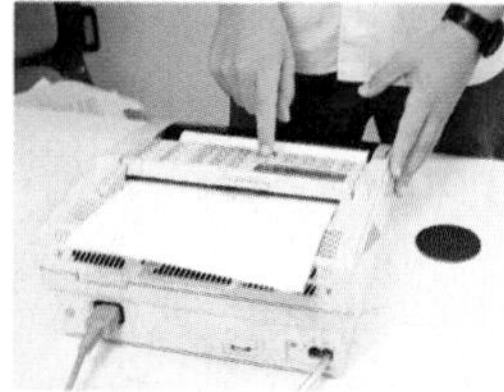

2. 

3. 

Élève B Ask your partner the following questions. Correct answers are in parentheses.

1. Tu as un dictionnaire sur CD-ROM?
   (Oui, j'ai un dictionnaire sur CD-ROM.)
2. Tu cliques sur l'icône du logiciel avec quoi?
   (Je clique sur l'icône du logiciel avec la souris.)
3. Tu tapes tes devoirs sur quoi?
   (Je tape mes devoirs sur le clavier.)

Activity 10

CHAPITRE 4, Mots 1, pages 98–99

Élève A Ask your partner the following questions. Correct answers are in parentheses.

1. Quelles lignes desservent Mitry-Claye et Les Noues?
   (Les Lignes de Banlieue)
2. Quelle lignes desservent Londres et Lille?
   (Les Grandes Lignes)
3. La voiture du train a un couloir central?
   (Oui, la voiture du train a un couloir central.)
4. Il y a deux sièges de chaque côté?
   (Oui, il y a deux sièges de chaque côté.)

Élève A Answer your partner's questions based on the picture below.

M. et Mme Dubois **Madame Delacroix**

Élève B Answer your partner's questions based on the pictures below.

1–2.

3–4.

Élève B Ask your partner the following questions. Correct answers are in parentheses.

1. Madame Delacroix est assise?
   (Oui, elle est assise.)
2. M. et Mme Dubois sont dans un compartiment?
   (Non, ils sont dans le couloir.)
3. Le compartiment est complet?
   (Oui, le compartiment est complet.)
4. M. et Mme Dubois sont assis?
   (Non, ils sont debout.)

Activity 11

CHAPITRE 5, Mots 1, pages 142–143

Élève A Ask your partner the following questions. Correct answers are in parentheses.

1. Marie a de l'argent liquide?
   (Oui, elle a de l'argent liquide.)
2. Elle dépense tout son argent?
   (Non, elle met de l'argent de côté.)
3. Sophie est au bureau de change?
   (Non, elle est au distributeur automatique.)
4. Elle retire de l'argent?
   (Oui, elle retire de l'argent.)

Élève A Answer your partner's questions based on the pictures below.

1–3.

4.

Élève B Answer your partner's questions based on the pictures below.

1–2.

3–4.

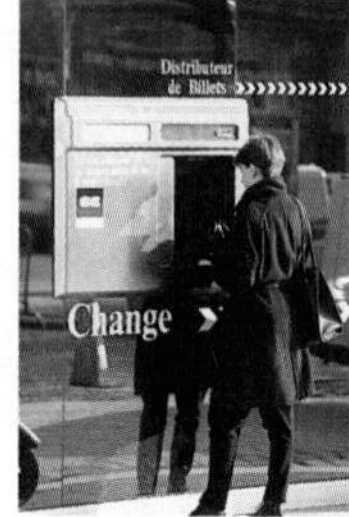

Élève B Ask your partner the following questions. Correct answers are in parentheses.

1. La touriste est allée au bureau de change?
   (Oui, elle est allée au bureau de change.)
2. Elle a changé des dollars?
   (Oui, elle a changé des dollars.)
3. Le caissier lui a donné des euros?
   (Oui, il lui a donné des euros.)
4. Elle a mis les pièces où?
   (Elle a mis les pièces dans son porte-monnaie.)

VERBES RÉFLÉCHIS		VERBES AVEC CHANGEMENTS D'ORTHOGRAPHE	
INFINITIF	**se laver** *to wash oneself*	**acheter**[1] *to buy*	**appeler** *to call*
PRÉSENT	je me lave tu le laves il se lave nous nous lavons vous vous lavez ils se lavent	j'achète tu achètes il achète nous achetons vous achetez ils achètent	j'appelle tu appelles il appelle nous appelons vous appelez ils appellent
IMPÉRATIF	lave-toi lavons-nous lavez-vous	achète achetons achetez	appelle appelons appelez
PASSÉ COMPOSÉ	je me suis lavé(e) tu t'es lavé(e) il s'est lavé nous nous sommes lavé(e)s vous vous êtes lavé(e)(s) ils se sont lavés	j'ai acheté tu as acheté il a acheté nous avons acheté vous avez acheté ils ont acheté	j'ai appelé tu as appelé il a appelé nous avons appelé vous avez appelé ils ont appelé
IMPARFAIT	je me lavais tu te lavais il se lavait nous nous lavions vous vous laviez ils se lavaient	j'achetais tu achetais il achetait nous achetions vous achetiez ils achetaient	j'appelais tu appelais il appelait nous appelions vous appeliez ils appelaient
FUTUR	je me laverai tu te laveras il se lavera nous nous laverons vous vous laverez ils se laveront	j'achèterai tu achèteras il achètera nous achèterons vous achèterez ils achèteront	j'appellerai tu appelleras il appellera nous appellerons vous appellerez ils appelleront
CONDITIONNEL	je me laverais tu te laverais il se laverait nous nous laverions vous vous laveriez ils se laveraient	j'achèterais tu achèterais il achèterait nous achèterions vous achèteriez ils achèteraient	j'appellerais tu appellerais il appellerait nous appellerions vous appelleriez ils appelleraient
SUBJONCTIF PRÉSENT	que je me lave que tu te laves qu'il se lave que nous nous lavions que vous vous laviez qu'ils se lavent	que j'achète que tu achètes qu'il achète que nous achetions que vous achetiez qu'ils achètent	que j'appelle que tu appelles qu'il appelle que nous appelions que vous appeliez qu'ils appellent

[1] *Verbes similaires:* **emmener, se lever, peser, se promener, soulever**

VERBES AVEC CHANGEMENTS D'ORTHOGRAPHE				
INFINITIF	commencer[2] *to begin*	manger[3] *to eat*	payer[4] *to pay*	préférer[5] *to prefer*
PRÉSENT	je commence tu commences il commence nous commençons vous commencez ils commencent	je mange tu manges il mange nous mangeons vous mangez ils mangent	je paie tu paies il paie nous payons vous payez ils paient	je préfère tu préfères il préfère nous préférons vous préférez ils préfèrent
IMPÉRATIF	commence commençons commencez	mange mangeons mangez	paie payons payez	préfère préférons préférez
PASSÉ COMPOSÉ	j'ai commencé tu as commencé il a commencé nous avons commencé vous avez commencé ils ont commencé	j'ai mangé tu as mangé il a mangé nous avons mangé vous avez mangé ils ont mangé	j'ai payé tu as payé il a payé nous avons payé vous avez payé ils ont payé	j'ai préféré tu as préféré il a préféré nous avons préféré vous avez préféré ils ont préféré
IMPARFAIT	je commençais tu commençais il commençait nous commencions vous commenciez ils commençaient	je mangeais tu mangeais il mangeait nous mangions vous mangiez ils mangeaient	je payais tu payais il payait nous payions vous payiez ils payaient	je préférais tu préférais il préférait nous préférions vous préfériez ils préféraient
FUTUR	je commencerai tu commenceras il commencera nous commencerons vous commencerez ils commenceront	je mangerai tu mangeras il mangera nous mangerons vous mangerez ils mangeront	je paierai tu paieras il paiera nous paierons vous paierez ils paieront	je préférerai tu préféreras il préférera nous préférerons vous préférerez ils préféreront
CONDITIONNEL	je commencerais tu commencerais il commencerait nous commencerions vous commenceriez ils commenceraient	je mangerais tu mangerais il mangerait nous mangerions vous mangeriez ils mangeraient	je paierais tu paierais il paierait nous paierions vous paieriez ils paieraient	je préférerais tu préférerais il préférerait nous préférerions vous préféreriez ils préféreraient
SUBJONCTIF PRÉSENT	que je commence que tu commences qu'il commence que nous commencions que vous commenciez qu'ils commencent	que je mange que tu manges qu'il mange que nous mangions que vous mangiez qu'ils mangent	que je paie que tu paies qu'il paie que nous payions que vous payiez qu'ils paient	que je préfère que tu préfères qu'il préfère que nous préférions que vous préfériez qu'ils préfèrent

[2] *Verbe similaire:* **effacer**
[3] *Verbes similaires:* **changer, exiger, nager, voyager**
[4] *Verbes similaires:* **appuyer, employer, essayer, essuyer, nettoyer, tutoyer**
[5] *Verbes similaires:* **accélérer, célébrer, espérer, oblitérer, récupérer, sécher, suggérer**

VERBES IRRÉGULIERS				
INFINITIF	**pouvoir** *to be able to*	**prendre**[4] *to take*	**recevoir** *to receive*	**savoir** *to know*
PRÉSENT	je peux tu peux il peut nous pouvons vous pouvez ils peuvent	je prends tu prends il prend nous prenons vous prenez ils prennent	je reçois tu reçois il reçoit nous recevons vous recevez ils reçoivent	je sais tu sais il sait nous savons vous savez ils savent
IMPÉRATIF	(pas d'impératif)	prends prenons prenez	reçois recevons recevez	sache sachons sachez
PASSÉ COMPOSÉ	j'ai pu tu as pu il a pu nous avons pu vous avez pu ils ont pu	j'ai pris tu as pris il a pris nous avons pris vous avez pris ils ont pris	j'ai reçu tu as reçu il a reçu nous avons reçu vous avez reçu ils ont reçu	j'ai su tu as su il a su nous avons su vous avez su ils ont su
IMPARFAIT	je pouvais tu pouvais il pouvait nous pouvions vous pouviez ils pouvaient	je prenais tu prenais il prenait nous prenions vous preniez ils prenaient	je recevais tu recevais il recevait nous recevions vous receviez ils recevaient	je savais tu savais il savait nous savions vous saviez ils savaient
FUTUR	je pourrai tu pourras il pourra nous pourrons vous pourrez ils pourront	je prendrai tu prendras il prendra nous prendrons vous prendrez ils prendront	je recevrai tu recevras il recevra nous recevrons vous recevrez ils recevront	je saurai tu sauras il saura nous saurons vous saurez ils sauront
CONDITIONNEL	je pourrais tu pourrais il pourrait nous pourrions vous pourriez ils pourraient	je prendrais tu prendrais il prendrait nous prendrions vous prendriez ils prendraient	je recevrais tu recevrais il recevrait nous recevrions vous recevriez ils recevraient	je saurais tu saurais il saurait nous saurions vous sauriez ils sauraient
SUBJONCTIF PRÉSENT	que je puisse que tu puisses qu'il puisse que nous puissions que vous puissiez qu'ils puissent	que je prenne que tu prennes qu'il prenne que nous prenions que vous preniez qu'ils prennent	que je reçoive que tu reçoives qu'il reçoive que nous recevions que vous receviez qu'ils reçoivent	que je sache que tu saches qu'il sache que nous sachions que vous sachiez qu'ils sachent

[4] *Verbes similaires:* **apprendre, comprendre**

VERBES IRRÉGULIERS				
INFINITIF	**servir**[5] *to serve*	**suivre** *to follow*	**venir**[6] *to come*	**vivre** *to live*
PRÉSENT	je sers tu sers il sert nous servons vous servez ils servent	je suis tu suis il suit nous suivons vous suivez ils suivent	je viens tu viens il vient nous venons vous venez ils viennent	je vis tu vis il vit nous vivons vous vivez ils vivent
IMPÉRATIF	sers servons servez	suis suivons suivez	viens venons venez	vis vivons vivez
PASSÉ COMPOSÉ	j'ai servi tu as servi il a servi nous avons servi vous avez servi ils ont servi	j'ai suivi tu as suivi il a suivi nous avons suivi vous avez suivi ils ont suivi	je suis venu(e) tu es venu(e) il est venu nous sommes venu(e)s vous êtes venu(e)(s) ils sont venus	j'ai vécu tu as vécu il a vécu nous avons vécu vous avez vécu ils ont vécu
IMPARFAIT	je servais tu servais il servait nous servions vous serviez ils servaient	je suivais tu suivais il suivait nous suivions vous suiviez ils suivaient	je venais tu venais il venait nous venions vous veniez ils venaient	je vivais tu vivais il vivait nous vivions vous viviez ils vivaient
FUTUR	je servirai tu serviras il servira nous servirons vous servirez ils serviront	je suivrai tu suivras il suivra nous suivrons vous suivrez ils suivront	je viendrai tu viendras il viendra nous viendrons vous viendrez ils viendront	je vivrai tu vivras il vivra nous vivrons vous vivrez ils vivront
CONDITIONNEL	je servirais tu servirais il servirait nous servirions vous serviriez ils serviraient	je suivrais tu suivrais il suivrait nous suivrions vous suivriez ils suivraient	je viendrais tu viendrais il viendrait nous viendrions vous viendriez ils viendraient	je vivrais tu vivrais il vivrait nous vivrions vous vivriez ils vivraient
SUBJONCTIF PRÉSENT	que je serve que tu serves qu'il serve que nous servions que vous serviez qu'ils servent	que je suive que tu suives qu'il suive que nous suivions que vous suiviez qu'ils suivent	que je vienne que tu viennes qu'il vienne que nous venions que vous veniez qu'ils viennent	que je vive que tu vives qu'il vive que nous vivions que vous viviez qu'ils vivent

[5] *Verbe similaire:* **desservir**
[6] *Verbes similaires:* **devenir, revenir, se souvenir**

	VERBES IRRÉGULIERS		VERBES IMPERSONNELS	
INFINITIF	voir *to see*	vouloir *to want*	falloir *to be necessary*	pleuvoir *to rain*
PRÉSENT	je vois tu vois il voit nous voyons vous voyez ils voient	je veux tu veux il veut nous voulons vous voulez ils veulent	il faut	il pleut
IMPÉRATIF	vois voyons voyez	veuille veuillons veuillez		
PASSÉ COMPOSÉ	j'ai vu tu as vu il a vu nous avons vu vous avez vu ils ont vu	j'ai voulu tu as voulu il a voulu nous avons voulu vous avez voulu ils ont voulu	il a fallu	il a plu
IMPARFAIT	je voyais tu voyais il voyait nous voyions vous voyiez ils voyaient	je voulais tu voulais il voulait nous voulions vous vouliez ils voulaient	il fallait	il pleuvait
FUTUR	je verrai tu verras il verra nous verrons vous verrez ils verront	je voudrai tu voudras il voudra nous voudrons vous voudrez ils voudront	il faudra	il pleuvra
CONDITIONNEL	je verrais tu verrais il verrait nous verrions vous verriez ils verraient	je voudrais tu voudrais il voudrait nous voudrions vous voudriez ils voudraient	il faudrait	il pleuvrait
SUBJONCTIF PRÉSENT	que je voie que tu voies qu'il voie que nous voyions que vous voyiez qu'ils voient	que je veuille que tu veuilles qu'il veuille que nous voulions que vous vouliez qu'ils veuillent	qu'il faille	qu'il pleuve

VERBES AVEC ÊTRE AU PASSÉ COMPOSÉ	
aller *(to go)*	je suis allé(e)
arriver *(to arrive)*	je suis arrivé(e)
descendre *(to go down, to get off)*	je suis descendu(e)
entrer *(to enter)*	je suis entré(e)
monter *(to go up)*	je suis monté(e)
mourir *(to die)*	je suis mort(e)
naître *(to be born)*	je suis né(e)
partir *(to leave)*	je suis parti(e)
passer *(to go by)*	je suis passé(e)
rentrer *(to go home)*	je suis rentré(e)
rester *(to stay)*	je suis resté(e)
retourner *(to return)*	je suis retourné(e)
revenir *(to come back)*	je suis revenu(e)
sortir *(to go out)*	je suis sorti(e)
tomber *(to fall)*	je suis tombé(e)
venir *(to come)*	je suis venu(e)

la **critique** review
croire to believe, think, 7.2
le **croisement** intersection, **7.2**
se **croiser** to cross, intersect, **10.1**
la **croissance** growth
le **croissant** croissant, crescent roll, 5.1
le **croque-monsieur** grilled ham and cheese sandwich, 5.1
la **crosse** hockey stick
la **cuillère** spoon, 5.2
cuire to cook, **6.2**
la **cuisine** kitchen, 4.2; cuisine *(food)*
faire la cuisine to cook, 6
le **cuisinier, la cuisinière** cook, **6.2**
la **cuisinière** stove, **6.1**
cuit(e) cooked
bien cuit(e) well-done *(meat)*, 5.2
le **cuivre** copper
cultiver to cultivate; to grow; to farm (land), **11.2**
la **culture** culture, growing
culturel(le) cultural
curieux, curieuse odd
le **curriculum vitae (C.V.)** résumé, **14.2**
le **cyclisme** cycling, bicycle riding, 10.2
le/la **cycliste** cyclist, bicycle rider
cycliste bicycle, cycling *(adj.)*, 10.2
les **cymbales** *(f. pl.)* cymbals, **12.1**

d'abord first, 12.1
d'accord okay, all right *(agreement)*
être d'accord to agree, 2.1
la **dame** lady
les dames checkers

dangereux, dangereuse dangerous
dans in, 1.2
la **danse** dance
danser to dance, **1.1**
le **danseur, la danseuse** dancer, **1.1**
la danseuse ballerina, **1.1**
d'après according to
dater de to date from
la **datte** date
le **dattier** date palm
d'autres some other, 2.2
de from, 1.1; of, belonging to, 1.2; about
de bonne heure early
de près close, **11.1**
de temps en temps from time to time, occasionally
le **débarquement** landing, deplaning
débarquer to get off *(plane)*, **4.2**
débarrasser la table to clear the table, 12.2
debout standing, 9.2
le **début** beginning
au début in the beginning
le/la **débutant(e)** beginner, 11.2
débuter to begin
le **décalage horaire** time difference
la **décapotable** convertible, **7.1**
le **déchet** waste
décider (de) to decide (to)
déclarer to declare, call
le **décollage** takeoff *(plane)*, **4.2**
décoller to take off *(plane)*, 8.1
décorer to decorate
la **découverte** discovery
découvrir to discover
décrire to describe
décrocher (le téléphone) to pick up the (telephone) receiver, **3.2**
dedans into it

dédié(e) dedicated
défaire to unpack, **9.1**
le **défilé** parade, **12.1**
défiler to march, **12.1**
définir to define
déformer to distort
se **dégager** to be given off
dehors outdoors
au dehors de outside
déjà already; ever; yet, BV
déjeuner to eat lunch, 3.1
le **déjeuner** lunch, 5.2
le petit déjeuner breakfast, 5.2
délicieux, délicieuse delicious
demain tomorrow, BV
À demain. See you tomorrow., BV
demander to ask, to ask for, 3.2
demeurer d'accord to agree, **L4**
demi(e) half
et demie half past *(time)*, BV
le **demi-cercle** semi-circle; top of the key *(on a basketball court)*, 10.2
le **demi-frère** half brother, 4.1
la **demi-heure** half hour
la **demi-sœur** half sister, 4.1
le **demi-tarif** half price
le **demi-tour** about-face
faire demi-tour to turn around, **11.1**
la **demoiselle d'honneur** maid of honor, **12.2**
le **dénouement** ending
la **dent** tooth, 12.1
le **dentifrice** toothpaste, 12.1
le **départ** departure, 8.1
le **département d'outre-mer** French overseas department
dépasser to pass, **L1**
se **dépêcher** to hurry, 12.1
dépendre (de) to depend (on)

dépenser to spend *(money)*, **5.1**
depuis since, for, 9.2, **10.2**
le **dérangement** disturbance
dernier, dernière last, 10.2
derrière behind, **11.1**
désagréable disagreeable, unpleasant
descendre to get off *(train, bus, etc.)*, 9.2; to take down, 9; to go down, 9; to take downstairs, **9**; to stay at *(hotel)*
descendre à la prochaine to get off at the next station, **10.1**
la **descente** getting off, **10.2**
le **désert** desert
désert(e) deserted
désespéré(e) desperate, L4
le **désir** desire; wish
désirer to want, 5.1
désolé(e) sorry, **3.2, 13.2**
désormais from then on
le **dessert** dessert
desservir to serve, go to *(transp.)*, **4.1**
le **dessin** drawing, illustration; design
le dessin animé cartoon, **1.1**
dessiner to design, draw
dessus on it
le/la **destinataire** addressee
la **destination** destination
à destination de to *(destination)*, 8.1
destiné(e) à intended for
la **destinée** destiny
déterrer to unearth
détester to hate, 3.1
déverser to spill
deux: tous (toutes) les deux both
deuxième second, 4.2
devant in front of, 8.2, **11.1**
développer to develop
devenir to become, **4**
deviner to guess
la **devinette** riddle
la **devise** currency
le **devoir** homework *(assignment)*
faire les devoirs to do homework, 6
devoir to owe, 10; must, to have to (+ *verb*), 10.2
dévoué(e) devoted
d'habitude usually, 12.2
le **diagnostic** diagnosis, **2.2**
le **diamant** diamond
dicter to dictate
le **dictionnaire** dictionary
difficile difficult, 2.1
la **difficulté** problem, difficulty
être en difficulté to be in trouble
diffuser to spread, to propagate
la **dinde** turkey
le **dindon** turkey
le **dîner** dinner, 5.2
dîner to eat dinner, 5.2
le **diplôme** diploma
diplômé(e): être diplômé(e) to graduate
dire to say, tell, 9.2
Ça me dit! I'd like that!
le **directeur (la directrice) des ressources humaines (D.R.H.)** director of human resources, **14.2**
diriger to manage, **14.1**
le **discours** speech
discuter to discuss
disparaître to disappear
disparu(e) disappeared, lost
disponible available, **4.1**
le **disque** record
la **disquette** diskette, **3.1**
distinguer to distinguish, to tell apart
distribuer to distribute, **5.2**
le **distributeur automatique** ATM, **5.1;** stamp machine, **5.2;** ticket machine, **10.1**
divers(e) various
diviser to divide
le **djellaba** djellaba *(long, loose garment)*
le **doigt** finger, **8.1, 13.1**
le doigt de pied toe, **8.1**
le **dolmen** dolmen
le **domaine** domain, field
le **domicile: à domicile** to the home
dominer to overlook
donc so, therefore
les **données** *(f. pl.)* data, **3.1**
donner to give, 4.1
donner à manger à to feed
donner un coup de fil to call on the phone, **3.2**
donner un coup de pied to kick, 10.1
donner une fête to throw a party, 4.1
donner sur to face, overlook, 4.2
dont of which, whose
doré(e) golden
dormir to sleep, 8.2
le **dortoir** dormitory
le **dos** back, **L2**
le **dossier du siège** seat back, **4.2**
la **douane** customs, **4.2**
doublé(e) dubbed *(movies)*, **1.1**
doubler to pass, **7.2**
la **douche** shower, 12.1
douloureux, douloureuse painful
le **doute** doubt
douter to doubt, **14**
la **douzaine** dozen, 6.2
le **drame** drama, **1.1**
le **drap** sheet, **9.2**
le **drapeau** flag, **12.1**

dribbler to dribble *(basketball)*, 10.2
le **droit** right
droite: à droite right, **7.2**
la **drôle de tête** strange expression
du coin neighborhood *(adj.)*
dur(e) hard
la **durée** duration
durer to last

E

l' **eau** *(f.)* water, 6.2
l'eau minérale mineral water, 6.2
l' **échange** *(m.)* exchange
échanger to exchange
s' **échapper** to escape
l' **écharpe** *(f.)* scarf, 11.2
éclaté(e) burst
l' **école** *(f.)* school, 1.2
l'école primaire elementary school
l'école secondaire secondary school, 1.2
écologique ecological
l' **économie** *(f.)* economics, 2.2
faire des économies to save money, **5.1**
économiser to save money
écouter to listen (to), 3.1
l' **écouteur** *(m.)* earphone, headphone, **L3**
l' **écran** *(m.)* screen, 8.1, **3.1**
écrasé(e) crushed
écrire to write, 9.2
l' **écriture** *(f.)* writing
l' **écrivain** *(m.)* writer *(m. and f.)*, L2, **14.1**
l' **édifice** *(m.)* building
efficace efficient
égal(e): Ça m'est égal. I don't care.; It's all the same to me., **1.1**
également as well, also
égaliser to tie *(score)*
l' **église** *(f.)* church, **11.1, 12.2**
égoïste egotistical, 1.2
égyptien(ne) Egyptian
l' **électricien(ne)** electrician, **14.1**
l' **électroménager** *(m.)* home appliances
l' **élevage** *(m.)*: **faire de l'élevage de chevaux** to raise horses
l' **élève** *(m. et f.)* student, 1.2
élevé(e) high
bien élevé(e) well-behaved, **13.1**
mal élevé(e) impolite, **13.1**
éliminer to eliminate
éloigné(e) distant, remote
éloigner to distance
l' **embarquement** *(m.)* boarding, leaving
embarquer to board *(plane, etc.)*, **4.2**
s' **embrasser** to kiss (each other), **12.2, 13.1**
l' **émission** *(f.)* program, show *(TV)*, 12.2
emmagasiner to store
emmener to send, L4; to take, **8.1**
l' **emploi** *(m.)* use; job, **14.2**
l'emploi du temps schedule
l' **employé(e)** employee, **14.1**
l'employé(e) des postes postal employee, **5.2**
l' **employeur, l'employeuse** employer, **14.2**
emprisonné(e) imprisoned
l' **emprunt** *(m.)* loan
emprunter to borrow, **5.1**
en in, 3.2; by, 5.2; as; on
en avance early, ahead of time, 9.1
en avion plane *(adj.)*, by plane
en ce moment right now
en classe in class
en face de across from, **11.1**
en fait in fact
en général in general
en l'honneur de in honor of
en particulier in particular
en plein air outdoors
en plus (de) besides, in addition
en première (seconde) in first (second) class, 9.1
en provenance de arriving from *(flight, train)*, 8.1
en retard late, 9.1
en solde on sale, 7.1
en vain in vain
en voiture by car, 5.2
encaisser to cash
l' **enceinte de résidences** compound, **L2**
enchanté(e) delighted, **13.2**
encore still, 11; another; again
s' **endetter** to go into debt
s' **endormir** to fall asleep
l' **endroit** *(m.)* place
énervé(e) irritable
l' **enfance** *(f.)* childhood
l' **enfant** *(m. et f.)* child, 4.1
enfermer to shut up
enfin finally, at last, 12.1
l' **ennemi(e)** *(m. et f.)* enemy
ennuyeux, ennuyeuse boring
l' **enquête** *(f.)* inquiry, survey
enragé(e) rabid
enregistrer to tape, 12.2
(faire) enregistrer to check *(baggage)*, 8.1
enrhumé(e): être enrhumé(e) to have a cold, **2.1**
l' **ensemble** *(m.)* outfit; whole, entirety
ensemble together, 5.1
ensuite then *(adv.)*, 12.1

entendre to hear, 9.1
enthousiaste enthusiastic, 1.2
entier, entière entire, whole
l' **entracte** *(m.)* intermission, **1.1**
entre between, among, 3.2
l' **entrée** *(f.)* entrance, 4.2; admission
entreposer to store, **11.2**
l' **entreprise** *(f.)* firm, company, **14.2**
entrer to enter, 7.1
l' **entretien** *(m.)* interview, **14.2**
l' **enveloppe** *(f.)* envelope, **5.2**
environ about
envoyer to send, 10.1, **3.1**
l' **épée** *(f.)* sword, L3
épeler to spell
éperdument madly
l' **épice** *(f.)* spice
épicé(e) spicy
l' **épicerie** *(f.)* grocery store, 6.1
les **épinards** *(m. pl.)* spinach, 6.2
éplucher to peel, **6.2**
l' **époque** *(f.)* period, times
épuisé(e) exhausted
épurer to purify
l' **équateur** *(m.)* equator
l' **équilibre** *(m.)* balance
équilibré(e) balanced
l' **équipe** *(f.)* team, 10.1
l' **équipement** *(m.)* equipment
l' **erreur** *(f.)* error; wrong number (phone), **3.2**
l' **escale** *(f.)* stopover, **4.2**
l' **escalier** *(m.)* staircase, 4.2
l'escalier mécanique escalator, **10.1**
l' **escalope** *(f.)* **de veau** veal cutlet, **6.2**
l' **espace** *(m.)* space
les grands espaces open spaces
l' **espagnol** *(m.)* Spanish *(language)*, 2.2
les **espèces** *(f. pl.)*: **payer en espèces** to pay cash, **9.2**
espérer to hope, **6.2**
l' **esprit** *(m.)* spirit; mind
essayer to try on, 7.2; to try
l' **essence** *(f.)* gas(oline), **7.1**
essuyer to wipe, **L2**
s'essuyer la bouche to wipe one's mouth, **13.1**
et and, BV
l' **étable** *(f.)* stable, **11.2**
établir to establish
l' **établissement** *(m.)* establishment
l' **étage** *(m.)* floor *(of a building)*, 4.2
l' **étal** *(m.)* stand, stall
l' **étape** *(f.)* stage, lap
l' **état** *(m.)* state
les **États-Unis** *(m. pl.)* United States
l' **été** *(m.)* summer, 11.1
en été in summer, 11.1
éteindre to turn off *(appliance)*, 12.2, **3.1**
éternuer to sneeze, **2.1**
étonné(e) surprised, **13.2**
étonner to surprise
s'étonner to be surprised
étranger, étrangère foreign, **1.1**
être to be, 1.1
être d'accord to agree, 2.1
être enrhumé(e) to have a cold, **2.1**
ne pas être dans son assiette to be feeling out of sorts, **2.1**
l' **être** *(m.)* being
l'être humain human being
l' **étudiant(e)** *(university)* student
l' **étude** *(f.)* study
étudier to study, 3.1
l' **euro** *(m.)* euro, 6.2
s' **évader** to escape, L4
l' **événement** *(m.)* event
évidemment evidently
évident(e) obvious, **14**
l' **évier** *(m.)* kitchen sink, 12.2
éviter to avoid, 12.2
évoquer to evoke
exagérer to exaggerate
l' **examen** *(m.)* test, exam, 3.1
passer un examen to take a test, 3.1
réussir à un examen to pass a test
examiner to examine, **2.2**
l' **excursion** *(f.)* excursion, outing
excuser to excuse
exécuter to execute, carry out
l' **exemple** *(m.)*: **par exemple** for example
l' **exercice** *(m.)* exercise
exigeant(e) demanding
exister to exist, to be
l' **expéditeur, l'expéditrice** sender
expliquer to explain
exposer to exhibit
l' **exposition** *(f.)* exhibit, show, **1.2**
l' **express** *(m.)* espresso, black coffee, 5.1
exprimer to express
expulser to expel, banish
exquis(e) exquisite
l' **extrait** *(m.)* excerpt

la **fable** fable
la **fabrication** manufacture
fabriquer to build
fabuleux, fabuleuse fabulous
la **face** side *(of paper)*, **3.1**
face écrite non visible face down *(paper)*, **3.1**
face écrite visible face up *(paper)*, **3.1**

se **fâcher** to quarrel
facile easy, 2.1
facilement easily
faciliter to facilitate
la **façon** way, manner
d'une façon générale generally speaking
le **facteur, la factrice** mail carrier, **5.2**
la **facture** bill
facultatif, facultative optional
faible weak, L1
faim: avoir faim to be hungry, 5.1
faire to do, make, 6.1
s'en faire to worry, **8.1**
Ça fait mal. It (That) hurts., **2.1**
faire du (+ nombre) to take size (+ number), 7.2
faire des achats to shop
faire un appel to make a (phone) call, **3.2**
faire attention to pay attention, 6; to be careful, 11.1
faire du cheval to go horseback riding, **11.2**
faire des courses to go shopping, 7.2
faire les courses to do the grocery shopping, 6.1
faire la cuisine to cook, 6
faire les devoirs to do homework, 6
faire des économies to save money, **5.1**
faire enregistrer to check (luggage), 8.1
faire escale to stop *(plane)*, **4.2**
faire des études to study
faire du français (des maths, etc.) to study French (math, etc.), 6
faire du jogging to jog
se faire mal to hurt oneself, **8.1**
faire la monnaie de to make change for *(bill)*, **5.1**
faire la navette to go back and forth, make the run
faire le numéro to dial the number, **3.2**
faire une ordonnance to write a prescription, **2.2**
faire un pansement to bandage, **8.1**
faire partie de to be a part of
faire un pas to take a step, **L2**
faire de la planche à voile to go windsurfing, 11.1
faire le plein to fill up the gas tank, **7.1**
faire une promenade to take a walk, 11.1
faire la queue to wait in line, 9.1
faire du ski nautique to water-ski, 11.1
faire un stage to intern, **14.2**
faire du surf to go surfing, 11.1
faire la vaisselle to do the dishes, 12.2
faire les valises to pack (suitcases), 8.1
faire un voyage to take a trip, 8.1
Il fait quel temps? What's the weather like?, 11.1
Vous faites quelle pointure? What size shoe do you take?, 7.2
Vous faites quelle taille? What size do you take (wear)?, 7.2
fait(e) à la main handmade
la **famille** family, 4.1
le nom de famille last name
le/la **fana** fan
la **fanfare** brass band, **12.1**
la **farce** stuffing
la **farine de sorgo** sorghum flour
fatigué(e) tired
fauché(e) *(slang)* broke, **5.1**
faut: il faut (+ *inf.*) one must, it is necessary to, 8.2
il faut que one must, it is necessary to, **12.2**
la **faute** fault, mistake
le **fauteuil roulant** wheelchair, **8.1**
faux, fausse false
le faux pas social blunder
favori(te) favorite, 7.2
le **fax** fax; fax machine, **3.1**
la **femelle** female
la **femme** woman, 7.1; wife, 4.1
la femme de chambre maid *(hotel)*, **9.2**
la **fenêtre** window
côté fenêtre window *(seat) (adj.)*, 8.1
la **fente** slot, **3.2**
la **ferme** farm, **11.2**
fermer to close, **9.1**
à clé to lock, **9.1**
le **fermier, la fermière** farmer, **11.2**
la **fête** party, 4.1; holiday, **12.1**
de fête festive
la fête des Lumières Festival of Lights, Chanouka, **12.2**
le **feu** heat, **6.2;** traffic light, **7.2, 11.1;** fire, **L2**
le feu doux low heat, **6.2**
le feu vif high heat, **6.2**
le feu d'artifice fireworks, **12.1**
la **feuille de papier** sheet of paper, 3.2
le **feutre** felt-tip pen, 3.2
les **fiançailles** *(f. pl.)* engagement, L4

la **fiche** registration card, **9.1**
le **fichier** file *(computer)*
fictif, fictive fictional
fier, fière proud
la **fièvre** fever, **2.1**
avoir une fièvre to have a fever, **2.1**
la **figue** fig
la **figure** face, 12.1
la **file de voitures** line of cars, **7.2**
le **filet** net *(tennis, etc.)*, 10.2; string bag
le filet de sole fillet of sole, **6.2**
la **fille** girl, 1.1; daughter, 4.1
le **film** film, movie, **1.1**
le film d'amour love story, **1.1**
le film d'aventures adventure movie, **1.1**
le film comique comedy, **1.1**
le film étranger foreign film, **1.1**
le film d'horreur horror film, **1.1**
le film policier detective movie, **1.1**
le film de science-fiction science-fiction movie, **1.1**
le film en vidéo movie video, **1.1**
le **fils** son, 4.1
la **fin** end
financier, financière financial
la **fine herbe** herb, **6.1**
finir to finish, 8.2
fixe fixed
fixement: regarder fixement to stare at
fixer un rendez-vous to make an appointment
la **flèche** arrow, **7.2**
la **fleur** flower, 4.2
fleuri(e) in bloom, L2; decorated with flowers
fleurir to bloom
le **fleuve** river
la **flûte** flute
le **foie** liver
avoir mal au foie to have indigestion
la **fois** time *(in a series)*, 10.2
à la fois at the same time
deux fois twice
la **fonction** function
le/la **fonctionnaire** civil servant, **14.1**
le **fonctionnement** functioning
fond: au fond in the background
respirer à fond to breathe deeply, **2.2**
au fond de at the bottom of
fonder to found
le **foot(ball)** soccer, 10.1
le football américain football
la **force** strength
forcément necessarily
le **forgeron** blacksmith, **L2**
former to form; to train
le **formulaire** form, **8.2**
la **formule** phrase
fort hard *(adv.)*; very
fort(e) strong, 2.2
fort(e) en maths good in math, 2.2
fou, folle crazy; insane
la **fouille** dig *(archaeol.)*
se **fouler** to sprain, **8.1**
le **four** oven, **6.1**
le four à micro-ondes microwave oven, **6.1**
la **fourchette** fork, 5.2
la **fourmi** ant
la **fourniture** supply
les fournitures scolaires school supplies, 3.2
la **fracture** fracture *(of bone)*, **8.2**
la fracture compliquée compound fracture, **8.2**
frais: Il fait frais. It's cool. *(weather)*, 11.2
les **frais** *(m. pl.)* expenses; charges, **9.2, 13.1**
la **fraise** strawberry, 6.2
le **français** French *(language)*, 2.2
francophone French-speaking
frapper to hit, L3; to knock, L4, **L2**
freiner to break *(slow down)*, **7.1**
fréquemment frequently
fréquenter to frequent, patronize
le **frère** brother, 1.2
la **fresque** fresco
le **fric** *(slang)* money, **5.1**
le **frigidaire** refrigerator, 12.2, **6.1**
le **frigo** "fridge," **6.1**
les **frissons** *(m. pl.)* chills, **2.1**
les **frites** *(f. pl.)* French fries, 5.1
froid(e) cold
Il fait froid. It's cold. *(weather)*, 11.2
le **fromage** cheese, 5.1
la **frontière** border
frugal(e) light, simple
le **fruit** fruit, 6.2, **6.1**
les fruits de mer seafood, **6.2**
la **fumée** smoke
fumer to smoke, **4.2**
le **funiculaire** funicular
furieux, furieuse furious, **13.2**
le **futur** future, L2

le/la **gagnant(e)** winner, 10.2
gagner to earn; to win, 10.1
la **gamme** range
le **gant** glove, 11.2
le gant de toilette washcloth, 12.1, **9.2**

le **garage** garage, 4.2
le **garçon** boy, 1.1
le garçon d'honneur best man, **12.2**
garder to guard, watch; to keep
le **gardien** guard, L4
le gardien de but goalie, 10.1
la **gare** train station, 9.1
la gare routière bus terminal (Africa)
se **garer** to park, **7.1**
gastronomique gastronomic, gourmet
le **gâteau** cake, 4.1
gâter to spoil
gauche: à gauche left, **7.2**
le **gaz** gas
le gaz carbonique carbon dioxide
le gaz GPL liquefied petroleum gas
le/la **géant(e)** giant
geler to freeze
Il gèle. It's freezing. *(weather)*, 11.2
le **genou** knee, **8.1**
le **genre** type, kind, **1.1;** genre
les **gens** *(m. pl.)* people
gentil(le) nice *(person)*, 6.2
gérer to manage
le **gigot d'agneau** leg of lamb, **6.2**
le **gilet de sauvetage** life vest, **4.2**
la **glace** ice cream, 5.1; ice, 11.2; mirror, 12.1
glisser to slip, **8.1**
la **gomme** eraser, 3.2
le **gommier** Caribbean flat-bottomed fishing boat
la **gorge** throat, **2.1**
avoir mal à la gorge to have a sore throat, **2.1**
la **gousse d'ail** clove of garlic, **6.1**

le **goût** taste
le **gouvernement** government
gouverner to govern
grâce à thanks to
le **gradin** bleacher *(stadium)*, 10.1
la **graisse** fat
le **gramme** gram, 6.2
grand(e) tall, big, 1.1; great
le grand magasin department store, 7.1
de grand standing luxury *(adj.)*
la grande surface large department store; large supermarket
grandir to grow (up) *(children)*
la **grand-mère** grandmother, 4.1
le **grand-père** grandfather, 4.1
les **grands-parents** *(m. pl.)* grandparents, 4.1
la **grange** barn, **11.2**
gratter to scratch, **2.1**
gratuit(e) free
grave serious, **3.2**
Ce n'est pas grave. It's not serious., **3.2**
le **grec** Greek *(language)*
la **Grèce** Greece
la **griffe** label
le **griot** griot *(African musician-entertainer)*
la **grippe** flu, **2.1**
gris(e) gray, 7.2
gros(se) big, large, **14.2**
la **grotte** cave, L4
guérir to cure, **L4**
la **guerre** war, L3
le **guerrier** warrior, L3
le **guichet** ticket window, 9.1, **10.1;** box office, **1.1;** counter window *(post office)*, **5.2**
le **guide** guidebook; guide

guillotiné(e) guillotined
le **gymnase** gymnasium
la **gymnastique** gymnastics, 2.2

habillé(e) dressy, 7.1
s' **habiller** to get dressed, 12.1
l' **habitant(e)** inhabitant
habiter to live *(in a city, house, etc.)*, 3.1
hacher to grind, **6.2**
le **hall** lobby, 8.1, **9.1**
le **hameau** hamlet
handicapé(e) handicapped
le **hangar** shed, **11.2**
la **Hanouka** Hanukkah, **12.2**
les **haricots** *(m. pl.)* **verts** green beans, 6.2, **6.1**
la **harpe** harp
haut(e) high, **11.1**
en haut de at the top of
haut de gamme state of the art
le **hautbois** oboe
l' **herbe** *(f.)* grass, **11.2**
la fine herbe herb, **6.1**
le **héros** hero
l' **heure** *(f.)* time *(of day)*, BV; hour, 3.2
à l'heure on time, 8.1
à quelle heure? at what time?, 2
À tout à l'heure. See you later., BV
de bonne heure early
les heures de pointe rush hour, **10.1**
heureusement fortunately
heureux, heureuse happy, **13.2**
hier yesterday, 10.1
avant-hier the day before yesterday, 10.2

hier matin yesterday morning, 10.2
hier soir last night, 10.2
l' **histoire** *(f.)* history, 2.2; story
l' **hiver** *(m.)* winter, 11.2
la **H.L.M.** low-income housing
le **homard** lobster, **6.2**
l' **homme** *(m.)* man, 7.1
honnête honest
les **honoraires** *(m. pl.)* fees *(doctor)*
l' **hôpital** *(m.)* hospital, **8.1**
l' **horaire** *(m.)* schedule, timetable, 9.1
l' **horloger, l'horlogère** clockmaker
l' **horodateur** *(m.)* time-stamp machine, **11.1**
l' **horreur** *(f.)* horror
l' **hôtel** *(m.)* hotel, **9.1**
l'hôtel de ville city hall
l' **Hôtel-Dieu** hospital
l' **hôtesse** *(f.)* **de l'air** flight attendant *(f.)*, 8.2
l' **huile** *(f.)* oil, 6.1
l'huile d'olive olive oil, **6.1**
l' **huître** *(f.)* oyster, **6.2**
humain(e) human
la **hutte** hut
l' **hydrate** *(m.)* **de carbone** carbohydrate
l' **hymne** *(m.)* anthem, **12.1**
hyper: J'ai hyper faim. I'm super hungry.
l' **hypermarché** *(m.)* large department store, supermarket
l' **hypothèque** *(f.)* mortgage

l' **icône** *(f.)* icon
idéal(e) ideal
l' **idée** *(f.)* idea
idée fixe fixed idea; obsession
identifier to identify
il: il y a there is, there are, 4.1
il y a dix ans ten years ago
l' **île** *(f.)* island, L4
illisible illegible
l' **immeuble** *(m.)* apartment building, 4.2
s' **implanter** to be established
impoli(e) impolite
impressionné(e) impressed
les **impressionnistes** *(m. pl.)* Impressionists *(painters)*
l' **imprimante** *(f.)* printer, **3.1**
imprimer to print
inaugurer to inaugurate
inconnu(e) unknown
l' **inconvénient** *(m.)* disadvantage
incroyable incredible
l' **indicatif** *(m.)*: **l'indicatif du pays** country code, **3.2**
l'indicatif régional area code, **3.2**
l' **indication** *(f.)* cue
indiquer to indicate, to show
l' **individu** *(m.)* individual
inférieur(e) lower
infini(te) infinite
l' **infirmier, l'infirmière** nurse, **8.1**
l' **informaticien(ne)** computer expert, **14.1**
l' **information** *(f.)* information; data
les informations *(f. pl.)* news *(TV)*
l' **informatique** *(f.)* computer science, 2.2
l' **ingénieur** *(m.)* engineer *(m. and f.)*, **14.1**
innombrable countless
l' **inquiétude** *(f.)* worry
s' **installer** to settle
l' **instant** *(m.)* moment, **3.2**
l' **institut** *(m.)* institute
l'instrument *(m.)* **à clavier** keyboard instrument
l'instrument à cordes string instrument
l'instrument à vent wind instrument
interdit(e) forbidden, **4.2**
intéressant(e) interesting, 1.1
intéresser to interest
s'intéresser à to be interested in
l' **intérêt** *(m.)* interest
intérieur(e) domestic *(flight)*, 8.1
interne internal
l' **interprète** *(m. et f.)* interpreter
l' **interro(gation)** *(f.)* quiz
interurbain(e): appel interurbain toll call
intervenir to step in
l' **intervention chirurgicale** operation
intime intimate
intitulé(e) entitled
introduire to insert
inventer to make up; to invent
l' **invité(e)** guest
inviter to invite, 4.1
isoler to isolate
l' **issue** *(f.)* **de secours** emergency exit
l' **italien** *(m.)* Italian *(language)*, 2.2
l' **Ivoirien(ne)** *(m. et f.)* Ivorian *(inhabitant of Côte d'Ivoire)*

jaloux, jalouse jealous
jamais ever
ne... jamais never, 11.2
la **jambe** leg, **8.1**
le **jambon** ham, 5.1
janvier *(m.)* January, BV
japonais(e) Japanese
le **jardin** garden, 4.2

jaune yellow, 7.2
Je vous en prie. You're welcome. *(form.)*, BV
le **jean** jeans, 7.1
jeter to throw, L4
le **jeu** game
jeune young
la **jeunesse** youth
les **jeunes** *(m. pl.)* young people
le **jogging: faire du jogging** to jog
la **joie** joy
joli(e) pretty, 4.2
la **joue** cheek, **13.1**
jouer to play, 3.2; to show *(movie)*; to perform, **1.1**
jouer à (un sport) to play (a sport), 10.1
jouer de to play a musical instrument
le **jouet** toy
le **joueur, la joueuse** player, 10.1
le **jour** day, BV
huit jours a week
le jour de l'An New Year's Day, **12.2**
de nos jours today, nowadays
quinze jours two weeks
tous les jours every day, **1.2**
le **journal** newspaper, 9.1
le journal télévisé TV news, **6.1**
le/la **journaliste** reporter, **14.1**
la **journée** day, 3.1
Belle journée! Have a nice day!, 4.2
joyeux, joyeuse joyous
Joyeux anniversaire! Happy birthday!
Joyeux Noël! Merry Christmas!
le/la **juge** judge, **14.1**
juif, juive Jewish, **12.2**
le **jumeau, la jumelle** twin, L1
la **jupe** skirt, 7.1
le **jus** juice, 5.1
jusqu'à (up) to, until, 10.2
jusqu'où? how far?
juste just, 2.1
juste à sa taille fitting (him/her) just right
juste là right there
tout juste just barely
jusques ici up to now
justement exactly

le **kilo(gramme)** kilogram, 6.2
le **kilomètre** kilometer
le **kiosque** newsstand, 9.1
le **kleenex** tissue, **2.1**

là there; here, **3.2**
là-bas over there, **10.1**
là-haut up there
le **lac** lake
la **lagune** lagoon
laisser to leave *(something behind)*, 5.2; to let, allow
le **lait** milk, 6.1
la **laitue** lettuce
lancer to throw, to shoot *(ball)*, 10.2, **12.1**
le **langage: en langage courant** commonly known as
la **langue** language, 2.2
la langue maternelle mother tongue
le **lapin** rabbit, **11.2**
large loose, wide, 7.2
la **larme** tear, **L2**
le **laurier** bay (leaves), **6.1**
le **lavabo** (bathroom) sink
la **lavande** lavender
laver to wash, 12
se **laver** to wash oneself, 12.1
le **lave-vaisselle** dishwasher, 12.2
la **leçon** lesson, 11.1
la leçon de conduite driving lesson, **7.1**
le **lecteur, la lectrice** reader
le lecteur de disquettes diskette drive, **3.1**
la **lecture** reading
le **légume** vegetable, 6.2, **6.1**
lever to raise, 3.1
lever la main to raise one's hand, 3.1
se lever to get up, 12.1
la **lèvre** lip, **13.1**
libérer to free; to vacate, **9.2**
la **liberté** freedom
libre free, 5.1; available, **14.2**
le **lieu** place; setting, **14.1**
au lieu de instead of
avoir lieu to take place, **12.1**
le lieu de travail workplace, **14.1**
la **ligne** line, **4.1**
les grandes lignes main lines *(train)*, **4.1**
les lignes de banlieue commuter trains, **4.1**
la **limitation de vitesse** speed limit, **7.2**
la **limite** limit
la **limonade** lemon-lime drink, BV
la **lipide** fat
le **liquide** liquid
l'argent liquide cash, **5.1**
en liquide in cash, **9.2**
lire to read, 9.2
le **lit** bed, **9.1, L2**
le **litre** liter, 6.2
la **livre** pound, 6.2
le **livret de caisse d'épargne** savings passbook
le **livre** book, 3.2

le **logement** housing
loger to house
le **logiciel** software, **3.1**
loin far (away)
loin de far from, 4.2
plus loin further
le **long: le long de** along
long(ue) long, 7.1
longtemps (for) a long time, 11.1
trop longtemps (for) too long, 11.1
la **longueur** length
le **look** style
louer to rent, **1.1;** to reserve
les **lunettes** *(f. pl.)* **de soleil** sunglasses, 11.1
la **lutte** fight, battle, L3
lutter to fight, L3
luxueux, luxueuse luxurious
le **lycée** high school, 2.1
le/la **lycéen(ne)** high school student

la **machine** machine, **10.2**
Madame (Mme) Mrs., Ms., BV
Mademoiselle (Mlle) Miss, Ms., BV
le **magasin** store, 3.2, **14.1**
le grand magasin department store, 7.1
le **magazine** magazine, 9.1
le **Maghreb** Maghreb
le **magnétoscope** VCR, 12.2
magnifique magnificent
le **mail** e-mail, **3.1**
le **maillot** jersey
le maillot de bain bathing suit, 11.1
la **main** hand, 3.1, **13.1**
fait(e) à la main handmade
maintenant now, 2.2
le **maire** mayor, **12.1**
la **mairie** town hall, **12.2, 14.1**
mais but, 2.1
Mais oui (non)! Of course (not)!
la **maison** house, 3.1
la maison d'édition publishing house
la **maisonnette** cottage
le **maître, la maîtresse** elementary school teacher
la **majorité** majority
mal badly, **2.1**
avoir mal à to have a(n) . . . -ache, to hurt, **2.1**
Ça fait mal. It (That) hurts., **2.1**
Pas mal. Not bad., BV
le/la **malade** sick person, patient, **2.2**
malade ill, sick, L1, **2.1**
la **maladie** illness, disease
le **mâle** male
malheureusement unfortunately
malheureux, malheureuse unhappy
malin (maligne): C'est malin! Very clever! *(ironic)*
la **maman** mom
la **mamie** grandma
la **Manche** English Channel
la **manche** sleeve, 7.1
à manches longues (courtes) long- (short-) sleeved, 7.1
le **mandat** money order
manger to eat, 5.1
la **manifestation culturelle** cultural event
la **manœuvre: instructions pour la manœuvre** operating instructions
le **manteau** coat, 7.1
se **maquiller** to put on makeup, 12.1
le/la **marchand(e) (de fruits et légumes)** (produce) seller, merchant, 6.2
la **marchandise** merchandise
le **marché** market, 6.2
bon marché inexpensive
le marché aux puces flea market
marcher to walk, **8.1**
le **mari** husband, 4.1
le **mariage** marriage; wedding, **12.2**
le **marié** groom, **12.2**
la **mariée** bride, **12.2**
se **marier** to get married, L4, **12.2**
le **marin** sailor, L4
le **Maroc** Morocco
marocain(e) Moroccan
la **marque** brand, **7.1;** sign, **L4**
marquer un but to score a goal, 10.1
marron *(inv.)* brown, 7.2
marseillais(e) from Marseille
martiniquais(e) from or of Martinique
le **masque à oxygène** oxygen mask, **4.2**
masqué(e) masked, **12.1**
un groupe masqué group of masqueraders, **12.1**
le **mat** *(fam.)* morning
le **match** game, 10.1
le **matériel** equipment, **11.2**
la **matière** subject *(school),* 2.2; matter
le **matin** morning, BV
du matin A.M. *(time),* BV
mauvais(e) bad; wrong, 2.2
Il fait mauvais. It's bad weather., 11.1
le **médecin** doctor *(m. and f.),* **2.2**
chez le médecin at (to) the doctor's office, **2.2**
le **médicament** medicine, **2.1**
meilleur(e) better, **8**
le **mélange** mixture
même *(adj.)* same; very, 2.1; *(adv.)* even

tout de même all the same, 5.2
mener to lead
mensuel(le) monthly
le **menuisier** carpenter, **14.1**
la **mer** sea, 11.1
la mer des Antilles Caribbean Sea
la mer des Caraïbes Caribbean Sea
la mer Méditerranée Mediterranean Sea
merci thank you, thanks, BV
la **mère** mother, 4.1
la **merveille** marvel, wonder
merveilleux, merveilleuse marvelous
le **messager, la messagère** messenger
la **messe de minuit** midnight mass, **12.2**
la **mesure** measurement
mesurer to measure
le **métier** trade, profession, **14.1**
le **mètre** meter
le **métro** subway, 4.2, **10.1**
la station de métro subway station, 4.2, **10.1**
mettre to put (on), to place, 7.1; to turn on *(appliance)*, 7
mettre le contact to start the car, **7.1**
mettre de côté to save, to put aside, **5.1**
mettre une lettre à la poste to mail a letter, **5.2**
mettre la table to set the table, 7
les **meubles** *(m. pl.)* furniture
le **microbe** microbe, germ
la **micropuce** microchip
midi *(m.)* noon, BV
le **miel** honey
mieux better, 7.2
aimer mieux to prefer, 7.2
aller mieux to feel better, **2.2;** to be better, **8.1**
il vaut mieux it is better, **13.2**
le **milieu** middle, **10.2**
mille (one) thousand, 3.2
le **million** million
mimer to mime
la **ministère** ministry
minuit *(m.)* midnight, BV
la **minute** minute, 9.2
la **mi-temps** halftime *(sporting event)*
la **mode: à la mode** in style
le **mode** means
la **moelle épinière** spinal cord
moi de même the same with me, **13.2**
moi-même myself
moins less, fewer, 7.1; minus
le **mois** month, BV
le **monde** world
beaucoup de monde a lot of people, 10.1
tout le monde everyone, everybody, 1.2
le **moniteur** *(computer)* monitor
le **moniteur, la monitrice** instructor, 11.1
la **monnaie** change *(money)*; currency, **5.1**
la pièce de monnaie coin
Monsieur *(m.)* Mr., sir, BV
le **mont** mount, mountain
la **montagne** mountain, 11.2
monter to go up, 4.2; to get on, get in, 9.2; to take (something) upstairs, **9.1**
monter une pièce to put on a play, **1.1**
la **montre** watch, **L1**
montrer to show
le **morceau** piece, **6.2**
le **morse** Morse code
la **mort** death
la **mosquée** mosque
le **mot** word
le mot apparenté cognate
le **motard** motorcycle cop, **7.2**
la **moto** motorcycle, **7.1**
le **mouchoir** handkerchief, **2.1**
la **moule** mussel, **6.2**
mourir to die, 11
la **moutarde** mustard, 6.2
le **mouton** mutton; sheep, **11.2**
moyen(ne) average, intermediate
le **moyen de transport** mode of transportation
multicolore multicolored
la **multinationale** multinational corporation, **14.2**
multiplier to multiply
muni(e) de with
la **municipalité** city government
les **munitions** *(f. pl.)* ammunition
le **mur** wall, L4
le **musée** museum, **1.2**
la **musique** music, 2.2
musulman(e) Moslem
mystérieux, mystérieuse mysterious

nager to swim, 11.1
le **nageur, la nageuse** swimmer
naître to be born, 11
la **nappe** tablecloth, 5.2
la **natation** swimming, 11.1
nature plain *(adj.)*, 5.1
naturel(le) natural
le **navarin** mutton stew
la **navette: faire la navette** to go back and forth, make the run
naviguer sur Internet to surf the Net

ne: ne... jamais never, 11.2
ne... pas not, 1.2
ne... personne no one, nobody, 11
ne... plus no longer, no more, 6.1
ne... que only
ne... rien nothing, 11
né(e): elle est née she was born
la **nécessité** necessity
de première nécessité essential
la **négritude** black pride
la **neige** snow, 11.2
Il neige. It's snowing., 11.2
nerveux, nerveuse nervous
n'est-ce pas? isn't it?, doesn't it (he, she, etc.)?, 2.2
le **neveu** nephew, 4.1
le **nez** nose, **2.1**
avoir le nez qui coule to have a runny nose, **2.1**
ni... ni neither . . . nor
niçois(e) of or from Nice
la **nièce** niece, 4.1
le **niveau** level, **7.1**
le **Noël** Christmas, **12.2**
noir(e) black, 7.2
le **nom** name; noun
le nom de famille last name
le **nombre** number
nombreux, nombreuse numerous, many
peu nombreux few
nommer to name, mention
non no; not
non plus either, neither
non-fumeurs non-smoking *(section)*, 8.1
le **nord** north
nord-africain(e) North African
les **notables** *(m. pl.)* dignitaries, **12.1**
la **note** note; grade; bill *(hotel)*, **9.2**
nourrir to feed
la **nourriture** food, nutrition
nouveau (nouvel), nouvelle new, 4.2
à nouveau again
la **nouvelle** short story
les nouvelles news, **L3**
la **Nouvelle-Angleterre** New England
la **Nouvelle-Orléans** New Orleans
le **nuage** cloud, 11.1
la **nuit** night
nul(le) *(slang)* bad
le **numéro** number, **5.2**
le bon numéro right number, **3.2**
composer/faire le numéro to dial the number, **3.2**
le mauvais numéro wrong number, **3.2**
numéroté(e) numbered

ô oh
l' **objet** *(m.)* object
obligatoire mandatory
obtenir to obtain, get
l' **occasion** *(f.)* opportunity
occidental(e) western
occupé(e) occupied, taken, 5.1; busy
Ça sonne occupé. The line's busy, **3.2**
occuper to occupy, take up
s'occuper de to take care of
l' **œuf** *(m.)* egg, 6.1
l'œuf à la coque poached egg
l'œuf brouillé scrambled egg
l'œuf sur le plat fried egg
l' **œuvre** *(f.)* work(s) *(of art or literature)*, **1.1**
offrir to offer
l' **oignon** *(m.)* onion, 5.1, **6.1**
l' **oiseau** *(m.)* bird
l' **omelette** *(f.)* omelette, 5.1
l'omelette aux fines herbes omelette with herbs, 5.1
l'omelette nature plain omelette, 5.1
on we, they, people, 3.2
On y va? Let's go.; Shall we go?
l' **oncle** *(m.)* uncle, 4.1
opérer to operate
l' **or** *(m.)* gold, L4
l' **oranger** *(m.)* orange tree, L2
l' **ordinateur** *(m.)* computer, **3.1**
l' **ordonnance** *(f.)* prescription, **2.2**
faire une ordonnance to write a prescription, **2.2**
l' **ordre** *(m.)* order
l' **oreille** *(f.)* ear, **2.1**
avoir mal aux oreilles to have an earache, **2.1**
l' **oreiller** *(m.)* pillow, **4.2**
organiser to organize
l' **orgue** *(m.)* organ *(musical instrument)*
oriental(e) eastern
originaire de native of
l' **origine** *(f.)*: **d'origine américaine (française, etc.)** from the U.S. (France, etc.)
orner to decorate
l' **os** *(m.)* bone, **8.2**
ou or, 1.1
où where, 1.1
d'où from where, 1.1
oublier to forget, **7.2**
l' **ouest** *(m.)* west
oui yes, BV
l' **outil** *(m.)* tool
ouvert(e) open, **1.2**

l' **ouvrage** *(m.)* work
l' **ouvrier, l'ouvrière** worker, **11.1**
ouvrir to open, **2.2, 13.2**

le **paiement** payment
le **pain** bread, 6.1
le pain complet whole-wheat bread
le pain grillé toast
la tartine de pain beurré slice of bread and butter
la **paire** pair, 7.1
la **paix** peace
le **palais** palace
le **palet** puck
le **palmier** palm tree
le **pamplemousse** grapefruit, **6.1**
le **panier** basket, 10.2
réussir un panier to make a basket, 10.2
la **panne** breakdown, **7.1**
le **panneau** road sign, **7.2**
le **pansement** bandage, **8.1**
le **pantalon** pants, 7.1
la **papeterie** stationery store, 3.2
le **papier** paper, 3.2
la feuille de papier sheet of paper, 3.2
le papier hygiénique toilet paper, **9.2**
le **Pâques** Easter
le **paquet** package, 6.2
par by, through
par conséquent as a result
par exemple for example
par semaine a (per) week, 3.2
le **parc** park
parce que because
le **parcmètre** parking meter, **11.1**
par-dessus over *(prep.)*, 10.2
le **pare-brise** windshield, **7.1**
paresseux, paresseuse lazy
parfait(e) perfect
le **parfum** flavor
le **parking** parking lot, **11.1**
parler to speak, talk, 3.1
parler au téléphone to talk on the phone, 3.2, **L3**
parmi among
les **paroles** *(f. pl.)* words, lyrics
la **part:**
C'est de la part de qui? Who's calling?, **3.2**
d'autre part on the other hand
de part et d'autre on each side
de sa part on his (her) part
partager to share, **13.1**
particulier, particulière private *(room, house, etc.)*
la **partie** part
faire partie de to be a part of
partir to leave, 8.1
partout everywhere
pas not, 2.1
pas du tout not at all, 3.1
Pas mal. Not bad., BV
Pas question! Out of the question! Not a chance!
le **pas** step, **L2**
faire un pas to take a step, **L2**
le **passage pour piétons** crosswalk, **11.1**
le **passager, la passagère** passenger, 8.1
la **passe** pass
le **passeport** passport, 8.1
passer to spend *(time)*, 3.1; to go (through), 8.1; to pass, 10.1
passer à la douane to go through customs, **4.2**
passer un examen to take an exam, 3.1
se passer to happen
se **passionner** to become enthusiastic
la **patate douce** sweet potato
les **pâtes** *(f. pl.)* pasta, **6.1**
le **patin** skate; skating, 11.2
faire du patin à glace to ice-skate, 11.1
la **patinoire** skating rink, 11.2
le/la **patron(ne)** boss
le **pâturage** pasture
pauvre poor, L1, **2.1**
le **pavillon** small house, bungalow
payer to pay, 3.2
le **pays** country, 8.1
le **paysage** landscape, **4.1**
le/la **paysan(ne)** peasant, L1
le **péage** toll, **7.2**
la **pêche** fishing
le **pêcheur, la pêcheuse** fisherman (-woman)
le **peigne** comb, 12.1
se **peigner** to comb one's hair, 12.1
peindre to paint
le **peintre** painter, artist *(m. and f.)*, **1.2**
le peintre (en bâtiment) (house) painter, **14.1**
la **peinture** painting, **1.2**
pendant during, for *(time)*, 3.2
la **péniche** barge
penser to think
la **pente** slope
perdre to lose, 9.2
le **père** father, 4.1
le Père Noël Santa Claus, **12.2**
perfectionner to perfect
la **période** period
la **périphérie** outskirts
la **perle** pearl
permettre to permit, allow, let
le **permis de conduire** driver's license, **7.1**

le **persil** parsley, **6.1**
le **personnage** character *(in a story)*
la **personne** person
ne... personne no one, nobody, 11
le **personnel de bord** flight crew, 8.2
peser to weigh, **5.2**
petit(e) short, small, 1.1
le petit ami boyfriend
la petite amie girlfriend
le petit déjeuner breakfast, 5.2
les petits pois *(m.)* peas, 6.2
la **petite-fille** granddaughter, 4.1
le **petit-fils** grandson, 4.1
les **petits-enfants** *(m. pl.)* grandchildren, 4.1
le **pétrole** oil
le **pétrolier** oil tanker
peu (de) few, little
à peu près about, approximately
un peu a little, 2.1
en très peu de temps in a short time
très peu seldom, 5.2
peur: avoir peur to be afraid, L1, **13.2**
peut-être perhaps, maybe
le/la **pharmacien(ne)** pharmacist, **2.2**
la **phrase** sentence
le/la **physicien(ne)** physicist
la **physique** physics, 2.2
physique physical
la **pie** magpie
la **pièce** room, 4.2; play, **1.1;** coin, **5.1**
le **pied** foot, 10.1, **8.1**
à pied on foot, 4.2
donner un coup de pied to kick, 10.1
être vite sur pied to be better soon, **2.1**

la **pierre** stone
la pierre précieuse gem, L4
le **piéton, la piétonne** pedestrian, **11.1**
le/la **pilote** pilot, 8.2
piloter to pilot, to fly
le **pilotis** piling
piquer to sting, **2.1**
la **piqûre** injection, **8.2**
la **pirogue** pirogue (dugout canoe)
la **piscine** pool, 11.1
la **piste** runway, 8.1; track, 10.2; ski trail, 11.2
pittoresque picturesque
le **placard** closet, **9.2**
la **place** seat *(plane, train, movie, etc.)*, 8.1; place; square
à ta place if I were you, **7.1**
la **plage** beach, 11.1
la **plaine** plain
le **plaisir** pleasure
le **plan** street map, **7.2**
le plan du métro subway map, **10.1**
la **planche à voile: faire de la planche à voile** to windsurf, 11.1
le **plat** dish *(food)*; serving dish, **6.1**
le **plateau** tray, 8.2
le **plâtre** cast, **8.2**
plâtrer to put in a cast, **8.2**
plein(e) full, 10.1, **13.1**
avoir plein d'argent *(slang)* to have a lot of money, **5.1**
pleurer to cry, L1
pleut *(inf.* **pleuvoir): Il pleut.** It's raining., 11.1
plissé(e) pleated, 7.1
le **plombier** plumber, **14.1**
le **plongeon** dive
plonger to dive, 11.1
la **pluie** rain
la **plupart (des)** most (of), 9.2

plus plus; more, 7.1
de plus en plus more and more
en plus de in addition to
ne... plus no longer, no more, 6.1
plus ou moins more or less
plus tard later
plusieurs several
plutôt rather
le **pneu** tire, **7.1**
le pneu à plat flat tire, **7.1**
la **poêle** frying pan, **6.2**
la **poésie** poetry
le **poids** weight
le **poignet** wrist, **13.1**
le **point** period; dot
le point de suture stitch, **8.2**
à point medium-rare *(meat)*, 5.2
la **pointure** size *(shoes)*, 7.2
Vous faites quelle pointure? What (shoe) size do you take?, 7.2
la **poire** pear, 6.2
le **poisson** fish, 6.1, **6.2**
la **poissonnerie** fish store, 6.1
la **poitrine** chest
le **poivre** pepper, 6.1
le **poivron rouge** red pepper, **6.1**
poli(e) polite, **13.1**
malpoli(e) impolite, **13.1**
la **police** police
appeler police secours to call 911, **8.1**
poliment politely, **9.2**
la **politesse** courtesy, politeness, BV
polluant(e) polluting
pollué(e) polluted
le **polo** polo shirt, 7.1
la **pomme** apple, 6.2
la tarte aux pommes apple tart, 6.1
la **pomme de terre** potato, 6.2, **6.1**

le/la **pompiste** gas station attendant, **7.1**
le **pont** bridge
le **porc** pork, 6.1, **6.2**
le **portable** mobile phone, laptop computer, **3.2**
la **porte** gate *(airport)*, 8.1; door, L4, **9.1, L2**
le **porte-monnaie** change purse, **5.1**
porter to wear, 7.1; to bear, carry, **L2**
porter un toast à to toast
se porter bien to be in good health, **L4**
portugais(e) Portuguese
poser sa candidature to apply for a job, **14.2**
poser une question to ask a question, 3.1
posséder to possess, own
la **poste** mail; post office, **5.2**
le bureau de poste post office, **5.2**
mettre une lettre à la poste to mail a letter, **5.2**
la poste par avion airmail
le **poste** job, **14.2**
le **pot** jar, 6.2; drink
le **pouce** thumb, **13.1**
la **poule** hen, **11.2**
le **poulet** chicken, 6.1
le **pouls** pulse, **8.2**
le **poumon** lung
pour for, 2.1; in order to
pour cent percent
le **pourboire** tip *(restaurant)*, 5.2
pourquoi why, 6.2
pourquoi pas? why not?
pousser to push, **10.2**
pouvoir to be able to, can, 6.1
pratique practical
la **pratique** practice
pratiquer to practice
le **pré** meadow, **11.2**
précaire precarious
précis(e) specific
préféré(e) favorite
préférer to prefer, 6
premier, première first, 4.2
en première in first class, 9.1
prendre to have *(to eat or drink)*, 5.1; to take, 5.2; to buy
prendre un bain (une douche) to take a bath (shower), 12.1
prendre un bain de soleil to sunbathe, 11.1
prendre des kilos to gain a few pounds
prendre le petit déjeuner to eat breakfast, 5.2
prendre possession de to take possession of
prendre rendez-vous to make an appointment
prendre le métro to take the subway, 5.2
le **prénom** first name
près: de près close, **11.1**
près de near, 4.2
prescrire to prescribe, **2.2**
la **présentation** introduction, **13.2**
présenter to present; to introduce, **13.2**
se présenter to occur
presque almost
la **pression** pressure, **7.1**
prestigieux, prestigieuse prestigious
prêt(e) ready
prêter to lend, **5.1**
prie: Je vous en prie. You're welcome., BV
primaire: l'école *(f.)* **primaire** elementary school
le **printemps** spring, 11.1
au printemps in the spring
le **prisonnier, la prisonnière** prisoner, L4
privé(e) private
le **prix** price, cost, 7.1
le prix forfaitaire flat fee
le **processus** process
prochain(e) next, 9.2
descendre à la prochaine to get off at the next station, **10.1**
proche close
procurer to provide
se procurer to obtain, get
le **produit** product
le/la **prof** teacher *(inform.)*, 2.1
le **professeur** teacher *(m. and f.)*, 2.1
profiter de to take advantage of
la **programmation** programming
le **progrès** progress; improvement
le **projet** plan
se **prolonger** to be prolonged, **L3**
la **promenade: faire une promenade** to take a walk, 11.1
la **promesse** promise
promotion: en promotion on special, on sale
prononcer to pronounce
propos: à propos de on the subject of
proposer to suggest
propre clean, **9.2**
le/la **propriétaire** owner
la **propriété** property
protéger to protect
provenance: en provenance de arriving from *(train, plane, etc.)*, 8.1
provençal(e) of or from Provence
la **province** province
en province outside Paris
les **provisions** *(f. pl.)* food
prudemment carefully, **7.2**
la **publicité** commercial *(TV)*, 12.2; advertisement
publier to publish
les **puces** *(f. pl.)*: **le marché aux puces** flea market

le **pull** sweater, 7.1
punir to punish
purifié(e) purified

le **quai** platform *(railroad)*, 9.1, **10.1**
quand when, 4.1
la **quantité** amount, number
le **quart: et quart** a quarter past *(time)*, BV
moins le quart a quarter to *(time)*, BV
le **quartier** neighborhood, district, 4.2, **11.1**
le quartier d'affaires business district, **11.1**
quatrième fourth
québécois(e) from or of Quebec
quel(le) which, what
Quel(le)... ! What a . . . !
quelque some *(sing.)*
quelque chose something, 11
quelque chose de spécial something special
quelque chose à manger something to eat, 5.1
quelque part somewhere
quelquefois sometimes, 5.2
quelques some, a few *(pl.)*, 9.2
quelqu'un somebody, someone, 10.1
quelqu'un d'autre someone else, **L3**
qu'est-ce que what, **8**
qu'est-ce qui what, **8**
la **question** question, 3.1
Pas question! Out of the question! Not a chance!
poser une question to ask a question, 3.1
la **queue** line, 9.1
faire la queue to wait in line, 9.1
qui who, 1.1; whom, 10; which, that
qui que ce soit anyone at all
quitter to leave *(a room, etc.)*, 3.1
Ne quittez pas. Please hold. *(telephone)*, **3.2**
quoi what *(after prep.)*
quotidien(ne) daily, everyday

raccrocher to hang up (telephone), **3.2**
raconter to tell (about)
radieux, radieuse dazzling
la **radio** radio, 3.2; X-ray, **8.2**
la **radiographie** X-ray, **8.2**
le **raisin** grape(s), **6.1**
le raisin sec raisin
la **raison** reason
ralentir to slow down, **7.1**
ramasser to pick up, 8.2
le **randonneur, la randonneuse** hiker
le **rang** row, **12.1**
le **rap** rap *(music)*
râper to grate, **6.2**
rapide quick, fast
rapidement rapidly, quickly
rappeler to call back; to call again, **3.2**
se rappeler to remember
le **rapport** relationship; report
rapporter to bring back
se **raser** to shave, 12.1
le **rasoir** razor, shaver, 12.1
se **rassembler** to gather
rassurer to reassure
rater to miss *(train, etc.)*, 9.2
ravager to devastate
le **rayon** department *(in a store)*, 7.1
le rayon des manteaux coat department, 7.1
réaliser to achieve; to create
récemment recently
la **réception** front desk, **9.1**
le/la **réceptionniste** desk clerk, **9.1**
la **recette** recipe, **6.1**
recevoir to receive, 10.2
la **recherche** research
à la recherche de in search of
la **récolte** harvest, **11.2**
recommander to recommend
reconnaître to recognize
la **récré** recess, 3.2
la **récréation** recess, 3.2
recueillir to pick up
récupérer to claim *(luggage)*, **4.2**
le **recyclage** recycling
la **rédaction** composition
la **réduction** discount
réfléchir to think
le **réfrigérateur** refrigerator, 12.2, **6.1**
le/la **réfugié(e)** refugee
regarder to look at, 3.1
regarder fixement to stare at
le **régime** diet
faire un régime to follow a diet
réglable adjustable, **4.1**
la **règle** ruler, 3.2; rule
régler to order, plan; to set, **L1**
régler la circulation to direct traffic, **11.1**
regretter to be sorry, 6.1, **13.2**
la **reine** queen
la **relation** relationship
le **relevé** statement *(bank)*
se **relever** to get up (again)
relier to connect
religieux, religieuse religious, **12.2**
remarquer to notice

rembourser to pay back, reimburse
remercier to thank
remettre un os en place to set a bone, **8.2**
le **rempart** rampart
remplacer to replace
remplir to fill out, 8.2, **8.2**
remuer to stir, **6.2**
rencontrer to meet
le **rendez-vous** meeting, appointment, **10.2**
prendre rendez-vous to make an appointment
rendre to give back, **5.1**
rendre bien service to be a big help
rendre visite à to visit
renommé(e) renowned
rénover to renovate
les **renseignements** *(m. pl.)* information
rentrer to go home; to return, 3.2
renvoyer to return *(a ball)*, 10.2
réparer to repair
le **repas** meal, 5.2
répéter to repeat
le **répondeur automatique** answering machine, **3.2**
répondre (à) to answer, 9.2
la **réponse** answer
le **reportage** news article
reposer to lie
réputé(e) reputed
le **réseau** network
la **réserve: mettre en réserve** to store
réservé(e) reserved
réserver to reserve, **9.1;** to have in store
le **réservoir** gas tank, **7.1**
respecter to abide by, **7.2, 11.1**
la **respiration** breathing; respiration
respirer to breathe, **2.2**
respirer à fond to take a deep breath, **2.2**
resquiller to cut in line, **13.1**
ressembler à to resemble
ressortir to leave
le **restaurant** restaurant, 5.2
la **restauration** food service
la restauration rapide fast food
rester to stay, remain, 11.1
il reste there remains
rester en contact to keep in touch
les **restes** *(m. pl.)* leftovers
le **restoroute** roadside restaurant
le **résultat** result(s)
le **retard** delay
avec une heure de retard one hour late, **4.2**
avoir du retard to be late *(plane, train, etc.)*, 8.1
en retard late, 9.1
retirer to remove; to take out, **3.1;** to withdraw, **5.1**
le **retour** return
le **retraite** retreat, retirement
se retrouver to get together, **13.1**
réuni(e) reunited
réussir to succeed, 10.2
réussir un panier to make a basket, 10.2
réussir à un examen to pass an exam
le **rêve** dream
réveillé(e) awake
se **réveiller** to wake up, 12.1
le **réveillon** Christmas Eve or New Year's Eve dinner, **12.2**
réveillonner to celebrate Christmas Eve or New Year's Eve, **12.2**
revenir to come back, **4**
la **revue** magazine, L2
le **rez-de-chaussée** ground floor, 4.2
le **rhume** cold *(illness)*, **2.1**
rien nothing
ne... rien nothing
rien à voir avec nothing to do with
rigoler to joke around, 3.2
Tu rigoles! You're kidding!, 3.2
rigolo(tte) funny, 4.2
la **rigueur** harshness
la **rime** rhyme
rincer to rinse
risquer to risk
la **rivière** river, **L2**
le **riz** rice
la **robe** dress, 7.1
le **rocher** rock, boulder, L3
le **roi** king, L3
le **rôle** role
romain(e) Roman
le **roman** novel, **L1**
le roman policier mystery
le **romancier, la romancière** novelist, **L1**
le **romansch** Romansh
le **romarin** rosemary
rond(e) round
la **rondelle** round (piece), **6.2**
le **rond-point** traffic circle, **7.2, 11.1**
rose pink, 7.2
le **rôti de bœuf** roast beef, **6.2**
la **roue de secours** spare tire, **7.1**
rouge red, 7.2
le **rouleau de papier hygiénique** roll of toilet paper, **9.2**
rouler (vite) to go, drive, ride (fast), 10.2, **7.2**
la **route** road, **7.2**
le **rubis** ruby
la **rue** street, 3.1, **5.2, 11.1**
la rue à sens unique one-way street, **11.1**
russe Russian

le **sable** sand
le **sac** bag, 6.1
le sac à dos backpack, 3.2
sage wise; well-behaved, **12.2**
saignant(e) rare *(meat)*, 5.2
la **saison** season
la **salade** salad, 5.1; lettuce, 6.2
le **salaire** salary, **14.2**
sale dirty, **9.2**
la **salle** room
la salle à manger dining room, 4.2
la salle d'attente waiting room, 9.1
la salle de bains bathroom, 4.2
la salle de cinéma movie theater, **1.1**
la salle de classe classroom, 2.1
la salle d'opération operating room, **8.2**
la salle de séjour living room, 4.2
saluer to greet, **L1**
Salut. Hi.; Bye. BV
la **salutation** greeting
les **sandales** *(f. pl.)* sandals, 7.1
le **sandwich** sandwich, BV
le **sang** blood
sans without
sans escale nonstop *(flight)*, **4.2**
sans que without
la **santé** health, **2.1**
le **sapin** fir tree, **12.2**
satisfaire to satisfy
la **saucisse** sausage, **6.1**
la saucisse de Francfort hot dog, BV
le **saucisson** salami, 6.1
sauf except (for), **1.2**
le **saumon** salmon, **6.2**
sauvegarder to safeguard; to save, **3.1**
sauver to save
le **savant** scientist
savoir to know *(information)*, **1.2**
le **savoir-vivre** good manners
le **savon** soap, 12.1, **9.2**
scintiller to sparkle
scolaire school *(adj.)*, 3.2
la **scolarité** schooling, education
le **sculpteur** sculptor *(m. and f.)*, **1.2**
la **séance** show(ing) *(movie)*, **1.1**
sec, sèche dry
sécher to dry
se sécher to dry oneself, **9.2**
le **secours** help, aid, **8.1**
le/la **secouriste** paramedic, **8.1**
le **séjour** stay, **9.1**
le **sel** salt, 6.1
selon according to
la **semaine** week, 3.2; allowance
la semaine dernière last week, 10.2
la semaine prochaine next week
par semaine a (per) week, 3.2
semblable similar, L1
le/la **Sénégalais(e)** Senegalese *(person)*
le **sens** direction, **7.2**; meaning
dans le bon (mauvais) sens in the right (wrong) direction, **11.1**
le **sentiment** feeling
se **sentir** to feel *(well, etc.)*, **2.1**
séparer to separate
sérieux, sérieuse serious, 7
le **serpentin** streamer, **12.1**
serré(e) tight, 7.2
se **serrer la main** to shake hands, **13.1**
le **serveur, la serveuse** waiter, waitress, 5.1
le **service** service, 5.2
le service radio radiology department
le service des urgences emergency room, **8.1**
Le service est compris. The tip is included., 5.2
la **serviette** napkin, 5.2, **13.1;** towel, 11.1, **9.2**
servir to serve, 8.2; 10.2
se servir de to use, **3.2, L4**
seul(e) alone, 5.2; single; only *(adj.)*
tout(e) seul(e) all alone, by himself/herself, 5.2
seulement only *(adv.)*
le **shampooing** shampoo, 12.1
le **shopping** shopping, 7.2
le **short** shorts, 7.1
si if; yes *(after neg. question)*, 7.2; so *(adv.)*
le **sida (syndrome immuno-déficitaire acquis)** AIDS
le **siècle** century, **L4**
le **siège** seat, 8.2
siffler to (blow a) whistle, 10.1, **L1**
le **sifsari** type of veil worn by Tunisian women
la **signification** meaning, significance
signifier to mean
simplement simply
sinon or else, otherwise, 9.2
la **sinusite** sinus infection, **2.2**
le **sirop** syrup, **2.1**
le **site** site; Web site
situé(e) located
le **ski** ski, skiing, 11.2
faire du ski to ski, 11.2
faire du ski nautique to water-ski, 11.1
le ski alpin downhill skiing, 11.2
le ski de fond cross-country skiing, 11.2

le **skieur, la skieuse** skier, 11.2
le **snack-bar** snack bar, 9.2
sociable sociable, outgoing, 1.2
la **société** company; corporation, **14.2**
la grosse société large corporation, **14.2**
la **sœur** sister, 1.2
soi oneself, himself, herself
soif: avoir soif to be thirsty, 5.1
soigner to take care of, **8.1, L4**
soigneusement carefully, **9.1**
le **soin** care
de soins polyvalents general care *(adj.)*
prendre soin de to take care of, **L4**
le **soir** evening , BV
ce soir tonight
du soir in the evening, P.M. *(time),* BV
le soir in the evening, 5.2
le **sol** ground, 10.2
le **soldat** soldier, L3, **12.1**
le **solde** balance
les soldes sale *(in a store),* 7.1
la **sole** sole, **6.2**
le **soleil** sun, 11.1
au soleil in the sun, 11.1
Il fait du soleil. It's sunny., 11.1
sombre dark
la **somme** sum
le **sommet** summit, mountaintop, 11.2
le **son** sound, L3
le **sondage** survey, opinion poll
sonner to ring *(telephone),* **3.2**
Ça sonne occupé. The line's busy, **3.2**
sonner du cor to blow a horn, L3
la **sonnerie** ringing
la **sorte** sort, kind, type
la **sortie** exit, **7.2**
sortir to go out; to take out, 8.2
sortir victorieux (victorieuse) to win (the battle)
la **souche** tree stump
dormir comme une souche to sleep like a log
soudain suddenly
souffrir to suffer; to be hurt, to be in pain, **2.2**
souhaiter to wish, **9.1, 12.2**
le **souk** North African market
soulever to lift up
le **soulier** shoe, **12.2**
la **soupe** soup, 5.1
la soupe à l'oignon onion soup, 5.1
la **source** source; spring
la **souris** mouse, **3.1**
sous under, 8.2
les **sous-titres** *(m. pl.)* subtitles, **1.1**
soustraire to subtract
souterrain(e) underground
le **souvenir** memory
souvent often, 5.2
le sport collectif team sport
le sport d'équipe team sport, 10.2
sport *(inv.)* casual *(clothes),* 7.1
sportif, sportive athletic
le **squelette** skeleton
le **stade** stadium, 10.1
le **stage** internship, **14.2**
faire un stage to intern, **14.2**
le/la **stagiaire** intern, **14.2**
standing: de grand standing luxury
la **station** station, 4.2, **10.1;** resort
la station balnéaire seaside resort, 11.1
la station de métro subway station, 4.2
la station de sports d'hiver ski resort, 11.2
la station thermale spa
stationner to park, **11.1**
la **station-service** gas station, **7.1**
la **statue** statue, **1.2**
le **steak frites** steak and French fries, 5.2
le **steward** flight attendant *(m.),* 8.2
stimuler to stimulate
stocker to store
le **studio** studio (apartment)
le **stylo-bille** ballpoint pen, 3.2
le **sucre** sugar
le **sud** south
suffisant(e) enough
suggérer to suggest
suivant(e) following
suivre to follow, **11.1**
suivre une voiture de trop près to tailgate, **11.1**
le **sujet** subject
au sujet de about
super terrific, super
supérieur(e) higher
le **supermarché** supermarket, 6.2
le **supplément** additional charge
supporter to tolerate
sur on, 4.2
sûr(e) sure, certain
le **surf: faire du surf** to go surfing, 11.1
le **surfeur, la surfeuse** surfer, 11.1
surgelé(e) frozen, 6.2
surtout especially, above all; mostly

surveiller to watch, keep an eye on, **7.2**
le **survêtement** warmup suit, 7.1
la **survie** survival
survoler to fly over
le **sweat-shirt** sweatshirt, 7.1
sympa *(inv.)* nice (*abbrev. for* **sympathique**), 1.2
sympathique nice *(person)*, 1.2
le **symptôme** symptom
le **syndicat d'initiative** tourist office

le **tabac: le bureau de tabac** tobacco shop
la **table** table, 5.1
à table at the table, **13.1**
le **tableau** painting, **1.2;** chart; arrival/departure board *(train)*, **4.1**
le tableau noir blackboard
la **taille** size *(clothes)*, 7.2
juste à sa taille fitting (him/her) just right
la taille au-dessous next smaller size, 7.2
la taille au-dessus next larger size, 7.2
Vous faites quelle taille? What size do you take/wear?, 7.2
le **tailleur** suit *(woman's)*, 7.1
le **tambour** drum, **12.1**
la **tante** aunt, 4.1
taper to type; to keyboard, **3.1**
tard late, 12.1
plus tard later
le **tarif** fare
la **tarte** pie, tart, 6.1
la tarte aux pommes apple tart, 6.1
la **tartine** slice of bread with butter or jam
la **tasse** cup, 5.2
le **taux** level
le taux d'intérêt interest rate
la **techno** techno *(music)*
la **télécarte** phone card, **3.2**
télécharger to download
la **télécommande** remote control, 12.2
la **télécopie** fax, **3.1**
le **télécopieur** fax machine, **3.1**
le **téléphone** telephone, 3.2, **3.1**
le numéro de téléphone telephone number
le téléphone à cadran rotary phone
le téléphone à touches touch-tone telephone, **3.2**
téléphoner to call (on the telephone)
le **télésiège** chairlift, 11.2
la **tempe** temple
tempéré(e) temperate
temporaire temporary
le **temps** weather, 11.1; time; tense
de temps en temps from time to time, 11.1
l'emploi *(m.)* **du temps** schedule
en très peu de temps in a short time
Il fait quel temps? What's the weather like?, 11.1
se **tenir** to behave, **13.1**
la **tension** blood pressure, **8.2**
le **terme** term
le **terminus** last stop, **10.2**
le **terrain de football** soccer field, 10.1
la **terrasse** terrace, patio, 4.2
la terrasse d'un café sidewalk café, 5.1
la **terre** earth, land, **11.2**
à terre on the ground
tester to test
la **tête** head, 10.1
avoir mal à la tête to have a headache, **2.1**
le **TGV (train à grande vitesse)** high-speed train, **4.1**
thaïlandais(e) Thai
le **thé** tea
le **théâtre** theater, **1.1**
le **thon** tuna
le **thym** thyme, **6.1**
le **ticket** bus or subway ticket, **10.1**
tiens! hey!
timide shy, timid, 1.2
le **timbre** stamp, **5.2**
tirer to take, to draw
la **toilette: faire sa toilette** to wash
les toilettes *(f. pl.)* bathroom, toilet, 4.2
le **toit** roof
le toit de chaume thatched roof
tomber to fall, 11.2, **8.1**
tomber malade to get sick, L1
tomber en panne to break down, **7.1**
la **tonalité** dial tone, **3.2**
se **tordre** to twist (one's knee, etc.), **8.1**
tôt early, 12.1
totalement totally
la **touche** button, key, **3.1**
toucher to touch, 10.2; to cash, **5.1**
toujours always, 4.2; still, **10.2**
la **tour** tower, **11.1**
le **tour: à son tour** in turn
À votre tour. (It's) your turn.
tourner to turn, **7.2**
tourner en rond to go around in a circle
le **tourniquet** turnstile, **10.1**
tous, toutes *(adj.)* all, every, 2.1, 8

tous (toutes) les deux both
tous les jours every day, **1.2**
tousser to cough, **2.1**
tout *(pron.)* all, everything
C'est tout. That's all., 6.1
en tout in all
pas du tout not at all, 3.1
tout droit straight ahead, **7.2**
tout le monde everyone, everybody, 1.2
toutes les cinq minutes every five minutes, **10.1**
tout *(adv.)* very, completely, all, 4.2
À tout à l'heure. See you later., BV
tout autour de all around *(prep.)*
tout compris all inclusive, **9.1**
tout de même all the same, 5.2
tout près de very near, 4.2
tout(e) seul(e) all alone, all by himself/herself, 5.2
tout de suite right away
toxique toxic
la **tradition** tradition
traditionnel(le) traditional
la **tragédie** tragedy, **13.1**
tragique tragic
le **train** train, **9.1**
le **trait** characteristic
la **traite** monthly payment
le **traitement** treatment
traiter to treat
le **trajet** trip, **10.2**
la **tranche** slice, 6.2
tranquillement peacefully
transmettre to transmit, **3.1**
les **transports en commun** mass transit
transporter to transport
le **travail** work
travailler to work, 3.1, **14.2;** to practice
travailler à mi-temps to work part-time, **14.2**
travailler à plein temps to work full-time, **14.2**
traverser to cross, **11.1**
très very, BV
le **trésor** treasure, L4
le **tribunal** court, **14.1**
la **tribune** grandstand, **12.1**
triste sad, L1, **13.2**
troisième third, 4.2
le **tronc cérébral** brain stem
le **trône** throne
trop too *(excessive)*, 2.1
trop de too many, too much
le **trottoir** sidewalk, **11.1**
le **trou** hole, L4
le **trouble digestif** indigestion, upset stomach
se **troubler** to become flustered, **L3**
le **troupeau** flock, herd, **11.2**
trouver to find, 5.1; to think *(opinion)*, 7.2
se trouver to be located
le **t-shirt** T-shirt, 7.1
tuer to kill
le **tutoiement** the use of *tu*, **13.1**
tutoyer to call someone *tu*, **13.1**
le **type** type; guy *(inform.)*
typique typical

l' **un(e)... l'autre** one . . . the other
un(e) à un(e) one by one
unique single, only one
uniquement solely, only
l' **unité** *(f.)* unit
l' **université** *(f.)* university
urbain(e): appel urbain local call
l' **urgence** *(f.)* emergency
l' **usine** *(f.)* factory, **11.1**
utile useful
utiliser to use, **3.1**

les **vacances** *(f. pl.)* vacation
en vacances on vacation
les grandes vacances summer vacation
la **vache** cow, **11.2**
la **vague** wave, 11.1
le **vaisseau sanguin** blood vessel
la **vaisselle** dishes, 12.2
faire la vaisselle to do the dishes, 12.2
valable valid
la **valeur** value
valider to validate, **10.1**
la **valise** suitcase, 8.1
faire les valises to pack, 8.1
la **vallée** valley
la **vanille: à la vanille** vanilla *(adj.)*, 5.1
vaut: il vaut mieux it is better, **13.2**
le **veau** veal, **6.2;** calf, **11.2**
la **veille** eve, **12.2**
la **veine** vein
le **vélo** bicycle, bike, 10.2
le **vélomoteur** lightweight motorcycle, **7.1**
la **vendange** grape harvest
le **vendeur, la vendeuse** salesperson, 7.1
vendre to sell, 9.1
vengé(e) avenged
la **vengeance** vengence
se **venger** to get revenge
venir to come, **4.2**
venir chercher (quelqu'un) to meet; to pick up, **4.2**

venir de to have just (done something), **10**
le **vent** wind, 11.1
Il y a du vent. It's windy., 11.1
le **ventre** abdomen, stomach, **2.1**
avoir mal au ventre to have a stomachache, **2.1**
vérifier to check, verify, 8.1
vérifier les niveaux to check under the hood, **7.1**
véritable real
la **vérité** truth
le **verre** glass, 5.2
vers toward
le **vers** verse
verser to deposit, **5.1;** to pour, **6.2**
verser des arrhes to pay a deposit, **9.1**
le **verso** back *(of a paper)*
vert(e) green, 5.1
la **veste** (sport) jacket, 7.1
les **vestiges** *(m. pl.)* remains
les **vêtements** *(m. pl.)* clothes, 7.1
la **viande** meat, 6.1, **6.2**
vide empty, **7.1**
la **vidéo** video, 3.1
la cassette vidéo videocassette, 12.2
le film en vidéo movie video, **1.1**
la **vie** life
en vie alive
vieux (vieil) vieille old, 4.2
mon vieux buddy
le **vignoble** vineyard, **11.2**
la **villa** house
le **village** village, small town
la **ville** city, town, 8.1, **5.2, 11.1**
en ville in town, in the city, **11.1**
le **vin** wine
le **vinaigre** vinegar, 6.1
la **virgule** comma
visionner to view
visiter to visit *(a place),* **1.2**
vite fast *(adv.)*, 10.2
la **vitesse** speed, **4.1**
à grande vitesse high-speed, **4.1**
la **vitrine** (store) window, 7.1
vivant(e) living
Vive... ! Long live . . . !, Hooray for . . . !
vivre to live, **11**
voici here is, here are, 4.1
la **voie** track *(railroad),* 9.1; lane *(highway),* **7.2**
voilà there is, there are; here is, here are *(emphatic),* 1.2
le **voile** veil
voir to see, 7.1
rien à voir avec nothing to do with
voir en rose to look on the bright side
le/la **voisin(e)** neighbor, 4.2
la **voiture** car, 4.2
en voiture by car, 5.2; "All aboard!"
la **voix** voice
le **vol** flight, 8.1
le vol intérieur domestic flight, 8.1
le vol international international flight, 8.1
le vol sans escale nonstop flight, **4.2**
voler to fly, **L3**
le **volley(-ball)** volleyball, 10.2
le/la **volontaire** volunteer
la **volonté** willpower
vouloir to want, 6.1
le **vouvoiement** the use of *vous*
le **voyage** trip, 8.1; voyage
faire un voyage to take a trip, 8.1
voyager to travel, 8.1
le **voyageur, la voyageuse** traveler, passenger, 9.1
vrai(e) true, real, 2.2
vraiment really, 1.1
la **vue** view

le **wagon** *(railroad)* car, 9.2
le **wagon-restaurant** dining car
le **week-end** weekend
le **western** Western movie
le **wolof** Wolof (West African language)

le **yaourt** yogurt, 6.1
les **yeux** *(m. pl; sing.* **œil***)* eyes, L1, **2.1**
avoir les yeux qui piquent to have itchy eyes, **2.1**

zapper to zap, to channel surf, 12.2
la **zone** zone
la zone de conflit war zone
Zut! Darn!, BV

cabaret le cabaret
cabin *(plane)* la cabine, 8.1
café le café, BV
cafeteria la cafétéria
cake le gâteau, 4.1
calcium le calcium
calculator la calculatrice, 3.2
calendar le calendrier
calf le veau, **11.2**
call *(telephone)* l'appel *(m.)*, **3.2**
  local call l'appel urbain
  toll call l'appel interurbain
to **call** appeler; *(on the telephone)* téléphoner; donner un coup de fil, **3.2**
  to call a penalty déclarer un penalty
  to call back rappeler, **3.2**
  to call 911 appeler police secours, **8.1**
calm calme
calorie la calorie
Camembert cheese le camembert
campaign la campagne
can pouvoir, 6.1
can of food la boîte de conserve, 6.2
Canadian *(adj.)* canadien(ne), 6
to **cancel** annuler, **4.2**
candelabra le chandelier, **12.2**
candle la bougie, 4.1, **12.2**
cap la casquette, 7.1
capital la capitale
car la voiture, 4.2; *(railroad)* le wagon
  by car en voiture, 5.2
  dining car le wagon-restaurant
  sleeping car le wagon-couchettes (lits)
carbohydrate la glucide; l'hydrate *(m.)* de carbone
carbon dioxide le gaz carbonique
card la carte
  credit card la carte de crédit, **9.2**
  greeting card la carte de vœux, **12.2**
cardboard le carton
cardiac cardiaque
care le soin
to **care: I don't care.** Ça m'est égal., **1.1**
career la carrière, **14.2**
Careful! Attention!, 4.2
carefully prudemment, **7.2;** soigneusement
Caribbean Sea la mer des Caraïbes, la mer des Antilles
carnival *(season)* le carnaval, **12.1**
carpenter le charpentier; le menuisier, **14.1**
carrot la carotte, 6.2
to **carry** porter, **L2**
carry-on luggage les bagages *(m. pl.)* à main, 8.1
to **carry out** exécuter; assurer
cartoon le dessin animé, **1.1**
case le cas
  in case of en cas de
cash l'argent liquide, **5.1**
  cash register la caisse, 3.2
  in cash en liquide, **9.2**
  to pay cash payer en espèces, **9.2**
to **cash** toucher, **5.1**
cashier le caissier, la caissière, **5.1**
cassette la cassette, 3.1
cast le plâtre, **8.2**
  to put in a cast plâtrer, **8.2**
castle le château
casual *(clothes)* sport, 7.1
cat le chat, 4.1
catalog le catalogue
to **catch** attraper
to **cause** causer
cave la grotte, L4
CD le CD, 3.1
CD-ROM le CD-ROM, **3.1**
to **celebrate** célébrer, L4
  to celebrate Christmas Eve or New Year's Eve réveillonner, **12.2**
cell la cellule, L4
Celtic celte, celtique
center le centre
century le siècle, **L4**
cereal les céréales *(f. pl.)*
ceremony la cérémonie, **12.2**
certainly certainement
chairlift le télésiège, 11.2
champion le/la champion(ne)
change *(money)* la monnaie, **5.1**
  change purse le porte-monnaie, **5.1**
  to make change for faire la monnaie de, **5.1**
to **change** changer (de), 9.2
channel *(TV)* la chaîne, 12.2
  to channel surf zapper, 12.2
character *(in a story)* le personnage
characteristic la caractéristique; le trait
charge: in charge of chargé(e) de
charges les frais *(m. pl.)*, **9.2, 13.1**
charm le charme
charming charmant(e)
to **chat** bavarder
check le chèque, **5.1;** *(in restaurant)* l'addition *(f.)*, 5.2
  traveler's check le chèque de voyage
to **check** vérifier, 8.1; contrôler, **4.1**
  to check *(luggage)* (faire) enregistrer, 8.1
  to check under the hood vérifier les niveaux, **7.1**
cheek la joue, **13.1**
cheese le fromage, 5.1

chemical chimique
chemist le/la chimiste
chemistry la chimie, 2.2
chest la poitrine; le coffre, L4
chewing gum le chewing-gum
chic chic *(inv.)*
chicken le poulet, 6.1
child l'enfant *(m. et f.)*, 4.1
childhood l'enfance *(f.)*
chills les frissons *(m. pl.)*, **2.1**
chimney la cheminée, **12.2**
Chinese chinois(e)
chocolate le chocolat; *(adj.)* au chocolat, 5.1
choir le chœur
to **choose** choisir, 8.1
choppy *(sea)* agité(e)
Christmas le Noël, **12.2**
Christmas carol le chant de Noël, **12.2**
Christmas Eve dinner le réveillon, **12.2**
Christmas gift le cadeau de Noël, **12.2**
Christmas tree l'arbre *(m.)* de Noël, **12.2**
church l'église *(f.)*, **11.1, 12.2**
circle le cercle
traffic circle le rond-point, **7.2, 11.1**
circuit le circuit
circus le cirque
to **cite** citer
city la ville, 8.1, **5.2, 11.1**
city hall l'hôtel *(m.)* de ville
in the city en ville, **11.1**
civil civil(e)
civil servant le/la fonctionnaire, **14.1**
civilization la civilisation
civilized civilisé(e)
to **claim** *(luggage)* récupérer, **4.2**
clarinet la clarinette
class *(people)* la classe, 2.1; *(course)* le cours, 2.1
in class en classe
in (French, etc.) class en cours de (français, etc.)
classical classique
classified ad la petite annonce, **14.2**
classroom la salle de classe, 2.1
clean propre, **9.2**
clearly clairement
to **clear the table** débarrasser la table, 12.2
clever: Very clever! *(ironic)* C'est malin!
to **click** cliquer, **3.1**
climate le climat
clinic la clinique
close *(adv.)* de près, **11.1;** *(adj.)* proche
to **close** fermer, **9.1**
closet le placard, **9.2**
clothes les vêtements *(m. pl.)*, 7.1
cloud le nuage, 11.1
clove of garlic la gousse d'ail, **6.1**
clown le clown
coach l'autocar *(m.)*
coast la côte
coat le manteau, 7.1
code le code, 4.2
coffee le café, 5.1
black coffee l'express *(m.)*, 5.1
coffee with cream *(in a café)* le crème, 5.1
coin la pièce, **5.1**
cola le coca, 5.1
cold froid(e) *(adj.); (illness)* le rhume, **2.1**
to have a cold être enrhumé(e), **2.1**
collection la collection
color la couleur, 7.2
What color is . . . ? De quelle couleur est… ?, 7.2
comb le peigne, 12.1
to **comb one's hair** se peigner, 12.1
to **come** venir, **4.2**
to come back revenir, **4**
Come on! Allez!, 9.2
comedy la comédie, **1.1;** le film comique, **1.1**
musical comedy la comédie musicale, **1.1**
comfortable confortable
comic comique, **1.1**
commercial *(TV)* la publicité, 12.2
to **commit** commettre
common commun(e); courant(e)
in common en commun
to **communicate** communiquer
communication la communication
community la communauté
commuter trains les lignes de banlieue, **4.1**
company la société, **14.2;** l'entreprise, **14.2**
in the company of en compagnie de
to **compare** comparer
compartment le compartiment, **4.1**
complete complet, complète
to **complete** compléter
completely complètement
complicated compliqué(e)
composed of composé(e) de
composer le compositeur, la compositrice
composition la composition; la rédaction
compound enceinte de résidences, **L2**
compound fracture la fracture compliquée, **8.2**
computer l'ordinateur *(m.)*, **3.1**
computer expert l'informaticien(ne), **14.1**
computer science l'informatique *(f.)*, 2.2
concept le concept
concert le concert

concisely brièvement
condition la condition
conductor *(train)* le contrôleur, 9.2
to **connect** connecter; relier
connection *(between trains)* la correspondance, 9.2, **10.1**
to **conspire** comploter
to **consult** consulter
contamination la contamination
to **contain** contenir
contest la compétition, le concours
continent le continent
to **continue** continuer
contrary: on the contrary au contraire
to **control** contrôler, **4.1**
convent le couvent
conversation la conversation, **L3**
to **converse** converser
convertible la décapotable, **7.1**
cook le cuisinier, la cuisinière, **6.2**
to **cook** faire la cuisine, 6; cuire, **6.2**
cooked cuit(e)
cool frais, fraîche 11.2
copper le cuivre
corner le coin, **10.1, 11.1**
on the corner au coin, **11.1**
corporation la société, **14.2**
large corporation la grosse société, **14.2**
correspondence la correspondance
corridor le couloir, 8.2
cosmopolitan cosmopolite
cost le prix, 7.1
to **cost** coûter, 3.2
to **cough** tousser, **2.1**
counselor le conseiller, la conseillère
count le comte, L4
to **count** compter, **5.1**
counter le comptoir, 8.1
counter window *(post office)* le guichet, **5.2**
country le pays, 8.1
country code *(tel.)* l'indicatif *(m.)* du pays, **3.2**
country(side) la campagne, **11.2**
courage le courage
courageous courageux, courageuse
course le cours, 2.1
of course bien sûr; mais oui
of course not mais non
court la cour; le tribunal, **14.1**
courtesy la politesse, BV
courtyard la cour, 3.2
cousin le/la cousin(e), 4.1
to **cover** couvrir
covered couvert(e)
cow la vache, **11.2**
crab le crabe, 6.1, **6.2**
crazy fou, folle
cream la crème
coffee with cream *(in a café)* le crème, 5.1
to **create** créer; réaliser
credit card la carte de crédit, **9.2**
Creole *(language)* le créole
crepe la crêpe, BV
criminal le/la criminel(le), L4
critic le/la critique
croissant le croissant, 5.1
to **cross** traverser, **11.1; se** croiser, **10.1**
crosswalk le passage pour piétons, **11.1**
crushed écrasé(e)
crutch la béquille, **8.1**
to **cry** pleurer, L1
cucumber le concombre
to **cultivate** cultiver, **11.2**
cultural culturel(le)
cultural event la manifestation culturelle
culture la culture
cup la tasse, 5.2
winner's cup la coupe, 10.2
to **cure** guérir, **L4**
currency la devise; la monnaie, **5.1**
current courant(e)
customer le/la client(e)
customs la douane, **4.2**
to go through customs passer à la douane, **4.2**
to **cut** couper, **6.2**
to cut (one's finger, etc.) se couper, **8.1**
to cut in line resquiller, **13.1**
cycling le cyclisme, 10.2; *(adj.)* cycliste
cyclist *(in race)* le coureur (la coureuse) cycliste, 10.2
cymbals les cymbales *(f. pl.)*, **12.1**

dad papa
daily quotidien(ne)
dairy store la crémerie, 6.1
dance la danse
to **dance** danser, **1.1**
dancer le danseur, la danseuse, **1.1**
dangerous dangereux, dangereuse
dangerously dangereusement, **7.2**
dark sombre
dark haired brun(e), 1.1
Darn! Zut!, BV
data les données *(f. pl.)*, **3.1**
date la date; *(fruit)* la datte
date palm le dattier
What is today's date? Quelle est la date aujourd'hui?, BV
to **date from** dater de
daughter la fille, 4.1
day le jour, BV; la journée, 3.1
the day before yesterday avant-hier, 10.2

every day tous les jours
Have a nice day! Belle journée!, 4.2
dear cher, chère
death la mort
debt: to go into debt s'endetter
December décembre *(m.)*, BV
to **decide (to)** décider de
decision la décision
the decision is made la décision est prise
to **declare** déclarer
to **decorate** orner; décorer
dedicated dédié(e)
to **defeat** battre
delay le retard
delicatessen la charcuterie, 6.1
delicious délicieux, délicieuse
delighted enchanté(e), **13.2**
demanding exigeant(e)
dentist le/la dentiste
deodorant le déodorant
department *(in a store)* le rayon, 7.1; *(in a company)* le service
coat department le rayon des manteaux, 7.1
department head le chef de service, **14.1**
department store le grand magasin, 7.1
departure le départ, 8.1
to **depend (on)** dépendre (de)
deplaning le débarquement
deposit les arrhes *(f. pl.)*, **9.1**
to pay a deposit verser des arrhes, **9.1**
to **deposit** verser, **5.1**
descendant le/la descendant(e)
to **describe** décrire
description la description
desert le désert
deserted désert(e)
to **design** dessiner
designer (clothes) le couturier
to **desire** désirer, 3.2
desk clerk le/la réceptionniste, **9.1**
desparate désespéré(e), L4
dessert le dessert
destination la destination
destiny la destinée
detail le détail
to **devastate** ravager
to **develop** développer
devoted dévoué(e)
diagnosis le diagnostic, **2.2**
to **dial** *(phone number)* composer, **3.2;** faire le numéro, **3.2**
dial tone la tonalité, **3.2**
dialect le dialecte
diamond le diamant
dictionary le dictionnaire
to **die** mourir, 11; crever, **L4**
diet l'alimentation *(f.)*; le régime
to follow a diet faire un régime
difference la différence
different différent(e), 8.1
difficult difficile, 2.1
difficulty la difficulté
with difficulty difficilement
dig *(archaeol.)* la fouille
to **dig** creuser, L4
dignitaries les notables *(m. pl.)*, **12.1**
dining car la voiture-restaurant
dining hall *(school)* la cantine, 3.1
dining room la salle à manger, 4.2
dinner le dîner, 5.2
to eat dinner dîner, 5.2
diploma le diplôme
direction la direction, **10.1;** le sens, **7.2**
in the right (wrong) direction dans le bon (mauvais) sens, **11.1**
directly directement
director of human resources le directeur (la directrice) des ressources humaines (D.R.H.), **14.2**
to **direct traffic** régler la circulation, **11.1**
dirty sale, **9.2**
disadvantage l'inconvénient *(m.)*
disagreeable désagréable
to **disappear** disparaître
discount la réduction
to **discover** découvrir
discovery la découverte
to **discuss** discuter
disease la maladie
dish *(food)* le plat
dishes la vaisselle, 12.2
to **do the dishes** faire la vaisselle, 12.2
dishwasher le lave-vaisselle, 12.2
diskette la disquette, **3.1**
diskette drive le lecteur de disquettes, **3.1**
to **distinguish** distinguer
to **distribute** distribuer, **5.2**
district le quartier, 4.2, **11.1;** *(Paris)* l'arrondissement *(m.)*
business district le quartier d'affaires, **11.1**
dive le plongeon
to **dive** plonger, 11.1
to **divide** diviser
to **do** faire, 6.1
to do the grocery shopping faire les courses, 6.1
doctor le médecin *(m. et f.)*, **2.2**
at (to) the doctor's office chez le médecin, **2.2**
document le document, **3.1**
documentary le documentaire, **1.1**
dog le chien, 4.1
domain le domaine
domestic *(flight)* intérieur(e), 8.1
donkey l'âne *(m.)*

door la porte, L4, **9.1, L2**
dormitory le dortoir
to **doubt** douter, **14**
to **download** télécharger
downtown le centre-ville, **11.1**
dozen la douzaine, 6.2
drama le drame, **1.1**
drama club le club d'art dramatique
drawing le dessin
dream le rêve
dress la robe, 7.1
dressed: to get dressed s'habiller, 12.1
dressy habillé(e), 7.1
to **dribble** *(basketball)* dribbler, 10.2
to **drink** boire, 10.2
drink la boisson; la consommation, 5.1; le pot
to **drive** conduire, **7.1, 11.1**
driver l'automobiliste *(m. et f.)*, **7.1;** le conducteur, la conductrice, **7.1;** le chauffeur
driver's license le permis de conduire, **7.1**
driving lesson la leçon de conduite, **7.1**
driving school l'auto-école *(f.)*, **7.1**
drugstore la pharmacie, **2.2**
druid le druide
drum le tambour, **12.1**
dry sec, sèche
to **dry** sécher
dubbed *(movie)* doublé(e), **1.1**
duck le canard
duration la durée
during pendant, 3.2
dynamic dynamique, 1.2

each *(adj.)* chaque, **4.1**
each (one) chacun(e), 5.2
ear l'oreille *(f.)*, **2.1**
earache: to have an earache avoir mal aux oreilles, **2.1**
early en avance, 9.1; de bonne heure; tôt, 12.1
to **earn** gagner
earphone l'écouteur *(m.)*, **L3**
earth la terre, **11.2**
easily facilement
Easter le Pâques
eastern oriental(e)
easy facile, 2.1
to **eat** manger, 5.1
ecological écologique
ecology l'écologie *(f.)*
economics l'économie *(f.)*, 2.2
egg l'œuf *(m.)*, 6.1
fried egg l'œuf sur le plat
poached egg l'œuf à la coque
scrambled egg l'œuf brouillé
egotistical égoïste, 1.2
Egyptian égyptien(ne)
elbow le coude, **13.1**
electric électrique
electrician l'électricien(ne), **14.1**
electronic électronique
element l'élément *(m.)*
elevator l'ascenseur *(m.)*, 4.2
to **eliminate** éliminer
elsewhere ailleurs
e-mail l'e-mail *(m.)*, le mail, **3.1**
emergency l'urgence *(f.)*
emergency exit l'issue *(f.)* de secours
emergency medical technician le/la secouriste, **8.1**
emergency room le service des urgences, **8.1**
emission l'émission *(f.)*
emotion l'émotion *(f.)*, **13.2**
employee *(m. and f.)* l'employé(e), **14.1**
employer l'employeur, l'employeuse, **14.2**
employment office le bureau de placement, **14.2**
empty vide, **7.1**
encyclopedia l'encyclopédie *(f.)*
end la fin; le bout
ending le dénouement
enemy l'ennemi(e) *(m. et f.)*
energetic énergique, 1.2
energy l'énergie *(f.)*
engagement les fiançailles *(f. pl.)*, L4
engineer l'ingénieur *(m.)*, **14.1**
England l'Angleterre *(f.)*
English anglais(e)
English *(language)* l'anglais *(m.)*, 2.2
English Channel la Manche
enormous énorme
enough assez, 1.1
to **ensure** assurer
enriched enrichi(e)
to **enter** entrer, 7.1
enthusiastic enthousiaste, 1.2
entire entier, entière
entitled intitulé(e)
entrance l'entrée *(f.)*, 4.2
envelope l'enveloppe *(f.)*
equipment l'équipement *(m.)*; le matériel, **11.2**
equivalent l'équivalent *(m.)*
eraser la gomme, 3.2
escalator l'escalier mécanique, **10.1**
to **escape** s'échapper; s'évader, L4
especially surtout
espresso l'express *(m.)*, 5.1
essential essentiel(le); de première nécessité, indispensable
to **establish** établir
establishment l'établissement *(m.)*
euro l'euro *(m.)*
Europe l'Europe *(f.)*

European *(adj.)* européen(ne)
eve la veille, **12.2**
evening le soir, BV
event l'événement *(m.)*
ever jamais
every tous, toutes, 2.1, 8; chaque, **4.1**
every day *(adj.)* tous les jours, **1.2**
every five minutes toutes les cinq minutes, **10.1**
everybody tout le monde, 1.2
everyday *(adj.)* quotidien(ne)
everyone tout le monde, 1.2
everything tout
everywhere partout
evidently évidemment
exact exact(e)
exactly exactement; justement
to **exaggerate** exagérer
exam l'examen *(m.)*, 3.1
to pass an exam réussir à un examen
to take an exam passer un examen, 3.1
to **examine** examiner, **2.2**
example: for example par exemple
excellent excellent(e)
except excepté(e); sauf, **1.2**
exception l'exception *(f.)*
exceptional exceptionnel(le)
exchange l'échange *(m.)*
exchange rate le cours du change, **5.1**
to **exchange** échanger; changer, **5.1**
excursion l'excursion *(f.)*
exclusively exclusivement
to **excuse** excuser
excuse me pardon
to **execute** exécuter
exercise l'exercice *(m.)*
exhausted crevé(e); épuisé(e)
to **exist** exister
exhibit l'exposition *(f.)*, **1.2**
existence l'existence *(f.)*
exit la sortie, **7.2**
to **expel** expulser
expenses les frais *(m. pl.)*, **9.2, 13.1**
expensive cher, chère, 7.1
experience l'expérience *(f.)*
expert *(adj.)* expert(e)
to **explain** expliquer
explanation l'explication *(f.)*
explosion l'explosion *(f.)*
to **express** exprimer
expression l'expression *(f.)*
exquisite exquis(e)
exterior l'extérieur *(m.)*
extraordinary extraordinaire
extreme extrême
extremely extrêmement
eye l'œil *(m., pl.* yeux*)*, **2.1**
to have itchy eyes avoir les yeux qui piquent, **2.1**
eyes les yeux *(m. pl.)*, L1

fable la fable
fabulous fabuleux, fabuleuse
face la figure, 12.1
face down *(paper)* face écrite non visible, **3.1**
face up *(paper)* face écrite visible, **3.1**
to **face** donner sur, 4.2
to **facilitate** faciliter
factory l'usine *(f.)*, **11.1**
fairly assez, 1.1
fall *(season)* l'automne *(m.)*, 11.2
to **fall** tomber 11.2, **8.1**
to fall asleep s'endormir
false faux, fausse
to **falsify** falsifier
family la famille, 4.1
famous célèbre; connu(e), **1.1**
fan le/la fana
fantastic fantastique
far (away) loin
far from loin de, 4.2
fare le tarif
farm la ferme, **11.2;** *(adj.)* agricole, **11.2**
to **farm** *(land)* cultiver, **11.2**
farmer l'agriculteur, l'agricultrice, **11.2;** le fermier, la fermière, **11.2**
fast *(adj.)* rapide; *(adv.)* vite 10.2
to **fasten** attacher, 8.2
fast-food *(adj.)* de restauration rapide
fast-food restaurant le fast-food
fat la graisse; la lipide
father le père, 4.1
fault la faute
favorite favori(te); préféré(e)
fax le fax; la télécopie, **3.1**
fax machine le fax; le télécopieur, **3.1**
February février *(m.)*, BV
to **feed** nourrir; donner à manger
to **feel (well, etc.)** se sentir, **2.1**
to feel better aller mieux, **2.2**
to feel like avoir envie de
to feel out of sorts ne pas être dans son assiette, **2.1**
feeling le sentiment; la sensation
fees *(doctor)* les honoraires *(m. pl.)*
felt-tip pen le feutre, 3.2
female la femelle
festival le festival
Festival of Lights la fête des Lumières, **12.2**
festive de fête
festivity la festivité
fever la fièvre, **2.1**
to have a fever avoir de la fièvre, **2.1**
few peu (de); peu nombreux

nothing to do with rien à voir avec
to **notice** remarquer
novel le roman, **L1**
novelist le romancier, la romancière, **L1**
November novembre *(m.)*, BV
now maintenant, 2.2
right now en ce moment
nowadays de nos jours; actuellement
number le nombre; le numéro, **5.2**
right number le bon numéro, **3.2**
telephone number le numéro de téléphone
wrong number l'erreur *(f.)*; le mauvais numéro, **3.2**
numbered numéroté(e)
numerous nombreux, nombreuse
nurse l'infirmier, l'infirmière, **8.1**

oboe le hautbois
object l'objet *(m.)*
to **oblige** obliger
to **observe** observer
obsession l'idée *(f.)* fixe
to **obtain** obtenir; se procurer
obvious évident(e), **14**
occupied occupé(e)
to **occupy** occuper
ocean l'océan *(m.)*
o'clock: It's . . . o'clock. Il est… heure(s)., BV
October octobre *(m.)*, BV
odd curieux, curieuse
of *(belonging to)* de, 1.2
of course bien sûr
Of course (not)! Mais oui (non)!
to **offer** offrir
office le bureau, **11.1, 14.1**
official officiel(le)
often souvent, 5.2
oil l'huile *(f.)*, 6.1; le pétrole
oil tanker le pétrolier
okay *(health)* Ça va.; *(agreement)* d'accord, BV
Okay! Bon!, 6.1
old vieux (vieil), vieille, 4.2; âgé(e); ancien(ne)
How old are you? Tu as quel âge? *(fam.)*, 4.1
older l'aîné(e), L1
olive oil l'huile *(f.)* d'olive, **6.1**
omelette (with herbs/plain) l'omelette *(f.)* (aux fines herbes/nature), 5.1
on sur, 4.2
on board à bord de, 8.2
on foot à pied, 4.2
on sale en solde, 7.1
on time à l'heure, 8.1
on Tuesdays le mardi, **1.2**
one by one un(e) à un(e)
oneself soi
one-way street la rue à sens unique, **11.1**
one-way ticket l'aller simple *(m.)*, 9.1
onion l'oignon *(m.)*, 5.1, **6.1**
only seulement; uniquement; *(adj.)* seul(e)
open ouvert(e), **1.2**
to **open** ouvrir, **2.2, 13.2**
opera l'opéra *(m.)*
comic light opera l'opéra bouffe
light opera l'opéra comique
to **operate** opérer
operating room la salle d'opération, **8.2**
operation l'opération *(f.)*; l'intervention *(f.)* chirurgicale
opinion l'avis *(m.)*, 7.2
in my opinion à mon avis, 7.2
opponent l'adversaire *(m. et f.)*
opponents le camp adverse, 10.1
opportunity l'occasion *(f.)*
to **oppose** opposer, 10.1
opposing adverse, 10.1
opposite le contraire
optional facultatif, facultative
or ou, 1.1
or else sinon, 9.2
orange *(fruit)* l'orange *(f.)*, 6.2, **6.1;** *(color)* orange *(inv.)*, 7.2
orange tree l'oranger *(m.)*, L2
orchestra l'orchestre *(m.)*
symphony orchestra l'orchestre symphonique
order: in order to pour
to **order** commander, 5.1
ordinary ordinaire
organ *(of the body)* l'organe *(m.)*; *(musical instrument)* l'orgue *(m.)*
to **organize** organiser
orthopedic surgeon le chirurgien-orthopédiste, **8.2**
other autre
in other words autrement dit
on the other hand par contre; d'autre part
some others d'autres, 2.2
otherwise sinon, 9.2
outing l'excursion *(f.)*
outdoors en plein air; dehors
outgoing sociable, 1.2
outfit l'ensemble *(m.)*
outside *(n.)* l'extérieur *(m.)*; *(adv.)* à l'extérieur, dehors; *(prep.)* au dehors de
to work outside the home travailler à l'extérieur
outskirts la périphérie
oven le four, **6.1**
microwave oven le four à micro-ondes, **6.1**
over *(prep.)* par-dessus, 10.2
over there là-bas, **10.1**
to **overlook** donner sur, 4.2; dominer

overseas *(adj.)* d'outre-mer
ox le bœuf, **11.2**
oxygen l'oxygène *(m.)*
oxygen mask le masque à oxygène, **4.2**
to **owe** devoir, 10
to **own** posséder
owner le/la propriétaire
oyster l'huître *(f.)*, **6.2**

P

to **pack** *(suitcases)* faire les valises, 8.1
package le paquet, 6.2; le colis, **5.2**
packed *(stadium)* comble, 10.1; *(train)* bondé(e), **10.1**
pain in the neck *(slang)* casse-pieds
painful douloureux, douloureuse
to **paint** peindre
painter l'artiste peintre *(m. et f.)*, le/la peintre, **1.2**
house painter le peintre en bâtiment, **14.1**
painting la peinture, **1.2;** le tableau, **1.2**
pair la paire, 7.1
pal le copain, la copine, 2.1
palace le palais
palm tree le palmier
pancake la crêpe, BV
pants le pantalon, 7.1
paper le papier, 3.2
sheet of paper la feuille de papier, 3.2
parade le défilé, **12.1**
paragraph le paragraphe
parents les parents *(m. pl.)*, 4.1
Parisian *(adj.)* parisien(ne)
park le parc
to **park** se garer, **7.1;** stationner, **11.1**
parking lot le parking, **11.1**
parking meter le parcmètre, **11.1**
parsley le persil, **6.1**
part la partie
to be part of faire partie de
to **participate (in)** participer (à)
party la fête, 4.1
to throw a party donner une fête, 4.1
pass la passe
to **pass** passer, 10.1; doubler, **7.2**
to pass an exam réussir à un examen
passage le passage
passageway le passage
passbook *(bank)* le livret de caisse d'épargne
passenger le passager, la passagère, 8.1
passport le passeport, 8.1
passport check le contrôle des passeports, **4.2**
past passé(e)
pasta les pâtes *(f. pl.)*, **6.1**
pasture le pâturage
pâté le pâté
patience la patience, 9.2
to lose patience perdre patience, 9.2
patient le/la malade, **2.2;** *(adj.)* patient(e), 1.1
patio la terrasse, 4.2
to **pay** payer, 3.2
to pay attention faire attention
to pay back rembourser
to pay cash payer en espèces, **9.2**
to pay a deposit verser des arrhes, **9.1**
payment le paiement
peace la paix
pear la poire, 6.2
peas les petits pois *(m. pl.)*, 6.2
peasant le/la paysan(ne), L1
pedestrian le piéton, la piétonne, **11.1**
to **peel** éplucher, **6.2**
pen: ballpoint pen le stylo-bille, 3.2
felt-tip pen le feutre, 3.2
penalty *(soccer)* le penalty
pencil le crayon, 3.2
penicillin la pénicilline, **2.1**
people les gens *(m. pl.)*
pepper le poivre, 6.1
percent pour cent
perfect parfait(e)
to **perfect** perfectionner
perfectly parfaitement
to **perform** jouer, **1.1**
perhaps peut-être
period l'époque *(f.)*; la période; le point
to **permit** permettre
person la personne
personal personnel(le)
personality la personnalité
personally personnellement, **1.2**
pharmacist le/la pharmacien(ne), **2.2**
pharmacy la pharmacie, **2.2**
phenomenon le phénomène
phone card la télécarte, **3.2**
photograph la photo
physical physique
physicist le/la physicien(ne)
physics la physique, 2.2
to **pick up** ramasser, 8.2; recueillir; venir chercher (quelqu'un), **4.2**
to pick up the (telephone) receiver décrocher (le téléphone), **3.2**
pickup truck le pick-up
picnic le pique-nique
picturesque pittoresque
pie la tarte, 6.1
piece le morceau, **6.2**
pig le cochon, **11.2**
pill le comprimé, **2.2**
pillow l'oreiller *(m.)*, **4.2**
pilot le/la pilote, 8.2
pink rose, 7.1
pizza la pizza, BV
place l'endroit *(m.)*; la place, le lieu

to take place avoir lieu, **12.1**
to **place** mettre, 7.1
plain la plaine
plan le projet
plane l'avion *(m.)*, 8.1, **L3**
by plane en avion
plant la plante
plastic le plastique
plate l'assiette *(f.)*, 5.2
platform *(railroad)* le quai, 9.1, **10.1**
to **play** jouer, 3.2
to play *(a sport)* jouer à, 10.1, jouer de (instrument), **12.1**
play la pièce (de théâtre), **1.1**
to put on a play monter une pièce, **1.1**
player le joueur, la joueuse, 10.1
playwright l'auteur *(m.)* dramatique
pleasant agréable
please s'il vous plaît *(form.)*, s'il te plaît *(fam.)*, BV
pleasure le plaisir
pleated plissé(e), 7.1
plot l'argument *(m.)*
plumber le plombier, **14.1**
plus plus
p.m. de l'après-midi; du soir, BV
pocket money l'argent *(m.)* de poche
poem le poème
poet *(m. and f.)* le poète
police la police
police officer l'agent *(m.)* de police, **11.1**
polite poli(e), **13.1**
politely poliment
politeness la politesse, BV
political politique
polluted pollué(e)
pollution la pollution
polo shirt le polo, 7.1
pool la piscine, 11.1
poor pauvre, L1, **2.1**
pop *(music)* pop
popular populaire, 1.2
pork le porc, 6.1, **6.2**
la côtelette de porc pork chop, **6.2**
port le port
Portuguese portugais(e)
position la position
to **possess** posséder
possession la possession
possibility la possibilité
possible possible
postal postal(e)
postal employee l'employé(e) des postes, **5.2**
postcard la carte postale, 9.1, **5.2**
poster l'affiche *(f.)*
post office la poste, **5.2;** le bureau de poste, **5.2**
pot la casserole, **6.2**
potato la pomme de terre, 6.2, **6.1**
pound la livre, 6.2
practical pratique
to **practice** pratiquer; travailler
to **prefer** préférer, 6
prehistoric préhistorique
to **prepare** préparer
to **prescribe** prescrire, **2.2**
prescription l'ordonnance *(f.)*, **2.2**
to write a prescription faire une ordonnance, **2.2**
present le cadeau, 4.1
to **present** présenter
to **press** appuyer sur, **3.1**
pressure la pression, **7.1**
prestigious prestigieux, prestigieuse
pretty joli(e), 4.2
prevalent prévalent(e)
price le prix, 7.1
priest l'abbé *(m.)*
principal principal(e)
to **print** imprimer
printer l'imprimante *(f.)*, **3.1**
prison la prison, L4
prisoner le prisonnier, la prisonnière, L4
private individuel(le); privé(e)
problem le problème; la difficulté
product le produit
profession la profession
professional professionnel(le)
program le programme; *(TV)* l'émission *(f.)*, 12.2; *(computer)* le logiciel
programming la programmation
progress le progrès
promise la promesse
promotion l'avancement *(m.)*
to **pronounce** prononcer
property la propriété
protein la protéine
proud fier, fière
public public, publique
to **publish** publier
pulse le pouls, **8.2**
to **punish** punir
purchase achat *(m.)*
to **push** pousser, **10.2;** *(button, etc.)* appuyer sur, **3.1**
to push and shove bousculer, **13.1**
to **put (on)** mettre, 7.1
to put on makeup se maquiller, 12.1
to put on a play monter une pièce, **1.1**

quality la qualité
to **quarrel** se fâcher
Quebec: from or of Quebec québécois
queen la reine
question la question, 3.1
to ask a question poser une question, 3.1
quick rapide
quickly rapidement

quite assez, 1.1
quiz l'interro(gation) *(f.)*

rabbit le lapin, **11.2**
race *(human population)* la race; *(competition)* la course, 10.2
bicycle race la course cycliste, 10.2
radio la radio, 3.2
railroad le chemin de fer
rain la pluie
to **rain: It's raining.** Il pleut., 11.1
to **raise** lever
to raise one's hand lever la main, 3.1
raisin le raisin sec
rap *(music)* le rap
rapidly rapidement
rare *(meat)* saignant(e), 5.2; rare
rather plutôt
razor le rasoir, 12.1
to **read** lire, 9.2
reading la lecture
ready prêt(e)
real vrai(e), 2.2; véritable
reality la réalité
really vraiment, 1.1
rear l'arrière *(m.)*, 8.2, **10.2**
rear guard l'arrière-garde *(f.)*
reason la raison
to **reassure** rassurer
to **receive** recevoir, 10.2
recently récemment
recess la récré(ation), 3.2
recipe la recette, **6.1**
to **recognize** reconnaître
to **recommend** recommander
record le disque
recycling le recyclage
red rouge, 7.1
referee l'arbitre *(m.)*, 10.1
refrigerator le frigidaire, 12.2; le réfrigérateur, 12.2, **6.1;** le frigo *(slang)*, **6.1**
region la région
registration card la fiche, **9.1**
police registration card la fiche de police, **9.1**
regular régulier, régulière
to **reimburse** rembourser
religious religieux, religieuse, **12.2**
to **remain** rester, 11.1
remains les vestiges *(m. pl.)*
to **remember** se rappeler
remote éloigné(e)
remote control la télécommande, 12.2
to **renovate** rénover
renowned renommé(e)
to **rent** louer, **1.1**
to **repair** réparer
to **replace** remplacer
reporter le/la journaliste, **14.1**
to **represent** représenter
research la recherche
to **resemble** ressembler à
to **reserve** réserver, **9.1**
respective respectif, respective
respiratory respiratoire
responsible responsable
restaurant le restaurant, 5.2; le resto *(inform.)*
result le résultat
as a result par conséquent
résumé le curriculum vitae (C.V.), **14.2**
return le retour
to **return** rentrer, 3.2; *(volleyball)* renvoyer, 10.2
reunited réuni(e)
revolution la révolution
revolutionary révolutionnaire
rhyme la rime
rhythm le rythme
rice le riz
rich riche
ridiculous ridicule
right le droit; *(adv.)* à droite, **11.1**
right away tout de suite
right there juste là
to **ring** *(telephone)* sonner, **3.2**
ringing la sonnerie
to **rinse** rincer
river le fleuve; la rivière, **L2**
Riviera *(French)* la Côte d'Azur
road la route, **7.2;** le chemin
road map la carte (routière), **7.2**
road sign le panneau, **7.2**
roast beef le rôti de bœuf, **6.2**
rock le rocher, L3; *(music)* le rock
role le rôle
roll of toilet paper le rouleau de papier hygiénique, **9.2**
Roman romain(e)
romantic romantique
roof le toit
thatched roof le toit de chaume
room *(in house)* la pièce, 4.2; la salle; *(in hotel)* la chambre, **9.1**
dining room la salle à manger, 4.2
living room la salle de séjour, 4.2
rooster le coq
rosemary le romarin
round rond(e)
round (piece) la rondelle, **6.2**
round-trip ticket le billet aller-retour, 9.1
route le chemin
routine la routine, 12.1
row le rang, **12.1**
royal royal(e)
ruin la ruine
to **ruin** ruiner
rule la règle
rules of the road le code de la route, **11.1**
ruler la règle, 3.2
to **run a red light** brûler un feu rouge, **7.2**
runner le coureur, 10.2

running shoe la basket, 7.1
runway la piste, 8.1
rural rural(e)
rush hour les heures *(f.)* de pointe, **10.1**
Russian *(language)* le russe

sad triste, L1, **13.2**
sailor le marin, L4
salad la salade, 5.1
salami le saucisson, 6.1
salary le salaire, **14.2**
sale: on sale en solde, 7.1; en promotion
salesperson le vendeur, la vendeuse, 7.1
salmon le saumon, **6.2**
salt le sel, 6.1
same même, 2.1
  all the same tout de même, 5.2
  It's all the same to me. Ça m'est égal., **1.1**
  the same goes for me moi de même, **13.2**
sand le sable
sandals les sandales *(f. pl.)*, 7.1
sandwich le sandwich, BV
Santa Claus le Père Noël, **12.2**
sardine la sardine
to **satisfy** satisfaire
Saturday samedi *(m.)*, BV
sauce la sauce, **6.2**
sauerkraut la choucroute, **6.1**
sausage la saucisse, **6.1**
to **save** sauver; sauvegarder, **3.1;** *(money)* faire des économies, **5.1;** économiser; mettre de côté, **5.1**
saxophone le saxophone
to **say** dire, 9.2
scale la balance, **5.2**
scarf l'écharpe *(f.)*, 11.2
scene la scène, **1.1**
schedule l'emploi *(m.)* du temps; l'horaire *(m.)*, 9.1
school l'école *(f.)*, 1.2; *(adj.)* scolaire, 3.2
  elementary school l'école primaire
  junior high/high school l'école secondaire, 1.2
  high school le lycée, 2.1
  school supplies la fourniture scolaire, 3.2
schooling la scolarité
science les sciences *(f. pl.)*, 2.1
  natural sciences les sciences naturelles, 2.1
  social sciences les sciences sociales, 2.1
scientific scientifique
scientist le savant
to **score a goal** marquer un but, 10.1
to **scratch** gratter, **2.1**
screen l'écran *(m.)*, 8.1, **3.1**
sculptor le sculpteur *(m. et f.)*, **1.2**
sculpture la sculpture, **1.2**
sea la mer, 11.1
  by the sea au bord de la mer, 11.1
seafood les fruits de mer, **6.2**
seashore le bord de la mer, 11.1
seaside resort la station balnéaire, 11.1
season la saison
seat le siège, 8.2; la place *(plane, train, movie, etc.)*, 8.1
  seat back le dossier du siège, **4.2**
  seat belt la ceinture de sécurité, 8.2, **7.1**
seated assis(e), 9.2
second *(adj.)* deuxième, 4.2; second(e)
  in second class en seconde, 9.1
secret *(adj.)* secret, secrète; *(noun)* le secret
secretary le/la secrétaire, **14.1, L3**
security (airport) le contrôle de sécurité, 8.1
to **see** voir, 7.1
  See you later. À tout à l'heure., BV
  See you soon! À bientôt!, BV
  See you tomorrow. À demain., BV
seldom très peu
self-employed: to be self-employed être à son compte, **14.2**
to **sell** vendre, 9.1
to **send** envoyer, 10.1, **3.1;** emmener, L4
sender l'expéditeur, l'expéditrice
separate séparer
September septembre *(m.)*, BV
serious sérieux, sérieuse, 7; grave, **3.2**
to **serve** servir, 8.2; 10.2; *(go to)* desservir, **4.1**
service le service, 5.2
serving dish le plat, **6.1**
to **set** régler, **L1**
  to set a bone remettre un os en place, **8.2**
  to set the table mettre la table, 7; mettre le couvert
to **settle** s'installer
several plusieurs
to **shake hands** se serrer la main, **13.1**
Shall we go? On y va?
shampoo le shampooing, 12.1
shape la forme
to **share** partager, **13.1**
to **shave** se raser, 12.1
shaver le rasoir, 12.1
shed le hangar, **11.2**
sheep le mouton, **11.2**
sheet le drap, **9.2**
  sheet of paper la feuille de papier, 3.2
shepherd le berger
to **shine** briller
shirt la chemise, 7.1

shoe la chaussure, 7.1; le soulier, **12.2**
to **shoot** *(ball)* lancer, 10.2
shop la boutique, 7.1
to **shop** faire des achats
shopkeeper le/la commerçant(e), **14.1**
shopping le shopping, 7.2
to do the grocery shopping faire les courses, 6.1
to go shopping faire des courses, 7.2
shopping cart le chariot, 6.2
shopping center le centre commercial, 7.1
short petit(e), 1.1; court(e), 7.1
in a short time en très peu de temps
short story la nouvelle
shorts le short, 7.1
to **shout** crier, L4
show *(TV)* l'émission *(f.)*, 12.2
show(ing) *(movies)* la séance, **1.1**
to **show** montrer; *(movie)* jouer
shower la douche, 12.1
to take a shower prendre une douche, 12.1
shrimp la crevette, 6.1
shy timide, 1.2
sick malade, **2.1,** L1
to get sick tomber malade, L1
sick person le/la malade, **2.2**
side le côté, **4.1;** *(in a sporting event)* le camp, 10.1
sidewalk le trottoir, **11.1**
sidewalk café la terrasse (d'un café), 5.1
sign le signal; la marque, **L4**
to **sign** signer
signal le signal
similar semblable, L1
simply simplement
since *(time)* depuis, 9.2, **10.2**
to **sing** chanter, **1.2**
singer le chanteur, la chanteuse, **1.1**
single unique; seul(e)
sink *(kitchen)* l'évier *(m.)*, 12.2; *(bathroom)* le lavabo
sinus infection la sinusite, **2.2**
sir monsieur, BV
sister la sœur, 1.2
to **sit: Where would you like to sit?** Qu'est-ce que vous voulez comme place?, 8.1
site le site
size *(clothes)* la taille; *(shoes)* la pointure, 7.2
the next larger size la taille au-dessus, 7.2
the next smaller size la taille au-dessous, 7.2
to wear size (number) faire du (nombre), 7.2
What size do you wear? Vous faites quelle taille (pointure)?, 7.2
skate le patin, 11.2
to **skate (ice)** faire du patin (à glace), 11.1
to go skating faire du patin, 11.1
skating rink la patinoire, 11.2
skeleton le squelette
ski le ski, 11.2
ski boot la chaussure de ski, 11.2
ski cap le bonnet, 11.2
ski jacket l'anorak *(m.)*, 7.1
ski pole le bâton, 11.2
ski resort la station de sports d'hiver, 11.2
ski trail la piste, 11.2
to **ski** faire du ski, 11.2
skier le skieur, la skieuse, 11.2
skiing le ski, 11.2
cross-country skiing le ski de fond, 11.2
downhill skiing le ski alpin, 11.2
skirt la jupe, 7.1
skull la boîte crânienne
sky le ciel, 11.1
to **sleep** dormir, 8.2
sleeping car le wagon-couchette
sleeve la manche, 7.1
long-(short-)sleeved à manches longues (courtes), 7.1
slice la tranche, 6.2
slice of bread with butter or jam la tartine
to **slip** glisser, **8.1**
slope la pente
slot le fente, **3.2**
to **slow down** ralentir, **7.1**
small petit(e), 1.1
smoke la fumée
to **smoke** fumer, **4.2**
snack la collation, **4.2**
snack bar *(train)* le snack-bar, 9.2
sneaker la basket, 7.1
to **sneeze** éternuer, **2.1**
snow la neige, 11.2
to **snow: It's snowing.** Il neige., 11.2
snowman le bonhomme de neige
so alors, BV; donc; si *(adv.)*
soap le savon, 12.1, **9.2**
soccer le foot(ball), 10.1
soccer field le terrain de football, 10.1
sociable sociable, 1.2
social social(e)
social blunder le faux pas
social sciences les sciences sociales *(f. pl.)*, 2.1
social worker l'assistant(e) social(e), **14.1**
sock la chaussette, 7.1
software le software, **3.1;** le logiciel, **3.1**
soldier le soldat, L3, **12.1**
sole le sole, **6.2**
solely uniquement
solid solide

solution la solution
some quelques, 9.2; certains
some other d'autres, 2.2
somebody quelqu'un, 10.1
someone quelqu'un, 10.1
someone else quelqu'un d'autre, **L3**
something quelque chose, 11
something else autre chose
something special quelque chose de spécial
sometimes quelquefois, 5.2
somewhere quelque part
son le fils, 4.1
song la chanson
soon bientôt
See you soon. À bientôt., BV
sore throat: to have a sore throat avoir mal à la gorge, **2.1**
sorry désolé(e), **3.2, 13.2**
to be sorry regretter, 6.1, **13.2**
I'm sorry. Désolé(e)., **3.2**
so-so comme ci, comme ça
sound le son, L3
soup la soupe, 5.1
source la source
south le sud
south-east le sud-est
South America l'Amérique *(f.)* du Sud
space l'espace *(m.)*
open spaces les grands espaces
spaghetti les spaghettis *(m. pl.)*
Spanish espagnol(e)
Spanish *(language)* l'espagnol *(m.)*, 2.2
spare tire la roue de secours, **7.1**
to **sparkle** scintiller
to **speak** parler, 3.1
to speak to s'adresser à
special spécial(e)
specialty la spécialité
specific précis(e)
spectator le spectateur, la spectatrice, 10.1
speech le discours
speed la vitesse, **4.1**
speed limit la limitation de vitesse, **7.2**
to **spell** épeler
to **spend** *(time)* passer, 3.1; *(money)* dépenser, **5.1**
spice l'épice *(f.)*
spicy épicé(e)
to **spill** déverser
spinach les épinards *(m. pl.)*, 6.2
spinal cord la moelle épinière
spirit l'esprit *(m.)*
splendid splendide, **4.1**
to **spoil** gâter
spoon la cuillère, 5.2
sport le sport, 10.2
sports car la voiture de sport, **7.1**
team sport le sport collectif; le sport d'équipe, 10.2
to **sprain one's ankle** se fouler la cheville, **8.1**
spring *(season)* le printemps, 11.1; *(water)* la source
square la place
stable l'étable *(f.)*, **11.2**
stadium le stade, 10.1
stage *(of a race)* l'étape *(f.)*
staircase l'escalier *(m.)*, 4.2
stall *(market)* l'étal *(m.)*
stamp le timbre **5.2**
stamp machine le distributeur automatique (de timbres), **5.2**
to **stamp (a ticket)** composter, 9.1
stand l'étal *(m.)*
standing debout, 9.2
to **stare at** regarder fixement
to **start** commencer, 9.2
to start the car mettre le contact, **7.1**
state l'état *(m.)*
state of the art haut de gamme
statement *(bank)* le relevé
station la station, 4.2, **10.1**
gas station la station-service, **7.1**
station wagon le break, **7.1**
subway station la station de métro, 4.2
stationery store la papeterie, 3.2
statue la statue, **1.2**
stay le séjour, **9.1**
to **stay** rester, 11.1
steak and French fries le steak frites, 5.2
step le pas, **L2**
to take a step faire un pas, **L2**
to **step in** intervenir
stepfather le beau-père, 4.1
stepmother la belle-mère, 4.1
still toujours, **10.2;** encore, 11
to **stir** remuer, **6.2**
stitch le point de suture, **8.2**
stomach le ventre, **2.1**
stone la pierre
stop l'arrêt *(m.)*, 9.2, **10.2**
bus stop l'arrêt d'autobus, **10.2**
to **stop** s'arrêter, 10.1; cesser; *(plane)* faire escale, **4.2**
stopover l'escale *(f.)*, **4.2**
store le magasin, 3.2, **14.1**
department store le grand magasin, 7.1
to **store** stocker; emmagasiner; entreposer, **11.2;** mettre en réserve
story l'histoire *(f.)*
short story la nouvelle
stove la cuisinière, **6.1**
straight ahead tout droit, **7.2**
strategy la stratégie
strawberry la fraise, 6.2
streamer le serpentin, **12.1**

street la rue, 3.1, **5.2, 11.1**
one-way street la rue à sens unique, **11.1**
street map le plan, **7.2**
strength la force
stretcher le brancard, **8.1**
to **stretch out** allonger
strict strict(e), 2.1
strong fort(e), 2.2
student l'élève *(m. et f.)*, 1.2; l'étudiant(e) *(university)*
studio (artist's) l'atelier *(m.)*
studio (apartment) le studio
study l'étude *(f.)*
to **study** étudier, 3.1; faire des études
to study French (math, etc.) faire du français (des maths, etc.), 6
stuffing la farce
stupid stupide
stupid thing la bêtise
style le look
in style à la mode
subject le sujet; *(in school)* la matière, 2.2
on the subject of à propos de
subtitles les sous-titres *(m. pl.)*, **1.1**
to **subtract** soustraire
suburbs la banlieue, **4.1, 11.1**
subway le métro, 4.2, **10.1**
subway map le plan du métro, **10.1**
subway station la station de métro, 4.2, **10.1**
to **succeed in (doing)** arriver à (+ *inf.*), 9.1
success le succès
suddenly soudain
to **suffer** souffrir, **2.2**
sugar le sucre
to **suggest** proposer; suggérer
suit *(men's)* le complet; *(women's)* le tailleur, 7.1
suitcase la valise, 8.1
sum la somme
summer l'été *(m.)*
in summer en été, 11.1
summit le sommet, 11.2
sun le soleil, 11.1
to **sunbathe** prendre un bain de soleil, 11.1
sunburn le coup de soleil, 11.1
Sunday dimanche *(m.)*, BV
sunglasses les lunettes *(f. pl.)* de soleil, 11.1
sunny: It's sunny. Il fait du soleil., 11.1
suntan lotion la crème solaire, 11.1
super super
superbe superbe
supermarket le supermarché, 6.2
supply la fourniture
school supplies les fournitures scolaires, 3.2
sure sûr(e)
surfer le surfeur, la surfeuse, 11.1
surfing le surf, 11.1
to go surfing faire du surf, 11.1
to **surf the Net** naviguer sur Internet
surgeon le chirurgien, **8.2**
orthopedic surgeon le chirurgien-orthopédiste, **8.2**
surprise la surprise
to **surprise** étonner
surprised étonné(e), **13.2**
survey le sondage, l'enquête *(f.)*
survival la survie
to **swallow** avaler, **2.2**
sweater le pull, 7.1
sweatshirt le sweat-shirt, 7.1
sweet potato la patate douce
to **swim** nager, 11.1
swimmer le nageur, la nageuse
swimming la natation, 11.1
sword l'épée *(f.)*, L3
symphony la symphonie
symptom le symptôme
syrup le sirop, **2.1**
system le système

table la table, 5.1
table setting le couvert, 5.2
tablecloth la nappe, 5.2
to **tailgate** suivre une voiture de trop près, **11.1**
to **take** prendre, 5.2; *(someone somewhere)* emmener, **8.1**
to take care of s'occuper de; soigner, **8.1, L4;** prendre soin de, **L4**
to take down descendre, 9
to take an exam passer un examen, 3.1
to take the. . . line *(subway)* prendre la direction… , **10.1**
to take off *(airplane)* décoller, 8.1
to take out retirer, **3.1**
to take place avoir lieu, **12.1**
to take possession of prendre possession de
to take size (number) faire du (nombre), 7.2
to take the subway prendre le métro, 5.2
to take a trip faire un voyage, 8.1
to take up occuper
to take (something) upstairs monter, **9.1**
to take a walk faire une promenade, 11.1
What size do you take? Vous faites quelle taille (pointure)?, 7.2
taken occupé(e)

takeoff *(plane)* le décollage, **4.2**
talent le talent
to **talk** parler, 3.1
to talk on the phone parler au téléphone, 3.2, **L3**
tall grand(e), 1.1
to **tan** bronzer, 11.1
tape la cassette, 7.1
to **tape** enregistrer
tart la tarte, 6.1
apple tart la tarte aux pommes, 6.1
taste le goût
tea le thé
to **teach (someone to do something)** apprendre (à quelqu'un à faire quelque chose)
teacher le/la prof *(inform.)*, 2.1; le professeur, 2.1
elementary school teacher le maître, la maîtresse
team l'équipe *(f.)*, 10.1
teammate le coéquipier, la coéquipière, 10.1
tear la larme, **L2**
techno (music) la techno
technology la technologie
teenager l'adolescent(e)
telephone le téléphone, 3.2, **3.1;** *(adj.)* téléphonique, **3.2**
telephone booth la cabine téléphonique, **3.2**
telephone call l'appel (téléphonique), **3.2;** le coup de téléphone
telephone card la télécarte, **3.2**
telephone directory l'annuaire *(m.)*, **3.2**
telephone number le numéro de téléphone
touch-tone telephone le téléphone à touches, **3.2**
to **tell** dire, 9.2
to tell (about) raconter
temperate tempéré
temperature la température
temple la tempe
temporary temporaire
tendon le tendon
term le terme
terrace la terrasse, 4.2
terrible terrible
terrific super; terrible
test l'examen *(m.)*, 3.1
to take a test passer un examen, 3.1
to pass a test réussir à un examen
text le texte, **3.1**
Thai thaïlandais(e)
thank you merci, BV
thanks merci, BV
thanks to grâce à
that ça; ce (cet), cette; cela
that is (to say) c'est-à-dire
that one celui-là, celle-là, **11.2**
That's all. C'est tout., 6.1
That's it., That's right. C'est ça.
thatched roof le toit de chaume
theater le théâtre, **1.1**
theme le thème
then alors, BV; ensuite, 12.1
there là, **3.2**
over there là-bas, **10.1**
there are il y a, 4.1
there is il y a, 4.1
therefore donc
thing la chose
to **think** penser; croire, 7.2; *(opinion)* trouver, 7.2; réfléchir
thousand mille, 3.2
throat la gorge, **2.1**
throat infection l'angine *(f.)*, **2.1**
through par
to **throw** lancer, 10.2, **12.1**
to throw a party donner une fête, 4.1
thumb le pouce, **13.1**
Thursday jeudi *(m.)*, BV
thyme le thym, **6.1**
ticket le billet, 8.1
bus or subway ticket le ticket, **10.1**
one-way ticket l'aller (simple), 9.1
round-trip ticket le billet aller (et) retour, 9.1
ticket machine le distributeur automatique, **10.1**
ticket window le guichet, 9.1, **10.1**
traffic ticket la contravention, **7.2**
to **tie** *(score)* égaliser
tie la cravate, 7.1
tight serré(e), 7.2
time *(of day)* l'heure *(f.)*, BV; *(in a series)* la fois, 10.2; le temps
(for) a long time longtemps, 11.1
at the same time à la fois
at what time? à quelle heure?, 2
in a short time en très peu de temps
it's time that il est temps que, **13**
on time à l'heure, 8.1
time difference le décalage horaire
times l'époque *(f.)*
What time is it? Il est quelle heure?, BV
timetable l'horaire *(m.)*
tip le bout; *(restaurant)* le pourboire, 5.2
to leave a tip laisser un pourboire, 5.2
The tip is included. Le service est compris., 5.2
tire le pneu, **7.1**
flat tire le pneu à plat, **7.1**
spare tire la roue de secours, **7.1**
tired fatigué(e)
tissue le kleenex, **2.1**
to à, 3.1; à destination de *(plane, train, etc.)*, 8.1; *(in order to)* pour
(up) to jusqu'à

toast le pain grillé
to **toast** porter un toast à
tobacco shop le bureau de tabac
today aujourd'hui, BV; de nos jours
toe le doigt de pied, **8.1**
together ensemble, 5.1
to get together with retrouver
toilet paper le papier hygiénique, **9.2**
toll le péage, **7.2**
toll call l'appel interurbain
tomato la tomate, 6.2
tomorrow demain, BV
See you tomorrow. À demain., BV
tonight ce soir
tonsillitis l'angine *(f.)*, **2.1**
too *(also)* aussi, 1.1; *(excessive)* trop, 2.1
tool l'outil *(m.)*
tooth la dent
toothbrush la brosse à dents, 12.1
toothpaste le dentifrice, 12.1
totally complètement; totalement
to **touch** toucher, 10.2
to be in touch with être en contact avec
touch-tone telephone le téléphone à touches, **3.2**
tourist le/la touriste
tourist office le bureau de (du) tourisme; le syndicat d'initiative
toward vers
towel la serviette, 11.1, **9.2**
tower la tour, **11.1**
town la ville, 8.1, **5.2, 11.1;** le village
in town en ville, **11.1**
small town le village
town hall la mairie, **12.2, 14.1**
toxic toxique
toy le jouet

track la piste, 10.2; *(railroad)* la voie, 9.1
track and field l'athlétisme *(m.)*, 10.2
trade le métier, **14.1;** le commerce
tradition la tradition
traditional traditionnel(le)
traffic la circulation
traffic circle le rond-point, **7.2, 11.1**
traffic jam le bouchon, **7.2**
traffic light le feu, **7.2, 11.1**
traffic ticket la contravention, **7.2**
tragedy la tragédie
tragic tragique
train le train, 9.1
train station la gare, 9.1
train station restaurant le buffet, 9.1
traitor le traître, la traîtresse
to **transform** transformer
to **transmit** transmettre, **3.1**
to **transport** transporter
transportation le transport
traveler le voyageur, la voyageuse, 9.1
tray le plateau, 8.2
treasure le trésor, L4
to **treat** traiter
treatment le traitement
tree l'arbre *(m.)*, L3
trigonometry la trigonométrie, 2.2
trip le voyage, 8.1; le trajet, **10.2**
to take a trip faire un voyage, 8.1
trombone le trombone, **12.1**
tropical tropical(e)
trouble: to be in trouble être en difficulté
truck le camion, **7.1**
small truck la camionnette
true vrai(e), 2.2
trumpet la trompette, **12.1**
truth la vérité

to **try on** essayer, 7.2
T-shirt le t-shirt, 7.1
Tuesday mardi *(m.)*, BV
tuna le thon
tunic la tunique
Tunisian tunisien(ne)
tunnel le tunnel
turkey le dindon; la dinde
turn signal le clignotant, **7.2**
to **turn** tourner, **7.2**
to turn around faire demi-tour, **11.1**
to turn off *(appliance)* éteindre, 12.2, **3.1**
to turn on *(appliance)* mettre, 7; allumer, 12.2, **3.1**
turnstile le tourniquet, **10.1**
TV la télé, 12.2
on TV à la télé, 12.2
twin le jumeau, la jumelle, L1
to **twist** *(one's knee, etc.)* se tordre, **8.1**
type le type, la sorte, le genre, **1.1**
to **type** taper
typical typique
typically typiquement

uncle l'oncle *(m.)*, 4.1
under sous, 8.2
underground souterrain(e)
to **understand** comprendre, 5
to **unearth** déterrer
unemployed au chômage, **14.2**
unemployed person le chômeur, la chômeuse, **14.2**
unemployment le chômage, **14.2**
unfortunately malheureusement
unhappy malheureux, malheureuse

unit l'unité *(f.)*
United States les États-Unis *(m. pl.)*
university l'université *(f.)*
unknown inconnu(e)
to **unpack** défaire, **9.1**
until jusqu'à
up there là-haut
upset stomach le trouble digestif
use l'emploi *(m.)*
to **use** utiliser, **3.1;** se servir de, **3.2, L4**
useful utile
usually d'habitude, 12.2

to **vacate** libérer, **9.2**
vacation les vacances *(f. pl.)*
on vacation en vacances
summer vacation les grandes vacances
valid valable
to **validate** valider, **10.1**
valley la vallée; le val
value la valeur
vanilla *(adj.)* à la vanille, 5.1
varied varié(e)
variety la variété
various divers(e)
VCR le magnétoscope, 12.2
to **vary** varier
veal le veau, **6.2**
veal cutlet l'escalope *(f.)* de veau, **6.2**
vegetable le légume, 6.2, **6.1**
veil le voile
vein la veine
vengence la vengeance
to **verify** vérifier, 8.1
very très, BV; tout
very near tout près, 4.2
very well très bien, BV
victorious victorieux, victorieuse
victory la victoire
video la vidéo, 3.1
movie video le film en vidéo, **1.1**
videocassette la cassette vidéo, 12.2
Vietnamese vietnamien(ne), 6
view la vue
village le village
vinegar le vinaigre, 6.1
vineyard le vignoble, **11.2**
violin le violon
viral viral(e)
virus le virus
visit la visite
to **visit** *(a place)* visiter, **1.2;** *(a person)* rendre visite à
vitamin la vitamine
voice la voix
volleyball le volley(-ball), 10.2
volunteer le/la bénévole; le/la volontaire
voyage le voyage

to **wait (for)** attendre, 9.1
to wait in line faire la queue, 9.1
waiter le serveur, 5.1
waiting room la salle d'attente, 9.1
waitress la serveuse, 5.1
walk la promenade, 11.1
to take a walk faire une promenade, 11.1
to **walk** marcher, **8.1**
walkway le passage piéton
wall le mur, L4
to **want** désirer, vouloir, avoir envie de
war la guerre, L3
war zone la zone de conflit
warm chaud(e)
warmup suit le survêtement, 7.1
warrior le guerrier, L3
to **wash** se laver, 12.1; faire sa toilette
to wash one's hair (face, etc.) se laver les cheveux (la figure, etc.), 12.1
washcloth le gant de toilette, 12.1, **9.2**
waste le déchet
watch la montre, **L1**
to **watch** surveiller, **7.2**
Watch out! Attention!, 4.2
water l'eau *(f.)*, 6.2
to **water-ski** faire du ski nautique, 11.1
way la façon
weak faible, L1
weapon l'arme *(f.)*
to **wear** porter, 7.1
weather le temps, 11.1
Web site le site
wedding le mariage, **12.2**
wedding ring l'alliance *(f.)*, **12.2**
Wednesday mercredi *(m.)*, BV
week la semaine, 3.2
a week huit jours
a (per) week par semaine, 3.2
last week la semaine dernière, 10.2
next week la semaine prochaine
two weeks quinze jours
weekend le week-end
to **weigh** peser, **5.2**
weight le poids
welcome le/la bienvenu(e)
Welcome! Bienvenue!
You're welcome. Je t'en prie. *(fam.)*, BV; Je vous en prie. *(form.)*, BV
well bien, BV; eh bien; ben *(slang)*
well then alors, BV
well-behaved bien élevé(e), **13.1;** sage, **12.2**

well-done *(meat)* bien cuit(e), 5.2
well-known connu(e), **1.1**
well-mannered bien élevé(e), **13.1**
well-to-do aisé(e)
west l'ouest *(m.)*
western occidental(e)
western *(movie)* le western
wheat le blé, **11.2**
wheelchair le fauteuil roulant, **8.1**
when quand, 4.1
where où, 1.1
from where d'où, 1.1
which quel(le), 6
to **whistle** siffler, 10.1, **L1**
white blanc, blanche, 7.2
who qui, 1.1
whole *(adj.)* entier, entière; *(n.)* l'ensemble *(m.)*
whole-wheat bread le pain complet
whom qui, 10
why pourquoi, 6.2
why not? pourquoi pas?
wide large, 7.2
wife la femme, 4.1
to **win** gagner, 10.1; sortir victorieux (victorieuse)
wind le vent, 11.1
window *(seat)* (une place) côté fenêtre, 8.1
window *(store)* la vitrine, 7.1
windshield le pare-brise, **7.1**
windsurfing la planche à voile, 11.1
to go windsurfing faire de la planche à voile, 11.1
windy: It's windy. Il y a du vent., 11.1
wine le vin
winner le/la gagnant(e), 10.2
winner's cup la coupe, 10.2
winter l'hiver *(m.)*, 11.2
to **wipe** essuyer, **L2**
wise sage
wish le désir
to **wish** souhaiter, **9.1, 12.2**
with avec, 3.2; auprès de; muni(e) de
to **withdraw** retirer, **5.1**
without sans; sans que
woman la femme, 7.1
wood le bois
word le mot
words *(of song, etc.)* les paroles *(f. pl.)*
work le travail; *(of art or literature)* l'œuvre *(f.)*, **1.1;** l'ouvrage *(m.)*
to **work** travailler, 3.1, **14.2**
to work full-time (part-time) travailler à plein temps (à mi-temps), **14.2**
worker l'ouvrier, l'ouvrière, **11.1**
workplace le lieu de travail, **14.1**
world le monde
worry l'inquiétude *(f.)*
to **worry** s'en faire, **8.1**
wound la blessure, **8.1**
wounded blessé(e)
wrist le poignet, **13.1**
to **write** écrire, 9.2; rédiger
to write a prescription faire une ordonnance, **2.2**
writer l'écrivain *(m.)*, L2, **14.1**
wrong mauvais(e), 2.2
What's wrong? Qu'est-ce qui ne va pas?
What's wrong with him? Qu'est-ce qu'il a?, **2.1**
wrong number l'erreur *(f.)*; le mauvais numéro, **3.2**

x-ray la radio(graphie), **8.2**

year l'an *(m.)*, 4.1; l'année *(f.)*
yellow jaune, 7.2
yes oui, BV; si *(after neg. question)*, 7.2
yesterday hier, 10.1
the day before yesterday avant-hier, 10.2
yogurt la yaourt, 6.1
young jeune
young people les jeunes *(m. pl.)*
younger le cadet, la cadette, L1
youth la jeunesse
youth hostel l'auberge *(f.)* de jeunesse

to **zap** zapper, 12.2
zero zéro
zip code le code postal, **5.2**
zone la zone
zoology la zoologie

Credits

COVER (top to bottom)Bro Brannhage/Panoramic Images, (b)Mark Segal/Panoramic Images, (c)Sylvain Gradadam, (students)Philippe Gontier; **iv** José Fuste/The Stock Market; **v** (l)K. N'Dour/Liaison Agency, (r)AFP/CORBIS; **vi** (tl)Timothy Fuller, (tr)Ch. Viojard/Liaison Agency, (b)Curt Fischer; **vii** (l)A. Schroeder/Reporters-DIAF, (r)P. Dannic/DIAF; **viii** (t)Marge/Sunset, (b)Aaron Haupt; **ix** (tl b)Larry Hamill, (tr)Michael Agliolo/International Stock; **x** (tl)Leyreloup/Wallis Phototheque, (tr)Larry Hamill, (b)J.D. Sudres/DIAF; **xi** Tom Craig/FPG; **xii** (l)Michael Krasovitz/FPG, (r)Winston Fraser; **xiii** (l)Macduff Everton/The Image Works, (r)Steven Ferry; **xiv** (l)Mark Antman, (r)Tony Savino/The Image Works; **xv** (t)Camille Moirenc/DIAF, (b)PhotoDisc; **xvi** (tl)Jacques Brinon/AP/Wide World Photos, (tr)A. Ramey/PhotoEdit, (b)Melissa Gerr; **xvii** (l)Stuart Cohen/The Image Works, (r)Timothy Fuller; **xviii** Coo Lwa-Dann Tardif/The Stock Market; **xix** Dave G. Houser; **xxxvi–R1** Robert Fried; **R2** (tl br)Catherine et Bernard Desjeux, (tr)Aaron Haupt, (cl cr bl)Curt Fischer; **R3** (t)Wayne Rowe, (b)John Evans; **R4** (t)José Fuste/The Stock Market, (b)Matt Meadows; **R5** (l)Everton/The Image Works, (r)Sylva Villerot/DIAF; **R6** The Purcell Team/CORBIS; **R7** (t)Robert Fried, (b)Beryl Goldberg; **R8** (t)Timothy Fuller, (b)Owen Franken/CORBIS; **R9** (t)Michael Yamashita/CORBIS, (b)Tim Courlas; **R10–R11** Guy Durand/DIAF; **R12** (t)Stuart Cohen/The Image Works, (c)Jorge Ramirez/International Stock, (b)Michelle Chaplow; **R13** (t)Pictor, (cl)Amanita Pictures, (cr)Curt Fischer; **R14** (t)Morton Beebe, SF/CORBIS, (bl)Catherine et Bernard Desjeux, (br)Matt Meadows; **R15** Duchene/Wallis Phototheque; **R16** Mark Antman; **R17** Steven Needham/Envision; **R18** Beryl Goldberg; **R20–R21** Michael Busselle/CORBIS; **R22** (l)Robert Fried, (r)Catherine et Bernard Desjeux; **R23** Robert Holmes/CORBIS; **R24** (t)Roberto Soncin Gerometta/Photo 20–20/PictureQuest, (b)Matt Meadows; **R25** Brooks Walker/Envision; **R26** O. Baumgartner/Sygma CORBIS; **R27** (t)Robert Fried, (b)Curt Fischer; **R28–R29** SuperStock; **R30** (t c)Larry Hamill, (bl)Icone/The Image Works, (br)Larry Hamill; **R31** (l)courtesy Air France, (r)D. Cordier/Sunset; **R32** (l)B.B. Holding/Sunset, (r)Larry Hamill; **R33** Courtesy Air France; **R34** Larry Hamill; **R35** José Nicolas/Hèmisphéres Images; **R36–R37** J. Langevin/Teamsport/Sygma CORBIS; **R38** (tl)Pawel Wysocki/Hèmisphéres Images, (tr)Garufi/Wallis Phototheque, (c)Charlier/Wallis Phototheque, (bl)Amwell/Stone, (br)J. Christophe Pratt/DIAF; **R39** (l)SuperStock, (tr)Patrick Somelet/DIAF, (br)Amwell/Stone; **R40** (l)Larry Hamill, (r)Stone; **R41** Alain Gaveau; **R42** (t)Camille Moirenc/DIAF, (b)Tim Gibson/Envision; **R43** Chris Harvey/Stone; **R44** (t)Iconos/DIAF, (b)Ron Angle/Liaison Agency; **R45** J.Ch. Gerard/DIAF; **R46–R47** David Simson/Stock Boston/PictureQuest; **R48** (tl tr)Larry Hamill, (b)R. Sidney/The Image Works; **R49** (t)Stuart Cohen/The Image Works, (b)Larry Hamill; **R50** Larry Hamill; **R51** John Evans; **R54** J. Sierpinski/DIAF; **R56** (t)Rick Souders/Index Stock, (b)Larry Hamill; **R58** British Museum, London/Bridgeman Art Library, London/SuperStock; **R58–1** Mark Burnett; **2** Timothy Fuller; **3** (t)Timothy Fuller, (bl)SuperStock, (br)Pictor; **4** (t)Timothy Fuller, (b)John Evans; **5** Mark Burnett; **7** Timothy Fuller; **8** Giraudon/Art Resource, NY; **9** ©Photo RMN—Hervé Lewandowski/Musée D'Orsay; **10** Jacques Sierpinski/DIAF; **11** Scala/Art Resource, NY; **12** Timothy Fuller; **13** (l)file photo, (r)Monika Graff/The Image Works; **14** Yann Arthus-Bertrand/CORBIS; **15** (l)Monika Graff/The Image Works, (r)Peter McCabe/The Image Works; **16** (t)J. Marc Laccerand/Wallis Phototheque, (b)©Photo RMN—Hervé Lewandowski/Musée D'Orsay; **17** Vanni/Art Resource, NY; **18** Larry Hamill; **20** (l)Derek Croucher/The Stock Market, (r)Larry Hamill; **21** (t)AFP/CORBIS, (c)Ramsay/Wallis Phototheque, (b)Gérard Lacz/Sunset; **22** (t)Jason Laure, (b)Hilarie Kavanagh/Stone; **23** (tl)Neal Preston/CORBIS, (tr)Mark Burnett, (b)K. N'Dour/Liaison Agency; **24–25** (bkgd)Steve Cole/PhotoDisc; **25** (t)Robbie Jack/CORBIS, (c)AFP/CORBIS, (b)Stéphane Cardinale/Sygma CORBIS; **26** (t)Robert Fried, (b)Larry Hamill; **27** Timothy Fuller; **29** Curt Fischer; **30** (l)Robbie Jack/CORBIS, (tr)Mark Burnett, (br)Larry Hamill; **31** (tl bl)Greg Bond, videographer, South Park Productions, Inc., (r)Zefa/Index Stock; **32** Roger-Viollet, Paris/Bridgeman Art Library; **32–33** Stefano Bianchetti/CORBIS; **34** (tr br)Aaron Haupt, (tc)John Evans, (others)Timothy Fuller; **35** Timothy Fuller; **36** Curt Fischer; **37** Mark Burnett; **38** Timothy Fuller; **39** (tl tr)Larry Hamill, (others)Timothy Fuller; **40** (t)John Evans, (b)Timothy Fuller; **42** (l r)Catherine et Bernard Desjeux, (c)Image Club Graphics; **44** (t)Timothy Fuller, (b)Larry Hamill; **47** Ken Karp; **49** (t)Adina Tovy/Photo 20-20, (bl)Monika Graff/The Image Works, (br)Ken Karp; **50** Timothy Fuller; **51** (l)Monika Graff/The Image Works, (r)Ken Karp; **52 54** Timothy Fuller; **55** (l)Ch. Vioujard/Liaison Agency, (r)SuperStock; **56** (cl)Curt Fischer, (cr)Mark Burnett, (b)Clasen/Wallis Phototheque; **56–57** (bkgd)Mitch Hrdlicka/PhotoDisc; **57** (t)Catherine Panchout/Stone, (b)Larry Hamill; **59** (t)Larry Hamill, (b)P. Wysocki/Explorer; **60** Curt Fischer; **62** (t)Timothy Fuller, (bl)John Evans, (br)Mark Burnett; **63** (tl bl)Greg Bond, videographer, South Park Productions, Inc., (r)Mark Burnett; **64** Galerie Daniel Malingue, Paris/Bridgeman Art Library; **64–65** P. Savin/CORBIS Sygma; **66 67 68** Larry Hamill; **69** (t)Curt Fischer, (b)Larry Hamill; **70** (cell phone)PhotoDisc, (coins)Mathias Kulka/The Stock Market, (others)Larry Hamill; **71** Larry Hamill; **72** (t)Larry Hamill, (b)Mark Burnett; **73** A. Schroeder/Reporters-DIAF; **76** Travelpix/FPG; **77** (t)C. Vaisse/Hoa Qui, (b)Patrick Somelat/DIAF; **78** Aaron Haupt; **79** (t)Roger-Viollet, (b)Larry Hamill; **81** Grant V. Faint/The Image Bank; **82 83** Larry Hamill; **84** (l)Sylva Villerot/DIAF, (c r)Larry Hamill; **85** Larry Hamill; **86** (t)Hallé/Marco Polo, (c)Larry Hamill, (b)Suzanne Murphy-Larronde; **87** Larry Hamill; **88** file photo; **88–89** PhotoDisc; **89** (t c)P. Dannic/DIAF, (b)Larry Hamill; **90** (l)A. Schroeder/DIAF, (r)Larry Hamill; **91** Vincent Gauvreau; **92** (t)Curt Fischer, (b)Timothy Fuller; **95** (tl bl)Greg Bond, videographer, South Park Productions, Inc., (r)Duprat/Wallis Phototheque; **96** (b)Musée d'Orsay, Paris/AKG, Berlin/SuperStock; **96–97** Georgia Bowater/The Stock Market; **98** (t)Patrick Bedout, (c)Robert Fried, (b)Larry Hamill; **99** David Barnes/The Stock Market; **100** (t)Dave Bartruff/CORBIS, (b)Mark Burnett; **102** (t)Barret/Wallis Phototheque, (others)Larry Hamill; **103** Stéphane Frances/Hèmisphéres Images; **104** Larry Hamill; **105** Tom Hussey/The Image Bank; **106** Patrick Ward/CORBIS; **107** (t)Manfred Mehlig/Stone, (b)Mark Antman/The Image Works; **108** Andre Jenny/Focus Group/PictureQuest; **110** Andrew Payti; **112** Peetit/Wallis Phototheque; **114** (t)Michele Burgess/The Stock Market, (b)Alain Choisnet/The Image Bank; **115** Guido A. Rossi/The Image Bank; **116** (t)Peter Turnley/CORBIS, (bl br)Aaron Haupt; **117** Stéphane Frances/Hèmisphéres Images; **118** Marge/Sunset; **119** (t)Paul Almasy/AKG London, (b)Marge/Sunset; **120** (t)Art Wolfe/Stone, (c)Cosmo Condina/Stone, (b)Hans Wolf/The Image Bank; **121** (t)Stéphane Frances/Hèmisphéres Images, (b)Olivier Blaise/Liaison Agency; **122** D. Thierry/DIAF; **122–123** (bkgd)CORBIS; **123** (t)José F. Poblete/CORBIS, (bl)Roger Wood/CORBIS, (br)SuperStock; **124** (l)David Ball/Stone, (r)Larry Hamill; **127** Wayne Rowe; **128** (t)David Barnes/The Stock Market, (bl)Manfred Mehlig/Stone, (br)Alain Choisnet/The Image Bank; **129** (tl bl)Greg Bond, videographer, South Park Productions, Inc., (r)Index Stock Imagery; 130 Larry Hamill; **132** (l)Stuart Cohen/The Image Works, (r)Reunion des Musées Nationaux/Art Resource, NY; **135** Larry Hamill; **136** (tl)Bruno De Hogues/Stone, (tr)Todd Gipstein, National Geographic Image Collection, (bl)Bob Handelman/Stone, (br)Francois Ducasse/Rapho/Photo Researchers; **136–137** (bkgd)Bruce Dale, National Geographic Image Collection; **137** (t)Kell-/Mooney Photography, (b)Michael Busselle/CORBIS; **138** (tl)Michael Busselle/Stone, (tr)Michel Viard/Peter Arnold, Inc., (bl)Herve Donnezan, (br)Michael Boys/Stone; **138–139** (bkgd)Pictor; **139** (l)Ric Ergenbright/Stone, (r)Pictor; **140** Kunsthaus, Zurich/Giraudon, Paris/SuperStock; **140–141** Matthieu Colin/Hèmisphéres Images; **142** (tl)Peter Weber/Stone, (tc tr bl)Larry Hamill, (br)Icone/The Image Works; **143** Larry Hamill; **144** (t)Larry Hamill, (b)William Whitehurst/The Stock Market; **145** (t)Larry Hamill, (b)Stéphane Frances/Hèmisphéres Images; **146** Larry Hamill; **147** (tl)Wayne Rowe, (tr bl br)Larry Hamill;

148 (tl)Curt Fischer, (tc b)Larry Hamill, (tr)Mark Burnett, (c)Catherine et Bernard Desjeux; **150 151** Larry Hamill; **152** (t)Sylvain Grandadam/Stone, (bl br)Monika Graf/The Image Works; **153** Robert Fried; **154** Aaron Haupt and Jeff Malony/PhotoDisc; **156** Richard Laird/FPG; **157 158** Larry Hamill; **159** Diagentur/Sunset; **160** Larry Hamill; **161** (l)Mark Burnett, (r)Larry Hamill; **162** (t)Paul Thompson/International Stock, (b)Michael Agliolo/International Stock; **163** (t)Stuart Cohen/The Image Works, (b)Larry Hamill; **164** (t)file photo, (b)Bernard Regent/DIAF; **164–165** (bkgd)file photo; **168** (tl tr)Peter Weber/Stone, (b)Larry Hamill; **170** Larry Hamill; **171** (tl bl)Greg Bond, videographer, South Park Productions, Inc., (r)Werner Forman/CORBIS; **172** Hermitage Museum, St. Petersburg/SuperStock; **172–173** Jean-Claude Amiel/Saula/Liaison Agency; **174** (t)Stan Ries/International Stock, (bl br)Larry Hamill; **175** Larry Hamill; **176** (t)Larry Hamill, (b)Rita Maas/The Image Bank; **177 178 179** Larry Hamill; **180** (l)Larry Hamill, (r)Tina Buckman/Index Stock; **181** (t)Larry Hamill, (b)Simeone Huber/Stone; **183** (t)Victor Scocozza/FPG, (b)Judy Buie/Bruce Coleman, Inc.; **184** J.D. Sudres/DIAF; **186** Larry Hamill; **188** Andrew Payti; **190** Catherine et Bernard Desjeux; **192** Larry Hamill; **193** (l)Larry Hamill, (r)J.D. Sudres/DIAF; **194** (l)Larry Hamill, (r)Michael Boys/CORBIS; **195** Larry Hamill; **196** (t)Hulton Archives/Stone, (b)Giraudon/Art Resource, NY; **196–197** (bkgd) file photo; **197** (t)Reunion des Musées Nationaux/Art Resource, NY, (b)H. Gyssels/DIAF; **198** Leyreloup/Wallis Phototheque; **199** Jeanetta Baker/Photobank/Sunset; **201** Rosine Mazin/DIAF; **202** Larry Hamill; **203** (tl bl)Greg Bond, videographer, South Park Productions, Inc., (r)Melissa Gerr; **204** AKG London; **204–205** Edouard Berne/Stone; **206** (tl)IPA/The Image Works, (tr)Dean Siracusa/FPG, (cl)Stuart Cohen/The Image Works, (cr)Alain Gaveau, (b)Larry Hamill; **207** Steven Ferry; **208** (cl)J.M. Leligny/DIAF, (others)Larry Hamill; **209** (t)T.H. Werbung/Sunset, (b)Mark Burnett; **211** Mark Burnett; **212** (tr)Hans Wolf/The Image Bank, (br)Gerard Gsell/DIAF, (others)Mark Burnett; **213** Mark Burnett; **215** (t)Gail Mooney/CORBIS, (b)Max Hunn/FPG; **218** Andrew Payti; **219** Mark Burnett; **221** Ken Karp; **222** Patrick Bedout; **223** Curt Fischer; **224** Joachim Messerschmidt/FPG; **225** (t)Mark Burnett, (b)Pete Turner/The Image Bank; **226** (t)Holt Studios/Sunset, (b)T.H. Werbung/Sunset; **227** (t)Bertrand Rieger/Hèmisphéres Images, (b)Lorne Resnick/Stone; **228–229** (bkgd) Kent Knudson/PhotoLink/PhotoDisc; **229** Tom Craig/FPG; **230** (t)Daniel Perret/La Photothéque, (b)Mark Burnett; **233** Wayne Rowe; **234** Larry Hamill; **235** (tl bl)Greg Bond, videographer, South Park Productions, Inc., (r)Yann Arthus-Bertrand/CORBIS; **236** (t)Steven Ferry, (b)Gilles Bassignac/Liaison Agency; **238** Joe Carini/The Image Works; **240** Arthur Beck/The Stock Market; **241** Xavier Yestelin/Liaison Agency; **242** (tl)Rohan/Stone, (tr)Hans Georg Roth/CORBIS, (bl)Lonely Planet Images, (br)Frances Linzee Gordon/Lonely Planet Images; **242–243** (bkgd)Wolfgang Kaehler/CORBIS; **243** (t)Paul Stepan-Vierow/Photo Researchers, (b)Sidi Brahim/Woodfin Camp & Associates; **244** (tl tr)Nik Wheeler/CORBIS, (bl)John Beatty/Stone, (br)Sandro Vannini/CORBIS; **244–245** (bkgd)Nicholas DeVore/Stone; **245** (t)G. Boutin, Explorer, (b)Glen Allison/Stone; **246** Giraudon/Art Resource, NY; **246–247** P. Moulu/Sunset; **248** Steven Ferry; **249** (t)John Evans, (bl br)Aaron Haupt; **251** J.P. Porcher/Sunset; **252** (tl tr)Steven Ferry, (others)Aaron Haupt; **253** (t)V. Audet/Sunset, (b) Yoav Levy/PhotoTake; **254** Michael Krasowitz/FPG; **255** B. Yarvin/Sunset; **257** Mark Burnett; **258** Curt Fischer; **259** (bl)Peter McCabe/The Image Works, (others) Ken Karp; **260** (l)Peter McCabe/The Image Works, (r)Ken Karp; **262** Larry Hamill; **263** TRIP/P. Rauter; **264** Steven Ferry; **265** (t)Steven Ferry, (b)Infra/La Photothéque; **266** (l)Ulrike Welsch, (r)Steven Ferry; **267** (b)Mark Burnett; **268** Frank Fournier/Contact Press/PictureQuest; **270** (t)Mark Burnett, (b)The Image Works; **270–271** (bkgd)PhotoLink/PhotoDisc; **271** (t)Jean-Loup Charmet/Science Photo Library/Photo Researchers, (b)Ch. Viojard/Liaison Agency; **272** Winston Fraser; **276** B. Yarvin/Sunset; **277** (tl bl)Greg Bond, videographer, South Park Productions, Inc., (r)Ch. Vioujard/Liaison Agency; **278** Portal Gallery Ltd/Bridgeman Art Library; **278–279** Wolfgang Kaehler/CORBIS; **280 281 282** Steven Ferry; **284** (t)Catherine et Bernard Desjeux, (bl)Photo FERNAND/Sunset, (br)Steven Ferry; **285** Steven Ferry; **286** Peter Vanderwarker/Stock Boston; **287** (t)Macduff Everton/The Image Works, (b)M. Ajuria/Sunset; **289** Gerald Buthaud/Woodfin Camp & Associates; **290** Steven Ferry; **292** Photo Gabrielle/Treal/Liaison Agency; **294** Steven Ferry; **296** (t)Bruno Bebert/Liaison Agency, (b)Nik Wheeler/CORBIS; **297** (t)Joachim Messerschmidt/FPG, (b c)SuperStock; **298** Bruno Bebert/Liaison Agency; **299** Robert Fried/Stock Boston; **300** (l)Stuart Cohen/The Image Works, (r)Maurice Smith/La Photothéque SDP; **300–301** (bkgd)CORBIS; **301** (t)Mark Burnett, (bl)Beryl Goldberg, (br)David Barnes/La Photothéque SDP; **302** Camille Moirenc/DIAF; **303** Larry Hamill; **305** Mark Antman; **306** M. Ajuria/Sunset; **307** (tl bl)Greg Bond, videographer, South Park Productions, Inc., (r)Peter Menzel/Stock Boston; **308** Manu Sassoonian/Art Resource, NY; **308–309** Betty Press/Woodfin Camp & Associates/PictureQuest; **310** Steven Ferry; **311** (l)Robert Holmes/CORBIS, (r)Catherine et Bernard Desjeux; **312** (tl)Franck Dunouau/SDP-DIAF, (tr)Stephen Studd/Stone, (bl br)Larry Hamill; **314** Philippe Gontier/The Image Works; **315** (tl tr)Steven Ferry, (b)Catherine et Bernard Desjeux; **316** Larry Hamill; **317** (t)Larry Hamill, (bl)Rosine Mazin/DIAF, (bc)Tom Craig/FPG, (br)Marc Verin/DIAF; **319** (t)Larry Hamill, (b)Steven Ferry; **320** (t)Andrew Payti, (b)G. Martin Raget/Wallis Phototheque; **322** Larry Hamill; **323** SuperStock; **324** Curt Fischer; **325** (tl)Pierre Schwartz/Sunset, (tr)Gerard Gsell/DIAF, (bl)Toyohiro Yamada/FPG, (br)Jon Lawrence/Stone; **326** (l)Peter Gridley/FPG, (r)Jacques Kerebel/DIAF; **328** (t)Tony Savino/The Image Works, (b)Sandro Vannini/CORBIS; **329** Andrew Payti; **330** (t)F. Astier/Sygma CORBIS, (c)Doug Armand/Stone, (b)Larry Hamill; **330–331** (bkgd)Neil Beer/PhotoDisc; **331 332** Larry Hamill; **335** Mark Antman; **336** (l)Rosine Mazin/DIAF, (c)Philippe Gontier/The Image Works, (r)SuperStock; **337** (tl bl)Greg Bond, videographer, South Park Productions, Inc., (r)Steven Ferry; **338** Charles Lenars/CORBIS; **338–339** Joe Cornish/Stone; **340** (tl)P. Moulu/Sunset, (tr)S. Chatenay/Sunset, (c)D. Ermakoff/The Image Works, (b)Stuart Cohen/The Image Works; **341** (tl b)Timothy Fuller, (tr cl)Robert Fried, (cr)Paul Almasy/CORBIS; **342** Robert Fried; **343** (t)Telegraph Colour Library/FPG, (b)Gerard Lacz/Sunset; **344** (tl)B. Rowland/The Image Works, (tr)Serge Coupe/La Photothéque SDP, (bl)Ian Shaw/Stone, (br)Robert Fried; **345** (tl tr)Timothy Fuller, (c bl br)PhotoDisc; **346** (t)Alain Marcay/La Photothéque, (b)STF/Sunset; **347** Leroy H. Mantell/The Stock Market; **349** (l)Esbin-Anderson/The Image Works, (r)Larry Hamill; **350** Suzanne & Nick Geary/Stone; **351 352** Larry Hamill; **353** (t)Capel/Sunset, (bl)Camille Moirenc/DIAF, (br)Walter Bibikow/FPG; **354** (l)Larry Hamill, (r)John Elk III; **355** (t)Lanthiez/Wallis Phototheque, (b)Frances S/Photo Researchers; **356** (l)Michael Dwyer/Stock Boston, (r)Gilles Rouget/La Photothéque; **357** (tl)Phillippe Renault/Hèmisphéres Images, (tr)Dave G. Houser, (b)SuperStock; **358** Camille Moirenc/DIAF; **358–359** Roger K. Burnard; **359** David Turnley/CORBIS; **360** Robert Fried; **361** (l)Earl Kogler/International Stock, (r)Farrell Grehan/CORBIS; **363** Curt Fischer; **364** (l)STF/Sunset, (r)Leroy H. Mantell/The Stock Market; **365** (tl bl)Greg Bond, videographer, South Park Productions, Inc., (r)Gerard Gsell/DIAF; **366 367** Timothy Fuller; **368** (t)Charlie Waite/Panoramic Images, (b)Aaron Haupt; **369** (t)Nik Wheeler/CORBIS, (b)John Elk III; **370** (tl)Michael Yada, (tr)Robin Hill/Southern Stock/PictureQuest, (bl)Philip Gould/CORBIS, (br)Andre Jenny/Focus Group/PictureQuest; **370–371** (bkgd)Andre Gallant/The Image Bank; **371** James P. Blair; **372** (tl)Philip Gould/CORBIS, (tr)Robert Fried/Stock Boston/PictureQuest, (bl)Paul Thompson/Eye Ubiquitous/CORBIS, (br)B. Stichelbaut/Masterfile; **372–373** (bkgd)Marc Garanger/CORBIS; **373** (t)Bob Krist/CORBIS, (b)Christopher Morris/Black Star/PictureQuest; **374** Bridgeman Art Library; **374–375** Kelly-Mooney Photography/CORBIS; **376** (tl)Remy de la Mauviniere/AP//Wide World Photos, (tr)Vince Streano/CORBIS, (cl)Curt Fischer, (cr)AFP/CORBIS, (b)Ary Diesendruck/

Credits

Stone; **377** (l)Reuters/Eric Gaillard/Archive Photos, (tr)TRIP/N. Ray, (br)Charles Lenars/CORBIS; **378** (tl)Phyllis Picardi/Stock Boston, (tc)Gail Mooney/CORBIS, (tr)Beryl Goldberg, (bl)PhotoDisc, (br)AFP/CORBIS; **379** (l)Philip Gould/CORBIS, (r)Rosine Mazin/DIAF; **380** (tl)Owen Franken/CORBIS, (tr)Patrick Somelet/DIAF, (c)Mark Antman, (b)M. Rougemont/Sygma CORBIS; **381** (rings)Bernsau/The Image Works, (others)Timothy Fuller; **382** (l)Japack/Sunset, (r)E. Rossolin/Wallis Phototheque; **383** (t)Michael Shay/FPG, (b)Tom McCarthy/PhotoEdit; **386** (t)G.Guittot/DIAF, (b)Bernard Boutrit/Woodfin Camp & Associates; **387** Chris Duranti/Wallis Phototheque; **389** O. Nicolas/Sygma CORBIS; **390** (t)J. Sierpinski/DIAF, (b)Timothy Fuller; **391** Bob Daemmrich/The Image Works; **392** (r)Robert Fried, (l)Mark Antman/The Image Works; **393** (t)A. Ramey/PhotoEdit, (b)Timothy Fuller; **394** (t)J.J.Ch. Gerard/DIAF, (b)Melissa Gerr; **395** (t)Nathan Benn/CORBIS, (c)Mark Antman/The Image Works, (b)Melissa Gerr; **396** (l)FPG, (r)Dave G. Houser; **396–397** (bkgd)Aaron Haupt; **397** (t)North Wind Picture Archives, (b)John Elk III; **398** (l)J.J.Ch. Gerard/DIAF, (r)D. Cordier/Sunset; **399** Jean du Boisberranger/Hèmisphéres Images; **400** (tl tr br)Mark Antman, (bl)Curt Fischer; **401** Jacques Brinon/AP/Wide World Photos; **402** (t)Philip Gould/CORBIS, (b)Bernsau/The Image Bank; **403** (tl bl)Greg Bond, videographer, South Park Productions, Inc., (r)Pratt-Pries/DIAF; **404** AKG London; **404–405** Larry Hamill; **406 407** Timothy Fuller; **408** (t)Timothy Fuller, (b)Larry Hamill; **409** (t)Stuart Cohen/The Image Works, (b)Robert Fried; **411** Timothy Fuller; **412** (t)Stuart Cohen/The Image Works, (c)Timothy Fuller, (others)Mark Burnett; **413** Terry Sutherland; **415** (t)Timothy Fuller, (b)Thomas Jullein/DIAF; **417** (t)Mark Burnett, (b)Larry Hamill; **420** Timothy Fuller; **422** (l)Timothy Fuller, (r)Larry Hamill; **423** (t)Catherine et Bernard Desjeux, (b)Patrick Ward/Stock Boston/PictureQuest; **424** (t)David Hall/Masterfile, (b)Timothy Fuller; **425** Alex Wasinski/FPG; **426** Mark Burnett; **426–427** (bkgd)CORBIS; **429** (l)Larry Hamill, (r)Mark Burnett; **430 431** Wayne Rowe; **432** (t c)Timothy Fuller, (b)Stuart Cohen/The Image Works; **433** (tl bl)Greg Bond, videographer, South Park Productions, Inc., (r)Timothy Fuller; **434** SuperStock; **434–435** P. Thompson/Sunset; **436** (director) PhotoFest, (journalist)Beryl Goldberg, (others)Timothy Fuller; **437** Timothy Fuller; **439** (t)L. Zylberman/DIAF, (b)H. Gyssels/DIAF; **440 441** Timothy Fuller; **442** Coo Lwa-Dann Tardif/The Stock Market; **443** (t)Arnaud Fevrier/DIAF, (b)Timothy Fuller; **444** PhotoDisc; **445** (tl tr)Ken Karp, (bl)Victor Englebert, (br)Owen Franken/CORBIS; **446** SuperStock; **447** Pierre Goraz/DIAF; **448** Fotografia, Inc./CORBIS; **450** Timothy Fuller; **451** Sygma CORBIS; **452** (l)Beryl Goldberg, (r)The Peace Corps; **453** The Peace Corps; **454** (l)Vince Streano/CORBIS, (r)Margot Granitsas/The Image Works; **455** (t)Timothy Fuller, (cl)Aaron Haupt, (cr)PhotoDisc, (b)Mark Steinmetz; **456** (l)Timothy Fuller, (r)Alaine Le Bot/DIAF; **456–457** (bkgd)John A. Rizzo/PhotoDisc; **457** (l)Alaine Le Bot/DIAF, (r)L. Wiame/Sunset; **458** TRIP/B. Turner; **461** Brigit Koch/DIAF; **462** (t)Timothy Fuller, (b)L. Zylberman/DIAF; **463** (tl bl)Greg Bond, videographer, South Park Productions, Inc., (r)Owen Franken/CORBIS; **464 465** Timothy Fuller; **467** Robert Fried; **468** Curt Fischer; **469** (t)Monika Graf/The Image Works, (b)Ken Karp; **470** (tl)Gerard Del Vecchio/Stone, (tr)Macduff Everton, (bl)Rapa/Explorer, (br)Craig Aurness/CORBIS; **470–471** Tony Craddock/Stone; (t)Antoine Lorgnier/Masterfile, (b)Farrell Grehan/CORBIS; **472** (tl)Oliver Benn/Stone, (tr)Jodi Cobb, (bl)Cotton Coulson, (br)Alain Morovan/Liaison Agency; **472–473** Rapa/Explorer; **473** (l)Hideo Kurihara/Stone, (r)Wysocki/Explorer/Photo Researchers; **474–475** Dave G. Houser; **477** Henry Guttmann Collection/Hulton Archive; **478** file photo; **479** Timothy Fuller; **482** (t)file photo, (b)Marc & Evelyne Bernheim from Rapho-Guillumette/Woodfin Camp & Associates; **483** Chuck Cecil/Words & Pictures/PictureQuest; **484** Schomburg Center, The New York Public Library/Art Resource, NY; **484–485** Annabelle Lee Washington/SuperStock; **488** Hulton/Archive Photos; **489** Reuters New Media Inc./CORBIS; **490** Tom Hulce/PhotoFest; **491** Timothy Fuller; **493** Curt Fischer; **494** Bulloz; **495 496** Roger-Viollet; **497** (t)Larry Hamill, (b)Owen Franken/CORBIS; **498–H1** (bkgd)PhotoDisc, (bridge)SuperStock; **H2** (t)Timothy Fuller, (c)Pictor, (b)John Evans; **H3** H6 H7 Timothy Fuller; **H10** (t)Timothy Fuller, (cl cr)Larry Hamill, (bl br)Curt Fischer; **H12** (t c)Larry Hamill, (b)Icone/The Image Works; **H13** (t)Larry Hamill, (b)Stan Ries/International Stock; **H17** Larry Hamill; **H18** (t)Gerard/DIAF, (cr)Timothy Fuller, (cl bl br)PhotoDisc; **H19** Rosine Mazin/DIAF; **H20** (b)Timothy Fuller, (others)Mark Burnett; **H32** Sitki Tarlan/Panoramic Images.

In appreciation

Special thanks to the following for their cordial assistance and participation in the photo illustrations:

Aeroport Charles De Gaulle; Affinage du Val d'Yerres, Montgeron, Air Afrique, Air France, Banque de France, Café Les Deux Magots, Paris, Cafeteria Flunch Evry, Centre Commercial des Halles, Paris, Club Hyppique, Varennes Jarcy, Colleg de Montois, Donnemarie-Dontilly, College Pasteur de Brunoy, Cora Boussy Saint Antoine, Crep' Yerres, Creperie au Mystere de Carnac, Montgeron, Cuisines AJ, Yerres, Docteur Ponnoussamy, Electro Star, Bonneuil, Espace Photo, Vigneux, Fermelec de L'essonne, Galeries Lafayette, Hippopotamus, Horizon F.M., International School of Paris, Kosque du Palais Royal, Paris, Laboratoire d'Analyses Medicales des Godeaux, Le Restaurant Mona Lisa, Lycee Janson de Sailly, Lycee Louis-le-Grand, Maison de la Presse Montgeron, Maison de la Presse S.G.E.C., Evry, Marche des Champs Elysees, Musée d'Orsay, Paris, Musée du Louvre, Paris, Nicolas Dupont-Aignan/Depute Maire de Yerres, Pharmacie des Godeaux, Yerres, Pharmacie Laurence Dony, Yerres, Piscine de Brunoy, RATP, Relais-H Gare de Lyon, Restaurant Chez Paul, Restaurant le Clos Saint Jacques, Paris, Restaurant Procope, SAMU de Paris, SNCF-TGV, Yerres Ecole National de Musique et de Danse.

Glencoe would like to acknowledge the artists and agencies who participated in illustrating this program: Domenick D'Andrea; Fanny Mellet Berry represented by Anita Grien; Paul Casale; Jane McCreary; Ortelius Design; Shannon Stirnweis; Carol Strebel; Joseph Hammond, Susan Jaekel, Renate Lohmann, and DJ Simison represented by Ann Remen-Willis.